PLATE VI

THE ORGAN

OF THE

TWENTIETH CENTURY

A MANUAL ON ALL MATTERS RELATING
TO THE SCIENCE AND ART OF ORGAN
TONAL APPOINTMENT AND DIVISIONAL
APPORTIONMENT WITH COMPOUND
EXPRESSION

BY

GEORGE ASHDOWN AUDSLEY

DOVER PUBLICATIONS, INC.
Mineola, New York

THE ORGAN

The Organ—grandest instrument the hand
Of man has placed in Music's galaxy:
In which all Nature's wondrous sounds are linked
In golden chains of countless harmonies.
Responsive to the touch of man's weak hands
As if a giant's fingers swept its keys
And called concordant voices from the depths,
The diapason of the storm-struck sea,
The thunder's peal, the wind's wild whistling wail,
The songs of swift-winged warblers in the air,
And the soft sighing of the ambient breeze.
Temple of Tone art thou! The shrine supreme
Of Sound's mysterious powers and richest gifts.
God-given thought alone could have inspired
The human mind to frame so grand a work:
Great Organ—Monarch of all Instruments!

G. A. A.

Bibliographical Note

This Dover edition, first published in 1970 and reprinted in 2004, is an unabridged republication of the work originally published by Dodd, Mead and Company, New York, in 1919.

Library of Congress Cataloging-in-Publication Data

Audsley, George Ashdown, 1838-1925.
  The organ of the twentieth century : a manual on all matters relating to the science and art of organ tonal appointment and divisional apportionment with compound expression / by George Ashdown Audsley.
     p. cm.
  Originally published: New York : Dodd, Mead, 1919.
  Includes index.
  ISBN 0-486-43575-X (pbk.)
  1. Organ (Musical instrument)–Construction. I. Title: Organ of the 20th century. II. Title.

ML552.A95 2004
786.5'192–dc22

2003067490

Manufactured in the United States of America
Dover Publications, Inc., 31 East 2nd Street, Mineola, N.Y. 11501

BOIS LE DUC   J. HILL, DEL.

PROEM

INCE the year 1865 my interest in all matters connected with the construction and tonal appointment of the Organ has been deep and never-flagging. Fostered during the years in which my chief and almost only amusement was the construction of an Organ; and throughout the years in which my frequent travels in Continental countries were enriched by the inspection and study of notable Organs,—landmarks in the history of organ-building,—and made pleasant and profitable by acquaintanceship and communion with many distinguished masters of the art, my love for the Organ and the many problems its construction and tonal development presented grew steadily; until, with the exception of the imperative calls of my exacting profession, the study of the Organ as a musical instrument, with its seemingly infinite possibilities of scientific and artistic development, became the most absorbing one to my mind.

Under such circumstances it was only natural that I should take up pen and pencil to add something, however humble, to the literature of the Organ; especially at a time when so little of any real value was being said, and so little indicative of scientific and artistic advance was making its appearance in the organ-building world.

My first essays in this direction appeared in the years 1886-8, in a series of articles published in the *English Mechanic and World of Science;* in which, for the first time in the literature of the Organ, an attempt was made to differentiate, in their proper tonal appointments, the Church Organ, the Concert-room Organ, and the Chamber Organ. These were followed by lectures and articles on the Swell in the Organ; in which, for the first time, the necessity of imparting powers of flexibility and expression to all the Manual Divisions and the Pedal Organ was advocated on logical and artistic grounds.

In the year 1905 " The Art of Organ-Building " was offered to the organ-loving world. Since then my studies in tonal matters have been continued; their results furnishing the sole apology for the appearance of the present work, which I have ventured to entitle THE ORGAN OF THE TWENTIETH CENTURY.

With the exception of the first Chapter, which is given to the artistic treatment of the Organ-case in different countries, the work is devoted to the all-important subject of the General Appointment and Divisional Apportionment of the Tonal Forces of the Organ; and also to such formative and operative matters and details as are directly connected with Tone Production, its Control, and its Flexibility and Expression. These latter matters have rendered it necessary for much that is said in " The Art of Organ-Building " to be again gone over, to render the present work sufficiently self-contained; notably with regard to scientific and artistic stop-formation and the characteristics of labial and lingual pipes.

Purely constructive matters connected with the wind collecting and distributing portions of the Organ; and all mechanical devices and systems of transmission, extending between the appliances of the console, immediately commanded and operated by the performer, and the sound-producing divisions of the instrument, form no part of the matter presented in this volume. All such may be left to the care and ingenuity of the organ-builder and electrician of to-day, who have, in association, carried this branch of the art of organ construction to a high degree of excellence.

Generally, in the direction of Tonal Appointment, and, specially, in that of Divisional Tonal Apportionment, this work is of too revolutionary a character to meet with anything approaching general approval. While at times I may seem unduly dogmatic, I can assure the reader that this essay has not been written in any such spirit.

That I have strong opinions on many matters connected with organ construction and tonal appointment is well known: but these opinions —widely at variance with those commonly held by the organ-building world—are the result of half a century of study and investigation, such as probably no other man alive to-day has undertaken with an unbiassed mind; free from all trade traditions and interests on the one hand; and likewise free, on the other hand, from such personal leanings and prejudices as are commonly found in the minds of performers on the Organ, familiar only with a certain type of instrument, and the limited range of tonal effects possible thereon. Added to this, my personal experience in practical organ matters has not been altogether a small one.

It is not to be expected that organ-builders, and especially those in high places, will be influenced, or in any way moved out of their well-worn and smooth trade grooves, by anything advanced in this work. They naturally object to being addressed on the subject of their art by an outsider—an amateur who cannot claim even the dignity of being an organist—and, accordingly, it would be too great a condescension to admit that they could be taught anything in their time-honored art. Therefore it is not to the organ-builder that I can appeal for the due and unprejudiced consideration of what I advance and advocate in this essay: but rather to the accomplished and open-minded musician who can dispassionately weigh each tonal proposition,—pro and con,—judging it on its individual merits, and, what is of still greater importance, with respect to its relation to the complete tonal scheme, in which no part is specially independent.

In all probability I shall not be spared to see my ideas carried out in anything approaching their entirety; but that they will form the foundation of the Organ of the Twentieth Century I feel assured. The necessity for the introduction of more than one Expressive Division in an Organ; the improvement, along practical lines, of the Pedal Clavier; and the imperative call for the introduction of a distinct, properly constituted, and expressive String-toned Division —all first advanced by me—have been either wholly or partially adopted in certain Organs recently constructed. So I may reasonably hope that, in the course of time, the other necessary improvements I have suggested; and the radical system of Divisional Tonal Apportionment, involving the new principles of tonal contrast and compound flexibility and expression,—not hitherto recognized in organ appointment,—and the introduction of Ancillary or Floating

Organs, which are destined to be productive of remarkable and hitherto unknown tonal effects in organ music—all as set forth in the present work—will commend themselves to the accomplished and progressive musician, to whom the Organ of the Twentieth Century will open to his " imagination quite a vista of new. and previously impossible effects in organ playing."

One Chapter is devoted to a very important subject, which has never before been touched upon by any writer on the Organ, but which at the present time deserves very serious consideration. I allude to the Organ Specification, and the absolute necessity of attention being paid to the proper preparation of so important a document, in the interest of both the producer and the purchaser of an Organ, and more especially the latter. I commend the Chapter to the earnest consideration of every one contemplating the purchase of an Organ.

In conclusion, I have to express my sincere thanks to those whose names are mentioned in the following pages, from whom I have received valuable information; and especially to Mr. Arthur George Hill, B.A., F.S.A., of London, whose kind permission to reproduce a selection of the drawings which adorn his sumptuous work, " The Organ-cases and Organs of the Middle Ages and the Renaissance," in my previous work, " The Art of Organ-Building," has enabled me to repeat their presentation in this volume.

GEORGE ASHDOWN AUDSLEY.

BLOOMFIELD, NEW JERSEY,
APRIL, 1919.

CONTENTS

CHAPTER I.

CONTENTS

CHAPTER XII.

CHAPTER XIII.

CHAPTER XIV.

CHAPTER XV.

CHAPTER XVI.

CHAPTER XVII.

CHAPTER I.

ART IN ORGAN-BUILDING

T is only in recent times that Ornamental Art has been largely divorced from organ-building, and this is due to certain causes. Primarily, to the want of knowledge of and interest in organ matters on the part of the large majority of architects. Secondly, to the very general want of taste and skill in ornamental design on the part of organ-builders. Thirdly, to the parsimony of those for whom Organs are constructed. The result has been the production of the most lamentable failures and tasteless constructions in the form of organ-cases the world has ever seen. A few essays have certainly been made by accomplished architects to follow in the footsteps of the old designers; and several very satisfactory results have been produced, for which all lovers of the Organ should be grateful. It is to be hoped, however, as taste and knowledge increase, that the numerous monstrosities which disgrace so many modern churches and concert-rooms will be replaced by works of true ornamental art, in which the spirit of the old designers and art-workmen will again appear.

During the later periods of the Middle Ages and throughout the Renaissance, the exterior of the Organ was made a thing of beauty, and upon it were lavished artistic thought and labor unstinted. Fortunately, for our inspiration and emulation, many beautiful works of these art-epochs have been preserved, as will be shown on the following pages. It is to be regretted, however, that among the numerous organ-cases that remain there are comparatively few mediæval examples. Those which have survived the ruthless hands of the religious fanatic and natural decay are so suggestive, that one cannot help devoutly wishing that more had been spared for the guidance of the modern ecclesiastical architect and art-workman. Of the organ-cases of the Renaissance many fine examples remain on the Continent of Europe and a few in England. From these one may gather a knowledge of the artistic feelings and methods prevalent at the times of their construction, and, notwithstanding the many somewhat meretricious features in their designs, valuable lessons may be learnt and suggestions obtained to guide the designers of organ-cases of to-day.

Unfortunately there are no remains of Organs in England, constructed during the mediæval periods, to give us any idea of the art displayed on their exteriors, for what existed at the time of the Reformation were ruthlessly destroyed. But, judging from the artistic work that exists in other directions, notably in richly carved and painted screen-work, there is no doubt that the Organ received its full share of artistic adornment. A few remarks in the "Ancient Rites and Monuments of the Monastical and Cathedral Church of Durham," published by Davis in 1672, give us a slight idea on the subject:—

"There were three pair of Organs belonging to the said quire, for maintenance of God's service, and the better celebrating thereof. One of the fairest pair of the three stood over the quire door, only opened and play'd upon on principal feasts, the pipes being all of the most fine wood, and workmanship very fair, partly gilt upon the inside, and the outside of the leaves and covers up to the top, with branches, and flowers finely gilt, with the name of JESUS gilt with gold. There were but two pair more of them in all England of the same making, one in York, and another in Paul's.

"The second pair stood on the north side of the quire, being never play'd upon, but when the four Doctors of the Church were read, viz., Augustine, Ambrose, Gregory, and Jerome, being a pair of fair large Organs, called the *Cryers.*"

These particulars are interesting, speaking as they do of an Organ, the pipes of which were "all of most fine wood, and workmanship very fair," and the case of which had, in the almost universal mediæval fashion, folding "leaves and covers up to the top," richly decorated with colors and gold, in the manner then prevalent, as shown by the decorated woodwork still preserved in English churches. Owing to the general destruction of Organs in the time of Cromwell, we have no conception of the richness of England in Church Organs during the fifteenth and sixteenth centuries. The more beautiful and richly decorated the Organs were, the more completely were they destroyed, and their pipes melted down to make bullets.

When we turn to certain Continental countries, we fortunately find some notable examples of ornamental art applied to mediæval Organs,

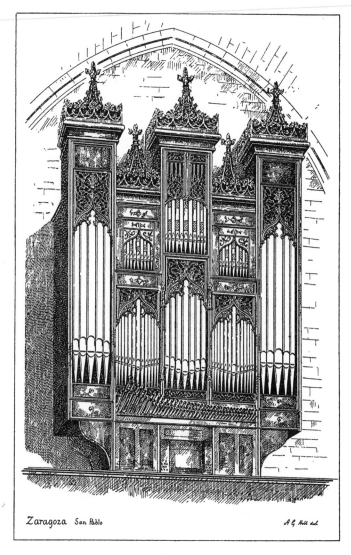

Zaragoza San Pablo   A G Hill del

FIG. I.

late in style, as might be expected. For the earliest examples of any note we have to go to Spain. In the Cathedral of Zaragoza, there is a noteworthy Organ constructed in the year 1413. The beautiful Gothic case of this important instrument is shown in the accompanying Plate I. The design presents three quadrangular towers, surmounted by bold cornices and concave pyramidal roofs, ornamented with crockets and finials, and separated by curtains surmounted by boldly molded and carved crestings. In all likelihood, similar carved-work ornamented the cornices of the towers. The flat treatment of the front, with its five compartments on a vertical plane, is characteristic of a certain type of Gothic organ-cases. It was evidently adopted to allow of folding shutters being conveniently applied. The manner in which such shutters are fitted to a three-towered, flat case is shown in Fig. XI., which depicts the Organ in the Church of St. George, at Nördlingen, with its shutters closed. The manner in which the five large compartments, filled with displayed pipes, are enriched with arched, cusped, carved, and traceried pipe-shades is beautiful and full of pure Gothic feeling. The smaller compartments are treated in a similar manner, on necessarily a smaller scale. All the carved- and tracery-work is gilded solid; but the rich coloring which doubtless accompanied the gilding has been covered by a coating of brown paint. The TRUMPETS and CLARION *en chamade* are additions to the original design, the treatment not having been adopted so early as the beginning of the fifteenth century.

In the Church of San Pablo, in Zaragoza, there is another fine Organ, the exterior of which is shown in the preceding illustration, Fig. I. This instrument was constructed about the year 1420. It will be seen that in general design this case closely resembles that of the Organ in the Cathedral, while it is much richer in the finish of the towers and curtains, all of which have elaborately carved crestings, and traceried, crocketed, and finialed rooflets. The case is not perfect: the upper panels of the lateral towers have lost their carvings or tracery-work; and the upper divisions of the curtains are certainly not portions of the original design. These portions were evidently treated, with cusped arches and spandril tracery, in accord with the lower divisions. Here, again, we observe the later addition of the reed stops *en chamade,* characteristic of Spanish Organs of the Renaissance.

The cases of both the Organs just described furnish admirable studies for modern adoption. They present the simplest form of general construction, and their carved-work and arched and traceried pipe-shades may be either imitated or simplified, according to taste or means. A case so designed and illuminated with gold and colors would present a very beautiful appearance in a Gothic church. So decorated, it would not call for the use of expensive wood. The displayed pipes may be simply gilded, or gilded and diapered, in black or brown, with suitable Gothic patterns: no other colors should be used on the pipes.

In the Chapel of San Bartolomé, adjoining the old Cathedral of Salamanca, is the Organ represented in the illustration, Fig. II. This

PLATE I

Zaragoza. Cathedral

A.G. Hill del.

is, so far as is commonly known, the earliest important example of a Gothic case preserved, having been constructed during the last quarter of the fourteenth century. It was evidently the then prevailing form,

FIG. II.

on which the later and elaborate cases previously described were modeled. The present example is severe in general character, and, with the exception of its five richly-carved and traceried pipe-shades, is entirely devoid of ornament. The simple battlemented tops of the towers and curtains, and the disposition of the displayed pipes of irregular lengths, indicate the early character of the work. It will be observed that the several groups of pipes graduate toward the left or bass side of the instrument, for what reason it is difficult to surmise. The painted shutters, which have been preserved (probably of later date), have a very striking effect. Here, again, the designer of to-day may find suggestions of value.

The finest example of Italian mediæval art, so far as the Organ is concerned, exists in the Church of San Petronio, Bologna. This noteworthy Organ which is the work of Maestro Lorenzo di Giacomo da Prato, was begun in 1470,* and was finished, in all probability, in 1472. The original case is shown in the central portion of the accompanying illustration Fig. III. The debased Renaissance work, freely sketched, which surrounds the case was executed in 1674. Nothing could well be simpler or lighter in construction than the general framework of this remarkable case, perfectly flat, and devoid of a single molding, yet how admirably it lends itself to the lavish display of Gothic tracery. The composition presents seven quadrangular compartments containing groups of large and small displayed pipes, graduated and arranged in the fashion characteristic of old Italian organ-cases. The central and largest pipes of the four smaller groups are embossed. Respecting this example, Mr. Hill remarks: " The case was most probably designed by one of the numerous artists who worked from time to time upon the decoration of the basilica. The traceried pipe-shades are of extreme beauty, and in the delicacy of their geometrical patterns are strongly influenced by more northern feeling, if indeed, they are not the work of foreign artists." These shades should inspire modern designers.

In France important Organs were constructed during the fifteenth and sixteenth centuries, and fine cases are still preserved of these periods. For our present purpose it is only necessary for us to describe and illustrate two representative and highly suggestive examples, constructed in the opening years of the sixteenth century. The first, which exists in the Cathedral of Perpignan (Pyrénées Orientales), is depicted in Fig. IV., but without its large painted shutters, which are merely

---

* " In the May of that year the authorities of the city determined to erect an Organ in their basilica which should be worthy of the church upon which so much art and labour had been expended. For this purpose letters were sent to Maestro Lorenzo requiring him to come to Bologna. In the fabric rolls of S. Petronio the following entry occurs: ' 1470. *Die secunda Junii Ant. pred. det. Maestro Laurentio Jacobi di Prato organiste lib. quinque et sol. duodecim gt. pro resto expensarum illi promissarum veniendo a Civitate Senarum ad Civitatem Bononiae.*'

" It appears from the archives that Lorenzo accepted this invitation and arrived at Bologna within a few weeks, and the Organ is stated to have been nearly completed in 1471, the following year. . . .

" The organ builder worked during this time in the church itself, and not in his factory; and this was the custom of most craftsmen in the olden times. The *Fabriceria* (or committee of works connected with the fabric), moreover, supplied him with wood, lead, tin, and other materials necessary for his craft, which seems to have been customary at the time." Hill— " Organ-cases and Organs of the Middle Ages and Renaissance." London 1883.

indicated where they are hinged to the case. These shutters are covered with paintings representing the Adoration of the Magi, the Baptism of

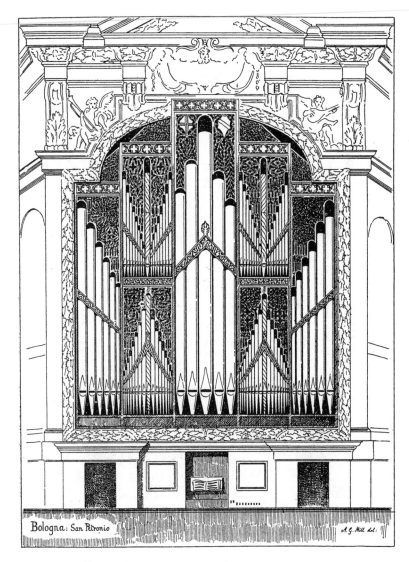

Bologna: San Petronio

FIG. III.

our Lord, and the four Evangelists. In general outline, the case re-sembles that of the Organ in the Church of San Petronio; but in its ornamental details, and in the number and disposition of its compartments containing the displayed pipe-work, it differs considerably. In the lower central compartment we meet with the peculiar and objection-able feature of inverted pipes, introduced, along with a corresponding series of upright pipes, as a surface decoration of a painted panel. All

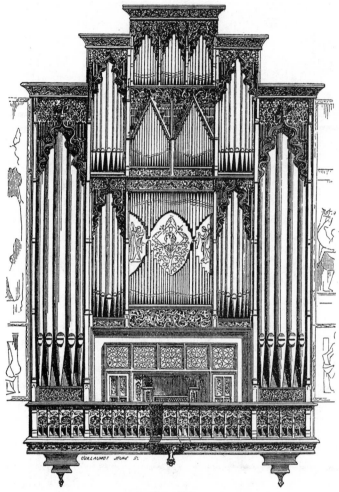

Fig. IV.

the pipe-shades are richly carved, molded, and elaborately traceried; and all the panels and the balustrade are carried out in an equally rich manner. The whole of the woodwork is of oak and beautifully ex-ecuted. Though Perpignan is now a French town, it originally belonged to Spain; and this accounts for the organ-case being thoroughly Spanish in general form and detail. The Organ stands in a tribune, over an arch about half-way down the nave, and about sixteen feet above the floor. The case is twenty-three feet wide and forty-five feet high. The two lateral compartments contain pipes of the 32 ft. stop. The impress-

FIG. V.

ive character of this superb case may be imagined from its great dimensions.

In Fig. V. is given an illustration of the Gothic case of the Organ in the Church of Hombleux (Somme), constructed about the year 1500. This case presents a treatment which seems to have been favored by the organ-builders of the period.   The Gothic case shown in Fig. I., and the cases of the Organs in the Cathedral of Strasbourg and the Marien-kirche, at Dortmund, present the same overhanging treatment at their sides.   It also appears, in a pronounced form, in the Organ in the Church of St. George, at Nördlingen.   It was also adopted by the designers of the Renaissance in many important Organs.

The Hombleux case, as it at present exists, has undergone some "restoration" at the hands of Renaissance workmen, which accounts for the incongruity obtaining in the carved and pierced pipe-shades in the several compartments.   Those of the central and lateral compart-ments belong to the Gothic period; while those of the intermediate com-partments, containing emblazoned shields, are Renaissance.   The orna-mentation of the paneling in the lower portion of the case is also of the Renaissance period.   Taken altogether, this case affords valuable sug-gestions for a moderately sized Organ.*   Large and dignified Gothic cases can be designed by an extension of the treatment it presents, as is shown in the fine modern case of the Organ in the Church of St. Bartholomew, at Armley, England, an illustration of which is given in Plate XV.

One of the finest Gothic organ-cases extant is that in the Cathedral of Strasbourg (Alsace-Lorraine) of which a view is given in Plate II. This case was constructed in the year 1497.   The rich and beautifully carved wings which flank the main case are Renaissance additions, and were probably made to replace the painted shutters with which the case was originally furnished.   The pipe-shades of the adjoining compart-ments are evidently of the same period, differing widely from those of the central portion.   The Organ is on the north side of the nave, pro-jected out in front of the triforium and clerestory.   The tribune or organist's gallery is a Gothic *cul-de-lampe,* the carved ribs of which are richly cusped, and spring from a sculptured boss.   In front of the gallery is projected the Positif or Choir Organ—Gothic in all save its small carved wings.   The late German Gothic details are highly char-acteristic and display the wandering vagaries of the style.   Placed in such an admirable position, the whole composition has a most imposing effect.   Its height from the boss of the *cul-de-lampe* to the top of the cresting is about fifty feet.   The tin pipes of the Pedal Organ MONTRE, 16 FT., occupy the central portion of the case.

The treatment throughout deserves careful study by the modern designer, and only calls for a more refined style of Gothic detail.   It was this Organ that the late Sir George Gilbert Scott took as his model when he designed the beautiful case which is projected from the tri-forium of the choir of Ely Cathedral.

---

* It would be desirable, if not absolutely necessary, to have the bellows located away from the instrument.

PLATE II

Strasbourg

a. g. Hill del.

PLATE III

Jutfaas

A. G. Hill del.

We have now to consider another magnificent mediæval organ-case, still preserved in the Marienkirche, at Dortmund, Westphalia. Like the preceding example, it is situated in a gallery placed high over the nave

Dortmund

FIG. VI.

arcade. This beautiful case, which is shown in the accompanying illustration, Fig. VI., was constructed about the year 1485, and fortunately has escaped the hands of the Renaissance "restorer." It is a fine example of the overhanging treatment, and presents the unusual features, in a Gothic design, of semicircular towers. These are treated in a highly artistic manner, and the way in which they are corbeled out is very satisfactory. The treatment of the overhanging supports is extremely good. While, for the most part, the composition is consistent and artistic, we are of opinion that it would have been greatly improved had the lateral towers been carried higher than the adjoining curtains or flats, and had the central tower been made somewhat less in diameter. All the tracery, pipe-shades, crestings, and panel decorations are full of spirit and beautifully executed. This is another organ-case full of suggestions to the organ-designer of the present time, who has the good sense to take lessons from what true artists have done in the past, to help him in his work in the present, for the adornment of the Organ of the Twentieth Century.

Another remarkable Gothic organ-case—the most complete and elaborate one in existence—is to be seen in the Church at Jutfaas, in Holland. This originally belonged to the Nieuwerszÿds-Kapel, at Amsterdam, from which it was removed in 1871 and re-erected at Jutfaas. This case is shown in Plate III., reproduced from Mr. Hill's copy of a drawing by Mr. P. J. H. Cuypers, of Amsterdam. The style of the case is the florid and impure one which obtained in North-western Europe in the opening years of the sixteenth century, except in France and Great Britain, when Gothic architecture had reached its last stage. The plan of the case is unique, being based on rather more than a semicircle—a form badly suited for the internal economy of the Organ, and one not likely to be followed in modern work. The whole is supported on a richly molded and traceried *cul-de-lampe,* which occupies a spandril between two arches, as indicated, and rises to the height of about thirty-five feet. The lower part of the case immediately above the *cul-de-lampe,* and in which is disposed all the displayed pipe-work, is formed of three semicircular and two V-shaped towers, placed alternately, and divided by four segmental curtains, as indicated on the small plan given. The curtains have pipes arranged in two stages, while the towers contain large pipes only. The towers are carried above the pipes in tall and richly detailed canopy-work of several stages, and the intermediate segmental compartments are finished with foliated pipe-shades, molded arches, and pedestals supporting angels holding shields. The standards at the junctions of the towers with the curtains terminate upward in tall and slender, crocketed pinnacles. The central tower is the highest; the lateral ones being of two lower dimensions. From the center of all rises a lofty and very elaborately treated polygonal lantern-like structure, terminating in an open, traceried, and crocketed spire of unusual design. The whole composition is extravagant: and although we do not recommend any portion of it for imitation, the designer of to-day can obtain some suggestive hints from a study of its more severe details.

In Plate IV., is given an illustration of the Grand Organ in the Marienkirche, at Lübeck. The case of this instrument presents a noteworthy example of the flat treatment characteristic of Gothic design in connection with the Organ; and apparently due to the practice of providing the cases with protecting shutters. Describing this important work, Mr. Hill says: "It is placed in a gallery at the west end, some forty feet from the ground, and the case itself is nearly eighty feet high and is forty feet wide. The church is 125 feet to the apex of the vaulting. This case was erected in the year 1504, though the Choir Organ is later, the date 1561 being carved upon it. The case consists essentially of five flats of pipes, of which three are carried up to form towers, the spaces between them at the top being filled in with elaborate tracery and carving. The way in which the crocketed pinnacles are twisted about [in the erratic manner obtaining in late German Gothic] should be noticed. Upon the cornice moldings of the three towers scrolls have been lately placed, bearing the inscription ' GLORIA IN EXCELSIS DEO.' Above the center tower is a figure of the Blessed Virgin Mary with the Infant, and over the two lower flats are figures of prophets with texts inscribed on scrolls. These three figures appear to be of the same date as the Organ, but the angels with expanded wings, at the sides, are of Renaissance workmanship. The design of the Choir Organ is very elaborate. . . . Like most old Organs, this has little depth, being only 7 feet from back to front." The seven pipes in the central tower are the lower notes of the GROSS PRINCIPAL, 32 FT., of the Pedal Organ, and are made of pure tin. The smaller pipes of the same stop occupy the lateral towers.

We have now to enter the period of the Renaissance; and treat, so far as our very limited space permits, of the art expended during that period on the adornment of the Organ. Italy may, very properly, provide the first examples. In the opening years of the sixteenth century several important Organs were erected in Italian churches; and in the designs of these, although Gothic feeling had not entirely disappeared, we find Renaissance treatment firmly established. An early example is furnished by the Organ erected, in the year 1500, in the Chapel of the Palazzo Publico, at Siena, an illustration of which is given in Fig. VII. The case was designed by Baldassare Peruzzi, who also designed the Organs in the Duomo and in the Ospedale della Scala, in the same city. The treatment is dignified and highly characteristic of the somewhat eclectic style which obtained in Tuscany at the close of the fifteenth century. The carving throughout is rich and effective, and the entire case is decorated with colors and gold. The introduction of pipes of their actual speaking lengths is noteworthy, and highly to be commended on artistic and tonal grounds. The total absence of pipe-shades shows a radical departure from mediæval models. This case deserves the

Siena: Palazzo Publico   A.G. Hill del.

Fig. VII.

attention of modern designers, showing the square architectural treatment characteristic of Italian Renaissance in this branch of art.

PLATE IV

PLATE V

Another interesting example is furnished by the Organ in the Church of Santa Maria della Scala, at Siena, illustrated in Plate V. Speaking of this case, Mr. Hill remarks: "The organ-case under consideration was erected, most probably, about the year 1510, and is a very elaborate and fine piece of work. It is placed in a gallery or tribune at some height from the ground, the gallery being likewise much ornamented. It will be seen that the pipes in the organ-case are kept clear of the canopies or arcades, while they are cut to their natural speaking length without regard to exactitude of rake. All the details of this case are extremely well designed and executed, and the entire front is illuminated in blue and gold, red being very sparingly used. The frieze of the entablature and the panels of the columns are richly carved, the raised portions being gilded and the ground colored blue. In the side circles are figures representing the Annunciation." The design of the filling-in, between the angle pilasters, is of a very curious character, but highly effective in the actual work. The entablature is surmounted by a composition of a very artistic and pleasing description, on the highest part of which stands a figure of the Blessed Virgin and Child. The irregular treatment of the pipes, characteristic of both Spanish and Italian organ-cases, is here very marked and is certainly not without its charm. One can easily imagine what a magnificent case could be produced on the lines of this design, supposing it to be devised by an artist, executed by a master-hand, and illuminated with gold and harmonious colors, like so much of the gorgeous Italian furniture and woodwork of the fifteenth and sixteenth centuries.

We may conclude our brief remarks on Italian organ-cases by directing attention to that of the Organ in the Church of Santa Maria di Carignano, Genoa, a reduced copy of Mr. Hill's clever drawing of which is given in the accompanying illustration, Fig. VIII. This remarkably elaborate and beautiful case, executed about the year 1660, is, as Mr. Hill informs us, "the work of Georges Heigenmann in its main features, the carvings being executed by Guilio Lippi, G. B. Hola, and Santino Guintino. The paintings on the shutters and the gilded decorations were carried out by Paolo Brozzi and Domenico Piola, the brother of the celebrated Pellegro." With such a galaxy of talent, one cannot wonder at the artistic result produced. When again will such a combination be brought together over the production of an organ-case? Yet, with some such desire, the introduction of an altogether unnecessary and sometimes ridiculous number of stops might well be abandoned in favor of having a beautiful and thoroughly artistic exterior. The craze for monster Organs, without one evidence of artistic feeling, growing to-day, is a huge mistake: there is no excuse for it.

Referring to the case under review, it may be remarked that although both designed and executed in Italy, it cannot be pronounced a specimen

of Italian Renaissance art.   It bears unmistakable evidence of Northern
influence, due, doubtless, to Heigenmann who must have been a German.
The manner in which the flanking towers are designed, the center portion
is relieved by semicircular and V-shaped projecting features, the pipe-

FIG. VIII.

work is arranged, and the pipe-shades are treated, leaves nothing to be
desired.   As it stands on an elevated gallery, and with its painted
shutters outspread, this Organ has a magnificent effect.
     Several very beautiful organ-cases, constructed during the Renais-

sance period, adorn Spanish cathedrals and churches; two of which we are able to illustrate through the courtesy of Mr. Arthur G. Hill; and

FIG. IX.

two which, to the best of our knowledge, have never before been illustrated in any work on the Organ.

First, in date of construction, is the beautiful case of the Organ in

of the designers of the organ-cases of the twentieth century. On the frieze of the intermediate entablature is this appropriate inscription: OMNIS SPIRITVS LAVDET DOMINVM. The principal entablature is thoroughly Classical in character and detail, with the exception of the enrichment of the frieze. From the sides of this stage extend the two immense shutters "with majestic effect . . . well painted on canvas with representations of the Adoration of the Magi and the Resurrection."

The third or upper stage is, in every sense, an admirable crowning to the entire composition. Here again Classical feeling predominates, and seems to repeat, on a larger scale, the Choir Organ design, but with a more suitable form of pediment. The whole of the architectural features are covered with elaborate, carved ornamentation, and the three compartments have beautiful pipe-shades, according in all respects with those below. Four statues adorn this stage, as indicated. The entire woodwork of the case is of oak darkened by age, and entirely unrelieved by colors or gilding.

The two other very important Spanish Organs which we are fortunately able to give illustrations of are those on the north and south sides of the *coro,* in Seville Cathedral. These differ widely both in style and general treatment from the preceding examples, all traces of flatness disappearing, and a much greater massiveness combined with exuberance of carved ornament and large sculptured figures of angels, etc., being employed. So elaborate and complicated are the designs that an adequate description is impossible, but from the illustrations given a fair idea can be gained of the general treatments and details.

In Plate VI. is shown the south front of the Organ on the north side of the *coro;* the corresponding front of the Organ on the south side of the *coro* being practically identical, except as regards the seated figure above the central group of pipes, which is that of a Pope. The composition is faulty, being overloaded with the upper portion, which is entirely out of scale with the main body of the case. The disposition of the displayed pipes is good; but the pipe-shades are much too clumsy and overdone for elegance. Refinement and artistic repose are generally absent from the entire composition.

In Plate VII. is shown the south front of the south Organ, or that toward the south aisle of the cathedral. While in the main portion of the case, including the disposition of the displayed pipes, there is no essential difference from that of the front toward the *coro,* the upper portion differs in several of its features. This Plate shows the organist's gallery and the very elaborate ornamentation of the lower portions of the Organs. The design of the small Organ, projected from the gallery, is worthy of special notice. Reed stops *en chamade* appear on all the four fronts of these Organs.

Examples of organ-cases of the same school of design, but much less

PLATE VII

extravagant in ornamentation, are to be seen in the Cathedral of Mexico. In these the absurd practice of displaying inverted pipes is carried to the extreme. We actually find large pipes inverted, and carrying heavy, architectural entablatures on the tips of their long conical feet. It would be difficult to imagine a greater monstrosity in organ-case design. There are no fewer than seventy inverted pipes in one

FIG. XI.

front alone; while, in the same front, there are only one hundred and nineteen displayed pipes in their proper position.

Before directing attention to organ-cases of Renaissance design executed in Germany in the seventeenth and eighteenth centuries, we may refer to the example in the Church of St. George, at Nördlingen. The case, shown in Fig. XI., does not present any features of special interest; and is only illustrated with the view of showing the manner in

PLATE **X**

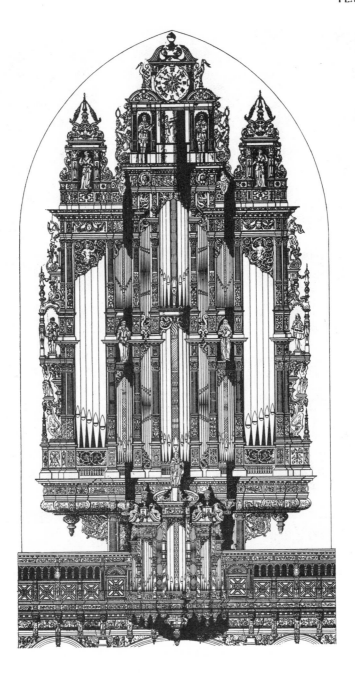

ment is carried in the main case to the extreme limit, but confined to the portions that slope back. It will be observed that the central pipes in six of the compartments are embossed. The Choir Organ and the gallery are extremely rich and beautiful in design. Indeed, the entire work deserves the closest study by the organ-case designers of the twentieth century. Mr. Hill, from whose beautiful drawing our Plate has been made, correctly says: "The whole composition is one of extreme magnificence and size. The work is probably without equal for its date, and the general design exhibits none of the architectural decay which would be observable in productions of the same period in more southern districts of Europe."

The Organ stands at the west end of the nave of the church. It is forty feet in width, and the case rises to the height of one hundred feet from the floor of the nave.

In Plate XI. is given a view of the Organ which stands at the west end of the Cathedral of St. Bavon, at Haarlem. It is, perhaps, not too much to say that no Organ ever constructed has earned so world-wide a reputation as this; and, thanks to the wise care that has been bestowed upon it, it still remains practically in the state it was left by its talented builder, who certainly produced a noble work of art from every point of view. It was constructed by Christian Müller, of Amsterdam, who commenced the work on the 23rd day of April, 1735, and completed it on the 13th day of September, 1738. The Organ stands in an elevated gallery, the front of which is of white marble, supported on columns and pilasters of a Composite order. From the center of the gallery is projected the Choir Organ, containing fourteen stops. The main Organ towers behind almost to the vault of the nave—a work, considering the state of ornamental art at the time of its construction, which is singularly successful in its design. Exception must be taken to the crowning composition, which is completely out of scale with the case-work below. The disposition of the displayed pipes in the semicircular and V-shaped features is highly satisfactory, but the lavish introduction of very small pipes in the twelve dividing compartments goes far to weaken the design, but here the objectionable introduction of inverted pipes has been wisely avoided. All the exposed pipes are of pure English tin, burnished. The CCCC pipe of the SUB-PRINCIPAL, 32 FT., standing in one of the lateral towers, measures about 39 feet in length by 15 inches in diameter. What may be designated the architectural features of the cases are well designed and carefully executed; and the numerous figures are full of character and spirit. Our visit to St. Bavon's, and the pleasure of seeing and hearing its magnificent Organ can never be forgotten so long as life lasts.

Three examples of Renaissance organ-cases constructed in France will be sufficient for the purposes of the present Chapter. The first, in order of date, is that in the Church of La Ferté Bernard (Sarthe), illustrated in Fig. XIII. Speaking of this interesting example, Mr.

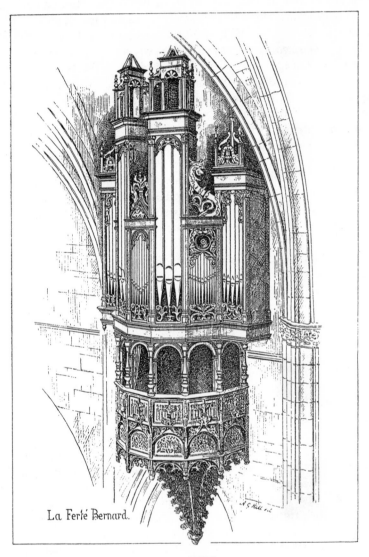

La Ferté Bernard.

Fig. XIII.

Hill remarks: " No one with any appreciation of art can fail to recognize the beauty of this design, which, so far as we know, is unique. Originally, no doubt, there were many Organs of fifteenth-century

PLATE XI

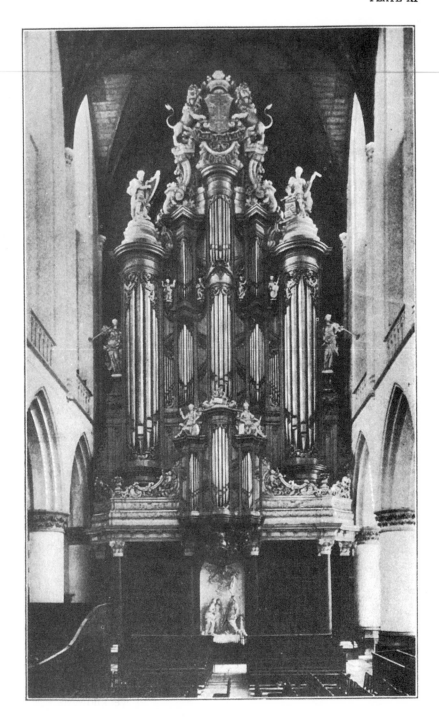

workmanship suspended from the triforium in this manner; but few now remain, those at Strasbourg and Dortmund being notable exceptions. It will be seen that the *cul-de-lampe,* or tribune, is of earlier date than the Organ above, the former being Gothic and the other Renaissance, without any trace of Gothic spirit. This is all the more curious, because it is known that the organ-case proper was made only thirty-five years after the *cul-de-lampe,* and yet the styles of the two parts have hardly anything in common. The beautiful Gothic gallery was designed by Everard Baudot, organ-builder and organist, and the work was executed by him in 1501. The buffet or organ-case above is one of the masterpieces of Pierre Bert, organ-builder, of Le Mans, who executed it in 1536 from the designs of Sainctot Chemin, an eminent artist. . . . The organ-case is an admirable example of early Renaissance work, and both the design and execution of it are remarkable. . . . The woodwork is entirely of oak, and has become very dark with age.''

While we readily admit the beauty of the tribune with its pendant *cul-de-lampe,* we must say we fail to join Mr. Hill in his unqualified admiration of the case, which, in the point of design, leaves something to be desired. The separation of the two tall towers by the central and most ineffective feature of the composition is insufficient according to the canons of good design. The details, including the pipe-shades, are poor in comparison with those of the cases previously illustrated. The whole is, however, highly suggestive; and the expert designer or architect of to-day can see how the whole could be translated into Gothic language, in strict accord with the tribune.

The finest example of an early French Renaissance organ-case is that in the beautiful Church of Saint-Maclou, at Rouen (Seine-Inférieure), an illustration of which is given in Plate XII. No work of its class or period deserves more careful study than this fine case —fine both in design and execution. Critical as one may be, it would seem difficult to find fault with any portion of this remarkable work of French Renaissance art. Mr. Hill furnishes the following particulars: " The work is chiefly by the hand of Nicholas Castel, and dates from the years 1518-21, while fifteen years later Martin Guibert, and his assistants, Mancel, Guillaume Dubost, and Robert Carolus, executed further work at a cost of 180 livres, being aided by the advice of Antoine Jousselme, organ-builder, who received 140 livres. . . . Nicholas Quesnel, image maker, executed the figures of angels on the case. The whole work was originally decorated in gold and color, from a design furnished by Gougeon [Jean], and executed by Jacques de Seéz, painter, at a cost of 300 livres. This has, unfortunately, been removed of late years, and the woodwork entirely cleaned. This is greatly to be regretted, as the decoration was, no doubt, of high excellence." We heartily join Mr. Hill in this expression of regret; for while we examined the actual case in its present condition, we realized, in our knowledge of polychromic decoration, how much it must have gained by its embellishment under the direction of so accomplished a master as Jean Gougeon.

The general architectural disposition, and the relative proportions of the several features of the case are admirable. The arrangement of the displayed pipes in the lateral towers and intermediate projecting features is perfect, and given just the necessary relief by the quiet treatment of the pipes in the four flat compartments. The detail throughout is extremely rich, and beautifully executed. The terminations to the towers and intermediate features are very superior to those commonly found in Renaissance cases. Compare them with the terminations shown in the preceding example, Fig. XIII. The Choir Organ, projected from the gallery, does not, while of very pleasing design, correspond in all details with the main Organ; we should pronounce it a later work by a different designer. Every part of this very beautiful case claims most careful study by the designer of to-day.

In the Cathedral of Saint-Brieuc (Côtes-du-Nord) there is in an elevated gallery at the west end of the nave, an imposing Organ, the main case of which is of Renaissance design, executed (with the exception of certain careful and accurate restorations) about the year 1540. The case was, according to M. Cavaillé-Coll, brought from England in the year named, but there certainly is no evidence of either English design or workmanship to be seen in it. At this date, Late Pointed architecture still obtained in England, and, although debased, it had not assumed a Renaissance garb such as covers every feature of this organ-case. This interesting Organ is shown in the accompanying Plate XIII. The manner in which the five salient portions of the case are adjusted in height, for the evident purpose of leaving the circular Flamboyant window unobstructed, goes far to prove that, wherever the case was made, it was designed for the place it occupies at present. Occasions may arise when designers will find it desirable to follow the precedent this case establishes and, accordingly, may study it with advantage.* The width of the case is about 23 feet, so the dimensions of the several parts can be readily approximated. The details throughout are good and well executed. The Choir Organ is modern, having been constructed in 1848, when M. Cavaillé-Coll restored the main Organ.

---

* In designing the case for the Organ in the Church of Our Lady of Grace, Hoboken, N. J., we had precisely the same conditions to meet; and, although the window was too low down to be entirely exposed, the case interferes with it very slightly—hardly any when viewed from the sanctuary of the church. This case is illuminated in colors and gold, and the pipes are gilded and, for the most part, covered with Gothic diaper-work executed in black and brown. The design was made to accord with the architecture of the interior of the church, which we had previously decorated. The case is illustrated in the Chapter on The Organ Specification.

PLATE XII

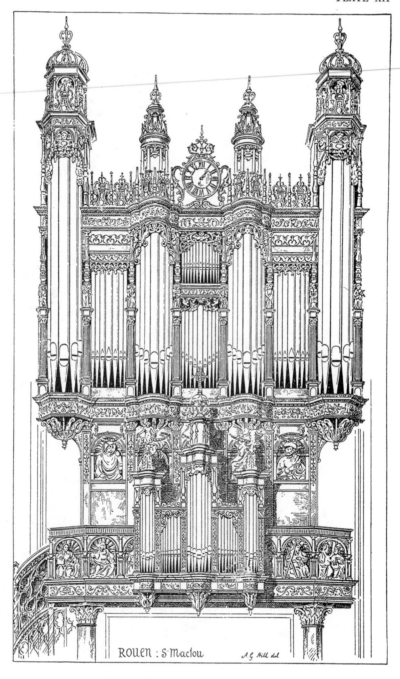

ROUEN : S· Maclou   A.G. Hill del

PLATE XIII

Of the three examples of English Renaissance organ-cases, which we are able to illustrate through the courtesy of Mr. Hill, the earliest is that in the magnificent Chapel of King's College, Cambridge, shown

Fig. XIV.

in Fig. XIV. This case is one of the oldest and most perfect examples of its class in England. It stands on a grand Renaissance screen of wood which divides the chapel into two portions. The Organ was built between the year 1606-09; but nothing of the original work save the case remains: fortunately it has been preserved, when one sees the artless abominations that are now being perpetrated in the direction of organ-cases. Both in France and England some beautiful and appropriate cases have been designed by able architects, but they are few and far between.

The organ-case now under consideration is dignified in its simplicity of outline, and in the characteristic manner in which the displayed pipes are arranged and the ornament is distributed. Originally, the more important pipes were embossed, and must have added greatly to the beauty of the work. The arms, crowns, and the Tudor badges—the portcullis and rose—have been introduced in sympathy with the architectural details of the chapel. The Choir Organ case is beautiful and in perfect keeping with the main case, and harmonizes perfectly with the superb stall-work below. As Mr. Hill remarks respecting the main case: "The case is kept low in the middle, so as to allow of a better view of the chapel [with its marvellous fan-traceried vault of stone] from end to end. It is of a comparatively small size, and a great portion of the present Organ is placed within the screen."

Of all the old examples preserved in England, we specially commend the case illustrated in Plate XIV. to the attention of the architect and designer of to-day. This Organ was built by Harris for Magdalen College, Oxford, in the year 1637; and one hundred years later was transferred to Tewkesbury Abbey, where it now stands.

The principal details of the case are in the early Renaissance style developed in England, commonly designated Elizabethan; and these go far to show what an admirable style it is for the ornamental woodwork of the organ-case. Almost numberless fine examples of art-woodwork of this period exist in the mansions throughout England; and as accurate drawings of these can be found in several books devoted to the art and architecture of the period, designers need not be at a loss for inspiration and suggestions. The general treatment of the woodwork of the case and its ornamentatal details are admirable; and the arrangement of the displayed pipes is good and effective. Here we find the embossed pipes introduced which were much in favor at the time. The lower entablature with its pendant arches is a fine and characteristic piece of work.

The Renaissance organ-case in Exeter Cathedral, constructed in 1665, presents an entirely different treatment, as shown by the view of its east front given in Fig. XV. Like the Organ in King's College Chapel, it stands on the center of the choir-screen. While the composition presents some good features, as a whole its teaching is largely of a negative character. The raising of the principal groups of pipes on a bracket above the level of all the other principal groups is an

PLATE XIV

Tewkesbury Abbey

A. G. Hill del.

by Wren [the greatest architect of his day], but there is no record of his having done so. If not Wren, probably the organ-builder was the designer of the case as well as of the Organ." We are inclined to say that the case itself is sufficient *record of Wren not having done so*. It is essentially an organ-builder's case, and an extraordinarily good one.

Numerous organ-cases of a refined and appropriate character were designed by English architects during the Gothic Revival, notably those for instruments of moderate dimensions. The larger cases, such as those in Chester Cathedral and the Church of St. Mary, Nottingham, are of a very elaborate description, but can hardly be pronounced entirely satisfactory. In these more important works there is a restlessness of treatment and a straining after effect which somewhat impairs their dignity. Simplicity and breadth of treatment in large cases, which have of necessity to be viewed from a considerable distance, are more effective and satisfactory than the most lavish display of broken-up features and carved enrichments. One may tolerate, or even approve of, the absence of repose, and the presence of an excess of elaboration, in a Renaissance design, but hardly in a pure Gothic one. Of the more artistically treated large organ-cases in English churches, that in the Church of St. Bartholomew, at Armley, illustrated in Plate XV., may be considered the most satisfactory. It is extremely effective in work, and enshrines one of Edmund Schulze's choicest instruments. The Organ stands on an arcaded and vaulted stone gallery in the north transept of the church, the arch of which it almost fills. The case is of oak throughout, boldly traceried and carved. Its general design and the disposition of its several parts are appropriate and harmonious, many of the details furnished by ancient organ-cases and mediæval woodwork of late date having been skilfully made use of. Light bands of ornamental wrought-iron are introduced to support the displayed pipes. Two figures of angels holding musical instruments surmount the canopies at the angles of the projection portion of the case. These angle features, containing three large pipes each, are supported, as it were, by large figures of angels carrying stringed instruments. Severe criticism might pronounce these figures out of place; certainly their omission would in no way injure the architectural propriety of the work. The three triplets of large pipes give strength to the composition, and are well disposed. The overhanging wings are boldly and artistically designed; while the compartments, filled with comparatively small pipes, on each side of the central feature, are beautifully and correctly treated. All the details are pure in style, and are executed in the true Gothic spirit. The organist's seat is in the central advanced portion of the elaborately traceried oak screen-work which surmounts the stone gallery, and gives so much value, in an architectural sense, to the entire composition.

Special notice must be taken of the organ-cases which stand at the north and south ends of the choir-screen in Westminster Abbey, one of which is illustrated in Plate XVI. While differing in general treatment from the Armley case, these cases are equally fine examples of Gothic design, and are well worthy of a place in the magnificent interior of the abbey church. They stand, as shown, against arches of the main arcade, and rise from the top of the choir-screen to the level of the beautiful triforia. Confining our attention to the case illustrated: the general disposition of all the leading features, and especially those in the upper portion of the case and including the lateral towers, leaves nothing to be desired; and the carved and pierced pipe-shades, the crestings, and the angel figures are beautifully designed and admirably executed. The large, projecting wings are also fine pieces of work. The lower portion of the case, between the towers, which has the appearance of a Choir Organ, but in this example closely attached, does not seem to join very happily with the rest of the composition. It would serve as a separate organ-case, but even then it would not be quite satisfactory. It is worthy of note that, in the true spirit of Gothic art, there is no repetition of design in any of the pipe-shades, pierced work, or surface carving. The crestings alone form necessary exceptions. The case was constructed from the design prepared by the late talented ecclesiastical architect, Mr. Pearson, R.A., of London.

Without a series of elaborate illustrations it would be profitless to attempt to describe the representative Gothic organ-cases which have been designed by the leading ecclesiastical architects of England, and notably those which have been designed by the late Mr. G. F. Bodley, A.R.A., of London. Unfortunately we are unable to give any illustrations of the beautiful works of this master. One example may be given to show what has been accomplished in the shape of a small Chancel Organ. In Plate XVII. is given a sketch of the Organ in Northington Church, Hants, designed by Mr. T. G. Jackson. It is obvious that, although this case is carried out in pure English Gothic, such cases as those of the Organs in the Cathedral of Zaragoza and the Marienkirche, at Lübeck, have been studied by the architect. The general effect of the case is good; and the treatment throughout is perfectly in accord with the material used in its construction. The organist sits behind the open portion of the screen. This is a very objectionable position as it renders it extremely difficult for him to realize the effect of the Organ and hear the voices of the choir.

We cannot close our brief remarks on modern Gothics organ-cases without directing attention to the remarkable and absolutely unique conception of the late Mr. William Burges, the distinguished and learned English architect. The case alluded to is illustrated in Fig. XVI. It is designed in a style of early Gothic of which Mr. Burges was a past master, and was intended for the Organ in the Cathedral of Lille (Nord). The idea which he had in his mind—he invariably had some leading idea controlling or pervading each artistic work he essayed—

Fig. XVI.

was evidently that of a Castle of Sound and Music. The strong resemblance in the leading features to the castellated architecture of the Middle Ages, and the remarkable system of pictorial decoration applied throughout, certainly support our opinion respecting the artist's motive.

PLATE XVI

PLATE XXI

adjuncts to organ-cases. In all instances these must be artistically introduced; and modeled in a style of simplicity and severity. Nothing in the shape of the grotesque and sprawling figures to be seen in many of the Organs on the Continent of Europe must be contemplated under any circumstances. In Church Organs, figures of angels playing musical instruments may occupy elevated positions on the tops of angle posts or canopies, or in niches or arcades designed to receive them; or with outspread wings, and carrying musical instruments or inscribed scrolls, at advanced angles or other salient points. While these and other appropriate figures may be executed in the same wood as the case and left plain, they will be much enhanced in value, for decorative purposes, if painted after the fashion of middle age sculpture. The treatment of the case generally will to a large extent dictate the method of decorating the figure work. For important positions in the case, other figures, such as King David with his attribute the harp, St. Cecilia bearing a Regal or Portative, St. Genesius with the violin, and St. Dunstan with his harp, are appropriate enrichments.

For the decorations of the cases of Concert-room and Chamber Organs, allegorical figures, representations of mythological personages connected with music, and statues of the great masters of organ music, may appropriately be introduced.

It is of course impossible to give rules of universal application for the decorative painting of Organs; but there is one piece of advice that may be given here, worthy of being remembered by decorators—Never overdo the work, but rather confine the decoration to that which is necessary to accentuate and harmonize all the features of the design; err on the side of simplicity rather than on that of over-elaboration; and employ only colors of refined and subdued tones, using gilding chiefly with the view of defining the leading structural and ornamental forms of the case. Gold is, however, not necessary, and unless used with great taste and judgment is better omitted; but this latter remark applies with equal force to all decorative painting.

The amount and style of decoration on the cases of Concert-room Organs will largely, if not entirely, be dictated by the decoration of the rooms in which they stand. The decorative painting should not be a very difficult matter if the cases have been designed in strict harmony with the architecture which surrounds them.

Great liberty is given in the decorative painting of Chamber Organs; and as it is comparatively small in extent, and will be closely viewed, it should be of the most beautiful and accurately executed character. Figure subjects painted in quiet colors upon gold grounds are desirable decorations. The framework and ornamental features may be of some rich wood, or stained black and relieved with gilding. The pipes may in all cases be delicately painted or of burnished tin, as individual taste may direct. A pleasing effect of soft color may be obtained by the use of woods of different tints, ranging from the soft white of holly to the black of ebony. Gilding may be again introduced to add richness to the design.

Decorative painting so far as Organs are concerned is, as a general rule, confined to the displayed pipe-work, true or sham, being used on pipes formed of zinc or common pipe-metal. Pipes formed of fine materials—tin or rich spotted metal—are rarely decorated. To decorate an organ pipe in a refined and thoroughly artistic manner requires careful study and no little ingenuity and skill; for it must always be remembered that the decoration must not appear to disturb the true form or construction of the pipe, on the contrary, it ought to accentuate its form. No words are sufficiently strong to condemn the meaningless and tasteless class of decorative painting almost universally met with in modern Organs, in which the coarseness of the patterns used is only surpassed by the vulgarity of the coloring.

Circular metal pipes are more difficult to decorate in an effective manner than quadrangular wooden ones; yet the latter are comparatively seldom, and in our opinion far too seldom, used for decorative purposes. In metal pipes, the foot and mouth present some difficulties in their treatment, and seem to demand a style of design which is out of sympathy with that most suitable for the cylindrical body. Diaper-work, band-work, and powderings, which are, generally speaking, suitable patterns for the body of a pipe, do not lend themselves to the conical surface of the foot or the conventional form of the mouth. This difficulty is overcome by having the foot and lower part of the body, up to a short distance above the upper lip of the mouth, either of plain gold or some quiet color, having a horizontal band of a simple pattern carried round its upper edge, so as to clearly mark the two divisions of the pipe. The cylindrical body, above this band, may be enriched in a great variety of ways, all of which group themselves under the three general classes of decoration above alluded to; namely, diaper-work, band-work, and powderings. Diaper-work includes all designs or patterns of a connected character, which repeat at regular intervals, and may be carried over any extent of surface. The most beautiful patterns of this class are those suggested by the rich velvets, cloths of gold, and silk brocades, of the fourteenth, fifteenth, and sixteenth centuries. Band-work includes those patterns which are composed of plain or ornamental bands or ribbons, disposed horizontally, vertically, diagonally, or in zigzag or chevronwise, or in any of these ways combined. The mural paintings and the illuminated manuscripts of the Middle Ages furnish good models for this class of decoration. Powdering is that class of ornamentation which, as its name implies, consists of detached devices, powdered or disposed at regular intervals over a plain ground. For Church Organs, powderings of symbols, emblems, and monograms are highly suitable; while for other Organs any devices are available that taste may suggest.

In the decoration of pipes, any of the above classes may be used alone on all surfaces suitable for their reception; but the introduction of horizontal bands along with either diapering or powdering has a good effect. In these compound treatments, colors must be introduced with caution so as not to produce disturbed and bizarre effects. Diaper patterns will, of necessity, be executed on plain grounds, either of color or gold. Black or dark brown diaper-work, of some evenly distributed and flowing design, executed on a mat gold ground has a singularly rich and refined effect. If a quieter and somewhat antique effect is desired—resembling that of old gilded leather decoration—the brightness of the gold ground should be toned down by the application of a tawny or light brown lacquer or varnish. A great amount of artistic taste and skill may be displayed in such high class pipe decoration.

Band-work and powderings may be applied to either gold or colored grounds, or to the bright surface of tin or spotted-metal. A very pleasing effect is produced by gilding the lower portion of a spotted-metal pipe, banding it at the top edge of the gold (as previously directed), and then powdering the upper surface of the body with a conventional floral or symbolical device, executed in bright colors and gold outlined with black. We have decorated towers of large pipes in this manner with most satisfactory results. To preserve the decorations and gilding, and also to prevent the surface of the spotted-metal becoming tarnished and dull, we varnished the whole with a single coat of fine French oil varnish. After twenty years of exposure, and repeated washings with clean cold water, we found the surface of the pipes as perfect as the day they were finished. For this class of decoration, we prefer pipes made of a metal having a large and boldly-marked spot to the finer confluent variety which almost resembles pure tin in appearance.

Quadrangular wood pipes are not so difficult to decorate as cylindrical metal ones. This is owing to their having uniform flat surfaces with defined edges, and, under usual conditions, presenting only the front surface for ornamentation. Besides this, they have neither the awkwardly-shaped mouths nor the long conical feet of the metal pipes; indeed, such feet as they have are rarely shown in such a way as to require anything beyond plain painting. The mouths of wood pipes, which consist (except when inverted) of a plain sloped part within quadrangular lines, are best treated in a perfectly plain manner, either gilded, or colored some appropriate tint, contrasting with the rest of the painting. The caps, below the mouths, may be decorated in various ways. They should, to start with, be formed with a view to their ultimate decoration, having some simple mouldings worked upon them, horizontally, for the reception of lines of color. It is hardly necessary to say that in flats, formed of quadrangular pipes, the decoration should be such as to produce a satisfactory general effect; that is, all the pipes should be treated alike in design and coloring. Sometimes pipes have been painted in two designs, alternating; but, except in small groups, say of three or five, this treatment is rarely successful. Whatever description of pattern is selected for the pipes, it must be graduated in all its measurements and details to suit the different sizes of the same. There will, accordingly, require to be as many drawings, stencils, etc., as there are pipes to be decorated. We have tested this system of decoration with an eminently successful result. A flat of fifteen small-scaled Bourdon pipes was decorated with a graduated diaper and band design, executed in black and brown upon gold grounds; brighter tints appearing only on the mouldings of the caps and the stopper handles. The diaper pattern began and ended in precisely the same manner on every pipe, being accurately drawn to suit the different lengths and widths in all cases.*

Powderings and banded patterns are more easily graduated to fit the different sizes of pipes than diaper designs; but they do not produce effects of so pleasing a character. Bands, whether applied to cylindrical metal or quadrangular wood pipes, should never be placed spirally or diagonally, like the bands on a barber's pole; for, so disposed, they produce an unpleasant and restless effect, destructive of all dignity and artistic propriety. On metal pipes, they should be placed only horizontally or in chevron fashion; and on wood pipes, they should be chiefly used in the horizontal position; but in certain designs, for large pipes, vertical bands, close to the angles of the pipes, have a satisfactory appearance. The golden rule in organ-pipe decoration is: Use no designs which tend to destroy the true forms of the pipes, and select those which are simple in their forms and combinations. Avoid all loud and vulgar coloring, and a great variety of colors.

* In the Chamber Organ designed and constructed by the author of this treatise, the front swell-box (there are two in the instrument) is most elaborately treated. It comes forward to within about nine inches of the front line of the case below, and has only a single rank of stopped wood pipes in advance of it. These pipes fall downward in a curve to the center so as to allow the upper part of the swell-box to be seen. The box is enriched at each end with arched paneling, fully decorated; and is surmounted by a deep moulded cornice and battlemented cresting, also richly decorated. The louvres, horizontally placed, in front, are painted with a conventionalized rose-tree spreading over a gold trellis, the horizontal bars of which fall at the lower edges of the louvres. The wooden pipes, in advance of this, fifteen in number, are entirely gilded on their exposed surfaces and decorated with a quaint, 15th-century, diaper executed in black and brown: their caps are moulded and accentuated with quiet coloring. As the pipes are stopped and their stopper-handles are ornamental and shown, it is obvious that all the fifteen are of different lengths. This irregularity has been studied, and imparts a pleasing feeling of freedom to the front. The pipes have been so carefully scaled and regulated that their heights graduate in a symmetrical manner, and exactly the same amount of each stopper-handle appears. The diaper pattern is correctly graduated, so that all the pipes are alike as regards the number of repeats in length and width. The effect produced by these gold and black pipes against the rose-trellis background of the swell-box is extremely rich and refined. The sides of the central portion of the Organ and its lateral extensions are fronted by the wooden pipes of the Pedal Organ Contra-Basso, 16 ft., and the Diapason, 16 ft. These are decorated with plain gold, and gold ornamentation upon black grounds. This Organ is illustrated on Plate V., Vol. I., p. 340 of "The Art of Organ-Building."

It is to be regretted that the art of decorating metal pipes by means of embossing has been so largely neglected; entirely so by American organ-builders. Attempts have been made by certain English architects to revive the art; and under the directions of the late Mr. G. F. Bodley, embossed pipes have been introduced in his beautiful organ-cases. They appear in the Organs in the Churches of St. Paul, Burton-on-Trent, and St. John the Baptist, Tue Brook, Liverpool: both designed by this consummate artist. Numerous old examples are still preserved from which suggestions for appropriate and easily executed patterns can be obtained.

In a general treatise, like the present, it is quite impossible to discuss a complex subject, such as the artistic decoration of the Organ, in any degree of completeness; and no detailed description of decorative systems would be understood without an elaborate series of colored designs, which is quite beyond the limits of this Work. Enough has been said, perhaps, to induce those really interested in organ-building and its artistic development to pay more attention to the proper decoration of the different classes of instruments. At present the art is in a most neglected state; and we fear it will remain so until the Organ is once more looked upon as worthy of the highest consideration by architects and decorative artists of eminence and skill.

MEDIÆVAL PORTATIVE.

SMALL ORGAN OF THE FIFTEENTH CENTURY:
FROM ENGRAVING BY ISRAEL VAN MECKENEM.

CHAPTER II.

THE TONAL STRUCTURE OF THE ORGAN.

UCH of the unsatisfactory character of the majority of modern Organs may safely be attributed to imperfections or shortcomings in their Tonal Structure. This is the conclusion arrived at after careful study of a great number of representative instruments constructed by European and American builders; and the conviction is, accordingly, forced upon us that the true acoustical laws directly bearing on the tonal structure of the Organ are either generally misunderstood or insufficiently worked upon by organ-builders. It is not too much to say that it is hopeless to expect an Organ to be entirely satisfactory unless the laws which govern the production of refined compound musical sounds are fully recognized and carefully followed in the development of its tonal structure. To direct the reader's attention to these laws, so far, at least, as they have a direct bearing on the stop appointment of the Organ, is the purpose of the present Chapter.

Our attention was first directed to the acoustical phenomena resulting from the combination of the tones of organ-pipes of different pitches about forty-five years ago, by the great French organ-builder Aristide Cavaillé-Coll. This scientific builder entertained us in his studio, in Paris, with a long and instructive disquisition on the phenomena, illustrated by a very ingenious apparatus of his own invention, by means of which the several acoustical effects produced by the combination of the tones of organ-pipes were made evident, in a striking manner, to the ear. Since then we have fully investigated the subject, satisfying our mind on the great importance of its proper recognition in the scientific and artistic tonal appointment of the Organ.

It is not universally known that all the stops, or ranks of pipes, higher in pitch than the prime or fundamental tones of the instrument, are introduced in the Organ in strict accordance with the natural laws of sound; and that the octave, and all the higher mutation tones are introduced, with the view of substantiating or corroborating similar tones naturally present, but in an undesirably weak condition, in the prime tones of the foundation unison stops, and of building up a complete harmonic structure, pregnant with tonal vitality and brilliancy. Such, however, is the case.

It is not proposed in this treatise to go into a lengthy scientific dissertation on the subject just introduced; but enough must be said to make its particular bearings clear to the reader.

It has long been known to certain physicists and special investigators that the ear, in attentively listening to the sounds produced by stringed and other musical instruments, realizes the presence of tones higher in pitch than those which are known as the fundamental or prime tones; and that it is owing to the perfect proportion and combination of these over-tones with the prime tones that the resultant compound sounds of the musical instruments are rich and beautiful to our sense of hearing. Theoretically the series of over-tones has a great, if not a limitless, upward range; but practically, it is bounded by the very circumscribed powers of the human ear. The over-tones forming this series are known as *harmonics, harmonic upper partial tones, upper partials,* or *over-tones* of the prime tone. The prime tone is designated, in addition to the simple term *prime,* the *fundamental tone,* the *ground tone,* and the *prime partial tone.* The prime tone is the lowest and most powerful and assertive of all the partial tones, and by it we judge the pitch of the whole compound tone. The term *compound tone* is used to designate the musical tone compounded of the predominant prime partial and all the upper partial tones it embraces. The upper partials bear a definite relationship to the prime tone; and this relationship is invariably the same in the compound tones produced by musical instruments. The complete series of upper partials is, however, not invariably present in such compound tones; their presence or absence, as well as their relative degrees of strength or assertiveness, determining the quality or *timbre* of the compound tones of which they are constituents. These are important facts in musical acoustics which should never be lost sight of by the artist in tone-production. Before proceeding farther it is desirable to lay before the reader particulars respecting the upper partial tones necessary to be recognized by the organ-builder in the tonal structure of the Organ.

The *First Upper Partial Tone* is that generated by twice the number of vibrations required to produce the prime or fundamental tone. Thus, if the prime tone is CC, yielded by an open pipe of say 8 feet speaking length, which, for the sake of argument, may be accepted as having 64 vibrations per second, the first upper partial is C, the prime tone yielded by an open pipe of say 4 feet speaking length, having 128 vibrations per second. Accordingly, in the tonal structure of

great a degree of brilliancy, or harmonic complexity and richness of coloring, may be imparted to it by the addition of numerous higher tones, its true prime pitch must not be disturbed. There must be no screaming quality, no flutter of acute tones as if they were endeavoring

DIVISIONS OF STRING YIELDING PARTIAL TONES.	NOTATION OF THE PARTIAL TONES.	THEORETICAL LENGTHS OF OPEN ORGAN PIPES.		NUMBER OF DOUBLE VIBRATIONS PER SECOND.
Full length	Prime tone.	8 feet	—	64
$\frac{1}{2}$ length	1st Upper partial.	4 "	—	128
$\frac{1}{3}$ "	2nd Upper partial.	$2\frac{2}{3}$ "	—	192
$\frac{1}{4}$ "	3rd Upper partial.	2 "	—	256
$\frac{1}{5}$ "	4th Upper partial.	$1\frac{3}{5}$ "	—	320
$\frac{1}{6}$ "	5th Upper partial.	$1\frac{1}{3}$ "	—	384
$\frac{1}{7}$ length. Between	6th Upper partial.	$1\frac{1}{7}$ feet	—	448
$\frac{1}{8}$ "	7th Upper partial.	1 "	—	512
$\frac{1}{10}$ "	9th Upper partial.	$\frac{4}{5}$ "	—	640
$\frac{1}{12}$ "	11th Upper partial.	$\frac{2}{3}$ "	—	768
$\frac{1}{16}$ "	15th Upper partial.	$\frac{1}{2}$ "	—.	1024

to drag the prime tone upward in pitch; on the contrary, the prime tone must be more firmly established and more satisfactory to the musical ear with the entire harmonic structure added than when heard without it. This most desirable result can only be attained by the accurate proportionment of all the upper partial tones to the prime.

The first upper partial tone, commonly furnished by the OCTAVE, or so-called PRINCIPAL, 4 FT., must be distinctly secondary in power to the prime tone, and of a sympathetic or mixing quality. Speaking in a general way, and in the full knowledge that circumstances alter cases, if we accept the strength of the prime tone to be equal to 100, we may accept the proportionate value of the first upper partial tone as 70. The effect produced by sounding a single note of the OPEN DIAPASON and the OCTAVE, 4 FT., combined, must be distinctly different from that produced by the same note and its octave on the OPEN DIAPASON alone. This marked difference of tonal effect will not, under proper conditions, be due only to the different strengths of the tones of the two octaves; but to the fact that the independent OCTAVE correctly corroborates the first upper partial tone of the DIAPASON prime, and that it loses its individuality in that prime tone, enriching, without affecting, its pitch.

The second upper partial tone represented by the TWELFTH, $2\frac{2}{3}$ FT., must be softer and lighter than the first upper partial; otherwise a disturbing and *timbre-altering* effect will be apparent. A perceptible difference will, however, be sufficient to secure tonal homogeneity and a rich musical coloring. Still accepting the value of the prime tone as 100, the second upper partial may have the proportionate value of 60. This and the first upper partial tone are the two most prominent harmonic over-tones commonly observed in the compound sounds produced by bowed strings and the small-scaled organ-pipes of the VIOL family. Accordingly, such harmonics call for a more decided reinforcement or corroboration than any of those which are higher in pitch.

The third upper partial tone ranks next in importance; but should, in the tonal structure of the Organ, where it is represented by the SUPER-OCTAVE or FIFTEENTH, 2 FT., be considerably softer and less assertive in its tonality than the preceding upper partial. Its proportionate value may be accepted as 50, or just one-half the strength of the fundamental or prime tone. This and the two preceding upper partial tones may be correctly classified as harmonics of the first order.

The fourth upper partial tone, represented by the TIERCE or SEVEN-TEENTH, $1\frac{3}{5}$ FT., must be decidedly weaker than the third upper partial; its proportionate value being about 40. When the TIERCE is inserted of too great a strength of tone it produces a somewhat harsh effect, giving to the harmonic a false or unnatural relation to the prime tone, rather than simply corroborating it and imparting a fulness to the compound tone.

The fifth upper partial tone, represented by the NINETEENTH or LARIGOT, $1\frac{1}{3}$ FT., must be slightly softer than the fourth; its proportionate value in relation to the prime tone may be accepted as 35. This is also a somewhat uncommon stop in a complete and separate form, although, like all the following more acute harmonic-corroborating ranks, it frequently appears in the composition of MIXTURES or compound stops.

The sixth upper partial tone, which, in the complete tonal structure of the Organ, is furnished by the SEPTIÈME, $1\frac{1}{7}$ FT., requires to be most skilfully proportioned in strength of intonation. This is essential from the fact that it is the first dissonant interval in the harmonic series—the so-called "sub-minor seventh." This stop has seldom been introduced by organ-builders, doubtless on account of the difficulties which beset its scientific adjustment.

The most noteworthy instances of the introduction of the SEPTIÈME we know of are furnished by the Grand Organ in the Cathedral of Notre-Dame, at Paris, constructed by M. Cavaillé-Coll, in 1868. In this noble instrument the SEPTIÈME is introduced in the 32 feet, 16 feet, and 8 feet harmonic series, being respectively stops of $4\frac{4}{7}$ feet, $2\frac{2}{7}$ feet, and $1\frac{1}{7}$ feet speaking lengths.

The sixth upper partial is naturally weak; accordingly, the SEPTIÈME must be of very small scale and delicate intonation. As it corroborates an over-tone of comparatively small importance, it may be omitted except in Organs of the first magnitude in which completeness of tonal structure is aimed at. Its effect in the Notre-Dame Organ is highly satisfactory. The presence of this stop necessitates the introduction, in a complete form, of the stop which corroborates the next higher upper partial tone. The sixth must invariably be covered by the seventh upper partial tone.

The seventh upper partial tone, represented in the tonal structure of the Organ by the TWENTY-SECOND, 1 FT., the most acute stop ever introduced in a complete form,—that is, throughout the entire range of the manual clavier,—must be rather more assertive than the SEPTIÈME, being a perfect consonant of the prime tone. Its proportionate value may be accepted as being about 30. The TWENTY-SECOND, as a distinct and complete stop, appears in a few English, German, Dutch, and French Organs, but its general adoption seems to have met with little favor. Of course it appears in the Organ of Notre-Dame, where its presence is compulsory on account of the SEPTIÈME. In all instruments of any pretension to completeness the TWENTY-SECOND appears, in certain parts of the compass, as a rank in one or more of the MIXTURES.

It will be sufficient for our present purpose to speak of the higher upper partial tones as invariably represented, in a broken manner, in the tonal structure of the Organ by ranks of the compound stops or MIXTURES. The upper partials commonly corroborated by these ranks are the ninth, eleventh, and fifteenth, under the names, respectively, of TWENTY-FOURTH, TWENTY-SIXTH, and TWENTY-NINTH. In rare instances the still higher upper partial tones; namely, the nineteenth, twenty-third, and thirty-first, are corroborated by the ranks known respectively as the THIRTY-FIRST, the THIRTY-THIRD, and THIRTY-SIXTH. Owing to the small size of the pipes required for such high-pitched ranks, it is obvious that they can only be introduced in the bass octave of the manual compass. As a separate Chapter is specially devoted to the consideration of all important questions appertaining to the MIX-TURES, it is unnecessary to enlarge here on the subject of the upper partial tones they are intended to corroborate, beyond stating, emphatically that, in accordance with the natural phenomena of musical sounds, they must be softer than all the preceding upper partial tones, and be relatively softer as they rise in pitch.

From what has already been said in the present Chapter, the reader will have grasped much that is essential to be understood relative to the harmonic structure of the Organ; and the reasons for the introduction, throughout the compass of the instrument, of certain mutation ranks of pipes, which on first impressions might appear to be entirely out of place, and productive of discord rather than that solidity and grandeur of tone which places the Organ at the head of all musical instruments fabricated by man.

It has been very generally held by those who have not made the subject of compound-tone production a special study, that the tone of the DIAPASON of the Organ is in itself complete and satisfying to the ear; but this is correct to a certain extent only, beautiful and unique as is the tone of the true fundamental DIAPASON in its most characteristic form. Stops of this species, even in their best form, are naturally deficient in upper partial tones, yielding very few that are appreciable by the unaided ear, and, accordingly, have a decided tendency to become heavy and dull in tone when used alone in harmony, especially in the bass and tenor octaves. The use of two or more unison stops of the same class in combination only increases the evil, and proves the inherent shortcomings of the genus. The trained musical ear can never be altogether satisfied with the tone of a simple OPEN DIAPASON: the almost total absence of that quality which makes the compound tones of bowed instruments so rich and gratifying is realized by the ear with a feeling of dissatisfaction. The purer and grander the OPEN DIAPASON is, viewed from the position it should occupy in the tonal structure of the Organ, the less it will satisfy the musical sense when used alone in harmony. A melodic succession of single notes will, on the other hand, be pleasing so far as it goes. Like single tones produced by tuning-forks, the single notes will not strike the ear with any feeling of incompleteness: their near approach to simplicity now becomes an element of beauty. But it is foreign to the true office of the OPEN DIAPASON to be used or considered as a solo stop: to all intents and purposes it is the foundation of the tonal structure of the Organ, incomplete without its appropriate superstructure, just as the foundation of a building is incomplete or valueless without the walls and roof which are destined to give it purpose and the reason for being.

In the foregoing remarks we have briefly treated of the acoustical theory on which the tonal structure of the Organ is based, and have pointed out the only method, in strict accordance with the phenomena of sound, by which a satisfactory compound tone can be given to a series of organ-pipes. It now becomes expedient to enter on the consideration of the subject of the present Chapter in a more extended manner. Hitherto, in speaking of the harmonic series of stops, we have confined it to its relation to the fundamental OPEN DIAPASON, yielding the prime tone. This has been done purposely with the view of impressing the reader with the fact that the harmonic series of stops yielding the upper partial tones of the prime must be schemed with reference to the tonal strength of the *one stop*, producing the prime tone, *which is the foundation of the true organ-tone* in whatever division of the Organ it may be located.

It is a very common impression, shared, as has been shown, by the writer of the remarks above quoted, that the harmonic-corroborating stops of the Organ can and should only be used when something approaching the full organ is drawn in combination. This has evidently been a hard and fast conviction among organ-builders for a long period, hence the screaming and unduly-pronounced character of all their harmonic-corroborating stops, simple and compound. We hold a widely different view to this, and unhesitatingly affirm that, while the harmonic-corroborating stops should be proportioned with direct reference to the fundamental unison of the division in which they appear, they should be so far independent of that unison as to be available in combination with one or more of the other unison stops also. Many valuable tonal effects can be obtained by the judicious and artistic combination of such stops, when they are scientifically schemed; while similar combinations of such stops as are commonly met with in Organs of the ordinary class are practically valueless for musical purposes. It must be obvious to every one who gives the subject consideration, that if four or five stops (probably embracing eight or ten ranks of pipes) are placed in any division of an Organ, which can only be properly used when the full division is drawn, their utility is, to say the least of it, undesirably circumscribed; and, accordingly, an absence of variety and flexibility becomes apparent in the tonal structure of the entire division.

It may be asked at this point: If all the harmonic series of stops, yielding the upper partial tones, is calculated from the OPEN DIAPASON alone, and is so scaled and voiced as to be perfectly satisfactory when drawn with that stop only, what is the state of affairs when the same series is employed with the full power or resources of the division of the instrument which contains it? In answering this question, we may point

and it now becomes expedient to enlarge somewhat on the rôle played by the Octave in the acoustics of the Organ. It may be accepted as having three important offices in the tonal structure of the instrument. First, it introduces the most necessary upper partial tone of the prime organ-tone. Secondly, it corroborates the same upper partial which exists, in a weak condition, in the compound tones of certain unison stops. Thirdly, it very decidedly augments and enriches, by the production of the *differential tone,* the prime tone with which it is associated. Of the first and second offices we have already spoken to some length; of the third we have still to speak.

It has long been observed by those engaged in the investigation of the properties of musical sounds, that when two loud tones of different pitches are sounded simultaneously there is heard a combinational tone distinct from both the generating tones. The pitch of this combinational tone is, as a rule, different from that of the generating tones and their upper partials. There is a notable exception, however, to this rule in the combinational tone produced by the simultaneous sounding of a prime tone and its first upper partial or octave.

Sorge discovered that when two tones of different vibrational numbers are sounded together a third is produced, whose vibrational number is exactly the sum of the difference of the vibrational numbers of the two generating tones. This third tone has, accordingly, been appropriately designated the *differential tone* of the two tones which create it.* In addition to this differential tone there is another tone generated by the simultaneous and prolonged sounding of two musical tones of different pitches. This combinational tone was first discovered by Helmholtz, and called by him the *summational tone,* because the number of its vibrations is the sum of the vibrations of both the generating tones. With this latter combinational tone we do not profess to have much to do in our present essay; but we are not prepared to say that it is not a somewhat important factor in the tonal structure of a well-balanced Organ. To the differential tones and their obvious influence on the tonal structure of the Organ we have to devote considerable attention.

Let us first investigate the differential tone of two tones which stand in the relationship of a perfect octave to each other. Under these conditions the differential tone has the same vibrational number as the lower of the two generating tones, thus:—

Generating Tones.		Differential Tone.
CC 8 ft. — C 4 ft.	. . .	CC 8 ft. tone
64 128		64 vibrations

* During the visit to the studio of M. Cavaillé-Coll, alluded to in the opening remarks in the present chapter, we were clearly shown the great importance of the *differential tones* produced by organ pipes. This was demonstrated on the ingenious apparatus constructed on scientific lines by M. Cavaillé-Coll. During the experiments, not only the existence but also the

The bearing of this acoustical phenomenon on the tonality of the Organ cannot be disputed; for it must be recognized that the differential tone has an existence outside the generating tone of its own pitch, and that it does not lose itself in that generating tone, but is added to it and proportionately enriches or augments its volume. This fact is proved by analogy. The great value of the OCTAVE stops, in their dual office in the tonal structure of the Organ, is thus made evident.

Helmholtz remarks: "On investigating the combinational tones of two compound musical tones, we find that the primary and upper partial tones may give rise to both differential and summational tones. In such cases the number of combinational tones is very great. But it must be observed that generally the differential are stronger than the summational tones, and that the stronger generating simple tones produce stronger combinational tones. The combinational tones, indeed, increase in a much greater ratio than the generating tones, and diminish also more rapidly. Now since in musical compound tones the prime generally predominates over the partials, the differential tones of the two primes are generally heard more loudly than all the rest, and were consequently first discovered. They are most easily heard when the generating tones are less than an octave apart, because in that case the differential is deeper than either of the two generating tones." *

The most striking proof of this latter fact that can be given, in connection with the tonal structure of the Organ, is the creation of the so-called "acoustic bass," of 32 ft. pitch, by the simultaneous sounding of two pipes of 16 ft. and 10⅔ ft. speaking length respectively. It will be found that the differential tone is an octave lower in pitch than the deeper of the two generating tones, thus :—

GENERATING TONES.		DIFFERENTIAL TONE.
CCC 16 FT. — GGG 10⅔ FT.	. . .	CCCC 32 FT. TONE
32 48		16 vibrations

Considerable use has been made of this differential tone in the stop apportionment of large Pedal Organs; and although the deep bass tone so produced cannot be compared to that yielded by an independent stop of 32 ft. pitch, it is of some value in its power of enriching and adding gravity to the tonality of the Pedal Organ.

In speaking of the differential tone in connection with the manual stops, we pointed out the importance of the OCTAVES, or stops of 4 ft.

prominence of the *differential tones,* produced by the simultaneous sounding of pairs of organ pipes of different pitches, were made evident to the unaided ear. In some cases the *differential tones* were almost as loud as the voices of the pipes which generated them. That the presence of such tones in an Organ must exercise a great influence on its general tonality is beyond question: and the subject deserves more attention than has as yet been accorded to it.

* "On the Sensations of Tone." London, 1875. p. 230.

pitch: let us now see what good office is fulfilled by those harmonic-corroborating stops which stand at the interval of a perfect fifth apart. At the outset, we find that the two ranks of pipes which corroborate the two most important upper partials of the fundamental unison prime are the OCTAVE and TWELFTH, a perfect fifth apart. The differential tone produced in this case is, as in that above given, an octave below the deeper of the two generating tones, and, accordingly, in unison with the prime tone, thus :—

PRIME TONE.	GENERATING TONES.		DIFFERENTIAL TONE.
CC 8 FT.	C 4 FT. —	G 2⅔ FT.	CC 8 FT. TONE
64	128	192	64 vibrations

Carrying our investigations just one step farther, we come to the differential tone produced by the simultaneous sounding of the ranks which represent the second and third upper partials of the unison prime; namely, the TWELFTH and SUPER-OCTAVE or FIFTEENTH. These ranks of pipes stand at the interval of a perfect fourth apart; and their differential tone is precisely the same as that produced by both the pairs of ranks previously spoken of, and which stand, respectively, at the intervals of a perfect octave and a perfect fifth apart. Accordingly we find the differential tone of the TWELFTH and FIFTEENTH is in unison with the prime tone, thus :—

PRIME TONE.	GENERATING TONES.		DIFFERENTIAL TONE.
CC 8 FT.	G 2⅔ FT.—	c^1 2 FT.	CC 8 FT. TONE
64	192	256	64 vibrations

It is, perhaps, unnecessary to go much farther with this analysis, interesting as it is from the scientific point of view. Although there is no doubt that the differential tones of all the stops of different pitch exert an influence on the general tonality of the Organ, more or less appreciable to the cultivated ear, those which we have above noted are of the greatest importance from a practical point of view. We have directed attention to the fact that the ranks of pipes which yield the unison or prime tone, and the first, second, and third upper partials of that tone, and which stand toward each other, respectively, in couples, at the intervals of a perfect octave, a perfect fifth, and a perfect fourth, produce differential tones which are all alike so far as their vibrational numbers are concerned, and which go to the improvement of the prime or foundation tone. It only remains for us to direct attention to the fact that the entire series of differential tones, resulting from the simultaneous sounding of any couple of ranks, standing respectively at the intervals of a third, fourth, fifth, octave, twelfth, fifteenth, nineteenth, and twenty-second, either accentuate the foundation tone or one or other of its upper partial tones.

The following Table, given for ready reference, explains and summarizes what has been said. The letters following those which indicate the pitch or position of the notes in the musical scale signify: foundation or prime tone [P.T.]; first upper partial [1, U.P.]; second upper partial [2, U.P.]; third upper partial [3, U.P.]; fourth upper partial [4, U.P.]; fifth upper partial [5, U.P.]; sixth upper partial [6, U.P.]; seventh upper partial [7, U.P.].

TABLE OF DIFFERENTIAL TONES GENERATED BY THE PRIME AND UPPER PARTIAL TONES, REPRESENTED BY THE DIAPASON, 8 FEET, AND THE HARMONIC-CORROBORATING STOPS OF THE ORGAN.

Generating Tones.		Differential Tones.
CC [P. T.] —— C [1, U. P.]	. . .	CC [P. T.]
64 vibrations 128 vibrations		64 vibrations
CC [P. T.] —— G [2, U.P.]	. . .	C [1, U. P.]
64 " 192 "		128 "
CC [P. T.] —— c¹ [3, U. P.]	. .	G [2, U. P.]
64 " 256 "		192 "
CC [P. T.] —— e¹ [4, U. P.]	. . .	c¹ [3, U. P.]
64 " 320 "		256 "
CC [P. T.] ·—— g¹ [5, U. P.]	. . .	e¹ [4, U. P.]
64 " 384 "		320 "
CC [P. T.] —— c² [7, U. P.]	. . .	Septième [6, U. P.]
64 " 512 "		448 "

C [1, U.P.]—— G [2, U.P.]	. . .	CC [P. T.]
128 " 192 "		64 "
C [1, U.P.]—— c¹ [3, U. P.]	. . .	C [1, U. P.]
128 " 256 "		128 "
C [1, U.P.]—— e¹ [4, U. P.]	. . .	G [2, U. P.]
128 vibrations 320 vibrations		192 vibrations
C [1, U.P.]—— g¹ [5, U. P.]	. .	c¹ [3, U. P.]
128 " 384 "		256 "
C [1, U.P.]—— c² [7, U. P.]	. . .	g¹ [5, U. P.]
128 " 512 "		384 "

G [2, U.P.]—— c¹ [3, U. P.]	. . .	CC [P. T.]
192 " 256 "		64 "
G [2, U.P.]—— e¹ [4, U. P.]	. . .	C [1, U. P.]
192 " 320 "		128 "
G [2, U.P.]—— g¹ [5, U. P.]	. . .	G [2, U. P.]
192 " 384 "		192 "
G [2, U.P.]—— c² [7, U. P.]	. . .	e¹ [4, U. P.]
192 " 512 "		320 "

c^1 [3, U.P.]—— e^1 [4, U.P.]	. . .	CC [P. T.]
256 " 320 "		64 "
c^1 [3, U.P.]—— g^1 [5, U.P.]	. . .	C [1, U. P.]
256 " 384 "		128 "
c^1 [3, U.P.]—— c^2 [7, U.P.]	. . .	c^1 [3, U. P.]
256 " 512 "		256 "

---

e^1 [4, U.P.]—— g^1 [5, U. P.]	. . .	CC [P. T.]
320. " 384 "		64 "
e^1 [4, U.P]—— c^2 [7, U.P.]	. . .	G [2, U P.]
320 " 512 "		192 "

---

g^1 [5, U.P.]—— c^2 [7, U. P.]	. . .	C [1, U P.]
384 " 512 "		128 "

In the above Table no notice has been taken of the sixth upper partial, represented in the tonal structure of the Organ by the SEPTIÈME, beyond the fact that it appears as the differential tone of the prime and its seventh upper partial (c^2). When the SEPTIÈME is inserted as a stop in the Organ it enters into the general scheme in the same favorable manner as do all the other harmonic-corroborating stops. This will be realized from the subjoined Table:

TABLE OF DIFFERENTIAL TONES GENERATED BY THE PRIME AND SEVERAL UPPER PARTIAL TONES AND THE SIXTH UPPER PARTIAL TONE REPRESENTED BY THE SEPTIÈME, 1¼ FEET.

GENERATING TONES.		DIFFERENTIAL TONES.
CC [P. T.]—— [SEPTIÈME]	. . .	g^1 [5, U. P.]
64 vibrations 448 vibrations		384 vibrations
C [1, U.P.]—— [SEPTIÈME]	. . .	e^1 [4, U. P.]
128 " 448 "		320 "
G [2, U.P.]—— [SEPTIÈME]	. . .	c^1 [3, U. P.]
192 " 448 "		256 "
c^1 [3, U.P.]—— [SEPTIÈME]	. . .	G [2, U. P.]
256 " 448 "		192 "
e^1 [4, U.P.]—— [SEPTIÈME)	. . .	C [1, U. P.]
320 " 448 "		128 "
g^1 [5, U.P.]—— [SEPTIÈME]	. . .	CC [P. T.]
384 " 448 "		64 "
[SEPTIÈME] —— c^2 [7, U.P.]	. . .	CC [P. T.]
448 " 512 "		64 "

It must surely be realized, on a careful consideration of all the foregoing data, that the tonal structure of the Organ is a matter of great importance both in its theoretical and practical aspects; and that it is one the organ-builder who desires to become an artist in his calling cannot afford to ignore or even neglect.   There can be no doubt, as has already been said, that the shortcomings and self-evident crudities in the tonality of too many Organs are due to the ignorance or wilful neglect of the acoustical principles or laws which should govern their stop appointment and all matters relating thereto.   M. Cavaillé-Coll was the only organ-builder known to us who systematically approached the stop appointment of the Organ from the scientific side; and his tonal schemes, though not invariably all that could be wished, may be studied with great advantage.

In the present Chapter, in giving the vibrational numbers of the different tones, we have used the scale adopted by the French physicists, and in accordance with which the beautiful acoustical apparatus constructed by Dr. Kœnig, of Paris, is adjusted.   This physical and untempered scale gives middle c^1 512 single vibrations per second according to the French method of counting the forward motion of a swinging body as one vibration, and the backward as another.   English acousticians count the backward and forward motion as a single vibration.   We have, accordingly, adopted the latter method, giving middle c^1 256 vibrations per second.   The pitch of the scale adopted by the German physicists, at the suggestion of Scheibler, in 1834, gives 440 double vibrations to the note a^1, and to middle c^1 264.   This pitch is the one followed by Prof. Helmholtz throughout his work " On the Sensations of Tone."

Before concluding the present brief dissertation, a few words may appropriately be said on the limits of the human ear with reference to musical sounds.   It is somewhat difficult to determine the point, in the downward range, at which the musical character of sounds may be said to cease.   Helmholtz, whose accuracy of observation, so far as the phenomena of sound are concerned, can hardly be called in question, places the point about the lowest note of the four-stringed Double Bass of the orchestra; namely, EEE of 41·25 vibrations per second.   He remarks that the musical character of all tones below this note " is imperfect, because we are here near the limit of the power of the ear to combine vibrations into musical tones.   These lower tones cannot therefore be used musically except in connection with their higher octaves, to which they impart a character of greater depth without rendering the conception of the pitch indeterminate."   The common impression, among persons interested in organ matters, is that musical sounds of determinate character descend to the 32 ft. note,—CCCC of 16·5 vibrations per second,—and some go so far, in direct opposition to known facts, as to believe that certain notes in the 64 ft. octave can be appreciated by the ear as musical sounds.   It is difficult to understand on what grounds, theoretical or practical, such a monster as the 64 ft. reed stop in the pedal department of the Organ in the Centennial Hall, Sydney, was ever constructed: it is in its lower octave as devoid of musical tone as the rattling of a Venetian shutter.

That the sound yielded by an open pipe of 32 ft. speaking length can be heard as a low rumbling we freely admit; but that it has *per se* a determinate musical character we unhesitatingly deny, and we are supported in this firm opinion by all the weight of Helmholtz's investigations. We have no intention of advocating, on these grounds, the disuse of the 32 ft. octave in the Organ, but we must impress upon all interested in the science and art of organ-building the absolute necessity of associating with the DOUBLE OPEN DIAPASON, 32 FT., a fairly complete harmonic series, so that its grave sounds may be helped and enriched. But, in the name of science and common sense, let there be no groping amidst the sound tombs of the 64 ft. Octave, where nothing more musical can be heard than the rhythmical rattling of the bones of skeletons. There is quite enough to be done, in more fertile fields, to improve the tonal structure of the Organ, to render it advisable to neglect the production therein of unmusical noise.

The ear can appreciate sounds very much higher in pitch than any producible by organ-pipes. Despretz has asserted that he has heard the sound of d^8 of 38016 vibrations in a second. This extremely high sound he produced from a tuning-fork excited by a violin bow. Helmholtz remarks: " The musical tones which can be used with advantage and have clearly distinguishable pitch, have therefore between 40 and 4000 vibrations in a second, extending over seven Octaves. Those which are audible at all have from 20 to 38000 vibrations, extending over eleven Octaves. This shows what a great variety of different vibrational numbers can be perceived and distinguished by the ear."

CHAPTER III.

THE COMPOUND HARMONIC-CORROBORATING STOPS.

T is greatly to be regretted that during late years the Compound Harmonic-corroborating Stops, commonly known as MIXTURES, have been so deliberately and systematically neglected by organ-builders and others interested in the construction of Organs. It is to be regretted, because such harmonic-corroborating stops are elements of the highest value, and hold an important place in the scientific tonal structure of the Organ, and are essential to the production of the higher and more beautiful qualities of pure organ-tone. The cause for their neglect in modern, and especially in recently constructed, Organs is not based on any argument of the slightest value or importance,—scientifically or artistically,—for, granted that such compound harmonic-corroborating stops are properly made, no valid argument against their introduction in the tonal structure of the Organ has been, or even can be, urged against their legitimate use in tone-production. No,—the only apparent reason for their neglect, in the organ-building world, obtains in the minds of unscientific and inartistic organ-builders, who, for trade reasons, dislike such stops; the manufacture, voicing, regulating, and tuning of which are attended by considerable trouble and the expenditure of considerable time, especially if they are properly made and artistically finished. All this labor and trouble has a profit-lowering effect. Besides, with their several ranks and, accordingly, numerous pipes,—frequently numbering between three and four hundred,—such stops appear in the organ specification no more prominently than any other stops of only sixty-one pipes; and necessarily make little show on paper. When an Organ is being contracted for, and when the purchaser is ignorant of tonal matters beyond the familiar limit, the organ-builder realizes the importance of making as big a show as possible on the pages of the specification.

He knows that a PICCOLO makes just as much show on paper as a MIXTURE of V ranks; and he can better afford to furnish two stops of the former class than one of the latter. A five-rank MIXTURE properly designed, scaled, and voiced, and scientifically graduated and regulated in tone throughout, will cost about as much as three PICCOLOS of ordinary make. Under such circumstances is it to be wondered at that in the organ-builder's competitive specification or *list of stops,* MIXTURES are studiously omitted? The dollar wins the day against the teaching of science and art; and will continue to do so while trade methods are allowed to dominate scientific and artistic tonal appointment.

There is another aspect of this matter which gives rise to the pertinent question: Why has the organ-loving and musical world been agreeable to the elimination of the compound harmonic-corroborating stops from the tonal appointment of the Organ, after the centuries of their use in lands noted for the highest musical knowledge and culture, and especially the land that gave birth to the organ-giant, Bach? The question seems difficult to answer satisfactorily; but, on careful consideration, we have been forced to the conclusion that disregard for such important compound voices has arisen from the objectionable character of the stops which modern organ-builders have put in their instruments, under the name of MIXTURES—loud, screaming, and coarsely voiced stops, intolerable with any combination save the full organ, and often objectionable with that. Be this as it may; we are satisfied that in the representative Organs of the Twentieth Century the compound harmonic-corroborating stops will again occupy proper positions in their tonal structures.

It is unnecessary, after what has been said in the preceding Chapter, to enlarge on the reasons for the introduction of harmonic-corroborating stops here; but we may remark that all the statements made respecting the single complete ranks of pipes which represent the chief upper partial tones of the foundation or prime tone of the PRINCIPAL or DIAPASON, 8 FT., apply, in every particular, to the ranks composing the compound stops described in the present Chapter.

The compound stops, as the term implies, consist of two or more ranks of pipes which yield certain upper partial tones of the prime tone. The numbers of ranks generally found in well-appointed Organs vary from three to eight, but MIXTURES having a greater number of ranks have frequently been made by German and other European builders. The greatest number we have found in a British Organ is fourteen—the "HARMONIC MIXTURE" in the Organ of the Edinburgh University. It is quite a common thing to meet with compound stops in which the numbers of the ranks vary in different portions of their compass; and in certain classes of MIXTURES—notably those of the Pedal Organ—this treatment is to be recommended. Both the number and pitch of the ranks will, in scientific tonal appointment, depend upon the number and pitch of the independent and complete harmonic-corroborating stops inserted in the same division of the Organ.

Probably in no branch of stop appointment can the organ-designer or organ-builder of to-day display scientific knowledge and sound musical sense more clearly than in the correct composition and adjustment of his compound harmonic-corroborating stops. Is this fact generally or properly realized?

The old builders who, in many instances, appear to have resorted to mixture-work to obtain power and excessive brilliancy of tone, introduced into their Organs a superabundance of compound-work, both in number of ranks and loudness of intonation. In proof of this, we may direct attention to the Great and Choir divisions of the Organ in the Old Church, at Amsterdam, finished in 1686. The Great, which contains sixteen stops, has three stops of 16 ft. pitch and only three of 8 ft., while there are three compound stops having, collectively, eighteen ranks; namely, a SESQUIALTERA, IV. ranks, a MIXTURE, VI., VII., and VIII. ranks, and a SCHARF, VI. ranks. The Choir Organ contains twelve stops, including five stops of 8 ft. pitch, and has also eighteen ranks in its three compound stops; namely, a SESQUIALTERA, IV. ranks, a MIXTURE, VII. and VIII. ranks, and a SCHARF, VI. ranks. These stops, comprising thirty-six ranks of pipes, are, as in all old Dutch and German Organs, made of comparatively large-scaled pipes, and loudly voiced, in defiance of the teaching of the phenomena of musical sounds: their effect is, accordingly, unduly assertive. Probably observing the objectionable results attending the excessive use of such assertive stops, later organ-builders went, when left to their own devices, too far in the opposite direction, omitting compound stops in their small Organs, and inserting one, or two at most, in the most important division of those of larger dimensions. In scheming a compound harmonic-corroborating stop for the foundation division of an Organ, it is essential, if a perfect result is to be obtained, to look upon the foundation-work and its superstructure as a grand MIXTURE; first tabulating all the single through ranks, and then completing the tonal structure by the addition of the higher harmonic upper partials in the ranks of the compound stop or stops, scientifically graduated in strength of tone in accordance with the phenomena of musical sounds. No other mode of procedure can be attended with a satisfactory result so far as the foundation division of the Organ is concerned.

The compound stops of the Organ are designated by several names, only few of which have any direct reference to their constitution or their special tonal character. The most common name is MIXTURE, under which, strictly speaking, all the compound stops may be included. The following are the names commonly found in English and American Organs: MIXTURE, SESQUIALTERA, CORNET, FURNITURE, and ACUTA.

In German and Dutch Organs we find the names MIXTUR, CORNET, SESQUIALTERA, CYMBEL, SCHARF, SCHERP, RAUSCHQUINTE, and GLOCKENSPIEL. In French Organs the following names occur: CORNET, SESQUIALTERA, FOURNITURE, CYMBALE, PLEIN-JEU, and CARILLON. In Italian Organs the general name for the compound stops is RIPIENO; and in Spanish instruments, LLENO.

Compound stops appear in three classes: 1. Those which extend throughout the compass of the clavier without any break. 2. Those which extend through a portion of the compass of the clavier only. 3. Those which extend throughout the compass of the clavier, having one or more breaks.

The first class of compound stops seldom appears in the manual divisions of the Organ for harmonic-corroborating purposes; while in the Pedal Organ it is the proper class to adopt, unless some special effect is aimed at,—the large size of the pipes representing the desirable upper partial tones of the prime (16 feet) tone of the pedal department, combined with the short compass of that department, rendering it altogether unnecessary to have breaks in the MIXTURE. This fact has probably done much to discourage the introduction of the harmonic-corroborating ranks in the form of compound stops, preference being shown —when they are introduced at all—for them as separate stops. We unhesitatingly say that no Pedal Organ, of any pretension toward tonal completeness, should be without a compound harmonic-corroborating stop, commensurate with its general stop apportionment. Organbuilders of to-day, however, cannot be looked to to support this contention, for obvious reasons.

The most important and complete Pedal Organ compound stops which, so far as our knowledge extends, have been constructed by European builders are those in the Organs in the Votive Church, at Vienna, and the Cathedral of Riga. The stop in the latter Organ is labeled " GRAND BOURDON " and its ranks corroborate or furnish the first, second, third, fourth, and seventh upper partial tones of the 32 ft. harmonic series.* It is composed of five complete ranks, as follows:

I. PEDAL ORGAN MIXTURE—GRAND BOURDON—V. RANKS.

PRINCIPAL, 16 FT.——QUINT, 10⅔ FT.——OCTAVE, 8 FT.——TIERCE, 6⅖ FT.——
SUPER-OCTAVE, 4 FT.

In the Organ in the Church at Mühlhausen the pedal department has a MIXTURE, of X. ranks. In the pedal department of the Concert-room Organ in St. George's Hall, Liverpool, there is a MIXTURE, of III. ranks,

---

* All the pipes of this MIXTURE are of wood; the scales and particulars of which are given in the Chapter on the Timbre-creating Compound Stops.

and FOURNITURE, of V. ranks. It is, however, extremely rare to find a
MIXTURE of any description in the pedal department of an Organ of
recent construction, but one remarkable example must be recorded. In
the immense Organ erected in the Wanamaker Store, in Philadelphia,
Pa., the pedal department, which has, according to our original Specification, a COMPENSATING MIXTURE, of VI. ranks, has recently received
the addition of the most remarkable MIXTURE which has ever been inserted in an Organ. It is composed of ten ranks of open metal pipes of
the DIAPASON family, voiced on a wind-pressure of eleven inches. The
ranks are as follows:

1. DIAPASON	. .	Metal.	16 feet	6. SUPER-OCTAVE .	.	Metal.	4 feet
2. QUINT.	. . .	"	10⅔ "	7. OCTAVE TIERCE.	.	"	3⅕ "
3. OCTAVE.	. . .	"	8 "	8. TWELFTH.	. .	"	2⅔ "
4. TIERCE.	. . .	"	6⅖ "	9. FIFTEENTH	. .	"	2 "
5. OCTAVE QUINT	.	"	5⅓ "	10. NINETEENTH. .	.	"	1⅓ "

This stupendous harmonic-corroborating stop belongs to the 32 ft. series,
and when drawn with the DOUBLE OPEN DIAPASONS, 32 FT., produces a
majestic harmonic tonal structure impossible on any other Pedal Organ
in existence. Heard alone, the tone of this MIXTURE is that of a magnificent reed, so perfectly are its constituents balanced and regulated.*

It is hardly necessary in any Pedal Organ to have a harmonic-corroborating stop belonging to the 32 ft. prime; but, on the other hand, it
is most desirable, when space and funds are adequate, to introduce a
MIXTURE belonging to the 16 ft. harmonic series. Such a stop to be
agreeable to the ear and generally useful in all possible combinations,
should be formed of pipes of medium scales carefully graduated in
strength of tone, in accordance with the laws set forth in the preceding
Chapter, and so as not to give undue prominence to the higher notes of
the Pedal Organ. A full MIXTURE of this class may properly be composed of the following complete ranks:

II. PEDAL ORGAN MIXTURE—VI. RANKS.

CCC to G . . . OCTAVE, 8 FT.——TWELFTH, 5⅓ FT.——FIFTEENTH, 4 FT.——
SEVENTEENTH, 3⅕ FT.——NINETEENTH, 2⅔ FT.——TWENTY-SECOND, 2 FT.

The effect of a compound stop of this class, provided it be scientifically scaled and regulated, would be extremely beautiful with the
DIAPASON, 16 FT., or with a full-voiced VIOLONE, 16 FT.; producing in
both cases compound tones of a richness absolutely unknown in the
ordinary Pedal Organs of to-day. This stop, owing to the accommo-

---

* This stop was schemed by and constructed under the direction of Mr. William Boone
Fleming, who superintended the construction of the original Organ in the factory of The Los
Angeles Art Organ Company.

dating nature of properly-proportioned harmonic-corroborating stops, would prove sufficient for the full tone of the largest pedal department ever likely to be provided in an Organ. In the construction of the Mixture, four perfectly legitimate courses are open to the artistic builder. 1. The ranks may be made of full-scaled metal pipes of the Dulciana or Dolce class, whose refined and singing tones will blend perfectly with the voice of the Diapason, 16 ft., the Dulciana, 16 ft., or, indeed, with that of any other unison stop. 2. The ranks may be formed of softly voiced metal pipes of the Viol family, yielding a tone, richer in harmonics, which will form a brilliant combination with the solid voice of the Diapason, 16 ft.; and will assimilate perfectly with the kindred voice of the Violone, 16 ft. 3. The ranks may be formed throughout of wood (as in the Riga Cathedral Organ) either of the Melodia or Lieblichgedeckt family, producing a beautiful superstructure of sympathetic flute-tone. 4. The ranks may be varied in tonal character by the introduction of pipes of different classes—wood or metal, open or stopped—according to the judgment or artistic aim of the designer, who should be guided in his selection by the general stop appointment of the Pedal Organ.

There is another Pedal Organ compound stop on which we place great value, and to which we desire to direct the organ-designer's and organist's special attention, for it is one that should find a place in every Organ of any pretensions toward tonal completeness. We allude to the compound stop to which we have given the English name Compensating Mixture. The principal peculiarity of this stop is that all its ranks vary in their compass or number of notes, while only one may, in some cases, extend throughout the compass of the pedal clavier. This invaluable stop has been fully tested in two important Organs designed by us, and has been proved all that musical sense can desire in such a direction.

The first stop of this class was schemed by Musikdirektor Wilke, of Neu-Ruppin, to which he gave the name Compensationsmixtur. It was inserted in the pedal department of the Organ in the Church of St. Catherine, at Salzwedel, constructed by F. Turley, in 1838. We were so greatly struck by Seidel's remarks, that we lost no opportunity of testing the value of Wilke's happy thought. Seidel says: "Its purpose is to give to the lower notes of the Pedal Organ the promptest and most distinct intonation possible; and to impart to the pedal department throughout such an even power of tone that rapid passages can be rendered thereon, with an equal roundness and distinctness from the lowest to the highest notes of the compass." The stop, when properly constructed, does all this and more. It imparts to the naturally dull and bald tones of the lower portion of the Pedal Organ, a brilliance of tonality and a richness of harmonic structure absolutely unknown in the

Pedal Organs of the ordinary organ-builder type: at the same time it in no way interferes with the gravity so desirable in the Pedal Organ. The stop, as originally constructed, is in our opinion quite unsuited for insertion in an Organ designed to meet the musical demands of the twentieth century. Its composition is as follows:

1. A TIERCE, 3⅕ FT., extending from CCC to GGG, comprising only eight pipes; the intonation of which from DDD is gradually reduced until almost inaudible at GGG.
2. A QUINT, 2⅔ FT., extending from CCC to AAA, comprising ten pipes, the tone of which diminishes from EEE in like manner.
3. A PRINCIPAL, 2 FT., extending from CCC to GGG♯, comprising nine pipes, the tone of which diminishes from DDD.
4. A QUINT, 1⅓ FT., extending from CCC to FFF♯, comprising seven pipes, the tone of which diminishes from CCC♯.
5. A SIFFLÖTE, 1 FT., extending from CCC to FFF, comprising six pipes, the tone of which diminishes from CCC♯.

This stop was both unscientifically and inartistically conceived; and while it doubtless ameliorated, to some extent, the dull and groaning tones of the lower octave of the heavy pedal department of the Salzwedel Organ, in which it was placed, it could not have proved satisfactory from a musical point of view. It, however, pointed the way to what seemed highly desirable; and induced us to give the matter earnest thought, and to test practically the possibilities it foreshadowed. We can truthfully say that the results have proved eminently satisfactory.

Of the musical value of a properly scaled and tonally graduated COMPENSATING MIXTURE, in even a Pedal Organ of small dimensions, there can be no question: of that we are thoroughly convinced; for not only has it the effect of imparting life and clearness to the necessarily dull and largely indeterminate tones of the lower notes of the Pedal Organ (especially when a DOUBLE PRINCIPAL, 32 FT., is speaking), but it creates a harmonic superstructure of great richness and effectiveness. It also renders a pedal solo very distinct without interfering with the true pitch.

We give for the consideration of the expert the following composition for a COMPENSATING MIXTURE of six ranks, suitable for a Pedal Organ of the first magnitude:—

III. PEDAL ORGAN COMPENSATING MIXTURE—VI. RANKS.

CCC to G, SUPER-OCTAVE, 4 FT.	32 notes.
CCC to D, TIERCE, 3⅕ FT.	27 "
CCC to BB, OCTAVE QUINT, 2⅔ FT. . . .	24 "
CCC to GG, TWENTY-SECOND, 2 FT. . . .	20 "
CCC to EE, TWENTY-SIXTH, 1⅓ FT. . . .	17 "
CCC to CC, TWENTY-NINTH, 1 FT.	13 "

The scales of the several ranks should be relatively smaller as they rise in pitch; and their scale ratio should be such as to place the half diameter on the thirteenth pipe.   In addition to this quick reduction in scale, it is essential to the true office of the stop that the voice of each rank be gradually reduced in strength as it ascends the scale, so as to render the cessation of its voice practically imperceptible to the ear.   As the sole purpose of the stop is to corroborate or impart the higher harmonic upper partials of the 16 ft. prime, and by that means impart a sensible degree of life and distinctness to the grave and somewhat droning tones of the foundation unisons and doubles of the department, the pipes should be of metal, of scales commensurate with the foundation work of the department, and the strength of voice required.

As a COMPENSATING MIXTURE of six ranks is much too large for the ordinary run of modern Pedal Organs, which usually comprise between five and ten stops (unless wholesale borrowing from the manual department is resorted to—a practice becoming too prevalent in certain quarters), we give the composition of a desirable three-rank stop:—

IV. PEDAL ORGAN COMPENSATING MIXTURE—III. RANKS.

CCC to D,	SUPER-OCTAVE, 4 FT.	27 notes.
CCC to GG,	OCTAVE QUINT, 2⅔ FT.	20 "
CCC to DD,	TWENTY-SECOND, 2 FT. . . .	15 "

We are strongly of opinion that similar principles of construction and tonal treatment might with advantage be followed in the formation of a special class of compound harmonic-corroborating stops, suitable for insertion in the manual divisions of the Organ.   We are supported in our opinion by Prof. Helmholtz, who, after commenting on the influence of the " resonance box " of a bowed instrument on its compound tones, remarks: " A similar effect is attained in the Compound Stops of the Organ, by making the series of upper partial tones, which are represented by distinct pipes, less extensive for the higher than for the lower notes of the stop.   Thus each digital opens six pipes for the lower octaves, answering to the first six partial tones of its note; but in the two upper octaves, the digital opens only three or even two pipes, which give the Octave and Twelfth, or merely the Octave, in addition to the Prime."   It is a noteworthy fact that, contrary to the phenomena of musical sounds, MIXTURES have been devised in which the lowest octave of the manual compass has only two pipes to each note, the tenor octave three pipes to each note, and the higher octaves four pipes to each note. This method is widely different from that recommended by Helmholtz; and that followed in the COMPENSATING MIXTURE.   Example V. is the MIXTURE, of two, three, and four ranks, included by Edmund Schulze,

be carefully observed here as in all other Mixtures. The Fourniture appears in many of the Organs by French builders. Confining our remarks to instruments constructed by Aristide Cavaillé-Coll, of Paris, we find a Grosse Fourniture of four ranks in the Grand-Chœur of the Organ in the Church of Saint-Sulpice, Paris; a Fourniture of five ranks in the Grand-Orgue of the Organ in the Church of Saint-Sernin, Toulouse; a Fourniture of five ranks in the Bombarde of the Organ in the Church of Saint-Owen, Rouen, and a Fourniture of five ranks in the Grand-Orgue of the Concert Organ in the Albert Hall, Sheffield, constructed in 1873.

THE SESQUIALTERA

The compound harmonic-corroborating stop called the Sesquialtera or Sexquialtera is found in numerous old and modern Organs. Correctly composed, this stop should have two ranks only and extend throughout the manual compass without a break. The original Sesquialtera, as used by the old German organ-builders, was of two ranks, composed of a fifth-sounding and a third-sounding rank, the former being the lowest in pitch: the two ranks sounding a major sixth, as G—e^1 on the CC key.* The sizes of the two ranks were usually 2⅔ ft. and 1⅗ ft., which, accordingly, correspond with the Twelfth and Tierce. When of this size, the stop should be carried throughout the compass without a break, the Tierce being voiced softer than the Twelfth, to prevent any tendency toward a harsh effect. Notable examples of this form of Sesquialtera exist in German, Swiss, and Dutch Organs.

In manual divisions in which there are both a Twelfth, 2⅔ ft., and a Tierce, 1⅗ ft., as through and independent stops, it is unnecessary to insert a Sesquialtera; but when these complete stops do not appear in the tonal scheme, a Sesquialtera is strongly to be recommended. It is important that the second and fourth upper partial tones should be corroborated if a full compound organ-tone is aimed at, as it should be in every Organ worthy of the name. When two compound stops are inserted in an important division, one should be a Sesquialtera or a Mixture in which there is a third-sounding rank in every break; the

---

* The name given to this compound stop does not seem to be entirely satisfactory. The Latin word *sesquialtera* (fem. of *sesquialter*) signifies "one half more," and on that account it is difficult to reconcile its use as the name of a stop the ranks of which bear no relation to the ratio 1:1½. Reference to different authorities does not clear the way.

Sir John Stainer says in "A Dictionary of Music," "The origin of the term Sesquialtera, as applied to an organ stop, is rather obscure. . . . On the whole it may be safely said that the word Sesquialtera was originally used for the purpose of showing that the stop contained pipes having ratios other than 2:1, or other than an octave-series."

Dr. Hopkins, in "The Organ," tells us that the two ranks which compose the stop sound together a major sixth "hence the name Sesqui-altera, from Sexta, a sixth."

In "The Century Dictionary" we find "Sesquialtera—in music, an interval having the ratio 1:1½ or 2:3—that is a *perfect fifth*. In organ-building a variety of mixture.

"Sext, sexte—In music the interval of a sixth. In organ-building a mixture-stop of two ranks separated by a sixth—that is, consisting of a Twelfth and a Seventeenth."

other being a MIXTURE composed of octave- and fifth-sounding ranks. The only complete SESQUIALTERAS are those of the original German class, composed throughout of a TWELFTH, 2⅔ FT., and a SEVENTEENTH, 1⅗ FT.; or, better still, of three unbroken ranks—TWELFTH, 2⅔ FT.— FIFTEENTH, 2 FT.—SEVENTEENTH, 1⅗ FT. The Pedal Organ SES- QUIALTERA, of three ranks, belonging to the 16 ft. harmonic series, is composed of a TWELFTH, 5⅓ FT.—SUPER-OCTAVE, 4 FT.—TIERCE, 3⅕ FT.

The so-called SESQUIALTERAS, introduced in old English and Con- tinental Organs, and which were composed of several ranks of pipes, requiring two or more breaks in their compass, were only correct in certain parts of their compass. A representative example is furnished by the stop inserted by Snetzler in the Organ he constructed, in the latter part of the eighteenth century, for St. Mary's Church, Nottingham. The composition of this stop is given in Example XVII.

XVII. SESQUIALTERA—IV. RANKS.

CC to G	15 —17 —19 —22.
G♯ to g¹	12*—15 —17*—19.
g♯ to top	8 —12*—15 —17*.

XVIII. SESQUIALTERA—V. RANKS.

CC to c¹	19*—22 —24*—26 —29.
c♯¹ to top	8 —12*—15 —17*—19.

XIX. SESQUIALTERA—IV. RANKS.

CC to F	15 —19*—22 —24*.
F♯ to f¹	12*—15 —17*—19.
f♯¹ to c³	8 —12*—15 —17*.
c♯³ to c⁴	1 — 5*— 8 —10*.

These three Examples practically cover the SESQUIALTERA in its many-ranked and broken form, as found in the better works of the old and some few modern organ-builders. In each the asterisks mark the sexts. Example XVIII. gives the composition of a true five-ranked SESQUIALTERA, as inserted in the Organ in the old Parish Church of Doncaster, constructed by Harris and Byfield, of London, in 1740. The list of the stops in the Great division of this Organ constructed by builders so justly celebrated in their day must be interesting, as showing how complete old English Organs were in their harmonic appointment:

1. OPEN DIAPASON	.	8	Feet.	7. TIERCE	. . .	1⅗	Feet.
2. OPEN DIAPASON	.	8	"	8. SESQUIALTERA	.	V.	Ranks.
3. STOPPED DIAPASON	.	8	"	9. CORNET (Middle c¹)	V.		"
4. PRINCIPAL	. .	4	"	10. TRUMPET	. .	8	Feet.
5. TWELFTH	. .	2⅔	"	11. TRUMPET	. .	8	"
6. FIFTEENTH	. .	2	"	12. CLARION	. .	4	"

The SESQUIALTERA, Example XVIII., is given in modern compass: in the Harris Organ its compass was GGG to d³. A generally useful stop can be obtained by omitting the acute fifth-sounding rank in both breaks. In Example XX. is given a SESQUIALTERA of six ranks, bright in the lower, and full and rich in the upper octaves, admirably suited for a large Swell Organ (as commonly appointed in other directions): in it all the ranks belong to the 8 ft. harmonic series. If considered too acute, the highest rank in each break can be omitted. In Example XXI.

XX. SESQUIALTERA—VI. RANKS.

CC to E♯	.	.	15 —17 —19 —22 —26 —29.
G to f♯¹	.	.	12*—15 —17*—19 —22 —26.
g¹ to f♯²	.	.	8 —12*—15 —17*—19 —22.
g² to c⁴	.	.	1 — 8 —12*—15 —17*—19.

is given the composition of a SESQUIALTERA of four ranks and of full intonation, designed by the late W. T. Best, of Liverpool, and recommended by him for the Great Organ, and to be specially used when the DOUBLE DIAPASON, 16 FT., is drawn. It will be observed that the ranks

XXI. SESQUIALTERA—IV. RANKS.

CC to C	.	.	.	.	.	15 —17 —19 —22.
C♯ to B	.	.	.	.	.	17 —19 —22 —26.
c¹ to b♭¹	.	.	.	.	12 —15 —19*—24*.
b¹ to b²	.	.	.	.	.	5*— 8 —10*—15.
c³ to c⁴	.	.	.	.	.	1 — 5*— 8 —10*.

on the two higher breaks—from b¹ to c⁴—belong to the 16 ft. harmonic series, imparting breadth and fulness to the treble. It will also be noticed that the intervals peculiar to the SESQUIALTERA appear only in the treble of the stop. The addition of a TWELFTH, 2⅔ FT., as a complete and independent stop, would create the necessary sexts in the bass and tenor-octaves, and Mr. Best certainly contemplated such an addition, covering it as usual, in proper appointment, with the independent SUPER-OCTAVE, 2 FT. We may here remark that the certain or possible addition of complete mutation ranks must always be taken into consideration in the composition or the judging of compound stops.

The value of the SEVENTEENTH cannot well be overrated, yet this natural and by no means weak or ineffective harmonic is shunned by modern organ-builders who do not study how to treat it scientifically, or proportion it properly in scaling, voicing, and regulating.

In the tonal structure of the Pedal Organ the SEVENTEENTH or TIERCE, either in the 32 ft. or 16 ft. harmonic series, is most effective, adding a desirable brightness to the somewhat dull and colorless foundation tones of the department. Two instances of its introduction will be sufficient here. In Example XXII. is given the composition of the SESQUIALTERA belonging to the 32 ft. harmonic series, in the Haupt-Pedal of the Organ in the Cathedral of Riga. Example XXIII. is the composition of the SESQUIALTERA, of five ranks, formed of metal pipes,

XXII. PEDAL ORGAN SESQUIALTERA—II. RANKS.

CCC to D, . . . QUINT, 10⅔ FT.——TIERCE, 6⅖ FT.

XXIII. PEDAL ORGAN SESQUIALTERA—V. RANKS.

CCC to F, ... 12*——15——17*——19——22.

in the pedal department of the Concert Organ in the Music Hall, in Cincinnati, constructed by E. & G. G. Hook & Hastings, of Boston, in 1878. The stop belongs to the 16 ft. harmonic series, the TWELFTH rank being 5⅓ ft. It is labeled CORNET, but it is strictly a SESQUI-ALTERA.

THE TERTIAN

The compound harmonic-corroborating stop which may in proper order be considered at this point is that designated the TERTIAN. It is simply an inversion of the SESQUIALTERA, the third-sounding rank being lower in pitch than the fifth-sounding one. The accompanying Example, XXIV., shows the composition of the stop in the 8 ft. harmonic series :—

XXIV. TERTIAN—II. RANKS.

CC to c⁴, . . . SEVENTEENTH, 1⅗ FT.——NINETEENTH, 1⅓ FT.

In the 16 ft. harmonic series the TERTIAN is composed of a TENTH, 3⅕ FT., and a TWELFTH, 2⅔ FT. In old German Organs it is met with of three ranks, the latter stop having a SUPER-OCTAVE, 4 FT., added to it. Constructed of small-scaled pipes—DULCIANA, DOLCE, or SPITZFLÖTE—voiced and regulated so as to have the fifth-sounding rank slightly softer than the octave-sounding rank, and the third-sounding rank decidedly softer than the fifth-sounding rank, the TERTIAN becomes a valuable addition to any softer-toned manual division of the Organ, enriching the voice of any unison stop—labial or lingual.

THE CORNET

The term CORNET was used by the old German and French organ-builders to designate a compound and incomplete stop, usually inserted in the principal manual division of the Organ. Respecting this now obsolete stop we cannot do better than give Seidel's description :—

"Cornet, or 'Cornetto,' is a mixture of a very wide measure, which begins generally at c¹ or at the G below, and goes through the upper octaves of the manual. It has a strong intonation, and a horn-like tone, which is well adapted for filling out. Sometimes, when hymns are to be sung with a melody which is not familiar to the congregation, this register will be found very efficient for the purpose of making the melody prominent, since the right hand plays the melody upon that manual which contains the Cornet, while the left hand plays the accompaniment upon some other manual, for which weaker registers are drawn. This Mixture has sometimes five ranks, 8, 4, 2⅔, 2, and 1⅗ feet; sometimes four ranks, 8, 4, 2⅔, and 1⅗ feet; and sometimes three ranks, 4, 2⅔, and 1⅗ feet. In France, the lowest rank of this register is nothing but a Rohrflöte, 8 ft. Wilke deems it best to construct the Cornet with three ranks only, but so that the lowest of them is a fifth, and next an octave, and the last a third,—5⅓ ft., 4 ft., and 3⅕ ft., or 2⅔ ft., 2 ft., and 1⅗ ft. The latter arrangement is better suited for small Organs, the former for large ones."

The Cornet of the old builders was formed of metal pipes larger in scale than the corresponding pipes of the Diapason or Principal, 8 ft., of the division in which it was placed, and voiced to yield a very full and dominating pure organ-tone. It comprised, commonly, from three to five ranks, but this larger number was often exceeded considerably, as in the Organ at Weingarten. As the large-scaled and numerous pipes required considerable space for their accommodation, they were frequently planted on a special small wind-chest, elevated above the pipework of the main wind-chest, and connected with the grooves of the latter by metal conveyances. The stop is termed Mounted Cornet.

The term Cornet seems to be applied without any definite signification by modern organ-builders, although it is most commonly applied to a Mixture or Sesquialtera, composed of five or more ranks of small-scaled pipes, voiced to yield a bright, singing quality of pure organ-tone. Such, at least, should be' the aim of the artist organ-builder.

Compound harmonic-corroborating stops, composed of several ranks of very small-scaled and delicately voiced pipes, are of the greatest value and beauty, producing a fascinating quality of compound tone in combination with soft-toned labial and lingual stops. Of this fact we have had satisfactory proof in our own Chamber Organ, in which is a Cornet formed of five ranks of Dulciana pipes, carefully voiced on wind of 2⅜ inches. Its composition is given in Example XXV. This

XXV. Dulciana Cornet—V. ranks.

CC	to	BB	. . . . .	19——22——24——26——29.
C	to	B	. . . . .	12——15——17——19——22.
c¹	to	b¹	. . . . .	8——12——17——19——22.
c²	to	g³	. . . . .	1—— 8——10——12——15.

stop is so scientifically graduated in strength in all its ranks and breaks, and is so delicate and refined in its character, that it can be used with a single DULCIANA, 8 FT.; while as a harmonic-corroborating stop it is sufficient when combined with the compound expressive Great Organ of thirteen stops. Speaking of this CORNET (labeled in the Organ RIPIENO DI CINQUE), Mr. F. E. Robertson, in " A Practical Treatise on Organ-Building," remarks: " Mr. Audsley had a very beautiful Chamber Organ of his own building,* the specification of which was as follows: [The specification is given.] Wind 2⅜". The scale of the OPEN DIAP. is 5¼" dia. A V-rank MIXTURE in an Organ of that size [Nineteen speaking stops] would, in the ordinary acceptation of the word, be a monstrosity, but to DULCIANA scale, and with every pipe [280 in number] regulated and voiced with the utmost care, it has a beautiful effect." This tribute, from a distinguished authority on organ construction, amply proves that MIXTURES can be made valuable and beautiful tone-producers.

In Example XXVI. is given the composition of a DOLCE CORNET, of five ranks, as included in the Roosevelt standard collection of compound stops. It may be seen that it would produce a much fuller effect than the preceding composition. In all save its top break it is a true SESQUIALTERA. It may be effectively formed of DOLCE or SPITZFLÖTE pipes.

XXVI. DOLCE CORNET—V. RANKS.

CC to ff¹	12*—15 —17*—19 —22.
f♯¹ to f¹	8 —12*—15 —17*—19.
f♯² to c³	1 — 8 —12*—15 —17*.
c³ to c⁴	1 — 8 —10 —12 —15.

In the Swell division of the Concert Organ in the Music Hall, in Cincinnati, is a DOLCE CORNET, of six ranks, the composition of which is given in Example XVII. This composition points to considerable brill-

XXVII. DOLCE CORNET—VI. RANKS.

CC to BB . . .	15—19—22—26—29—36.
C to B	12—15—19—22—26—29.
c¹ to b¹ . . .	8—12—15—19—22—26.
c² to c⁴ . . .	1— 5— 8—10—12—15.

iancy of tonal effect in the two lower octaves; to richness in the middle octave; and to singular fulness in the higher octaves. It will be observed

---

* This Organ was purchased by Lord Dysart in 1891, and is now in Ham House, on the Thames, near Richmond, England.

that all the ranks in the two higher octaves belong to the 16 ft. harmonic series, corroborating the first, second, third, fourth, fifth, and seventh upper partial tones; and that a third-sounding rank is only introduced in these octaves. A MIXTURE of this nature demands, beyond pipes of small scales, most artistic voicing, and scientific graduation of tone throughout the ranks in all the breaks. These remarks, however, apply equally to all compound harmonic-corroborating stops.

THE CYMBALE

Another compound stop, formed of several ranks of high-pitched pipes, and commonly having from four to seven ranks, is designated the CYMBALE, CYMBAL, CYMBEL, or CIMBALO. It has derived its name, seemingly, from the fancied resemblance of its compound tone to the clang of the orchestral cymbals. This stop seems to have been favored by the great French organ-builder, Aristide Cavaillé-Coll. There are CYMBALES, of four ranks, in his Organs in the Church of Saint-Sernin, Toulouse, and in the Albert Hall, Sheffield; and one, of six ranks, in the Organ in the Church of Saint-Sulpice, Paris. The remarkable composition of this stop given in Example XXVIII. is that of the CYMBALE, of seven ranks, in the Great division of the Organ in the Music Hall, Cincinnati. It contains no fewer than 427 pipes. Such

XXVIII. CYMBALE—VII. RANKS.

```
CC to BB  .  .   15——19——22——26——29——33——36.
C  to B   .  .   12——15——19——22——26——29——33.
c¹ to b¹  .  .    8——12——15——19——22——26——29.
c² to b²  .  .    1—— 5—— 8——12——15——19——22.
c³ to c⁴  .  . DOUBLE— 1—— 5—— 8——12——15——19.
```

a stop very few organ-builders of the present century will care to venture on; for if carefully made and voiced, and scientifically regulated throughout, it will demand much skill, study, and time—scarce things in the organ-building world to-day.

THE CARILLON

Many attempts appear to have been made to produce MIXTURES, the compound tones of which shall imitate the sounds peculiar to bells. The results have, owing largely to the absence of the percussion effect, been only moderately successful, and far from generally so. Stops of this class are commonly called CARILLONS. The characteristic features of these stops lie in the scales and voicing of their pipes, and in their composition presenting three ranks—octave-, third-, and fifth-sounding.

Example XXVIII. is a CARILLON of this class; and Example XXIX. is one specified by Mr. W. T. Best. It will be observed that the bell effect is confined to the tenor and lower treble octaves, just where it would prove most effective. CARILLONS, of I. and III. ranks, are to be found

XXVIII. CARILLON—III. RANKS.

CC	to F	.	.	.	.	.	.	.	.	17——19——22.
F♯	to f	.	.	.	.	.	.	.	.	15——17——19.
f♯¹	to f	.	.	.	.	.	.	.	.	12——15——17.
f♯²	to c⁴	.	.	.	.	.	.	.	.	10——12——15.

XXIX. CARILLON—III. RANKS.

CC	to BB	.	.	.	.	.	.	.	.	15——19——22.
C	to B	.	.	.	.	.	.	.	.	12——17——22.
c¹	to b¹	.	.	.	.	.	.	.	.	12——15——17.
c²	to a³	.	.	.	.	.	.	.	.	8——12——15.

in the Organ in the Town Hall of Manchester, constructed by Cavaillé-Coll. It has a fifth-sounding rank from CC to F♯; and a fifth-, a third-, and an octave-sounding rank from G to c⁴. All the pipes are of large scale, having wide and low mouths, and languids finely and closely nicked. There is a stop of four ranks, of this class in the Echo division of the Organ in the Centennial Hall, Sydney, N. S. W., under the German name, GLOCKENSPIEL. CARILLONS, of II. or III. ranks, are to be found in several Dutch Organs and also in a few German instruments. It must be observed that while these characteristic compound stops are, from the nature of the ranks which compose them, harmonic-corroborating, they are chiefly valuable on account of their *timbre-creating* qualities. In the Sheffield Organ, we observed a remarkable bell-like effect when the combination, in the Solo Organ, of the FLÛTE HARMONIQUE, 8 FT., the DOUBLETTE, 2 FT., and the TIERCE, 1⅗ FT., was played *staccato*. In the CARILLON, the third-sounding rank has not to be softened, as is desirable in other compound stops.

THE ACUTA

A MIXTURE composed of high-pitched ranks, called by German organ-builders SCHARF, and by others ACUTA. It has, in different examples, three, four, or more ranks of pipes, having a keen, bright quality of tone of carefully graduated strength. It is designed to impart additional brilliancy to the general tone of the division in which it is inserted, without being unduly piercing. It is valuable, when artistically made, in the production of varied tone-colorings or *timbres*. The ACUTA should invariably comprise a third-sounding rank through-

out its compass, for its true character and office depend on its introduction. Example XXX. may be accepted as a representative compos-

XXX. Acuta—III. ranks.

CC	to	B	.	.	.	.	.	.	.	22——24——26.
c^1	to	b^1	.	.	.	.	.	.	.	17——19——22.
c^2	to	b^2	.	.	.	.	.	.	.	15——17——19.
c^3	to	c^4	.	.	.	.	.	.	.	12——15——17.

ition of three ranks, each break comprising an octave-, a third-, and a
fifth-sounding rank. In a four-rank stop the first break should com-
mence with c^2—e^2—g^2—c^3, or with c^3—e^3—g^3—c^4; and in a five rank stop
with g^2—c^3—e^3—g^3—c^4. The Acuta strictly belongs to the Great
Organ, where it should appear with other harmonic-corroborating stops
of graver pitch. In Dutch Organs, the stop appears under the name
Scherp.

THE PLEIN-JEU

It is only necessary to describe particularly one other compound
harmonic-corroborating stop of pure organ-tone, called by the French
organ-builders Plein-Jeu. An example, of five ranks, occurs in the
Positif of the Organ of the Church of Saint-Ouen, at Rouen; but a
very important stop of the class, by Cavaillé-Coll, is to be found in the
Concert Organ in the Town Hall of Manchester. The composition of
this Plein-Jeu is given in Example XXXI. It has no special feature
to distinguish it from an ordinary Mixture in which octave- and
fifth-sounding ranks alone are introduced, except in its extreme richness of tonality, and the introduction of the Doubles and Double
Quint, in the upper breaks.

XXXI. Plein-Jeu—VII. ranks.

CC	to	E	.	.	15—— 19——22——26——29——33——36.
F	to	e^1	.	.	8—— 12——15——19——22——26——29.
f^1	to	e^2	.	.	1—— 8——12——15——19——22——26.
f^2	to	b^2	.	.	1—— 5—— 8——12——15——19——22.
c^3	to	f^3	.	double—— 1—— 5— 8——12——15——19.
f♯^{3}	to	c^4	.	double—double quint— 1—— 5— 8——12——15.

It may be remarked that in the manual division—Grand Orgue—in
which this great Mixture is placed, there are three stops of 16 ft. pitch,
which fact accounts for the presence of the Doubles in the higher
breaks, as well as the larger fifth-sounding ranks in the three higher
breaks. The largest Plein-Jeu known to us is that of ten ranks in

the Grand division of the Organ in the Madeleine, Paris, It is the only compound stop in the division.

In the scaling, voicing, and regulating of all the compound harmonic-corroborating stops great knowledge (acoustical), skill, and musical taste are required; and unless the organ-builder is prepared to give both careful study and painstaking attention to all matters connected with their formation and tonal adjustment, he had much better omit them altogether from his schemes. It is preferable to have no MIXTURES than to have bad ones; for bad ones will destroy what may, in their absence, be fairly good. Proof of this has been afforded by too many Organs. The chief fault lies in the practice of ignoring the true offices of the compound stops; and this leads to all manner of mistakes, notably the mistake of making them much too loud and penetrating. It was the old practice of making such stops loud and screaming that led Seidel, of Breslau, to pen these words: " We find sometimes MIXTURES with from six to eight, and in old Organs even from ten to sixteen, ranks, both in the manual and the pedal departments. A MIXTURE of so many ranks is a most absurd thing; for by the horrible noise it produces, the other stops lose their gravity and dignity, and the full organ produces nothing but a benumbing, stupefying noise." Seidel was right as regards the effect produced, but he was wrong respecting the cause. It was not the number of ranks in the old MIXTURES, so much as their large scales and coarse voicing, and unscientific and unsympathetic regulation, that produced the " horrible noise " he wrote about. He failed utterly to grasp the true facts of the case; for he says, in his definition of a MIXTURE—in his treatise on the Organ,—that it is " a stop of tin or metal having the same scale as the PRINCIPAL, repeating generally in the two upper octaves." How he could expect a simple harmonic-corroborating stop, formed of several ranks of pipes of the same large scale as the pipes of the foundation unison (8 ft.), to produce anything " but a benumbing, stupefying noise," in combination with the other stops of the Organ, is difficult to divine. Without giving one the slightest information respecting the proper method of constructing a compound stop, he adds: " On the other hand, a well-constructed MIXTURE is a very useful stop, since it unites in itself several stops, as it were, neither of which could be used by itself, and thereby saves a deal of space. Besides, it gives to the tone of the Organ, especially the full organ, fulness and power; distinctness and sharpness to the lower tones, more especially distinctness; and to the whole mass of tone a silver-like quality." A " well-constructed MIXTURE " does all Seidel claims for it, and more; but such a stop is rarely found in any Organ, old or new.

It must be borne in mind by all interested in the scheming of Organs, that all compound stops must, if they are to be of real value, be scientifically proportioned with respect to the general tonal structure or

apportionment of the divisions in which they are to be placed.   A Mix-
TURE that may be perfectly satisfactory in one Organ will, in all probability, be quite unsuitable in another.   Under these circumstances, it is
obvious that every compound stop must be recognized as a distinct problem to be solved only on scientific and artistic lines.

The composition of compound stops along artistic lines has not
hitherto received proper study and attention.   Much remains to be done,
in the Organ of the Twentieth Century, to invest such stops with
special tone-colorings, by the introduction of different classes of pipes
in their separate ranks, and, under special circumstances, in their several
breaks.   Some tentative essays have been made in this direction with
fair success.   For instance, in the Swell division of the Concert Organ
in the Public Halls, Glasgow, Scotland, built by T. C. Lewis & Co., of
London, is an "Echo Dulciana Cornet," of six ranks, in which wood
and metal, and open and stopped pipes are associated together artistically.   In compound stops in which the ranks are carried throughout the
manual compass without a break, such as Mixtures composed of a
Twelfth and Seventeenth; of an Octave, Twelfth, Fifteenth,
and Seventeenth; or any other combination of such ranks, favorable
opportunities are afforded for the production of varied tonal colorings,
each rank having a special tonal tint.

It is a well known fact that unison stops of any tone can be modified
or altered in tonal coloring by their combination with harmonic-corroborating stops; and, such being the case, it becomes obvious that such
tonal coloring depends largely on the composition of the compound stops
and on the tonal character of the pipes of which they are formed.   Mix-
TURES formed of the same number of ranks and of the same intervals
will produce different tonal colorings if their pipes are of different
classes.   For instance a Mixture formed of the ordinary pipes, schemed
from the Diapason and yielding pure organ-tone, will produce a widely
different tonal effect in combination with any unison stop than will a
Mixture formed of Dulciana, Dolce, Salicional, Vox Angelica,
Gemshorn, Spitzflöte, Flauto d'Amore, Lieblichflöte, or Viol
pipes, or of any combination of any or all of these pipes.

At this point special mention must be made of a very uncommon
compound harmonic-corroborating stop which may be designated Viol
Mixture or Viol Cornet.   The former name is appropriate when the
stop is composed of high-pitched pipes, rendering some breaks necessary: the latter name is appropriate when all the ranks extend throughout the compass without a break.   We inserted a Viol Cornet in our
scheme for the String-toned division of the Third or Swell Organ of
the Grand Concert Organ, installed in the Festival Hall of the Louisiana
Purchase Exposition, St. Louis, Mo.   Not only to give the composition
of this compound stop, but to show its relation to the tonal appointment

of the division, we give the complete list of the stops with which it is associated as follows :—

THIRD OR SWELL ORGAN

SECOND SUBDIVISION—EXPRESSIVE

Inclosed in Swell-Box No. 3.

Contra-Basso	. .	Wood	16	Feet.	Violette	. . . . .	Tin	4	Feet.
Violoncello	. . .	Tin	8	"	Viol ⎱ Viol, muted.		"	2⅔	"
Viola	. . . . .	"	8	"	Cornet ⎰ Viol "		"	2	"
Violino	. . . .	"	8	"	IV. ⎱ Viol "		"	1⅗	"
Violino (tuned sharp)	"	8	"	Ranks. ⎰ Viol "		"	1	"
Tierce Viol	. . .	"	8	"	Corroborating Mixture		"	V. Ranks	
Quint Viol	. . .	"	5⅓	"	String-tone.				
Octave Viol	. . .	"	4	"					

No such String-tone division had ever been introduced in another Organ; and it is easy for the musician to realize the orchestral effect of so great a volume of string-tone, at the command of the organist, without resort to coupling, or in any way interfering with the First Subdivision of the Third Organ—of twenty-three stops—inclosed in swell-box No. 2. The String-toned Subdivision could be brought on or thrown off the Third Organ clavier by thumb-pistons, at the will of the performer. The only string-toned Mixture known to us, in a foreign Organ, is that in the small instrument in the Young Men's Christian Association Hall, at Stuttgart. It is a fairly satisfactory stop.

Notwithstanding all that has been done during the last two centuries, we are strongly of opinion that the making of mixture-work, both as harmonic-corroborating and timbre-creating, is in its infancy. Surely much more can be done in the Organ of the Twentieth Century than has yet been achieved. Directed by the results of the researches conducted by Professor Helmholtz in the realms of tone, the organ experts of to-day are in a position altogether superior and better equipped than that occupied by the old pioneers and masters of the art of organ-building. But seeing the little that has been attempted of a truly scientific and artistic character, it is difficult to divine what may be accomplished in the future, when highly educated and scientifically trained organ-builders realize the necessity of giving their serious attention to the scientific and artistic development of the tonal resources and powers of the Organ.

CHAPTER IV.

TIMBRE-CREATING COMPOUND STOPS.

 SUBJECT is touched upon in the present Chapter which deserves the earnest consideration and careful study of all interested in the tonal development of the Organ. It is a subject which has either never presented itself to, or has been strangely neglected by, the many writers on the Organ; for, outside our own writings, we are not aware of its ever having been touched upon in the entire range of organ literature. We allude to the production of new and exceptional timbres or qualities of tone by the scientific and artistic combinations of stops of contrasting tonalities. As we have said elsewhere: while a few tentative essays in this direction have been made by certain builders, no noteworthy results of systematic methods have as yet appeared in important Organs. The field is practically a virgin one, offering a wide scope for study and experiment: and it is to be hoped that the musicians and experts interested in the tonal development of the Organ of the Twentieth Century will give this interesting branch of tone-production the attention it deserves.

When it is fully recognized that the MIXTURES or compound stops are not merely harmonic-corroborating, but that they are also, under certain conditions, *timbre-creating,* it is not difficult to realize that much can be done, under the inspiration of acoustical science and musical sense, which has never been attempted under the methods of tonal appointment adopted by the old builders, and followed, more or less closely and blindly, by their successors.

It may be safely said that no stop in the Organ affords so fertile a field for the exercise of acoustical knowledge and the display of musical sense as the MIXTURE; and no single stop exerts so potent an influence for good or ill on the tone of the division in which it is placed.

We have, in the preceding Chapter, pointed out how the compound harmonic-corroborating stops should be constructed according to the teaching of the laws and phenomena of musical sounds. In the present Chapter we shall offer some suggestions for their further development along different lines; and also for the formation of dual timbre-creating stops. The latter subject deserves the earnest attention of organists and organ-builders seriously interested in the tonal development of the Organ.

While we maintain that all the harmonic-corroborating stops of the Organ should be so voiced and regulated as to yield tones in strict accordance with the natural laws of sound, we do not say that they should all be constructed alike. On the contrary, we go so far as to say that no two MIXTURES in the same Organ should be similar in their tonal character or office. In a large instrument, having three, four, or more separate manual divisions or subdivisions, every one of its several compound stops should be entirely different from the others; its predominant pitch, the number of its ranks, the number and positions of its breaks, and the tonal character of each of its ranks, being dictated by the tonal apportionment of the division or subdivision in which it is placed, and the office it has to fulfil therein. Speaking broadly, the compound stops may be grouped under two classifications; namely, *harmonic-corroborating* and *timbre-creating*. The former properly belong to the foundation-work, represented by the OPEN DIAPASONS, and find their proper place and office in the division in which the principal pure organ-toned stops are congregated—that commonly called the Great Organ. Here the compound stops, in their correct treatment, are of normal organ-tone, corroborating, and to a considerable extent introducing, the upper partial tones of the DIAPASON prime, to which they impart fulness and richness without changing its pure organ-tone. The *timbre-creating* compound stops, as the term implies, are those which have a distinctive and varied tonality, and which introduce a special tonal coloring into every combination of which they form a constituent. These compound stops have a dual office. In the first place, they enrich the harmonic structure of the divisions in which they are placed, by introducing the higher upper partial tones of the unison prime. In the second place, they create in combination with the several unison labial and lingual stops important and striking changes in tonal coloring,— imparting to certain stops or combinations an element of intense brilliancy; to others rich and vivid coloring; to others solidity of tone,— apparently altering their own tonal character with every change of the prime tones and their combinations.

The timbre-creating compound stops may be formed according to two methods, which may now be briefly described. In the first method of construction, all the ranks employed are of the same class of pipes, yielding the same quality of tone, and graduated in strength in accordance with the laws which govern the natural harmonic upper partial tones, as already dwelt upon. The pipes forming a timbre-creating compound stop, of the form now under consideration, may be all of metal or all of wood, and all open or all covered; and they may be of any tonality possible in labial pipes. Accordingly, we can have compound stops composed of pipes belonging to any of the following classes: LIEBLICHGEDECKT, ROHRFLÖTE, SPITZFLÖTE, HARMONIC FLUTE, ZAUBERFLÖTE, ZARTFLÖTE, GEMSHORN, DULCIANA, VOX ANGELICA, ÆOLINE, VIOLA DA GAMBA, VIOLA D'AMORE, VIOL, DOLCAN, and several others that will suggest themselves to the artist in quest of tone-colors. Compound stops constructed under this method have been introduced to some extent by certain builders, and invariably with encouraging results; but it is open to the artistic builders of the present century to carry their construction to the highest point of excellence, and to introduce them into the expressive divisions of their Organs. That the timbre-creating value of compound stops of different tonalities will ultimately be recognized by musicians we have very little doubt: and the general introduction of such stops, in scientifically and artistically appointed instruments, can only be retarded by the reluctance of organ-builders to depart from the old-fashioned and time-honored manner of tonal appointment.

When we approach the consideration of the compound stops constructed according to the second method, we enter upon ground all but unexplored,—at best, only pressed by the hesitating footsteps of those whose musical sense and artistic perception lead to a desire for better things than are commonly served up by the average organ-builder, or are dreamt of by the average organist. This second method of constructing the timbre-creating compound stops consists in forming their ranks of pipes of different tonalities. This method, as may be readily realized, opens up a wide and fertile field for study and experiment on the part of the organ-builder who will for a time forget the modern craze for mechanical complexity, and deign to turn his attention to the far more important matters of scientific and artistic tone-production and tonal appointment.

While it is imperative, in accordance with the natural laws of musical sounds, that the several ranks of a harmonic-corroborating compound stop be graduated in strength of tone, and softened as they rise in pitch; it is by no means necessary that the ranks of a purely timbre-creating compound stop should follow the same system of graduation. If, however, a harmonic-corroborating stop is composed of ranks of pipes of different tonalities, for the purpose of creating special tonal coloring, then the necessity of graduating the strength of tone of the several ranks comes into force. The dual office of such a stop must not be overlooked, nor must its harmonic-corroborating property be sacrificed.

When one realizes the advantage of making harmonic-corroborating stops also timbre-creating, one can readily see the musical value certain to accrue from an artistic introduction of stops of contrasting tonalities into their ranks. MIXTURES so composed would, apart from their harmonic-corroborating properties, introduce a new and valuable element into the tonal structure of the Organ, and lend themselves to the production of varied compound tones at the present time entirely unknown in the Organ. In compound stops of this class it is desirable to avoid unnecessary breaks in the ranks, and the necessary breaks should be made in the several ranks at different parts of their compass, so as to cover them as much as possible. Ranks that can be carried throughout the compass should not be broken; and the more assertive qualities of tone should be selected for these unbroken ranks. In the more important class of timbre-creating stops no breaks are required, as will be shown farther on.

We will suppose a timbre-creating MIXTURE, of four or five ranks, to be introduced in an expressive division of an Organ, each rank of which is formed of pipes having a distinct and contrasting tonality; and that unison stops of similar tonalities are present in the same division, or in other divisions which can be coupled with that containing the MIXTURE. Now, any one well versed in the subject of tonal combinations of organ stops can easily imagine the immense variety of *timbres* that would result from the combination of such a MIXTURE with the unison stops, individually or in groups. Each unison stop would find only one rank in the MIXTURE yielding tones strictly belonging to its own family of harmonics; while the tones of all the other ranks, falling in—in pitch only—with the sequence of the harmonic upper partials of the prime unison tone, would create special, and frequently remarkable and beautiful, effects of tonal coloring—effects absolutely impossible to obtain in the Organ by any other expedients. Such effects—which may be compared to the wonderful hues produced by the painter on his many-tinted palette —would be practically inexhaustible in Organs of moderate dimensions, while in Concert-room Organs of the first magnitude they would be absolutely inexhaustible.

It is not practicable to formulate any rules for the tonal structure of these timbre-creating compound stops, simply because it depends upon the tonal appointment of the divisions of the Organ in which they are placed and the peculiar tonal coloring aimed at. In deciding the treatment to be adopted, the following matters have to be taken into careful consideration. First, the number of ranks have to be decided on. Secondly, the pitches of the ranks have to be selected, with respect to the general tonal apportionment of the division in which the stop is to be placed. Thirdly, the different tones to be congregated have to be selected in accordance with the special purposes of the stop. Fourthly,

—and this is a question of great moment,—the apportionment of the selected tones to the different ranks. In the case of a Mixture of five ranks this apportionment can be varied to almost any extent, each one producing a distinct tonal coloring.

Compound stops of the Cornet class, formed of ranks which can be carried throughout the manual compass without a break, afford admirable opportunities for effective timbre-creation; and should be introduced, in one or more of the expressive manual divisions in every important Concert-room Organ. These timbre-creating Cornets, having no direct harmonic-corroborating office to fulfil, do not require to be graduated in strength of tone in the same manner as the purely harmonic-corroborating Mixtures. Each rank of the Cornet may be treated as a separate stop and regulated in the usual manner. The relative strengths of tone of the several stops forming the ranks must depend on the tonal character of the stops, and also on the influence they are destined to exercise on the compound tone the Cornet is schemed to produce. Should a stop of high pitch be introduced, the pipes of which become too small to be carried to the top note of the compass, it should be discontinued where practically necessary, and not continued with larger pipes, after the fashion of a break in an ordinary Mixture. In a compound timbre-creating stop, composed of four or more ranks, the omission of the highest octave of pipes in one or even two of the higher pitched ranks will not seriously affect the tonal value of the stop.

In a timbre-creating Cornet, such as has been alluded to, the principal rank should, as a rule, be formed of a stop of 4 ft. pitch, which may be open, covered, or half covered, as the tonal coloring of the complete stop may dictate. While it will be generally desirable to form the other ranks of stops of higher harmonic pitches, it may be found, for the production of certain tonal colorings, necessary to introduce two stops, preferably, though not necessarily, of 4 ft. pitch—an open and a covered stop being desirable for the sake of contrast. As a suggestion, we may here give the composition for a five-rank, timbre-creating Cornet, suitable for insertion in any manual division, save the First or Foundation Division, of an important Concert-room Organ.

Timbre-creating Cornet—V. ranks.

RANK.			PITCH.			CHARACTER OF STOP.
I.	.	.	Octave, 4 ft.	.	.	Lieblichgedeckt.
II.	.	.	Tenth, $3\frac{1}{5}$ ft.	.	.	Gemshorn.
III.	.	.	Twelfth, $2\frac{2}{3}$ ft.	.	.	Viol.
IV.	.	.	Fifteenth, 2 ft.	.	.	Harmonic Piccolo.
V.	.	.	Nineteenth, $1\frac{1}{3}$ ft.	.	.	Dolce.

Any organ expert versed in tonal matters can readily see how such a Cornet could be altered in its timbre-creating properties by either simply altering the positions and pitches of the component stops, or by substituting others of different tonalities in any or all of the ranks. A less number of ranks can also be adopted.

In the concluding portion of the preceding Chapter we speak of the subject to which this Chapter is devoted, and allude to the desirability of introducing different classes of pipes in the separate ranks of MIX-TURES, mentioning the fact that the ECHO DULCIANA CORNET in the Swell division of the Concert Organ in the Public Halls, at Glasgow, constructed by Messrs. T. C. Lewis & Company, is composed of six ranks of metal and wood, open and covered, pipes artistically associated. The tonal effect of this compound stop is extremely beautiful and satisfactory. Mr. Lewis, who was a distinguished bell-founder as well as organ-builder, was the only English builder known to us who devoted serious attention to the science of acoustics so far as the production of compound musical sound is concerned,—in this direction rivaling his French confrère, M. Cavaillé-Coll,—and the construction of the compound stop just commented on was a result of his investigations. It is to be regretted that there are not more men of his attainments in the organ-building world to-day, to raise the Organ out of its dull monotony of tonal appointment.

In the preceding Chapter are given particulars of the largest compound harmonic-corroborating stop ever constructed, the MIXTURE of ten ranks in the Pedal Organ of the large instrument in the Wanamaker Store in Philadelphia. This gigantic stop, being composed throughout of pipes of the DIAPASON class, cannot well be placed among timbre-creating stops. Another important Pedal Organ compound stop is mentioned, which may claim to be classed as timbre-creating; namely the GRAND BOURDON in the Organ in the Cathedral of Riga. Through the courtesy of the distinguished builders, Messrs. E. F. Walcker & Company, of Ludwigsburg, we are able to give the measurements of the CCC pipes of the several ranks forming this stop. The pipes are of wood throughout and varied in tonality in each rank. The TIERCE, 6⅖ FT., is formed of conical pipes, doubtless for the purpose of securing a special light and bright singing quality in this somewhat assertive upper partial tone. The stop belongs to the 32 ft. harmonic series.

MEASUREMENTS OF THE CCC PIPES OF THE GRAND BOURDON—
V. RANKS, IN THE ORGAN OF RIGA CATHEDRAL.

PRINCIPAL, 16 FT. . . .	Width, 220 mm.	Depth, 280 mm.
QUINT, 10⅔ FT.	" 110 "	" 153 "
OCTAVE, 8 FT.	" 108 "	" 131 "
TIERCE, 6⅖ FT. At mouth, .	" 74 "	" 106 "
" " At top, . .	" 48 "	" 64 "
SUPER-OCTAVE, 4 FT. . . .	" 65 "	" 80 "

Certain individuals who claim to be authorities in organ-building matters have pronounced an opinion that, under the modern or their special manner of stop appointment, MIXTURES are unnecessary and undesirable. It is practically a waste of words to discuss the arguments, if arguments they can be called, that these persons have advanced; for, after the researches of Prof. Helmholtz, the value of the harmonic-corroborating stops cannot well be questioned, even if one is disposed to forget all that past experience has proved, and to ignore the opinions of the many musicians who have advocated their introduction and recognized their importance in the tonal appointment of the Organ. We are disposed to believe that those who dispute the importance and utility of the harmonic-corroborating stops in tone-creation have given very little, if any, serious attention to the acoustical phenomena involved. That a certain class of organ-builders should be willing to meet the wishes of those who object to the introduction of MIXTURES is not to be wondered at. However many ranks a MIXTURE may comprise, it appears in an Organ Specification as a single stop; and this, when a builder is estimating for an Organ on the many-stop basis, is a decided drawback in his estimation. Besides this, an organ-builder, unless he is a consummate artist, looks upon MIXTURES unfavorably, because they are usually unsatisfactory in their tonal effects through unscientific treatment; and because they are expensive and troublesome to make, and still more troublesome to regulate, tune correctly, and keep in order. Such considerations, however, should not influence the musician who realizes the proper office and true value of the harmonic-corroborating stops.

The opinions alluded to in the preceding paragraph will doubtless retard to a considerable extent the development and introduction of timbre-creating compound stops, just as they have largely discouraged, during late years, the introduction of purely harmonic-corroborating compound stops in many important Organs. There is a conviction in the minds of certain organ experts and organ-builders—doubtless the wish is largely father to the thought—that the introduction in the Organ of labial and lingual stops of unison pitch, the voices of which are in themselves rich in harmonic upper partials, renders the addition of compound harmonic-corroborating stops altogether unnecessary—unnecessary only so far as such individual stops are concerned. It may be readily conceded that so far as the pungent string-toned stops, introduced during late years, are affected, there is no call for direct aid from harmonic-corroborating mixture-work: but the reverse is the case with timbre-creating compound stops, which are calculated to produce with such string-toned stops many beautiful and hitherto unknown qualities of compound tone. It must not be forgotten, however, that the majority of the unison stops of the Organ have voices which are essentially weak in, if not entirely devoid of, harmonic over-tones; and that for the production of many beautiful and highly effective varieties of timbre or tone-color, these important unison stops have to be associated with other stops—simple or compound—of different tonalities, strengths of voice, and pitch.   For this purpose no stops could be more efficient or fertile in the production of such desirable varieties of tone-color than properly-formed timbre-creating compound stops; comprising in their structure more or less active harmonic-corroborating qualities.

In concluding this branch of our subject we can safely say that no section of the tonal forces of the Organ calls for more scientific knowledge, more painstaking investigation, more careful experimentation, and a more highly cultivated musical sense, than the section which embraces the compound stops—harmonic-corroborating and timbre-creating—yet at the present time there is no section so systematically neglected, even by those who profess to be artistic organ-builders.   By some, such compound stops are held to be of little importance and may be altogether dispensed with, while the fact is they are of great importance and value, affecting to a marked degree the entire tonal character of the Organ. They are factors of immense influence in the production of varied timbres and rich compound tones, which would simply be unproducible without their aid.

Notwithstanding all that has been achieved in the organ-builder's art during the past two centuries, it would be a rash thing to say that the Organ has reached its highest point of excellence tonally: indeed, on the contrary, we are convinced that much remains to be done before the Organ of the Twentieth Century, as a perfect musical instrument, can be said to exist.   We are strongly of opinion that much will depend, so far as tonal excellence, variety, and charm are concerned, upon the scientific and artistic development of timbre-creating compound stops, both of the many-ranked class previously commented on, and the simpler but hardly less important dual class we have now to briefly consider.

TIMBRE-CREATING DUAL STOPS

While it is a common practice in ordinary organ registration to combine two stops of different tonalities, using such stops as are available in the tonal apportionment of the division performed on, for the purpose of obtaining varied compound tones; very little attention has been paid by organ experts and organ-builders to the construction of dual stops, scientifically and artistically devised, for the permanent production of entirely new and valuable compound voices; such as can, under no conditions, be yielded by a single rank of pipes, or produced under the ordinary system of tonal appointment in which the necessary elements are not provided.   We are strongly of opinion that timbre-creating dual stops will occupy an important place in the tonal appointment of the perfect Organ of the Twentieth Century. They have already taken their place, in some force, in one very important Concert Organ, as will be shown later on.

There are certain stops at present in the Organ, chiefly of the lingual class, the characteristic voices of which require for their imitative development the addition of what may be designated *helpers* or *auxiliary stops*. This is notably the case with the lingual stop called the Vox Humana, which yields a voice of a falsetto character, strongly nasal in the majority of examples, and one which calls for a supporting and body-giving tone to enrich its imitativeness. From close observation we know that the late W. T. Best never used the fine Vox Humana, in the St. George's Hall Organ, without drawing a soft-toned unison stop along with it to give it volume—chest-voice quality—and to cover, as much as possible, the nasal intonation peculiar to it and all Vox Humanas. No hard and fast rule can be laid down with regard to the stop to be associated with a Vox Humana, simply because its voice varies considerably in different examples, and is very rarely agreeable and sympathetic, especially when constructed with short resonators. Accordingly, each Vox Humana must be specially studied, so as to determine the best quality of tone to be yielded by its helper. Generally, we have found that a soft and round unimitative flute-tone, of unison pitch, is the one best adapted for combination. In an Organ of any importance the Vox Humana should certainly appear as a dual stop; as specified by us for the Vox Humanas in the Third and Fifth Organs of the instrument installed in the Festival Hall of the Louisiana Purchase Exposition. Each Vox Humana was associated with a wood stop of a flute tonality.

While a dual Vox Humana requires the aid of the Tremolant to impart to its voice the imitative character required, it should not be forgotten that if the stop is properly made and voiced it forms, without the tremolo effect, a valuable stop that can be used in full chords and in ordinary combinations. This is especially the case when the lingual stop is properly constructed with long, covered and slotted resonators.

There are other lingual stops which appear in the tonal appointment of almost every Organ of importance, and which call for a dual treatment to establish their imitative voices. Chief among these is the Orchestral Clarinet, 8 ft. Although in the best examples of this stop the imitation of the true orchestral instrument is very close, it never fails to be greatly improved by association with a sympathetic helper. Helmholtz has analyzed the tones and musical character of the orchestral Clarinet, and has found that the tones dependent on the length of the cylindrical column of air within the instrument correspond to the sounds proper to a covered organ-pipe. This fact leads conclusively to the adoption of a covered stop of unison pitch as the most suitable helper to the organ CLARINET; and actual experimental tests have proved this conclusion to be correct. By careful trials and observation we have found the most suitable helper to be a DOPPELFLÖTE, 8 FT., of small scale and medium strength of voice. Its tone combines perfectly with that of the CLARINET, imparting to it the peculiar full and woody quality, so to speak, of the orchestral instrument, and especially of the Bass Clarinet, the grave tones of which have to be imitated in the organ stop of full compass.

The CORNO DI BASSETTO, 8 FT., is another lingual stop that can be greatly enhanced in tonal character and beauty by being treated artistically as a dual stop. While it may be supposed to imitate the voice of the orchestral instrument of the same name, which is in reality a Tenor Clarinet in F, as an organ stop it properly yields a tone fuller and rounder than that of the ORCHESTRAL CLARINET, commented on above. The normal voice of the lingual CORNO DI BASSETTO can be added to and modified to any desirable degree by the character of the auxiliary stop associated with it. When both a CLARINET and a CORNO DI BASSETTO are introduced in an Organ, care should be taken to give the latter a tonality markedly dissimilar from that of the CLARINET. This is done to a certain extent in the lingual stop itself, by enlargement of scale and special voicing; but much more can be done by its helper. Our practical tests have induced us to favor the addition of a full-toned QUINTATEN, 8 FT.,* which, in effectively corroborating the second upper partial tone, greatly improves the characteristic timbre of the stop. Care must be taken to adjust the strength of the tone of the QUINTATEN to the dominating voice of the CORNO DI BASSETTO, so as to obtain a perfectly smooth compound tone of a rich timbre. Much art and musical taste can be displayed in this direction.

There are other lingual stops which could be considerably improved by association with labial helpers of suitable tonality; the most important being the ORCHESTRAL HORN, 8 FT., which has never yet been made fully imitative of the peculiar tone of the orchestral instrument. Careful tests can alone be depended on to solve the question of the most suitable combination to produce a satisfactory imitative voice, after the best possible result has been reached in the lingual stop alone. The field is open for investigation and experiment, and is well worthy of the artist-voicer's earnest study.

We have now to consider dual stops of another description in which labial stops, open and covered, are alone used in combination.

Two dual stops which are both timbre-creating and harmonic-cor-

---

* Commonly, but less correctly, termed QUINTADENA. The name QUINTATEN is derived from the Latin words *quintam tenentes*, and is properly used to designate covered stops which yield compound tones, in which the second upper partial is almost as prominent as the prime tone. Helmholtz remarks: " Narrow stopped pipes let the twelfth be very distinctly heard at the same time with the prime tone; and have hence been called *Quintaten (quintam tenentes).*"

roborating may first be dwelt upon. The first is the SESQUIALTERA, formed of a QUINT, $5\frac{1}{3}$ FT., and a TIERCE, $3\frac{1}{5}$ FT., which stand at the interval of a major sixth apart. In this grave pitch, the dual stop belongs to the 16 ft. harmonic series; so, as a timbre-creating stop, it can be introduced in any manual division of an important Organ in which a stop of 16 ft. tone is inserted. The SESQUIALTERA can be varied in its timbre to almost any desired extent; for there are no conditions imposed on the respective tonalities of the stops selected to compose it, save that the TIERCE must, for the production of an agreeable compound tone, be less assertive than the QUINT. Both stops may be of open or covered pipes, or one may be of open and the other of covered or half-covered pipes, and either or both may be of metal or wood. Such being the case, the timbre-creating opportunities provided by this dual stop are practically limitless. In combination with either unison or double labial or lingual stops of full intonation, the SESQUIALTERA, as suggested, would produce remarkable tonal effects, unproducible on any Organ of ordinary construction to-day.

No SESQUIALTERA of this grave tonality has ever, to our knowledge, been introduced into a manual division of an Organ, nor has one of any pitch been devised as a timbre-creating stop. It, accordingly, furnishes one of the opportunities in tone-production which should not be overlooked in the tonal appointment of the Organ of the Twentieth Century, in which every element of refined musical sound should be provided.

The second dual stop which is both timbre-creating and harmonic-corroborating is the TERTIAN, formed of a TIERCE, $6\frac{2}{5}$ FT., and a QUINT, $5\frac{1}{3}$ FT., standing at the interval of a major third apart, hence its name. In this grave pitch the dual stop, in its capacity of harmonic-corroborator, belongs to the 32 ft. harmonic series. In that direction it strictly belongs to the Pedal Organ in which the 32 ft. tone is provided: but in a manual division the stop is valuable on account of its timbre-creating powers, which, as in the case of the SESQUIALTERA, can be developed to almost any extent. In the TERTIAN the component stops may either be of open or covered pipes, and either or both may be of metal or wood; accordingly, it is possible to produce remarkable *timbres* in great variety by associating stops of analogous or of contrasting tonalities. In this dual stop it is not so necessary to subdue the tone of the TIERCE as in the case of the SESQUIALTERA, as the character of the compound tone will depend principally on the voice of the third-sounding rank in its relation to that of the higher fifth-sounding rank. The problem of timbre-creation is in this case an extremely interesting one, and both musical taste and artistic skill have a wide field for their display.

It is needless to remark that both the SESQUIALTERA and the TERTIAN must be subordinate in strength of tone to the principal unison stops of the divisions of the Organ in which they are introduced.

There is another and very important class of timbre-creating dual labial stops which remains to be described. In all the stops belonging to this class the principal component stop is invariably of unison (8 feet) pitch, while the other is a mutation stop. Of dual stops so composed we are able to give existing examples which have been skilfully devised and constructed by a noted expert. The use of the unison stop leads to the production of a large family of beautiful timbre-creating stops, which are eminently suited for solo effects, and for combination with other labial and with lingual stops of both unison and double pitch. The solo voices produced by these dual stops surpass in richness and variety everything possible to be produced by the ordinary single stops, hence their great value in the tonal appointment of important Organs. That they have so long been neglected is far from being creditable to those who have claimed to have the tonal development of the Organ at heart. Expense may be urged as an excuse; but it is hardly a valid one in this age of monster Organs, comprising between two and three hundred speaking stops.

The most noteworthy examples of timbre-creating dual stops which have come under our observation are the very effective ones recently devised by an expert engaged in the reconstruction and extensive enlargement of the Organ originally designed by us, and exhibited at St. Louis in 1904, now in the great Wanamaker Store in Philadelphia, Pa. The particulars respecting the combinations and tonalities of these stops cannot fail to be of service to those interested in the creation of new and valuable voices in the Organ. We are able to furnish them through the courtesy of Mr. Rodman Wanamaker and the expert by whom the stops were devised and constructed.

The manual dual stops are five in number and are named, respectively, QUINT FLUTE, 8 FT., TIERCE FLUTE, 8 FT., NASARD FLUTE, 8 FT., NASARD GAMBA, 8 FT., and UNDA MARIS, 8 FT. These are inserted in different divisions of the Organ.

QUINT FLUTE, 8 FT.—This is located in the so-called Etherial Organ, where it speaks on wind of 25 inches pressure. It is, so far as our knowledge extends, the most noteworthy timbre-creating dual stop of 8 ft. pitch ever constructed, and one that could only be properly introduced in Organs of the first magnitude, and under favorable conditions. It can be realized from the following particulars that its compound voice is of considerable grandeur, while its tonality surpasses in richness of color that of any other flute-toned stop known to have been produced.

The first and principal rank is a CLEAR FLUTE, 8 FT., formed of open wood pipes from CC to c⁴, to which are added twelve open metal pipes for octave coupling. Both the scale of the pipes and the treatment of their mouths vary at different portions of the compass, showing a keen appreciation of tone-value by the designer and voicer.

Scale of the Clear Flute.

	WIDTH INSIDE.	DEPTH INSIDE.	HEIGHT OF MOUTH.
CC	8 inches.	$10\frac{1}{2}$ inches.	$3\frac{7}{8}$ inches.
C	$5\frac{3}{16}$ "	$6\frac{5}{16}$ "	$2\frac{1}{2}$ "
F	$4\frac{1}{4}$ "	5 "	2 "
c^1	$3\frac{1}{4}$ "	$3\frac{7}{8}$ "	$1\frac{1}{2}$ "
b^1	$2\frac{1}{4}$ "	$3\frac{3}{16}$ "	$\frac{15}{16}$ "
c^2	$2\frac{1}{8}$ "	3 "	$1\frac{3}{16}$ "
c^3	$1\frac{3}{8}$ "	$1\frac{3}{4}$ "	$\frac{9}{16}$ "
c^4	$\frac{7}{8}$ "	$1\frac{1}{8}$ "	$\frac{1}{4}$ "

The pipes from CC to E—17 notes have the usual mouths, level blocks, and the windway formed in hollowed caps. From F (where ratio changes) to b^1 the blocks are slightly sunk save near the lower lip, the mouths are of the ordinary form, and the windway formed in hollowed caps. From c^2 to c^4 the pipes have inverted mouths, sunk blocks, and windway formed in hollowed caps. The thickness of the upper lips ranges from ⅜ths of an inch at CC to ⅛th at c^4. All are fully rounded save in the inverted mouths. The mouths of the pipes CC to GG♯ have rounded harmonic-bridges.

The metal pipes from $c♯^4$ to c^5 are harmonic, of double length, and pierced. Their diameters range from 1 inch to $\frac{7}{16}$ inch; and their mouths range in height from ⅜ inch to ¼ inch, and are rounded out and arched.

The second and subordinate rank is a Quint, $5\frac{1}{3}$ ft., formed of covered wood pipes from CC to $f♯^2$—43 notes, and open metal pipes from g^2 to c^5—30 notes: all voiced to yield a normal tone.

Scale of the Quint.

	WIDTH INSIDE.	DEPTH INSIDE.	HEIGHT OF MOUTH.
CC	$3\frac{1}{4}$ inches.	$4\frac{1}{4}$ inches.	$1\frac{1}{8}$ inch.
C	$2\frac{1}{8}$ "	$2\frac{3}{4}$ "	$\frac{3}{4}$ "
G	$1\frac{5}{8}$ "	$2\frac{1}{8}$ "	$\frac{9}{16}$ "
c^1	$1\frac{1}{3}$ "	$1\frac{3}{4}$ "	$\frac{1}{2}$ "
c^2	$\frac{7}{8}$ "	$1\frac{1}{8}$ "	$\frac{5}{16}$ "
d^2	$1\frac{3}{16}$ "	$1\frac{1}{16}$ "	$\frac{9}{32}$ "
$f♯^2$	$\frac{3}{4}$ "	$\frac{15}{16}$ "	$\frac{1}{4}$ "

In this scale, the ratio shows halving on the 20th pipe, closely approaching the ratio $1:2.3$, which halves on the 21st pipe. The pipes have ordinary mouths with upper lips of moderate thickness, well rounded. The blocks are level on top. In the CC octave the windway is formed in the blocks, while from C to $f♯^2$ the windway is cut in hollowed caps.

From g^2 to c^5 the pipes are of open metal: the scale of g^2 being

15/16ths inch in diameter, with a mouth 3/8ths inch high. The c^5 pipe is 3/8ths inch in diameter, with a mouth 3/32nds inch high.

TIERCE FLUTE, 8 FT.—This timbre-creating dual stop is inserted in the Choir Organ, where it speaks on wind of the high pressure of 15 inches. The stop is unique; for it is safe to say that such a stop has never been even contemplated in the preparation of any tonal scheme for an Organ hitherto constructed. We know of no existing Organ in which the component parts of the stop appear in any single manual division.

The first and pitch-determining rank is a HARMONIC FLUTE, 8 FT., formed of metal pipes throughout; the pipes from c^2 to c^5 being of double length and pierced; and have segmental mouths.

SCALE OF THE HARMONIC FLUTE.

	DIAMETER.	HEIGHT OF MOUTH.	
CC . .	5 inches . . .	1 5/8 inches.	
C . .	3 1/2 "	1 3/16 "	
c^1 . .	2 3/16 "	11/16 "	
c^2 . .	1 3/4 "	9/16 "	—HARMONIC.
c^3 . .	1 1/2 "	7/16 "	"
c^4 . .	1 1/16 "	1/4 "	"
c^5 . .	11/16 "	1/8 "	"

The second and subordinate rank is a TIERCE, 3 1/5 FT., of open metal pipes throughout, yielding pure organ-tone. This mutation stop, strictly belonging to the 16 ft. harmonic series, is very seldom introduced in the manual divisions of Organs; never except the 16 ft. pitch is prominently present. In the case of the dual stop under consideration it is timbre-creating and has no direct harmonic-corroborating office. Its voice is so artistically combined with that of the HARMONIC FLUTE that it produces a solo voice of an absolutely new and striking tone-color, impossible to be produced from a single-ranked FLUTE, however made and voiced. This fact must be recognized.

SCALE OF THE TIERCE.

	DIAMETER.	HEIGHT OF MOUTH.
CC . .	3 3/8 inches . . .	7/8 inch.
C . .	2 "	9/16 "
c^1 . .	1 3/16 "	5/16 "
c^2 . .	3/4 "	5/32 "
c^3 . .	1/2 "	3/32 "
c^4 . .	5/16 "	5/64 "

c^5—Top twelve pipes repeated.

NASARD FLUTE, 8 FT.—This timbre-creating harmonic dual stop is located in the Great Organ, where it speaks on a wind of 5 inches pressure. Its quality of tone, owing to its unique composition, is necessarily and essentially different from that of any single FLUTE hitherto introduced in organ appointment; and it is reasonable to assert that it never can be produced from a single rank of pipes, however constructed. The existence of such a dual stop multiplies to an undreamt-of extent the resources of the flute-toned forces of the Organ, when used in combination. This fact has been proved by actual tone tests; and plainly shows the value and art-importance timbre-creating dual stops must assume in the tonal appointment of the perfect Organ of the Twentieth Century.

The first and principal rank is a HARMONIC FLUTE, 8 FT., of open metal pipes. From c² to c⁴ the pipes are double length and pierced, and have arched mouths with rounded lips.

SCALE OF THE HARMONIC FLUTE.

	DIAMETER.		HEIGHT OF MOUTH.	
CC	5 inches.		1⁷⁄₁₆ inches.	
C	3³⁄₃₂ "		1⁵⁄₁₆ "	
c¹	1¹⁵⁄₁₆ "		⁹⁄₁₆ "	
c²	1⁷⁄₁₆ "		⁹⁄₁₆ "	—HARMONIC.
c³	1⁵⁄₁₆ "		⁵⁄₁₆ "	"
c⁴	⁹⁄₁₆ "		³⁄₁₆ "	"

The second and subordinate rank is a HARMONIC NASARD or TWELFTH, 2⅔ FT., of metal, the pipes of which are double length and pierced from C to top. Mouths arched.

SCALE OF THE NASARD.

	DIAMETER.		HEIGHT OF MOUTH.	
CC	2¼ inches.		1¹⁄₁₆ inch.	
C	1⅝ "		⁹⁄₁₆ "	—HARMONIC.
c¹	1⁵⁄₁₆ "		³⁄₈ "	"
c²	⁹⁄₁₆ "		³⁄₁₆ "	"
c³	⁹⁄₃₂ "		⅛ "	"

NASARD GAMBA, 8 FT.—This remarkable timbre-creating dual stop is placed in the Swell Organ, where it speaks on wind of 15 inches pressure. It is an entirely new addition to the family of string-toned stops; and it points the way to further developments, even within the necessarily restricted field imposed by the combination of stops of the same tonality. A much wider field is open for the artist in tone-production through the association of stops of widely different character and of different pitches: and we firmly believe that many very beautiful voices, hitherto unknown, will enrich the tonal appointment of the Organ of the Twentieth Century, when the value of timbre-creating dual stops is fully realized, and organ-builders and experts find it desirable to become painstaking artists in their production.

The first and pitch-determining rank is a GAMBA, 8 FT., of metal throughout, all pipes from c^1 to c^5 being of tin. The mouths of all pipes from CC to $a\sharp^3$ are fitted with harmonic-bridges. This stop is voiced to yield a powerful string-tone, so as to strongly assert the unison pitch.

SCALE OF THE UNISON GAMBA.

		DIAMETER.			HEIGHT OF MOUTH.
CC	. .	$3\frac{3}{16}$ inches.	.	.	$\frac{3}{4}$ inch.
C	. .	2 "	.	.	$\frac{9}{16}$ "
c^1	. .	$1\frac{3}{16}$ "	.	.	$\frac{5}{16}$ "
c^2	. .	$\frac{3}{4}$ "	.	.	$\frac{3}{16}$ "
c^3	. .	$\frac{7}{16}$ "	.	.	$\frac{1}{8}$ "
c^4	. .	$\frac{5}{16}$ "	.	.	$\frac{3}{32}$ "
c^5	. .	$\frac{1}{4}$ "	.	.	$\frac{1}{16}$ "

The second and subordinate rank is a NASARD GAMBA, $2\frac{2}{3}$ FT., constructed of tin throughout. The mouths of all pipes from CC to $a\sharp^2$ are fitted with harmonic bridges. This stop is voiced to yield a somewhat subdued but clear string-tone, which combines perfectly with the voice of the unison GAMBA, and produces a compound tone of wonderful beauty and color-value : it is unlike anything hitherto yielded by a single string-toned stop.

SCALE OF THE NASARD GAMBA.

		DIAMETER.			HEIGHT OF MOUTH.
CC	. .	$1\frac{1}{4}$ inches.	.	.	$\frac{1}{4}$ inch.
C	. .	$\frac{3}{4}$ "	.	.	$\frac{3}{16}$ "
c^1	. .	$\frac{1}{2}$ "	.	.	$\frac{1}{8}$ "
c^2	. .	$11\frac{1}{32}$ "	.	.	$\frac{3}{32}$ "
c^3	. .	$\frac{1}{4}$ "	.	.	$\frac{1}{16}$ "
c^4	. .	$\frac{5}{32}$ "	.	.	$\frac{1}{32}$ "

c^5—Pipes from $c\sharp^3$ to c^4 repeated for this octave.

UNDA MARIS, 8 FT.—This timbre-creating dual stop is placed in the Choir Organ, where it speaks on wind of the pressure of 5 inches. This stop differs from the four preceding examples in so much as both its ranks are of unison pitch. The name given to the stop is somewhat misleading to those conversant with stop-formation and nomenclature. The name has long been an established one, and is correctly applied to a single rank of pipes yielding a soft organ-tone, and tuned slightly flatter than the true pitch of the Organ; so that when drawn with some other softly-voiced unison stop it produces an undulatory effect in the combined tone, which has been compared to the gentle wave-motion of the sea, hence the name UNDA MARIS. It would seem difficult, however, to find a truly appropriate and expressive name for this dual stop, for it yields a compound tone distinct from any recognized standard tonality. It is true, however, that owing to one of its ranks being tuned a few beats per second flat, an undulatory effect is imparted to its compound tone. This fact doubtless suggested the name.

The stop is formed of a GEMSHORN, 8 FT., and a string-toned rank or GAMBA, 8 FT. The former rank is constructed of open wood pipes from CC to BB, and from C to c⁴ of spotted-metal pipes, tapered in the usual manner. The mouths of the twelve wood pipes are furnished with harmonic-bridges, and are so voiced as to carry down the GEMSHORN tone in close imitation. The GAMBA starts from Tenor C, and, accordingly, has only 49 pipes, all of which are of tin.

SCALES OF THE GEMSHORN.

WOOD PIPES.	WIDTH INSIDE.	DEPTH INSIDE.	HEIGHT OF MOUTH.
CC	3½ inches.	4½ inches.	1 3/16 inches.
GG	2¾ "	3½ "	⅞ "
BB	2⅜ "	3 "	9/16 "

METAL PIPES.	DIAMETER AT MOUTH.	DIAMETER AT TOP.	HEIGHT OF MOUTH.
C	3 inches.	1½ inches.	9/16 inch.
c^1	1¾ "	⅞ "	5/16 "
c^2	1 1/16 "	9/16 "	3/16 "
c^3	11/16 "	13/32 "	⅛ "
c^4	13/32 "	¼ "	1/16 "

These metal pipes are tuned flat, producing about three undulations per second at C, and gradually increasing to about double the number in the top octave.

SCALE OF THE GAMBA.

	DIAMETER.	HEIGHT OF MOUTH.
C	2¼ inches.	7/16 inch.
c^1	1 5/16 "	5/16 "
c^2	13/16 "	3/16 "
c^3	7/16 "	⅛ "
c^4	5/16 "	1/16 "

The four dual stops just described should, on account of their unquestionable success in timbre-creation, urge other organ experts to enter the field which, though new, is certain to become a fruitful one in the tonal appointment of the Organ of the Twentieth Century. It is certainly to the advantage of organ-builders that dual stops should be encouraged; but they are desirable only when they are scientifically and artistically compounded and relatively voiced, resulting in the production of new and beautiful voices, enriching the tonal appointment of the Organ.

The present range of tonalities, furnished by the existing array of labial and lingual stops, each producing varied tonal characteristics, due to different scales, wind-pressures, and the necessary modifications in voicing, forms a richly set palette of beautiful colors which the tonal artist can combine with wonderful results. We have long advocated the introduction of timbre-creating compound stops; and it is very gratifying to see that at last an artist in tone-production has entered the prolific and theoretically inexhaustible field which he has inaugurated by the formation of the dual stops inserted in the great Wanamaker Organ. The proper introduction of new and effective timbre-creating dual stops, such as those described, in the coming Organs of the Twentieth Century will clearly indicate who are the artistic and who are the merely tradesmen organ-builders of the period. It must be recognized, however, that both limited money and limited space for the accommodation and construction of an Organ will necessarily militate against the introduction of many or any dual stops such as have been commented on in this Chapter.

SINGLE STOPS HAVING DUAL INTONATION

This Chapter would be still more incomplete than it must necessarily be without some allusion to those stops which yield dual tones. At the present time such stops are very few in number, but, as has recently been proved, their production is not necessarily ended.

The stop of this class most commonly known and introduced in the Organ is the QUINTATEN, also known by the common and less expressive names QUINTADENA and QUINTATON. This is a stop formed of covered pipes, so blown and voiced as to yield in addition to the prime tone the second upper partial tone or octave quint, sufficiently strong to impart a distinct duality to the resultant tone. The QUINTATENS, of both 16 ft. and 8 ft. pitch, are, when skilfully voiced, very valuable timbre-creating stops which may, with great advantage, be introduced in both the pedal and manual divisions of the Organ, and especially in those in which no coloring stop of the QUINT class is provided. It may be remarked that the natural dual tonality of the QUINTATEN is altogether different from that produced by the artificial combination of two independent stops,—a unison and octave QUINT,—the peculiar relationship in relative strengths of tone being, of necessity, entirely different.

The most refined form of the QUINTATEN introduced up to the present time is the stop invented by the late William Thynne, of London, and named by him ZAUBERFLÖTE. The stop, commonly of 4 ft. pitch, is formed of covered metal pipes, double length and harmonic from tenor C to the top. To prevent these pipes speaking the prime tones proper to their lengths, they are pierced with small holes, after the manner followed in the open pipes of the HARMONIC FLUTES. The duality of the voice of the ZAUBERFLÖTE is distinctly pronounced and the compound tone is refined and beautiful.

The most effective and remarkable stop of dual tonality, of which we have any knowledge, has recently been invented by Mr. George W. Till, of Philadelphia, Pa. This stop may, appropriately, be termed OCTATEN, from the fact that its pipes yield the prime tone and its first upper partial in almost equal assertiveness. The dual tone produced is remarkable on account of its penetrating and traveling quality without any undesirable loudness. The effect of tone upon the ear is one of restrained power; and it is not difficult to realize the tonal value of such a stop in combination with both labial and lingual stops of imitative character. The pipes forming the OCTATEN are of wood, open, slightly tapered in one direction, slotted, with mouths having upper lips of thick pipe-metal, projecting ears, and cylindrical bridges. The form of the pipes is shown and described in the Chapter on the Forms and Construction of Wood Pipes. Mr. Till has named this stop DUOPHONE.

Both the QUINTATEN and OCTATEN are very valuable timbre-creating stops, and point the way to further developments in dual tonality. This branch of stop formation deserves the earnest attention of pipe designers and voicers.

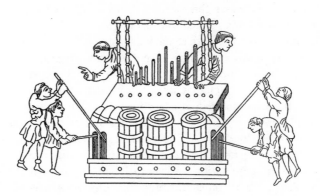

ORGAN OF THE ELEVENTH CENTURY, FROM A MS.
IN THE LIBRARY OF TRINITY COLLEGE, CAMBRIDGE.

CHAPTER V.

THE TONAL APPOINTMENT OF THE ORGAN.

N Chapter II., on The Tonal Structure of the Organ, we deal chiefly with the different pitches of organ-pipes; and the acoustical phenomena and natural laws connected with them, both in their association with, and their relation to, each other. In the present Chapter we treat of the Tonal Appointment of the Organ, or the grouping of pipes or stops, chiefly with reference to their individual and distinctive qualities of tone. The correct and artistic appointment of an Organ is a matter of the greatest importance, and one that calls for the exercise of some scientific knowledge and considerable judgment and musical taste.

While the voices of the Organ are numerous and varied in their tonality and assertiveness, they seem naturally to group themselves into more or less sharply defined and distinctive classes. We have found it convenient and satisfactory to divide the entire range of the tonal forces at the disposal of the modern organ-builder into two primary groups, subdividing each into four secondary groups. By so doing we obtain the following :—

FIRST GROUP.	SECOND GROUP.
Organ-Tone.	Orchestral-Tone.
Unimitative Quality.	*Imitative Quality.*
1. PURE ORGAN-TONE.	1. ORCHESTRAL FLUTE-TONE.
2. FREE ORGAN-TONE.	2. ORCHESTRAL STRING-TONE.
3. FLUTE ORGAN-TONE.	3. ORCHESTRAL REED-TONE.
4. VIOL ORGAN-TONE.	4. ORCHESTRAL BRASS-TONE.

Although all these tones must be adequately represented in the tonal appointment of a complete and resourceful modern Organ, devised for the rendition of both legitimate organ works and orchestral transcriptions, the four tones forming the first group are the only ones that are essential to the constitution of the Organ proper. The purely imitative voices are, however, of the greatest value, and should be introduced to some extent in instruments of every class. In the properly appointed Concert-room Organ, the orchestral-tones are indispensable, and should be represented to the fullest extent called for by the size of the instrument. Indeed, the introduction and apportionment of these voices, under compound expression, form a problem of great importance, and one of profound interest to the organist and student of organ construction. In the Chamber Organ, which should, in all possible cases, be schemed on the Concert-room Organ model, the imitative voices are also indispensable up to the possible or desirable limit. Care must be taken to give them a refined and sympathetic quality suitable for chamber music. In the true and properly appointed Church Organ, the imitations of orchestral instruments are of less importance and may be sparingly introduced. They should never be introduced at the sacrifice of the foundation organ-tone and its harmonic structure. The purely imitative voices are not so well adapted as the several organ-tones for the support and accompaniment of the voices of a choir or congregation, or for the production of the solemn, dignified, and refined tones which should characterize the music of the Church.

Pure organ-tone is essentially unimitative in character, and is that which is peculiar to the Organ—no other instrument can supply it. It is produced by open metal pipes, commonly of large scale, copiously blown by wind of moderate pressure. Such pipes when properly voiced yield singularly full and round tones that are practically simple in their nature; for, under proper and usual conditions, no harmonic upper partial tones are pronounced in them: indeed, the only upper partial tones that produce any sensible effect on the prime tone are the first and second, the latter very slightly, if audible at all. It is from the stops formed of such pipes that the Organ derives its distinctive character and the chief elements of its grandeur. Of such stops those known as the DIAPASONS or PRINCIPALS are the most important; and they form the true foundation of every properly appointed Organ. As Helmholtz remarks: " Wide pipes, having larger masses of vibrating air and admitting of being much more strongly blown [than smaller-scaled, open cylindrical pipes] without jumping up into a harmonic, are used for the great body of sound on the Organ, and are hence called *Principal stimmen* [Principal voices]. For the above reasons they produce the prime tone alone strongly and fully, with a much weaker retinue of secondary tones."

These principal or foundation stops are of 16 ft. pitch in the pedal and 8 ft. pitch in the manual departments. The tones of such stops, pure, full, and commanding as they are, produce, if massed together and depended upon alone, too cloying and heavy an effect to be perfectly satisfying to the musical ear. As before stated, these foundation voices are essentially deficient and weak in harmonic upper partial tones, therefore it is found desirable, in accordance with the phenemona of compound musical sounds, to associate with them other and higher voices, calculated to create a perfectly satisfactory compound tone, rich, bright, and jubilant in its quality. The higher tones so introduced corroborate and supply a desirable number of the upper partials of the prime tones.

The harmonic-corroborating stops associated with the DIAPASONS are, like them, formed of open cylindrical metal pipes, yielding pure organ-tones of different degrees of assertiveness. These stops must be properly scaled with reference to the scales of the DIAPASONS, and voiced so as to combine with, or be absorbed in, the prime tones, without asserting undue prominence individually.

The more important associated harmonic-corroborating stops are the OCTAVE, TWELFTH, FIFTEENTH, SEVENTEENTH, NINETEENTH, and TWENTY-SECOND. They corroborate the 1st, 2nd, 3rd, 4th, 5th, and 7th upper partial tones of the unisons. In addition to these, other open cylindrical metal stops, yielding pure organ-tone, and belonging to the foundation-work, bear the following names in English and American Organs: DOUBLE DIAPASON, 32 FT. (in the Pedal Organ), DOUBLE DIAPASON, 16 FT. (in the manual department), FLAT TWENTY-FIRST, TWENTY-FOURTH, TWENTY-SIXTH, TWENTY-NINTH, THIRTY-THIRD, and THIRTY-SIXTH. The FLAT TWENTY-FIRST, which corroborates the 6th upper partial of the unison, is very rare in English Organs, although it has appeared in certain MIXTURES; but under the name SEPTIÈME it appears in the form of a complete and separate stop in certain French Organs. In the Grand Organ in the Cathedral of Notre-Dame, Paris, constructed by A. Cavaillé-Coll, there is a SEPTIÈME, $1\frac{1}{7}$ FT., in the Grand-Chœur; in the Bombardes a SEPTIÈME, $2\frac{2}{7}$ FT., belonging to the 16 ft. harmonic series; and a SEPTIÈME, $4\frac{4}{7}$ FT., belonging to the 32 ft. harmonic series, in the Pédalier. We have not met with any instance of the SEPTIÈME being introduced in a French MIXTURE. While all the other harmonic-corroborating stops above the FIFTEENTH, 2 FT., commonly appear in the several breaks of the compound stops, the SEVENTEENTH, NINETEENTH, and TWENTY-SECOND sometimes appear as complete stops, as in the Grand-Chœur of the Notre-Dame Organ. In the Pedal Organ they should appear complete, as they would belong to the 16 ft. harmonic series.

In the above list is a practically complete series of stops and ranks of pipes yielding pure organ-tone, from which a great variety of more or less satisfactory Pedal and Great or First Organ apportionments can be made, but the only perfect apportionment, from a scientific point of view, is that in which every member of the series is represented in due relation to the prime or foundation unisons. The advantage of having in a large Organ a practically complete tonal structure and apportionment in at least the pedal department and one manual division cannot be overestimated, for by that means the true foundation—the pure organ-tone—of the instrument is firmly laid. An interesting example of such an apportionment is furnished by the Grand-Chœur of the Organ in Notre-Dame, showing Cavaillé-Coll's scientific leanings in his art, and his appreciation of what has just been stated. The apportionment is as follows:—

1. PRINCIPAL	. .	8	pieds.	7. LARIGOT	. . .	1⅓	pieds.
2. BOURDON .	. .	8	"	8. SEPTIÈME	. .	1⅐	"
3. PRESTANT	. .	4	"	9. PICCOLO	. . .	1	"
4. QUINT	. . .	2⅔	"	10. TUBA MAGNA .	.	16	"
5. DOUBLETTE	. .	2	"	11. TROMPETTE	. .	8	"
6. TIERCE	. . .	1⅗	"	12. CLARION	. . .	4	"

We have stated that pure organ-tone is that produced by open cylindrical metal pipes, of large scale, copiously blown by wind of moderate pressure: these are furnished with plain, wide, and moderately high mouths. The purest organ-tone is yielded by the true English DIAPASON, formed of such pipes of a scale ranging between 5½ inches and 7 inches in diameter at the CC, or 8 ft. pipe,* and blown by wind of from 3 inches to 5 inches pressure. It is never desirable, for the production of a refined and pure organ-tone, to exceed the latter pressure; for when it is exceeded, the purity and sympathetic quality of the tone suffers. The CC pipe of the fine DIAPASON, 8 FT., by Bernard Smith, in the Organ of Trinity College, Cambridge, measures 6 inches in diameter; while the large DIAPASON, 8 FT., by Schulze, in the Organ in Leeds' Parish Church, Yorkshire, probably the grandest stop of its class in Great Britain, and the finest known to us, has its CC pipe only 6¼ inches in diameter. The latter stop is very copiously blown by wind of only 3¾ inches pressure. Although both scales and wind-pressures are factors of great importance, the art of the voicer, directed by a fine musical sense, is a factor of more direct importance than either; and it is through its skilful and painstaking exercise that one must look for the perfection of pure organ-tone; and, indeed, for tonal perfection in the Organ of the Twentieth Century.

It is extremely difficult to define the boundary lines, in practice, between the several divisions of organ-tone: in written description it is

---

* Stops ostensibly of the DIAPASON class have been made of much larger scales and blown with wind of high pressures. Doubtless their voices are extremely grand, heard under the acoustical advantages which obtain in spacious cathedrals and large vaulted churches: but it is questionable if such stops can be strictly held to belong to the true diapason-work, for their tones, if properly analyzed, are more likely to place them in the flute-work of the Organ.

practicably impossible.   Between pure organ-tone and what we mean by free organ-tone there is a very fine line of demarkation.   On the boundary line stands the true DULCIANA, the tone of which is only distinguishable from pure organ-tone by its extreme delicacy and singing quality.   This beautiful stop is formed of cylindrical pipes of small scale and lightly blown.   Like the DIAPASON, the DULCIANA, 8 FT., may be attended by its family of harmonic-corroborating stops, producing very lovely compound tones of the greatest value in the apportionment of the Choir Organ, and especially of the Chamber Organ.   The members of the family most useful are the OCTAVE DULCIANA, 4 FT.; DULCIANA QUINT, $2\frac{2}{3}$ FT.; SUPER-OCTAVE DULCIANA, 2 FT.; and the DULCIANA CORNET or SESQUIALTERA, as described in the preceding Chapter. In the apportionment of the Pedal Organ, a DULCIANA, 16 FT., should in all possible cases be inserted.   The value of a stop of this class, to furnish an appropriate bass to soft manual stops and combinations, cannot be overrated.   For the sub-octave voice in the Choir Organ, no stop can supersede the DOUBLE DULCIANA, 16 FT.; but it is only in the largest Organs that its lowest octave can be inclosed in the swell-box. It is, however, one of the stops which can be uninclosed, and used among the pipe-work displayed in the case-work of the instrument.   Allowing, as is desirable, that the Choir or Second Organ is divided and inclosed in two swell-boxes, the uninclosed DULCIANA will place, along with them, on the commanding clavier *three independent divisions—two expressive and one unexpressive.**

Still more delicate in tone than the DULCIANA is the so-called VOX ANGELICA, 8 FT.; and much more assertive are the SALICIONAL and KERAULOPHON, both of unison pitch.   It is somewhat difficult to class these stops, because their tones vary considerably under different systems of voicing.   The SALICIONAL has sometimes an unimitative string-tone more or less pronounced, and the KERAULOPHON yields a horn-like tone, yet they may properly be classed as producing free organ-tone. The DOLCAN, 8 FT., formed of inverted conical pipes of either metal or wood, and the DOLCE, 8 FT., properly formed of small-scaled inverted conical pipes of metal, are stops yielding free organ-tone of a quiet and somewhat plaintive character.   Among the few wood stops which yield free organ-tone are the MELODIA, 8 FT., and the HARMONICA, 8 FT. These voices are valuable on account of their special character and good mixing properties.   Of loudly voiced stops yielding free organ-tones of great assertiveness may be mentioned the HORN DIAPASON, 8 FT., the BELL DIAPASON, 8 FT., and the STENTORPHONE, 8 FT.   The last named, when blown with high-pressure wind, is the loudest labial stop in the Organ and is properly included in the dominant voices suitable for the

* Just the arrangement we placed on the first clavier of the Chamber Organ we constructed in 1865-72, and which obtains in no other Organ hitherto constructed.

apportionment of the Solo Organ in large instruments.   Other varieties of free organ-tone are produced by conical metal pipes, such as those of the GEMSHORN series of stops, and also the stops which stand on the boundary line between free organ-tone and flute organ-tone, known as the SPITZFLÖTES, of 8 ft., 4 ft., and 2 ft. pitch.   The examples given are sufficient to indicate the wide range of free organ-tone, and to show the number and importance of the stops producing its several varieties. In the tonal appointment of the Organ the great value of such voices must not be overlooked, for they supply qualities that the pure organ-tone is deficient in.   Certain stops yielding free organ-tone have their voices comparatively rich in upper partial tones; and these are very effective in combination with the DIAPASONS, adding brightness and richness to their dignified voices.   Alluding to the SALICIONAL, GEMS-HORN, and SPITZFLÖTE stops, Helmholtz says: "These pipes have, I find, the property of rendering some higher partial tones, from the fifth to the seventh,* comparatively stronger than the lower.   The quality of tone is consequently poor but peculiarly bright."   Such physical facts as these show the great importance of a scientific as well as an artistic tonal appointment.

By almost imperceptible gradations the voices of the Organ pass from what we have designated free organ-tone into flute organ-tone. The stops which produce the latter are numerous and valuable.   They are formed of both metal and wood pipes of different forms and pro-portions, and are either open, half-covered, or covered.   All these stops are described in the Chapters on the Forms and Construction of Wood and Metal Pipes; it is, therefore, only necessary to allude to repre-sentative examples here.

By the term flute organ-tone we signify that wide and varied range of fluty tone, produced by organ-pipes, which is not strictly imitative of the clear tones of the orchestral Flutes.   The pipes which yield flute organ-tone may be classified, so far as their forms and materials are concerned, into seven groups, as follows: 1. Open cylindrical metal pipes of ample scales and of standard speaking lengths.   2. Open cylindrical metal and quadrangular wood pipes, of medium scales, and double the standard speaking lengths: these are known as harmonic pipes, produc-ing tones proper to half their lengths by being perforated near their centers and overblown.   3. Half-covered cylindrical metal pipes, of large and medium scales.   4. Stopped or covered cylindrical metal pipes of large and medium scales.   5. Open quadrangular and triangular wood pipes, of large, medium, and small scales.   6. Half-covered quadrangul-ar wood pipes of medium and small scales.   7. Covered quadrangular

* These are the sixth to the eighth *upper* partial tones.   When the term *partial tones* is used the fundamental tone is included, it being the *prime partial tone* of the compound tone. All the partials above and exclusive of the prime are, correctly speaking, *upper partial tones.*

wood pipes, of large, medium, and small scales. With all these forms of pipes, and with the further differences created by the various styles and proportions of mouths, methods of voicing, the varied wind supply, and different pressures of wind, it is not difficult to realize the production of an immense range of tones in this single division.

As a general rule, the flute organ-tones are weak in upper partials, and are, accordingly, somewhat dull; but in certain varieties, yielded by open pipes, and especially by those rendered harmonic, the upper partial tones are distinct, numerous, and assertive, producing better qualities of tone. Of all the stops which produce flute organ-tone, the least important are those formed of open cylindrical metal pipes of standard speaking lengths. Their fluty tones are forced by the necessary system of blowing and voicing. Pipes of this class are chiefly useful in forming the lower portion of the metal harmonic stops.

The HARMONIC FLUTES, invented and first introduced by Cavaillé-Coll, and which are formed of medium-scaled open cylindrical metal pipes, of double the standard speaking lengths, furnish valuable voices in the Organ. They are made of 8 ft., 4 ft., and 2 ft. pitch; and their voices are singularly clear and penetrating. These valuable voices should never be overlooked in the appointment of important Organs, for they are highly suitable for the Swell Organ or chief expressive division.

The stops formed of half-covered cylindrical metal pipes produce bright fluty tones owing to the presence of the fourth upper partial tone, or the higher major third of the prime tone, in a comparatively strong state. The principal stops of this class are the German ROHR-FLÖTE, either of metal or wood, and of 8 ft., 4 ft., and 2 ft. pitch; and the French FLÛTE À CHIMINÉE. The latter is made of large-scaled cylindrical metal pipes, furnished with a sliding cap, from the center of which rises a small tube communicating with the internal air-column. Pipes of this form are occasionally used in the higher octaves of the BOURDON, 16 FT., as in the Great division of the Organ in the Manchester Town Hall, where the stop has half-covered pipes from c^2 to the top. By difference of scale, variation in the length and diameter of the small tube or *chiminée,* variety in the form and proportions of the mouth, special styles of voicing, and the adoption of different pressures of wind, many valuable qualities of flute organ-tone can be obtained from such half-covered pipes. The COR DE NUIT of the French, or the NACHTHORN of the German organ-builders, is a variation of this stop. When not too powerful, the stop furnishes a valuable voice in the Choir or accompanimental division of the Church Organ.

Stopped metal pipes were frequently used for the treble octaves of the STOPPED DIAPASON, 8 FT., by the old English organ-builders. Sometimes they formed the entire stop of metal. In modern French Organs the BOURDON, 8 FT., is formed of metal pipes of large scale, covered with sliding caps. Stopped metal pipes of medium and small scales, voiced on low and moderate pressures, yield charming qualities of flute organ-tone. Stops so formed are commonly called LIEBLICHGEDECKTS, and are made of 8 ft., 4 ft., and 2 ft. pitch. It is usual to make the bass octave of the unison stop of wood pipes.

In the wood stops which yield flute organ-tone there is a most important and valuable series of voices—a series that has not been properly recognized by French and English builders for reasons that have no reference to their tonal value.* German builders have largely, and American builders have to some extent, paid attention to the claims of wood stops, and the tonal character of their Organs has gained accordingly.

There are several very important stops formed of open wood pipes which yield flute organ-tones, and these deserve to be carefully considered in the tonal appointment of the Organ. They are specially valuable on account of their good mixing qualities, and for the solidity and fulness they impart to the somewhat thin and piercing voices of both the lingual stops and the metal labial stops whose tones are rich in the higher upper partial tones. As representatives of this latter class may be named the GROSSFLÖTE, CLARABELLA, HOHLFLÖTE, WALDFLÖTE, and the so-called PHILOMELA. The GROSSFLÖTE and CLARABELLA produce fluty tones of a full and agreeable character and perfect mixing quality. The CLARABELLA, 8 FT., should be carried throughout the manual compass in open pipes, although it usually has its bass octave of stopped pipes. The octave stop of this class—the CLARABEL FLUTE, 4 FT.—is a most desirable adjunct to the CLARABELLA. The BASS FLUTE, 8 FT., of the Pedal Organ, is, in its best form, a large-scaled CLARABELLA. The HOHLFLÖTE, of 8 ft., 4 ft., and 2 ft. pitch, is formed of either quadrangular or triangular pipes. Its tones are of a hollow and rather dull character, owing to the weakness or absence of the higher upper partial tones. The WALDFLÖTE, 4 FT., is an open wood stop of medium scale, having a full and clear tone, in good examples approaching an imitative quality. The German builders construct this stop of 8 ft., 4 ft., and 2 ft. pitch, wisely forming practically a complete family of valuable voices. The importance of introducing special families of stops in different divisions of the Organ has not been sufficiently recognized by modern builders; but it will have to be realized in the artistic appointment of the Organ of the Twentieth Century.

* Certain English and French organ-builders have shown a decided disposition to abandon the use of wood pipes. For instance, in the manual divisions of the large Organ in the Royal Albert Hall, South Kensington, London, built by Henry Willis, there is only one wood stop. The tonality of this instrument has, accordingly, suffered seriously. Willis claimed that he could produce a better wood-tone from metal pipes. In the Organ in the Church of the Sacred Heart, Montmartre, Paris, there are no stops of wood throughout in the manual divisions. Wood pipes only appear in some few bass octaves. The FLÛTE, 32 FT., and the SOUBASSE, 32 FT., in the Pedal Organ, are the only complete wood stops in this Organ of seventy-four speaking stops. The instrument was constructed by M. Charles Mutin, successor to M. Cavaillé-Coll.

There are very few half-covered wood stops to be found in existing Organs; but, judging from the beautiful tonal quality of those with which we are acquainted, it is to be regretted that pipe makers and voicers have not given this class of stops serious attention. The most important stop at present introduced is the ROHRFLÖTE, 8 FT., which, as already mentioned, is also made of metal. When made by a master hand, the wooden ROHRFLÖTE yields a tone of a pure singing quality which mixes well with all the medium and softer voices of the Organ.

There is at the present time a decided deficiency of soft and refined voices, of distinct tonality, in the ordinary Organ; indeed, the tendency on the part of the organ-builders of to-day, and also on the part of a large majority of organists who prepare lists of stops, called "Organ Specifications," is toward the production of as much loud sound as there is money to pay for, and as much high-pressure pipe-wind as can be produced by a noisy power-blower. All this is a grave mistake, and especially so in instruments designed to accompany the human voice. The student of the science and art of organ appointment should never overlook the value of the delicately toned stops in the appointment of Organs of all sizes and classes. We have invariably found, among persons of refined musical taste, that the softly voiced stops have been those most admired. In the loud stops, power of tone goes far to destroy that individuality and variety so essential in an instrument like the Organ, in which musical expression is so largely dependent on the varied qualities and strengths of its voices.

We now come to the consideration of the valuable qualities of tone produced by wholly covered wooden pipes. When such pipes are of large scale, and are blown by wind of moderate pressure, they yield tones almost free from upper partials: but when of smaller scales, and blown by wind of higher pressure, or are copiously blown, they yield tones in which the second upper partial, or twelfth, of the prime tone is present in a more or less pronounced degree: so much so in certain stops as to earn them the name QUINTATEN. With wind of still higher pressure these pipes also give the fourth upper partial tone, or higher major third. Covered pipes cannot give the *uneven* upper partial tones, such as the first or octave and the third or super-octave, etc. Even with such passing remarks as these, the student of organ construction must surely realize that there is much more to be considered in the tonal appointment of an Organ, than merely inserting the names of some familiar stops in his Specifications, simply as a matter of taste or fancy. The tonal appointment of an Organ is a problem in science as well as in art. The instant an instrument is constructed with more than one rank of pipes, science asserts itself and must be recognized.

The most important covered wood stops are the STOPPED DIAPASON, BOURDON, DOPPELFLÖTE, LIEBLICHGEDECKT, and QUINTATEN. When made and voiced by a master hand, the STOPPED DIAPASON, 8 FT., has a quiet fluty voice of a beautiful singing quality. It is a valuable voice in the Choir Organ. It should be borne in mind that while the STOPPED DIAPASON may produce a tone as free from upper partials as the OPEN DIAPASON, it has a distinct quality which holds its own in combination, chiefly from the absence of acoustical sympathy. The STOPPED DIAPASON can be carried down to CCC (16 ft.), when the stop becomes suitable for the Pedal Organ.

The BOURDON, in English and American Organs, is usually a Pedal Organ stop of 16 ft. pitch, formed of large-scaled pipes in all essentials similar to those of the STOPPED DIAPASON, 16 FT., but on account of their much larger scale and the different treatment of their mouths, produce a heavier and duller tone—too often objectionable. In the true BOURDON the second upper partial tone, or twelfth, is distinctly produced along with the prime, and in this respect it approximates to the characteristic *timbre* of the QUINTATEN, while it is more drone-like. These variations in tonal character should be carefully considered in the appointment of an Organ.

Perhaps the most valuable and beautiful flute organ-tone produced by covered pipes is that of the DOPPELFLÖTE, 8 FT. This stop, on account of its fine and remarkably solid tone, should be inserted in every Organ of any pretensions. While it is suitable for any manual, it is specially valuable in the Solo Organ and in the division in which stops of orchestral reed-tone are apportioned, where its enriching and filling-up quality is extremely effective. In combination with the CLARINET, 8 FT., the BASSOON, 8 FT., and the CONTRAFAGOTTO, 16 FT., it produces striking orchestral colorings. The true quality of the DOPPELFLÖTE rarely extends below tenor C, at which the double-mouthed pipes commence and extend to the top. The DOPPELFLÖTE has very rarely been made by English organ-builders; indeed, we believe it was introduced for the first time in England when we inserted one in our own Chamber Organ (in 1883) under the name FLAUTO PRIMO, 8 FT.

We now come to the very beautiful family of flute organ-toned stops known as the LIEBLICHGEDECKTS. These stops in their most refined and characteristic tonal character, are composed of small-scaled wood pipes, although their treble octaves are frequently formed of metal pipes, simply because they are more easily made and voiced. The unison (8 ft.) stop loses much by this labor-saving method. In the octave (4 ft.) stop, the two upper octaves can safely be made of covered metal pipes. Of course the LIEBLICHGEDECKT, 16 FT., should be made of wood throughout. There is no acknowledged standard for the tones of these stops, but the best qualities are those in which the second and fourth upper partial tones are just sufficiently strong to brighten and enrich the prime tone. The LIEBLICHGEDECKTS mix perfectly with all the other stops of the Organ. With the CLARINET, one of unison pitch adds greatly to the imitative character of the stop, imparting to its rather thin tones fulness and depth without impairing their special quality. The LIEBLICHGEDECKT, 16 FT., forms a valuable DOUBLE in the Choir Organ, and also in small Swell Organs, where it will not have power sufficient to disturb the balance and prominence of the unison tone. It is likewise a valuable stop in any Pedal Organ, but especially in one in which there is no DULCIANA, 16 FT. It may be remarked that a free use may advantageously be made of the complete LIEBLICHGEDECKT family, hitherto greatly overlooked.*

The stop known as the QUINTATEN differs only from the LIEBLICH-GEDECKT in its tone having the second upper partial (twelfth) more distinct; so much so that in good examples of the QUINTATEN it approaches the strength of the prime tone. The QUINTATEN has been made of 32 ft., 16 ft., and 8 ft. pitch; the last being the stop suitable for introduction in the manual divisions of the Organ. In certain cases the QUINTATEN, 16 FT., forms an effective DOUBLE on the manuals. The unison stop is specially valuable in a division in which there is no TWELFTH, 2⅔ FT., to corroborate the second upper partial of the unison tone. It is also extremely valuable in a division which contains several stops of string-tone, even when there is a separate TWELFTH, 2⅔ FT., present. In such a case it is highly effective in the softer combinations, imparting solidity to the imitative voices, and affording means of producing a great variety of tonal effects with stops of different classes and colorings. In the apportionment of the Pedal Organ, the QUINTATEN, 16 FT., should receive careful consideration.

There are several stops introduced in the Organ which yield tones partaking more or less of the character of those produced by bowed instruments; and when not strictly imitative these voices fall into the First Group, as organ-tones. We have introduced the term viol organ-tone to distinguish the voices of these useful stops from the other classes of organ-tones, and from the voices of the purely imitative string-toned stops which belong to the Second Group. This quality of organ-tone is commonly known as *gamba-tone,* but we consider so senseless a term inappropriate, and have, accordingly, adopted the appropriate term *viol* as more expressive.

The most important stop yielding viol organ-tone is that known as the GEIGENPRINCIPAL, or VIOLIN DIAPASON, 8 FT. This stop produces, among others, the second upper partial tone in so pronounced a manner, in combination with its fine prime tone and first upper partial, that a well-defined string- or viol-tone is the result. When this stop is

---

* In the Organ in the Church of Our Lady of Grace, Hoboken, N. J., designed by us, there are in the First Expressive Division of the Second Organ a LIEBLICHGEDECKT, 16 FT., a LIEBLICHGEDECKT, 8 FT., and a LIEBLICHFLÖTE, 4 FT.—the principal members of the family.

introduced in place of a true DIAPASON, 8 FT.,—as it well may be in any division save the foundation one—its crisp viol-tone may with advantage be subdued in favor of a more pronounced prime tone; but, on the other hand, when there is, in the same division, also a unison DIAPASON present, the full tonality of the GEIGENPRINCIPAL should be retained. The GEIGENPRINCIPAL is made of 16 ft., 8 ft., and 4 ft. pitch, and all the stops are valuable. On the Second Manual of the Organ in the Cathedral of Riga there is a GEIGENPRINCIPAL, 16 FT., and on the Third Manual there are others of 8 ft. and 4 ft. pitch.

We have introduced the term GRAND VIOL, 8 FT., to indicate a stop still richer in harmonics and, accordingly, in string-tone than the usual GEIGENPRINCIPAL. We inserted a GRAND VIOL, 8 FT., in the First Division (unexpressive) of the First Organ in the Organ in the Church of Our Lady of Grace, Hoboken, N. J.

Next in importance is the stop commonly known as the GAMBA, composed of medium-scaled cylindrical open metal pipes. When properly formed and artistically voiced, this stop yields a full tone in which the first five upper partial tones are commonly audible. The strength of these, in relation to the prime tone, varies considerably in different examples of the stop; and it is, accordingly, possible to adapt the tone to the special requirements of any division of the Organ. When the upper partial tones are of moderate strength, and decrease considerably as they rise in pitch, the compound voice of the GAMBA is full and rich; but when the upper partials are relatively strong, and are heard distinctly up to the fifth, or octave 12th of the prime tone, the compound voice becomes somewhat more harsh and cutting.

There are several stops of different forms and scales which belong to the family yielding viol organ-tone, and some have voices so strongly imitative in character that it is sometimes difficult to classify them. This is the case with such characteristic stops as the VIOLA DA GAMBA and VIOLA D'AMORE. These, when at their best, may be considered imitative stops, and their place would seem to be among those yielding orchestral string-tone, but when compared with the modern stops that imitate so closely the assertive and complex tones of the orchestral Violin, Violoncello, and Contra-Basso, their timid voices fall back into what may be correctly considered organ-tone.

Several names have been introduced to distinguish different forms of GAMBA pipes, and to indirectly convey some ideas respecting their tonal characters. Among these names we find CONE GAMBA, BELL GAMBA, and GERMAN GAMBA. It is well known that the shape of a pipe has a great influence on its tonal character, chiefly by altering the number, nature, and relative intensity of the upper partials which, in combination with the prime, go to create its compound tone. Such being the case, we find each of the GAMBAS named to have voices of a more or less distinctive tonality. Of course, further differences of tone are created by changes in the manner of voicing, and blowing by wind of different pressures. The GERMAN GAMBA is formed of cylindrical metal pipes voiced to yield a full unimitative string-tone. In its original slow-speaking form it has disappeared from the modern Organ. The BELL GAMBA and CONE GAMBA have practically disappeared in face of the more modern and more efficient system of voicing by means of harmonic-bridging. The softest stop yielding viol organ-tone is the ÆOLINE, 8 FT. It is formed of small-scaled, open cylindrical pipes (preferably of tin), voiced to produce a delicate, singing string-tone. It is suitable for the Chamber Organ and in the expressive Choir division of the Church Organ. Walcker has placed it on the Fourth Manual of the Riga Organ, where it is associated with several stops of a soft and refined tonality, such as the BOURDON DOUX, 8 FT., VOIX CÉLESTE, 8 FT., VOX ANGELICA, 4 FT., and HARMONIA ÆTHERIA.

In the appointment of the Organ, the tonal value of the stops yielding viol organ-tone should be fully recognized; but they must, on account of their pungent and penetrating voices, be introduced with great judgment and care. They must be selected with due reference to their strength of tone and the nature of their compound voices, so as to harmonize with the complete tonal scheme of the division of the Organ in which they are placed. It is not too much to say that a badly proportioned or unsuitable string-toned stop will destroy the tonal balance of a division. In matters of this kind scientific knowledge, experience, and a refined musical sense can alone guide the organ-builder and expert. How often are these acquirements exercised in the tonal appointment of the Organ?

We have now to consider briefly the organ stops which belong to the Second Group, the pipes of which are constructed and voiced with the sole aim of producing tones imitating, as closely as possible, those of the principal string and wind instruments of the orchestra.

The old builders were satisfied with very few and indifferent imitative stops; and, indeed, it is only within the last sixty years or so, or since the inception of the true Concert-room Organ, that leading organ-builders and clever voicers have given serious attention to the production of organ equivalents of the principal voices of the orchestra. Every step made in this direction was a gain; and to-day the tonal resources at the disposal of the expert in organ appointment and the organist are extensive and very varied. What is now chiefly needed by the organ architect or expert is scientific knowledge, obtained by research and careful observation, and an artistic taste, to so devise and dispose these tonal forces in the suitable divisions of the Organ—preferably the Concert-room Organ—that their fullest powers, separately, in artistic contrast, and in combination, may be placed at the command of the player.

Opinions differ respecting the liberal introduction of strictly imitative voices into the Organ; and those who are adverse to their holding a prominent place in the tonal economy of the instrument point, in support of their objection, to the famed Organs of the old masters, notably those of Germany and the Netherlands. Reference to old Organs, however, carries no weight, simply because only a very few, isolated stops of an imitative character were known at the times of their construction; and even the best of these fell far short of being satisfactory. Such being the case, the old builders did wisely in confining themselves to the stops they could make successfully, and which proved sufficient for all the demands made by the organ music of the time. The old Church Organ had its own special office to fulfil, and did not call for the introduction of orchestral-toned stops; and we are willing to admit (much as we admire the results of modern ingenuity and skill) that the average Church Organ of to-day requires more that belongs to the Organ proper than to imitations of orchestral instruments. The perfect Church Organ of the Twentieth Century has yet to be designed and constructed. Size is not to be the principal factor. Countless Church Organs have been spoiled by the unreasoning desire on the part of the inexperienced schemers of their so-called Specifications to have some ear-tickling or favorite imitative stops provided, at the sacrifice of the correct and complete tonal structure, and the general utility, dignity, and artistic beauty of the instruments. The usual organ-builders' and organists' " Specifications," produced every day, are masterpieces of incompetence, if not something worse in some cases. The old German organ-builders were not guilty of such folly, although even they did some ridiculous things in connection with the Organ. A glance, however, at their Pedal Organ schemes shows what masters they were of tonal appointment in a direction now so largely neglected. The orchestral-toned stops are of the highest value, and should never be overlooked in the tonal appointment of large instruments; but it must be borne in mind that they are only a means to a special end; and that, in all save perhaps the grand Concert-room Organ, they are of secondary importance to the true organ-toned stops.

Notwithstanding the fact that the stringed instruments have always formed the foundation of the orchestra, the orchestral string-toned stops of the Organ have, until very recently, received comparatively little attention, indeed it was not until such masterly voicers as the late Edmund Schulze, of Paulenzelle, and William Thynne, of London, demonstrated what could be done in the direction of imitative string-toned stops, that one fully realized their importance and could form some conception of the place they are destined to occupy in the properly appointed Concert-room Organ of the future; and of the tonal resources they will place at the command of the organ virtuoso in the rendition of orchest-

ral scores and transcriptions; furnishing him with tone-colors for his
loftiest flights of artistic improvisation—the glory of the accomplished
organist. Much will be done in the Organ of the Twentieth Century
when the scientific and artistic tonal appointment of the King of Instruments is better understood.

The stringed instruments whose complex harmonic-laden tones have
been wonderfully imitated by the voicers alluded to are the Violin,
Violoncello, and Contra-Basso. Under the name VIOLE D'ORCHESTRE,
8 FT., Mr. Thynne produced small-scaled, open metal stops, the tones of
which almost exactly imitated those of the Violin. In the Organ in
Tewkesbury Abbey the Solo VIOLONCELLO, 8 FT., voiced by the same
master-hand, reproduces in a marvellous manner the characteristic tones
of the true Violoncello.* This fine stop is of metal and wood. Of the
many imitative string-toned stops voiced by the renowned Schulze, we
know of none that surpasses the Pedal Organ VIOLONE, 16 FT., of the
Organ in the Church of St. Peter, Hindley, Lancashire; the tones of
which imitate those of the Contra-Basso in a surprising manner, even
to the rasp of the bow. Knowing that such stops are possible and can
be created by accomplished voicers—for what has been done can be
done again—it is greatly to be regretted that so many important Concert-room Organs in England, in this country, and elsewhere, are so
lamentably deficient in imitative string-toned stops, in family apportionment, foreshadowed in our apportionment of the string-toned, Second
Expressive Subdivision of the Third Organ, in the Grand Organ originally installed in the Festival Hall of the Louisiana Purchase Exposition, St. Louis, Mo. The list of the stops in this Subdivision is given
in the concluding Appendix. As this was the *first essay* in this direction in the history of organ-building, it may well be accepted as
tentative; but we venture to believe that it points the way to what must
become an important feature in the tonal appointment of the Concert
Organ of the Twentieth Century, as we shall show in our Chapter on
the Concert-room Organ.

Let us take a representative of the usual state of affairs, and one of
the finest Concert Organs in existence. If we glance at the long list
of the stops of the Organ in St. George's Hall, Liverpool, in its latest
and improved (?) condition we find that in the Great Organ there is a
VIOLONCELLO, 8 FT., and VIOLA, 4 FT.; in the Choir Organ a VIOLA DA
GAMBA, 8 FT., and a GAMBA, 4 FT.; in the Swell Organ a VIOLA DA
GAMBA, 8 FT., and an OCTAVE VIOLA, 4 FT.; and in the Solo Organ a
VIOLA DA GAMBA, 8 FT. In all seven ranks of string-toned pipes in an
Organ of one hundred speaking stops, which include no fewer than

* During the Dedication of this Organ, at which we were present, the most beautiful
number was a Sacred Song, accompanied by that stop alone. The effect produced by the pure
soprano voice and the sympathetic VIOLONCELLO was one not easily forgotten by an organ-lover.

thirty-five reed stops.   Now, what is specially to be lamented in regard
to this otherwise remarkable Organ, apart from the almost entire absence of true imitative tone in the seven stops named, is the absolute
impossibility of massing the stops together for any solid string effect,
without crippling the claviers, for the time being, for any other effect.
Without coupling two claviers, it is impossible to have a combination of
even two unison string-toned stops.   Nothing can be advanced in de-
fense of such a short-sighted, unscientific, and inartistic system of departmental apportionment.   We have had—what few men alive to-day
have had—the advantage of realizing, under the best possible conditions,
the absurdity of the prevailing dispersive system of tonal appointment.
We have, during the thousands of public recitals given throughout a
period of a quarter of a century, observed the late Mr. W. T. Best's
futile attempts to obtain sufficient combinations of string-tone on the
St. George's Hall Organ for the orchestral compositions he so frequently
and so wonderfully performed.   We had ample opportunity of realizing
how unsatisfactory the instrument proved in this direction even under
his consummate manipulation.   Little has been done systematically by
organ-builders to better this *dispersive malappointment* in their large
Concert instruments.

The tones of the organ stops which so closely imitate the Violin,
Viola, Violoncello, and Contra-Basso of the orchestra are due to the
presence of an extended series of upper partials—a more extended series
than is present in the compound voices of any other labial stops.   In
the sounds of the bowed instruments the upper partial tones are distinctly audible up to the ninth or tenth, while by the aid of scientifically-
constructed resonators still higher harmonics can be recognized by the
sensitive ear.   Helmholtz remarks: " The prime in the compound tones
of bowed instruments is comparatively more powerful than in those
produced on the pianoforte or guitar by striking or plucking the strings
near their extremities; the first upper partials are comparatively weaker;
but the higher upper partials, from the sixth to about the tenth, are much
more distinct, and give those tones their cutting character."   In the compound sounds of the ordinary string-toned stops, Helmholtz found upper
partial tones as high as the fifth; as he says: " On forcibly blowing the
narrow cylindrical pipes of the Organ we hear a series of upper partials
distinctly and powerfully accompany the prime tone, giving them a more
cutting quality, resembling a Violin."   This investigator does not appear
to have had any opportunity of examining such imitative string-toned
pipes—wood and metal—as those produced by Schulze or Thynne, previously to the appearance of his " Sensations of Tone."   Had such pipes
come under his observation, he would have found a higher series of
upper partials in their compound voices than those discovered, by the
aid of resonators, in the string-toned pipes used in his investigations.

The imitative tones of the VIOLE D'ORCHESTRE or ORCHESTRAL VIOLIN, 8 FT., the ORCHESTRAL VIOLONCELLO, 8 FT., and the ORCHESTRAL CONTRA-BASSO, 16 FT., are produced by open metal and wood pipes of small scales, the mouths of which are furnished with the harmonic bridge * or some form of the *frein harmonique*. The VIOLONE, 16 FT., in Schulze's Organ, at Hindley, has its CCC pipe only 5½ inches square internally. Pipes of this imitative class speak with the greatest purity, and unstrained in tone, on winds of moderate pressures; although for solo stops of brilliant intonation wind of 6 inches may be employed. The dimensions and acoustical properties of the hall or room in which the Organ is to be placed will to a large extent dictate the wind-pressures, up to the desirable limits only, for these imitative as well, indeed, as all other stops. Stops of less powerful and cutting intonation than those just named, which imitate the singing and somewhat plaintive tones of the old string-instruments, the Viola da Gamba and Viola d'Amore, are most valuable in the tonal appointment of the Organ, especially in the Church Organ, where they are more suitable than the very assertive stops of the imitative orchestral class are, as a rule. There is a very beautiful VIOLA, 8 FT., formed of small-scaled wood and metal pipes, in the Choir division of Schulze's Hindley Organ; and there is also, in the same division, a fine VIOLE D'AMOUR, 4 FT. Stops of this delicate, accompanimental character produce their most beautiful and sympathetic tones on wind of about 2½ inches—a pressure favored by Schulze for his Choir Organ stops, as in his fine Organ in the Church of St. Bartholomew, Armley, Yorkshire.

In the tonal appointment of a Concert-room Organ of any importance, and of Organs installed in places of public amusement in which the services of an orchestra are to be largely or altogether dispensed with, the provision of a sufficient volume of orchestral string-tone to meet all demands in the rendition of the largest orchestral transcriptions must not be neglected. And it is essential that this volume, scientifically built up, be immediately, and at all times, available in one, and the most convenient, division of the instrument, and endowed with independent powers of expression; so that all the other divisions in the tonal appointment, commanded by the different claviers, are entirely free for the other necessary tonal effects and combinations. On this important subject we have more to say. It is, in our opinion, essential that in the Organ of the Twentieth Century a completely new departure must be made from the aimless, old-fashioned system of tonal appointment and apportionment; and, as we have said elsewhere, it is hopeless to look to tradesmen organ-builders for any steps toward this departure. One

---

* This appliance is commonly, illogically, and incorrectly termed the "beard." In either form or position it bears no relation to a mouth, and the stupid term should be abandoned in favor of the scientific and appropriate term.

thing seems highly desirable, and to our mind necessary; namely, that for the production of distinctive groups or combinations of tone-colors, as little resort to coupling claviers should be made as possible. On all ordinary occasions every clavier should remain independent, for its special work in the tonal scheme of the instrument. Coupling in the Organs of to-day is more resorted to for the production of noisy effects than for the production of beautiful tone-color. In scheming the tonal appointment and apportionment of an important Organ, the necessity for couplers should be largely discounted.

Although the voices of the orchestral string-toned stops of unison pitch contain the extended series of harmonic upper partials sufficient to create their individual imitative tones, such unison stops are not sufficient alone, even when multiplied, to produce the extremely rich and complex musical effect of the string division of the grand orchestra. Such being the case, it is desirable to associate along with the unison stops other and higher-pitched ranks of pipes, preferably of soft viol-tone, to add fulness to the upper partials of the unison tones, and generate others of still higher pitch, so as to build up the required volume of characteristic and invaluable musical sound, and construct a complete string-toned division of the Organ.

Little requires to be said on the subject of orchestral flute-tone, because there are only three stops of a strictly imitative character that furnish it satisfactorily; namely, the ORCHESTRAL FLUTE or FLAUTO TRAVERSO, 8 FT., the FLAUTO TRAVERSO, 4 FT., and the ORCHESTRAL PICCOLO, 2 FT. The pipes of these stops are made of both wood and metal, but the former material is preferable, in the hands of an artist, and should always be used for the unison and octave stops. The finest examples of the ORCHESTRAL FLUTES have the pipes of their middle and higher octaves made of hardwood, turned out of the solid and bored, and furnished with small mouths and caps of a special form. These cylindrical pipes are harmonic; that is, they are made double the standard speaking lengths, and are perforated near the center of their tubes, in the usual manner, and as described and illustrated in our Chapter on The Forms and Construction of Wood Pipes. The tones produced by these cylindrical pipes are highly satisfactory imitations of those produced by the orchestral instruments, and ably represent them in the tonal appointment of the Organ. Edmund Schulze and other German organ-builders have been very successful with stops of this imitative form. Fine examples by Schulze exist in the Organs in the Parish Churches of Leeds and Doncaster, Yorkshire. Very satisfactory ORCHESTRAL FLUTES have been made of small-scaled, open, quadrangular wood pipes, harmonic from about f^1 in the unison, and an octave lower in the stops of 4 ft. pitch: the lower pipes, in both cases, being of open wood of the standard speaking lengths. The ORCHESTRAL

FLUTES, of 8 ft. and 4 ft. pitch, and the ORCHESTRAL PICCOLO, 2 FT., are stops of the first importance in organ appointment, representing, as they do, an effective section of the " wood-wind " of the orchestra. While in the Concert-room Organ the three FLUTES should certainly find a place in the manual division devoted specially to the stops which represent the wood-wind forces of the orchestra, it is desirable to place ORCHESTRAL FLUTES, preferably of clear and somewhat powerful intonation, in the division specially reserved for solo voices; so that Flute passages can be rendered at any moment, without crippling the important tonal combinations or accompanimental effects that may be provided in the other divisions of the instrument. All such matters must be very carefully considered, from all points of view, in working out the scheme of tonal apportionment in an Organ on which compositions of an orchestral character will be systematically performed; and on which orchestral scores will be rendered. It is all-important that in the performance of the most complex compositions all the claviers should be kept as independent of each other as possible.

The instruments of the orchestra which are more or less closely imitated by the stops of the Organ yielding orchestral reed-tone are the Clarinet, Fagotto, Oboe, Corno di Bassetto, Saxophone, and Cor Anglais. All the stops which bear these names yield, when artistically made and voiced, tones of great beauty and value.

Of all the stops of the Organ which imitate the tones of orchestral reed instruments, the CLARINET, 8 FT., may be said to be the most satisfactory. When made by a master-hand, and used in combination with a soft-toned covered wood stop of unison pitch, such as a DOPPEL- FLÖTE, 8 FT., it produces an almost perfect imitation of the orchestral instrument in its best register. The resonant tubes of the CLARINET are, like the tube of the orchestral instrument, cylindrical. The tube of the orchestral Clarinet is of the nature of a stopped pipe, producing in addition to the prime, the second, fourth, sixth, and higher even upper partial tones. Such being the case, the CLARINET of the Organ natur- ally derives considerable benefit, tonally, by having associated with it a covered stop which has in its voice the same progression of har- monics. We accordingly strongly recommend that the ORCHESTRAL CLARINET, 8 FT., in the Concert-room Organ, be composed of two ranks, namely, the reed stop and a small-scaled covered stop, preferably a DOPPELFLÖTE. The latter may also be arranged to draw alone for general combinational purposes. Speaking of the Clarinet, Berlioz remarks : " It is the one of all the wind instruments which can best breathe forth, swell, diminish, and die away its sound. Thence the precious faculty of producing *distance,* echo, an echo of *echo,* and a *twilight* sound. What more admirable example could I quote, of the application of some of these shadowings, than the dreamy phrase of the

Clarinet, accompanied by a tremolo of stringed instruments, in the midst of the Allegro of the Overture to *Freischütz?*" And yet, in utter ignorance or disregard of these remarkable properties of the orchestral instrument, we find the thoughtless organ-builders and framers of so-called Organ Specifications perpetually placing the CLARINET in an exposed Choir or some other uninclosed and *unexpressive* division of the Organ. It appears, under the name CREMONA, 8 FT., in the unex-pressive Choir division of the Organ in St. George's Hall, Liverpool.

In the tonal appointment of a Concert-room Organ of importance, two ORCHESTRAL CLARINETS should, at least, be introduced: one occupy-ing a place in the manual division chiefly devoted to the " wood-wind "; and the other placed in the division devoted to the principal solo voices. The latter stop should be composed of two ranks, as suggested above, because its voice must be full and highly imitative.

The Corno di Bassetto is another fine orchestral instrument that is closely imitated by the somewhat uncommon organ stop of the same name. Its compass is from FF to c³; so the organ CORNO DI BASSETTO, 8 FT., has its top octave beyond the upward range of the orchestral instrument. The tone of the Corno di Bassetto is somewhat similar to, but richer than that of, the Alto Clarinet: its finest notes are in its lowest register. Mozart, realizing the value of this fine instrument, used it in two parts for darkening the coloring of his harmonies in his *Requiem*, and has assigned to it some important solos in his Opera *La Clemenza di Tito*. The imitative CORNO DI BASSETTO, 8 FT., is by no means a common stop, and the voicers of to-day seem to be content with common reed stops in ordinary demand. Perhaps the finest example of this stop in existence is that in the Solo Organ in the instrument in St. George's Hall, Liverpool. Another example obtains in the Solo division of the Organ in the Centennial Hall, Sydney. The CORNO DI BASSETTO, 8 FT., has very seldom been introduced in a Church Organ, but we find one in the Schwell-Pedal of the Organ in Riga Cathedral, and one in the large Pedal of the Organ in the Cathedral of Ulm, under the name BASSETHORN, 8 FT. As the voice of the CORNO DI BASSETTO closely resembles that of the ORCHESTRAL CLARINET, it should be placed in a manual division or subdivision which does not contain the latter stop.

The OBOE, 8 FT., is a stop commonly found in Organs of all dimen-sions. It is made in two forms: one yielding a tone fuller and rounder than that of the orchestral instrument of the same name, and, accord-ingly, not closely imitative; while the other, called the ORCHESTRAL OBOE, 8 FT., is made and voiced to produce a tone of a strictly imitative character. In the tonal appointment of the Concert-room Organ the ORCHESTRAL OBOE should be inserted in the division specially devoted to the " wood-wind." In an instrument of the first magnitude a second ORCHESTRAL OBOE may with advantage be inserted in the division reserved for solo voices: this one should be as imitative as practicable and rather more assertive than the other. The OBOE, 8 FT., as commonly made and voiced, is very desirable in the Church Organ, where a soft reed-tone of a distinctive character is particularly valuable in combinations, and occasionally in solo passages of a plaintive kind. It is unnecessary to say that it must always be placed in an expressive division of the Organ. This reed is also well suited for a small Chamber Organ, where, apart from its own valuable voice, it is of great use on account of its admirable mixing quality.

An OCTAVE OBOE, 4 FT., has been introduced in certain modern Organs. It appears in both the Choir and Solo divisions of the Sydney Organ, already alluded to, and on the Second Manual of the Riga Cathedral Organ. When not of a strictly imitative tonality, this stop will form a very suitable octave reed in the softer divisions of the Organ. In a Chamber Organ it should occupy the place of a CLARION, 4 FT.

Although there is no authority from the orchestra for the introduction of a CONTRA-OBOE, 16 FT., yet, as the tone of the unison stop is so satisfactory, there can be no good reason why a similarly toned stop of 16 ft. pitch should not be introduced in important Concert-room and Church Organs. Under the name CONTRA-HAUTBOY, 16 FT., a fine example is to be found in the Swell division of the Liverpool Organ. According to the particulars just given, it is shown that there are four OBOE stops available for the tonal appointment of the Organ; namely, the ORCHESTRAL OBOE, 8 FT., having a strictly imitative and solo voice, and the family of three of normal tone—the CONTRA-OBOE, 16 FT., OBOE, 8 FT., and OCTAVE OBOE, 4 FT. As we strongly advocate the association of the different families of important stops in separate divisions of the Organ, we suggest the desirability of keeping these three OBOES together in any expressive division it may be considered desirable to place them; but, above all others, in the wood-wind division or subdivision of the Concert-room Organ, should there be one. This appointment would, in all probability, be practicable in Organs of the first magnitude only.

The Cor Anglais, or Corno Inglese, is an orchestral instrument of the Oboe class: it is, so to speak, the Alto of the Oboe. Speaking of the Cor Anglais, Berlioz says: "Its quality of tone, less piercing, more veiled, and deeper than that of the Oboe, does not so well as the latter lend itself to the gaiety of rustic strains. . . . It is a melancholy, dreamy, and rather noble voice." The organ stop which has been designed to imitate the instrument, and which bears its name, may in its best form be accepted as suitable for a place in the tonal appointment of an important Concert-room or Church Organ. In its best form, the stop is a free-reed, furnished with resonant tubes of peculiar form. Its tone is distinct from that of the OBOE, and has valuable mixing and coloring qualities. We introduced a free-reed CORNO INGLESE, 8 FT.,

in our tonal apportionment of the expressive Second Organ of the Grand
Concert Organ erected in the Festival Hall, Louisiana Purchase Exposition.

The orchestral Fagotto or Bassoon is the true bass of the Oboe; and
the value of a good imitation of its characteristic voice, in the Organ,
may be realized from the following remarks by Berlioz: " The Bassoon
is of the greatest use in the orchestra on numerous occasions.   Its
sonorousness is not very great, and its quality of tone, absolutely devoid
of brilliancy or nobleness, has a tendency toward the grotesque. . . .
Its low notes form excellent basses to the whole group of wooden wind
instruments."   The FAGOTTO, 8 FT., as made by a master-hand, is a
very satisfactory stop, although only moderately imitative, and is extremely valuable in artistic tonal appointment.   In its best form, its
resonant tubes are of an inverted conical shape, of medium scale, and
of wood.   The stop correctly belongs to the wood-wind division of the
Organ, but is not necessarily confined to any division.   As the orchestral
instrument extends upward only to e², the FAGOTTO, 8 FT., proper, ceases
at that note, and is theoretically carried up by an OBOE, but practically
by pipes of similar form and tonality peculiar to the stop.

The Contrafagotto or Double Bassoon of the orchestra is to the
Fagotto or Bassoon, what the Contra-Basso is to the Violoncello.   The
compass of the Contrafagotto is from BBBB♭ to F—32 notes, and,
accordingly, the stop which represents it in the Organ properly belongs
to the pedal department, the compass of which simply cuts two notes
from its downward range.   When the CONTRAFAGOTTO, 16 FT., is inserted in a manual division it properly extends upward only to f¹, being
carried to e² in FAGOTTO, 8 FT., pipes, and thence to the top by pipes that
theoretically belong to the OBOE, 8 FT.   The stop is, however, carried
throughout in pipes of one formation, so as to secure perfect uniformity
of tonal character: and the same must be the case with the unison
FAGOTTO, 8 FT., when properly made.   There is nothing more objectionable, in the tonal appointment of an Organ, than stops which have
different intonations in different portions of their compass.   The CON-
TRAFAGOTTO, 16 FT., is, when properly scaled and voiced, a very valuable
and effective stop.   It appears in different divisions in important
Organs, and, except as regards its correct position in the Pedal Organ,
apparently without any special reference to the general tonal appointment of the divisions.   According to the prevailing aimless system of
tonal apportionment, that is what might be expected.   In the Sydney
Organ it appears in the Choir, Swell, Solo, and Pedal divisions.   In the
Liverpool Organ it appears in the Solo and Pedal divisions.   The CON-
TRAFAGOTTO is *par excellence* a Pedal Organ stop, and should be inserted in that department in every important instrument.   Its position
in the manual department will be, or should be, dictated by the special

tonal appointment and apportionment. In the average Church Organ it need not appear in any manual division; but when it does, it certainly should be in an expressive one. In the properly-apportioned tonal scheme of the Concert-room Organ, its proper place is in the wood-wind division. This rule we followed in the tonal apportionment of the Organ exhibited at the Louisiana Purchase Exposition. The CONTRA-FAGOTTO, 16 FT., was placed in the First Division (expressive) of the Third Organ; in which the corresponding wood-wind instruments were represented by the stops—FLUTE, 8 FT., FLUTE, 4 FT., PICCOLO, 2 FT., CONTRAFAGOTTO, 16 FT., FAGOTTO, 8 FT., CONTRA-OBOE, 16 FT., ORCHESTRAL OBOE, 8 FT., CLARINET, 8 FT., and CORNO DI BASSETTO, 8 FT. In the Organ in the Church of Our Lady of Grace, Hoboken, we placed the CONTRAFAGOTTO, 16 FT., in the Third Organ (expressive) along with these wood-wind stops—ORCHESTRAL FLUTE, 4 FT., ORCHESTRAL PICCOLO, 2 FT., ORCHESTRAL OBOE, 4 FT., and CORNO DI BASSETTO, 8 FT.

We have now to mention, in concluding our necessarily brief remarks on the organ stops yielding orchestral reed-tone, the beautiful family of orchestral single-reed instruments known as the Saxophones. They are six in number,—the High, Soprano, Alto, Tenor, Baritone, and Bass,—collectively covering a compass from BBB to f^3; practically the compass of the ordinary short claviers of the Organ being one note below the CC downward limit of all modern manual claviers, and only seven notes short of the upward limit of the five-octave claviers now universally adopted in important Organs. The organ SAXOPHONE, 8 FT., must in all cases be a complete stop, the fact that it extends a few notes above the High Saxophone of the orchestra being an advantage rather than otherwise. Only the note BBB of the Bass Saxophone has to be omitted.

Up to the present time few serious attempts have been made by organ-builders to produce stops having voices imitative of the orchestral Saxophones. No success has as yet attended attempts made in the direction of reed stops. Unquestionably the best, and we may say the only satisfactory, organ stop yet made that yields tones strictly imitative of those of the Saxophones, is the one invented and first introduced by Mr. W. E. Haskell. This beautiful and invaluable stop is illustrated and described in our Chapter on The Forms and Construction of Wood Pipes. Strange to say, it is not a reed, but a small-scaled open wood labial stop, voiced harmonically.

While the tubes of the orchestral Saxophones are of brass, their reeds are, like those of the Clarinets, formed of wood; accordingly, the Saxophones belong to the reed forces and the wood-wind division of the orchestra. These facts should dictate the appointing of the SAXOPHONE to the division of the Concert-room Organ most appropriate for its reception. Although there is not a Double-bass Saxophone in the orchestra, the introduction of a SAXOPHONE, 16 FT., of characteristic voice would be invaluable in the Organ and should be provided.*

The organ lingual stops which represent the "brass-wind" of the orchestra are not so successful in their imitative voices as the few stops previously mentioned. The orchestral brass instruments whose tones are more or less closely imitated are the Trumpet, Trombone, Ophicleide, and Bass Tuba. Others, such as the Horn, Euphonium, and Cornopean or Cornet à pistons, have not been nearly so successfully imitated in the Organ; indeed, it seems a difficult task to imitate the tones of the Horn by any kind of lingual pipes. We are convinced that if these tones are ever successfully imitated, labial pipes will be employed for the purpose. The beautiful and smooth tones of the Euphonium are certainly difficult to imitate, and they seem to be more closely allied to the tones produced by free-reed pipes than those yielded by the more generally used striking-reeds. The difficulty attending the satisfactory imitation of the characteristic and not altogether pleasing tones of the Cornopean is also great; and it is not too much to say that the CORNOPEAN, 8 FT., as commonly met with in the Organ, is by no means a satisfactory imitative stop. One of the commonest and most generally useful reed stops is the TRUMPET, 8 FT., and this is to be found in the tonal appoinment of every Organ of any pretensions, while in large instruments it appears in two or more divisions: for instance, in the Organ in the Centennial Hall, Sydney, it is introduced in four divisions—the Great, Swell, Solo, and Pedal Organs. This stop appears in some large Organs under two names; namely, TRUMPET and TROMBA, as in the instrument in the Auditorium, at Chicago, where there are TRUMPETS in the Great and Stage Organs, and a TROMBA in the Choir Organ. When two or more TRUMPETS are introduced in the same instrument, they should be made of different scales, and voiced to yield distinctive tones, suitable for the divisions in which they are placed. The ORCHESTRAL TRUMPET, 8 FT., the tone of which resembles, as closely as practicable, that of the Trumpet of the orchestra, finds its proper place in the division which contains the principal solo stops, or in that devoted to the stops which represent the brass-wind of the orchestra. The other TRUMPETS, whose tones are of the usual organ character, may be placed in the Great, Swell, and Pedal Organs, according to the demands of the general tonal appointment of the instrument. There is a manual stop of 16 ft. pitch, known as the DOUBLE TRUMPET, formed of pipes similar in form to, but smaller in scale than, the corresponding pipes of the unison TRUMPET. The tone of this double stop should be lighter than that of the TRUMPET, 8 FT., when both stops are placed in the same division, as in the Great division of the Organ in the Parish Church of Doncaster. TRUMPETS

* A free-reed CONTRA SAXOPHONE, 16 FT., occupied a place in the Pedal of our own Chamber Organ.

of powerful intonation are frequently introduced in large Organs, and are very effective when placed, as they always should be, in expressive divisions. The powerful intonation is chiefly due to the high-pressure wind employed, the scale of the pipes and the mode of forming and voicing the reeds being adapted to the requirements. The HARMONIC TRUMPET, 8 FT., when properly scaled and voiced, is perhaps the finest of the loud-toned TRUMPETS, and is accordingly highly to be recommended for insertion in the expressive Solo Organ. There is a TRUMPET, 8 FT., on wind of 22 inches, in the Solo division of the Organ in St. George's Hall, Liverpool; but unfortunately this magnificent stop has lost much of its value, from a true musical point of view, by being placed outside the swell-box which contains the larger number of the stops of the division. It is astonishing that the practice of placing the high-pressure reed stops beyond control and powers of expression was not long ago condemned by men of cultivated and refined musical taste. Organ-builders and organists generally advocate the apportionment of the more delicately voiced and comparatively ineffective stops to expressive divisions of the Organ,—in itself perfectly proper,—while they advocate, in a thoroughly inconsistent manner, the planting of the loudest and coarsest voiced stops in exposed positions, where it is impossible to modify or impart any light and shade to their voices. As they roar at first, so must they roar for all time. There is no authority in the orchestra for such unmusical treatment, nor the slightest authority furnished by any musical instrument outside the Organ. Every orchestral instrument is capable of producing a *crescendo* and *diminuendo*, at the will of the performer. Why, then, in the name of common sense, should the most assertive stops of the Organ, which are designed to reproduce the voices of important orchestral instruments, be denied, by the illogical organ-builder and the noise-at-any-price loving organist, these all-important powers of expression? Such questions must be answered in the coming Organ of the Twentieth Century.

The TROMBONES of the Organ, while they cannot be said to successfully imitate in their tones the fine Trombones of the orchestra, are majestic and most valuable stops. The compass covered by the Trombones extends from AAA to f♯²; accordingly, the organ TROMBONE, 8 FT.; can be accepted as imitative only up to the latter note; above that it is strictly a full-toned TRUMPET, to which no exception can be reasonably taken. The unimitative TROMBONES, of 16 ft. and 32 ft. pitch, are very important stops in the modern Organ; and, when voiced by a master-hand, produce tones of singular dignity and grandeur. Under the name of CONTRA-POSAUNE, there is a stop of 16 ft. pitch in both the Great and Pedal Organs of the instrument in the Centennial Hall, Sydney. TROMBONES, 16 FT., are to be found in the Great and Swell divisions of the Organ in St. George's Hall, Liverpool; and a POSAUNE,

32 FT., is in the Pedal Organ of the same grand instrument; while TROM-
BONES, 8 FT., are inserted in the Great and Swell Organs.   In Schulze's
large instrument in Doncaster Parish Church, there is a POSAUNE, 8 FT.,
in the Great Organ, and a POSAUNE, 16 FT., and a CONTRA-POSAUNE,
32 FT., in the Pedal Organ.   There is a TROMBONE, 16 FT., in the Pedal
Organ of the instrument in the Church of Our Lady of Grace, Hoboken.
In our tonal appointment of the Concert Organ in the Festival Hall
of the Louisiana Purchase Exposition, there are the following stops: a
CONTRA-BOMBARDE, 32 FT., BOMBARDE, 16 FT., and TROMBONE, 16 FT.,
in the Pedal Organ, and a BASS TROMBONE, 16 FT., and TROMBONE, 8 FT.,
in the expressive Fourth Organ, which contains the representatives of
the " brass-wind " instruments of the orchestra.   The BASS TROMBONES
are represented in French Organs by the BOMBARDES of 32 ft. and 16 ft.
In his tonal scheme for the Grand Organ for the Basilica of St. Peter,
at Rome, M. Cavaillé-Coll introduced in the Pedal department a CONTRE-
BOMBARDE, 32 FT., a BOMBARDE, 16 FT., and, in addition, a QUINT BOM-
BARDE, 10⅔ FT.   We are not aware of a reed stop of the last given pitch
ever having been made; but in a Pedal Organ, such as projected for St.
Peter's, containing five stops of 32 ft. and five stops of 16 ft. pitch, one
can understand the reason, on scientific grounds, for the addition of the
QUINT BOMBARDE.   Something of the kind will doubtless appear in the
Organ of the Twentieth Century, yet to come.   The tones of the French
BOMBARDES are much softer than the English TROMBONES, and on this
account are more generally useful in varied combinations.   TROMBONES
of an intonation, in strength, between the voices of the high-pressure
TROMBONES and the ordinary FAGOTTOS would be valuable in all modern
Organs.

The Ophicleides of the Orchestra cover a compass extending from
GGG to f²; accordingly, the Pedal Organ OPHICLEIDE, 16 FT., is only
extended downward seven notes below the Bass Ophicleide.   The manual OPHICLEIDE, 8 FT., exceeds the upward range of the Alto Ophicleide in F about an octave and a half.   While the tones of the
OPHICLEIDES of the Organ are not strictly imitative, they are, in good
examples, superior in musical quality and evenness to the orchestral
instruments.   In the Organ in St. George's Hall, Liverpool, there are
four fine OPHICLEIDES.   Three of 8 ft. pitch occupy places in the
Great, Swell, and Solo Organs; that in the last-named division speaking on wind of 22 inches, and being stupidly placed outside the swell-
box: this stop is practically a TUBA.   The fourth OPHICLEIDE, 16 FT.,
is in the Pedal Organ.   Accordingly, there is only one OPHICLEIDE
expressive in this noble instrument, whereas every one should have
been expressive and flexible.

There is no necessity to consider the claims of the OPHICLEIDE in
the tonal appointment of the Church Organ; but in the Concert-room

Organ its value must not be overlooked. In important and properly appointed instruments, a unison OPHICLEIDE should be inserted in the expressive division in which the brass-wind instruments of the orchestra are properly represented; while an OPHICLEIDE, 16 FT., may with advantage be placed in the Pedal Organ, especially if it has an expressive division.

Speaking of the Bass Tuba, Berlioz correctly says: "The Bass Tuba possesses an immense advantage over all other low wind instruments. Its quality of tone, incomparably more noble than that of the Ophicleides, Bombardons, and Serpents, has something of the vibration and quality of tone of Trombones. It has less agility than the Ophicleides; but its sonorousness is more powerful than theirs, and its low compass is the largest existing in the orchestra." The Bass Tuba has a compass of from $AAAb$ to ab^1. This majestic instrument deserves to be carefully studied with the view of its tones being imitated closely in the Organ. The BASS TUBA of the Organ is of course a reed stop of 16 ft. pitch, and its proper place, on account of the short compass upward, would appear to be the Pedal Organ, especially as the finest tones of the orchestral instrument lie within the compass of the Pedal; but where it has hitherto been introduced it occupies a place in one of the manual divisions. Under the name of CONTRA-TUBA, 16 FT., it is to be found in the Solo division of the Organ in the Centennial Hall, Sydney. The correct place for the imitative BASS TUBA, 16 FT., would be in an expressive pedal division; but otherwise in the expressive manual division specially devoted to the representatives of the brass-wind instruments of the orchestra, or among the solo stops.

The stops of 8 ft. pitch called TUBAS, apparently intended as organ representatives of the Sax-Tubas, vary very greatly in their qualities and strengths of tone, according to their scales, modes of voicing, and the pressures of wind on which they speak. These effective stops find their culmination in the high-pressure reed designated the TUBA MIRABILIS, of which several fine specimens exist in English Organs. The TUBA, 8 FT., of moderate intonation, may be inserted in the Swell or Solo divisions; but when of powerful intonation, its proper place is in the latter division, where it certainly should be inclosed and rendered expressive and flexible. There is a TUBA MIRABILIS, 8 FT., in the Solo division of the Organ in the Auditorium, at Chicago, which, according to Mr. Roosevelt's sensible treatment, is inclosed in the swell-box of the division. There are fine examples in the Solo Organs of the large instruments in the Royal Albert Hall, Kensington, and Westminster Abbey, London; but neither of these is expressive, while both speak on wind of very high pressures. The TUBAS in the solo division of the Organ in York Minster are most unwisely planted outside the swell-box. If there are any stops of the Organ that call for absolute control and powers of expression, the TUBAS are the ones. Nothing but a sheer love of noise, and absolute absence of true musical taste and sense, can account for the practice of placing such "roaring reeds" beyond control. Such a practice will be abandoned in the Organ of the Twentieth Century.

In addition to the TUBAS above described there is a stop of 4 ft. pitch, called the TUBA CLARION. This is properly a high-pressure reed of brilliant intonation. Examples are to be found in the Solo divisions of the Organs in the Royal Albert Hall, London, and the Centennial Hall, Sydney. In the same division of the Organ in St. George's Hall, Liverpool, there are two high-pressure reeds of this class and pitch,— an unnecessary duplication, unless for noise,—and both uninclosed, like the TUBA CLARIONS, 4 ft., in the preceding two Organs.

Unfortunately no entirely satisfactory imitation of the peculiar and beautiful tones of the orchestral Horn has been accomplished through the medium of organ-pipes. Indeed, the voice of this "noble and melancholy instrument," as Berlioz calls it, seems foreign to the sounds characteristic of all lingual pipes. The nearest approach to the voice of the Horn that we have ever heard in an Organ, was produced in the tenor and middle octaves of a labial stop of the KERAULOPHONE species. Notwithstanding the unimitative character of the organ stop commonly labeled HORN, 8 FT., there is no question that it is, when artistically voiced, a valuable voice in the Organ—even if we accept it as little more than a soft and smooth-toned TRUMPET. Reed stops of soft and smooth intonations are so rare in modern Organs, and during the general craze for high pressures, that their intonation should always be welcomed and encouraged by the musician. There are some satisfactory examples of the so-called HORN to be found in Organs by prominent builders who have made a careful study of reed-voicing, Willis in particular. In a HORN of a satisfactory character all brassy quality must be eliminated, and a smooth, velvety tone must be produced in which there is no trace of reed vibration. These desirable conditions are by no means fulfilled by reed pipes of the ordinary construction. How far the adoption of free-reeds would solve the problem has not yet been properly tried. Some form of the resonating tubes would, in all likelihood, go far to solve the problem. An ORCHESTRAL HORN, 8 FT., has recently been introduced by the Hook & Hastings Organ Co., of Kendal Green, Mass., which is remarkable for its production of an imitation of the closed tones peculiar to the orchestral Horn. A pipe of this fine stop is illustrated and described in the Chapter on the Forms and Construction of Lingual Pipes.

While the position of the HORN in an Organ may vary according to its tonal character and assertiveness, it is certainly proper, as in the case of all reed stops, that it should be placed in an expressive division.

The HORN has never, so far as we are aware, been introduced in any French or German Organ. It is evidently of English origin, and is believed to have been invented by Richard Bridge, and introduced for the first time in the Organ he built, in 1730, for Christ Church, Spital-fields, London.

Attempts have apparently been made to produce a stop, the tones of which imitate the fine tones of the Euphonium; but, as in the case of the Horn, the task seems difficult. Under the names EUPHONIUM and EUPHONE, free-reed stops of soft and pleasing intonation have been introduced in certain Organs. A EUPHONE, 16 FT., is to be found in the Positif of the Organ in the Church of Saint-Sulpice, Paris, and one of 8 ft. pitch is inserted in the First Manual division of the Riga Cathedral Organ.

When the EUPHONE is simply a soft-toned reed of an unimitative character, it may be placed in any manual divisions of the Organ where its voice would be of the greatest value in combination; but when its tone is rich, full, and strongly imitative of that of the Euphonium, it may properly take its place, under the name EUPHONIUM, in the Solo Organ, or, in a large Concert-room Organ, in the division representing the brass-wind portion of the orchestra. When of 16 ft. pitch, its most useful place is in the Pedal Organ, where the presence of a soft-toned reed of a distinctive character and good mixing quality is invaluable. This fact is generally overlooked in the tonal appointment of the Pedal Organ, along with many other facts connected with that all-important department, as we have attempted to show.

The CORNOPEAN, 8 FT., of the Organ, as usually made, cannot be considered an imitative stop in a strict sense. The proper tones of the CORNOPEAN lie between the brassy tones of the TRUMPET and the smooth round tones of the HORN, when imitative; and on that account they are desirable in a large Organ, imparting variety to the tonal coloring. In the generality of modern Organs, the CORNOPEAN is little better than a vulgar TRUMPET, blatant in tone. There is great scope for improvement in the voicing and intonation of this stop, and the voicer would do well to study the tones of the actual instrument as produced by an artistic performer. The CORNOPEAN, 8 FT., should invariably be placed in an expressive division.

Such, then, are the more important tonal forces at the disposal of the organ-designer and builder; and it is in their selection for, and apportionment in, the different divisions of the Organ of the Twentieth Century that the coming designers, and, we hope, the coming organ-builders, will display their scientific knowledge and musical sense and taste. But things move slowly in these inartistic and "money-grubbing" days. Dollars, not art, is the path to fame!

We have clearly shown, in the Chapters specially devoted to them, that there are three classes of Organs—the Church Organ, the Concert-room Organ, and the Chamber Organ—and have endeavored to prove that each of these, having a different office to fulfil, should be designed on special lines, so far, at least, as its tonal appointment is concerned. We do not hesitate to say that very many of the failures in modern organ-building are directly due to the fact that those interested in the art failed to fully realize the nature of the problems submitted to them. There is many a Church Organ that would be more properly placed in a concert-room; many a Concert-room Organ that would be more useful if placed in a church; while the majority of Chamber Organs are merely small instruments, on the ordinary Church Organ model, very much out of place in private residences. Such a state of affairs would not obtain if organ-designers and builders realized the obvious fact that in each case the Organ should be schemed from a different starting point, and developed on special lines.

It must never be forgotten that in the tonal appointment of the Organ two equally important matters demand careful study and consideration; namely, the selection of the complete series of speaking stops suitable for the special class of instrument and the chief work it has to do; and the proper disposition of the stops, so selected, in the different divisions of the instrument, so as to enable the performer to separate or combine the several varieties of tone, in the most convenient and effective manner, without having resort to an undesirable and perplexing use of mechanical appliances or helps; and likewise enable him to control the entire tonal forces at his disposal in the most direct and musicianly manner.

In apportioning the stops in the different divisions of the Organ, due attention must be paid to those which demand powers of expression and flexibility from those which may, with some degree of artistic propriety, be planted on uninclosed wind-chests: this necessary separation should exercise a decided influence on the selection of the entire series of stops. In a scientifically schemed instrument having practically full powers of expression, the series of stops will vary considerably from the series proper and desirable for an instrument with very limited expressive powers, or which (as is very common) may have only one division—the Swell Organ—inclosed in a swell-box. This self-evident fact appears, however, to be generally unrealized or ignored, judging from the present universal type of organ-builders' lists of stops, or so-called Specifications. Theoretically, and from a true musical standpoint, every speaking stop in the Organ should have expressive powers given it.

The division of the Organ, commonly called the Great Organ, which is, with the exception of a few advanced examples, left entirely uninclosed and expressionless, may, with great advantage from a musical or artistic point of view, have a considerable portion of its speaking stops rendered tonally flexible by being inclosed in a swell-box. It must be quite obvious to every one who has studied the tonal structure of the Organ, that the same stop apportionment would not be equally appropriate for an entirely uninclosed and for a partly inclosed Great Organ. In the latter a much greater latitude obtains in the selection of the stops, and a much more satisfactory harmonic structure may be built up. This is due to the great tonal flexibility imparted to the stops which properly form the inclosed section of the division. In short, the stops that would be proper for the inclosed section, in combination with the desirable uninclosed stops, such as the DIAPASONS, 8 FT., DOUBLE DIAPASON, 16 FT., and other full-tone labial stops of unison pitch, would not be altogether suitable for an entirely exposed Great Organ. In the former case the great variations of strength of tone in, and the flexible character of, the Great Organ, secured by its inclosed section, multiply ten-fold the tonal effects and *nuances* that are both possible and desirable from a strictly musical point of view.

While in the case of the Great Organ, or that manual division which is its equivalent, it is unnecessary and generally undesirable to inclose the double and unison labial stops which form the foundation of the entire Organ, it is, both on scientific and artistic grounds, most desirable to render flexible the stops which strictly belong to the harmonic-corroborating series. The inclosure of these stops renders the introduction of a practically complete tonal structure not only possible but highly desirable. The harmonic-corroborating series, including the octave stops, mutation stops, and compound stops, under the controlling influence of the swell-box, becomes so flexible as to be of value in every combination of the unison and double stops of the division. It is no longer necessary to confine the use of the mutation and compound stops to full or loud tonal effects : on the contrary, they may be most effectively used with the softest combinations possible in the division, or even with a single unison stop. The advantage of such an arrangement must surely be obvious to the musician. Both artistic skill and musical taste can be displayed in the proper gradation of the harmonic-corroborating tone in all the possible combinations ; and brilliant flashes of tonal coloring may be produced by the powers of expression the swell supplies.

The speaking stops which strictly belong to the Great Organ are those which yield pure organ-tone—the OPEN DIAPASONS and the stops derived therefrom; and in instruments of moderate dimensions which comprise three manual divisions it is unnecessary to add materially to these, beyond, perhaps, two or three unisons of varied qualities of tone. These may be a full-toned covered stop, a stop of viol organ-tone, and an effective reed, such as the DOPPELFLÖTE, 8 FT., the GAMBA, 8 FT., and the TRUMPET, 8 FT. While it may not be generally desirable to inclose the labial stops, the TRUMPET should certainly be placed in the swell-box. If an OCTAVE of either of these stops should be introduced, it ought to be inclosed so as to place its strength of tone under control.

The characteristic qualities which should mark the stop apportion-ment of the Great Organ are grandeur, dignity, and solidity of tone; and these can only be secured by accurately proportioned scales, artistic voic-ing, and a copious wind supply at a moderate pressure—a scientifically schemed harmonic structure being understood. The importance of the inclosed harmonic-corroborating series of stops is not confined to the Great Organ; for it will prove of the greatest value, in numerous com-binations, when coupled to the other divisions of the instrument which, in the usual order of things, are not furnished with anything approach-ing a complete harmonic structure. The value of the Great Organ flexible harmonic-corroborating series, in conjunction with combinations in the other divisions of the Organ, cannot well be realized by the ordinary performer who has had experience only with instruments of the usual old-fashioned description, in which only one flexible and expressive division—the Swell Organ—is introduced. Both in the con-struction and playing of the Organ there are possibilities hardly dreamt of at the present time. The organist of the twentieth century has a fertile field before him.

The second division of the Organ, or that very commonly termed, by English and American organ-builders, the Choir Organ, calls for a tonal apportionment widely different from that of the Great Organ. The tonal character of this second division should be distinctive, and present a decided contrast to that of the first division. While in the first division grandeur, dignity, and solidity should, as we have said, be the character-istic qualities of tone, in the Choir Organ stop apportionment mod-erate strength of tone, variety of character, and extreme refinement of intonation should obtain throughout. In the Church Organ this is essentially an accompanimental division, and this fact must be steadily held in view while scheming its tonal apportionment. The Choir Organ is at the present time almost invariably uninclosed, while as an accom-panimental division it is imperative that it should have powers of ex-pression and flexibility imparted to it. There has been a strong preju-dice against the multiplication of the swell, and even accomplished organists have objected, very illogically we maintain, to the inclosure of the Choir Organ in a swell-box. We met with notable examples of this illogical objection on the occasion of our address on the subject of " The Swell in the Organ " before the Royal College of Organists, in London.

In the Concert-room Organ, when systematically appointed, the sec-ond manual division can hardly be pronounced an accompanimental one. It correctly consists of a series of stops, softer and more varied in tonal character than those forming the Great or first division. It groups, under easy control by means of a special clavier, certain tonal forces, which are selected from the entire stop appointment for a well-conceived purpose, and with a definite aim. This second division should certainly be rendered entirely expressive, as in the case of the Organ in the Albert Hall, Sheffield, and the Organ in the Auditorium, Chicago. In the majority of existing Concert-room Organs the second, or so-called Choir, divisions are uninclosed. Accordingly, in both Church and Concert-room Organs there are two classes of Choir divisions,—the uninclosed and inclosed,—and these call for different stop apportionments. Much greater liberty may be exercised in the selection of the stops for an inclosed or expressive division than for one that has to be heard, at all times, at its full strength of tone; and this is especially the case when the exposed Choir Organ is schemed chiefly for accompanimental purposes.

Under no circumstances should a Choir or Second Organ be appointed as a miniature Great Organ; for duplication of any of the Great Organ stops, even though they be DIAPASONS of softer intonation, leads to an undesirable narrowing of tonal variety. In the case of very large instruments, however, this rule against duplication of similar qualities of tone may be to some extent relaxed in favor of the foundation stops of pure organ-tone, but no further. In small instruments no duplication should appear. It may be remarked that in certain cases the Choir Organ may be only partly inclosed; and this arrangement should certainly be adopted when there are any stops of a strictly solo character, and when there is a decided prejudice against rendering the entire division expressive. The CLARINET, 8 FT., has very frequently been inserted in the unexpressive Choir Organ; but this should never obtain in a properly schemed and appointed instrument. The CLARINET should invariably be placed in an expressive division: indeed, it may be accepted as a rule of general application that in a proper stop apportionment, no stop of a strictly solo character should be inserted in an unexpressive division of any Organ.

Beyond the directions given above no hard and fast rules of general application can be given for the stop apportionment of the Second or Choir Organ; for in this, as in all the other divisions, the apportionment entirely depends on the size, number of manual divisions, and the tonal appointment of the entire instrument. For further particulars respecting the stops suitable for the Choir division of the Church Organ and the corresponding manual division of the Concert-room Organ we must direct our readers to the Chapters on the Church and Concert-room Organs. The Chapter on the Chamber Organ may also be consulted.

In the tonal apportionment of the third division of the Organ—that commonly designated the Swell Organ, from the fact that in old and in the large majority of modern Organs it is the only division inclosed in a swell-box—considerable latitude obtains. In every instrument which has only one expressive division the Swell Organ should be both the largest and, tonally, the most varied division; and it should also be the most brilliant in its tonal effects. It becomes in this case the chief accompanimental division, simply because it alone is flexible and expressive. It is difficult, we venture to say, for the true musician to imagine any instrument suitable for the accompaniment of the human voice that is not endowed with powers of expression. If an accompaniment is to be of any artistic value it must follow, and in all instances accentuate, the tonal expression of the vocal music; and in an instrument of great strength of tone, like the Organ, flexibility and expression are absolutely essential properties. We lay great stress on these facts because they must never be lost sight of in scheming the tonal appointment of the Organ.

In addition to its being the chief accompanimental division in an Organ which has only a single swell-box, the Swell Organ is, or should be, the most important division for the production of solo effects; and this simply because it is essential that all purely solo voices should be endowed with powers of expression. But when an Organ has a fourth or Solo division, inclosed in a swell-box, the so-called Swell Organ should be appointed as a full accompanimental division, and that not only with reference to the human voice, but also with reference to the solo voices of the Solo Organ. The Swell Organ, in what may be considered its proper form, strictly belongs to the Church Organ; and as we have treated its apportionment at considerable length in the Chapter on the Church Organ, it is only necessary to pass a few remarks in addition here. Whether the Swell Organ is schemed as an accompanimental division only, or as both an accompanimental and a solo division, it should have a fairly complete tonal structure, founded on an OPEN DIAPASON, 8 FT., of a bright quality; or a GEIGENPRINCIPAL, 8 FT., of rich intonation, as dictated by the general tonal appointment of the Organ. This structure may in all favorable cases be richer in harmonic-corroborating stops than even that of the Great Organ; for, as we have already said, brilliancy should characterize the tonal effects of the Swell Organ; and this desirable brilliancy cannot easily be secured without the introduction of special mutation and compound harmonic-corroborating and timbre-creating stops. Further richness and brilliancy of tonal effect, combined with a general increase of body and weight, can be secured by the judicious introduction of unison stops which are in themselves rich in harmonic over-tones. In Organs of small dimensions every expedient, consistent with general tonal excellence, should be resorted to, to enrich the unison tone without the undue introduction of small stops. There are many solo stops, as already mentioned, which are comparatively rich in certain natural harmonics; and the introduction of such stops goes far to render, especially in small Organs and in certain divisions of large instruments, the addition of medium-pitched mutation stops unnecessary: but as such unison stops are somewhat weak in the higher upper partial tones, it is not generally desirable to depend upon them for the compound tonal effects which the MIXTURES are constructed to produce. The remarks made in this and the foregoing paragraph have special reference to the Church Organ.

The third division of a properly appointed and stop-apportioned Concert-room Organ is a very important one, furnishing effective accompaniments to the prominent solo voices of the fourth division, or so-called Solo Organ, and also, what is of equal importance, independent solo voices required for special orchestral effects and tonal combinations. The full apportionment of this division, or Third Organ of the Concert-room instrument, is considered in the Chapter specially devoted to the Concert-room Organ; but other satisfactory tonal apportionments may be schemed, on similar lines, for instruments of lesser size. As a rule, it is always desirable to scheme the stop apportionment of this division so that it may not only be distinctly marked from that of the other divisions, but that it may fill a clearly defined and special office in the tonal economy of the instrument. While in the ordinary Church Organ it is desirable, if not absolutely necessary, to have the Swell division complete in itself and practically independent, so that it may fulfil its accompanimental office in the most efficient manner; in the Concert-room Organ, which has two, three, or more of its manual divisions wholly or partly inclosed and expressive, the corresponding division does not call for a similar treatment. On the contrary, it should be tonally apportioned with strict reference to all the other divisions of the instrument—taking its place as simply a part of the grand tonal scheme; just as a division of the orchestra, organized for the production of special musical effects, is a portion of, and is dependent on, the entire tonal fabric of the orchestra.

In the case of a large Concert-room Organ, having only four manual claviers, it is well worth serious consideration whether or not the Third Organ, commanded by the third clavier, should be divided into two tonally-contrasting portions and given double expression; for the decision in this matter will materially influence the tonal apportionment of the division. This will be clearly seen on reference to our dissertation on the apportionment of the Third Organ in the Chapter on the Concert-room Organ. When the division is subdivided, each part should have a distinct tonal character, chiefly with the view of aiding the performer to readily produce special and important orchestral effects and masses of distinct tonal coloring, without objectionable resort to coupling, and without stultifying any other manual division for the time. It is essential that each subdivision be inclosed in a separate swell-box; and very important effects and *nuances* are obtainable by this system of compound expression.

In the properly appointed Concert-room Organ the third division, whether it be subdivided or not, should be strongly orchestral in its tonal character; and it appears, to our mind, to be the proper division in which to represent the string forces of the orchestra. String-toned stops should here be massed together, forming a rich harmonic structure, always ready at the command of the organist without drawing upon the resources of the other divisions in the slightest degree; and, when coupled to the other divisions, imparting to them a vast increase of brilliancy and variety, aided by the compound powers of expression. In this Third Organ may be properly and conveniently placed the stops representing the wood-wind forces of the orchestra, embracing both labial and lingual, and wood and metal stops. Such stops would furnish effective tonal contrasts to the string-toned stops, either permanently or temporarily associated with them in this third division of the Organ. On this important subject we have much to say in the Chapter on the Concert-room Organ, and in a direction not hitherto contemplated in the tonal appointment of the Organ in any of its forms.

The fourth division in all Organs having four manual claviers, and the fifth division in instruments having five manual claviers, may be considered, as the name commonly given to it implies, to be the division devoted to the stops of a decidedly solo character, and to those of a specially powerful intonation which are more suitable for pronounced solo effects and dominating musical passages than for the purpose of combination. Except in Concert-room Organs of the first magnitude, the Solo Organ need not contain many stops; but in all cases the stops must be carefully selected, so as to supply what may be markedly deficient in the other manual divisions of the instrument, and to furnish voices of an orchestral character, strongly imitative and assertive in their tonality. In a small Solo Organ there should be no duplication of stops that appear elsewhere in the instrument; while in large Solo Organs duplication is only admissible under very special tonal appointments, and for the necessary production of well-defined tonal effects. When a stop of any class is duplicated, care must be taken to give individuality to the voice of that inserted in the Solo Organ, so that it may have due prominence over the stop of the same name which is inserted in any other division. All the more important stops of the Solo Organ should be, as we have already remarked, of an imitative and orchestral character; and this division is the most appropriate one for the reception of those assertive stops which represent the brass-wind of the orchestra, and which speak on wind of high pressures. These remarks will be more clearly understood on reference to the stop apportionment of this division in our scheme given in the Chapter on the Concert-room Organ.

The Solo Organ should invariably be rendered entirely expressive by being inclosed in a special swell-box. Notwithstanding the present objectionable practice of certain organ designers, which places the high-pressure and dominant reed stops in an uninclosed position, such power-ful and commanding voices should never, in artistic tonal appointment, be placed beyond proper control or without expressive powers.

We have brought the matter of the swell somewhat prominently for-ward in the present Chapter, simply because its introduction or omission very materially affects the tonal appointment and apportionment of the Organ. It must be evident that between an exposed and an inclosed division of an Organ a wide difference of tonal apportionment should obtain, in the class of stops selected, and also with regard to their scaling and voicing, and the pressures of wind on which they are to speak. In the scientific and artistic tonal appointment of an Organ not a single thing affecting the tonality or voice of the stops should be overlooked. It must never be forgotten that a stop perfectly suitable for one pos-ition, or in one tonal scheme, may be quite out of place in another; and it is in such a matter that scientific knowledge, experience, and musical sense are required and display themselves. A survey of numerous schemes of ordinary tonal appointment, presented in the so-called Speci-fications of organ-builders and organists of to-day, goes to show the absence of all system, and the utter disregard of the teachings of science, and of the guidance of cultivated musical sense. A great change must take place in these directions, and much has to be done, before the Organ of the Twentieth Century makes its most welcome appearance; and its advent will not be due to the unaided efforts of the tradesman organ-builder. Scientific and artistic men, with keen musical sense and a knowledge of the orchestra, must come forward to instruct and direct the organ-builder and voicer. Then, and then only, will the Organ assume the unassailable position of the " King of Instruments."

The present Chapter would be incomplete without some allusion to one other manual division, sometimes introduced in large modern Organs; but which is of comparatively little importance, and is only resorted to for the production of ear-tickling effects, rarely if ever called for in legitimate organ music, and never required in the rendition of orchestral scores. We allude to the so-called Echo Organ, or the com-paratively small division usually located at some distance from the main portion of the Organ, and in a position calculated to impart to its tones the effect of distance and a somewhat mysterious character.

A manual division called the Echo appears in the works of the old European builders, which is simply a softly toned, uninclosed, division occupying the place ultimately taken (in England) by the Swell Organ. In the celebrated Organ in the Cathedral of Haarlem, built in the year

1738, the Echo comprises fifteen stops and 1,098 pipes. It presents a very complete tonal structure, having, in addition to its unison stops, two mutation stops and three compound stops, in all fourteen ranks of pipes. Its reed stops are the SCHALMEI, 8 FT., DULCIAN, 8 FT., and VOX HUMANA, 8 FT. The last usually found a place in the old Echo Organs. In many instances in old Dutch and German Organs the Echo was larger and more complete in its tonal apportionment than the Choir Organ. With old examples, however, we have nothing to do in the present Chapter, for the Echo division in modern organ appointment is a widely different thing.

Perhaps the most noteworthy Echo Organ, in a modern instrument, is that of the large Organ in the Auditorium, at Chicago. It is placed in an elevated locality, above the hall, more than one hundred feet from the console, is inclosed in a swell-box, and played from the fourth or Solo Organ clavier. The following is a list of its stops:—

1. QUINTATEN . . . . 16 feet.	7. FLAUTO TRAVERSO . . 4 feet.
2. KERAULOPHON . . . 8 "	8. HARMONIA ÆTHERIA. .IV. ranks.
3. DOLCISSIMO . . . . 8 "	9. HORN . . . . . . 8 feet.
4. UNDA MARIS . . . . 8 "	10. OBOE . . . . . . 8 "
5. FERNFLÖTE . . . . 8 "	11. VOX HUMANA . . . 8 "
6. DULCET . . . . . 4 "	— TREMOLANT.

The chief conditions required for a successful Echo Organ obtain in this example; namely, considerable distance from the player and audience, and inclosure in a swell-box. The tonal apportionment, in relation to the rest of the instrument, may be accepted as fairly satisfactory: it is certainly capable of producing many charming tonal effects.

Turning now to the larger modern Organ in the Centennial Hall, at Sydney, N. S. W., we find an expressionless Echo Organ, having the following rather peculiar stop apportionment:—

1. VIOLE D'AMOUR . . . 8 feet.	5. FLAGEOLET . . . . 2 feet.
2. UNDA MARIS, (II. ranks) 8 "	6. ECHO DULCIANA CORNET IV. ranks.
3. LIEBLICHGEDECKT . . . 8 "	7. GLOCKENSPIEL . . IV. "
4. VIOLE D'AMOUR . . . 4 "	8. BASSET HORN . . . 8 feet.

It is somewhat remarkable that this Echo division is not inclosed in a swell-box. To leave such a division without powers of expression, and beyond control so far as strength of tone is concerned, is surely an error of judgment.

In deciding the tonal apportionment of the Echo Organ, the office of the division should, at the outset, be clearly defined. The Echo Organ may either be independent of all the other manual divisions and be tonally complete in itself, or a dependent division schemed with the view of furnishing echo effects to several of the special solo stops in other manual divisions.   In the latter case it is, strictly speaking, an Echo Organ.   In all cases it should be inclosed in a swell-box and located in a position favorable to the production of distant effects.   Unless the Echo Organ can be properly treated, so as to yield artistic results, it should be entirely omitted.   It is by no means necessary in the tonal appointment of any instrument.

As the stop apportionment of the Pedal Organ, when correctly schemed, depends entirely on the appointment of the manual divisions of the instrument, nothing beyond a single rule need be given here.   Let the Pedal Organ stops carry down as many as practicable of the more important stops of the manual divisions, with due regard to variety of character and strength of tone, and by this means provide suitable basses for the most useful and effective manual combinations and solo voices. As the Pedal Organ has to furnish basses for *all* the manual divisions, separate and combined, it is obvious that its stop apportionment, so far as unison (16 ft.) stops are concerned, must have a considerable range in tonal strength.   It must not be forgotten that a soft bass is as valuable as a loud one; yet we find very few modern Church Organs, of medium size, provided with adequate Pedal Organs, or with those which contain soft unison stops.   On this important branch of our subject further remarks will be found in the Chapters on the Church and Concert-room Organs.   We desire the reader's special attention to what we say on the subject of the expressive Pedal Organ in the Chapters on the Concert-room Organ and the Swell.   The adoption of an expressive division will materially alter the desirable stop apportionment.

" MUSIC TYPIFIED " — FROM " MARGARITA PHILOSOPHICA NOVA." PRINTED IN 1508.

CHAPTER VI.

THE CONSOLE.

GOOD deal has been done in a practical direction, and much has been said and written, respecting certain improvements deemed desirable in the mechanical appointments of the organ console. Recently steps have been taken toward its standardization, chiefly with regard to the relative positions of the manual claviers and the draw-stop and coupler appliances— knobs, rocking-tablets, or drop-touches. For the standardization, a joint Committee of the American Guild of Organists and the National Association of Organists was appointed. During its few meetings certain resolutions were passed which will be recorded in the present Chapter.

THE MANUAL CLAVIERS.

As the forms and dimensions of the natural and sharp keys have for a long time been standardized it is unnecessary to discuss them here, accordingly our remarks may be confined to their relative positions. In different countries, at different times, and in the hands of different organ-builders, the positions of the claviers with respect to each other have varied greatly; and it has long been most desirable that a uniform system should obtain. With the view of arriving at a decision in this important matter the Committee on Standardization, just alluded to, was instituted. The Resolution, arrived at after a careful consideration of all the points involved is as follows:—

"RESOLVED—That the distance from the surface of one manual clavier to that of another, immediately above it, shall be two and three-eighths inches: and that the distance from the front edge of each clavier to that of the clavier immediately above it shall be four inches."

These relative measurements are accurately set forth in the accompanying Section, Plate XXII. With the moderate key-overhang of seven-eighths inch, the distance between the claviers is sufficient to give easy access to the combination pistons in the key-slips, as indicated at A. The cutting away of the back portion of the sharp keys—now commonly done—is also a convenience with respect to the pistons.

Regarding the touch of the manual claviers the following decisions were arrived at by the Committee on Standardization:—

" RESOLVED—That the fall of the manual keys at their front ends shall be three-eights of an inch and that the pressure required to depress them, under the touch of the fingers, shall be equal to the weight of four ounces laid upon the playing portion of the keys."

While no exception can well be taken to these Resolutions, it might be desirable for the console maker to provide means for readily adjusting the weight of the touch, throughout the claviers, to meet the wishes of the organist. It is probable that to some the touch may be too heavy, while to others it may feel too light. For general adoption, however, the four-ounce touch may be safely accepted by the console maker; care being taken to make it perfectly uniform and agreeable to the finger.

No allusion is made in the Resolutions regarding the order in which the manual claviers should be arranged, yet this is a matter deserving consideration. Probably the majority of the members of the Committee were of the opinion that the question had been decided by the practice prevailing in the American organ world, and that a Resolution respecting it was unnecessary. It is to be regretted, however, that the question was overlooked; for the proper arrangement of the claviers of the several manual divisions of the Organ is clearly a matter for standardization, seeing that both opinion and practice have long varied regarding it.

The almost universal method, followed in this country, of arranging the claviers, which places that of the Choir Organ under the Great Organ clavier, cannot be advocated on any logical grounds, or, indeed, on any practical ones of the slightest value. The order should be reversed. The Great Organ is the fundamental tonal division upon which all the other manual divisions are, or should be, based and built up; accordingly, its clavier should occupy the first or lowest position. Both the German and French organ-builders have realized this logical reasoning: so we find in their representative and modern Organs the *Hauptwerk* of the former and the *Grand-Orgue* of the latter commanded by the lowest clavier. A modification appears in certain French instruments, notably those in the Cathedral of Notre-Dame and in Saint-Sulpice, Paris. In both these important Organs we find the First clavier commanding the *Grand-Chœur* and the Second clavier the *Grand-Orgue*. But it must be understood that the *Grand-Chœur* is merely an

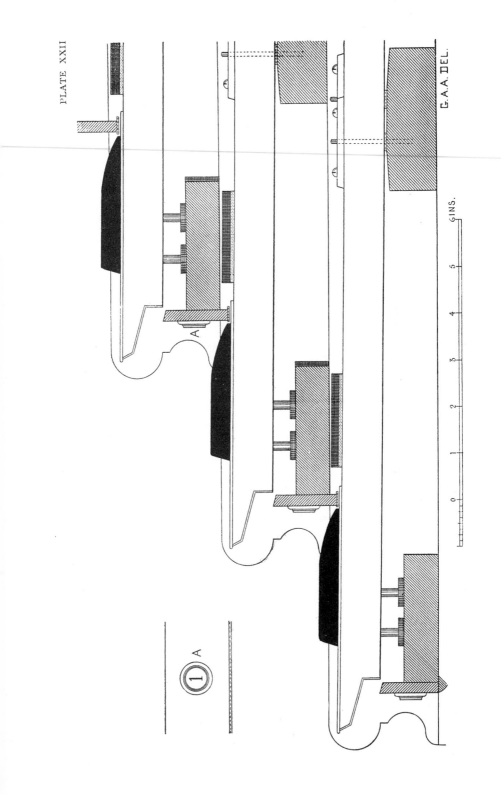

PLATE XXII

G.A.A. DEL.

6 INS.

integral part of the *Grand-Orgue,* separated from it for special manipulation. The office of the *Grand-Chœur* can be understood on referring to the tonal appointment of the Saint-Sulpice Organ, the *Grand-
Chœur* of which contains all the compound harmonic-corroborating and
all the seven lingual stops belonging to the tonal apportionment of the
Grand-Orgue. The following arrangement of the claviers properly obtains in the important Organs in the Basilique du Sacré-Cœur and the
Palais du Trocadero, Paris; and in the Concert Organ in the Albert Hall,
Sheffield, constructed by M. Cavaillé-Coll, under the late W. T. Best's
directions: First clavier—*Grand-Orgue.* Second clavier—*Positif.* Third
clavier—*Récit.* Fourth clavier—*Solo.* A slight variation takes place
when the *Clavier de Bombarde* is introduced, but the proper position
of the *Grand-Orgue* is never interfered with. In our opinion the only
correct position for the Great Organ clavier is below all the other
manual claviers in the console.

The natural keys should be covered with ivory not less than one-
tenth of an inch in thickness, and the sharps made of the finest deep-
black ebony. The overhanging portions of the natural keys to be plated
with ivory celluloid, as indicated in the illustration.

THE COMBINATION PISTONS.

It will be observed that in the Section in Plate XXII., the usual form
of projecting thumb-piston is not represented, which, in the perfected
electric action, is neither necessary nor desirable. The form of combination piston or touch we advocate is that resembling the electric-bell
push: it consists of an ivory disc, half-an-inch in diameter, set in a
nickel-plated ring, from which it projects not above one-eighth of an
inch. Its action only requires about that amount of play, under the
slight pressure of the thumb, to make the necessary electrical contact.
Both in utility and appearance this form of piston, shown in Front
and Side Views at A, A, Plate XXII. is greatly to be preferred: it is
pleasant to the touch and is never in the way of the fingers while
playing the sharp keys.

The Standardization Committee made no recommendations respecting the form of the combination pistons, but gave consideration to some
matters relating to their office, as the following Resolution shows:—

"Resolved—That all combination pistons shall be adjustable at the console.
"That each manual piston shall be capable of operating, or allowing to
remain neutral, the couplers and Pedal Organ stops.
"That the Pedal Organ shall have its own set of combination pistons."

It is, of course, imperative that in all properly constructed Organs
the adjustable combination action shall be under the direct command of

the organist seated at the console, and be easily manipulated by him. It is, accordingly, imperative that the means of adjustment be made as simple as skill can devise, demanding the least possible expenditure of time on the part of the performer. The importance of a perfect combination action, adjustable at the console, in a large modern Organ cannot be overrated.

The third clause of the Resolution properly directs that the Pedal Organ shall have its own set of combination pistons, but does not state where the pistons are to be placed in the console. It would seem logical, seeing that the pistons of the manual divisions are located immediately under the respective claviers, that the Pedal Organ combination pistons should be placed immediately adjoining the pedal clavier and within easy reach of the feet. Such being the case, the proper place for the pistons would seem to be on the toe-board of the pedal clavier, to be touched easily by the performer while playing. Instead of pistons, requiring a direct downward pressure, hinged tablets or small levers, merely requiring the touch of a passing toe, might be used with advantage. These should lie along the free part of the toe-board. It may be desirable, however, to have the Pedal Organ pistons placed, in a group, to the left of the pistons under the lowest manual clavier, as in the console illustrated in Plate XXV. These may be instead of, or in addition to, the toe-pistons or levers.

The second clause of the Resolution, which reads, "That each manual piston shall be capable of operating, or allowing to remain neutral, the couplers and Pedal Organ stops," may seem to be satisfactory so far as it goes; but it cannot be considered sufficient, as it does not touch on the desirable operations, separately and conjointly, of the draw-stop and combination piston actions. These should be clearly defined in the standardization of the console of the Organ of the Twentieth Century.

The Resolution offers no solution of the important question at issue between what is commonly known as the "Absolute" and the "Dual Combination Systems." Yet it is essential, if standardization is to mean anything, that this question be settled.

There has been considerable discussion respecting the claims of the two systems; and it has been quite obvious that personal and individual likes and dislikes have naturally and, perhaps, unwisely influenced the opinions or arguments advanced in favor of one or the other. But we venture to think that such an important question should be looked upon from an absolutely impersonal and unprejudiced point of view. It is hardly a matter for individual decision, but one properly to be decided on purely artistic and practical grounds. In these directions it should not be difficult to arrive at a decision as to which system offers the greater advantages to the performer in the preparation and production of desirable tonal effects and changes. It must be obvious to any one skilled in organ matters, and giving the subject at issue serious and unbiased consideration, that both systems—*absolute* and *dual*—cannot be equally efficient in the production of artistic tonal combinations and effects. And it is also obvious that, at this so-far developed stage in the art of organ-building, it is more than desirable that the question should be settled so as to further the correct standardization of the console.

To assist the reader in arriving at a conclusion on the question under consideration we may briefly describe what the two systems alluded to are, and what they do in stop control.

THE ABSOLUTE SYSTEM—Without approving of the name which has been commonly accepted to designate this system of stop combination and control, we shall not attempt to introduce another, even though it might be more appropriate. The term *absolute* seems to have been given to convey the information that the piston combination action, while in operation, holds absolute control of the draw-stop system of the Organ. That is, it operates directly through the general draw-stop system of the instrument, and in doing so moves the draw-stop knobs in the jambs of the console. Indeed, it seems to be the only strong argument advanced by those in favor of this old-fashioned system, that this corresponding movement of the draw-stop knobs is a direct and valuable aid to memory, by recording visibly the combination of stops drawn by any piston. This claim is, however, when duly weighed, of little value; for the organist is bound to remember every combination of stops he has set on the pistons, otherwise he could not unhesitatingly use them during the proper and connected rendition of an exacting composition. As he is, or should be, fully aware of what the tonal combination will be before he touches the commanding piston, it seems difficult to understand what great advantage the corresponding movement of the draw-stop knobs can be. In one sense, it would seem to be more distracting than otherwise.

There seems to be only one advantage connected with the movement of the recording draw-stop knobs, providing that, should they be changed by hand, they would temporarily dominate the piston combination; and so permit the performer, by direct manipulation of the knobs, to subtract from, or add to, the combination brought on by the piston for the time being; allowing another touch of the piston to reinstate the combination strictly belonging to it, or set upon it by the performer for a definite purpose.

Even should the draw-stop knobs, the operations of which are controlled by the combination piston, not move, it should be possible for the performer to *enrich* the combination by drawing any knobs not already affected in their operation by the piston movement. On the other hand, it will be impossible, by any manipulation of the piston-controlled, unmoved knobs, to *reduce* the piston combination.

THE DUAL SYSTEM—This system, as the name implies, comprises two practically independent combination actions—that commanded by the draw-stop knobs, rocking-tablets, or other devices, and that commanded by the pistons located under or adjoining the claviers. These combination actions can be used separately or conjointly, as the performer may desire; a convenient means being provided to combine or separate them—preferably by double-acting pistons or touches set in the cheeks of the claviers. Under such conditions, the operation of the pistons in no case moves the draw-stop knobs or devices; nor does it affect in any way the tonal combination prepared on the knobs or draw-stop devices. These are important advantages belonging to a properly constituted dual combination system.

It will be understood that unless the piston release belonging to a clavier has been operated, the combination pistons of that clavier are active; and that their respective tonal combinations will remain available, at the command of the performer, regardless of whatever stop or combination of stops belonging to the clavier may be drawn by means of the knobs or draw-stop devices. This is an important condition.

Now, if the two combination actions belonging to a clavier are separated, by means of the double-acting pistons alluded to above, the draw-stop combination will be cut off from the clavier, and all the piston combinations will be available without any tonal alteration. Then, should the performer reverse the double-acting pistons, so as to unite the two combination actions, the tonal combination provided on the draw-stop knobs or devices will immediately speak on the clavier, along with the tonal combination on any piston of the clavier that the performer may operate. While this connection obtains, any addition to or subtraction from the draw-stop combination can be made, by the manipulation of the knobs or devices, at the will of the performer. The value of these methods of producing varied combinational effects with ease and certainty cannot well be overrated, be the Organ small or large. They render possible the instantaneous changes of tonality, producing powerful or other pronounced effects, or imparting a special tonal coloring, by the addition of one or more voices, to all the piston combinations that may be brought on the clavier. Now, if the piston release is operated, the draw-stop combination, whatever it may be, will alone remain active on the clavier. Let the reader versed in stop-registration give this whole matter careful consideration, and we feel convinced he will realize the great possibilities and value, from an artistic point of view, of the dual combination system. We are decidedly of opinion that this system should be adopted in the standardized console of the Organ of the Twentieth Century.

THE DRAW-STOPS.

Like other details connected with console appointment, the forms and positions of the draw-stops have been the subject of considerable discussion and diversity of opinion. At the present time it is impossible to find any indications of an approach toward standardization. Draw-stop knobs of different materials, forms, and sizes; rocking-tablets of different proportions and treatment; pendant touches, hinged at their upper ends, and resembling huge teeth; and stop-keys after the clavier form, are all to be found in the consoles constructed by organ-builders in this country, and in accordance with the personal tastes of different organists.

Difference in console construction and appointment has evidently been, of late years, one of the chief aims of rival organ-builders; and much ingenuity has been displayed by them in the forms and disposition of the draw-stop appliances. This is as it should be, provided such efforts are looked upon as tentative, leading ultimately to the general recognition and acceptance of the treatments most suitable and convenient for Church and Concert-room Organs of different dimensions. We are of opinion, however, considering the various sizes of Organs and the purposes for which they are constructed, that a generally accepted standardization in this draw-stop matter will be a very difficult if not an impossible achievement. Turning now to the Resolutions of the Console Standardization Committee we find the following:

"RESOLVED—When Draw-Stops are used they shall be placed in vertical stop-jambs at an angle of 45° with the ends of the key-desk. The groups of draw-stops shall be placed in vertical columns. The Swell and Pedal draw-stops shall always be placed on the left of the manuals, and the Great, Choir, and Solo draw-stops on the right.

"Regarding the placing of the families of Stops, the Committee recommends their being grouped in the following order, reading downwards: Reeds, both chorus and solo; Mixtures and Mutation Stops, Strings and soft 8 ft. Stops; Diapasons; 16 ft. Stops.

"The Tremolant draw-stops shall be placed at the bottom of the groups to which they belong."

According to this Resolution, the employment of the ordinary, direct-faced, draw-stop knobs is implied, for no other form would be suitable, arranged in vertical columns on vertical jambs. The arrangement is sanctified by long usage, and has been favored by numerous organ-builders, especially in England, and even for large instruments requiring more than one hundred draw-stop knobs. It is to be found in the Organs, constructed by Willis, in St. George's Hall, Liverpool, and in the Royal Albert Hall, London; and in the still larger Organ, constructed by Hill & Son, in the Centennial Hall, Sydney, N. S. W. For Organs of moderate size the arrangement may be accepted as generally convenient; but for large instruments its suitability is more than questionable.

The placing of the draw-stop knobs in horizontal rows in stepped jambs, either in a direct line with the claviers or at an angle with them, has been frequently adopted, and has seemed to have some advantages. This disposition led to the introduction and use of oblique-faced knobs.

M. Cavaillé-Coll, of Paris, realizing the inconvenience that attended the old-style vertical stop-jambs for large Organs, devised stepped jambs of a quadrant form, and introduced them in the console for the Grand Organ in the Cathedral of Notre-Dame. A sketch of this console is given in the accompanying illustration, Fig. XVII. The convenience of this arrangement of draw-stop knobs is obvious, for

Fig. XVII.

it disposes them all in full view and within easy reach of the performer while seated properly at the console. The console of the Grand Organ, constructed by M. Charles Mutin, successor to M. Cavaillé-Coll, and erected a few years ago in the Basilique du Sacré-Cœur, Montmartre, Paris, has quadrant jambs of five stepped tiers. On these are arranged the ninety-eight draw-stop knobs, commanding the seventy-four Speaking Stops, three Tremolants, and the several *Registres de combinaison*. The disposition of the different series is peculiar and sufficiently interesting to be described here. On the first or lowest tier of both quadrants are placed, in duplicate for convenience, the knobs commanding the *Registres de combinaison*. On the second tier of both right and left quadrants are disposed the knobs drawing sixteen of the stops of the *Pédale*. On the third tier of both quadrants are disposed the eighteen stops of the *Grand-Orgue:* the first knob in the left quadrant drawing the FLÛTE, 32 FT., and the corresponding first knob in the right quadrant drawing the BOMBARDE, 32 FT., of the *Pédale.* On the fourth tier of the left quadrant are arranged the knobs drawing seven of the labial stops of the *Positif Expressif;* and also five knobs controlling Couplers. On the fourth tier of the right quadrant are arranged the knobs drawing eight of the labial stops of the *Récit Expressif;* and also four knobs controlling Couplers. On the fifth tier of the left quadrant are arranged the knobs drawing six of the stops of the *Solo Expressif;* six stops (embracing the four lingual stops) of the *Positif Expressif;* and a Tremolant. On the fifth tier of the right quadrant are arranged the knobs drawing the remaining six stops of the *Solo Expressif;* the three lingual and two harmonic-corroborating stops of the *Récit Expressif;* and two Tremolants. The disposition of the entire series of draw-stop knobs is remarkable and, so far as our observation extends, unique.*

Jambs of the tiered quadrant form were adopted for the console of the large Concert-room Organ installed in the Festival Hall of the Louisiana Purchase Exposition, in 1904. A view of this important console is given in the accompanying Plate XXIII. Following the French model, draw-stop knobs were adopted throughout all the tiers; and to assist the eye, all the knobs had inclined faces, as indicated. The couplers were commanded by the thirty-six rocking-tablets above the highest clavier.

Up to this point the remarks on the draw-stops have been confined to the projecting knob variety, the use of which is evidently implied, as we have said, by the Resolution of the Console Standardization Committee: but it has been evident for some time that for Organs of considerable size other forms of draw-stops have been found to be more compact in grouping and, accordingly, more easily manipulated. The most desirable form is that of an oblong or domino-shaped tablet, faced with ivory, pivoted in the center, and adjusted to rock easily under the touch of a finger. This form of draw-stop, disposed in convenient positions as close as practicable to the manual claviers, is, in our opinion, the one that will be most frequently adopted in properly appointed consoles for large Organs; while it is perfectly suitable for those of instruments of any dimensions. Numerous examples of the employment of rocking-tablets are already in existence, and one, very noteworthy, will be specially alluded to further on: these go far to prove the practical efficiency and ease of manipulation of this form of draw-stop.

* Organ-builders and organ-experts, who may feel a special interest in this noteworthy console, will find it graphically set out in the Appendix to Mr. Wallace Goodrich's admirable work, "The Organ in France." Boston, 1917. In this work much valuable information is given respecting French Organs.

The positions occupied by the tablets naturally vary in different consoles; dictated, on the one hand, by the number of speaking stops to be commanded, and, on the other hand, by the judgment or caprice of the console designer. The only essential conditions necessary to be observed in placing the several series of tablets commanding the different divisions of the Organ, are that they shall be in full view and within easy reaching distance of the performer seated at the claviers. The tablets should be grouped in the manner recommended for the draw-stop knobs by the Console Standardization Committee; and so secure the desirable uniformity of disposition. It is, however, impossible to formulate a rule for the placing of the tablets in the jambs of the console, or for the form of the jambs themselves: these matters will, of necessity, largely depend on the number of the tablets required and the dimensions and form of the console.

Respecting the other forms of draw-stops which have been used during late years in a certain class of Organ little need be said, for there is very little likelihood of their coming into general use in the Organ of the Twentieth Century. The form which consists of a narrow strip of ivory (or celluloid probably), hinged at the upper end, and projecting in a pendant fashion and at an angle from some parts of the console, in rows like gigantic, grinning teeth, is, to our mind, very objectionable. The form may be suitable for the unimportant type of Theatre Organ; but we would be very sorry to see it appear in either the Church or Concert-room Organ. It appears in a certain type of instrument to which no further allusion will be made in these pages.

Certain treatments have been adopted with the desirable view of rendering the draw-stops of the different divisions of the Organ distinct from each other, thereby assisting the performer in their prompt manipulation. When the draw-stops are arranged in vertical columns on vertical jambs, as recommended by the Standardization Committee, the proper labeling and a distinct separation of the columns are sufficient to effectively distinguish the different divisional groups; and all the draw-stops may be of the same form, materials, and color. When less evident grouping obtains, as when the draw-stops are disposed in horizontal tiers in jambs of any form, it will generally be found desirable to adopt some distinguishing feature in the draw-stops. In the case of draw-stop knobs, it has been a practice to form them of wood of different colors, faced with ivory for the inscriptions. This practice cannot be followed when tilting-tablets or their equivalents are used; accordingly, staining, in different tints, of the ivory face-plates has been resorted to with satisfactory results. This system has been carried to the fullest development in the draw-stop appointment of the finest console that up to the present year (1918) has ever been con-

PLATE XXIII

structed. In its groups of draw-stop tablets and couplers nine distinguishing colors are used. This remarkable console is described further on.

THE COUPLERS.

It may be safely said that no matter connected with the appointment of the console has called forth more diverse opinions in both the organ-building and organ-playing worlds than that relating to the form and disposition of the coupling appliances; and it seems very probable that diversity of opinion in the matter will continue to obtain. We may properly open the subject here by giving the Resolution passed by the majority of the members of the Console Standardization Committee on June 9th, 1917.

"Resolved—The Couplers shall be placed above the highest manual clavier, and shall be grouped as follows :—

"All Couplers coupling to the Pedal Organ shall be placed on the left of those coupling to the Great, Swell, Choir, Solo, and Echo Organs, which shall be placed in the order given.

"The Tablet for each coupler shall contain the name of the division of the Organ which is being coupled, and, immediately below the name, the octave at which it is being coupled. It shall omit the name of the division to which the coupling is made. This name shall appear directly below its own group of couplers, on a label, in distinct lettering. The order of the couplers shall be as follows :—

"To the Pedal Organ :—Great, Swell, Choir, Solo, Echo.

"To the Great Organ :—Swell, 8 ft., Swell, 16 ft., Swell, 4 ft.—Choir, 8 ft., Choir, 16 ft., Choir, 4 ft.—Solo, 8 ft., Solo, 16 ft., Solo, 4 ft.—Echo, 8 ft., Echo, 16 ft., Echo, 4 ft.—Great, 16 ft., Great, 4 ft.

"To the Swell Organ :—Solo, 8 ft., Solo, 16 ft., Solo, 4 ft.—Echo, 8 ft., Echo, 16 ft., Echo, 4 ft.—Swell, 16 ft., Swell, 4 ft.

"To the Choir Organ :—Swell, 8 ft., Swell, 16 ft., Swell, 4 ft.—Solo, 8 ft., Solo, 16 ft., Solo, 4 ft.—Echo, 8 ft., Echo, 16 ft., Echo, 4 ft.—Choir, 16 ft., Choir, 4 ft.

"To the Solo Organ :—Swell, 8 ft., Swell, 16 ft., Swell, 4 ft.—Solo, 16 ft., Solo, 4 ft.—Echo, 8 ft., Echo, 16 ft., Echo, 4 ft.

"It is recommended that the Unison Release or Separation be located in the right-hand cheek of each manual clavier."

The position of the couplers is that now commonly adopted; and while it is questionable if it is desirable that all the couplers should be confined to that distant position, perhaps, under ordinary conditions in Church Organs, no serious objection can be advanced against it. We are, however, strongly in favor of certain of the more frequently used couplers being located or duplicated, in the form of thumb-pistons, under their respective claviers: thereby preventing the necessity of the performer frequently removing his hands to so great a distance from the clavier on which he may be playing. This arrangement we feel sure will commend itself to every experienced organist. We feel that we are performing a pleasant duty, in connection with the present subject, in recording in these pages the valuable suggestions, founded on long experience, made by the distinguished organist, Mr. Alfred Pennington, in an article which appeared in *The Console* for May, 1916. He says:—

"Without a detailed enumeration of the course of my experiments I shall give now the arrangement of the pistons adjusted to operate couplers only, which I decided on in the first six months—an arrangement which I have never changed in the five succeeding years. First let me say that the pistons are divided into five groups of eight pistons each, a group under each of the four manuals, and the fifth over the Solo manual. The pistons occupy a central position under the keyboards, are about three-quarters of an inch apart, and are, therefore, touched easily by the thumb of each hand from that part of the manual most played upon.

"The row of pistons under a given manual performs two kinds of registration for that manual. Certain of the pistons are devoted to coupler changes only, certain others to changes in sounding-stops. The upper row of pistons is divided in its duties, supplementing the other rows. The pistons operating the couplers are to the extreme left, beginning with piston No. 1.

"In arranging the pistons for couplers, I looked upon a piston that isolates a given manual from all other manuals, and brings on the Pedal coupler to that manual, as deserving first place. Consequently piston No. 1 under each of the four manuals performs that office for that manual. When one desires, for example, the Great Organ isolated from the other manuals, and with the Great to Pedal only, it is evident that any or all of the following couplers that are on must go off; Swell to Great Unison, Swell to Great Octaves, Swell to Great Sub-Octaves, Choir to Great Unison, Choir to Great Octaves, Choir to Great Sub-Octaves, Solo to Great Unison, Solo to Great Octaves, Swell to Pedal, Swell to Pedal at Octaves, Choir to Pedal, and Solo to Pedal. And the Great to Pedal must come on. Here we have thirteen couplers moving into their proper positions to produce the isolated Great manual with its Pedal coupler.

"The isolated Choir manual places upon piston No. 1 of the Choir the duty of withdrawing seven manual couplers operative from that manual (including the Octaves and Sub-Octaves on itself), and four Pedal couplers, besides drawing Choir to Pedal. Like duties are performed for the Swell and Solo manuals by their No. 1 pistons, as I have indicated.

"Great piston No. 2 insures the coupler combination so much used—Swell to Great, Great to Pedal, and Swell to Pedal, drawing and withdrawing to produce it exactly.

"Great piston No. 3 insures the coupler combination of Choir to Great, Great to Pedal, and Choir to Pedal.

"Choir piston No. 2 insures the combination Swell to Choir, Choir to Pedal, and Swell to Pedal.

"Choir piston No. 3 insures the combination Swell to Choir Unison, Swell to Choir Octaves, Swell to Choir Sub-Octaves, Choir to Pedal, and Swell to Pedal.

"Swell piston No. 2 insures the combination Solo to Swell, Swell to Pedal, and Solo to Pedal.

"Piston No. 1 in the top row insures Solo to Choir, Choir to Pedal, and Solo to Pedal.

"Here we have ten pistons devoted entirely to fundamental coupler control, and, with only one exception, every piston is under its corresponding manual, immediately to the left, and forming part of the row of pistons devoted to sounding-stop combinations for the same manual. And what is the advantage of this? A tremendous advantage, namely; that as the hands are moving to a given manual to play upon that manual the thumb of the left hand drops down to the proper coupler piston and the thumb of the right hand drops down to the sounding-stop piston, both are pressed at exactly the same instant and the player proceeds on his way. Neither the couplers nor the sounding-stops are regarded in the least, the player's only care being to press the two pistons required.

"'I observe,' says one, 'that when you couple two manuals together with a piston you make it draw the Pedal couplers to both manuals. How would you manage the couplers if you wished to play a solo on the Choir, with Swell coupled, and the accompaniment on the Swell, with Swell to Pedal?' Easily enough. I would first press Choir piston No. 2, then Swell piston No. 1. Either of the other manuals could be chosen for the accompaniment by pressing piston No. 1 of that manual.

"The reversible Great to Pedal should always be retained, since it is extremely useful in rapid alternations between the Great and another manual. It will be observed that there is no provision for coupling the Solo to Great by means of a piston. This is accomplished by a reversible pedal. There is also a reversible Solo to Pedal."

It will be observed, according to the system of coupling advocated by Mr. Pennington, that it is unnecessary to have couplers actuated by the stop-combination pistons. He pertinently remarks: " It would be advantageous in every case to have the full complement of eight pistons to every manual for sounding-stop combinations, besides the pistons for couplers. In no case do the pistons operate Pedal stops. They are drawn by the combination pedals, and by five pedals acting on Pedal stops only." Mr. Pennington's scheme, in all its essential features, has our earnest approval; and we further agree in what he says: " Much has been said at the present time about the ' standardization of the organ console,' but any scheme which will omit the easy and logical control of the couplers in the way I have explained will, I am convinced, be wide of the mark."

It must not be understood from what has been recommended that the series of independent couplers, arranged above the highest clavier, should be either omitted or interfered with.

The number of the couplers provided in the Report of the Standardization Committee is ample for the largest desirable and properly appointed Church Organ: and, indeed, we are of opinion that those operating on the same clavier may well be dispensed with; although we are well aware that our opinion will not be shared by the majority of organists who love musical noise at any price. Any one, who has studied tone-production from both scientific and artistic points of view, must know that it is undesirable to add to a prime unison tone either a sub-octave or octave tone of precisely the same quality and intensity of voice; yet this is invariably done when the sub-octave and octave couplers of any clavier on itself are drawn. We have systematically omitted these undesirable couplers in every organ scheme over which we have had any control. These couplers are a mild, but none the less undesirable, reflection of the hideous system of tonal construction, in which half a hundred so-called stops of different pitches are derived from perhaps ten or fifteen stops of long compass; with the result of a complete confusion in tonal balance, and only as many varieties of tone as there are long-compass stops. The musical monster in the Auditorium, at Ocean Grove, N. J., is a representative example of this outrageous system of tonal appointment.

To our mind it has long seemed possible that through a more artistic and effective system of tonal apportionment in the several divisions of the Organ a much less lavish resort to couplers could be rendered necessary. It is obvious that their use between claviers must, to a considerable extent, result in the undesirable loss of clavier independence for the time being. We have proved to our own satisfaction that by an artistic system of tonal apportionment in the divisions of the Organ, commanded by the different claviers, the necessity for frequent coupling can be largely discounted. So long, however, as the prevailing or, indeed, we may say, universal want of a systematic tonal apportionment in the several divisions obtains, the constant resort to couplers will be necessary; for otherwise there are no means of producing many desirable combinations of stops either of similar families or of special tonal colorings.

In the remarks just made we have alluded to the coupling of the manual claviers; but similar remarks are applicable to the coupling of the manual claviers to the pedal clavier. Unquestionably, it is due to the prevailing insufficiency of the tonal apportionment of the Pedal Organ in modern instruments that resort to coupling has been found necessary. If the Pedal Organ be appointed in a proper manner, commensurate with the appointment of the manual department, the coupling of the manual claviers to the pedal clavier will be seldom required. The cheap and altogether insufficient system of Pedal Organ stop-apportionment, now followed in certain organ-building quarters, in which all the stops, more or less complete, are directly derived from stops belonging to the manual divisions, with the addition of only two or three octaves of special deep pitched pipes to carry down certain of the derived stops, renders the question of Pedal Organ coupling somewhat open and difficult to decide. It seems absurd to couple manual stops to pedal stops when the stops may be identical. So far, at least, coupling is valueless.

A tonally independent pedal part is desirable, if not on artistic grounds imperative, in the proper rendition of high-class organ compositions. Such being the case, an adequate tonal apportionment should be

given to the Pedal Organ, rendering coupling of the manual divisions
to it unnecessary save, perhaps, for very special effects and solo passages
of an orchestral character.

In important Organs, in which a system of distinctive coloring is
applied to the several groups of knobs or rocking-tablets commanding
the speaking stops of the different tonal divisions, in the manner already
alluded to, it is desirable that the same system be applied to the couplers
belonging to the respective divisions.

THE EXPRESSION LEVERS.

Several forms of Expression levers, or so-called swell-pedals or
expression pedals, have been introduced by organ-builders at different
times and in different countries. For a long time in England the only
form used, in Organs having a single swell-box, was a lever that returned
of its own accord, under the action of a spring or weight, as the foot of
the performer reduced its pressure upon it; and which could be hitched
and held at several stages of its movement until released by some
simple action of the foot. This form is known as the "recovering"
or "hitch-down" lever or pedal. As we have said elsewhere, it is unnecessary to enlarge on this form, for it is full time the hitch-down
lever be placed among the antiquated curiosities of organ-building, notwithstanding the fact that there are many good old-time organists whose
feet cling lovingly to it still.

The French expression lever, also known as the balanced expression
lever, is the only form now used in properly appointed consoles. The
balanced lever is most efficient in its control of the swell-box shutters,
and, accordingly, of the *crescendo* and *diminuendo* effects, when it is
associated with a direct mechanical action. With such an action, every
motion, however slight and gradual, is faithfully conveyed to the swell
shutters. This is an artistic condition that no electro-pneumatic action
hitherto devised can justly lay claim to. In the present Chapter we have
nothing to do with the operations of the expression levers, and, accordingly, may confine our remarks to the form, proportions, and positions
of those most desirable in the standard console. As a starting point in
the subject, the Resolutions of the Console Standardization Committee
may be given, as follows :—

" RESOLVED—That the Swell Organ Expression pedal shall be placed opposite
the gap between the DD♯ and FF♯ keys of the Pedal Organ clavier, and that
the Choir Organ pedal shall be placed to the left and the Solo Organ pedal
to the right of it.

"That the Crescendo pedal shall be placed to the right of the Expression
pedals, and separated by being raised slightly above their line.

"That the width of each Expression pedal shall be four inches; and the
distance between the pedals shall be half-an-inch.

" That a curved toe-stop shall be placed at the top of each of the Expression pedals, forming a guide in which the toe can rest."

When three expression levers are required, as is usual in the best appointed Church Organs having four manual divisions, the positions set forth in the Resolution are quite satisfactory; but no suggestions are made respecting the desirable arrangement of a greater number of expression levers. Many Organs of modern construction have four expressive divisions, and, in all probability, many Concert Organs of the Twentieth Century will have a greater number, which will require special expression levers. In addition to these, a balanced crescendo lever will be required; and in the fully appointed Concert Organ console a sforzando lever will be called for, the value of which is neither understood nor recognized at the present time. Under such conditions, seven balanced levers may have to be arranged conveniently in the console. It does not seem possible to formulate any rule of general application beyond that set forth in the Resolution, simply because both the number and tonal character of the divisions of the Organ, for which the console is designed, will dictate both the number and relative positions of the expression levers. The crescendo lever will retain its position on the right of the group of expression levers; and the sforzando lever, when introduced, will occupy a position still more to the right.

Balanced expression levers of different shapes have been devised—plain and ornamental—but those of a right-angled parallelogram and a shoe form have been most frequently adopted. The former shape is, however, the most suitable one from every practical point of view, and is evidently the one contemplated in the Resolution. The dimensions and surface treatments of this shape of lever vary somewhat, according to the views held by different organ-builders and organists: yet it should not be a difficult matter to arrive at a standard size and treatment. As regards the width, four inches are recommended, and this seems suitable, under general conditions, and for the average size of a man's shoe. When five or more balanced levers are required, the reduction of a half or even a quarter of an inch in the width would effect a desirable reduction in the length of the series. The distance apart is also a matter for consideration. Half-an-inch is recommended in the Resolution, and this is ample with levers four inches wide. Regarding the length of the expression lever nothing is said in the Resolution; but nine or ten inches will be ample for easy operation. We would, accordingly, recommend a balanced lever 4 inches by 10 inches to be accepted in the standardized console. The treatment of the surface of the lever is of considerable importance; and in considering that, the ordinary curvature of the sole of the shoe of the performer should be recognized. While about the front two-thirds of the surface should be flat, the remaining

PLATE XXIV

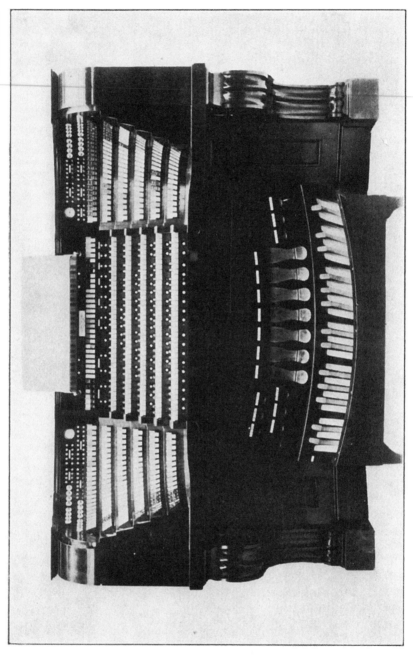

portion, on which front part or toe of the shoe rests, should be curved upwards so as to meet the shape of the sole and the natural action of the foot of the player. This is a very desirable provision and should not be neglected. At the extreme end of the lever a slightly raised straight stop should be provided, against which the tip of the shoe can rest in proper position. A " curved " toe stop is recommended in the Resolution, " forming a guide in which the toe can rest ": this form is, in our opinion, not convenient, as it interferes with the quick and easy lateral movement of the foot in gliding from one lever to another; or while the foot is operating two adjacent levers simultaneously, as will often have to be done in a properly schemed and tonally appointed Organ.

As a smooth surface is not agreeable on a balanced lever upon which the foot has to feel secure, it is desirable to have it covered with slightly roughened or corrugated, white, vulcanized rubber, of the finest quality and of sufficient thickness to insure durability. This must be securely cemented to the surface of the lever and otherwise attached if necessary. The action of all balanced levers must be perfectly uniform, offering a pleasant degree of resistance to the foot, but absolutely devoid of any motion of a jerky character. If considered desirable, each white rubber surface-covering can be inlaid with a bold figure indicating the number, or with a contraction of the name of the tonal division of the Organ to which the lever belongs. When two divisions are affected by one ex- pression lever, two numbers or contractions will be necessary. A due attention to all the details and matters recommended above will insure a perfectly satisfactory balanced expression lever.

The shoe-formed expression lever is shown in the consoles illustrated in Plates XXIII. and XXIV.; but as it cannot, on any practical grounds, be considered for universal adoption, it is unnecessary to dwell upon it here. It may have a neat appearance, and that is all that can be urged in its favor.

As the Pedal Organ clavier—a very important adjunct to the console —is fully treated of in the Chapter devoted to it, it is unnecessary to comment upon it here.

A NOTEWORTHY CONSOLE.

In the accompanying Plate XXIV. is given a view of the console recently constructed for the large Concert Organ installed in the great Wanamaker Store in Philadelphia, Pa. It is truly a notable console, and the most beautiful specimen of the organ-builder's art that has ever come under our observation. A brief description of the work will form a fitting conclusion to the present Chapter.

The general form and the disposition of the numerous features of this remarkable console can be realized from the illustration, but it can convey no adequate idea of the dignity and perfect workmanship of the reality. The evidence of a master-hand is present in every detail.

The five manual claviers commanding seven tonal divisions of the Organ are arranged in the following order: the first and lowest clavier commands the expressive Choir Organ of thirty-eight speaking stops (3,131 pipes); the second clavier commands the partly expressive Great Organ, of thirty-three stops (3,038 pipes); the third clavier commands the Swell Organ, of fifty stops (4,346 pipes); the fourth clavier commands the Solo Organ, of seventeen stops (1,330 pipes); and the fifth clavier commands the Echo Organ, of twenty-two stops (2,062 pipes). The expressive Ethereal Organ, of nineteen stops (1,594 pipes), is commanded by the fourth and fifth claviers; and the small portable Chorus Organ, of eight stops (732 pipes), is played from the second clavier.

Under the claviers are fifty-nine combination thumb-pistons, divided and arranged in the following manner. Under the first clavier, toward the left are nine pistons, for combinations on the stops of the Pedal Organ; and toward the right are seven pistons, for combinations on the stops of the Choir Organ. Under the second clavier are two groups of five pistons, for combinations on the stops of the First and Second Divisions of the Great Organ. Under the third clavier are two groups; one of six pistons, for combinations on the stops of the First Division; and one of ten pistons, for combinations on the stops of the Second and Third Divisions of the Swell Organ. Under the fourth clavier are two groups of six pistons; that on the left, for combinations on the stops of the Solo Organ, and that on the right, for combinations on the stops of the Ethereal Organ. Under the fifth clavier are five pistons, for combinations on the stops of the Echo Organ.

The entire stop combination system is adjustable by the performer at the console; all the adjusting appliances being systematically and conveniently arranged above the top rows of the draw-stop tablets in the quadrant jambs. These appliances are clearly shown in the View of the claviers and jambs given in Plate XXV. The appliances embrace adjusting pistons, corresponding in number and in groups to the combination thumb-pistons under the different manual claviers: to these are added series of general combination dials, each dial having five active divisions operated on by a movable hand or pointer. These dials are disposed in nine groups of four each, and are placed adjoining the groups of adjusting pistons, as shown in the Plate. The operations of these combination dials are commanded by the four general pistons situated on the left immediately above the fifth or Echo Organ clavier.

In setting a combination on a thumb-piston, all that is necessary, on the part of the performer, is to draw the stops required on the rocking-

PLATE XXV

tablets and then press the corresponding adjusting piston in the group in the jamb: a light in the small disc directly above the piston indicates that the combination set by that piston is in operation. A glance at the light discs immediately tells the player what thumb-piston is in operation on any tonal division of the Organ. The operations of the combination thumb-pistons do not move the draw-stop tablets; nor do they neutralize the action of the tablets, which remains independent. Accordingly, any stop addition can be made by the tablets without interfering with a piston combination. Here is exemplified the perfect dual system of stop control.

The four general pistons, situated above the fifth clavier, which are in connection with the series of dials, are for the general combination of separate thumb-piston combinations. While it is possible to set thirty-six combinations on the four general pistons at one time, thereby making thirty-six changes with four movements, it does not exhaust the possible combinations that can be made on the four pistons: any selection from any series of combination pistons can be put on any one of the four general pistons. A good feature obtaining in connection with the general pistons is that they are not mechanically fixed. Accordingly, if, after the thumb-piston combinations of different tonal divisions are set on one of the four general pistons, a change in any direction is desired, there is nothing to prevent any one of the thumb-piston combinations being altered without disturbing the others. For example, if the combinations set on thumb-piston No. 3 of the Great Organ and thumb-piston No. 2 of the Swell Organ are both set on general piston No. 1, by pressing any other thumb-piston of the Great Organ, the general piston combination can be so far changed without disturbing the combination of the Swell piston No. 2. The same advantage obtains throughout the piston combinations of the Organ. It can be plainly seen that through the compound operations of the four general pistons, facilities for instantaneous changes of combination on several claviers simultaneously are given the performer, which otherwise would be impossible without several distinct movements, involving time that could not properly be given during a connected rendition of exacting and complex compositions.

The nine pistons, under the six labels, toward the right immediately above the fifth clavier are for the cancellation of the several Organs and their divisions, giving further facilities for important tonal changes.

Turning now to the quadrant jambs, one finds on them the surprising display of two hundred and fifty-four rocking-tablets, commanding the vast tonal forces of Organ. These tablets are disposed, in a perfectly symmetrical manner, in six stepped tiers on each side of the claviers. Accordingly, every one of the tablets, bearing its proper inscription, is in full view and within easy reach of the performer while seated at the instrument. As pieces of workmanship, apart from other points of merit, the draw-stop jambs throughout are superb: and we are satisfied that it would be impossible to find anything finer in the entire organ world. The View given in Plate XXV. shows their general treatment and appearance, but fails to convey any clear idea of their actual impressiveness and beauty.

On the left jamb are the draw-stop tablets disposed in the following order from the bottom upward :—

In the first and second tiers are thirty-four tablets commanding speaking stops of the Pedal Organ: those for the labial stops being colored black and those for the lingual or reed stops being colored red; all having inscriptions in white.

In the third tier are sixteen tablets commanding the speaking stops of the Third Division of the Swell Organ: those for the labial stops being colored blue and four for the lingual stops being colored red. The Tremolant tablet is white. In this tier there are also three black tablets belonging to the Pedal Organ, one bringing on the bass of the Piano.

In the fourth tier are twenty-three tablets; twenty commanding the speaking stops of the Second Division of the Swell Organ: those for the labial stops being colored blue and those for the lingual stops red. The tablets for the wood-wind section are in this tier. Three spare tablets are provided.

In the fifth tier, starting from the left, are four tablets for Echo Organ stops, colored yellow: these are followed by two, colored black, drawing the Echo Pedal Organ stops. Then sixteen tablets, colored blue, command the stops of the First Division (string-toned) of the Swell Organ. The tier is completed on the right by the tablet commanding the Third Division Tremolant and two tablets that bring the Piano on to the Swell and Pedal Organ claviers. There are, in all, twenty-five rocking-tablets in this tier.

In the sixth tier there are nineteen tablets commanding speaking stops of the Echo Organ: those for the labial stops being colored yellow and those for the four lingual stops red; one spare red tablet being provided along with two spare yellow ones for future additions. The tier is completed by a tablet, colored yellow, commanding the Harp stop; one, parti-colored yellow and brown, bringing the Ethereal Organ on the Echo Organ clavier; and a white tablet, drawing the Tremolant. There are, in all, twenty-five rocking tablets in this tier.

On the right jamb are the draw-stop tablets disposed in the following order from the bottom upward :—

In the first tier there are fourteen tablets commanding the labial stops of the Second Division of the Choir Organ: these are colored light green. A white tablet, drawing the Tremolant, and a spare tablet complete this tier.

In the second tier there are three tablets, completing the series belonging to the Second Division of the Choir Organ; and fourteen tablets, colored green and red, commanding the labial and lingual stops of the First Division of the Choir Organ. A white tablet, drawing the Tremolant of this division, completes this tier.

In the third tier there are, toward the right, six green tablets commanding the remaining labial stops of the First Division of the Choir Organ. The fourteen pure white tablets, completing this tier, command the labial stops of the Second Division of the Great Organ.

In the fourth tier there are, toward the right, one red and five white tablets commanding the remaining stops of the Second Division of the Great Organ. Then follow the ten white and three red tablets commanding the labial and lingual stops of the First Division of the Great Organ. Two white tablets, bringing on the Tremolant and the Gongs, and two spare tablets complete this tier.

In the fifth tier there are thirteen purple and four red tablets commanding the labial and lingual stops of the Solo Organ. To these are added eight tablets colored dark green, inscribed in white, commanding the stops of the Chorus Organ.

In the sixth tier there are twenty tablets colored brown and red commanding the manual labial and lingual stops and Chimes of the Ethereal Organ; four black tablets, drawing the Ethereal Pedal Organ stops; and one white table, bringing on the Tremolant.

The Coupler rocking-tablets, thirty-four in number, situated above the fifth clavier, are, with a few exceptions, parti-colored, indicating in a very effective manner the different organs that are coupled. The tablets 1 to 6, commencing from the left, are Pedal Organ couplers, and are parti-colored black and white, black and blue, black and light green, black and purple, black and brown, and black and yellow. The seventh tablet is white, octave coupling the Great Organ on itself. Tablets 8, 9, 10 are parti-colored white and blue, coupling Swell to Great in the sub-octave, unison, and octave. Tablets 11, 12 are colored blue, coupling the Swell in the sub-octave and octave on itself. Tablet 13 is parti-colored light green and blue, coupling Swell to Choir. Tablets 14, 15, 16 are parti-colored white and light green, coupling Choir to Great in sub-octave, unison, and octave. Tablets 17, 18 are colored light green, coupling the Choir in the sub-octave and octave on itself. Tablets 19, 20, 21 are parti-colored white and purple, coupling Solo to Great in the sub-octave, unison, and octave. Tablets 22, 23 are colored purple, coupling the Solo in the sub-octave and octave on itself. Tablet 24 is colored blue and purple coupling Solo to Swell. Tablets 25, 26, 27 are colored white and brown, coupling the Ethereal to Great in the sub-octave, unison, and octave. Tablets 28, 29 are colored brown, coupling the Ethereal in the sub-octave and octave on itself. Tablet 30 is parti-colored blue and brown, coupling Ethereal to Swell. Tablets 31, 32 are colored white and yellow, coupling Echo to Great in the unison and octave. Tablet 33 is colored yellow, coupling the Echo in the octave on itself. Tablet 34 is parti-colored blue and yellow, coupling Echo to Swell.

From the particulars given above, and from an examination of the Plate, it will be observed that on each of the parti-colored tablets the organ to be coupled to is indicated by its special color being placed on its lower half—the part the finger presses in bringing the coupler into operation. This is, of course, the proper system, and obtains throughout the series of these tablets. It is questionable, however, if the general arrangement of the couplers is the most desirable one. It will be noticed that the tablets, fifteen in number, which belong to the Great Organ, are distributed in five groups, divided by other tablets from each other. We are of opinion that it would have been more logical and convenient to bring all these tablets together into one distinct group, just as the six Pedal Organ couplers are grouped at the left end of the row. The same system could have been carried through the entire series; the couplers strictly belonging to the several organs following the order recommended in the Resolution of the Console Standardization Committee.

The general system of coloring employed to distinguish the several tonal portions of the Organ, and to separate, to the eye, the lingual from the labial stops, is, so far as our observation extends, the most effective that has been introduced up to the present time. One could imagine a more symbolical or expressive series or disposition of colors, for sounds and colors have been symbolically and poetically associated: but, after all, the main consideration is the distinct separation, to the eye, of the different divisional tonal forces, to assist to the largest extent possible the performer in the manipulation of the draw-stops and couplers. This end has been successfully reached in the present remarkable console.

It is somewhat strange the French and other European organ-builders have not adopted color schemes in the consoles of their large Organs, and especially in those in which several horizontal tiers of draw-stop knobs are arranged. Perhaps the advantage, if not the necessity, of having resort to distinctive coloring will occur to them when they are called upon to construct consoles for instruments containing more than two hundred speaking stops.

The balanced expression levers of the Organ proper, five in number, situated immediately above the Pedal Organ clavier, are arranged in the following order from left to right. Expression lever to swell-chamber of the Ethereal Organ; expression lever to swell-box of Solo Organ; expression lever to swell-box of Great and Choir Organs; expression lever to swell-box of the Swell Organ; and expression lever to swell-chamber of the Echo Organ. The position of the group is thrown considerably toward the right by placing the first or Ethereal Organ lever over the DD key and the Swell Organ lever over the AA♯ and BB keys of the clavier. The positions and arrangement of the expression levers of the Choir, Swell, and Solo Organs differ widely from those recommended for general adoption by the Standardization Committee; but it did not take into consideration the positions and arrangement of more than three expression levers. The Piano lever situated on the extreme left, over the AAA key of the clavier, controls the Pianoforte dynamically, the instrument not being inclosed in a swell-box. The second balanced lever is the Crescendo lever occupying a very unusual position, preference and practice having long decided in favor of a position to the right of all expression levers. It may be safely said that the arrangement of the levers in this great console is unique.

The only mechanical accessories remaining to be mentioned are the nine toe-levers, indicated by labels and located to the left and right of the expression levers, as shown in Plate XXV. The three upper levers on the left are for the Double-touch of the claviers of the Choir, Swell, and Great Organs. The three lower levers are for General Release; Pedal Organ Ventil; and Great to Pedal Coupler. The three levers on the right are for Couplers; to Close all Swell-boxes; and to Open all Swell-boxes.

The dimensions of the Console are: Length 7 feet 6 inches; Depth 4 feet 7 inches; Height from floor 5 feet 1 inch. The Console weighs one ton.

The Console was designed by, and constructed under the direct superintendence of Mr. William Boone Fleming, the inventor of the electro-pneumatic action of the Organ.

CLAVIERS AND DRAW-STOPS OF EIGHTEENTH CENTURY
FRENCH ORGAN, FROM "L'ART DU FACTEUR D'ORGUES."

CHAPTER VII.

THE PEDAL CLAVIER.

T is somewhat remarkable that, while for a long time all matters relating to the form and standardization of the manual clavier have been, with general consent, recognized and adhered to, up to the present year of Grace, and after four centuries of slow development, the most desirable form, proportions, and general treatment of the pedal clavier remain unsettled among organ-builders and those much more immediately concerned—the host of able men who occupy the organ-seat in all parts of the world.

A recent essay was made toward a desirable standardization of the pedal clavier; but, as on previous attempts toward that end, no decided conclusions were arrived at. This is greatly to be regretted, for no one thoroughly acquainted with organ requirements can fail to see, while looking at such pedal claviers as are being daily fabricated by the numerous organ-builders at home and abroad, that a radical change for the better and some sort of uniformity are imperatively called for in the form and proportions of so important a feature. So long as it is left to the tender mercies of the organ-builder on the one hand, and so long as early-born individual prejudice obtains among organists on the other, it seems unlikely that, for some time at least, a standard form of pedal clavier, embracing all the features that are necessary to render it convenient for all classes of performers of both sexes, and adapted to the proper rendition of the most exacting pedal passages, will be universally acknowledged. It will, however, make its appearance in the perfect Organ of the Twentieth Century. Difference of opinion also obtains respecting the relative positions of the pedal and manual claviers.

One would naturally conclude, seeing that there can be only one proper position for the performer at the manual keys of every correctly constructed Organ, that there could be no question of any importance raised respecting the most desirable form and position for the pedal clavier, every key of which has to be so disposed as to be readily commanded by his feet, without rendering it necessary for him to change his position. It is surely obvious there can, under such circumstances, be only one *best form,* and only one *proper position,* for the pedal clavier: and it is our purpose, in the present Chapter, to arrive at a conclusion in these matters which shall appear satisfactory from all practical points of view. We shall, however, not attempt to combat opinions held by individuals, and which are born of custom or prejudice: such one-sided opinions, however stubbornly they may be held for a time, will die out, and what is right will ultimately obtain.

As even the little that is known regarding the origin and early history of the pedal clavier would be too long for insertion in this necessarily brief Chapter, we must be content to merely allude to and illustrate the earlier form, of fourteenth or fifteenth century date, of which any information has been handed down; and a more developed form which obtained in France during the eighteenth century. The former is illust-

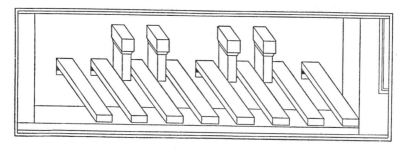

FIG. XVIII.

rated by Prætorius in his " Theatrum Instrumentorum seu Sciagraphia " as the pedal clavier of the celebrated old Halberstadt Organ, constructed in 1361 and renovated in 1495. This primitive clavier is depicted in Fig. XVIII. The eighteenth century form, as illustrated by Dom Bedos in his " L'Art du Facteur d'Orgues," is reproduced in Fig. XIX. This form is known as the " toe pedal board " from the manner in which it was played.

Turning now to the pages of the most important modern treatise on organ-building in the German language—" Die Theorie und Praxis des Orgelbaues "—we find prominence given to a pedal clavier which presents all the inconvenient features that could well be brought together. Such a clavier would not be tolerated for an hour by any one save an old-fashioned and long-suffering German organist. The keys are straight, short, and of the extreme width possible in the space allowed; and the playing parts of the sharps are only twice their width in length. It would be difficult to imagine a more inconvenient and objectionable arrangement; and the mode of construction represented is as faulty as the design. This work was published as late as 1888.

It is a noteworthy fact that, although the pedal clavier was adopted in England later than in Continental countries, and at first was nothing short of a manual auxiliary, pulling down the manual bass keys, it was in England that serious attention was first directed to the development of a thoroughly practical clavier.

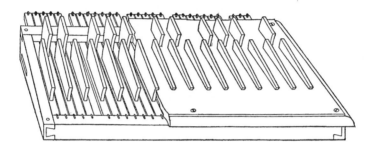

FIG. XIX.

Notwithstanding the fact that up to very recent times England was the only country in which concave pedal claviers were systematically constructed, it appears certain that their introduction there was due to a German organ-builder. Herr Schulze, of Paulinzelle, sent to the Great Exhibition of 1861 an Organ fitted with a concave pedal clavier; and we cannot find a record of an earlier appearance than this. We did not see this Organ; nor can we obtain any description of the pedal clavier, beyond the fact that its keys were parallel and arranged in concave fashion. We presume, as no mention has been made of any peculiarity in the sharp keys, that they were all of the same form and dimensions as in the ordinary German clavier of the time.

It has been stated, and apparently on good authority, that the principle of radiation was first applied in the construction of the pedal clavier by Elliott, the English organ-builder, in the year 1834. But it was left to the late Henry Willis, the most renowned English builder and an organist of consummate skill, to produce the most sensible and convenient pedal clavier that has been constructed up to now in England, by combining the radiating and concave principles of formation; giving to the world what is now commonly known as the "Willis pedal board." In the construction of this, Mr. Willis is said to have acted on the suggestion of Dr. S. S. Wesley: and under the direction of the latter it was applied to the Grand Organ in St. George's Hall, Liverpool, built in 1855. This clavier received the full approval of Mr. Best, although imperfect.

In the year 1881 the Royal College of Organists inaugurated a Conference of organists and organ-builders to consider and decide matters " with regard to greater uniformity in the external arrangements of Organs; " and as a result of this Conference, the College Council issued a series of Resolutions and Recommendations, which, so far as matters relating to the pedal clavier are concerned, have had most undesirable results. In the full knowledge of what had been done up to that time, it is difficult to understand on what logical arguments and practical grounds some of the Council's Resolutions were arrived at. Those relating to the pedal clavier are the following:—

" 1. That the compass of the pedals be from CCC to F, $i.\ e.,$ 30 notes.

" 2. That the pedals be parallel.

" 3. That the pedals be concave, with radial top facings; and that the concavity be the arc of a circle, having a radius of eight feet six inches.

" 4. That the length of the center natural key of the pedals be not less than twenty-seven inches.

" 5. That the fronts of the pedal short keys form an arc of a circle, having a radius of eight feet six inches; and that the length of the center short key of the pedals be not less than five and a half inches.

" 6. That the pedal scale be two and three-eights inches from center to center of two adjacent natural keys.

" 7. That a plumb-line dropped from the middle c^1 of the manuals fall on the center CC of the pedal board.

" 8. That a plumb-line dropped from the front of the Great Organ sharp keys fall two inches nearer the player than the front of the center short key of the pedal board.

" 9. That the height of the upper surface of the Great Organ natural key, immediately over the center of the pedal board, be 32 inches above the upper surface of the center natural key of the pedal board.

" 10. That the relationship between manuals and pedals be subservient to the fixed relative position of the Great Manual keyboard and the pedal board already defined; it being understood that the position of the Great Manual will determine the position of the other manuals.

" 11. That it is undesirable to alter the relative positions of the several manual keyboards as commonly found in English Organs, viz.: Swell above Great, Choir below Great, Solo above the Swell."

The Plan and Section given in Fig. XX accurately depict the pedal clavier constructed in conformity with the Resolutions 1 to 6 inclusive. It may be pointed out that Resolution 3 simply requires that the pedal keys are to have their " top facings," or playing surfaces, " radial," clearly implying that the key-bodies are not to be disposed radially to the center of concavity, but are to move vertically, as shown in the Section. This was a mistake on the part of the organists present, passed over, for obvious reasons, by the invited organ-builders. Perfectly smooth and practically frictionless action of the keys was prevented. However this may be, the clavier decided on was well received by organ-builders, but was strongly and wisely objected to by the advanced school of organists in England; and the Willis clavier continued in favor.

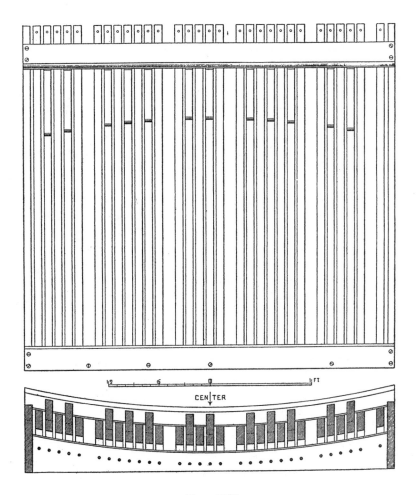

FIG. XX.

The pedal clavier, as first made in this country, was on the German model, flat throughout and with straight parallel keys. This had a great advantage in the estimation of the organ-builder—it was easy and cheap to make. The late distinguished American organ-builder, Hilborne L.

Roosevelt, essayed to improve this apology for a convenient pedal clavier, but he did not disturb its flat and parallel treatment, confining his improvements to the sharp keys, the fronts of which he properly set to the arc of a circle of about eight feet radius, and facing the naturals with hard white wood strips with a new form of playing surface, the advantage of which we altogether fail to see. In Fig. XXI. is given a Side View of a natural and sharp key: on the former is shown the applied strip or facing-piece. It will be observed that it is highest a little in advance of its center, sloping slightly toward the sharp key, and considerably so toward the heel-board.* This latter treatment is

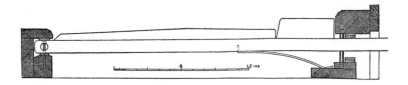

FIG. XXI.

exactly the reverse of what is logically and practically desirable. It will also be noticed that the playing surface of the sharp key is horizontal. When one bears in mind the forward swing of the leg from the knee, and the corresponding upward tilt of the foot, it must be recognized, we venture to think, that this form of sharp key is not to be desired. These may appear to the organ student to be small things. Granted; but it will be careful attention to these and other small things that will give birth to the *perfect pedal clavier,* worthy of the Organ of the Twentieth Century.

It is unnecessary to devote more space to the consideration of the parallel-keyed pedal clavier, which is destined before long to be classed among the curiosities of organ-building, and we may turn at once to the Willis clavier, which still holds the foremost position in the estimation of all organists of the advanced school in England.

The standard Willis Pedal Clavier is radiating and concave, having its keys radiating from a center 8 feet 6 inches distant from the front ends of the sharp keys, which follow the arc of this radius. The upper or playing edges of the natural keys are set to the arc of concavity, which has the similar radius of 8 feet 6 inches; the playing edges of the sharp keys following an arc struck from the same center. In the properly formed clavier, the bodies of all the keys are set radially to the center of concavity, so as to avoid undue friction.

The playing edges of the natural keys are horizontal from heel-board

---

* This illustration was prepared from a full-size drawing of the standard clavier, given by Mr. Roosevelt to the author.

to thumper-bar or toe-board, and perfectly straight along their surfaces.
Such, then, are all the important details of formation presented by the
Willis pedal clavier.

After a long study of the subject, and a careful consideration of the
many criticisms and certain valuable suggestions made by prominent
English organists, we have arrived at the conclusion, that while the
Willis clavier is at the present time the most convenient and sensible
one in use, it is both possible and desirable to modify and improve its
form and proportions to such an extent as to remove certain objections
and to recommend the radiating and concave pedal clavier for universal
adoption.

As the objection to the present radiating clavier which appears to
have the most weight, is that the distance between any two natural keys
varies to an inconvenient extent in the heel and toe direction, it seems
desirable that the radius which governs the radiation of the keys should
be of a much greater length than eight feet six inches,—the present
prevailing standard,—and that the keys should be made slightly thinner
at the heel end than where they adjoin the raised ends of the sharp keys.
It is also desirable that the keys should be made longer than is usual
at the present time, so as to render the touch more equal on the naturals.
The late Mr. W. T. Best was a strong advocate for thick and flat-faced
keys, and no performer on the Organ had a better right to speak authori-
tatively on such a subject. He required them to be one inch in thickness; and this dimension should be adopted for the keys at the toe-board
end, while they may conveniently be reduced to three-quarters of an
inch at the heel-board end. We have elsewhere said, " We do not
advocate the adoption of a shorter radius than eight feet six inches
for the arc of concavity," admitting, at the same time, that " players
with somewhat short legs might find pedal keys set to a smaller radius
more easily commanded." Further tests and a careful consideration of
all questions involved, have decided us in favor of a shorter radius for
general adoption, as we shall point out further on. It is a question,
however, just worthy of consideration, whether an arc of a circle is the
most suitable form for the concavity of the pedal clavier; and whether
a curve derived from an ellipse would not be more convenient and com-
fortable. If the latter curve were adopted, the central portion of the
clavier would be nearly flat, while its ends would rise somewhat higher
than in the case of a circular disposition. It would, perhaps, be a difficult matter to define a curve that would be in all respects desirable and
more convenient than the arc of a circle; it certainly would not be approved by the ordinary pedal clavier maker. On setting out the thirty-
two keys to several different elliptical curves, we have come to the conclusion that in any that could be adopted, the difference is so slight from
the arc of a circle as to render it unnecessary and undesirable to depart

from the accepted curvature. In this very important matter of concavity, it is proper (if a universal standard is to be established) to take
into consideration performers of both sexes who are not blessed with
long legs. From this point of view, we are satisfied that a shorter radius
than eight feet six inches is necessary. We have found it also convenient for long legs.

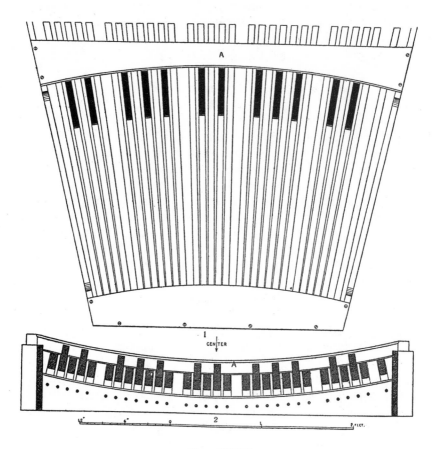

FIG. XXII.

In the accompanying illustration, Fig. XXII., are given the Top View
and Transverse Section of the Willis pedal clavier, accurately drawn to
scale, showing its radiation from a center 8 feet 6 inches from the fronts
of the sharp keys; and its concavity on the arc of a circle having a radius
of 8 feet 6 inches from the playing edges of the natural keys. Owing
to the necessary closeness of the keys at the heel-board, caused by the
short radius, their thickness rarely exceeded three-quarters of an inch.

In the Section, the keys are shown properly disposed on lines drawn from the center of concavity, and, accordingly, true to the arc.

We have sought in vain for the reason Willis had for the adoption of the radius of 8 feet 6 inches for both the radiation of the keys and the arc of their concavity. Looking at the radiation of his clavier, it would seem that he selected the shortest radius that would just escape bringing the heel ends of the keys into actual contact; and having adopted that short radius, by some form of reasoning, he considered the same radius would be suitable for the arc of concavity. In both directions, we have, from exhaustive tests, involving a study of the natural motions of the legs and feet in active pedalling, long come to the conclusion that he was wrong, in so much as his center of radiation was a great deal too close to the clavier, and that his radius of concavity was too long. In the Willis clavier of thirty notes, the arc of concavity is somewhat less inconvenient than it is in the present accepted clavier of thirty-two notes. Has the pedal clavier now reached its extreme compass? The short radius of radiation rendered it necessary for the keys to be made undesirably thin, to prevent their rubbing together, in contact, where pivoted under the heel-board. It is obvious, however, that the most objectionable feature of the Willis clavier is created by this very short radius; namely, the too great a difference which obtains between the centers of the natural keys at the different playing parts of their length. This called for a decided change of radius which had to be carefully decided. But this, as will be shown, is not the only desirable change necessary before the radiating and concave pedal clavier can be pronounced as even approaching perfection.

Judging by the numerous indifferently constructed pedal claviers that one sees, even attached to very expensive and important instruments, one is led to believe that the persons interested in the construction of Organs consider the pedal keys, because they are performed upon by the feet, unworthy of any special care or attention. Such, however, should not be the case. There is no reason why the pedal clavier should receive less careful workmanship than the manual claviers: and when one realizes the great importance of the Pedal Organ, when it is properly appointed tonally, one cannot overrate the importance of having its mechanical appointment as perfect as ingenuity and perfect workmanship can make it. The perfection of a pedal action, whatever its nature may be, should certainly commence with a properly designed and carefully constructed clavier. We think it safe to say that there would be better pedal-players among organists to-day had they given proper consideration to the character of the claviers on which they practiced, and had organ-builders thought it proper to expend some careful thought and skill on their form and construction. Perhaps much of this neglect has been due to the fact that in no treatise hitherto published on the

Organ has the subject of the pedal clavier received anything approaching proper attention.*

That the perfect pedal clavier has yet to be constructed may readily be conceded; and, in the meantime, the ideas of experienced and accomplished performers and organ experts are to be welcomed. But let it be remembered that mere difference of opinion, based on familiarity with this or that form of pedal clavier, is of little value: sound logical arguments must be advanced if proper and satisfactory results are to be attained. There can be only *one perfect pedal clavier*, which, if it is not at present in existence, has yet to be devised.

A careful examination of the numerous pedal claviers that have come under our observation during a fifty-years' study of organ construction in all the organ-building countries of the world, with the exception of Spain, which we have never visited, has satisfied us that the perfect pedal clavier has yet to be evolved. When and where is it to appear? Perhaps one should not be impatient, seeing that the evolution of the perfect manual clavier occupied centuries. Let us hope that some genius will arise and give the finishing touch to the pedal clavier, and render it worthy of the perfect Organ of the Twentieth Century when that instrument makes its appearance.

Without laying any claim to having devised a perfect pedal clavier, we submit for consideration, by the organ-playing world, the form which we have ventured to call the Audsley-Willis Pedal Clavier; the details of which are accurately shown, to scale, in the accompanying Plate XXVI. We shall fully describe this clavier, and for the sake of clearness shall do so under different heads.

RADIATION.—First, in importance, for consideration is the matter of key-radiation, which has been singularly neglected by those who should have given it serious attention. Although it was present in the Willis pedal clavier from the year 1855, it was systematically ignored by the Royal College of Organists, at its remarkable Conference in 1881; and, further, it has never, so far as our knowledge extends, been even alluded to by any of the writers on the Organ—German,

* That this statement is not without foundation is proved by the following facts: In "L'Art du Facteur d'Orgues," by Dom Bedos, sixty-eight lines only are devoted to the description of, and remarks on, the pedal clavier. In "Die Theorie und Praxis des Orgelbaues," by Töpfer-Allihn, only about one page is given to the construction of a very imperfect clavier. In "The Organ," by Hopkins and Rimbault, the subject of the pedal clavier is dismissed, so far as its construction is concerned, in a single page of forty-nine lines, illustrated by one small incorrect diagram. In "Organs and Organ-Building," by C. A. Edwards, the pedal clavier is treated at much less length, thirty-two lines only being devoted to it, accompanied by a diagram copied (reversed) from that in the preceding work. In "A Practical Treatise on Organ-Building," by F. E. Robertson, a better state of affairs obtains, for we find about a page and a half devoted to this important clavier, accompanied by a part Plan, Transverse Section, and Longitudinal Section of the Royal College of Organists pedal clavier. In "Organs and Tuning," by Thomas Elliston, the pedal clavier is dismissed in fourteen lines, unaccompanied by any illustration; and in "Organ Construction," by J. W. Hinton, M. A., Mus. Doc., neither a word of description nor a single complete illustration of a pedal clavier of any kind is given, truly a remarkable fact in connection with a work bearing so comprehensive a title. In a more recent work, entitled "Modern Organ-Building," by Walter & Thomas Lewis, Organ-builders,—a quarto of 164 pages,—the pedal clavier is dismissed in forty-seven words,

PLATE XXVI

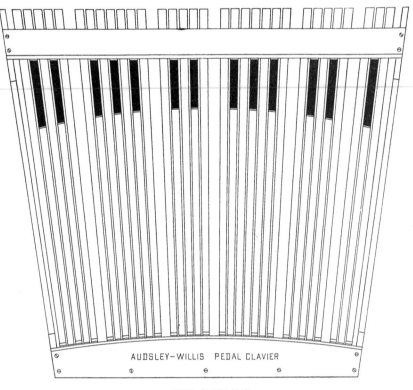

AUDSLEY—WILLIS PEDAL CLAVIER

— PLAN—SHOWN FLAT —

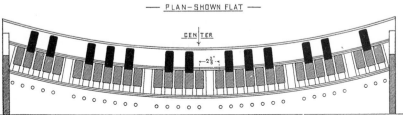

CENTER

2⅜"

— SECTION at TOE-BOARD —

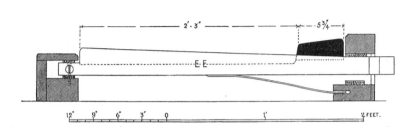

2'·3"

5¾"

E·E

12" 9" 6" 3" 0   1'   2 FEET.

French or English—beyond what we have written.* That key-radiation is essential to the proper and easy action of the legs and feet in
pedalling must be obvious to every one who has paid any attention to
the anatomy of the human frame. It is necessary that the organist,
steadily seated directly above the center of the pedal clavier, shall be
able to reach and properly depress the extreme keys—CCC and G—
without having to change his position in the slightest, or turn his body
in any unseemly fashion. Though radiation is not the only means to
this desirable end it is an all-important factor, and, accordingly, claims
careful consideration.

Viewing the Willis clavier from all practical points led us to the
apparently inevitable conclusion that at 8 ft. 6 ins. the point of radiation
was very much too near the keys, chiefly for the reason already given.
Then came the question: At what distance from the front of the DD$\sharp$
key should the center of radiation be fixed? After considerable study
and the drawing of full-sized diagrams of claviers, we decided on recommending, for general adoption, the radius of thirteen feet. That is correctly shown in the Top View or Plan in Plate XXVI., which may be
compared with the Willis clavier given in Fig. XXII. This decision
was arrived at many years ago, and to-day we can see no reason to
change it. The spaces between the natural keys, or the distances between their centers, throughout their playing surfaces are so slight as
to be hardly perceptible in pedalling—a matter of importance in a clavier
in which the natural keys assume a form different from that obtaining
in every other pedal clavier.

CONCAVITY.—Of no less importance than radiation is the matter
of concavity, indeed, in one direction it may be considered of more
importance. In determining the arc of concavity, the action of the
legs, as they swing laterally from the knee-joints, has to be carefully
considered, with the avoidance, as much as possible, of extreme movements of the thighs, which are not only undesirable in themselves, but
have the almost unavoidable effect of disturbing the rigid set of the
body, so desirable while playing.

In the Willis clavier of thirty notes, as originally devised, the long
radius of concavity may be found convenient by a player with long legs;
but for those of average length of legs, and especially for female
organists, the radius is much too long. In claviers of thirty-two notes,
the inconvenience of the Willis radius, of eight feet six inches, is considerably increased; and the desirability of bringing the extreme notes
of the pedal clavier—CCC and G—within easier reach of the player,
while centrally seated, becomes too obvious to be questioned. Our

* In " The Art of Organ-Building " twenty-eight pages are devoted to the Pedal Clavier.

studies from an anatomical point of view, combined with practical tests, have led to the conclusion that, in the thirty-two note pedal clavier, the longest radius of the arc of concavity should be seven feet. This is the arc shown in the Section given in Plate XXVI. We feel quite satisfied that for general adoption the seven feet radius will be found perfectly satisfactory: and we have no desire to have it altered in any clavier with which our name is in any way associated.

THE NATURAL KEYS.—In all the pedal claviers which have come under our observation, with the single exception of the Roosevelt standard clavier, the natural keys have been straight and practically horizontal along their playing edges. This seemingly common-sense treatment would naturally suggest itself in the absence of the due consideration of the player's requirements. Roosevelt evidently came to the conclusion that something had to be done in this direction; and, accordingly, introduced the form already alluded to and illustrated in Fig. XXI.; a form, as we have pointed out, that we consider the reverse of that which ought to be adopted.

The late George Cooper * (1820-1876)—one of the distinguished English organists of his day—in an article in the *Musical World* for April 14th, 1855, suggested that the natural keys of the pedal clavier should be formed with an *upward slope* on their playing surface, so that at the heel-board they should be an inch higher than at the line of the sharp keys. Notwithstanding this valuable suggestion by a man who knew what he was talking about, and who distinctly stated the treatment he advocated, " to wonderfully facilitate the performance of pedal passages requiring an extensive use of the heel," no notice seems to have been taken of it by organ-builders, and none is known to have been taken at the remarkable Conference of the Royal College of Organists. The only recognitions of Mr. Cooper's suggestion which have come under our notice, and unattended by any allusion to its author, are the crude and worthless woodcuts given in " The Organ," by Hopkins and Rimbault, and in " Organs and Organ-Building," by C. A. Edwards; the latter being merely a reversed copy of the former. Both are uncommented on so far as the form of the key is concerned. The advantage of this peculiar treatment of the natural keys is so obvious that we have unhesitatingly incorporated it in the Audsley-Willis clavier, as accurately shown in the Side View of the EE key, given in Plate XXVI.

---

* " Cooper did much to familiarise his hearers with the works of Bach and other great composers, which he played in a noble style. His ' Organ Arrangements,' ' Organist's Manual,' and ' Organist's Assistant,' are well known, and so is his ' Introduction to the Organ,' long the only work of its kind in England.
" When 11 years old he often took the service at St. Paul's for his father, and at the Festivals of the Sons of the Clergy it was Attwood's delight (then chief organist) to make him extemporise. . . . At Attwood's death [in 1838] he became assistant organist of St. Paul's. . . . On the death of Sir George Smart [1867] he was appointed organist of the Chapel Royal."—Grove's " Dictionary of Music and Musicians."

The keys of the clavier now under consideration, measured at the toe-board or thumper-bar, have a finished thickness of one inch, and as they follow the radiation, they measure full three-quarters of an inch at their hinged ends under the heel-board. In the Willis clavier, the keys were frequently made only about three-quarters of an inch thick and rounded along their playing surfaces. This practice was condemned by Mr. Best, who insisted on the desirability of having them one inch in thickness, and no one knew better than he did what was conducive to clean and smooth pedalling. He also, very wisely, insisted on their playing surfaces being flat, their sharp angles only being removed to prevent chipping. This treatment, in the Audsley-Willis clavier, is indicated in the Section. The distance from center to center of the keys is 2⅜ inches.

The keys are set radially to the center of the arc of concavity, and, accordingly, their playing surfaces are true to the arc, as shown in the Section. This disposition gives the greatest ease to the feet, through direct motion with equal and slight friction. The fall of the natural keys, six inches from the front of the sharps, is three-quarters of an inch. The manner of pivoting or hinging the keys, and giving them the most agreeable touch, is indicated in the drawing of the EE key. The spring is shown below the key. This method is not liked by many modern organ-builders, as it entails too much careful work and adjustment; so pivoting is abandoned, and a simple and cheap tail-spring is used—anything to save time and money is the order of the day. The minimum length of the natural key from the front of the DD♯ key to the heel-board is 2 feet 3 inches: this length gives a fairly equal touch to all the keys along their playing portions. The keys should be made of good beech or some equally close-grained hardwood that will not splinter. Facing them with holly or some suitable white wood is not at all necessary.

THE SHARP KEYS.—The sharp keys in the pedal claviers made by inartistic and money-saving organ-builders of to-day are radically bad in form and size, and are practically no better than the toe-pedals of the early part of the eighteenth century, as shown in Fig. XIX. Such round-nosed apologies for keys should be condemned by every organist who aspires to become a perfect pedalist.

No sharp key should be less than 5¾ inches in length; and in the pedal clavier illustrated in Plate XXVI. that minimum length falls on the DD♯ key. As the toe-board is in this case straight, all the other keys, which have their fronts set to an arc of a circle, are elongated, the extreme keys CCC♯ and F♯ being about 8 inches. In important electro-pneumatic Organs, toe-pistons or touches are commonly placed on the toe-board, and this practice favors the adoption of a segmental toe-board or thumper-bar, following the arc of the key-fronts, in the manner shown in Fig. XXIII. This treatment calls for a correspondingly curved front-board in the console, also advantageous for the lever movements placed therein. The playing surface of the keys should have a decided slope upwards, so that the feet may fall upon them as they do on the natural keys. This form is adopted in the Audsley-Willis

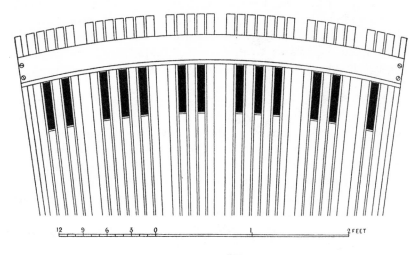

FIG. XXIII.

clavier, as shown in the Side View of the DD♯ key in the Plate. The common short, bull-nosed variety of key should be condemned by every organist who aspires to become an accomplished pedalist. The radius of the arc to which the fronts of the sharps are set is 7 feet 6 inches. The radius recommended by the Royal College of Organists' Resolutions is 8 feet 6 inches: this we are of opinion is too long, and have adopted the shorter one, as it brings the extreme sharps within easier reach of the generality of players, male and female.

During a discussion, respecting desirable improvements in the Willis radiating and concave clavier, which appeared, some years ago, in the columns of "The Organist and Choirmaster," certain suggestions were made by experienced organists. Although no action seems to have followed these suggestions, they, at least, deserve recognition here, in our desire to see the pedal clavier in every way perfect and worthy of the organists and Organ of the Twentieth Century.

The first suggestion of importance is that made by "Tuba," who advocates the lengthening of the sharp keys. He says: "It seems to me an anomaly, that while we are able to use both toe and heel on the white keys, we can only, at present, use our toes on the sharp keys. Therefore I would suggest lengthening the latter to nine or ten inches instead of six and a half as in the present Willis board. This would enable one to play such passages as the following quite smoothly and rapidly :—

and in fact make the sharp keys quite as easy as the white in every combination, because one could play either group of these sharp notes with the heel and toe of one foot. It would not do to lengthen the keys in the direction of the player, as that would preclude him from using his heels on the white keys, and would destroy his balance; but the sloping (Willis) pedal might be carried over the frame right up to the front board of the instrument. It would possibly entail an increase in the angle of slope of key, but I believe Mr. Willis himself thinks that this might be done to his present board, with advantage, to the extent of an inch."

While we have not had a clavier made, so as to arrive at a definite conclusion on the question, we have considered it of sufficient importance to bring it before our readers and to give, in Fig. XXIV., an illustration showing the sharp keys 9½ inches in length. Such an addition would necessitate throwing the front board of the console 3½ inches further from the performer. The sharp keys would require to have an upward slope to suit the natural position of the feet. Some progressive organ-builder should put this suggestion to an absolute test.

A writer who signs himself " W. E. B." suggests making the concavity of the pedal clavier " an arc of a lesser circle than at present, *i. e.,* to give a greater rise at each end, say another inch." The same writer adds: " As a means of overcoming the difficulty of playing three short pedal keys in succession, may I suggest the A♭ be brought forward ¼ or ⅜ of an inch more than G♭ or B♭? In general playing, the slight projection would be no obstruction, but in playing large intervals the organist's foot, which acquires an unusual sensibility, would ' find ' it directly."

In connection with this latter subject, Dr. Charles Vincent makes a suggestion which deserves the consideration of organists and organ-builders. He says: " All organists have doubtless experienced the difficulty of executing smoothly on the pedals the three notes F sharp, G sharp, and A sharp (or their harmonic equivalents) when following one another in ascending or descending passages. The G sharp, or A flat, is always a difficult pedal to put down in whatever passage it occurs, and only the most experienced performers are able to play this note with certainty, when the music is in a quick *tempo*. By a simple contrivance I find these difficulties can be entirely overcome, and G sharp instead of being the most difficult pedal to play becomes the easiest.

"The contrivance consists of a slight addition to the pedal board which can be made by any one in a very short time. Cut out two pieces of wood about 4½ inches long, 2 inches wide, and ¾ of an inch thick; screw these to the two G sharp pedals, at the end beneath the stool; these pedals will then have raised portions at both ends; the piece of wood to be fixed need not be as large as the ordinary raised portion

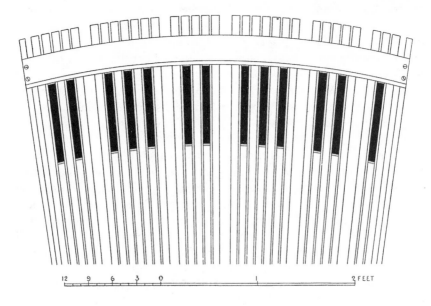

FIG. XXIV.

of a sharp or flat key. By adopting this device the difficult passages quoted at the beginning can be executed smoothly by alternate feet with the greatest ease, and all skips to the A flats or G sharps can be made with certainty. "I venture," concludes Dr. Vincent, "to make this suggestion for the consideration of organists who have found that F sharp or B flat *will* sometimes sound, when the player only intended the foot to strike G sharp or A flat."

There is no reason why this expedient, suggested by so accomplished an organist and musician as Dr. Vincent, should not be properly tested, and, if found advantageous, generally adopted. It would only require each of the G♯ keys to have a playing formation at its heel end similar to that at present on its front or toe end. Such an addition to be

carried as far forward as practicable without interfering with the passing of the feet, one under the other, on the natural keys in ordinary
pedalling.   In such a position, the added portions, which may be called
the rear keys or heel keys, could be readily operated by the feet drawn
back.

The materials used for the sharp keys, largely for the sake of distinction, in the better class of pedal claviers are ebony, rosewood, and
lignum vitæ. All of these are suitable, but ebony is preferable. In cheap
work stained wood is used.

Though much has been written and said respecting the relative positions of the manual and pedal claviers, it is only necessary to record
here the Resolutions on the subject, passed in 1917, by the Combined
Console Standardization Committee of the American Guild of Organists,
and the National Association of Organists.

"1. Resolved, that the distance of the manual claviers from the pedal clavier
shall be as follows: Take a line one-half way between the tops of the natural keys
of the lowest and highest manual claviers, and this line shall always be 32 inches
above the middle natural key of the pedal clavier. On a two manual and four
manual console, the medial line shall be half-way between the Great and Swell
claviers. On a three manual console, the medial line shall coincide with the top of
the central or Great Organ clavier.
"2. Resolved, that the front of the central sharp key of the pedal clavier shall
be 8½ inches back from a plumb-line dropped from the front of the natural key
to the lowest manual clavier."

While this latter Resolution may be accepted for general practice, it
may be remarked that the distance of which it treats has been the subject
of considerable diversity of opinion among English organ-builders and
organists; but it is quite unnecessary to give particulars of this diversity
here.

There is only one other question connected with the pedal clavier that
claims attention; namely, that which created a keen discussion among
English organists on the publication of the Royal College of Organists'
Resolutions. The seventh Resolution says:

"That a plumb-line dropped from the middle c^1 of the manuals fall on the
center CC of the pedal board."

Limited space renders it as impossible as it is unnecessary to go into
details of this discussion; and, especially as there is only one logical
and practical conclusion to come to on the question, we may be content
to give it a sufficient answer in the words of a distinguished organist.
Mr. Charles F. South, Organist of Salisbury Cathedral, remarked: "I
am sure there are many organists who thought that the 'R. C. O.' came
to a most unwise decision when they settled—so far as they could—that

the middle CC of the pedals should be under the middle c^1 of the
manuals. It has been amusing to me to read that such and such an
Organ has been built according to the 'R. C. O. suggestions.' What
an enormous amount of harm has been done! The unfortunate players
of these instruments have to struggle to get the upper note on the pedal
board in a way that is quite unnecessary. Surely a player ought to
sit over the center of the pedals so that the extreme notes will be
equidistant."

The correct relative positions of the manual and pedal claviers are
those which place them truly central to each other.

ORGAN IN A GALLO-ROMAINE SCULPTURE OF
THE FOURTH CENTURY.

CHAPTER VIII.

THE SWELL.

VER since the time we seriously turned our attention to matters connected with the art of organ construction and tonal appointment, we have held the firm conviction that the importance of the Swell in the Organ has been much underrated and to a considerable extent misunderstood with special regard to its dual office by those who should be deeply interested in the artistic and scientific development of the " King of Instruments." More than forty years ago we worked out the problem of the swell in connection with the different tonal divisions of the Organ to our own satisfaction; and up to the present time we have found no reason to depart from the conclusions then arrived at, although they involved a radical departure from the established practice in organ-building. At the time alluded to, one swell was considered ample for the largest Organ, even of the concert-room type, as in the Organ, of one hundred speaking stops, in St. George's Hall, Liverpool. Our studies led us to the conviction that not one only, but every tonal division—manual and pedal—called for powers of flexibility and expression to the fullest possible extent afforded by swell-boxes or satisfactory equivalents.*

Before entering on artistic and practical matters it will not be out

---

* " The chief advocate for the extended introduction of the swell-box in this country is Mr. G. A. Audsley, who has not only urged it on logical grounds in his treatise on ' Concert, Church, and Chamber Organs,' published in the columns of the *English Mechanic* (1886-8), and his recent lectures on the ' Swell in the Organ,' but has practically proved the great advantages to be secured by the multiplication of expressive departments in the Organ. About twenty-five years ago he schemed and constructed his own Chamber Organ, which was when finished, and still remains, for its size, the most flexible and expressive pipe organ existing. This can easily be understood when it is known that out of its nineteen speaking stops fifteen are rendered expressive by being inclosed in swell-boxes. The two expressive divisions of the Great Organ, on the lower clavier, are inclosed in two independent swell-boxes; the only stop here uninclosed being the PRINCIPALE GRANDE (*Open Diapason,* 8 ft.). The upper or Choir manual being entirely expressive. The range of expressive effects and *nuances* secured by these means is remarkable, while the tone qualities of the stops remain unaffected, and their balance is under perfect control. Mr. Audsley now advocates inclosing a portion of the Pedal Organ to make the bass also expressive."—Third Cantor Lecture on " Musical Instruments: their Construction and Capabilities," delivered before the Society of Arts, London, February 9, 1891, by A. J. Hipkins, F. S. A.

of place to briefly touch upon the history of the Swell, which opens in England. It is not quite settled at what date the small division of the Organ known as the Echo was first introduced by English builders, but it seems certain that it was first used by them. In the description by Mace, in his " Musicks Monument," published in 1676, of his own Chamber Organ, we find the following particulars: " It is in Bulk and Height of a very Convenient, Handsom, and Compleat Table Seize; (which may Become and Adorn a Noble-Mans Dining Room) all of the Best sort of Wainscot. The Length of the leaf 7 foot and 5 inches; the breadth 4 foot and 3 inches; the Height 3 Foot, Inch, and Better. . . . The Leaf has in it 8 Desks, cut quite through very neatly, with Springs under the Edge of the Leaf, so contriv'd that they may Open and Shut at pleasure; which (when shut down) Joyn closely with the Table-Leaf; But (upon occasion) may be Opened and so set up (with a spring) in the manner of a Desk, as your Books may be set against Them. Now the Intent of Those Desks, is of far more Excellent use than for mere Desks; For without those Openings your Organ would be but of very slender use, as to Consort, by Reason of the Closeness of the Leaf; but by the help of them, each Desk opened, is as the putting in of another quickning or enliv'ning stop; so that, when all the 8 Desks stand open, the Table is like a Little Church Organ, so sprightfully lusty, and strong, that it is too loud for any ordinary private use; but you may moderate that, by opening only so many of those Desks as you may see fit for your present use. There are in this Table Six Stops, the first is an Open Diapason; the second, a Principal; the third, a Fifteenth; the fourth, a Twelfth; the fifth, a Two-and-Twentieth; and the sixth, a Regal. There is likewise (for a pleasure and light content) a Hooboy Stop, which comes in at any time with the foot; which stop (together with the Regal) makes the Voice Humane."

Now, although this highly interesting description appears in Dr. Rimbault's " History of the Organ," and accordingly has been under the notice of the organ-loving world for nearly half a century, we do not remember ever having seen it commented upon. Let us see if it is not worthy of a little study. Only extracts have been given from Master Mace's full description of this " Table Organ," which the writer claims as his own contrivance. He adds: " Two of such organs only are but as yet in Being in the World; They being of my own contrivance; and which I caus'd to be made in my own House, and for my own Use, as to the maintaining of Public Consorts, &c." In giving this description the consideration it deserves, one cannot avoid recognizing that Mace's instrument was the true starting point of the Swell Organ; and, with such an instrument before their eyes, it is a surprising thing that the organ-builders of the time did not catch the idea of the swell. We are told by Mace that the " Leaf," or top of his " Table Organ," had eight desks, which were so fitted as to be almost invisible when closed down, but which could be raised up and fixed open with springs, leaving openings in the leaf through which the sound from the pipe-work, inclosed in the body of the instrument, found egress. He tells us that these desks were " of far more Excellent use than for mere Desks; For without those Openings, your Organ would be but of very slender use, as to Consort, by Reason of the Closeness of the Leaf." In closing all the " desks," it stands to reason that the entire instrument became so subdued as to be an Echo Organ. " By the help of them," as Mace quaintly remarks, " each Desk opened, is as the putting in of another quickning or enliv'ning stop; so that, when all the 8 Desks stand open, the Table is like a Little Church Organ, so sprightfully lusty, and strong, that it is too loud for any ordinary private use; but you may moderate that," says this pioneer in artistic organ-building, " by opening only so many of those Desks as you see fit for your present use."

Master Mace, as he wrote those words, or surveyed, with feelings of pride, his curious and noteworthy " Table Organ," was standing on the threshold of a great discovery or invention. Had he abandoned the practice of opening and shutting those eight " Desks " by hand, and simply connected them by a system of levers to a single pedal, or foot-lever, he would have invented the true swell, and, at one step, have imparted powers of flexibility and expression to the Organ. Such an oversight—to call it by no harder name—seems to us, in this inventive age, almost impossible, and certainly unpardonable. There was the swell forcing itself on his observation every time he opened or closed one, two, three, or more of the desks to apportion the sound of the instrument to the requirements of the " Consort." It is self-evident that the organ-builders of the year of grace 1676 were just as slow of comprehension, and as adverse to radical departures from established custom, as are the organ-builders of to-day. But however this may be, it took nearly a century to carry the idea that lay hidden, in broad daylight, in Mace's movable desks and table top into anything like practical form. It seems quite probable that at the date Mace constructed his notable Chamber Organs, the closed division of the Church Organ, called the Echo, had been introduced; but, at the same time, it is quite evident that no such division existed in the Organ built by Robert Dallam, of London, in the year 1634, for the Cathedral of York. This land-mark in the history of English organ-building had only two divisions; namely, a Great Organ and a " Chair," or Choir Organ. The Echo was probably not known at so early a date. We need not dwell on the subject of the Echo Organ, as, beyond its being the precursor of the Swell Organ, it has little interest here. We shall accordingly pass on to the year 1712. Among the advertisements in the *Spectator*, issued on February 8, 1712, the following interesting announcement occurs:

" Whereas Mr. Abraham Jordan, senior and junior, have, with their own hands, joynery excepted, made and erected a very large Organ in St. Magnus' Church, at the foot of London Bridge, consisting of four sets of keys, one of which is adapted to the art of emitting sounds by swelling the notes, *which never was in any Organ before;* this instrument will be publicly opened on Sunday next, the performance by Mr. John Robinson. The above-said Abraham Jordan gives notice to all masters and performers, that he will attend every day next week at the said church, to accommodate all those gentlemen who shall have a curiosity to hear it."

This announcement fixes two facts practically beyond question; namely, that the invention of the Swell is due to Englishmen, and that its first introduction in an Organ took place, in London, in the year 1712. The invention, as introduced by the Jordans, consisted of a front to the old Echo-box, fitted with a sliding shutter, which was raised and lowered, at the will of the player, by means of a foot-lever. On depressing the lever the shutter was raised, the box opened, and the sound from the inclosed pipe-work permitted to issue forth more or less freely. On relieving the pressure on the lever the shutter fell and gradually closed the box. As Dr. Hopkins correctly remarks: " The *' nag's-head swell,'* as the above early kind of swell was called, was not well designed, nor happily adapted to its purpose in a mechanical point of view. The weight or resistance to be overcome by the pressure of the foot was so great that the shutter could be set in motion only with difficulty, and when it was in motion there was equal difficulty in regulating the rate or extent of its ascent; for it would then not unfrequently run up almost of itself. Its descent was similarly beyond control, and it would often fall with an audible noise. The nag's-head swell continued in use for upwards of half a century, till it was superseded by what has since been denominated the ' Venetian swell.' "

Passing on to the year 1738, we find not only that the swell has become (even in its primitive form) firmly established in England, but that it is described in glowing terms. In the Articles of Agreement entered into by John Harris, organ-builder, of London, for the construction of an Organ for the Parish Church of Doncaster, the following passage occurs relative to the Swell Organ:

" The Eccho Organ to contain the following Stops, which shall Eccho and Swell to express passion in degrees of Loudness and Softness, as if inspired by human breath (viz.) One open Diapason with twenty-seven Speaking pipes. One stop'd Diapason with twenty-seven pipes. One Principall with twenty-seven pipes. One Cornet of three Rows with eighty-one pipes. One Trumpet and one Hautboy with twenty-seven pipes to each. . . . The keys of the Ecchos and Swelling from C sol fa ut Cliff, to D la sol, in all being twenty-seven keys."

At this time the so-called "nag's-head swell" continued in use, and had only a very limited compass; namely from middle c^1 to d^3, or thereabout. In the year 1769, Burkat Shudi, a maker of Harpsichords, took out a patent for "A piece of mechanism or machinery by which the Harpsichord is very much improved." In his Specification he thus describes his invention: "A cover extending the breadth of the Harpsichord, and from the front board of the Harpsichord to the ruler, of an indefinite number of valves, which, with their frame, extend the breadth of the Harpsichord, and the length thereof from the ruler to the small end, which valves are opened and shut by a number of small levers equal to the number of valves inserted or fixed in an axis spindle or bar turned by a pedal." It is to be understood by this description that the instrument, instead of having a single solid top or cover, as we see in Handel's Harpsichord, preserved in South Kensington Museum, and in all the German Harpsichords, was furnished with an inner cover, formed of narrow pieces of wood suspended by centre-pins in a frame of the size and shape of the stringed portion, and made so as to open and shut all together by means of a series of small levers controlled by a foot-lever or pedal. When closed the cover presented a level surface, and the sound from the strings was very subdued; and, of course, when the pedal was depressed by the foot of the performer, and the narrow pieces of wood (about 3 inches wide), or the shutters, turned, more or less, on their centres so as to leave openings between their edges, the sound swelled forth. It will be observed that Shudi's invention was really shadowed forth in Mace's Chamber Organ, with its table-top and eight lifting desks or shutters. Only, as has been explained, these desks had to be raised or opened singly by hand, and were not under the direct control of the performer at the keys. These facts show how slowly ideas develop; for it was about thirty-six years after Mace's invention for controlling the sound of his Organs, that Jordan invented the nag's-head swell; and it took another long period of fifty-seven years before any appliance was introduced which pointed the way to the improvement of the organ swell-box. Shudi's invention was the precursor of the mechanical and effect-producing portion of the Swell Organ as we now have it.

The honor of having applied Shudi's system of moving shutters to the organ swell-box is accredited to Samuel Green, of London: and the swell as constructed by him was termed the "Venetian swell," probably on account of its resemblance to a Venetian blind or shutter. All who believe in the great importance of the swell in the Organ should hold Green's name in high respect; for, apart from his ingenious adaptation, he developed the entire department considerably beyond the limits adhered to by his predecessors. Indeed, he may justly be called the Father of the Swell Organ in its approved treatment. In the instrument he built for the Chapel of Greenwich Hospital, he carried the Swell Organ down to FF, only five notes short of its present full compass downward. This instrument was built in 1789.

From this time the swell came into common use in England, and no Organ of any importance appears to have been constructed without one, while many old Organs had swells added to them. In Germany and other Continental countries the swell met with no immediate approval. Dr. Burney, in his famous work entitled " Continental Tours," written fifty years after the Swell Organ had become common in England, expresses his great surprise to find the swell utterly unknown upon the Continent. It was only toward the end of the third quarter of the last century that the conservative organ-builders and organists of Germany became awake to the value of the swell in the Organ. Probably, nursing their pride in what they had accomplished in organ construction, they were reluctant to acknowledge the invention of an Englishman— an invention which, in their idea of the natural order of things, they should have had the honor of making.

The very limited space at our disposal prevents any further remarks of a historical nature; but what has been done in the development of the swell both in Europe and this country, from about the middle of the last century, is sufficiently well known in organ-loving quarters to render any addition to what has been said unnecessary.*

While there has arisen no objection to the general adoption of the Swell Organ, there has been and probably still is in some quarters a belief that the swell-box seriously impairs the sounds of the inclosed pipe-work; and this conviction, real or assumed, has been freely used as an argument against the extended introduction of the swell in the Organ. We are free to admit that such a belief has had in too many cases a good foundation; but a foundation that is anything but creditable to organ-builders on the one hand, and to the discernment and reasoning powers of those outside the organ-building trade on the other. Whilst the former, in these days of cheap and competitive organ-building, very rarely care, or can afford, to show the spirit of artists or pioneers in the direction of radical improvements, which involve a substantial outlay and the display of considerable skill; the latter seem to overlook the fact that there are good as well as bad swell-boxes; and freely base their arguments on the imperfect and insufficient specimens of the swell-box which organ-builders think proper to produce. We have often wondered if it ever occurred to interested purchasers of Organs that a properly designed, correctly proportioned, and substantially constructed swell-box costs considerably more, and is infinitely more satisfactory in every way, than one of the cramped and unscientifically-constructed

* Remarks of some interest respecting the introduction of the swell in representative English, French, and American Organs are given in " The Art of Organ-Building," vol. ii, pp. 40-45.

things which are too often introduced in Organs built on the competitive and commission-paying system, only too often followed at the present time, to the detriment of honest and artistic organ construction.

Perhaps it is unreasonable to condemn those who, although admirable performers on the imperfect instruments served out to them, have a very superficial knowledge of the true principles of construction and of the internal economy of the Organ generally; and especially as some persons who claim to be practical authorities on organ-building hold that *small* swell-boxes—just sufficient to contain the closely packed pipe-work and no more, with sloping roofs to do away with all *unoccupied space* inside, not to speak of the desirable *economy of wood*—are the most satisfactory. It is difficult to imagine upon what these worthies base such a belief, except it be on dollars and cents, for it is entirely unsupported by scientific teaching and common-sense.

There is, of course, no question that stops inclosed in swell-boxes undergo a certain modification in their tones; but it is also a fact (and here we speak of what we know) that when the swell-boxes are properly proportioned and constructed, and the stops correctly spaced, and skilfully voiced for their position, the slight modification is an improvement rather than the reverse, giving a further refinement of their tones. Of course, to organists who love noise in organ music in preference to every other quality; and who are never truly happy save when they have every available stop of their instruments drawn, every coupler on, and the swells fixed open to their full extent, such refinement is simply so much power lost, so much possibility for noisy and ear-splitting effects done away with. Such robust players hold up their hands as if to ward off some dire calamity when the inclosing of the TUBAS and other powerfully voiced reed stops is advocated. "What!" say they, "spoil our most effective stops by putting them in a swell-box? The powers forbid! Where would our grand climaxes, our immense effects, and our overwhelming crashes be?"

Well, we have no delight in such robust playing, to use a mild expression; and we do not believe that it is musicianly or artistic. Accordingly, we are resolved to advocate and support any legitimate means of discouraging such outrage on the musical ear—that is, if it can be discouraged. It must be said, however, that even the fullest possible introduction of swells in the Organ can only counteract such ear-splitting effects to an extremely limited degree, so long as the taste for stops voiced on excessive pressures of wind are favored by organ-builders and organists—we use the term organists, for we can hardly think the true and refined *musician* can favor such things, especially in their usual uncontrollable condition. Surely anything and everything conducive to refinement and flexibility of tone in our monster modern Organs should be hailed with delight by both players and listeners.

In approaching the practical aspect of matters connected with the formation of swell-boxes, it is desirable that, as musicians, we should arrive at some sort of logical conclusion on two points. First, what the tone of the inclosed stops should be when the swell-box is fully opened; and, Secondly, what the tone should be, relatively, when the box is completely closed. Or, in fewer words, what degree of *diminuendo* is necessary or desirable in any expressive division of the Organ. To settle this question from a purely musical standpoint, it would be well to put the influence of any Organs we are familiar with out of our minds, and seek elsewhere for inspiration and guidance.

In considering this important question respecting the desirable degree of reduction in tone, or *diminuendo,* in an organ swell, we must suppose the full contents of the swell drawn; for the reduction of tonal power by the manipulation of the stops is altogether another matter, and need not enter the question at all.

In this matter we shall be best helped by turning our attention to the Orchestra. Let us imagine a selection of the different orchestral instruments made, say ten or fifteen, of different tones and pitches, and sounded together in unison or harmony at what may be considered their *fortissimo,* or at the fullest strength possible without impairing their pure normal qualities of tone; and let us accept the full volume of sound so produced as representing the tonal effect of all the stops forming an expressive division, with the swell-box open to its full extent. Now, let us request the instrumentalists to perform a gradual *diminuendo* until they reach the *pianissimo,* or the softest tone consistent with the pure musical character of their respective instruments; and let us carefully record the result in our musical consciousness. When this *pianissimo* is reached we shall hear a comparatively soft effect in relation to the preceding loud one; but we shall still hear a full, rich, and perfect volume of pure tone, without any indication of that smothered, " bee-in-a-bottle," mile-away, emasculated kind of tone, which is generally accepted as the acme of the organ-builder's skill in swell-box construction. We have listened to closed swells which entirely destroyed the true and characteristic tones of the inclosed pipe-work; and we unhesitatingly condemn such swells as gross libels on scientific and artistic organ-building—the work of bunglers, and the natural mistakes of men who have blindly followed precedent, or who have, from first to last, misconceived the true use and value of the swell in the Organ.

There is another abomination lately conceived by organ-builders, for which we have invented the only too appropriate name *Annihilating Swell.* This masterpiece of the modern organ-builders' skill, when in its highest development, and with its shutters closed, absolutely annihilates the sound of the inclosed pipe-work. We know an Organ of the concert-room class in which this achievement is remarkable in its success: and we have heard of an organist who wisely refused to give a recital on an Organ, until means were taken to prevent the swell shutters closing completely. This requirement on the part of the artist organist we can easily understand.

The swell, when properly constructed, is a legitimate means, within reasonable limits, for securing two most desirable objects; namely, *flexibility* and *musical expression.* To exceed those reasonable limits, is to be guilty of a serious mistake, and to call forth a deserved condemnation from every true musician. We speak strongly because we feel strongly in this matter: and no one who loves the Organ as we do, and who knows what it is capable of becoming under thoughtful and artistic treatment, can help regretting and lamenting whilst he sees hundreds of thousands of dollars thoughtlessly expended every year on Organs without a single serious attempt being made to render them more *truly musical, flexible,* and *expressive.*

It will be realized from what has been said that we advocate so constructing the swell-box, of any division of the Organ, that when it is closed it shall not destroy, or even impair the tonal character of the inclosed pipe-work. The listener should at all times hear distinctly the true tones of the stops that are speaking. Further than this, we hold that the effect of the closed swell should not be a *distant* one, any more than the *pianissimo* of the Orchestra should produce that effect; but that it should be merely a *soft* and *pure* one—one that can be prolonged through an entire movement, if necessary, without producing an unsatisfactory impression in the player's or the listener's mind.

We know it is the common impression among organ-builders and organists, that unless the closed swell has a very *distant,* or what we should call a *bottled-up* effect, no satisfactory *crescendo* can be obtained; but we have practically tested this matter; and are satisfied that a full and perfect *crescendo* and *diminuendo* can be secured from a swell constructed on the lines we advocate. Apart from its proper construction, two conditions are essential to its success; namely, ample internal dimensions, and a proper position for the free egress of sound. We have, from actual test, proved that from a swell, constructed according to our specification, and fulfilling all the requisite tonal conditions, a perfect *crescendo* could be obtained of ninety seconds duration, and that without altering a stop. Using two swells, the *crescendo* was prolonged to three minutes.

Considerable objection has been raised against the extended introduction of the swell through the unskilful and unmusicianly way too many organists have used and still use it. What is commonly called "pumping the swell-pedal," or what, in more polite language, may be termed the restless, sentimental method of using the swell, is most objectionable from every point of view, and young players are specially fond of it. It rarely occurs to them that the swell has another office than that of producing an everlasting *crescendo* and *diminuendo*. We are of opinion that the form of swell-pedal, or expression lever, as we prefer to call it, commonly introduced in English Organs, has greatly tended to foster the restless or sentimental style of swelling above spoken of. We allude to the ordinary recovering, or so-called "hitch-down pedal," so undeservedly popular with old-fashioned English organists. We know that the Royal College of Organists has advocated this form in its conservative way; but we venture to disagree with its advocacy in this, as in certain other matters of organ-building,—doubtless, a very presumptuous thing to do.

We may state here that the old-fashioned "hitch-down pedal" cannot be used where the swell is fully developed and its proper functions are provided for. Some appliances have been introduced by English builders with the view of doing away with the inherent imperfections of the "hitch-down pedal," and for the purpose of enabling the performer to leave the pedal stationary at certain points of its downward or upward range; and such appliances clearly point to the inherent shortcomings of the said pedal, which they only partly remove. Conservative organists hesitate to approve of the self-evident advantages offered by such appliances. The correct, common-sense, and convenient form of expression lever is that known as the "French," or "balanced-pedal;" and this is the form which will alone be used in Organs constructed on the proper lines. It is already used, almost exclusively, by the leading builders of America and the Continent of Europe; and is advocated by all the distinguished organists of France and the United States.

We may now enter upon the consideration of the swell as applied to each separate division of the Organ. In doing so we shall touch upon all the offices of the swell, and point out its practical conditions and requirements at the same time. We have no intention of touching, in the present Chapter, on the tonal structure of the Organ, or of specially commenting on the somewhat complicated question of the proper disposition or apportionment of the tonal forces in the several divisions of the instrument: these important matters are fully treated in other Chapters. We shall, accordingly, speak of the application of the swell to the several divisions of the Organ without special reference to the inclosed speaking stops. So when we speak in this Chapter of the Great or First Organ, Choir or Second Organ, Swell or Third Organ, Solo or Fourth Organ, and Pedal Organ, no special reference will be made to any new or unusual stop apportionment. For the time being, the reader may look upon these divisions of the Organ as differing in no essential point, so far as their stop apportionments are concerned, from those existing in the best examples of European and American organ-building.

Whilst we do not anticipate a storm of opposition to the proposal to extend the application of the swell-box to such divisions of the Organ as the Choir and Solo, we are prepared to meet with a whirlwind of objections—unreasonable and illogical for the most part—against the proposal we have to urge to apply the swell-box to both the Great and Pedal Organs. But this whirlwind will not blow us away from the stand long study has induced us to take in so important a question; and we do not fear that we shall long remain unsupported by thinking musicians. To the ordinary organist the idea of inclosing any portion of the Great Organ in a swell-box, and thereby imparting to its tonal forces flexibility and expression, smacks of musical heresy, if it does not seem to him absolute absurdity. We shall see how far the charge of heresy or absurdity can stand under the light of sound reasoning and common-sense. At this point we make a simple statement, which may be new to the reader, but which we recommend to his serious consideration. It is this:

There is no more reason in making any division of the Organ unexpressive and invariably uniform in the strength of its tones, than there would be in destining any division of the Grand Orchestra to deliver its sounds at one unvarying strength and without any expression whatever.

To our mind this statement contains a perfectly logical proposition; and surely every thoughtful and unprejudiced musician must recognize it the instant its true bearing enters his mind. In a conversation we had some years ago with Dr. E. H. Turpin, the amiable and talented Honorary Secretary of the Royal College of Organists, immediately after an admirable lecture he had delivered on the "Instruments of the Modern Orchestra," he made the following highly suggestive and apt remark: "The Grand Orchestra may be considered as the Sun in the musical universe, whilst the Grand Organ may be looked upon as the Moon, shining with *borrowed light*." How we wish both organ-builders and organists would realize what this terse remark really means; and how much its acceptance and its logical teaching would benefit the art of organ-building.

In applying the swell to the Great Organ, it is with the view of making it flexible rather than for the purpose of imparting powers of expression to it. Only a very few stops suitable for this division call for expressive powers. We have used the terms *flexible* and *expressive* frequently in the foregoing remarks; and it is perhaps desirable that we should clearly define their meaning, and the distinction to be drawn between them so far as the Organ is concerned. When we speak of an Organ being *flexible*, we desire to convey the idea that it is capable of immediate and easy control, so far as the strength of tone of any division, or portion of any division, is concerned, at the will of the player. Under the present crude system of organ-building and tonal

apportionment, numerous stops are inserted which have a sharply defined and a very restricted use. Take all the harmonic-corroborating
stops, and it will be found, under the present stereotyped system, that
they are usable only in full effects, or when all the foundation-work is
drawn. For instance a Great Organ MIXTURE would be drawn when
or after all the stops below it in the harmonic structure are drawn. This
is what is ordered by the usual direction " Full to MIXTURES." Now,
we maintain that this method—perhaps the only one admissible under
the old-fashioned system of organ-building—is a most undesirable and
inartistic narrowing of the utility of all the compound stops. The same
remarks apply to the octave, super-octave, and mutation stops. We
should never think of applying the term *flexible* to a division of an
Organ in which there are stops whose use is rigidly defined; and which
cannot be drawn unless the full complement of stops is likewise drawn.
When a Great Organ is made flexible, the general utility of all its stops
is largely increased, and numerous charming tonal effects can be produced with perfect ease that are absolutely impossible on the same
division as usually schemed.

When we speak of the Organ as being *expressive,* we mean that each
and every one of its divisions is wholly or partly capable of *crescendo*
and *diminuendo* effects, and, under certain conditions, of good *sforzando*
effects also. Both flexibility and expression, in the sense we desire
them to be understood, can alone be procured by the proper application
of the swell in the Organ.

In applying the swell to the Great division, it is chiefly with the view,
as has already been said, of rendering it flexible. Such being the case,
we advocate the inclosure in the swell-box of only such stops as call
for special control and modification of tone. The double stop, whatever it may be, the DIAPASONS, probably all the unisons with the exception of the reeds, and the chief OCTAVE, should not be inclosed; but the
other OCTAVES, SUPER-OCTAVES, all the mutation and compound stops,
and the reed stops, should most certainly be inclosed in the swell-box.
This box should immediately adjoin the exposed stops; and be constructed with the largest possible area of shutters or louvres. When
fully open, there should be a refining effect on the tone only, without
any practical loss of strength. It need hardly be pointed out how flexible
such a Great Organ would be; for it must be seen at a glance that its
complete harmonic structure, under the control of the swell, commanded
by a balanced lever, would no longer be confined to full effects, but could
be used in combination with the softest exposed unison stop in the
division; or with any combination of stops in its own or any other
division of the instrument.

In addition to the pleasing and effective tonal results obtained by
means of the swell, striking and singularly rich effects can be produced

by either a gradual or instantaneous entry of the full chorus into the full volume of unison and double tone yielded by the foundation-work. This is done by simply opening the shutters of the swell-box. Of course, the chorus has been heard all the time, but only as a mysterious background of refined harmonic tones so long as the swell-box remained closed.

In the ordinary expressive direction, the use of the swell in the Great division may be said to be very limited; indeed it may be accepted as practically confined to such stops as the reeds, when they are used for melodic or solo passages, or when they are employed to reinforce the DIAPASONS or non-expressive foundation-work. In the latter case, the effect is that of a *crescendo* on the TRUMPET, or whatever the chief reed may be, within a rich and steady volume of pure organ-tone. Such effects as we have shadowed forth are not to be heard in any Great Organ, or, in fact, in any single, uncoupled division in any of the Church or Concert Organs in Europe at the present time. We may conclude our brief remarks on the Great Organ, by giving the tonal appointment of the division, as schemed by us for the Grand Concert Organ exhibited at the Louisiana Purchase Exposition, St. Louis, Missouri, 1904.

GREAT ORGAN.

Compass CC to c⁴—61 notes.

FIRST SUBDIVISION—UNEXPRESSIVE.

SUB-PRINCIPAL	Metal	32	FEET.	OPEN DIAPASON, Minor	Metal 8	FEET.
DOUBLE OPEN DIAPASON	"	16	"	OPEN DIAPASON	Wood 8	"
CONTRA-GAMBA	"	16	"	GRAND FLUTE	" 8	"
SUB-QUINT	Wood	10⅔	"	DOPPELFLÖTE	" 8	"
GRAND PRINCIPAL	Metal	8	"	GAMBA	Metal 8	"
OPEN DIAPASON, Major	"	8	"	OCTAVE, Major	" 4	"
				GAMBETTE	" 4	"

SECOND SUBDIVISION—EXPRESSIVE.

Inclosed in Swell-box No. 1.

GROBGEDECKT	Wood 8	FEET.	GRAND	SEVENTEENTH	Metal	1⅗	FEET.
HARMONIC FLUTE	Metal 8	"	CORNET	NINETEENTH	"	1⅓	"
QUINT	" 5⅓	"	IV.	SEPTIÈME	"	1⅐	"
OCTAVE, Minor	" 4	"	RANKS.	TWENTY-SECOND	"	1	"
HARMONIC FLUTE	" 4	"	GRAND MIXTURE			VII.	RANKS.
TIERCE	" 3⅕	"	DOUBLE TRUMPET	Metal	16		FEET.
OCTAVE QUINT	" 2⅔	"	HARMONIC CLARION	Metal	8		"
SUPER-OCTAVE	" 2	"	HARMONIC TRUMPET	Metal	4		"

The Expressive Subdivision is brought on and thrown off the Great Organ clavier by thumb pistons: and it is also commanded by the Double Touch of the clavier, at the will of the performer.

Many pages could be filled with a mere outline of the numerous beautiful tonal effects and colorings that this one Great Organ is capable of producing under the hands of a skilful organist—effects and colorings absolutely impossible on any undivided and uninclosed Great Organ, however large, hitherto constructed. We ask the reader, if he is an accomplished organist, to carefully analyze the Great Organ appointment given above, and work out for his own satisfaction some of the practically innumerable tonal combinations it presents, bearing in mind that, without any resort to expression, all the voices inclosed in the swell-box are capable of being fixed, according to his wish, at any degree of strength of tone, within the limits of their full power and the *pianissimo* created by the closed swell, as previously described. Let him realize that he is no longer tied in the use of the harmonic-corroborating stops in full organ effects; but, on the contrary, he can use the sixteen harmonic-corroborating ranks, inclosed in the swell-box, with any one of the unison stops in the uninclosed subdivision. This fact opens up infinite tonal possibilities.

We now come to the consideration of the application of the swell to the second manual division of the Organ, commonly and not very appropriately called the Choir Organ. This division, which appears alike in Church and Concert-room Organs, is in no direct way related to either an architectural or a vocal choir. We keep here to the old-fashioned terminology, so as not to run the risk of confusing the reader: but we do not approve of the term Choir Organ any more than of the term Swell Organ when used in connection with an instrument in which every division is wholly or partly inclosed and rendered expressive. Our views in this matter are shown in the Chapters on the Church and Concert-room Organs.

Whatever the tonal appointment of the so-called Choir Organ may be, and whether it is schemed as an accompanimental, or simply as a tonally contrasting, division of the entire instrument, there can be no objection, on musical or artistic grounds, advanced against its being endowed with flexibility and powers of expression. The first question is: Should *all* its tonal forces be inclosed in a swell-box, or should they be divided, as in the case of the Great Organ, and only one subdivision inclosed? We are strongly in favor of the entire division being rendered expressive. The late Messrs. Roosevelt followed this practice, placing all the Choir stops in the same swell-box with the expressive subdivision of the Great Organ. This was done on the score of economy of both space and material; and beyond that little can be advanced in its favor. If single expression is desired, then the Choir should have a special swell-box. It will be seen from the Chapters on the Church Organ, the Concert-room Organ, and the Organ Specification, that we strongly favor giving this second manual division compound powers of flexibility and expression, by subdividing its tonal forces and inclosing them in separate swell-boxes. It is impossible, on artistic grounds, to over-estimate the musical results obtainable by compound flexibility and expression under the command of a single and uncoupled clavier.

So far as the application of the swell-box is concerned, it is unnecessary to make a special plea for the division commonly known as the Swell Organ: but whatever its tonal appointment may be, and so long as it is undivided, it is, of course, essential that its swell-box be independent of the other swell-boxes in the instrument and controlled by a special balanced expression lever. But when this important division is subdivided in the manner recommended in the Chapter on the Church Organ, and as carried into effect in the Organ in the Church of Our Lady of Grace, Hoboken, N. J., the case assumes a different form. On the suggestion made elsewhere, in connection with the Concert-room Organ, as to the desirability of separating the tonal forces of this important division—not necessarily more important than any other division in a properly-schemed instrument—into two subdivisions, and of inclosing each in a separate and special swell-box, it is unnecessary to enlarge here. Such an arrangement will, in all probability, be adopted only in Concert-room Organs of the first magnitude. We believe we were the first to devise and advocate this radical departure from the old method. Our scheme for subdividing the so-called Swell Organ and inclosing the two subdivisions in separate swell-boxes was, for the first time in the history of organ-building, carried out in a special and effective form in the Grand Concert Organ erected in the Festival Hall of the Louisiana Purchase Exposition. The first subdivision comprised twenty-three complete stops, including all the stops representing the "wood-wind" of the orchestra, all of which were inclosed in swell-box No. 2. The second subdivision comprised fourteen complete stops and eighteen ranks of pipes, representing tonally the full string forces of the orchestra; all of which were inclosed in swell-box No. 3. This was the first instance of an essay being made to produce a concentrated effect of compound string-tone in all the pitches and with a proper harmonic series. Both the subdivisions could be separately brought on or thrown off the third clavier by thumb pistons; and the string subdivision was also commanded by the double-touch of the clavier. This arrangement fully exemplified the great value of departmental flexibility as well as expression—an arrangement, among others, which must characterize the Organ of the Twentieth Century, however much prejudice and self-interest may attempt to decry it.

We now come to the Solo Organ; and here we are in the presence of another important division of the modern Organ respecting which difference of opinion obtains in matters of flexibility and expression. And when one glances at the largest and finest Organs built by the greatest English builder, and finds their Solo divisions fixed and un-expressive, one may be pardoned in halting before insisting on the abso-lute necessity, from a musical point of view, of the application of the swell to the Solo Organ. "Great men have great failings;" and we venture to think that the neglect of the Solo Organ, in this matter of flexibility and expression, is a very great failing, in an artistic sense, in the builder of these large Concert Organs, and one that is as unexcusable as it is extraordinary.

The very name given to the division is surely enough to indicate that it should, even above and before every other division of the Organ, be furnished with the highest powers of flexibility and expression that skill and ingenuity can devise.

Imagine, ye Musicians, a *solo* of any description without light and shade, innocent of a *crescendo* or *diminuendo,* full of unyielding *forte,* and guiltless of a single *piano.* Can you reconcile such a thing to your musical sense? The organist, satisfied with matters as they are, with ears vitiated by the crudities of modern organ-building, may say: " I do not expect the refinements of an orchestral solo from the Solo Organ. What I want is plenty of free sound. Just imagine," he adds, " my beautiful TUBAS endowed with light and shade—heaven forbid that they should have their glorious stentorian voices afflicted with powers of ex-pression. Powers of expression forsooth! I want them, and all such stops, to enter into *my* music like bellowing bulls and as roaring lions; not like the approach of distant thunder or as the swelling voice of mighty Boreas; and I want them to *roar* at *all times* and in *all kinds of music* at their *full blast."* On the other hand, the organ-builder may say: " Inclose my solo reeds?—Reeds that I have voiced on wind of suf-ficient power to blow a blast-furnace, and which are sufficient to split your ears—Never! Expressive powers?—Humbug! If you cannot play the Organ as I choose to build it, you had better give it up and go into the vocal or orchestral line, where you can revel in expression to your heart's content."

Well, we shall willingly leave both the illogical and inartistic organist and organ-builder to nurse their own opinions; and take our stand in favor of the highest powers of expression that can be given to the Solo Organ. It is usual, and we may say correct, to place in the Solo division stops imitative of the more assertive instruments of the orch-estra, and those powerful labial and reed stops whose voices pierce through the entire volume of the Organ: but is it scientific or even sens-ible to leave such assertive and dominating voices absolutely without any means of modification and incapable of expression? Surely not.

Cannot we learn the true lesson from the orchestra here if our own musical knowledge and common-sense is insufficient to guide us?

It has been asserted, by lovers of noise, that to inclose such stops as the high pressure reeds is to destroy all their attack and grandeur. We unhesitatingly reply that their entry or attack requires a good deal of destroying; whilst anything that can tone down their so-called *grandeur—blatant blast* would, in many cases, be a more appropriate term —should be hailed as a blessing. But the truth is, inclosure in a properly constructed swell-box, would only very partially meet these desirable ends. When the box is closed, of course the tones of the TUBAS are softened to an extent which renders them agreeable; but when it is fully opened, they are practically heard at their full power: all that the swell-box can do is to slightly soften the unpleasant roughness of the vibrating tongues of the reeds, and this is decidedly a gain.

It is acknowledged by every educated organist that the heavily-blown reed stops, as inserted in modern Organs, can only be very sparingly used, and, in playing, have to be *led up to.* Now, admitting the value of such imposing voices, we consider this an objectionable and regrettable narrowing of their utility. If the stops now placed, in an exposed condition, in the Solo division of modern Organs, were inclosed in properly constructed swell-boxes, their value would be immensely increased; and the effect of their entry, by means of a *crescendo,* or quasi *sforzando,* would be impressive in the extreme, without being irritatingly startling, as it almost invariably is, to the sensitive musical ear, under the existing crude system.

One of the alterations made in the Grand Organ in St. George's Hall, Liverpool, during its recent reconstruction, is the inclosing of portion of the Solo division in a swell-box: but strange to relate, the four heavily-blown reeds—the OPHICLEIDE, TRUMPET, CLARION No. 1, and CLARION No. 2—are left exposed. We are certainly at a loss to understand such a proceeding; for it was the continued observation of the behavior of these identical stops, during the many years of our experience of the late Mr. Best's playing, that impressed us with the necessity of imparting full powers of flexibility and expression to the Solo Organ.

When any of the Solo Organ stops are used for solo or melodic passages, the necessity for powers of expression becomes unquestionable. Among the stops which, in our opinion, should find a place in the Solo division of a Concert Organ are the following: CONCERT VIOLIN, CONCERT VIOLONCELLO, CONCERT FLUTE, ORCHESTRAL TRUMPET, CORNOPEAN, ORCHESTRAL CLARINET, TROMBONE, OPHICLEIDE, BASS TUBA, TUBA MIRABILIS, HARMONIC TROMBA, and HARMONIC CLARION. Can any musician, with a spark of refinement in his soul, offer a single logical or artistical reason why such stops as these should be left in the Organ in a state beyond all control, and without powers of expression?

To those who accept the opinion that all the manual divisions of the Organ should be wholly or partly expressive, the proposition that the Pedal Organ should also have powers of expression and flexibility given to it will not only seem reasonable but perfectly logical. On the other hand, those (and their name is legion) who are satisfied with the old-fashioned style of organ-building will condemn the idea of having an expressive Pedal Organ as an absurdity, in no sense to be encouraged. The opinions of organists on this question will, of course, depend largely, if not entirely, on the way they look upon and use the Pedal Organ.

To throw a little common-sense into this matter we shall address a few words to the organist who is doubtful, and who has not made up his mind respecting the desirability of extending the application of the swell to the Pedal Organ.

We shall take it for granted that you are willing to admit that it seems desirable to have powers of expression given to the manual divisions of the Organ, and that you accept the idea, previously expressed, that the Organ shines with light borrowed from the orchestra. Now, let us glance at the orchestra and see if it can teach us anything in this Pedal Organ question. You naturally hold, after many years of experience as an organist, that there is no necessity for the Pedal Organ to be expressive or flexible; but at the same time you desire to be consistent and logical in all musical matters. Let us take a few instruments of the string family,—say a string quartet, which you know consists of first Violin, second Violin, Viola, and Violoncello or Bass, —and see if we can learn anything to guide our uncertain steps. You will admit that during the performance of a Quartet, the parts for the two Violins and the Viola must be rendered with all the expression and *nuances* the music demands: but, bearing the unexpressive Pedal Organ in view, you will very naturally say that the composer never intended the bass part to have any expression; and that before starting a Quartet by Beethoven or any other composer, the violoncellist should receive strict injunctions to play his part all through at the full strength of his bow, and without the slightest *diminuendo* or expression of any sort. You will tell him to take the bass division of the " King of Instruments " for his model, and go on, in the even tenor of his way, regardless of what the other instrumentalists are doing.

Now, take the full orchestra—" the Sun in the musical universe "— and see what can be done with it. The Conductor, before commencing a Symphony, will, of course, address his forces thus: " All the Violins, Violas, Flutes, Oboes, Clarinets, and all the treble and tenor instruments generally are to render their respective parts with the greatest refinement, delicacy, and expression, paying strict attention to the *piano* and *pianissimo* passages. But, on the other hand, all the Violoncellos,

Double Basses, Bassoons, Bass Trombone, and all the bass instruments generally, are to render their respective parts uniformly, throughout the Symphony, at their full power, and without the ghost of a *diminuendo,* even when all the rest of the orchestra is playing *pianissimo."*

We need not ask the musician what his opinion of such a performance would be, or what he would think of the Conductor who proposed such an outrageous proceeding: but we can assure him that we look upon a performance on an Organ in which all the powers of expression are confined to the manual department as equally objectionable and inartistic.

At this point it may interest the organ-lover to have the opinion of a celebrated musician and pianist on the value of expression in the Organ. In the year 1877, an important Organ was erected in the concert room of the Public Halls, at Glasgow, by Messrs. T. C. Lewis & Co., of London, from the Specification and under the direction of the late W. T. Best and Henry Smart. In the four manual divisions there are fifty-two speaking stops; and of these twenty-six are rendered expressive by being inclosed in swell-boxes. The disposition of the tonal forces in this Organ are as follows: The Great Organ, of eighteen speaking stops, is entirely exposed and is accordingly unexpressive; the Swell Organ, of seventeen stops, is inclosed and entirely expressive; the Choir Organ has ten stops, two of which—the CLARINET and VOX HUMANA —are inclosed in a special swell-box and rendered expressive; and the Solo Organ, of seven stops, is inclosed in an independent swell-box and is entirely expressive.

With reference to the great advantages, from the true musician's point of view, derived from even the limited powers of expression provided in the Glasgow Organ, the opinion may be recorded here of a master whose right to speak with authority on matters of musical expression no one will venture to question. Dr. Hans von Bülow says, in the *Glasgow Herald* of November 3, 1877:

" I never met with an Organ so good in Germany, the instruments there not having the same amount of expression and flexibility—most delicate and exquisite *nuances*—that hearing the *diminuendi* and *crescendi* was to me a new sensation. If I would longer listen to an Organ like this, and a player like Mr. Best, I would, were I not grown too old, jeopardise my pianistical career, and begin to study the Organ, where certainly I would be able to display much more eloquence as Beethoven's and Chopin's speaker. In short, despite having been exceptionally fatigued by your consecutive concerts and numerous rehearsals, I listened with the most eager attention from the first to the last note of Mr. Best's recital."

Surely no higher testimony than this can be required as to the great value of increased powers of expression by the only means available

in the Grand Organ : and yet we hear men who can just struggle through
a piece of organ music in a mechanical manner, and organ-builders
who can just manage to put an Organ together on the stereotyped lines,
condemn, in terms as emphatic as they are redolent of ignorance, the
practice of introducing the swell in more than one division of the Organ.

If Dr. Hans von Bülow felt tempted, for a moment, to jeopardise
his " pianistical career " and to " study the Organ," on hearing Mr.
Best's performance on the Glasgow Organ, with its very limited powers
of expression; and that mainly on account of its " flexibility and expression," its " most delicate and exquisite *nuances,*" and its " *diminuendi* and *crescendi;* " what would he have said had he heard the same
performer on an Organ such as we advocate, endowed with powers of
expression and made perfectly flexible throughout its entire tonal forces
and in every division?   Such an Organ would indeed be an instrument
for the *virtuoso*—on which he could interpret his deepest and most
refined musical thoughts; and on which he could produce the richest
effects of light and shade, vivid contrasts, and all those " delicate and
exquisite *nuances,*" which are now only heard in the orchestra.   But
to make the Organ an instrument for the *virtuoso* and profound musician, we are free to admit that more must be done than merely giving
it powers of expression and complete flexibility by means of the swell.
Its entire tonal forces must be classified and arranged upon a far more
artistic and scientific system than that which obtains at the present time.
For further remarks on this important subject, the reader is referred
to the Chapter on the Concert-room Organ.

Before closing the present Chapter it may not be out of place to give
the tonal scheme, as originally prepared by us, for the pedal division of
the Concert Organ exhibited at the Louisiana Purchase Exposition,
showing its unexpressive and expressive subdivisions.   While all the
specified stops were inserted in the actual Pedal Organ, the scheme was
deemed by the conservative organ-builders too advanced in its tonal
apportionment; and the necessity for imparting expressive powers to
any portion of its tonal forces was, in the usual groove-loving manner
observed in the trade, not recognised.   Accordingly, the grand opportunity of putting on record a notable advance in organ construction and
tonal appointment was then lost.   In an Organ of its importance and
size (136 speaking stops), and where there was no difficulty as regards
accommodation for the necessary swell-chamber, the neglect of so great
an opportunity was short-sighted in the extreme; and only goes to show
how difficult it is to move organ-builders out of the old time-worn trade
grooves.

A careful examination of this scheme of tonal appointment and
apportionment—unexpressive and expressive—will convince any one,
versed in Pedal Organ registration and its requirements in modern

organ music, of the immense value given to the entire division by the inclosure of so many of its important and assertive stops, and especially all the unison and higher pitched reeds. It is no exaggeration to say that, for all legitimate purposes, the inclosure of the reed stops, thereby

PEDAL ORGAN.

Compass CCC to G=32 Notes.

FIRST SUBDIVISION—UNEXPRESSIVE.

1. GRAVISSIMA (Resultant) . 64 FEET.		7. OCTAVE . . . Metal 8 FEET.	
2. DOUBLE DIAPASON . Wood 32 "		8. BASS FLUTE . . Wood 8 "	
3. CONTRA-BOURDON . Wood 32 "		9. COMPENSATING	
4. DIAPASON . . . Metal 16 "		MIXTURE . Metal VI. Ranks.	
5. DIAPASON . . . Wood 16 "		10. CONTRA-BOMBARDE Wood 32 FEET.	
6. GAMBA . . . . Metal 16 "			

SECOND SUBDIVISION—EXPRESSIVE.

11. VIOLONE . . . Metal 16 FEET.		19. SUPER-OCTAVE . Metal 4 FEET.
12. BOURDON . . Wood 16 "		20. OFFENFLÖTE . . Wood 4 "
13. CONTRA-FLAUTO Wood 16 "		21. CONTRA-POSAUNE Metal 16 "
14. QUINTATEN . Wood 16 "		22. BOMBARDE . . Metal 16 "
15. QUINT . . . Wood 10⅔ "		23. EUPHONIUM . . Metal 16 "
16. DOLCE . . . Metal 8 "		24. FAGOTTO . . . Metal 8 "
17. VIOLONCELLO . Metal 8 "		25. TROMBA . . . Metal 8 "
18. WEITGEDECKT . Wood 8 "		26. CLARION . . . Metal 4 "

AUXILIARY PEDAL ORGAN.

PARTLY EXPRESSIVE.

27. DOUBLE DIAPASON (From First Organ) . . . . Metal 32 FEET.
28. DULCIANA (Expressive, from Second Organ) . . Metal 16 "
29. LIEBLICHGEDECKT (Expressive, from Third Organ) . Wood 16 "
30. CONTRAFAGOTTO (Expressive, from Third Organ) . Wood 16 "

rendering them flexible in tone, multiplies their value tenfold. How very few Pedal Organs have a softly-toned reed stop in their appointments; yet the great value of such a stop has never been questioned, while many an artistic performer has sighed for one. Apart from the possibility of adjusting every inclosed stop to exactly the strength of tone required by the manual combinations drawn, the powers of expression provided impart a richness, refinement, and force of character to the pedal part absolutely unknown and unattainable in the case of such inflexible Pedal Organs as have hitherto appeared, even in the largest existing Concert-room instruments. Surely, in this organ-loving and organ-building epoch, it is time that some effective attention should be paid to the requirements of the all-important Pedal Organ. A flexible and expressive Pedal Organ will, of necessity, be one of the distinguishing features of the Organ of the Twentieth Century.

For the convenience of the performer, in addition to a special Pedal Organ expression lever, an action should be provided, by means of which he can, at will, connect the pedal swell shutters to any one of the balanced expression levers belonging to the manual divisions. With a properly-appointed and expressive Pedal Organ, the performer can readily obtain a suitable bass for all his expressive manual divisions: and his perfect control over the strength of tone of the pedal forces allows him to graduate his bass at all times to suit his manual tones. The swell when properly applied, increases the beauty and utility of the Pedal Organ tenfold. We commend what we have said in the present Chapter to the unbiased consideration of organists and musicians generally. They alone can compel the organ-builder to depart from his conservative and old-fashioned views and ways of doing things.

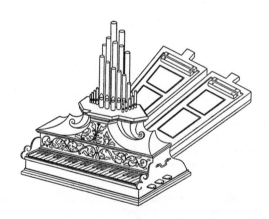

POSITIVE ORGAN OF THE SIXTEENTH CENTURY.

CHAPTER IX.

CONSTRUCTION OF THE SWELL-BOX.

HE proper construction of the Swell-box is a matter of the greatest importance, and yet it is very commonly misunderstood and very often neglected. Its importance becomes obvious when it is realized that a badly-proportioned and improperly-fabricated swell-box never fails to destroy much of the effect and beauty of the tonal forces inclosed therein. We have said in our Chapter on the Swell in the Organ that the belief, which prevails in certain quarters, that the swell-box is destructive of the sounds of the inclosed pipe-work is not without some foundation; and that the foundation for the belief has been furnished by the mistakes and misconceptions of organ-builders, and not by anything essentially inherent in the swell-box *per se*. We have also stated that stops inclosed in swell-boxes undergo a certain tonal modification; pointing out the fact that when the swell-boxes are properly proportioned and constructed, and the stops are correctly spaced and planted on wind-chests of ample size, and scientifically scaled and artistically voiced for the position they occupy, the slight modification their voices undergo is an improvement rather than the reverse.

We have invariably observed that the opinion respecting an injurious effect of a swell on the tonality of the inclosed stops, has been held and fostered by organists and organ-builders who have too long been accustomed to unexpressive Organs, and who have loved musical noise at any cost. The taste for loud sounds is a vitiated one, and once acquired is difficult to be got rid of; accordingly, to persons afflicted with such a taste anything that has an ameliorating and refining effect is unappreciated if not absolutely distasteful. It must not be overlooked that there is a loudness combined with coarseness and crudity, and a loudness combined with repose and refinement. The latter appeals to the true musician and the lover of sweet sounds.

It is somewhat remarkable that in the design and construction of the swell-box—a portion of the Organ which would naturally be expected to have long before this late date assumed a definite and well-established treatment—so many diverse and conflicting views and methods should obtain among organ-builders to-day. That all can be right is impossible, seeing that there can be only one correct mode of treatment in the case of an object which has practically only one office to fulfil, alike in every Organ, large or small.

There are certain causes for the unsatisfactory state of the swell-box in modern Organs, and these we shall briefly touch upon. First, the pretty general ambition on the part of church authorities and organists to have large Organs erected in places totally insufficient for the reception of instruments of moderate dimensions, has led to the cramming of numerous speaking stops into swell-boxes in every way inadequate for their proper accommodation. Not only, in such cases, are the swell-boxes too small, but the wind-chests which they inclose are so crowded with pipe-work that pure and effective intonation is out of the question. The combination of overcrowded pipe-work and small swell-boxes can only have one result—the serious impairment of the tonal qualities of the divisions of the Organ so maltreated. There are other, and external causes of failure, the chief of which will probably be the crowding of exposed pipe-work, belonging to the Great or some other uninclosed division of the Organ, directly in front of the shutters of the swell-box, materially interfering with the free egress of the sound that does issue from its overcrowded interior. These three adverse conditions obtain in a vast number of modern Organs; and when their internal economy is examined, it seems wonderful that they are capable of producing any expressive musical effects. It is in works of this inartistic and insufficient class that the objection to the extended introduction of the swell-box has had its origin.

Secondly, the very general impression that a swell-box should be so constructed as to impart, when closed, to the sounds of the inclosed stops the effect of great distance, almost, if not entirely, amounting to annihilation, has been attended by very objectionable results from an artistic point of view. Organ-builders have taxed their ingenuity and skill to produce swell-boxes or swell-chambers with thick composite walls, as impervious to sound as double layers of wood, packed with sawdust, felt, and other deadening materials, could make them: and of late, where conditions permitted, constructions of lath-and-plaster, brick-work, and reinforced-concrete have been introduced in the Organ; with the result of producing what we have stigmatized as the *annihilating swell*, the latest absurdity in modern organ-building. To such an extent is this mania being carried that one sees in a public advertisement of special steel-work the following: "Reinforcement for concrete swell-boxes." Not content with what sound-destroying brick and concrete walls can do, organ-builders must resort to double sets of shutters, with total disregard of the direct and obvious teaching of the grand orchestra and the string quartet, alluded to in the preceding chapter.

Thirdly, the conviction that, next to inordinately thick and deadened walls, it is most desirable to have every portion of the swell-box made and fitted as airtight as practicable, has combined with other mistaken ideas to foster wrong principles of construction. It stands to reason that in a confined space like that of a small swell-box, crammed full of pipes, and with tightly-closed shutters, a flatting effect must quickly show itself in the tones of the speaking pipes. Much more air, under a certain pressure, finds its way, through the pipe-work, into the swell-box, than can find its way out while the shutters remain closed: accordingly, it becomes almost impossible to use the inclosed division of the Organ without opening the shutters more or less. This fact in itself shows that there is something wrong in the construction of the swell-box, very seriously impairing its utility. The musical effect of a properly-constructed swell-box should be as satisfactory to the ear when the box is closed as when it is open; and every practical expedient should be resorted to, to secure this important result. This condition is essential in an Organ used for accompaniment to the voice; and it should be equally observed in all Concert Organs on which anything approaching a satisfactory rendition of orchestral scores is essayed. The most satisfactory performance of Mendelssohn's Overture to "A Midsummer Night's Dream" on the Organ—and we have heard it a dozen times rendered by Best on the St. George's Hall Organ, and as many times performed by the orchestra—was on an Organ in which the swell-boxes were entirely of wood less than two inches thick. Yet every *crescendo* and *diminuendo* and every refined *nuance* were rendered with rare artistic fidelity. But it must be said that the Organ was not coarsely voiced on the high-pressure wind system, now considered the acme of modern organ-building.

The golden rules of swell-box construction may be thus formulated:

I. *Let the swell-box be designed on as large a scale as the space available for the Organ will permit, and under no conditions let its height be denuded.*

A roomy swell-box is under all conditions an advantage; but it only reaches its highest excellence when it incloses a spacious wind-chest, on which the ranks of pipes stand a sufficient distance apart to allow them to speak freely and without strained intonation, and to admit of the unobstructed egress of their sounds. In Organs of important dimensions, the swell-box should be sufficiently large in plan to allow the pipe-work to stand perfectly free from its sides; and in all possible cases enough space should be provided around the pipe-work to permit easy access to all parts of the same for tuning, regulating, and cleaning. The banking up of the larger pipes (especially those of wood) against the woodwork of the box, preventing the desirable reflection of sound by the inner surface of the walls, is a practice to be strongly condemned on acoustical grounds. It is, unfortunately, almost unavoidable in small and overcrowded swell-boxes. Next in importance to ample space in plan is ample height above the larger pipe-work. This increases the acoustical property of the swell-box, prevents the flatting of the tones of the pipes, and permits the formation of a large area of shutter-work, thereby doing away with the objection, in one direction, which has been reasonably urged against badly-designed swell-boxes; namely, that they seriously impair the tonal quality of the inclosed stops. It is necessary, when the box is high, that the shutters be carried up to as near its roof as possible, so that there may be no locking in of sound above. The reed stops, especially, gain brilliancy by this treatment.

II. *Let the walls and roof of the swell-box be constructed of solid wood of the best quality and of proper thickness, without any packing or other expedient to render them dead and impervious to sound.*

Under this rule, we have to consider the wood most suitable for the construction of the swell-box; and also the thickness of the solid wood necessary to secure the maximum softness of effect, without any destruction of the tonal character of the inclosed speaking stops, when the swell is closed.

Of all woods the most suitable for the construction of the walls and roof of the swell-box is clean, straight-grained white pine; but the best straight-grained yellow or pitch pine is highly to be recommended. Both these woods can be depended upon when perfectly seasoned and free from sapwood, shakes, and other imperfections. For the shutters only the very finest and lightest kind of white pine should be used. Of the modes of constructing the walls, shutters, etc., we treat further on.

On the question of the thickness of the swell-box a considerable diversity of opinion obtains among organ-builders: but we feel sure if they would use more observation and independent judgment in matters connected with their art, this diversity of opinion would soon disappear. Several builders advocate the adoption of walls of inordinate thickness, formed of two layers of wood, stuffed between with sawdust, or separated by plies of coarse, thick felt. Such walls are made three or four inches thick, and are about as dead and impervious to sound as a brick wall. Such a thickness as the minimum above named would be bad enough if in solid wood, but in the composite form with sawdust or felt is absolutely fatal to the proper effect of the swell. When formed of solid white pine, the walls and roof should never, even in the largest swell-box likely to be made, exceed two and a half inches in thickness. In the case of a large swell-box, exposed on all sides, a special construction, involving the addition of a layer of thin felt in the paneling, may be adopted. For swell-boxes of ordinary dimensions, containing stops voiced on moderate pressures, closely-paneled walls of white pine two inches thick will be sufficient. If made of yellow pine, one and three-quarter inches will be ample. We believe we are correct in stating that the American organ-builder who first favored the multiplication of the swell in the Organ held the same views. The finest swell-box known to us, exposed on three sides, so far as acoustical and correct musical properties are concerned, is formed of white pine, one and a half inches in thickness.

III. *Let the swell-box have the largest area devoted to shutters consistent with the nature and office of the tonal forces inclosed by it.*

This rule provides for the proper proportion of shutter area to solid woodwork in the swell-boxes of the different divisions of the Organ to which powers of expression may be given. As we have shown in other Chapters, the swell-box may with great advantage be applied to sections of the pipe-work of the Great and Pedal Organs, and to the entire tonal forces of the Choir, Swell, and Solo Organs. Such being the case, we may now point out the fact that, while all that has been said under the first and second rules, above given, is applicable alike to all the swell-boxes that may be introduced in an Organ, the third rule directs that the area devoted to the shutters or louvres should vary in accordance with the nature and offices of the several divisions of the instrument.

In the First or Great Organ, only a section of the speaking stops should be inclosed; and the swell-box should have the largest area possible shuttered, so that when the box is fully open there should, beyond a slight refining effect on the tone, be no practical loss of power. Accordingly, when the position of the Great Organ permits, both the front and the ends of its swell-box should be shuttered to as large an extent as proper construction will admit of.

In the case of the Second or Choir Organ, we do not consider that a larger area than that presented by the front of its swell-box, when properly proportioned, is necessary to be shuttered, especially as the box is likely to be wide and high in proportion to its depth. When the Choir division is placed in the same swell-box with the expressive section of the Great Organ, it must accept the conditions imposed by the latter. It will, however, not greatly suffer, if it suffers at all, by those conditions.

In the Third or Swell Organ, full powers of expression are absolutely essential; and these can be secured in the case of a properly-constructed swell-box, of ample dimensions, by having its front entirely devoted to shutter-work, reaching from the level of the rack-boards to its roof.

For the swell-box of the Fourth or Solo Organ, the treatment just recommended for that of the Swell division may, under all ordinary circumstances, be adopted: but in Concert-room Organs of the first magnitude, the swell-box may with advantage have a greater shuttered area, so that the reed stops on wind of high pressure, which the Solo division may contain, can at the performer's will speak as freely as fully-exposed stops. In the case of an important and properly-placed Solo Organ, we strongly recommend that its swell-box be shuttered in front and back, and that its balanced expression-lever be given a compound action, operating on the back shutters only during the first half of its movement, and on both the back and front shutters during the remaining part of its movement, completely opening all the shutters at the limit of its movement. The result of such an action would be a very gradual and magnificent *crescendo,* with a corresponding *diminuendo.* This treatment can, of course, be applied to any other division.

The swell-chamber containing the expressive section of the Pedal Organ should have the maximum amount of shutter area, so that there may be no objectionable confinement of sound.

We now come to the consideration of certain details of construction, and may properly commence with those connected with the plain walls and roof of the swell-box. In the construction of these portions, beyond their proper thickness, the chief matter to be attended to is perfect solidity throughout, so that there may be no possibility of jarring or false vibration being set up in them while the larger inclosed pipes are speaking, or any lessening of their efficiency by the contraction of their component parts and the accompanying opening of joints. It is essential that only wood of the best quality, perfectly seasoned and dry, be used; otherwise imperfections are certain to show themselves when the work is subjected to the shrinking action of dry air for a length of time. Several modes of construction may be followed according to the dimensions of the box. Perhaps the most suitable, under general conditions, is that known as framed and flush paneled work. In this class of construction it is only necessary to have the framing securely mortised and tenoned, glued, and wedged; and the flush panels, of the same thickness as the framework, tongued into the frames and well glued in the manner shown in Section A in Fig. XXV.; or rebated, leathered, and firmly screwed to the framework, as indicated in Section B. In Section C is shown a heavier construction suitable for a large swell-box. The framework to be 2½ inches thick, with double panels 1⅛ inches thick, having a layer of soft felt between them, as indicated. Layers of strawboard, cut accurately to the openings may be used instead of felt.

In constructing the walls of the swell-box, provision must be made for easy access to the interior for tuning. A door about eighteen inches wide and about five feet high will be convenient. It must be of the same thickness as the wall of the box in which it is located, and be leathered or felted so as to prevent any vibration while the pipes are speaking. It should be secured by a lock and several turn-buttons, so as to hold it rigid in every part. When the swell-box is very large and is conveniently situated, entrance may be made through a trap-door formed in the floor of a passageway.

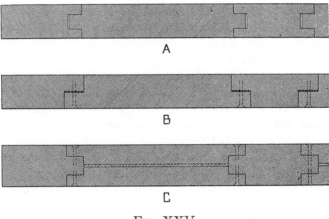

A

B

C

Fig. XXV.

From tests we have made, we are under the impression that a very efficient swell-box could be constructed with all its exposed and un-shuttered sides of specially thick, unpolished plate-glass, firmly fixed in wooden frames. The glass would furnish an admirable internal reflecting surface; while it would allow the pipe-work being illuminated from the exterior; thereby preventing any local heating of the pipe-work by internal lights during the process of tuning.

Although the roof of the swell-box is generally flat and laid horizontally, there may be occasions when it will be advisable or necessary to place it on an incline. The impression, which seems to have obtained in certain quarters, that the closer the top is to the inclosed pipe-work the better will be the acoustical properties of the swell, has led to the occasional adoption of a form of top which follows to a pronounced extent the pyramidal disposition of the pipes, the longest of which occupy the central portion of the box. This practice, founded on a misconception of the acoustical problem involved, should never be followed. If any inclination is to be given to the top, let it be such as will add to the height of the front or shuttered side of the box, and will aid in reflecting the sound in an outward direction, instead of throwing it back on the pipe-work from which it emanated. Much may be done by a scientific treatment and disposition of the roof of the swell-box to improve its acoustical properties; and this matter deserves the attention of all interested in scientific and artistic organ-building.

The entire internal surface of the walls, roof, etc., of the swell-box should either be painted with three coats of white-lead and linseed-oil paint and finished with hard enamel, or sized and varnished with three coats of best hard-drying floor varnish. By such means the wood is not only protected from the action of the atmosphere in all weathers, but it is given a hard and glossy reflecting surface, which materially aids the clearness and brilliance of the tones of the inclosed pipes. The exterior of the swell-box should also be protected by coats of oil paint or oil varnish. Thin coats of shellac varnish should never be depended on in a variable climate.

We have now to consider the mechanical portion of the swell-box, by means of which expression and flexibility are imparted to the inclosed tonal forces. This portion consists of a series of shutters or louvres, carefully fitted to each other and to the opening in the box, and supported on metal pins or centers so as to turn with the greatest freedom and without vibration. In old Organs, and also in modern ones in which the old-fashioned "hitch-down" or recovering "swell-pedal" is used, the shutters are hung horizontally; but in all properly-appointed instruments in which the balanced expression-lever is introduced, the shutters are supported vertically. It seems unnecessary to remark that in Organs of any pretensions toward completeness no other form of expression-lever should be used. Horizontal shutters belong to the past; and the recovering pedal, with its more or less awkward hitch-down or fixing arrangements, should be placed, for good and all, among the curiosities of organ-building. Strange to relate, there are organists to-day who prefer this old-fashioned and obviously insufficient appliance; and these are the men who wax eloquent against the extension of the swell in the Organ.

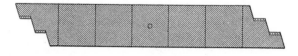

Fig. XXVI.

The shutters should be made of the finest and the lightest, straight-grained white pine that money can procure. Every precaution must be taken to prevent shrinking and warping. The practice followed by the late Messrs. Roosevelt is strongly to be recommended. The vertical shutters of their fine swell-boxes were formed of several longitudinal pieces of clear white pine glued together in the manner indicated in the Transverse Section of a shutter, Fig. XXVI. . Shutters should be of the same thickness as the walls of a properly-constructed swell-box, as above described; but under no circumstances need they exceed 2½ inches in thickness. Their width may vary from seven to ten inches, according to the size of the swell-box. The edges of the shutters may be formed in three ways. Two of these are shown in the Transverse Sections A, B, Fig. XXVII. The form shown at A is that which has

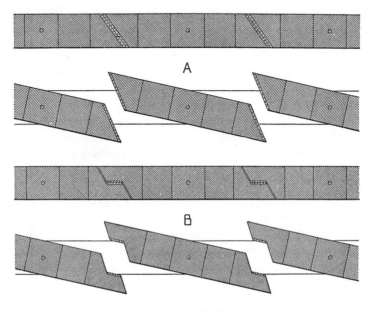

Fig. XXVII.

been almost invariably adopted for horizontal shutters, and very often for vertical ones. There are, perhaps, no serious objections to be advanced against its adoption providing the edges are accurately adjusted and covered with thick soft felt of good quality. The form shown at B is, however, to be preferred, requiring less felted surface, and furnishing a closer and freer contact. The third form is shown in the Roosevelt shutter, Fig. XXVI., the most desirable one in thick shutters. Two layers of felt must be used in all cases: one being glued and tacked to each surface, so that felt may strike felt when the shutters close. The unfelted edges must be fitted as closely as practicable, but under no conditions must they touch. The length of the shutters should be about ⅛ inch less than the height of the opening of the frame in which they are pivoted. Vertical shutters must be adjusted so as to turn without the slightest noise or apparent friction. Their lower pivots should be in the form of conical steel points, resting in corresponding sinkings in bell-metal plates. The upper pivots may be plain steel pins working in hardwood, well black-leaded.

Of equal importance to the proper fitting and pivoting of the shutters is the careful construction and adjustment of the action which operates them; so as to enable the performer to produce, with as little exertion as possible, a perfectly regular *crescendo* and *diminuendo*. This regular motion is a simple matter when a direct mechanical action connects the expression-lever with properly linked shutters: but so far as our observation extends, the same desirable sensitive movements and perfectly regular effects have not yet been obtained by an electro-pneumatic action. The problem of a perfectly satisfactory electric swell action has yet to be solved. It cannot be difficult, however, to make the action much more satisfactory than one finds it at present: in fact, there are several ways in which this can be done.

In the preceding remarks it has been clearly shown that we in no way join in the apparently growing craze for brick, reinforced-concrete, and lath-and-plaster constructions, called swell-chambers. They are purely late-day innovations, born of and fostered by a vitiated musical sense, and a false conception of the true and artistic office of the swell in the Organ. They have also been favored by those who have joined the craze for screaming, coarsely-voiced, high-pressure stops, which no properly constructed swell-box could control.

It is obvious that unless a church or concert-hall is specially furnished with such structural swell-chambers, it is practically impossible to construct them in any proper manner. Such massive and ponderous affairs require adequate foundations or supports, and these are not easily provided in elevated situations. An Organ having four or five brick-walled or reinforced-concrete swell-chambers would be a portentous affair, unless the church or concert-hall in which it was placed had been specially designed, with the chambers parts of the structure, and hidden or disguised. Then comes the important question: Would the chambers be in all respects satisfactory from artistic and musical points of view? We unhesitatingly answer, No!

It must be remembered that the grandest and most expressive Organs in the world to-day have wooden swell-boxes: and it is not within the realms of probability that any organ-builder in this country will, by the resort to brick or reinforced concrete chambers and screaming high-pressure stops, surpass or even equal such Organs.

CHAPTER X.

THE CHURCH ORGAN.

RIOR to about the middle of the last century the art of the organ-builder was almost exclusively concentrated on the fabrication of instruments for use in the church: and at the present day, although Church Organs cannot be said to embrace the largest or most representative instruments produced in recent times, they certainly continue, and in all likelihood will continue to form the most numerous, the most useful, and accordingly the most important class. Concert-room Organs, Organs for public places of amusement, and Chamber Organs, however much they may be advanced toward perfection or however beautiful they may become, will always remain comparatively few in number; and in point of general appreciation and utility will always occupy a subordinate place to those instruments which are constructed for public worship. Such being the case, it is obviously imperative on every one connected with the scheming and fabrication of Church Organs to devote earnest study to their scientific and artistic tonal appointment and apportionment.

How far the Church Organ of to-day, even in the most advanced form in which it is found in all the organ-building countries of the world, may be considered a satisfactory musical instrument; and how far it can lay claim, in the estimation of the accomplished musician, to be considered sufficient in tonal control and powers of expression, are questions deserving the attention of all students and lovers of the Organ. That it falls short of what it is capable of becoming, under proper development in tonal matters, we have for many years been convinced and have publicly affirmed. It must be quite evident to any one who gives the Organ serious attention and study, and who is gifted with a keen musical sense, that the Church Organ, as turned out to-day from the workshops of the groove-loving organ-builders, is a profoundly imperfect and unsatisfactory musical instrument, while it may be an example of consummate mechanical skill.

Both old and modern ingenuity and skill have furnished ample materials to work upon: what is required for the production of the Church Organ of the Twentieth Century is the application of more scientific knowledge; more artistic methods in tonal appointment and tonal grouping; more refinement in tonality; and largely extended powers of flexibility and expression—bringing the entire musical resources of the instrument more logically and consistently under control, without unduly taxing the exertions of the performer either mentally or physically. Simplicity is an element of beauty in an Organ as in every other work of art.

An unbiased review of the art of organ-building, so far, at least, as the Church Organ is concerned, leads to the unavoidable conclusion that since about the middle of the last century it has not progressed, in any decided manner, toward a more scientific, artistic, and logical system of tonal structure; toward a more effective and convenient system of divisional apportionment, and toward the production of a more flexible and expressive type of instrument. We do not deny that in the hands of some few leading organ-builders, both in this country and abroad, improvements have been made during recent years in the art of voicing; resulting in the production of a higher standard of tone in certain classes of stops: but these facts cause considerable regret that such improvements have not led to a deeper study of tonal matters with the view to the betterment of the Organ, throughout, as a musical instrument. Progress must not be confined to isolated evidences of genius in some few voicing-rooms; nor must it be looked for primarily in the organ factory.

Organ-builders work in grooves of their own or, what is more common, their predecessors' creating; and it is, accordingly, a matter of great difficulty, even backed by sound logical reasoning, to induce them to study new methods, or to depart from the ways of doing things which they and their grandfathers have been accustomed to. Many probably gave their allegiance to the traditional methods of their art when they did little more than make tapped-wires or sweep their masters' workshops. It can only be this tendency to go on year after year in old and well-beaten paths that accounts for the little progress and individuality displayed, during the last sixty or seventy years, by organ-builders of reputation in the general construction of Church Organs. Now, this adherence to traditional methods and ideas cannot but produce a certain degree of narrow-mindedness, and foster a conviction that there is nothing more to be learnt or done so far as the tonal appointment of the Church Organ is concerned. It is probable that in many cases (we know of some) organ-builders nurse their own conceit to such an extent as to look upon any attempt to convince them of errors of taste or judgment as a gross impertinence. When an artist, in any branch of art, is satisfied that he has reached the highest point of excellence, and has learnt everything, he has put his foot on the downward path. A true artist is always dissatisfied with his best endeavors, and is ever striving to achieve something above and beyond them.

The very general ignorance and apathy of the musical public have been important factors in the retardation of progress in the development of the Organ along tonal lines; and it can only be hoped that the coming generation of organists will look beyond the limitations of the console, and not be content just to take what the tradesmen organ-builders think proper to give them. We must look to these coming organists for The Organ of the Twentieth Century.

We have before us, as these words are written, a number of representative " specifications," or, more correctly speaking, dry lists of stops, for Church Organs, prepared either by the organ-builders or others interested in the construction of the instruments alluded to. And it is interesting to observe the remarkable similarity that obtains in their tonal schemes; and the almost total lack of individual thought and originality displayed in a right direction. The only signs of thought and originality lie in the ingenuity displayed in making a poor list of actual stops look a long and tempting list on paper. In this direction, the tonal appointment of the Pedal Organ should be specially scrutinized. Respecting the character and honest purpose of this display of originality, perhaps the less said the better. Purchasers of Organs who are not thoroughly conversant with organ matters and organ-builders' methods should obtain some reliable advice before blindly accepting organ-builders " specifications." On this subject the reader may glance at our Chapter on The Organ Specification.

A Church Organ to be thoroughly serviceable and appropriate, both from an artistic and a practical point of view, must be schemed and constructed to suit the place in which it is to be erected and the service it has to support. This is a golden rule which can never be wisely violated. A Church Organ must, therefore, be more or less powerful in tone in exact proportion to the internal dimensions and acoustical properties of the building in which it is placed; power being, in this case, understood to be volume and pervading character rather than loudness, in its simple state, which is of necessity accompanied by unmusical harshness and noise. A harshly-voiced and noisy Organ is an unmitigated abomination to the refined and musical ear. The leading characteristic of a Church Organ should be grandeur, combined with the greatest possible refinement of tone; so that it may be perfectly adapted for the appropriate accompaniment of choral and congregational singing, and the performance of voluntaries and other incidental music of a solemn and dignified character. It must never be forgotten that such an Organ is essentially, and before and above all, an accompanimental instrument; its capabilities for the display of florid skill in secular music on the part of the organist being an altogether secondary consideration, if it is a consideration at all. How often, however, do we find, on testing the tonal appointments of Church Organs, or carefully analyzing their lists of stops, that true dignity, grandeur, and usefulness have been sacrificed for the insertion of several ear-tickling and imitative stops for which many organists have so inordinate a predilection. An organist's Specification can generally be detected by the appearance of such fancy stops and the absence of that strictly accompanimental character which ought to distinguish the Church Organ. In the case of small, or even medium-sized, instruments this is fatal; but in large Organs there is generally ample material for both accompanimental and solo playing, although all may be deficient in flexibility and powers of expression. An English writer of evident knowledge and experience has made the following apposite remarks on this subject :—

"In the first place, the Organ should be of a size and power proportionate to the building and the congregation it will contain. We see in some churches, Organs erected out of all proportion to the requirements of the service; as an instance, let that of St. Mary at Hill, London, be adduced—a very fine instrument is to be found there; but it is far too large and noisy for the comparatively small church. This instrument, although possessing great merit, is not a Church Organ in its true sense. The same fault applies to the recently-erected Organ at St. Andrew's, Well-street, London; the instrument is far too large and noisy for the size of the church, placed, as it is, near the congregation. One more example, by way of contrast: take St. Alphage, London Wall; here is a small church, and an Organ designed for the church—a Church Organ *par excellence*. It is un-necessary to go farther into detail upon this point: a Church Organ is an Organ designed to accompany the voices, and to be at the same time capable of rendering with effect the voluntaries before and after service. When the musical demands of an ordinary Sunday service are considered, and the large proportion of accom-paniment to voice-singing in which it consists, it is certain that noise is not the attribute best suited to the Church Organ, but rather the more mellow tones of the foundation-stops—the DIAPASONS, and those registers which best accompany the voice. Now, the stops of this class are much more costly than the chorus and mutation stops, and a properly-constructed Organ of this type, with, say, twenty musical and well-balanced registers, would cost as much as an Organ of forty stops upon the quantity principle of endless small pipes. This may be explained more clearly by stating that the last twelve notes of the 8 ft. register on the key-board cost about as much as the remaining forty-eight pipes; and hence, in the cumbrous 'churchwarden's Organ,' it will be noticed how often the foundation-stops are cut off at tenor C, 4 ft., and grooved into a common bass, or left alto-gether incomplete, without any bass at all; while a number of ranks of small pipes are introduced without any proper counterbalance of the foundation tone either upon the Pedal Organ or keyboards. We now see why one specification of an Organ costing the same money may apparently represent a much more extensive instrument. Again, a Church Organ requires that in its design the tone of the Pedal Organ should be commensurate with the rest of the Organ; the Pedal Organ ought to carry down the last octave of the keyboard an octave lower without any very apparent break in the tone. Comparatively few of our present church instruments have any Pedal Organ at all. A single 16 ft. open wooden stop of a deep booming sound has to do duty alike for the full Chorus Organ and the soft Choir Organ vocal accompaniment. It is very rare to find a properly balanced Pedal Organ, even upon the most recently constructed Church Organs. The fact is, the cost of a proper Pedal Organ nearly equals that of the Organ it has to balance upon the keyboard. Our present Church Organs are, as a rule, ill-constructed instruments; and, more or less, are erected in a commercial spirit, and form a transaction like the placing of the bricks, stones, and mortar of the building. No one takes any special interest, partly from a want of the necessary knowledge, and partly because 'it is no one's business.' What is wanted is a portion of that pure artistic spirit which animated the 'Father Schmidts' and other builders and organists of former days: men whose aim was too high for mere money-getting, and who gloried in the progress of the sublimest of all the constructive arts." *Musical Standard,* June 23, 1877.

The strictures of this able and observant writer are perfectly just, and although written forty-one years ago they are equally applicable to the Church Organs erected up to the present day. With his remarks anent the general deficiency of Pedal Organs we cordially agree. But he had not become acquainted with organ-builders' latest methods of constructing Pedal Organs *on paper,* without the necessity of providing pedal stops in the actual Organs. This matter deserves the serious consideration of organists and others interested in the Organ, as a musical instrument, at this time of competitive organ-building.

It is perhaps unnecessary to point out that in approaching the subject of the proper tonal appointment of the Church Organ, one enters on the consideration of a problem widely different in its special bearings to those presented by the appointment of Concert-room and Chamber Organs. Between the true Church Organ and either of the instruments just named there are very few points in common beyond those which relate to general excellence of manufacture and refinement and purity of tone. Just as the three instruments are destined for different spheres of usefulness in the realms of music, so must they, when properly schemed and appointed, be widely different in their tonal resources, departmental treatment, and musical coloring. Excellence of workmanship, perfection of voicing, and the highest flexibility and powers of expression, are alike required in every class of Organ.

A Church Organ should be schemed throughout on the simplest and most thorough principles: there should be no ambition on the part of its designer to make a display in the form of a great number of speaking stops; but, on the contrary, a determination to have, in every possible way, a work of art—developed on the soundest lines, and true and perfect in materials and workmanship. The tonal structure of the instrument, be it small or large, should be characterized by gravity, dignity, and softness:—gravity, secured by an adequate and properly-balanced pedal department; dignity, by volume of foundation-tone in the basic divisions of the instrument; and softness and refinement, by skilful voicing with a copious wind stream at a moderate pressure.   Dignity combined with softness cannot be secured by insufficient and small-scaled foundation unisons in both pedal and manual departments, numerous ear-tickling and unnecessary stops, many ranks of high-pitched pipes, and blatant reeds, blown by high-pressure wind until they scream a coarse apology for their shortcomings.   Gravity combined with softness and refinement cannot be secured by a borrowed Pedal Organ, or by a single master-of-all-work pedal stop—a " booming " OPEN DIAPASON, 16 FT., or a large-scaled tubby-toned BOURDON, without control as regards strength of tone and expression.

A properly appointed Church Organ, containing nothing but complete stops of proper scales and an adequate pedal department, constructed of the best materials and by a conscientious builder, must of necessity be a somewhat costly affair; but it will fully represent the money expended, and prove a lasting satisfaction to all concerned in its fabrication and use.   Such an Organ, under proper care, should last for centuries.

Just a few words of advice to those who may be interested in the procural of a Church Organ, and we shall pass on to the consideration of matters of detail.   When an Organ is required, and the funds immediately available are limited (as is almost invariably the case), there are two straightforward and sensible modes of procedure, with reference to its construction, open to the purchaser.   First, if the church is small, do not aim at having an instrument out of all reasonable proportion to it; but be satisfied to accept the judgment of your organ architect, who has no interest in misleading you, and procure an Organ which will be amply sufficient to sustain, in refined and dignified accompaniment, the choir and congregation in all portions of the musical service.   Follow this course firmly, and intrust the work to a builder of proved taste, skill, and probity.   Remain persistently deaf to the expostulations of your enthusiastic organist, and the allurements of the *tradesman,* who, with a lengthy and fascinating list of small and short stops and specious promises, offers tempting and *apparently* substantial advantages.

Secondly, if the church is large, and the funds immediately forthcoming are obviously insufficient for the purchase of an Organ of the necessary size and tonal character, built as a Church Organ ought to be built, do not aim at having a complete instrument all at once,—cheap, badly constructed, and a continual source of trouble and disappointment. The best course to adopt is as follows: Call in a reliable expert; furnish him with full particulars regarding the music of your services; allow him to carefully inspect the church and test its acoustical peculiarities (every church differs in these) ; and instruct him to prepare a Specification for a true Church Organ, embodying all legitimate requirements and meeting all conditions, and of just sufficient volume and variety of tone for the church and the extreme demands of the most elaborate musical service ever likely to be held therein. Then state the present limit of your funds, and consult him as to the most desirable way of expending them on the projected instrument.

Let the scheme, so far as the bellows and their adjuncts, the wind-chests, the entire action and mechanical accessories, and the case, are concerned, be carried out in its entirety; and let preparation be made for all the tonal forces contemplated. The balance of the funds, after paying for the above, should be devoted to the procural of the foundation-stops and those most necessary for the simple accompaniment of the musical services. The remaining stops can be added subsequently and by degrees as money is obtained. Private generosity is ever at work in church matters, and an unfinished Organ is a favorable field for its operations. When it is known that the Organ has, so far, been constructed on the most perfect known lines, and that provision has been made for the reception of further speaking stops, the list of which can be inspected, one may calculate on the completion of the instrument at no very distant date. It will be a great and lasting satisfaction to all parties concerned to know that nothing has been done in a cheap and careless manner, and that all the work has been constructed of the proper materials, under experienced supervision. The voice of the Organ will speak for itself. The beginning has been wisely essayed; and the ending, albeit somewhat delayed, cannot but be entirely satisfactory.

Of course, when funds are ample all the difficulties hinted at above have practically no existence: but, in the name of art and common-sense, let the money be expended in procuring an Organ of the highest possible quality, constructed of the finest and most durable materials and with the best of workmanship, and containing the requisite number of properly-balanced and beautifully-voiced stops, suited for the highest class of ecclesiastical music; rather than a large and unwieldly instrument of inferior workmanship and materials, which will eventually prove a huge disappointment to every one connected with its procural and use, and which will entail a continual expenditure to keep it in working order. *The better an Organ is built the cheaper it will be in the end.* This is a fact to be added to the great advantages, in the musical direction, secured by the scientific and artistic treatment of the tonal forces.

GENERAL SCHEME OF THE ORGAN

DIVISIONS AND CLAVIERS.—The Church Organ, in its true form as an accompanimental instrument, should not have less than three, whilst it need not, under all ordinary conditions, have more than four independent tonal divisions; one, in both cases, being the Pedal Organ. When of three divisions, the two commanded by the manual claviers will be those commonly known as the Great and Swell Organs, and appropriately so when the latter division is alone expressive. When of four divisions, the three commanded by the manual claviers will, in like manner, be those commonly designated the Great, Choir, and Swell Organs. In the ordinary Church Organs, as at present tonally appointed, these terms may be retained: but in an advanced and more artistic system of tonal apportionment, having largely extended, or what may be considered complete, powers of flexibility and expression, the old-fashioned terms are neither expressive nor appropriate, and may with logical propriety be abandoned. The term Swell Organ, in a distinctive sense, becomes to a large extent meaningless, when all the divisions are either entirely or largely inclosed in independent swell-boxes, and become expressive divisions—as we maintain they should on both musical and artistic grounds. In a fully expressive accompanimental Church Organ, all its divisions should be Swell Organs and all its divisions Choir Organs. Accordingly, we advocate, in relation to a more artistic system of tonal appointment and apportionment, the adoption, for the manual divisions, of the simple terms First Organ, Second Organ, and Third Organ, retaining the old and appropriate name Pedal Organ; in the manner exemplified in the Grand Organ in the Church of Our Lady of Grace, Hoboken, N. J.* The compass of the manual claviers is now, properly and by common consent, five octaves—CC to c^4. The compass of the pedal clavier being thirty-two notes—CCC to G. In an Organ having two manual claviers, the Great or First Organ clavier should occupy the lower, and the Swell or Second Organ clavier the higher position. This is the accepted position at the present time. When there are three claviers, the lowest should command the fundamental division of the instrument—the Great or First Organ; the middle clavier the Choir or Second Organ; and the highest clavier the Swell or Third Organ. We strongly recommend this arrangement, especially in connection with the system of tonal apportionment we advocate, with its attendant compound powers of flexibility and expression. This logical arrangement of the claviers was invariably advocated and specified by the greatest organ-player of the last century, the late W. T. Best, of Liverpool; and that for both Church and Concert-room Organs. An example is furnished by the Organ in the Albert Hall, Sheffield, constructed by A. Cavaillé-Coll, under Mr. Best's directions. Both French and German builders have favored the arrangement. It is not, however, the old-fashioned one in this country, and will, accordingly, be objected

* See Chapter on " The Organ Specification."

to by groove-loving organ-builders and organists for some time to come.

We feel, that in advocating only three manual divisions, we shall be blamed by the whole world of ambitious organists, who are naturally proud of their executive abilities and desire Organs of the first magnitude,—of the Concert-room type, or at least, with all its resources,—whereon they can display, not their self-restrained and musicianly powers in the dignified and refined style of playing suited to ecclesiastical music, but the full extent of their powers as performers in *all classes* of music,—sacred and profane. It is quite certain if such organists cannot properly render, on a well-appointed three-manualed Organ, *all* the music that can be called for within the walls of a church, they will fail to do so on an instrument of four or five manuals. We cannot avoid, and do not seek to avoid, the condemnation of such performers. We adhere to the artistic and common-sense view of the matter, simply defining the true Church Organ as an instrument *sui generis;* unhesitatingly affirming that it is not a Concert Organ, and that it should not be impaired by any attempts to make it like one, with the inevitable result of rendering it insufficient for its chief, and, indeed, its only proper office. In an instrument of moderate size, schemed on the many-claviered, Concert-room type, a serious loss of grandeur and dignified volume of tone will be sacrificed to secure solo or " fancy " stops of indifferent mixing and building-up powers. A small Organ under such conditions becomes an " ear-tickler," rather than a solemn and noble-voiced instrument, fit for the appropriate accompaniment of the sacred songs of the Church. Of course, the simple multiplication of keyboards does not affect the sounds of the pipe-work; it merely cuts the instrument up into small, and often ineffective, divisions, and gives the performer facilities for making frequent and rapid changes of tonality,—changes by no means indispensable or generally desirable in the accompaniment of church music.

In English Church Organs of the first magnitude, designed for the accompaniment of the full cathedral service, four manual divisions are deemed sufficient; while the great majority of the finest Organs have only three manuals. In France, however, Church Organs of the largest size, built in recent times, have five manual divisions; for instance, the Grand Organs of the Cathedral of Notre-Dame and the Church of Saint-Sulpice, at Paris. Such instruments invariably occupy the west-end position, and are seldom, if ever, used for simple accompaniment. Another small and strictly accompanimental Organ is provided and placed in the choir in each instance. In the Church of the Madelaine, at Paris, the Grand Organ is elevated over the central entrance, while the Choir Organ (L'Orgue d'Accompagnement), an instrument dignified and refined in tone, is placed at the opposite end of the church, behind the high altar. The celebrated Organ in the Cathedral of Haarlem has only three manuals. In Germany, while several Church Organs which have been built or altered in recent times, have four manual claviers, the generality of the large Organs have only three. In the United States there are no lines of demarkation recognized between a Church and a Concert-room Organ; and, indeed, the fashionable and altarless American auditorium strongly resembles a concert-room, and much of the music performed therein lacks the true ecclesiastical character.

THE ACTION.—Four kinds of clavier action have up to the present time been used in the construction of Church Organs; namely, the early tracker action; the tracker and pneumatic-lever action; the tubular-pneumatic action; and the electro-pneumatic action, commonly called the electric action. So far as work of to-day is concerned, the two first-named actions may be passed over without further comment. The tubular-pneumatic action, which for a considerable time was held in high favor, and which has still, when properly constructed and applied under favorable conditions, much to recommend it, is now falling gradually out of use in many quarters. When it can be used with advantage, we have, from past experience, no hesitation in recommending its being considered. Ten years ago a very important Organ was constructed, with a tubular action throughout, from our Specification. Up to this moment of writing, the action has not shown a single defect or called for a single repair—a record few Organs can approach and still fewer surpass, whatever their actions may be.

Owing to the extensive use of electricity in almost all branches of manufacture and art at the present time; and the development that has recently taken place in the mechanical appointment of the Organ, in which electricity has become a potent factor, there can be no doubt that electro-pneumatic actions will soon be used exclusively in all Organs of any importance and for which current is available. Whether electro-pneumatic actions have now reached their highest point of excellence in simplicity and durability, it is impossible to say: but that *the action* of The Twentieth Century Organ is either with us in the hands of some clever inventor, or will soon be forthcoming, may be accepted as a certainty.

If the advantage of the electro-pneumatic action obtained only in the all-important fact that it admitted of the console of the Organ being placed anywhere most convenient for the organist to perform his duties as leader and accompanist of his choir, it would be sufficient in itself to establish its superiority, in connection with the Church Organ, over all other actions hitherto used. There is another advantage beyond that just mentioned; namely, that the action allows the console to be so located with respect to the sound-producing portion of the Organ, that the performer can at all times have a perfect knowledge of the musical effects he is producing, just as they are heard by others. It is no longer necessary for the claviers to be buried in the Organ; or for the console to be crowded against or placed close to, the sound-producing portions of the instrument. And, further, as the console is connected with the Organ by a flexible cable of any desirable length, it can be moved from place to place as circumstances may dictate.

COUPLERS.—According to the present prevailing unsystematic tonal appointment and divisional apportionment in Church Organs, the undesirable use of couplers between the manual claviers is necessary when the effective groupings of special families of tone-colors are desired: while in instruments tonally schemed on more artistic and logical lines, the use of couplers between the claviers is much less necessary. It must be borne in mind that the excessive resort to coupling seriously cripples the Organ, by interfering with the desirable independence of the claviers. Every care should be taken, in scheming the tonal appointment and apportionment, to impart special and distinctive coloring to the several manual divisions, so as to minimize the resort to coupling. The more artistically a Church Organ is tonally schemed, the less will couplers have to be resorted to for the production of beautiful and impressive effects.

There are three different classes of couplers which act on the manual claviers. First, those which connect one clavier with another in three ways,—the unison, the octave, and the sub-octave. Secondly, those which act on a single clavier uniting its notes in octaves and sub-octaves. Thirdly, those which connect the lower thirty-two notes of each manual clavier to the pedal clavier. The proper selection of the purely manual coupler is a matter of judgment and taste; but at the same time the selection should be made with due regard to the stop appointment of the different divisions of the instrument.

It is desirable that an ordinary Church Organ, with two manual claviers, should have all the following couplers, especially if the stops which the claviers command do not exceed twenty-five in number:

    I. Swell to Great, Unison coupler.
    II. Swell to Great, Octave coupler.
    III. Swell to Great, Sub-octave coupler.
    IV. Great to Pedal, Coupler.
    V. Swell to Pedal, Coupler.

In larger instruments, which may have a stop or stops of 16 ft. pitch in one or both of the manual divisions, the Swell to Great, Sub-octave coupler, may be omitted without any disadvantage. Some organists prefer the Octave coupler to affect the Great clavier only or the Swell clavier only; but we are convinced that in Organs of the class we advocate, the Swell to Great, Octave coupler, will be found to be more generally useful. It is true the Octave coupler on the Swell clavier only can also be commanded by the Great clavier when the Swell to Great, Unison coupler is drawn; but this involves the unison on the Swell in addition to the octave sounds, an effect not always desirable. This coupler question, so far as the true Church Organ is concerned, is not, however, one of paramount importance. A carefully schemed and well-balanced instrument will meet all legitimate demands made upon its musical resources even when it has only the Unison manual coupler and the two manual to pedal couplers.

In Church Organs with three manual claviers the following manual and pedal couplers are to be recommended:

      I. Swell to Great, Unison coupler.
     II. Swell to Great, Octave coupler.
    III. Swell to Choir, Unison coupler.
    IV. Choir to Great, Unison coupler.
     V. Choir to Great, Octave coupler.
    VI. Choir to Great, Sub-octave coupler.
   VII. Great to Pedal, Coupler.
  VIII. Choir to Pedal, Coupler.
    IX. Swell to Pedal, Coupler.

As in the preceding case, when there is a stop of 16 ft. pitch in the Great or Swell divisions, the Sub-octave coupler may be omitted; and, when the Choir Organ is an expressive division, a Choir to Great, Octave coupler, is a valuable addition. The resources of the Great clavier are materially increased by the Octave couplers, especially as they affect stops which are capable of being artistically adjusted to accord, in strength of tone, with the unison stops on the unexpressive clavier. When the Organ of three or four manual divisions is tonally appointed and apportioned in the advanced manner advocated and introduced by us, as a step toward the development of The Organ of the Twentieth Century, and in which compound expression is given to the several divisions, an extended system of couplers becomes necessary. An example of this system will be found in the Mechanical Appliances set forth in the description of the Church Organ given in the Chapter on The Organ Specification. In this example it will be observed that no Octave or Sub-octave coupler is introduced in any clavier, operating on itself. This we have avoided on scientific grounds. An Octave coupler operating on the same clavier as commands the unison tones, amounts to nothing more than direct borrowing in its effects; and operates in violation of the natural phenomena of compound musical sounds, which show that partial tones, higher in pitch than the foundation or prime tones, decrease in strength as they rise in pitch.

All the couplers which add to the tonal resources of any division of the Organ are strictly agents belonging to that division; and their draw-knobs, rocking-tablets, or touches may be correctly placed in the group commanding the speaking stops of the division. In many consoles this method has been followed: but at the present time the general opinion is in favor of locating the coupler control—preferably in the form of tablets or hanging touches—immediately above the upper clavier. There is much to recommend this latter arrangement, and it is almost certain to be universally adopted in connection with electro-pneumatic actions.

DRAW-STOP AND COMBINATION ACTIONS.—In all Church Organs, the draw-stop action will properly be of the same nature as the general action of the claviers, whether tubular-pneumatic or electro-pneumatic. When the action is tubular-pneumatic, draw-stop knobs of the usual approved form will in all probability be preferred: but when the action is electro-pneumatic, draw-knobs, rocking-tablets, or any desirable form of touches can be adopted with equal effect. On the other hand, while in the tubular-pneumatic action the position of the draw-knobs may, to a considerable extent, be dictated by the work they have to do; it is obvious, on account of the very little work, merely amounting to simple metallic contacts, that the electro-pneumatic action calls for, the positions occupied by the draw-knobs, rocking-tablets, or touches are entirely at the will of the organ architect or organ-builder, to be decided by taste and convenience. The positions most easily commanded by the eyes and hands of the performer, while properly seated at the claviers, will naturally be selected.

The dispositions of the draw-stop knobs, which have been adopted with the view to convenience, are as follows: 1. In vertical jambs, placed at about the angle of 45° from the left and right cheeks of the manual claviers, the knobs being arranged in groups; those commanding the stops of the Pedal and Swell Organs being conveniently disposed in the left jamb, and those commanding the stops of the Great and Choir Organs in the right jamb. 2. In straight, stepped tiers, practically continuing the lines of the claviers, the knobs being disposed in rows. 3. In straight, stepped tiers, carried at an angle from the cheeks of the claviers, the knobs being disposed in rows. 4. In stepped tiers, extending from the cheeks of the claviers in a quadrant form. When rocking-tablets are used, they can be attached to vertical or sloping jambs placed at any convenient angle from the left and right cheeks of the claviers; or they can be arranged in rows in a curved or quadrant form. Any description of projecting or hanging touches may be similarly disposed. In all forms of draw-stop actions, clear visibility and ease of manipulation are the essential elements of perfection. The console of the Grand Organ in the Cathedral of Notre-Dame, Paris, is illustrated in Fig. XVII. in

Chapter VI., in which is shown the stepped, quadrant form of jamb.

In addition to a perfectly satisfactory draw-stop action, every Church Organ, of any pretensions toward completeness, should have an adjustable combination action, commanded by thumb-pistons located directly under the claviers of the divisions on which they operate. The number of these pistons will vary according to the number of the speaking stops they can command. It is necessary, to make the combination action thoroughly efficient, that combinations can be set or changed on any or all of the pistons easily and quickly by the performer while seated at the claviers. The combination action should be such as to embrace the Pedal Organ stops, and the couplers operating on the several manual claviers. A set of combination pistons commanding all the Pedal Organ stops, independently of the manual pistons, should be provided. These may, conveniently, be placed under the bass octave of the lower clavier. Toe-pistons or levers should also be provided, duplicating the pistons, and located directly above the pedal clavier.

EXPRESSION LEVERS.—These rocking-levers, commonly, but not very appropriately, called swell-pedals, assume considerable importance in some modern Organs, and are destined to become still more important appliances in The Organ of the Twentieth Century. Their office is to open and close, in response to the pressure of the organist's foot, the shutters of the swell-boxes in which are inclosed the speaking stops of the divisions of the Organ which are thereby rendered expressive and flexible. The expression lever, now applied to all properly constructed Organs, is of the balanced form: that is, it is pivoted in the center, and is so connected with the shutters of the swell-box, that whilst it moves freely, in response to the pressure of the performer's foot in either opening or closing the swell-box, it remains balanced; and will retain any position the foot leaves it in. In an Organ in which there is only one swell-box, the expression lever should occupy the position immediately above the EE and FF keys of the pedal clavier, or over the FF and GG keys if preferred. When two expression levers are required, they should be placed side by side, with not more than half an inch of space between their inner edges: this space should be directly over the space between the EE and FF keys. When three expression levers are necessary, the central one, commanding the Swell Organ, to be placed directly over the space between the DD♯ and FF♯ keys; that commanding the Choir Organ, to be placed to the left; and that commanding the Solo Organ to the right of the Swell Organ lever. This arrangement implies an Organ of four manual divisions, the Great Organ having to be added, which, according to old-fashioned ideas, does not call for any powers of expression or flexibility. As the Solo Organ can well be dispensed with, save in the concert-room type of Church Organ, the three expression levers will command the swells of the Great or First Organ, the Choir or Second Organ, and the Swell or Third Organ; or such subdivisions as may be apportioned to the three swell-boxes under our system of compound expression. The expression levers should be about 10 inches long and 4 inches wide, placed ½ inch apart.

The crescendo lever to be in all cases located to the right of the expression levers, and to be treated in some slightly distinctive manner.

TREMOLANT.—When judiciously and artistically used, the TREMO-LANT imparts a pleasing effect to the voices of certain stops; but a too liberal and a tasteless employment of its *tremolo* is essentially vulgar and distressing to the educated ear. As its artistic use is far more uncommon than the reverse, many persons with refined musical sense have advocated the omission of the TREMOLANT from the Church Organ; but we do not consider their argument to be a good one. An Organ should be designed for the *artist* and not for the *bungler;* for it may be said, that under the hands of the latter not only the TREMOLANT but every stop and appliance in the instrument runs a great risk of being abused in some fashion.

No rule save a very general one can be given for the introduction or application of the TREMOLANT in the Church Organ; for, in the absence of a list of its speaking stops, it is impossible to say where the *tremolo* is required, or, indeed, if it is necessary at all. The general rule alluded to confines its application to manual stops inclosed in a swell-box; and when the division has more than one pressure of wind, to the portion in which the stops of a solo character are congregated. There is only one speaking stop in the Organ whose characteristic voice depends on the effect of the TREMOLANT: we allude to the VOX HUMANA. The introduction of this stop involves the application of the TREMOLANT.

Should there be more than one TREMOLANT in a Church Organ? This question can only be answered after an inspection of the scheme of the instrument. If there are two expressive divisions, and both contain soft and solo voices which are suitable for the *tremolo* effect, then each division may have a TREMOLANT affecting those stops.

SPEAKING STOPS.—The selection of the speaking stops for all classes of Organs is a matter of the greatest importance; and one which in all cases should be governed by the purposes for which the instruments are destined, and the demands which, in the proper order of things, are to be made on their musical resources. It is either from an entire misconception of the matter, or an equally serious neglect of the problem it involves, that so many modern Church Organs have been spoiled or rendered insufficient instruments. There is another cause for many failures. When the organist of a church is allowed to specify the contents of a new Organ, he is very apt to make it a personal matter, and either purposely or intuitively adapt the Specification to his own fancy and style of playing; forgetting that other organists are to come after him who are certain to disapprove of his arrangements. All this makes the advent of the independent organ expert highly desirable— the designer who will work on broad principles, born of science and art, and indulge in no personal whims and caprices.

Modern ingenuity has added numerous stops, chiefly of an imitative character, to the list of stops which was at the disposal of the organ builders of the eighteenth century and the beginning of the nineteenth; and, accordingly, the designer of Organs in the present day is subjected to considerable temptation when engaged in making a selection for any instrument. Unless he has a comprehensive knowledge of the nature and tonal qualities of all the organ stops at his disposal, and a practical acquaintance with their behavior on different pressures of wind; and unless he steadily holds in view the nature and uses of the instrument he is scheming, he is almost certain to make serious mistakes; sacrificing that which should be the governing feature in the tonal scheme, for what may be mere ear-tickling effects. There is little doubt that the ambition of organists to have the Church Organs schemed by them, adapted for solo or recital purposes, has done much to incapacitate instruments of small, or even moderate, dimensions for their true and legitimate office—the dignified and appropriate accompaniment of sacred song. When Organs are large, there is scope for the insertion of tonal materials for all classes of music: and so long as the Organ proper, in its true church aspect as an accompanimental instrument, is amply appointed, there need be no exception taken to the addition of stops suitable for solo playing or for the production of varied orchestral effects.

The most important stops, and, indeed, those upon which the whole tonal structure of the Organ is based and built up, are commonly classed under the general appellation of *Foundation-work*. The name is appropriate, and fully expresses the important office fulfilled by the stops in question. In the manual department of the Organ such stops are formed of open metal pipes of cylindrical form, yielding tones, peculiar to organ pipes, of great purity and volume. Their tones are, generally considered, of a simple nature, that is deficient in harmonic or upper partial tones. First in order of importance among the stops forming the foundation of the Organ are those known in English-speaking countries as the DIA-PASONS; and subordinate are those derived from, and strictly attendant on, the DIAPASONS, yielding voices which represent and corroborate the upper partial tones of the prime or unison tones. The most important of these corroborating stops are the OCTAVE, 4 FT., TWELFTH, $2\frac{2}{3}$ FT., and SUPER-OCTAVE, 2 FT. There can be no question that upon the proper scaling and voicing of the fundamental DIAPASONS, and upon the relative scaling and strengths of tone of all the derived harmonic-corroborating stops, the true and dignified Church Organ stands or falls as an instrument worthy of its place and office. First of all, therefore, it is imperative that these foundation stops should receive the greatest consideration in all matters connected with their materials, formation, and voicing. In all cases the richest " confluent-metal " or spotted-metal should be used in the fabrication of their pipes. In old times tin, almost pure, was commonly used. And it is essential that the metal should be of sufficient substance or thickness to render the pipes perfectly firm in their speech, and durable. Zinc pipes have come into use during late years, but beyond their relative cheapness they have nothing to recommend them. They should never be allowed in an Organ under four feet in speaking length.

When two or more DIAPASONS are planted in the same Organ, it is imperative that their scales should be different, and that their style of voicing should be markedly dissimilar. Not only does this treatment secure diversity of tone and different degrees of power, but it prevents a loss of volume in their combined tone through what may be called acoustical sympathy, the operation of which is not well understood. In very large Organs, or in instruments which have to prove efficient in large churches, perhaps not very good acoustically, it is desirable to add, in the foundation division, to the metal DIAPASONS a DIAPASON, 8 FT., of open wood pipes. The fine open wood DIAPASON pipes inserted by Schulze in his grand Organ in the Church of St. Bartholomew, at Armley, Yorkshire, clearly show what can be achieved in this direction.

In addition to the three harmonic-corroborating stops already mentioned, it is necessary in all instruments in which anything approaching completeness of tonal structure is aimed at, that further ranks of organ-toned pipes, associated in the form of MIXTURES, be inserted, to add richness and brilliancy to the foundation tone by corroborating the higher upper partials. Without the full complement (from the practical point of view) of the harmonic-corroborating stops, simple and compound, the Organ cannot be considered complete; and it will certainly not possess that rich and complex character of tone which is one of the chief elements of its beauty and impressiveness. It is, however, essential that all the harmonic-corroborating stops be rendered flexible, by being inclosed in a swell-box, so that they may be used in soft as well as in loud effects. A properly proportioned series of harmonic-corroborating stops cannot but add greatly to the musical value and beauty of the Organ; while, on the other hand, a badly proportioned series is fatal to the musical character of the instrument.

The greatest care and judgment must be exercised in all matters relating to the introduction of the compound stops, as all stops of the MIXTURE class may be generally termed; and, strange to say, little or nothing beyond negative teaching is to be derived from a study of the works of the old-organ builders. It is beyond all reasonable question that the early English and Continental builders and their immediate successors erred in making their MIXTURES far too assertive, by introducing inordinate scales and loud voicing, and by an unwise multiplication of them in their Organs. For instance, Father Smith inserted in his Temple Church Organ, which contained in all only twenty-three speaking stops no fewer than five MIXTURES. These comprised 713 pipes out of the total number of 1,715 pipes in the instrument. Again, in the Great division of the Organ built by Renatus Harris for the Church of St. Sepulchre, Snow Hill, London, three MIXTURES were included in the list of fifteen stops. Loudly-voiced MIXTURES, introduced in such numbers, go entirely beyond their province in the tonal structure of the Organ, and entirely upset the acoustical conditions which guarantee the introduction of such peculiar stops in proper form and proportion.

Next in importance to the foundation unisons and their harmonic-corroborating companions, come the so-called DOUBLES, or manual sub-octave stops of 16 ft. pitch. While it is necessary to be careful in the introduction of such grave voices, there can be no question as regards their great value in the Church Organ. Considering the instrument in its most important function,—that of accompaniment to a number of voices singing in harmony,—it will be observed that the unisons, combined with the octave and the higher harmonic-corroborating stops, sustain the Treble voices in a perfectly satisfactory manner; but that the Tenors and especially the Basses are not supported and enriched to the same degree. To meet this requirement a soft stop of 16 ft. pitch is required. Hence the importance of having at least one stop of the class in the manual department of every Church Organ of any pretension to completeness. In addition to the importance of having a sub-octave stop for ordinary accompanimental music, such a stop is of great value in imparting fulness and dignity beyond what is attainable by any multiplication of unison stops. Dr. Hopkins, speaking on this subject, remarks:—

" If a chord be played in the treble part of the Great Organ of an instrument in a large building, and not having any stops lower in pitch than the unison, there will be perceived a certain *smallness* of effect, which makes it evident that, although the treble may possess sufficient brightness and intensity, perhaps even amounting to shrillness, yet it lacks the amount of fulness and volume necessary to produce an ample and dignified tone. This arises from the fact of even the unison pipes in the treble being comparatively acute in their sound; and, therefore, in the very nature of things, unpossessed of stately impressiveness. It thus becomes obvious that the harmonic-corroborating series of stops alone do not present *all* the resources necessary to form a satisfactory Organ. Something that is essential appears to be wanting; and a fresh element is felt to be necessary to supply that absent property. The property wanting is *gravity;* which possesses a character peculiar to itself, and for the absence of which no amount of *intensity* in the other sounds will compensate. Of the traveling and filling-up character of grave sounds we have already spoken; and of the fact itself, a sufficient illustration is given in the circumstance of a chant sung by twenty tenor and bass voices, in unison, pervading a building more completely than if sung by thrice the number of trebles. Again, the deep tone of a pedal DIAPASON will travel through a building more entirely than a double chord of six or seven notes played on the manual DIAPASONS from middle c^1 upwards. Its sound will certainly not be nearly so well defined; but it will be of a more pervading character. The want felt, and above specified, however, is not a *substitute* for the harmonic sounds, but a new element, which, *added* to them, shall render the general tone larger and more ample. It is worth mentioning, that this want was so much felt, nearly three centuries and a half ago, abroad, that means were, even at that period, taken to supply the deficiency. It was about the year 1508, that a covered stop, of 16 ft. size of tone, was invented in Holland; and which, to some extent, imparted the necessary, deep, resonant, *humming* effect to the other stops, and was hence expressly called *Bourdon;* a name that means a hum or drone; and which stop has never ceased to be highly valued abroad to this day."

From the above remarks, the reader can hardly fail to realize the importance of one or more stops of 16 ft. pitch on the manuals; and it now remains for consideration what description of stop should be introduced in Organs of different sizes; and at what point, with reference to the contents of any manual division, so grave a voice becomes advisable if not imperative. The latter question may conveniently be taken first. So soon as sufficient unison, octave, and higher harmonic-corroborating tones are provided to accompany, in a fairly effective manner, the voices of the choir and congregation, then, and then only, should a stop of 16 ft. tone be contemplated; and it should be added in preference to any further multiplication of unison stops, or the introduction of stops of an orchestral or fancy character. When the manual divisions are furnished with the proper tonal forces to support, equally, all the voices in full harmony, then may imitative and fancy stops be inserted, with the view of further enriching the general tone, and securing the means of imparting variety of coloring and strength of tone to the lighter accompanimental and incidental music of the services. Speaking by way of general guidance, we recommend that every Church Organ be provided with a stop of 16 ft. tone in the manual department, even when that department comprises only a dozen stops in all. This number may be extended to twenty; but in larger instruments, the manual stops of which are distributed in two divisions, two stops of 16 ft. pitch should be introduced. In the fundamental and probably unexpressive divisions, a DOUBLE DIAPASON, DOUBLE DULCIANA, or CONTRA-VIOL (not too assertive in tone) should be inserted; while in the expressive division a small-scaled BOURDON or a full-toned LIEBLICH-

GEDECKT, 16 FT., should be introduced. This arrangement will be satisfactory, and will not require the swell-box to be of excessive dimensions. In still larger Organs having three manual divisions, two of which, at least, should be expressive, a stop of 16 ft. pitch should be planted in each: the third one, in this case, may with advantage be a medium-toned reed such as a CONTRAFAGOTTO, 16 FT. In the fundamental division, and especially if it is partly expressive (as it always should be), a DOUBLE TRUMPET, 16 FT., may be introduced to great advantage; but not unless a unison TRUMPET is also present in the same expressive subdivision. Then, to counteract the pulling-down effect of the DOUBLE stop, a CLARION or OCTAVE TRUMPET, 4 FT., will be required—completing that family of brass-tone.

It is scarcely necessary to point out that the Swell to Great, Sub-octave coupler, gives the organist ready means of adding several varieties and strengths of 16 ft. tone to any combinations in the Great Organ, down to Tenor C: and, further, that the same coupler furnishes the Great manual with a soft 32 ft. tone down to the same note, when the LIEBLICHGEDECKT or BOURDON in the Swell Organ is drawn. The utility of this coupler is thus made evident. Few Church Organs have a stop of 32 ft. pitch in any manual division. Two noteworthy instances may be mentioned:—the Organ in the Parish Church of Leeds has in its Great division a SUB-BOURDON, 32 FT., of wood and metal, down to Tenor C; and the Organ in the Parish Church of Doncaster has a stop of the same name, pitch and compass, in its Great division. Both these stops were made by the renowned Schulze, of Paulinzelle, who evidently believed in the value and beauty of grave tones in the manual department. We cannot, however, advocate the direct introduction of the 32 ft. tone, as furnished by an independent stop, in anything save Pedal Organs of important size. Should so grave a sound ever be required on the Great Organ clavier, it can be obtained, in sufficient volume for any legitimate musical effect, by the use of the Sub-octave coupler, as above mentioned.

On the subject of other labial stops which are desirable in the Church Organ little need be said here; nevertheless it must not be passed over altogether. Up to the present point we have, with the exception of the covered sub-octave stop suitable for the manual department, and the SUB-BOURDON as introduced by Schulze, spoken of open stops, or those important ranks of pipes which form the backbone of the Organ proper; now attention may be directed to another class of stops, secondary only in importance to the open foundation-work. We allude to the stopped or covered ranks known by the names, STOPPED DIAPASON, LIEBLICH-GEDECKT, ROHRFLÖTE, DOPPELFLÖTE, etc. All these stops, when of proper scales and artistically voiced, produce tones of good mixing and filling-up qualities; imparting to the tones of the open metal stops great roundness and increased solidity and sonorousness. This is due to the entire dissimilarity of their voices; and, accordingly, to the total absence of that acoustical sympathy which seems to reduce power by absorption. Of the stops just named, the DOPPELFLÖTE, 8 FT., is by far the most desirable and effective for the Great Organ, where a full volume of pervading tone is essential.

Next to the true organ-tone, as represented by the foundation-work, is that known as flute-tone; such tone as is yielded by the covered stops just enumerated, and by numerous other stops of both wood and metal, open and covered. Flute-tone, when of a refined quality, is extremely valuable for the accompaniment of the voice; and also for imparting that desirable variety in tonal coloring which may be resorted to in church music without any sacrifice of its general dignity. As a general rule, flute-tone should be kept strictly subordinate to the true organ-tone, for it is a quality the ear soon tires of; but in instruments of large size, such as those suitable for cathedrals or spacious churches, it will be expedient to insert two or more FLUTES of 8 ft. and 4 ft. pitch, having powerful and penetrating voices. We here allude to the HARMONIC FLUTES, the imitative ORCHESTRAL FLUTES, and such a stop as that introduced by Roosevelt in certain Church Organs, under the name of PHILOMELA. The last-named stop is formed of open wood pipes with two mouths; and when blown with wind of moderately high pressure has a voice of singular fulness and grandeur, both alone and in combination.

Stops producing sounds which imitate, more or less closely, the rich compound tones characteristic of the family of orchestral bowed instruments, although of less value in the Church Organ than those previously mentioned, may with great advantage be introduced in the chief expressive division. In instruments of moderate dimensions it is desirable to insert in the Swell Organ a VIOLONCELLO, 8 FT., of strictly imitative character. Such a stop, when skilfully used and played with appropriate expression, forms a beautiful accompaniment to a Tenor or Bass solo, while it furnishes most brilliant passages in combination with the higher voices. All the stops of the VIOL or so-called GAMBA class, on account of the specially rich harmonic structure of their sounds, enter into combination with all the other stops of the Organ but do not lose their individuality by absorption; accordingly, they produce bright and telling effects, and materially enrich the tonal resources of the instrument.

It is hardly necessary, in speaking of the Church Organ, to particularly allude to those stops which are justly classed as " fancy stops." Such may be allowed, or even considered desirable, in large, many-manualed instruments; but their value is questionable in the ordinary Church Organ, where, it is more than probable, their presence is secured at the sacrifice of stops of infinitely greater utility and importance. The craze which obtains among young and inexperienced organists, and a large section of the organ-loving public, for what may be called ear-tickling stops is highly injurious to the true art of organ appointment. The golden rule here is:—Let fancy stops be added to an otherwise perfect Organ, but never be depended upon to perfect an insufficient or faulty instrument.

When a Church Organ has been properly appointed with respect to its foundation-work and labial stops of the desirable classes, it requires but little aid from reed-work. Its presence, however, is desirable, for it imparts what may be called a golden sheen to the already richly colored embroidery of sounds. As Dr. Hopkins says: " Reed stops impart to the full organ stateliness and splendor, and in return receive fulness and brightness from the open series of stops."

In the ordinary Church Organ, the most important of all the manual reed stops is the TRUMPET, 8 FT.; and when properly scaled and voiced by a master hand it adds a highly desirable " stateliness and splendor " to all combinations into which it enters. It is also, when under the control of a swell, well adapted for solo passages of a pronounced character. In every Church Organ of any importance the TRUMPET ought to appear in one of the expressive divisions, or in the Swell Organ when there is only one expressive division. It is undesirable to place so potent a voice in an uninclosed position; but when it is so placed, it is advisable to modify and refine its tone. The Octave of this stop, called the CLARION, 4 FT., is a useful adjunct when the instrument reaches sufficient importance to require a very pronounced octave tone. The CLARION, as an attendant on, and the diminutive of, the TRUMPET, should follow it in tone and disposition. It should be of smaller scale and have a softer voice than the unison reed.

Next to the TRUMPET, in general usefulness comes the OBOE or HAUTBOY, 8 FT., a pleasant soft-toned reed. In small Organs placed in churches in which even a softly-voiced TRUMPET would prove too prominent, the OBOE is the most appropriate reed stop. Under these circumstances, the normal class of OBOE should be selected in preference to the thin-voiced, imitative stop known as the ORCHESTRAL OBOE, which is insufficient for, and out of sympathy with, the true Church Organ. The OBOE should invariably be placed in an expressive division.

In order of interest and utility, now comes the highly characteristic reed stop, the CLARINET, 8 FT. This is a reed of imitative and pleasing quality, which imparts an agreeable variety to the softer combinations, and a peculiar richness of coloring to all in which it may enter. In countless modern Organs, and especially in those of English construction, this stop appears in the unexpressive Choir Organ, or in some other unexpressive division; and that notwithstanding the obvious fact that of all the softer-toned reed stops it is the one which calls most clearly for powers of expression.*

Of the other unison reed stops suitable for Church Organs of average size, such as the HORN, CORNOPEAN, and BASSOON, little need be said in this place beyond pointing out that they should in all cases be placed in expressive divisions. The Vox HUMANA, of which so many vile examples exist in modern Church Organs, occupying the place of really important and badly-wanted stops, may safely be considered both useless and undesirable. It must be classed among the ear-ticklers already spoken of. It is, even when in its best form, of very limited use in solo music; while in legitimate accompanimental music it is of no use whatever.

When space will permit, and even in Church Organs of medium size, it may be found desirable to insert a reed stop of 16 ft. pitch in one of the manual divisions: this stop may be a small-scaled DOUBLE TRUMPET, 16 FT., a DOUBLE BASSOON, or a CONTRA-OBOE, 16 FT. It is hardly necessary to remark, after what has been said respecting other reed stops, that the selected one of 16 ft. must be placed in some expressive division, preferably the Swell Organ.

Except in instruments of the first magnitude, placed in cathedrals or very large churches, the introduction of reed stops voiced on high pressures is very undesirable. The dignity and grandeur of their voices cannot be disputed, and when skilfully used their effect is impressive; but they should invariably be looked upon as adjuncts to an otherwise complete Organ, rather than as integral parts of a necessarily circumscribed tonal structure. Such powerful voices really belong to the Concert-room Organ, in which they represent certain orchestral brass instruments.

These brief notes on the Speaking Stops may be appropriately closed with a few words on the more desirable stops belonging to the pedal department of the Church Organ. In the proper appointment of this most important department two difficulties very commonly present themselves; namely, circumscribed space for the accommodation of pipes of the necessary number and large dimensions; and insufficient funds for the purchase of the somewhat costly stops. An adequate Pedal Organ is, of necessity, a costly and cumbersome affair; but if a perfect, or even a thoroughly useful, instrument is aimed at, an adequate Pedal Organ must be provided. It is out of all reason to expect one or two stops of 16 ft. pitch to furnish a proper and satisfactory bass for all, or indeed any considerable portion of the manual department; yet the

---

* If the interested reader will refer to the list of Church Organs appended to Dr. E. J. Hopkins' work, " The Organ," he will observe of the one hundred Organs there specified only three have stops of the CLARINET species placed in the Swell division, whilst no fewer than ninety examples have the CLARINET (either so-called, or under such names as CREMONA, CORNO DI BASSETTO, KRUMMHORN) placed in the Choir Organ and, accordingly, without means of expression. So much for artistic organ appointment.

number of modern Church Organs which have one or perhaps two such stops forming their only pedal resources is legion.

The unison pitch of the Pedal Organ is 16 feet; and the most useful labial stops of this pitch are the OPEN DIAPASONS, metal and wood, the VIOLONE or DOUBLE BASS VIOL, DULCIANA, BOURDON, and LIEBLICH-GEDECKT. In all possible cases an OPEN DIAPASON, 16 FT., should be introduced, providing the foundation tone of the department and the true bass for the manual DIAPASONS. In large Organs a metal DIA-PASON, 16 FT., of medium scale may be added, in voice between the principal DIAPASON, 16 FT., and the DULCIANA, 16 FT., when the latter is inserted. The VIOLONE or DOUBLE BASS VIOL may be either of metal or wood, formed of open pipes of small scale, and voiced to imitate the tones of the orchestral Double Bass. This stop, when of a soft and refined quality, is invaluable in both accompanimental and solo music. The DULCIANA, 16 FT., is a very softly voiced metal stop, smaller in scale than the metal VIOLONE, yielding a pure organ-tone. As this in-valuable stop is all that can be desired for the bass of the softest accom-paniments, it should in every possible instance be inserted in the Pedal Organ. The BOURDON, 16 FT. TONE, a much abused and much over-used stop,—the delight of the cheap organ-builder,—is unquestionably a valuable stop in its correct place in the tonal structure of a complete Pedal Organ; but it should never, under ordinary circumstances, be depended upon for the principal unison tone of the department, even in the smallest Church instrument. The LIEBLICHGEDECKT, 16 FT. TONE, a small-scaled, covered wood stop, is extremely valuable; and when carefully voiced on a copious wind of medium pressure is suitable for insertion in the smallest Church Organs, when a stop of 16 feet speak-ing length can neither be afforded nor accommodated. It is preferable to the BOURDON on account of the purity and clear intonation of its voice.

Every Pedal Organ, however small it may be, should have an OCTAVE, 8 FT., of some description. In the case of instruments for which either space or funds are limited this OCTAVE may be borrowed from the unison stop, by means of an Octave coupler and the inexpensive addition of an upper octave of pipes. But in all possible cases an independent stop of 8 ft. speaking length should be inserted, either in the form of a BASS FLUTE of open wood, or a VIOLONCELLO of metal or wood. In the case of a borrowed OCTAVE it is, of course, impossible to have it softer in tone than the unison from which it is derived; and both scientifically and artistically considered this is an objection which deserves attention. When the OCTAVE is an independent stop, it should be voiced consider-ably softer in tone than the principal stop of 16 ft. pitch in the depart-ment.

In instruments of medium size, a QUINT, $10\frac{2}{3}$ FT., may be inserted.

When drawn in combination with an open stop of 16 ft., it produces, though somewhat faintly, an impression on the ear of the sub-octave or 32 ft. tone. The reason of the acoustical phenomenon is fully explained in the Chapter on The Tonal Structure of the Organ. In more important Organs a CONTRA-BOURDON, 32 FT. TONE, should be inserted and the QUINT omitted. It is of course, desirable to introduce an open stop of this pitch, the DOUBLE OPEN DIAPASON, 32 FT., but as this stop is expensive and demands considerable room and height for its accommodation, it is only to be contemplated for Organs of the first magnitude or exceptional character. It may be added that it is not really necessary to insert a stop of 32 ft. pitch in the Pedal Organ unless the Double, or 16 ft. tone, is amply represented in the manual department.

In addition to the unison and octave stops above alluded to, every complete Pedal Organ should contain several harmonic-corroborating stops, including a GRAND CORNET in which all the ranks are carried through the compass without breaks, scientifically graduated in strength of tone. Instead of this a less expensive and highly effective COMPENSATING MIXTURE may be inserted. All Pedal Organs, in which anything approaching completeness is aimed at, should have, at least, one reed stop of unison pitch. This may be either a BASS TROMBONE, 16 FT., or a full-tone CONTRAFAGOTTO, 16 FT.; and in large and properly appointed Pedal Organs an octave reed should be added to both or either of the unisons just mentioned, preferably in the form of a TRUMPET, 8 FT. A reed stop of 32 ft. pitch, such as the CONTRA-TROMBONE, CONTRE-BOMBARDE, or CONTRAPOSAUNE, is neither necessary nor desirable save in a large Cathedral Organ.

Other matters connected with the tonal appointment of the Pedal Organ are touched upon in the following section.

THE CHURCH ORGAN OF THE TWENTIETH CENTURY

In the following remarks we shall endeavor to point out to the organ-designer the manner in which, it seems to us, the Church Organ can, without resort to excessive size, be developed into a musical instrument much more artistic and satisfactory in its tonal appointment and divisional apportionment, and endowed with powers of flexibilty and expression largely in advance of the system which obtains in the organ-builders' Church Organ of the present time. We use the term organ-builders' Church Organ, advisedly, because, to all appearance, very little interest has been, or is being, taken in the tonal development of the Organ by organists or other musicians, who appear to be quite content to take what organ-builders think proper to give them. The general musical public and lovers of the Organ cannot be expected to do much in any effective direction, simply because they know little if anything

about the science and art of tonal appointment or the tonal structure of
the Organ. That the Organ can be greatly improved in several directions cannot be questioned: and we maintain that it must be improved
before it can lay claim to be considered The Organ of the Twentieth
Century.

FIRST OR GREAT ORGAN

The question that has to be decided before any steps can be taken
toward the solution of the problem of the scientific and artistic tonal
appointment of the First or Great Organ, is whether the division is to
be entirely unexpressive, partly expressive, or entirely expressive? At
the present time it is very rare indeed to find an organ-builder favoring
the idea of giving this most important division of the tonal forces of the
Organ any powers of flexibility and expression. This is hardly to be
wondered at; for ideas supported by centuries of usage are very difficult
to be abandoned, and especially as the ideas in this direction are favored
by the natural desire of the tradesman to save money wherever it can be
saved. A swell-box such as the stops of the First Organ would call for,
even if only a substantial portion of them were inclosed, would be an
expensive feature which would make no show in the organ-builder's
" specification "; and as such, its omission is to be desired, and would
be unobserved by the purchaser, not conversant with organ construction,
its present shortcomings, or its desirable improvements. All honor, we
say, to the late Hilborne L. Roosevelt, the greatest and most progressive
of American organ-builders, who was the first in this country to realize
the importance of imparting expressive powers to the Great Organ *—a
step in organ improvement we have advocated for half a century, and, in
a small way, put to actual proof forty years ago; before any organ-

* By way of illustrating what Mr. Hilborne L. Roosevelt accomplished in this direction,
we give the appointment of the Great division of the large Organ erected in Trinity Methodist
Episcopal Church, Denver, Colorado.

GREAT ORGAN.

UNEXPRESSIVE SECTION.

| 1. | DOUBLE OPEN DIAPASON, | 16 feet. | 3. | OPEN DIAPASON, | 8 feet. |
| 2. | DOUBLE MELODIA, | 16 " | 4. | OPEN DIAPASON, | 8 " |

EXPRESSIVE SECTION—IN CHOIR SWELL-BOX.

5.	GEMSHORN,	8 feet	12.	OCTAVE QUINT,	$2\frac{2}{3}$ feet.
6.	VIOLA DA GAMBA,	8 "	13.	SUPER-OCTAVE,	2 "
7.	PRINCIPALFLÖTE,	8 "	14.	MIXTURE,	IV. and V. ranks.
8.	DOPPELFLÖTE,	8 "	15.	SCHARF,	III. and IV "
9.	OCTAVE,	4 "	16.	OPHECLEIDE,	16 feet.
10.	GAMBETTE,	4 "	17.	TRUMPET,	8 "
11.	FLÖTE HARMONIQUE,	4 "	18.	CLARION,	4 "

It will be seen that only four stops out of the total number of eighteen contained in
this division are planted in an uninclosed position; namely, the two OPEN DIAPASONS and the
labial DOUBLES; all the remaining stops being planted in the swell-box in which the entire
Choir Organ, of twelve stops, is inclosed. Of the entire number of fifty-five manual stops
in this noteworthy instrument only the four above-named stops of the Great Organ are planted
outside the swell-boxes, of which there are three in the instrument.

builder in the world thought it desirable to extend powers of expression beyond the Swell Organ. We unhesitatingly assert that it is absolutely essential, before an Organ can be pronounced a properly appointed musical instrument, that the First Organ—the fundamental division—be endowed, to as large an extent as musical requirements and taste demand, with powers of flexibility and expression. There is not a single argument from an art or musical point of view that can be effectively advanced against this common-sense and logical treatment of the tonal forces of this all-important fundamental division.

The foundation of the tonal structure of the Organ is pure organ-tone—the tone, in its purity, that can be produced by no other musical instrument invented by man. This characteristic tonality must be made the fullest use of in the appointment of the First Organ. There and there alone it must reign supreme: the solid base upon which the tonal superstructure of the whole instrument must rest. This important fact seems to be systematically ignored in the tonal appointment of Church Organs to-day: the cause being either ignorance of the scientific tonal structure of the Organ, or merely a blind following of what has been so long accepted as satisfactory by groove-loving organ-builders, and unthinking and easily-pleased organists.

The Organ cannot be compared with any other musical instrument in existence; as an instrument under the control of a single performer it stands, and must ever stand, alone and unique. The only musical machine before which it assumes a subordinate position is the complete orchestra; and it is with this complex and animated piece of tonal mechanism alone that any comparison can be instituted, and from which any lessons can be learnt. Such being the case, we have, in building up the tonal structure and appointment of the Organ, to start from a perfectly novel foundation. That foundation is an adequate volume of pure organ-tone of unison pitch.

First of all, in the tonal appointment of the First Organ, it is necessary to select such stops as provide sufficient foundation tone upon which a practically complete harmonic structure can be built. This can only be done by means of the DIAPASONS, 8 FT., yielding pure organ-tone, which, when at its best, is almost entirely free from harmonic upper partials. In small Church Organs, one DIAPASON of full scale and intonation will be sufficient, supported, as it properly will be, by other unisons of varied tonality and strength of voice. In large instruments, two metal DIAPASONS will be necessary to provide the volume of foundation tone required in the division under consideration. These must be of different scales, as has been previously directed, for use separately and in combination. The first DIAPASON should be of large scale, voiced to yield a tone characterized by great volume and roundness—a tone forming, as one might say, a cushion of pure sound upon which all

other sounds of the division will rest in perfect repose. The second
DIAPASON should be smaller in scale, and voiced to yield a lighter and
brighter tone than the preceding. This diversity of tone is valuable on
two important grounds. First, it greatly enhances the mixing properties
of the two stops, and prevents any robbing of power in their combination: and, secondly, it renders them, severally and conjointly, valuable
for accompaniment and as foundations for many effective combinations.
As a rule, in modern Organs, when unison DIAPASONS are duplicated in
any manual division they are made too near each other in character and
strength of tone; and, accordingly, their independent utility is minimized,
and an unsatisfactory result attends their combination. As has been
previously remarked, in large Organs where more foundation tone is
required, an OPEN DIAPASON, 8 FT., of wood, constructed on the Schulze
model, should be added in preference to a third DIAPASON of metal.

Having provided in the first DIAPASON the foundation tone of the
entire harmonic structure of the Organ; the next step is to complete, as
far as practicable, that harmonic structure, by providing the series of
upper partial tones which create that rich and glowing volume of compound sound which is the crown and glory of the Organ. The first stop
to be added, and the most important in relation to the fundamental DIA-
PASON, is the OCTAVE, 4 FT., which furnishes the first and most assertive
upper partial tone of the unison prime. This stop must be smaller in
scale and softer in voice than the corresponding portion of the DIAPASON.
Care must be taken to keep the tone of this stop duly subordinate, especially when uninclosed. Organ-builders commonly overlook the true
office of the principal OCTAVE, and make it much too loud. When scientifically proportioned, the stop greatly enriches, brightens, and ennobles
the unison prime tone of the DIAPASON, without in any way disturbing
its pitch: but when of too powerful a voice, it imparts a hard and screaming character to the compound tone, a somewhat indeterminate pitch,
and goes far to disturb the desirable tonal balance of the foundation
work. There are points in every tonal structure beyond which the harmonic-corroborating tones must not go in their assertiveness; and he is
a true artist who knows the points and never oversteps them in his work.
The natural laws which govern and apportion musical sounds cannot
be disregarded with impunity. The OCTAVE must yield pure organ-tone
like the DIAPASON. It is the only stop of higher pitch than the unison
that may properly be left unexpressive.

The next stop called for in the harmonic structure, is that designated
the TWELFTH, 2⅔ FT.; furnishing the second upper partial tone of the
unison prime. It must be smaller in scale than the OCTAVE; and yield
a pure organ-tone of slightly less intensity. It is an inclosed stop. The
third upper partial is furnished by the FIFTEENTH or SUPER-OCTAVE, 2
FT.; also a pure organ-toned stop of about the same scale and strength of

voice as the TWELFTH. It is also properly an inclosed stop, and must always be introduced in Organs, even when the TWELFTH is omitted. The next stop, corroborating the fourth upper partial tone, is the TIERCE or SEVENTEENTH, 1⅗ FT. This stop must be smaller in scale and considerably softer in tone than the FIFTEENTH. In its complete and independent form, it is a stop little favored by English or American organ-builders, probably on account of the smallness of its pipes in the top octave. If properly graduated in tone, as all the high-pitched harmonic-corroborating stops should be, the top octave of pipes may be omitted. It appears in an independent form in Organs constructed by Cavaillé-Coll, as in the Positif of the Grand Organ in the Church of Saint-Sulpice, Paris.* The next stop, corroborating the fifth upper partial tone, is the NINETEENTH, 1⅓ FT. This, if inserted in an independent form, may be treated in the same manner as the SEVENTEENTH. It also appears in the Saint-Sulpice Organ as an independent stop. The only other harmonic-corroborating stop which has hitherto been made in an independent form, as in the Saint-Sulpice Organ, is (with the exception of the rare SEPTIÈME, 1⅐ FT.) the TWENTY-SECOND, 1 FT., corroborating the seventh upper partial tone of the fundamental prime.

Instead of attempting to introduce any one of the last named three high-pitched stops throughout the present adopted compass of sixty-one notes, in an independent or complete form, we strongly recommend introducing them in the form of a COMPENSATING CORNET of III. Ranks—a compound harmonic-corroborating stop, which, while quite easy to make, voice, and regulate satisfactorily, would be extremely valuable from a scientific and artistic point of view. We recommend the stop to be treated as follows:—

COMPENSATING CORNET, III. RANKS.

SEVENTEENTH, 1⅗ FT.	Compass CC to g³	
NINETEENTH, 1⅓ FT.	" CC to c³	
TWENTY-SECOND, 1 FT.	" CC to g²	

The NINETEENTH is to be softer in tone than the SEVENTEENTH, and the TWENTY-SECOND to, in like manner, be softer than the NINETEENTH. All the ranks to be voiced gradually softer upward, so as to prevent their cessation being very marked. The harmonic-corroborating series, so far complete, stands thus:—

OCTAVE, 4 FT. . . . . . CC to c⁴		SEVENTEENTH, 1⅗ FT. . . CC to g³	
TWELFTH, 2⅔ FT. . . . . CC to c⁴		NINETEENTH, 1⅓ FT. . . CC to c³	
FIFTEENTH, 2 FT. . . . . CC to c⁴		TWENTY-SECOND, 1 FT. . . CC to g²	

At this point, however, the harmonic structure is still incomplete,

---

* The compass of this Organ is CC to g³—56 Notes.

from the organ point of view, and calls for the corroboration of still higher upper partial tones. This is only possible in certain portions of the manual compass, and in the form of compound stops or MIXTURES. As a third-sounding rank has been provided in the COMPENSATING CORNET, it is neither necessary nor desirable to introduce another in the MIXTURE, the suitable composition of which is here given:—

FULL MIXTURE—VI. RANKS.

CC to BB	15——19——22——26——29——36.
C to B	12——15——19——22——26——29.
c¹ to b¹	8——12——15——19——22——26.
c² to c⁴ . . .	DOUBLE— I—— 5—— 8——12——15.

With the addition of this important compound stop, the foundation work of the Organ is practically completed: and to secure the full advantage of the harmonic structure in combination with the fundamental and any other exposed unison voices, it is absolutely necessary that all the harmonic-corroborating stops, with, perhaps, the exception of the OCTAVE, 4 FT., be inclosed in the swell belonging to the division.* The value of being at all times able to regulate the strength of the tones of the harmonic-corroborating stops, and impart expression to them, can only be realized by those endowed with keen musical sense, and who have had experience in this direction—very difficult to obtain under the present unscientific and inartistic system of organ construction.

Turning now to the completion of the tonal appointment of the First Organ; the first question that arises is, in what direction is it most desirable to add to the unison work provided by the DIAPASONS? In all possible cases it is most desirable to provide a sub-octave stop, preferably in the form of a medium-scaled DOUBLE DIAPASON, 16 FT., of metal, subordinate in power of voice to the fundamental DIAPASON, 8 FT. This stop should yield pure organ-tone. The unison stop in order of tonal value in combination with the DIAPASONS, is one of the unimitative VIOL class. This will be a desirable addition, giving varied tone-coloring to combinations for accompanimental purposes, and a clearness and crispness to the general labial unison tone of the division. If exposed, this stop should not be pronounced in its string quality, but when placed in the swell-box, as it ought to be, it should have a rich and full viol organ-tone, so as to be effective in flexibility and expression.

The next unison stop in order of importance is either a wood stop of the CLARABELLA or MELODIA class; or when there is a DIAPASON of wood, as before recommended, a covered stop, voiced to yield a tone of

* In Organs built by Roosevelt, it is usual to find the expressive portion of the Great Organ placed in the Choir Organ swell-box. This arrangement saved both space and money; but we do not advise this practice to be adopted; for it seriously interferes with that independence of the claviers which should always be retained.

good volume and filling-up quality. The best form of this latter is the DOPPELFLÖTE, 8 FT. This fine stop is peculiarly valuable in the First Organ, being of full intonation and mixing perfectly with the voices of the DIAPASONS and all other metal stops, and imparting a most desirable body and solidity to the tones of the reed stops. To be expressive.

Difference of opinion has a fair field concerning the other desirable unison stop or stops to be added to the expressive portion; because now general conditions may influence selection, and individual taste may exercise itself without much risk of injuring the true office and tonal character of the division. The stops which may be considered suitable are the GEMSHORN, 8 FT., KERAULOPHONE, 8 FT., and (if a subdued string-tone is desired) the VIOLA DA GAMBA, 8 FT. The selected stop or stops to be expressive.

When the First Organ is of a size rendering a second labial stop of 4 ft. pitch necessary or desirable for combination with the inclosed unison stops, it should be in the form of an open FLUTE of full and clear voice, but of much softer intonation than the DOPPELFLÖTE.

Little need be said with reference to the reed stops suitable for the First Organ. When the division is only sufficiently large to call for one stop of this class, preference should be given to the TRUMPET, 8 FT.; and in larger instruments the CLARION, 4 FT., should be added. In a division in which a full tonal appointment is aimed at a DOUBLE TRUMPET, 16 FT., should certainly be inserted, completing this desirable reed family. When these stops are planted on an uninclosed wind-chest, their scales should be small and their tones characterized by fulness and smoothness rather than by a brassy clang—a fault common in indifferent specimens of the stops. Like the harmonic-corroborating stops, these reeds are immensely enhanced in general usefulness and effectiveness when they are inclosed and rendered flexible and expressive. When inclosed, their scales may be full, and their tones of a brighter and more orchestral character. No stops of an essentially solo or orchestral character should be inserted in the First Organ, or, indeed, in any division, unless provision is made to impart powers of expression to them. This may be accepted as a golden rule in artistic organ appointment; largely ignored at present, simply because organ-builders are, with rare exceptions, no artists; and scientific and artistic organ-building is practically unknown to the tradesman organ-builder all over the organ-building world to-day.

It is to be understood from the foregoing particulars, that it is intended that all the stops constituting the tonal appointment of the First or Great Organ are to be inclosed in a special swell, which we shall designate swell-box No. 1, with the exception of the DIAPASONS, 8 FT. and 16 FT., and the OCTAVE, 4 FT. This last stop may properly be inclosed in the swell-box should it be desired to place its voice under control.

SECOND ORGAN.

In the old system of appointment, this subordinate second division would be designated the Choir Organ; and would comprise a general unclassified selection of stops, generally of a somewhat soft intonation, and chiefly suitable for accompanimental purposes. This would, especially, be the case when the division was exposed and entirely unexpressive, as, indeed, it continues to be in the majority of cases. In the new system, which we advocate, the term Choir Organ is practically meaningless; for all the divisions being expressive and under perfect control tonally, may be correctly classed as accompanimental; and the necessity for the selection of specially soft-toned stops no longer obtains in connection with the Second Organ.

What is required in the Second Organ is a tonal appointment and coloring entirely different from that of the fundamental First Organ. This is an essential condition if the maximum tonal value and contrasting effects are to be secured. In the system we urge for adoption, each manual division must have a definite and distinct tonal and contrasted coloring, and a definite office in the complete scheme of the instrument. Beyond what we have carried into effect, no essays seem to have been made in this direction; although a little careful study of the orchestra and its methods would naturally lead to the adoption of some such system of tonal appointment and apportionment as we have introduced.

We hold it is imperative that the Second Organ be entirely inclosed and expressive: and the only question that arises is to whether the expression shall be simple or compound;—single or double;—that is, whether all its stops shall be inclosed in one swell-box, and have simple expression; or, divided into two groups and inclosed in two independent swell-boxes, and have compound expression. In our scheme, compound expression, with the necessary attendant tonal flexibility, is an essential element necessary to obtain the desirable effects of contrast, and to secure the maximum tonal value of the stops.

To the organist who has had no knowledge or experience of the musical possibilities the compound expression of the separate manual divisions opens up to him, will probably arise the question as to the necessity for what, on first thoughts, may seem unnecessary complication. But a careful and unprejudiced consideration of the question will convince him of the utility and desirability of this advanced appointment. For many years we had the constant opportunity of observing the musical results obtained by the system, under the control of a great number of the most distinguished English and French organists, and can conscientiously recommend its adoption for all Organs in which refinements of expression and the maximum of flexibility are desired—and in what Church Organ can they not be desired? One of the most eminent cathedral organists in England, alluding to this system of compound expression, wrote thus respecting it: "It opened up to my imagination quite a vista of new and previously impossible effects in organ playing." That it does so we unhesitatingly affirm.

In the tonal appointment of the First Organ, we have directed the introduction of the foundation DIAPASON family with all its harmonic attendants, and the brass-toned family, represented by the TRUMPETS. So in the appointment of the Second Organ we advocate the introduction of another two families or groups of stops of contrasting qualities of tone, each group occupying a separate swell-box: both swells to be controlled by expression levers capable of being used separately or together at the will of the performer. To say that this arrangement multiplies the musical possibilities of all the stops in the division tenfold, does not fully convey an idea of the advantages secured. In the first place, it must be realized that the subdivisions, inclosed in the separate swell-boxes, are subject to any fixed and relative strength of tone desired by merely adjusting the shutters of the swells to the openings necessary, and allowing them to remain in that position while the division is being played without expression. In the second place, the arrangement allows of either of the subdivisions being fixed at any degree of strength of tone desired, while the other subdivision is under expressive control. In the third place, both the subdivisions can be played conjointly with uniform expression, as an undivided Second Organ. Lastly, the subdivisions can be played with alternating expression, producing most artistic effects of light and shade in the contrasting colorings. It must be borne in mind that all this is practicable on a single clavier, without resort to coupling and the consequent crippling of another clavier. Every legitimate and effective expedient, in a tonal direction, should be devised to render coupling the claviers as little necessary as possible. This is a golden rule in tonal appointment and apportionment.

In the general stop appointment, and in the special apportionment of the selected stops in the two subdivisions of the Second Organ, considerable skill and taste can be displayed by the organ expert or the builder. In this operation, the tonal appointment of the other divisions and especially that of the Third Organ must be carefully considered, so as to avoid anything approaching duplication, and so as to secure the spirit of contrast which should pervade the entire tonal scheme of the instrument. Under such conditions, the selection and apportionment of the stops representing the different families or tonalities assumes the dignity of an artistic and scientific problem: and the expert will do well to seek inspiration from the grand orchestra, notwithstanding the fact that the Church Organ should retain its true accompanimental characteristics, and not assume the orchestral and solo character of the Concert-room Organ.

The number of stops decided on for the Second Organ will, of necessity, influence their selection and grouping. Whatever their number may be, it is reasonable to suppose that if the division is subdivided, as we advocate, the stops will be apportioned equally, or as nearly so as desirable, to the two subdivisions; strict attention being paid to contrasting tonalities. In Chapter V., on The Tonal Appointment of the Organ, it is shown that the tonal forces or speaking stops of the Organ, in its widest sense, form two principal groups; one embracing those which strictly belong to the Organ, and, accordingly, are unimitative in their voices; and the other embracing those which are more or less closely imitative of the voices of orchestral instruments. Each of these principal groups embraces four sub-groups of different tonalities, valuable in contrasting apportionments. In the Church Organ, properly so-called, the first principal group, comprising the four classes of organ-tone, will be that made most use of; supplemented and enriched by a somewhat sparing introduction of the stops comprised in the four classes of imitative orchestral-tone. Accordingly, in scheming the appointment of the Organ, the artist expert has on his tonal palette eight practically distinct scales of color, from which to select his harmonies and contrasts for the several divisions and subdivisions of the instrument. On the skilful and artistic disposition of these colors depend the perfection and beauty of the Organ as a musical instrument; and also the facility essential to the performer in blending harmonies of analogy, and associating harmonies of contrast, on which so largely depend the beauty, indescribable charm, and striking effectiveness of organ registration.

We have suggested, for the tonal appointment of the Second Organ, that selection should be made, for the most part, from the stops yielding unimitative organ-tone. But as the stops of pure organ-tone have been properly apportioned to the fundamental First Organ, little if any resort need or should be made to stops of this class for insertion in the Second Organ; with, perhaps, the single exception of the DULCIANA, 8 FT., which, when of the proper quality of voice, is a diminutive DIAPASON. This soft-toned stop will be valuable in combination with the contrasting stops that may be selected for the division. The classes of stops from which selection should chiefly be made are those yielding free organ-tone, flute organ-tone, and viol organ-tone. For the first subdivision, to be inclosed in swell-box No. 2, we suggest representatives of the unimitative flute family, of which there are two branches; namely, open flute-work and covered flute-work, the latter embracing half-covered stops. In the open flute-work there are several stops, such as the CLARABELLA, MELODIA, HOHLFLÖTE, WALDFLÖTE, ZARTFLÖTE, FLAUTO AMABILE, and FLAUTO DOLCE. In the covered and half-covered flute-work there is a greater choice: among the available stops are the LIEB-LICHGEDECKTS, 16, 8, and 4 FT., LIEBLICHFLÖTE, DOPPELFLÖTE, BOUR-

DONALFLÖTE, ZAUBERFLÖTE, ROHRFLÖTE, DOPPELROHRFLÖTE, FLÛTE À CHIMINÉE, and FLAUTO D'AMORE. A desirable body of refined flute-tone, highly desirable for this first subdivision, is provided by the three LIEBLICHGEDECKTS of double, unison, and octave pitch; which, either used together, or separately in combination with contrasting stops, are always highly effective. The value of grouping stops of the same family in different pitches is not fully realized by organ designers: the craze for variety too often sacrifices richness, fulness, and dignity of tone. In the Church Organ, mere variety, for its own sake, should be avoided.

The chief unison stop in the first subdivision should have a voice in decided contrast to the flute-tone, and this will properly be of the viol organ-tone class; accordingly, no better stop can well be selected than the GEIGENPRINCIPAL, 8 FT. Instead of this, if a less powerful voice is desired, a SALICIONAL, 8 FT., of full tone, may be inserted with satisfactory effect. Should the subdivision be large enough to admit of a third unison a SPITZFLÖTE, 8 FT., will prove valuable; and a SALICET, 4 FT., may also be added, enriching the viol organ-tone. The stop apportionment of this subdivision should be completed by a DOLCE CORNET, V. RANKS, composed as follows:—

DOLCE CORNET—V. RANKS.

CC to F,	. . . . .	12——15——17——19——22.
F♯ to f²,	. . . . .	8——12——15——17——19.
f♯² to c³,	. . . . .	1—— 8——12——15——17.
c♯³ to c⁴,	. . . . .	1—— 8——10——12——15.

The stops apportioned to the first subdivision of the Second Organ are to be inclosed in swell-box No. 2.

In the stop apportionment of the second subdivision of the Second Organ, inclosed in swell-box No. 3, the chief consideration, from an artistic and effective point of view, is to institute throughout it a contrast of tone to that prevailing in the first subdivision, inclosed swell-box No. 2. This is essential if full advantage is to be derived from the double expression and flexibility. The stops required for this purpose would be just as necessary for the appointment of the Second Organ were it undivided and inclosed in a single swell-box. Such being the case, probably the best mode of procedure in scheming the tonal appointment of the Second Organ, is to prepare the full list of stops desirable for all reasonable requirements—looking upon the entire division as an effective Choir Organ—and then proceed to apportion the several stops to the two subdivisions according to the system of contrasted tonality here set forth.

Accepting the stop appointment of the first subdivision to be as suggested, we may complete a scheme for the entire Second Organ, by giving a suitable appointment for the second subdivision, inclosed in swell-box No. 3.   The combination forming an effective Second Organ thus :—

SECOND ORGAN—SECOND CLAVIER.

First Subdivision—Expressive.
Inclosed in Swell-Box No. 2.

1.	Lieblichgedeckt	. . . . .	Wood	16 Feet.
2.	Geigenprincipal	. . . . .	Metal	8 "
3.	Spitzflöte	. . . . . .	Metal	8 "
4.	Lieblichgedeckt	. . .	Wood and Metal	8 "
5.	Lieblichgedeckt	. . . . .	Metal	4 "
6.	Salicet	. . . . . .	Metal	4 "
7.	Dolce Cornet	. . . . . .	Metal	V Ranks.

Second Subdivision—Expressive.
Inclosed in Swell-Box No. 3.

8.	Dulciana	. . . . . .	Metal	8 Feet.
9.	Keraulophone	. . . . .	Metal	8 "
10.	Viola da Gamba	. . . . .	Metal	8 "
11.	Viola d'Amore (Tuned sharp)	. .	Metal	8 "
12.	Contra-Oboe	. . . . .	Metal	16 "
13.	Oboe	. . . . . .	Metal	8 "
14.	Clarinet	. . . . .	Metal	8 "
	Tremolant.			

Further remarks on the Second Organ are unnecessary, so we may proceed to speak of the apportionment of what may be considered the more important division, the Third Organ.

THIRD ORGAN.

Presuming, as has been suggested, that the Second Organ, just outlined, occupies the position in the present advanced scheme that the Choir Organ occupies in the old system: so the Third Organ in the present scheme of tonal appointment may be said to be represented in the old system by the Swell Organ.   The Third Organ is veritably a Swell Organ in every sense of the term; for not only is it, like the Second Organ, endowed with compound expression and flexibility; but it may be pronounced the most important expressive division of the instrument.   This Third Organ should not only contain the greatest number of stops, but those yielding the greatest and most distinctive variety of voices.   Here stops of characteristic organ-tone should be associated with those which imitate, as closely as practicable, certain orchestral instruments; selection being judiciously made from stops yielding orchestral flute-tone, string-tone, reed-tone, and brass-tone; all specially adapted for use in church and accompanimental music of a solemn and refined character: no attempt should be made to rival a properly appointed concert-room instrument. The Third Organ is to have its stop appointment divided into two tonally contrasting portions, in the same manner as the Second Organ: one being inclosed in swell-box No. 2, and the other in swell-box No. 3. This arrangement is satisfactory tonally, while it renders only three expression levers necessary for the manual divisions,—a great convenience to the performer.

In Church Organs, as commonly constructed by European builders, the Swell Organ is very rarely accorded its true dignity and proper position; traditions of earlier times still exerting a retarding influence, it would seem. This is especially the case with the German organ-builders, who in matters of construction and tonal appointment have been singularly conservative. Even when the Swell Organ is fairly well appointed, it is too often relegated to a locality in the depths of a chamber or some other disadvantageous place which proves fatal to its effectiveness. Serious complaints have been leveled against the swell-box, because the stops planted within it are believed to suffer a species of tonal annihilation. There may be good reason for such complaints in many cases, for, unquestionably, swell-boxes are too often very absurd affairs, constructed without proper regard to acoustical laws and with equal indifference respecting the office they have to fulfil. Greater care and better judgment are required in matters connected with the construction of the swell-box. In a properly proportioned and sensibly constructed swell-box we expect a perfectly pure and distinct tone both when its shutters are closed and open; with a well-marked and effective gradation from a clear *pianissimo* to a brilliant *forte* or the full strength of the division. The mile-away sound annihilation which too many organ-builders to-day seem to think is the acme of perfection in a closed swell is neither requisite nor at all desirable. This subject is treated more fully in the Chapter on The Swell in the Organ. The remarks just made apply to all the three swell-boxes called for in the scheme now under consideration.

The two subdivisions which have now to be considered must, according to the scheme already outlined, have their tonal apportionments contrast each other, and, at the same time, contrast to as great a degree as practicable and desirable the tonal apportionments of the subdivisions of the Second Organ. The general tone of the entire division must be fuller and more assertive than that of the Second Organ.. This will be largely due to the introduction of solo voices, which will find their accompaniments in the voices of either the First or Second Organs: and these solo voices will require combinational support and contrast in their own subdivisions.

In advocating the introduction of louder-voiced and more assertive stops in this division than in the Second Organ, it must not be imagined that we mean coarse, screaming stops, such as one too often hears in modern Church Organs. The stops we advocate are those of rich and refined intonation; having sufficient power, individuality, and clearness of voice to be effective even when the swells are closed, and full and brilliant in tone when the swells are fully open. These are essential conditions in the production of a satisfactory and efficient Swell Organ. Generally speaking, to secure the desirable results, a higher pressure of wind than that considered advisable for the First and Second Organs will be found necessary for this Third Organ. In large instruments two or more pressures will, in all probability, be considered desirable for the different classes of stops in so important a division; but extreme pressures should be avoided.

To impart firmness and solidity to the tonal structure of the Third Organ, a due proportion of foundation organ-tone should be introduced in the form of one or more unison stops of the DIAPASON class, with as many attendant harmonic-corroborating stops as circumstances will permit. It may here be desirable to remark that it is almost, if not quite, of as much importance that this division should have as complete a harmonic structure as the First Organ: but this can only be fully carried out in large instruments, for which there are sufficient accommodations and ample funds. To this foundation should be added, according to the size of the Organ and the legitimate calls to be made on its tonal resources, as many stops of unison and octave pitch of an imitative and solo character as can be accommodated, and one or two stops of 16 ft. pitch. It should be remembered that the tonal resources of this important division cannot well be too great.

In speaking of imitative and solo stops, we here allude to those which are specially calculated to impart a refined and distinctive coloring to all combinations into which they enter, and which can also be used alone or with varied accompaniments—stops which cast an orchestral brightness on the solid background of organ-tone, enriching without impairing its dignity. If only one stop of 16 ft. pitch is inserted, it should be in the form of an imitative reed, preferably a CONTRAFAGOTTO of full scale. A second stop of this pitch should be a small-scaled BOURDON, voiced to yield a tone having a string quality; or a large-scaled LIEBLICHGEDECKT of free organ-tone. It may be unnecessary to remark that when two stops of 16 ft. pitch are introduced they should be inserted in the different subdivisions, as contrasting voices.

In speaking of the scheming of the tonal appointment of the Second Organ, we advised first laying it out as an undivided whole, and then apportioning the stops to the two subdivisions according to our system of tonal contrast; and by so doing secure the maximum value and effect of the double swells in compound powers of flexibility and expression. We now recommend, with still greater force, the adoption of the same mode of procedure in scheming and apportioning the stops of the more important Third Organ. Much depends on the care, judgment, and skill with which all this is done. Even in preparing the complete scheme for the division, the apportionment of the ultimate subdivisions must be steadily kept in view, and the value of tonal contrast should never be lost sight of. This is easily done by one who has a clear knowledge of the true tonal character and combinational value of the various desirable stops.

The most important foundation stop should, of course, be a DIA-PASON, 8 FT., somewhat smaller in scale and brighter in tone than the first DIAPASON of the First Organ; and even more brilliant and penet-rating in character than the second DIAPASON. When two unison metal DIAPASONS are provided in the First Organ, of the tonal character described, the DIAPASON of the Third Organ should occupy a place, in scale and power of voice, midway between those of the First Organ. The DIAPASON, 8 FT., may, along with the labial stop of 16 ft. pitch, be inserted in the subdivision placed in swell-box No. 2: this may be called subdivision No. 1, of the Third Organ. Accordingly, if a har-monic structure is aimed at, probably including an OCTAVE, 4 FT., TWELFTH, 2⅔ FT., SUPER-OCTAVE, 2 FT., and CORNET or MIXTURE, it must attend the DIAPASON in subdivision No. 1. In this Third Organ, however, these harmonic-corroborating stops should assume different tonalities from the pure organ-toned harmonic stops of the same pitches in the fundamental First Organ; and, accordingly, they may be of free organ-tone, or of flute-tone and viol-tone unimitative or imitative as taste or circumstances may direct. The CORNET, of four or five ranks, may, with great advantage, be timbre-creating—that is, its ranks may be formed of open and covered pipes yielding different qualities of tone. This artistic treatment of a compound harmonic-corroborating stop has only too seldom been adopted; but it has proved productive of beautiful tonal effects in combination, absolutely unknown in the case of MIX-TURES, as commonly and inartistically made with pipes of one form and tonation. The tradesman organ-builder will, for obvious reasons, pro-fess to laugh at such refinements. That is to be expected, for he hates to be bothered with MIXTURES of any kind; but, nevertheless, both science and art come to the front in such tonal problems and remark-able results attend their successful solution.

As the DIAPASON, 8 FT., occupies the principal place in the apportion-ment of the first subdivision another unison stop, preferably of an un-imitative tonality, will be required in the second subdivision. The DUL-CIANA has been suggested for the second subdivision of the Second Organ, so that stop should not be duplicated; besides, it would not provide sufficient strength of voice or the desirable contrast of tone to the DIAPASON. If not introduced in the expressive subdivision of the

First Organ, a full-toned GEMSHORN, 8 FT.; will be highly suitable for the principal unimitative unison in the second subdivision, supplying, if properly voiced, an effective contrast to the DIAPASON in the first subdivision. Even should one be introduced in the First Organ it would be quite proper to place another GEMSHORN, of a different scale and brighter intonation, in the Third Organ. However desirable it may be to avoid duplicating stops in Organs appointed according to the system we advocate, it may not always be found expedient to do so. Valuable as tonal contrast and diversity are, they are not the only things that have to be taken into consideration. Should a still greater contrast of tone be desired in the principal unison of the second subdivision, and a flute tone be preferred, the FLAUTO MAGGIORE, 8 FT., or a refined GROSS-FLÖTE, 8 FT., may be selected. These are large-scaled open stops (preferably of metal) yielding a full and rich unimitative flute tone, contrasting distinctly and combining perfectly with the voice of the DIAPASON.

In completing the tonal appointment of the Third Organ, selection may be made from the following unimitative labial stops:—ROHRFLÖTE, 8 FT., STOPPED DIAPASON, 8 FT., MELODIA, 8 FT., HARMONICA, 8 FT., DOLCAN, 8 FT., HARMONIC FLUTE, 8 and 4 FT., FLAUTINO, 4 FT., and GAMBETTE, 4 FT. From the following imitative labial stops:—FLAUTO TRAVERSO, 8 FT., VIOLE D'ORCHESTRE, 8 FT., VIOLA, 8 FT., VIOLONCELLO, 8 FT., VIOLETTA, 8 FT., and FLAUTO PICCOLO, 2 FT. And from the following imitative reed stops:—CONTRAFAGOTTO, 16 FT., FAGOTTO, 8 FT., COR ANGLAIS, 8 FT., CORNO DI BASSETTO, 8 FT., FRENCH HORN, 8 FT., CORNOPEAN, 8 FT., BARYTONE, 8 FT., DULCIAN, 8 FT., and VOX HUMANA, 8 FT.*

It is highly desirable, if not essential, that in the tonal apportionment of the second subdivision a stop of 16 ft. pitch should be included; and as a BOURDON, 16 FT., has been recommended for the first subdivision, a no more satisfactory stop can well be selected than the CONTRAFAGOTTO, 16 FT. When properly scaled and voiced, this stop has a rich and refined tone which mixes admirably with all important unison stops and combinations. An imitative reed stop of a more assertive character is not desirable, especially as there is another stop of 16 ft. pitch provided in the first subdivision, which contrasts in tone perfectly with the CONTRAFAGOTTO. We have suggested a CONTRA-OBOE, 16 FT., for the double reed stop in the second subdivision of the Second Organ; and here, again, there is the desirable contrast of tonality between it and the CONTRAFAGOTTO, carrying out the principle we so strongly advocate in economic tonal appointment. A TREMOLANT will be a necessary adjunct to the second subdivision.

FOURTH OR SOLO ORGAN.

Notwithstanding what has been said respecting the unnecessary addition of a fourth manual clavier to the true and properly appointed Church Organ, our remarks would doubtless be considered incomplete by many organ-lovers without some direct allusion to the Fourth Organ in its capacity of a Solo Organ. This division is never really necessary in the properly appointed accompanimental Church Organ, which has sufficient imitative voices for all legitimate requirements provided in its Third Organ expressive subdivisions, as already directed. A Fourth or special Solo Organ need only be contemplated for instruments of the first magnitude; and then only for Organs which are certain to be used for very elaborate choral music, recitals of a secular character, etc. Under any conditions, the Fourth Organ need not be large, and must occupy a special swell-box, commanded by a special balanced expression lever, located to the right of the other expression levers.

It has been the general practice in what is supposed to be the *haut école* of Church Organ tonal appointment to insert in the Solo Organ, expressive or unexpressive, stops of very powerful intonation, voiced on wind of high pressures. This practice may be accepted as reasonable in the tonal appointment of the Concert-room Organ; but we very gravely question its wisdom in connection with a refined accompanimental instrument like the legitimate Church Organ. Notwithstanding the precedent furnished by several important Organs, such powerful voices, if inserted, should never be uninclosed.

What would seem to be most desirable in the tonal appointment of the Fourth Organ is a series of imitative string-toned stops, sufficient to produce the effect of several stringed instruments played together. One unison stop of the series may be tuned slightly sharp. The combined tone should be as imitative as practicable and characterized by richness, fulness, and refinement, without any approach to that ear-piercing quality so much affected by voicers of modern string-toned stops, and especially of those of very small scales. To such a body of string-tone may be added such solo stops as the Orchestral Flute, 8 ft., Orchestral Clarinet, 8 ft.,* Orchestral Oboe, 8 ft., Orchestral Trumpet, 4 ft. (harmonic), Harmonic Flute, 4 ft., and Harmonic Piccolo, 2 ft. Should a double stop be desired, a Euphonium, 16 ft., or a Trombone, 16 ft. (of medium power), may be inserted: the former is preferable in our estimation for a Church Organ. Should a Chimes be contemplated, it may properly find a place in the swell-box of this Organ, while it should be played from each manual clavier, at will; a Tremolant will be required.

---

* This stop should be of two ranks—a Clarinet, 8 ft., and a small-scaled Doppelflöte, 8 ft. While these should always be drawn together, the latter may be drawn alone.

PEDAL ORGAN.

It is unquestionably the fact that of all the divisions of the Church Organ, as it is commonly constructed in English speaking countries, the Pedal Organ is tonally the most deficient and fundamentally imperfect. The short-comings of this important division are attributable to several causes; such as want of a proper conception of its essential office in the tonal economy of the Organ; shortness of funds or unwise parsimony; deficiency of space for the reception of an adequate instrument, through blundering on the part of church architects; and ignorance of the science and art of true tonal appointment, combined with the blind following of established bad methods. It is obvious that for a long time the proper and legitimate office of the Pedal Organ has either been greatly misunderstood or wilfully ignored by English speaking organ-builders and designers; and that it has been systematically sacrificed and denuded of its necessary tonal resources for the sake of the manual divisions. Nothing could be more inartistic and short-sighted than such a mode of procedure.

There is, however, a still more serious and objectionable practice showing its head in certain organ-building quarters, which, in the name of art and common-sense, ought to be stamped out effectively. We allude to the practice of creating a Pedal Organ by a wholesale borrowing from the stops of the manual divisions; merely supplementing some of them by adding an octave of pipes, and, perhaps a single special stop. This is, of course, nothing but a miserable trade expedient to save labor and money; and a practice that lays the axe at the root of the true art of organ tonal appointment, and one that no one desirous of seeing the Organ retain its position as a truly efficient and noble musical instrument could sanction for a moment. We speak particularly of this pernicious practice in the Chapter on the Organ Specification, and need not dwell upon it here.

The true office of the Pedal Organ is to provide suitable basses for all the more important stops and combinations of stops in the manual divisions. To fulfil this office in a satisfactory and artistic manner, it is necessary that the Pedal Organ should be furnished with appropriate and well-chosen stops numbering not less than one-fifth of the entire series of speaking stops contained in the instrument. As will be seen by the following list of Organs in Germany and other Continental countries this proportion is substantially altered in favor of the Pedal Organ:—

	No. of Manual Stops.	No. of Pedal Stops.
Lutheran Church, Vienna	15	8
Lutheran Church, Warsaw	18	9

	No. of Manual Stops.		No. of Pedal Stops.
Catholic Church, Trebniz	22	———	11
St. Stephen, Vienna	28	———	13
SS. Peter and Paul, Goerlitz	36	———	19
Cathedral of Breslau	42	———	18
Parish Church, Mühlhausen	42	———	18
Cathedral of Haarlem	45	———	15
St. Paul, Frankfort	52	———	22
Cathedral of Merseburg	61	———	20
Cathedral of Schwerin	62	———	22
Cathedral of Ulm	71	———	31

Striking an average, roughly, of the above numbers, we find that the Pedal Organs contain closely upon five-twelfths of the number of stops contained in the manual Organs.

It may, at this point, be both instructive and interesting to give the list of the stops of the Pedal Organ of the instrument in the Cathedral of Schwerin, constructed by Friedrich Ladegast in 1871. The number of stops contained in the four manual divisions is sixty-two.

PEDAL ORGAN.

1. Violon	32 Feet.		12. Cello I.	8 Feet.
2. Untersatz	32 "		13. Cello II.	8 "
3. Principalbass . . .	16 "		14. Nasard	5⅓ "
4. Violon	16 "		15. Octave	4 "
5. Octavbass	16 "		16. Flötenbass	4 "
6. Salicettbass	16 "		17. Cornett	IV. Ranks.
7. Subbass	16 "		18. Posaune	32 Feet.
8. Terz	12⅘ "		19. Posaune	16 "
9. Nasard	10⅔ "		20. Dulcian	16 "
10. Bassflöte	8 "		21. Trompete	8 "
11. Octavbass	8 "		22. Trompete	4 "

It would be vain to seek for such a Pedal Organ as this in any American or English Organ having only sixty-two manual stops; and, indeed, in any Church Organ ever constructed in these countries. Its thirty-two feet and sixteen feet harmonic series are sufficiently complete for the most exacting calls: and with the substitution of a Dulciana, 16 ft., for either the Subbass, 16 ft., or the Octavbass, 16 ft., there would be little left to desire save powers of flexibility and expression— never contemplated by German organ-builders in their wildest flights of fancy.

All who have studied organ construction and appointment are aware that the large pipes necessary for the unison and double stops of the Pedal Organ are both cumbersome and costly; and that the mistakes of church architects on the one hand and shortness of funds on the other, have generally militated against a more liberal introduction of them. There is another and still more common cause for the shortcomings of

the Pedal Organ in church instruments—injudicious tonal apportionment. It is surely more advisable to scheme an Organ with *all* its divisions properly balanced and suited to each other, however modest in
size they may be, than to have the manual divisions unduly enlarged at
the expense, if not to the ruin, of the Pedal Organ; and, necessarily, to
the serious crippling of the instrument for every class of music.

Where is there an English or American Church Organ schemed on
such lines as those followed in the stop appointment of the moderately-
sized instruments in the Lutheran Churches of Warsaw and Vienna?
The former has eighteen manual stops and nine pedal stops; while the
latter has fifteen manual and eight pedal stops. Eight or nine pedal
stops are considered by English builders, from the highest to the lowest,
to be ample for Church Organs of from forty to fifty speaking stops.
There are a few exceptions which prove the rule. By far the greater
number of Church Organs in England have miserable pedal departments.
Four stops are considered a liberal allowance; while in instances too
numerous to be counted, one or two stops have to serve as the pedal
department in instruments containing many manual stops. It is the
height of absurdity to depend on one master-of-all-work, loud booming
Diapason, or, what is much worse, a tubby Bourdon, to furnish a
proper bass to fifteen or twenty manual stops. It is lamentable to note
the resorts organists are constantly put to in performing on Organs with
totally inadequate Pedals; and the expedients they adopt, in methods of
pedaling, to make some loud stop serve as the bass to some soft combination in the manual divisions, just, as a moment previously, it served
as the bass to the full organ, are worthy of all praise.

The matter which first claims attention in the tonal appointment of
the Pedal Organ, is the provision of several different strengths and
qualities of 16 ft. tone,—the unison pitch of the department,—and in no
case should there be fewer than three distinct strengths and qualities in
an instrument of any pretensions toward completeness or utility. The
total absence of anything in the nature of a softly-voiced unison stop in
this department has rendered the great majority of Church Organs in
England and America very unsatisfactory instruments. A softly-toned
bass is a *necessity* in every Organ used for accompanimental music, or,
indeed, music of any refined character; and we urge our readers never
to overlook this really important fact when engaged in designing or
purchasing Organs. For an instrument of small dimensions, having
only two stops in the pedal department, we recommend an Open Diapason, 16 ft., of wood, 10″ × 12″ scale, and a Dulciana or softly-
voiced Violone, 16 ft., of metal. With two such stops, three serviceable strengths of tone are available. At a small additional expense, an
Octave action or coupler and the extra top octave of pipes may be
provided in connection with the Dulciana or Violone, giving a valu-

able soft-toned OCTAVE, or VIOLONCELLO, 8 FT., as the case may be. Apart from the value of this OCTAVE, when used alone, it materially adds to the resources of the department both as regards variety and strength of tone. There is no reason why the Octave attachment should not be applied to the OPEN DIAPASON also, providing what may be called a BASS FLUTE, 8 FT. We strongly approve of any legitimate expedient whereby a small Pedal Organ may be improved; and we recommend the addition of the extra octave of small and inexpensive pipes and the Octave coupler in all cases in which either cramped space or shortness of funds renders a small Pedal Organ imperative. In proof of the utility of such additions in a department of two stops or ranks of pipes, such as has just been mentioned, we may state that while without the Octave attachments the tonal effects are limited to *three*, with the Octave attachments the possible effects are increased to *fifteen;* several, if not all, of which will be found useful. The same number of tonal effects are, of course, obtained by four independent stops; while with four stops and two Octave attachments no fewer than *sixty-three* tonal changes are possible.

It is unnecessary to again give a list of the stops desirable for the Pedal Organ, seeing that the matter has already been touched upon in our general remarks on the Speaking Stops: but before closing the subject we must again impress on all who are interested in the construction and tonal appointment of Church Organs the absolute necessity, on artistic grounds, of providing properly proportioned pedal divisions, with as complete harmonic structures as circumstances will permit. Let the idea which seems to have obtained in too many quarters that the Pedal Organ is an inferior division, or one of secondary importance to the Organs commanded by the manual claviers, be set aside for ever; and let it be recognized, in the tonal appointment and apportionment of the Organ of the Twentieth Century, that the Pedal Organ is quite as important in relation to the other divisions of the instrument, as the bass part of any musical composition is in relation to the upper parts thereof.

A word must be said respecting Borrowing with the view of augmenting the resources of the Pedal Organ. Borrowing is admissible under the following conditions only in artistic and efficient tonal appointment. When an adequate Pedal Organ has been legitimately provided, with proper and sufficient stops strictly belonging to it; then it is quite in order that it should be enriched by having an auxiliary division added to it by borrowing from any desirable stops in the expressive manual divisions, especially so when the Pedal Organ proper is not given any expressive powers.*

This leads to the important question of imparting to the Pedal Organ

* See example of this method of enriching the Pedal Organ in the Specification in the Chapter on The Organ Specification.

powers of flexibility and expression, by inclosing as many of its stops as practicable in a swell-box or swell-chamber—such stops as are of a harmonic-corroborating character, of a solo character, and all reed stops. In the Chapter on The Swell we have set forth our views and arguments in favor of an expressive Pedal Organ, and need not recapitulate them here. But we may briefly point out the advantages which attend the extension of powers of flexibility and expression to this important division of the Organ, in the artistic rendition of all classes of music—solo and accompanimental. First, respecting *flexibility;* the inclosure of the desirable portion of the Pedal Organ renders it possible to graduate the strength or assertiveness of the voices of the inclosed stops to any desired degree; thereby largely multiplying their tonal values. Any of the stops can, by simply adjusting the openings of the swell-shutters, have its voice modified from its full strength to any degree of softness called for by the music being rendered. This mere adjustment of tonality is an important advantage that can never be realized in an ordinary uninclosed Pedal Organ. Secondly, respecting *expression,* which is of equal importance to flexibility; there can be no question as to the necessity of having the bass practically as expressive as the tenor and treble in accompanimental, and, indeed in every class of refined and dignified music; and this artistic requirement can only be met in the Organ by imparting powers of expression to the Pedal Organ. The same system should be followed in selecting and inclosing the Pedal Organ stops as has been recommended in the apportionment of the stops of the First or Great Organ.

A special expression lever must be provided for the Pedal Organ swell; but, in addition, means must be provided for attaching the swell to the expression levers of the several manual divisions, at the will of the performer.

If the musician will carefully review all that has been presented for his consideration in the present Chapter; and work out all the advantages—the endless effects of light and shade and subtle *nuances*—such an Organ, tonally appointed and apportioned, supplemented by its system of compound expression and almost limitless powers of flexibility, as has been outlined, places at his disposal in the rendition of every class of church music, he can hardly fail to realize what the distinguished English cathedral organist meant in saying, in allusion to an Organ so tonally appointed: " It opened up to my imagination quite a vista of new and previously impossible effects in organ playing."

GRAND AND CHANCEL ORGANS.

A very few words will suffice on the subject of double Organs, that is, two Organs placed in one church. When two independent Organs are introduced, one commonly occupies an elevated, west-end, position, or what, for the sake of distinction, may be designated the west-end position, while the other is located in the neighborhood of the chancel or sanctuary. The former instrument, called the Grand Organ, is usually of important dimensions, and is used for incidental and, in some cases, for responsive music of a solemn and dignified character: and in the most notable examples it partakes, in its tonal character and resources, of the nature of the Concert-room Organ. Such Organs are to be found in the French cathedrals and large parish churches. The Organs in the Cathedral of Notre-Dame, the Madelaine, and the Churches of Saint-Sulpice and Saint-Eustache, at Paris, are among the best works of the class. The Organ which occupies the choir position is usually of moderate size, and is strictly of an accompanimental character, furnished with a carefully selected series of refined and softly-toned stops, chiefly of pure organ-tone, admirably adapted for the dignified and impressive accompaniment to the voices of the choir, and also as a support to the orchestral instruments frequently associated with it in fuller accompaniments. The Grand Organ supplies all the tonal qualities not strictly necessary for an effective accompaniment, while it is admirably fitted for the rendition of solo and incidental music. In the French churches the Choir or Sanctuary Organ, properly so called, is used for the accompaniment to plain-song; and its tones are full and rich, without any tendency to coarseness or a screaming character. The Orgue d'Accompagnement in the Madelaine is a representative example.

The practice of introducing a Choir or Sanctuary Organ, in addition to a main or Grand Organ, is gaining favor in this country in cases where the church services encourage such an arrangement, and the architectural conditions are suitable. A disposition very similar to that which obtains in the Madelaine and other French churches exists in the Church of Our Lady of Grace, Hoboken, N. J. There, carried out under our directions, a Grand Organ is placed on a gallery at the west end of the nave, while a Sanctuary Organ occupies a position immediately behind the altar in St. Joseph's Chapel adjoining the sanctuary. The latter Organ, after the French model, is purely accompanimental in character, inclosed in a general swell, and played from a console situated between the sanctuary and the chapel. Chancel Organs of considerable dimensions are to be found in certain large churches here and in England. A notable example is furnished by the divided Organ in the Church of St. Bartholomew, New York City. There are two complete Organs, one located in the chancel and the other on an elevated gallery at the end of the nave. The chancel Organ has fifty-two speaking stops apportioned as follows:—Pedal Organ nine stops; Great Organ twelve stops; Choir Organ thirteen stops; and Swell Organ

eighteen stops. The gallery Organ has seventy speaking stops apportioned as follows:—Pedal Organ fourteen stops, Great Organ seventeen
stops; Choir Organ ten stops; Swell Organ nineteen stops; and Solo
Organ ten stops. All the divisions are stop apportioned in the old-
established fashion.

ORGAN OF THE FOURTEENTH CENTURY.
MINIATURE IN A LATIN PSALTER.

CHAPTER XI.

THE CONCERT-ROOM ORGAN.

T is quite evident that up to the present time the absolute necessity—on both artistic and purely practical grounds—of the tonal appointment and apportionment of the Concert-room Organ differing radically from what is sufficient and proper for the true accompanimental Church Organ has not been fully realized either by organists or organ-builders. There has been too close adherence to tradition and old-fashioned ways of doing things, on the part of the latter; and a too willing belief that organ-builders' ideas of tonal appointment and divisional apportionment—if they can be said to have any logical ideas on the subject—are all-sufficient, on the part of the former.

At the present time nothing of any note is being done to clearly differentiate the Concert-room Organ, and perfect its tonal resources beyond increasing the number of its stops to such an extent as to render it necessary to cut them up into groups, forming distinct Organs, and to find localities for them here, there, or anywhere. The practice is as absurd and fatal to proper musical effects, as it would be to separate a large orchestra into groups and locate them in distant places—one in a gallery, one somewhere above the concert-room, one, perhaps, somewhere else, while the remaining group occupies the only legitimate position, the orchestra stage. An Organ so divided would no more be a complete and satisfactory instrument, than an orchestra, divided as suggested, would be a satisfactory musical machine.

The employment of electricity renders such an absurd, unnecessary, and undesirable distribution of separate Organs, or parts of an Organ, possible: and, in this direction, will probably foster the craze for aimless and unnecessarily large aggregations of stops, many of which could never be used in proper organ playing. The use of such divided and distributed Organs must ever perplex and annoy the lover of true and artistic music; who instead of listening to and enjoying the music of one complete and perfectly appointed Organ, will be continually wondering where the sounds are coming from—now in front of him, now to the right of him, now to the left of him, now far behind him, and now far above him.   Under such undesirable and distracting conditions, artistic, refined, and reposeful music will be impossible.   Let us hope that common-sense will step in, even if there is insufficient musical sense and artistic and scientific knowledge, to stem the present growing craze for monster divided Organs.

This craze is likely to flourish in a country of large fortunes like this; and will, of course, be encouraged by organ-builders, whose interest lies in piling up stops and accessories regardless of their necessity or where they are to be located—" The more the merrier."   The organ-builder's chief difficulty will be to find enough varieties of tone, old or new, or simple variations of familiar tones; and failing that, to concoct new names to swell up an immense list of stops, and so give some ostensible reason for its compilation.   The last mentioned difficulty is evidenced when, as a final resort, organ-builders have to create names for stops which have not the remotest relation to the sounds the stops produce or their means of production.   One remarkable example of this ridiculous nomenclature has recently appeared.   Wherein lies the value to the organist of such a nomenclature?   Surely the name of a stop should convey some idea of its tonality; or, at least, have some obvious foundation, either connected with its voice or the form of its pipes.

No one who loves the Organ and desires to see it advance along artistic lines can offer any objection to a proper and very liberal expenditure on its construction and tonal appointment.   But let the money be spent, not in an unmethodical manner, but in the most useful and artistic directions.   First of all, in securing the finest materials and the highest class of workmanship, doing away with all inferior and undesirable metals in pipe-construction—zinc and all the cheap and poor alloys, invariably used in competitive organ-building—and returning to the practice of the old masters of using pure tin and high-grade alloys.*   Also in using the finest hard and soft woods in pipe making, and for all the structural portions of the instrument.   Secondly, let money be liberally expended in securing the most artistic and careful voicing possible; and, what is almost of equal importance and almost as costly, perfect tonal regulation of every stop, large and small (a work of time, skill, and care as we have personally found), and particularly of the compound harmonic-corroborating stops.

---

* In the Organ in the Cathedral of Haarlem, all the displayed pipes, including the Sub-Principal, 32 ft., are of Cornish tin, burnished; and all the interior metal pipes are formed of an alloy of tin and lead in equal proportions. This is true organ-building.

Then, when all this has been provided for and secured, and generosity has still an open purse, let the Organ once again receive, externally, the attention it deserves, and which it invariably received in olden times. Let artistic skill in design and execution essay to surpass even such exteriors as those of the Organs in the Church of St. John, Bois le Duc, and the Cathedral of Tarragona. Then, and then only, with artistic and scientific tonal appointment, will the instrument deserve to be designated THE ORGAN OF THE TWENTIETH CENTURY—a work of delight to the ear and of beauty to the eye.

Every possible expedient should be resorted to to avoid dividing a Concert-room Organ and installing the divisions at a distance from each other, even to the extent of the different sides of the stage or orchestra platform. An instrument so divided is in every way objectionable: for, as it is necessary to locate its separate divisions, such as the First and Second Organs on one side, and the Third and Fourth Organs on the other, while the Pedal Organ stops may be distributed, in some fashion, on both sides, the sounds from the separated divisions will be perpetually heard issuing alternately from the opposite directions. The effect of such an arrangement is essentially bad and extremely annoying to the ear of a sensitive listener: once noticed, and the effect is continually listened for, until it becomes irritating and distracting. The bad effect is increased in proportion to the distance between the divisions of the Organ. None of the great Concert-room Organs in England are divided or buried in chambers at the sides of a stage.

We are aware that it is commonly due to the want of proper provision being made by architects in planning concert-rooms that Organs cannot be effectively placed therein. And this fact points to the desirability, when a concert-room is being planned, of the organ-builder or an organ-expert being associated with the architect, so far as the proper placing of, and accommodation for, the Organ are concerned, with the special view of avoiding the necessity of dividing it. The more closely associated the several divisions of an Organ are, the more connected and satisfactory will all its tonal effects be to the ear. Here, again, a lesson can be learnt from an orchestra, in which the instrumentalists are closely placed so as to secure, so far as possible, unity of sound.

As we desire to impress architects and all other interested parties with the importance of providing suitable accommodation for an Organ in a concert-room, in accordance with the proper conditions we have stated, we give, as an object lesson, the accompanying Plan, Fig. XXVIII., of the Organ in the Albert Hall, Sheffield, England, constructed by the late M. A. Cavaillé-Coll. The disposition of the several portions of this admirably arranged instrument may be briefly described. It is erected on an elevated floor, level with the highest tier of the orchestra seats, under which are located the bellows, reservoirs, and blowing mechanism. On the elevated floor is a somewhat low room *(rez-de-chaussée)* almost exclusively devoted to the pneumatic levers connected with the claviers and wind-chests, and the pneumatic draw-stop action. In this room are also placed the wind-chests for the lower octaves of the Principal-Bass, 32 ft., and the Contra-Bombarde, 32 ft., indicated at A on the Plan. Two circular staircases ascend to the upper stages of the instrument, as indicated at B,B. On the first stage,

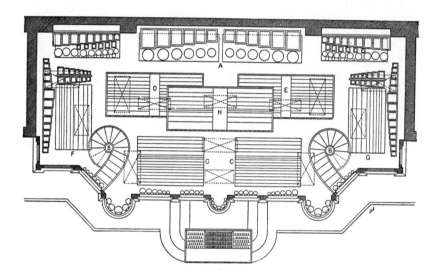

Fig. XXVIII.

immediately above the *rez-de-chaussée,* are placed, toward the front, the two large wind-chests, C,C, of the Grand Orgue; and behind them the wind-chests and swell-boxes of the Récit Expressif, D, and the Positif Expressif, E: ample space being provided all around them for easy access and the free emission of sound.* Here are also placed the remainder of the wind-chests of the Pédale, at F and G. On the second stage, which extends over the central portion of the instrument, are located the wind-chests and swell-box of the Solo, indicated at H. It would be difficult to devise a more compact and convenient arrangement under the condition imposed by the architects of the Hall. In all our long experience we have never known an Organ so convenient of access for inspection, tuning, and repairs. The external design of this interesting Organ—

---

* Free space around a swell-box is of great importance if the perfectly clear and singing quality of a proper *pianissimo* is to be secured. At present, among musical Philistines, the annihilating, brick-and-mortar or reinforced-concrete, swell is ignorantly considered the acme of perfection. The great Cavaillé-Coll knew both how to construct and how to place a swell-box.

thoroughly modern French in character—is shown in the accompanying illustration, Fig. XXIX.

It is invariably advantageous to arrange a Concert-room Organ on a wide and shallow plan: and in deciding the relative positions of the

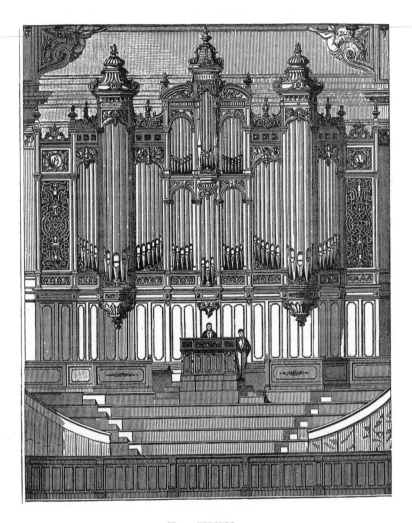

FIG. XXIX.

different tonal divisions, care should be taken to do justice to each one. Under no circumstances should one division be sacrificed for the sake of another, to the injury of the artistic balance of the Organ. The old European builders wisely favored a wide and shallow disposition in their important Church Organs, to their great advantage tonally: and the same disposition of the sound-producing portions of a Concert-room Organ should be aimed at; so as to prevent the necessity for forced and undesirable straining in voicing. The foolish and objectionable practice which has obtained of burying the Organ in a deep chamber on one side of the orchestra platform or stage, and further destroying its character and beauty of tone by inclosing it with a latticework or perforated screen across the only opening of the chamber, as in the Municipal Auditorium at Springfield, Massachusetts, should be universally condemned. It is purely a modern expedient, destructive of all artistic tonal balance, and only to be excused in photo-play houses, where music is of secondary importance.

Before submitting for the consideration of the organ-loving world our scheme for the tonal appointment, divisional apportionment, and compound expressive control of what we may venture to suggest as embryonic of the Concert-room Organ of the Twentieth Century, it is perhaps desirable to briefly define the nature and requirements of such an instrument, when in its true and perfect form.

It must be admitted by every thoughtful musician that no other class of Organ is called upon to meet so many and such varied demands on its resources as that designed for the Concert-room. A Chamber Organ, which, when of the first magnitude, may be considered most akin to the Concert-room Organ, has, at most, to meet very reasonable calls in solo and accompanimental or concerted music: while the Church Organ, in its true and legitimate office, has only to accompany the voices of the choir and congregation, and to lend itself to the rendition of a limited range of dignified solo music. On the other hand, the Concert-room Organ has a threefold office to fill, and that to the fullest extent possible in an Organ. It must be properly appointed for taking part, in conjunction with an orchestra, in the accompaniment of Oratorios and other important choral works. It should be equally suitable for the accompaniment of such works, furnishing an able substitute for the grand orchestra in the rendition of their full instrumental scores. It must furnish the musician with proper tone-colors, artistically and effectively grouped, and properly placed under his direct and easy control, for the clear and adequate rendition of the most refined and exacting compositions written for the Organ or the orchestra. In short, the Concert-room Organ should be a perfect Organ and an orchestra combined.

It must be obvious that to fulfil all these purposes, and to respond to the exacting demands of the accomplished musician and improvisatore, the Concert-room Organ must ever be an extremely elaborate instrument; yet both its tonal and mechanical structures should be founded upon systems so perfect, that simplicity will appear to characterize all matters connected with its control. We may assist the reader by explaining briefly what is meant by the remarks above. First, all the speaking stops in the different tonal divisions and subdivisions should be grouped on a definite and easily recognized system, widely different from the aimless method at present obtaining: when this is done, their number, however great, ceases to present the slightest element of confusion. Secondly, the means provided for the command of the several groups of stops, singly or in any desired combination, should be so perfect and so easily mastered that the mind of the performer is not severely taxed, and but a slight acquaintance with the instrument is necessary. Thirdly, each tonal division and subdivision should be flexible and expressive; and the mechanical means for controlling the several swells should be as simple as they are complete.

The musician must certainly acknowledge that all these conditions are simple, reasonable, and necessary; yet not one of the important Concert-room Organs constructed abroad, or existent in any concert-room, hall, or auditorium in this country, comprises them. Indeed, no systematic attempt had been made in the organ-building world to furnish such an instrument, until we schemed the Organ, constructed by the Los Angeles Art Organ Company, and installed in the Festival Hall of the Louisiana Purchase Exposition, in 1904. In preparing the scheme we were prevented, by the old-fashioned ideas of the builders, from carrying out our original system of tonal appointment and divisional apportionment, combined with compound expression, to its full development; and the same ideas defeated our purpose of providing an adequate flexible and expressive Pedal Organ. The new system devised by us for the tonal appointment and expressive equipment of the Concert-room Organ was set forth in a series of articles, published about thirty years ago, in the *English Mechanic and World of Science*. And therein, for the first time in the history and literature of the Organ, was the necessity for an expressive Pedal Organ urged on the notice of the organ-building and organ-loving world.

The instrument alluded to above was not only the largest and grandest Concert-room Organ in existence at the time of its construction, but it was the only one in which any systematic tonal apportionment was adopted; and it was the only one in which a complete and independent String Organ, endowed with full powers of flexibility and expression, was provided. Such an important addition to the tonal forces of the Organ seems to have never before been contemplated in the history of organ-building. Full particulars of the Organ, as schemed by us, will be found in the Appendix.

Subsequent to its removal from the Louisiana Purchase Exposition, the Organ was acquired by Mr. John Wanamaker, and is now installed in his great Store in Philadelphia, Pa., forming the groundwork for the immense divided Organ now completed there. The present instrument comprises two hundred and twenty-seven speaking stops and five of a percussion or mechanical character, including a pianoforte, distributed in seven main tonal divisions, two of which are located a considerable distance from the chief divisions of the instrument. The beautiful console of this Organ is described and illustrated in Chapter VI.

It is now our task to suggest what can yet be done to place the Organ still higher in position as a musical instrument—pointing the way to a tonal development along artistic lines which will justly earn for it the title THE ORGAN OF THE TWENTIETH CENTURY. The task is not a light one, nor do we undertake it without experiencing considerable responsibility. It is possible that our views may be wrong, and lead away from, instead of toward, the desired end. We venture, however, to unhesitatingly assert that the Concert-room Organ, as it has been schemed and constructed in the past by the most distinguished organ-builders, is radically imperfect in its tonal system; and that it has not been scientifically and artistically differentiated from the normal and old-established tonal appointment of the large Church Organ. Let any one take and compare any number of lists of stops of large Church Organs and Concert-room Organs, and discover, if he can, any difference (save, perhaps, in the element of size) between their systems of tonal appointment and divisional apportionment. Will one find that they have been thoughtfully schemed along definite and special lines, suited to the essentially different offices the specified Organs have to fulfil? We question it. Yet that they should bear in their tonal schemes unmistakable evidences of their different places in the musical world is unquestionable.

THE CONCERT-ROOM ORGAN OF THE FUTURE.

GENERAL REMARKS.

THE CLAVIERS.—The Concert-room Organ, as properly appointed, has its entire tonal forces commanded by a pedal clavier and five manual claviers. This number of claviers has, with common consent, been fixed only, however, because a greater number would be extremely difficult, if not impossible, to be operated upon by the performer properly seated at the console. A sixth manual clavier would be of great value in the Concert-room Organ for several reasons, but as such an addition is practically inadmissible, it remains for the organ expert and musician to devise a tonal appointment and apportionment which will impart to the five manual claviers the powers and facilities that would accrue were it possible to have a greater number of claviers: and this without impairing the independence of the five claviers, or rendering coupling of the claviers in any way necessary. A certain advantage is gained, which renders a sixth manual tonal division possible, by having it commanded by one or even two of the claviers specially connected with other divisions, as in the large Organ in the Wanamaker Store, in which the Ethereal Organ is played on either the Solo Organ or Echo Organ claviers. But in our conception of the Concert-room Organ of the Twentieth Century, the offices of the claviers commanding the tonal forces of the instrument must go very much further than this —much further than they have hitherto gone.*

While it would seem desirable to retain the old-established nomenclature of the manual divisions and claviers, which was apparently sufficiently expressive to be retained so long as the corresponding old system of tonal appointment obtained, it would be absurd to apply it to the claviers of the Concert-room Organ appointed and apportioned tonally under the advanced system we propose for adoption: in fact, it could not be retained with any semblance of consistency and expressiveness. It may just be remarked, however, that the single term Great Organ has much to recommend it, designating, as it properly does, that foundation division which should be fully appointed in its tonal structure in the Concert-room Organ, as in all other Organs of any importance, and upon which the rest of the tonal forces of the instrument should be scientifically and artistically schemed and built up.

We may pause here and ask: How often do we find, even among the best modern examples of organ tonal appointment, any evidences of this scientific and artistic building up? Do we not rather find a universal aim, in the tonal appointment of modern Organs, to make each division complete in itself, without any desire to make the several tonal divisions simply component parts of a grand whole? Surely an Organ should be one complete and united instrument; not merely a number of disconnected and more or less complete or self-contained Organs, without special coloring to adapt them for definite and relative offices in one grand tonal scheme, joined together, not by scientific and artistic tonal bonds, but by being brought under the control of a single performer through the means of associated claviers.

In the Concert-room Organ, developed according to the connected tonal scheme set forth in the present Chapter, the old terms, Great Organ, Choir Organ, Swell Organ, Solo Organ, and Echo Organ, could have no significance, indeed, if used, they would be altogether misleading and confusing. Such being the case, a more connected and relative terminology is required to individualize the main tonal divisions of the Organ and the claviers which command them. The simplest terms that can be employed, and those which are sufficiently expressive for all

* In these remarks we make no allusion to the common practice of making one console serve for two or more distinct Organs, situated at a distance from each other in a building. There is no tonal problem involved in such an economical arrangement; and it does not touch the tonal system we advocate here.

practical purposes, are First Organ, Second Organ, Third Organ, Fourth Organ, and Fifth Organ.

As there is only one tonal division in a properly appointed Organ that can justly claim supremacy and priority with respect to all the other divisions; that division deserves the name First Organ, and is logically and properly commanded by the First Clavier. This division comprises all the foundation stops of the instrument, and is that on which all the other divisions are reared as a musical edifice, perfect in proportions and replete with all the features which go to make a complete and effective temple of musical sound. As an architect and a student of sound production, we can picture to our mind a tonally perfect Organ; just as we can picture a perfect work of Gothic architecture, in which every detail, while subservient to the entire structure, has its special office and its own share of beauty, and from which nothing can be taken away without marring the consistency of the whole structure.

It is neither necessary nor desirable in these general remarks to allude to the tonal apportionments of the divisions commanded by the other manual claviers, for these will be found fully set forth in the sections of the present Chapter specially devoted to their consideration.

With respect to the compass of the manual claviers a very few words will suffice. The standard and now universally accepted compass in the Concert-room Organ is CC to c^4—61 notes; and there seems to be no call on any musical grounds to alter it in either the downward or upward range. It was not, however, always considered the most desirable compass for the Concert-room Organ; for the first important instrument of the class ever constructed—that in St. George's Hall, Liverpool—had originally the compass from GGG to a^3—63 notes. This has now been changed to the present standard compass. Particulars respecting the desirable relative positions of the claviers will be found in Chapter VI., on the Console.

Regarding the Pedal Organ clavier little need be said here, a full dissertation on its forms and dimensions being given in Chapter VII. The compass of the clavier now generally recognized as the standard for all properly appointed Organs is CCC to G—32 notes. A greater compass than this would be difficult for the performer to command without an undesirable movement of his body: and it is very unlikely that any music written for the Organ or any orchestral transcription will call for a greater compass.

THE ACTION.—For the Concert-room Organ there can, at the present stage of the organ-builder's art, be only one class of action employed—the electro-pneumatic. Though introduced, in a tentative form, in the latter part of the last century, it has only reached a satisfactory development in the present century. It would be difficult to say if it has reached its full development, for things move quickly in matters electrical. The advantages the electro-pneumatic action has already afforded are immense; and it is not too much to say that it has rendered possible, in the construction and appointment of the Concert-room Organ, what could never have been even contemplated under any of the older actions. The electro-pneumatic action belongs to the Organ of the Twentieth Century, meeting every requirement that can arise in matters of control and accommodation: it has overcome every difficulty in the operations and manipulation of the claviers, couplers, and draw-stop and combination appliances.

THE DRAW-STOPS.—There will, in all probability, be difference of opinion and taste regarding the form the draw-stops should assume in the console of an important, many-divisioned Concert-room Organ,

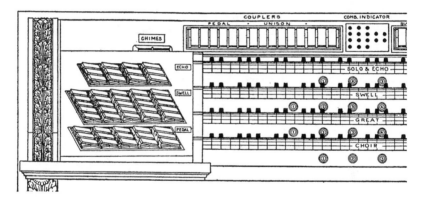

FIG. XXX.

and probably the choice will lie between the time-honored draw-knobs, as shown in the console illustrated in Plate XXIII., and the rocking-tablets shown in the console illustrated in Plates XXIV. and XXV. For an Organ of a hundred or more speaking stops, rocking-tablets should certainly be adopted in preference to any other form of draw-stops: they lie compactly, occupy little space, are easily disposed in full view of the performer, and are manipulated with the greatest ease and rapidity. In the case of a console such as that shown in Plates XXIV. and XXV., it would be extremely undesirable to adopt any other form or disposition of the draw-stops: and the type of console is unquestionably the best for a large Concert-room Organ. For an instrument of about a hundred speaking stops, quadrant jambs may be abandoned in favor of sloping jambs, carried at an angle, anywhere between 30° and 45°, from the cheeks of the claviers, in which the rocking-tablets are set in groups in the manner indicated in Fig. XXX. An Organ of one hundred and two speaking stops has been constructed, having a console fitted in this manner.

In our description of the remarkable console illustrated in Plates XXIV. and XXV. we have given the unique system of coloring applied to the draw-stop tablets to indicate the different tonal divisions of the Organ to which they belong. The utility of such a system of color-distinction is unquestionable, and should always be adopted in consoles of important Concert-room Organs. It is to be regretted that no attempt has been made to introduce a standard system of coloring, although it would be extremely difficult to devise one that would meet the demands of a many-divisioned and sub-divisioned Concert-room Organ, such as is projected in the present Chapter.

THE COUPLERS.—Next in importance to the draw-stops are the couplers, for while the former command the individual stops of the several tonal divisions of the Organ, the latter unite those divisions, commanded by the several claviers, in the unison, sub-octave, and octave, as the performer may find desirable for the production of the tonal combinations he requires, and which cannot be obtained in any division commanded by a single clavier. Accordingly, when properly and artistically used, the couplers are agents of great value.

The couplers now almost universally introduced in large modern Organs, constructed on the electro-pneumatic system, are very numerous, especially so in those having five manual claviers. But comparatively few of the couplers are of primal importance: certain of them are undesirable and, from a scientific point of view and, to a large extent, from an artistic one also, are positively objectionable. That this is not properly realized is evident from the examination of the series of couplers found in the majority of large modern Organs. The most undesirable coupler, which should never, on both scientific and artistic grounds, be introduced in a properly schemed Organ, is that which couples in the octave a manual tonal division on itself. To the organist who has been accustomed to use this coupler for the sake of the musical noise it creates, such a statement respecting it will seem absurd; yet none the less is it founded on the laws of musical sounds and common-sense. To add an octave of exactly the same quality and strength of tone to every note of a unison is against the laws of musical sounds, and is destructive of the true value of the unison tone. Any one with a keen perception of the value of compound tones must realize this, but the common introduction of the octave coupler, operating along with the unison on each clavier, in modern Organs, has done much to destroy the delicate musical sense of the performer who resorts to its use to gain increase of tone. We hear the organist who loves the octave coupler ask: Why object to coupling a manual division in the octave on itself, for have we not octave and super-octave stops in all the divisions? Yes: but these stops are not of the same tonal value, and probably not of the same tonal character, as the unison stops to which they stand in the relationship of upper partials or harmonic stops. Further, unless the octave stops have purely solo-voices, their tones will be less powerful than, and should be finely adjusted to, the tones of the unison stops in the same division.

Octave couplers operating between different manual divisions have a different office to fulfil in the tonal economy of the Organ, and are only second in importance to the unison couplers. Skilfully used these octave couplers produce many very beautiful and effective combinations of tone, largely assisted by the flexibility and expressive powers given to the coupled stops. There seems to be one important tonal division on which the octave coupler might occasionally operate with satisfactory effect, we allude to that of the Pedal Organ. Such a coupler would be required only in a Concert-room Organ of the first magnitude, and even there it might be confined to the more important stops, which would require to be carried up an additional octave—not a very great matter.

The sub-octave coupler operating on its own division is undesirable; while one operating on different divisions is of little value. In no instance is it productive of a properly balanced tone. In addition, it has the serious disadvantage of only affecting the compass of a manual clavier from tenor C to c^4, the bottom octave always remaining at the unison pitch. In a properly schemed Concert-room Organ, in which every manual division has one or more labial stops of 16 ft. pitch, it is very questionable if a sub-octave coupler is either necessary or desirable. The introduction of this coupler was due to the insufficient tonal appointment of the large majority of modern Organs, in which there were no labial stops of 16 ft. pitch in the manual divisions, while the desirability of having them was continually felt. Now, with the double tone fully supplied, there is little, if any, necessity for the sub-octave coupler.

While it is necessary that the Concert-room Organ should have the full complement of unison couplers, operating between all the tonal divisions commanded by the claviers, it is desirable and, indeed, of the greatest importance that they should have to be resorted to as little as possible. A proper and artistic tonal apportionment of the several divisions of the Organ will render, as we shall show further on, the frequent use of the couplers by the performer much less necessary than it has to be in Organs schemed tonally on the old-fashioned system, and that now followed by organ-builders at home and abroad. It must be realized that coupling largely destroys the desirable independence of the claviers: and for the proper rendition of compositions of a complex orchestral character, in which effects of the different classes of instruments have to be clearly brought out, it is essential that every clavier be free and charged with its special tonal office, either permanently or temporarily, as will be shown later on. For this desirable end, we may point out here, it is necessary that the tonal divisions commanded by the several claviers be artistically apportioned, not only with voices representing the organ proper, but also with those voices which represent all the important string and wind divisions of the grand orchestra, properly classified and grouped. Instead of such an economic apportionment, we find in Organs, as now universally schemed by organ-builders, general congeries of stops without any well-defined or special offices in their entire tonal appointments. This subject will be found fully treated on in the following pages of the present Chapter.

As we have recommended the adoption of draw-stops in the form of rocking-tablets, so do we advise the same form of tablets for the couplers in the Concert-room Organ. There are two positions that the couplers can occupy, as may be preferred by the designer of the console. The one most favored at present is that shown in the consoles illustrated in Plates XXIII. and XXIV.; and when the couplers are numerous, as in these consoles, it would seem that no better or more convenient place can be found for them, notwithstanding the fact that they are very far from the performer. They have the advantage, however, of always being in full view. The other position is one that has been strongly and logically advocated. This position places the couplers belonging to the several tonal divisions adjoining the draw-stops commanding the forces of those divisions. This would, of course, place them in the jambs of the console, and more within the reach of the performer. We are inclined to advocate placing certain of the more important and most frequently used couplers in both positions.

The means of readily distinguishing the couplers operating on the several divisions of the Organ have to be considered. The mere grouping and arranging them in a special order, as recommended in the Resolution of the Console Standardization Committee, is good so far as it goes, but it does not go far enough. The arrangement would be sufficient for a Church Organ of moderate size, such as would seem to be contemplated in the Resolution; but something more is necessary in connection with the series of coupler tablets of a large Concert-room Organ. It is evident that distinctive coloring must be resorted to, as in the case of the draw-stop tablets. In this direction, the system of parti-coloring adopted in the console described in Chapter VI., and illustrated in Plate XXV., can be studied with advantage. This system combined with proper grouping would seem to meet all requirements.

THE COMBINATION SYSTEM.—For the Concert-room Organ the combination system described and recommended in the Chapter on the Console should certainly be adopted, embracing, as it does, the readiest means of adjustment by the performer seated at the claviers, and the dual system, which secures independence, during a performance, of both the draw-stop tablets in the jambs and the thumb-pistons under the claviers. Accordingly, with what has been said in Chapter VI., it is unnecessary to enlarge on the combination system or appliances in our present general remarks.

THE EXPRESSION LEVERS.—In a Concert-room Organ which may comprise in its appointment nine or even ten separate tonal divisions endowed with flexibility and powers of expression, and which cannot be conveniently controlled by more than five expression levers (or six at the most), it is evident that certain new methods have to be adopted to meet the new conditions. Up to the present, and except in very rare instances, the largest number of expression levers required in the Concert-room Organ has been four, controlling the swell-boxes of the only expressive divisions, termed the Choir, Swell, Solo, and Echo Organs. In certain noteworthy instruments one of the levers has been made to control both the Choir and an expressive subdivision of the Great Organ, inclosed in one swell-box. In the large instrument in the Wanamaker store, in Philadelphia, there are five expression levers, one controlling the swell-box containing the subdivision of the Great and the entire Choir, and the remaining four controlling the separate swell-boxes and chambers of the Swell, Solo, Echo, and Ethereal Organs: the last named Organ being played from either the Solo or Echo claviers. This is as far as has been gone in legitimate organ construction up to the present time (1918). It may be remarked, that when two or more Organs, practically complete in themselves, and located at a distance from each other, are played from a single console, a single set of expression levers—four or five in number—will have to control all the expressive divisions in the separate instruments. The methods pointed out, efficient so far as they go, do not meet the problem that confronts us in the tonal scheme we have in view for a legitimate undivided Concert-room Organ of the first magnitude—a scheme never before contemplated in the organ-building world, and one that may not be readily recognized at its full value by the organist, content with the present old-fashioned system (if system it can be called) of tonal appointment and apportionment.

In our tonal scheme for the Concert-room Organ of the Twentieth Century, which we have developed on both scientific and artistic lines, we provide, in addition to the principal divisions, permanently commanded by the five manual claviers, certain ancillary or floating divisions, of special tonalities, and endowed with separate powers of flexibility and expression, which can instantly be brought, singly or collectively, on any one or more of the claviers, to be used alone or in combination with the tonal forces commanded by the claviers with which they are temporarily allied. These ancillary divisions can have their swell-boxes controlled by any of the expression levers, at the will of the performer. Such tonal adjuncts, used in combination with our system of tonal apportionment in the different principal divisions, and under compound expression, will be capable of producing musical effects of the most beautiful character, absolutely unknown in the Organ at the present time, and impossible on any one in existence to-day—musical resources and effects calculated to open up a new world to the improvisatore; and so tend to the development of the highest art to which the organist can aspire.

It is important that the performer shall have continually within full view a record of the state or position of all the expression levers. This should be provided in the form of a correct model of the set of levers; arranged to move exactly as the actual expression levers are moved by the feet of the performer. The model levers may be quite small—not larger than an ordinary draw-stop rocking-tablet—and they should occupy a central position immediately above the highest clavier, and under the couplers.

THE CRESCENDO AND SFORZANDO LEVERS.—A crescendo lever, similar in form to the balanced expression levers, must be provided and located immediately to the right of the series of expression levers, and about an inch distance from the same, so as to mark the distinction. If desired, a small metal plate or some form of stop may be projected upward near the center of the levers, so as to clearly indicate the separation and prevent the foot making a mistake. The crescendo lever, which is devised to draw, in proper order, a large proportion of the stops of the Organ, so as to produce a gradual and effective increase of tone on a single clavier, should be furnished with an adjunct by means of which any arrangement of the stops to be successfully brought on by the lever can be made as desired. A dial or other device should be provided in the console, in full view of the performer, indicating the position of the crescendo lever and, accordingly, the percentage of the stops brought on.

The sforzando lever, whereby an instantaneous increase of tone can be given to a single note or chord, producing the well-known *sforzando* effect in music, may conveniently be in the form of a small toe-lever located adjoining the crescendo lever. Its operation and utility are, however, so limited that its introduction is of questionable value even in the Concert-room Organ.

THE TREMOLANTS.—The number of these mechanical accessories necessary in the Concert-room Organ is dictated by the number of divisions and subdivisions, in the manual department, which require their aid. No TREMOLANT should be attached to the Expressive Subdivision of the First Organ. It is desirable to apply the TREMOLANT to such stops as are suitable for the *tremolo* effect, and to those only. On the other hand, it is undesirable to affect any of the foundation, mutation, and harmonic-corroborating stops. The only stop in the Organ which requires the TREMOLANT in the production of its characteristic voice is the VOX HUMANA. As the *tremolo* effect is chiefly required in short passages during the performance of a composition, convenient appliances should be provided, beyond the ordinary drawstop arrangements, whereby the organist can control the entry and exit of the TREMOLANT instantaneously and easily.

Much of the utility and beauty of the tremolant depends upon the character and speed of the *tremolo* it generates. Generally speaking, TREMOLANTS are both too powerful and too rapid. The result is unpleasant in the extreme; and the refined quality of the stops they affect is changed into a hooting or sobbing intonation. The action of a TREMOLANT should be only sufficient to impart a gentle wave-like ripple or undulation to the natural speech of the pipes, and that sufficiently slow to allow the ear to recognize their true musical tones.

With these general remarks and what has been set forth in preceding Chapters, we may pass over matters of minor importance here, and enter on the dominant subject of the present Chapter—the tonal appointment and apportionment of the Grand Concert-room Organ.

In speaking of claviers and tonal divisions, we have alluded to the necessity of abandoning the old nomenclature for the several divisions of the manual department in the class of Concert-room Organ now submitted for consideration. We cannot see how such a nomenclature could possibly be retained for the divisions of an instrument in the tonal appointment of which so much that is old-fashioned is swept away. The term Swell Organ, so appropriate in connection with an instrument having only one expressive division, can have no definite significance in relation to an instrument which has every one of its divisions wholly or partly inclosed in swell-boxes. No division is specially a Swell Organ, when the entire instrument may, under certain conditions, be correctly designated a Grand Swell Organ, and constituted such at the desire of the performer. Two other terms should also drop out of use; namely, Choir Organ and Echo Organ. The former is essentially meaningless in connection with any tonal division of the true Concert-room Organ, whilst the latter is simply absurd and has no *raison d'être* in relation to the modern Organ in its legitimate and dignified tonal development. There may not be the same objection to the retention of the terms Great Organ and Solo Organ; but these may very properly be abandoned.

Such being the case, we have decided to employ the simple, appropriate, and easily understood terms: First Organ (lowest clavier); Second Organ (second clavier); Third Organ (third clavier); Fourth Organ (fourth clavier); and Fifth Organ (fifth clavier). The term Pedal Organ, being perfectly applicable to the department commanded by the feet of the performer, is retained. The department embracing all the divisions enumerated above, commanded by the hands of the performer, may be termed the Manual Organ.

THE FIRST ORGAN.

The First Organ must be treated as the true foundation of the entire tonal scheme of the Manual Organ; forming, in conjunction with the foundation-work of the pedal department, the Organ proper. Its tonal structure and apportionment must be as complete and correctly proportioned throughout as science can direct and art accomplish. In the first place, the fullest desirable amount of pure organ-tone of 8 ft. pitch must be provided, to which must be added double, or 16 ft., tone in due subordination. Then both the eight and sixteen feet harmonic-corroborating series must be introduced, ordered conjointly, but having the elements strictly belonging to the sixteen feet series much less assertive in tone than those of the unison.

While it is desirable, in this most important manual division of the Organ, to have a due amount of 16 ft. tone and its harmonic upper partials, it must not be forgotten that the true manual pitch is that of 8 ft., and that nothing is gained by lowering the pitch an octave, and so assimilating it with the Pedal Organ unison pitch. Whatever stops of 16 ft. pitch are introduced in the First Organ, they must be both in strength and penetrating quality of tone strictly subordinate to the corresponding unison stops; and still more must those stops which strictly belong to the 16 ft. harmonic series, and corroborate certain upper partial tones of the 16 ft. tone, be subordinated to all stops near them in pitch which belong to the 8 ft. harmonic series. It may be mentioned that the only stops, or ranks of pipes in the compound stops, which will have to be considered, belonging to the 16 ft. series, are the QUINT, $5\frac{1}{3}$ FT., and the TIERCE, $3\frac{1}{5}$ FT. These stand in relation to the 16 ft. tone as the TWELFTH and SEVENTEENTH. The other intervals of this harmonic series are represented by stops of 8 ft., 4 ft., $2\frac{2}{3}$ ft., and 2 ft., but as all these intervals likewise belong to the more important 8 ft. harmonic series, the respective stops are provided and proportioned with regard to the foundation unison of the division, and not to the double or 16 ft. stop or stops. These are rules that must be observed if a well-established unison pitch and a perfect balance of tone are to be secured. There is one question that may present itself at this point. What character and strength of tone should the stop of 16 ft. pitch have with regard to the foundation DIAPASONS? From both a scientific and artistic standpoint there can be little doubt that the quality of tone should be similar, but considerably softer, so as to secure due subordination to the foundation unison when sounding in combination. Such being the case, the stop required is a DOUBLE DIAPASON, 16 FT., of open metal and medium scale. If a second stop of 16 ft. be desired, it may with advantage take the form of a soft, string-toned, open metal stop, properly designated CONTRA-VIOL, 16 FT. Such a double would prove most valuable in full combinations of pure organ-tone, brightening the dull effect which too often attends the use of pure organ-toned manual double stops.

Notwithstanding the practice which has been adopted by certain German builders of inserting a stop of 32 ft. pitch in the chief manual division of their large Church Organs, and which has been followed in the tonal appointment of two important Church Organs in England, it is just questionable how far it is desirable to insert so grave a stop in the manual department of the Concert-room Organ of the Twentieth Century. Whatever the opinion may be respecting its value from a tonal point of view; there can be no doubt that its introduction, as a special manual stop, will be rarely indulged in on one account, if on no other; namely, that of expense. Even should this be no obstacle, the height and floor-space required for its accommodation will always be difficult to provide, unless its larger pipes can be used as important features in the case. In these remarks we have contemplated an open stop of metal or wood, for in no instance would we recommend a covered stop of 32 ft. tone.

There appears, however, to be no valid reason why in a Concert-room Organ of the first magnitude, the manual department should be denied this element of supreme gravity. In the properly appointed pedal department of such an instrument, there will certainly be a softly-toned, open metal stop of 32 feet, preferably a CONTRA-DULCIANA; which, by extension, will provide a unison DULCIANA, 16 FT., and an OCTAVE DULCIANA, 8 FT.—all most desirable pedal voices. The extension will, necessarily, call for fifty-six pipes, and, accordingly, it will only be necessary to add five small pipes to furnish the manual compass. Such being the case, let the entire rank of pipes appear as an auxiliary stop to the First Organ, and so connected as to be commanded by the First Clavier at will, appearing on the draw-stop tablet under the name DOLCIANO PROFUNDO, 32 FT. We are not aware of anything of this nature having been carried into effect; but there is certainly no reason, under the facilities given by the electro-pneumatic action, why such an expedient as that suggested should not be adopted. The suggestion opens the question respecting the advisability of using other long-compass Pedal Organ stops as manual auxiliaries, for the production of special and striking tonal effects not otherwise possible in the manual department.   We commend this subject for consideration.   Old-fashioned ideas must give way to new thoughts—old methods to new devices in tone-production.

In all the manual divisions the fundamental 8 ft. tone must assert itself with overwhelming predominance, but in no division more so than in the one under immediate consideration.   The fundamental tone of the First Organ should be furnished by at least two DIAPASONS of metal, one of large scale and powerful intonation, with a voice full, round, and commanding; the other of contrasting quality, smaller in scale, and with a voice of rich and somewhat penetrating character.   This decided contrast, apart from variety, is of great value in preventing sympathy between the stops, and a consequent loss of power and volume in their combined voices.   In Organs of the first magnitude, a third DIAPASON, 8 FT., should be added, formed of wood pipes, as made and voiced by Schulze.*   This, again, with the view of materially increasing the variety and volume of unison tone, and avoiding any tendency toward sympathy. The next unison stop should be a covered stop of great body and filling-up quality.   No better stop than the DOPPELFLÖTE can be adopted, for its tone is characterized, when it is voiced by a master-hand, by great volume, dignity, and sonorousness: as a mixing stop it is singularly valuable.   With the four unisons already mentioned, the true foundation-tone of the First Organ is secured; but, leaving reeds and other inclosed unisons out of consideration for the moment, at least one other open metal stop of 8 ft. ought to be added, uninclosed; and this, to secure variety and contrast, should be a VIOL of a broad, normal string-tone, sufficiently pungent to assert itself through the whole pure organ-tone of the division.

We now enter on the important subject of the harmonic structure based on the foundation unison or diapason-tone.   There can be no doubt that the First Organ—the true Organ—should be characterized by as great a completeness as possible in its tonal structure; and all the facts that the science of acoustics has revealed must be carefully utilized in its development.   In the unison harmonic series, the first element, after the fundamental tone, is the OCTAVE, which furnishes the first and most important upper partial tone.   The stops which represent this tone are of 4 ft. pitch, and should be, to some extent, under control, so that the tone may be graduated in intensity to suit the strength of the different fundamenal unisons.   All the stops which corroborate the higher upper partial tones should be under control for a similar end.   These facts have, however, never been practically recognized by any European builder, if we judge by existing English and Continental Organs.   An

* Magnificent pipes of this class are to be found in the Organ, by Schulze, in the Church of St. Bartholomew, Armley, England.

Octave, 4 ft., formed of open metal pipes of about the same scale and strength of tone as the smaller Diapason, may with advantage be planted, along with the double and unison Diapasons, on an uninclosed wind-chest; but all the other loud-voiced stops of 4 ft. pitch and the two stops already named as belonging to the 16 ft. harmonic series, should unquestionably be inclosed and rendered flexible.

Let it be understood at this point that we advocate, in relation to the division of the Concert Organ now under consideration, the planting of the stops of 16 ft., the Diapasons, 8 ft., the other stops of 8 ft. pitch, as already mentioned, and at least one open metal Octave, 4 ft., on an uninclosed wind-chest; and that every other stop introduced in the division be planted on a wind-chest inclosed in a swell-box. By this treatment the First Organ becomes partly flexible and expressive, and has all its higher harmonic-corroborating stops and its reed stops under proper control. The unexpressive subdivision may be considerably added to in instruments of very large size.

The stops required to complete the 8 ft. harmonic series are as follows: 1. A small-scaled metal Octave, 4 ft., having a bright voice of medium strength. 2. A Twelfth, $2\frac{2}{3}$ ft., representing the second upper partial tone: this should be slightly softer than No. 1. 3. A Super-octave, 2 ft., representing the third upper partial tone: to be somewhat softer than No. 2. 4. A Tierce or Seventeenth, $1\frac{3}{5}$ ft., representing the fourth upper partial tone: this may be considerably softer than No. 2. 5. A Larigot or Nineteenth, $1\frac{1}{3}$ ft., representing the fifth upper partial tone: this should be slightly softer than the preceding. 6. A Septième, $1\frac{1}{7}$ ft., representing the sixth upper partial tone: this stop need only be introduced in Organs of large size; and when introduced it must be of small scale and of comparatively soft intonation. 7. A Twenty-second, 1 ft., representing the seventh upper partial tone: voiced softer than No. 5. Of course these remarks on the relative strength of tone must be accepted as of general application only. Every Organ should be carefully schemed and artistically balanced in its tonal structure; and this cannot be accomplished on paper, but only in actual work, under the cultivated ear and the artistic sense of the musician.

It may be objected by the organ-builder that it is inexpedient to introduce complete stops of so high a pitch as the Nineteenth, Septième, and Twenty-second, especially in an instrument which has a manual compass to c^4, on account of the difficulty of carrying up such small ranks to the top note. But this need be no barrier to their introduction, for they may be discontinued where their pipes become undesirably small, or break into the octave below at any convenient note in the top octave. The stops should be discontinued or broken on different notes. They may be associated together as a Cornet, but much will be gained by having them under independent control. It would be desirable, however, to have a rocking-tablet, through the single operation of which the SEVENTEENTH, NINETEENTH, SEPTIÈME, and TWENTY-SECOND could be drawn together. This tablet to be located adjoining the four tablets which draw the stops separately.

Notwithstanding the unusual completeness of the above scheme, the general harmonic structure of the First Organ will not be satisfactory without the addition of one or more compound harmonic-corroborating stops, which will carry the harmonic series of upper partial tones still higher throughout the lower octaves of the manual compass and considerably enrich the upper octaves. Such MIXTURES, when carefully schemed, and scientifically proportioned in strength of tone with regard to the other harmonic-corroborating stops, are of the greatest value, imparting a mysterious richness of tonal coloring, and a fascinating complexity of structure to the pure organ-tone, which no other class of stops can furnish.

Having devoted an entire chapter to the Compound Stops of the Organ, it is undesirable to do more here than convey a clear idea of what would be suitable for such a division of the Concert Organ as we have now under consideration. The two following compositions for full-toned MIXTURES may be accepted as representative:—

FULL MIXTURE—VI. and V. RANKS.

CC to B,	.	.	.	15——19——22——24——26——29.
c^1 to b^1,		.	.	8——12——15——17——19——22.
c^2 to b^2,		.	.	8——12——17——19——22.
c^3 to c^4,		.	.	1—— 8——10——12——15.

FULL MIXTURE—V. RANKS.

CC to e^1,	.	.	.	.	15——19——22——26——29.
f^1 to b^2,	.	.	.	.	8——12——15——19——22.
c^3 to c^4,	.	.	.	.	1—— 5—— 8——12——15.

The first MIXTURE comprises a third-sounding rank throughout, placed in the most favorable position for such an interval. From CC to b^1—36 notes, there are, in addition to the third-sounding rank, three octave- and two fifth-sounding ranks; and in the treble, from c^2 to b^2, there are, in addition to the continued third-sounding rank, two octave- and two fifth-sounding ranks; and from c^3 to c^4 there are one unison-, two octave-, one third-, and one fifth-sounding ranks. This last break theoretically belongs to the 16 ft. harmonic series, and on this account imparts fulness to the acute portion of the manual compass. The second MIXTURE has no third-sounding rank; octave- and fifth-sounding ranks alternating throughout. In both compositions, the highest rank of each break is octave-sounding, for that interval is unquestionably the best, tonally considered, in such a position. It is not, however, imperative that such an arrangement should obtain. In the scaling and voicing of these MIXTURES, and, indeed, every compound stop in the Organ, the builder must accept the teaching of the natural phenomena of sound as produced by the human voice and the more perfect orchestral instruments. Just as we find that in a rich, compound musical sound the upper partial tones decrease in strength as they ascend in pitch until they become inaudible, so must all the ranks of pipes inserted in the Organ with the view of corroborating the upper partial tones of the fundamental unisons be similarly graduated in strength of intonation. Probably no teaching of acoustical science has been more grievously misunderstood or more pertinaciously ignored by organ-builders than this. The early mediæval Organ was simply a large MIXTURE; but the higher-pitched ranks it comprised were not introduced for the purpose of corroborating upper partial tones. The series of pipes on each note formed a musical chord, and all the pipes were practically equal in strength of tone. When the Organ was developed from this early model, and large stops of an independent character were introduced, the MIXTURE was not abandoned; on the contrary, it was retained and occupied a very prominent position in the tonal appointment. Later it was discovered that stops of the MIXTURE class produced certain remarkable acoustic effects: but the early organ-builders seriously blundered in their treatment of these assertive stops, probably through imperfect knowledge, or a natural clinging to tradition or precedent. Their successors followed much on the same unscientific lines, for they had no observer like Helmholtz to teach them the true office of the compound stops and their scientific relationship to the prime tones of the Organ. So matters went on in the time-honored grooves century after century. The inartistic character, to use no stronger term, of all the old harmonic-corroborating stops, in their uncontrollable condition, has gradually induced some organ-builders, of observation and refinement, to restrict to an undesirable extent the introduction of MIXTURES and certain harmonic-corroborating ranks in their later Organs. We will not say that the pocket has had nothing to do with this modern spirit of restriction. Compound stops, if properly made, voiced, and regulated, are comparatively expensive and very troublesome; and few indeed are the organ-builders of to-day who are sufficiently artistic, or sufficiently well paid, to forget such facts. We may add that there are very few organ-builders who have studied acoustics and the phenomena of sound sufficiently to realize the importance of the harmonic-corroborating stops, or to treat them in a thoroughly scientific manner. In this, as in too many other tonal matters, the rule of thumb prevails in the organ-building world to-day. There are hopeful signs, however, of an improvement in scientific and artistic treatment. Let us hope, with our present knowledge of the phenomena of sound and the complex structure of the several varieties of musical tones, that nothing will be omitted from the tonal structure of the Concert-room Organ that is conducive to the production of pure organ-tone and imitative orchestral-tone. Prominent among the forces which aid in building up complex musical sounds in the Organ and which enter as potent factors in timbre-creation, stand the compound harmonic-corroborating stops.

One word more with reference to the harmonic-corroborating stops. It is understood that they are to be inclosed in a swell-box,—say swell-box No. 1,—and so placed under control as to be capable of having any desirable degree of softness given to them. Now comes the obvious question: What should their strength of tone be when heard at their full power, with the swell-box open? This is very easily answered. Let all the stops of the division which yield the fundamental unison organ-tone, and which are outside the swell-box, be drawn; then let all the stops which represent the 8 feet harmonic series be so voiced and regulated as to complete the desirable unison *compound tone* in the manner consistent with scientific teaching, and according to a true and refined musical sense. Let there be no scream, or crash like breaking glass, as the notes are put down by the fingers: on the contrary, let the whole complex structure combine in one grand volume of rich and refined sound, of which the sensitive ear feels assured it could never tire. When such a result is attained, the Organ in its proper form is safe; and the modifying operation of the swell may enter on its mission— to throw upon the several combinations of unison tone various garments of subtile and mysterious beauty, changing in musical texture and color at the will of the performer.

Such an Organ—call it a Great Organ if you will—is no longer the loud intractable thing one meets with in all instruments built on old lines, but a flexible and responsive division, bending itself to the will and requirements of the musician in a way unknown and scarcely foreshadowed in the present prevailing system of organ construction and appointment.

The First Organ, having its foundation-work and its harmonic structure complete, calls for only a few other stops for the purpose of imparting variety and richness to its numerous tonal combinations. Confining our remarks to the inclosed Subdivision, we would advise the insertion of another stop of 16 ft. tone; and this may preferably take the form of a QUINTATEN, of medium strength of voice, which would combine effectively with the inclosed harmonic-corroborating voices, and impart solidity to the lingual tones. One or two other labial stops, of 8 ft. pitch, should be inserted in this Subdivision. When two are inserted, they may appropriately be a full-toned GEMSHORN, 8 FT., and a

GROSSFLÖTE, 8 FT. When only one is inserted, preference may properly be given to the GEMSHORN. A stop of 4 ft. pitch, not belonging to the harmonic series, may be inserted in this Subdivision, preferably in the form of a HARMONIC FLUTE of large scale. The following three lingual stops, of unimitative tonality, may be sufficient in this Expressive Subdivision: DOUBLE TRUMPET, 16 FT., HARMONIC TRUMPET, 8 FT., and HARMONIC CLARION, 4 FT.

The following is the tonal scheme of the First Organ, based on the particulars and recommendations given above. It is suitable for a Concert-room Organ of the first magnitude.

FIRST ORGAN—FIRST CLAVIER.

PARTLY EXPRESSIVE—COMPASS CC TO c⁴—61 NOTES.

UNEXPRESSIVE SUBDIVISION.

1. DOUBLE DIAPASON	.	Metal. 16 Feet.	7. DIAPASON, MINOR	.	Wood. 8 Feet.
2. CONTRA-VIOL	. .	Metal. 16 "	8. HORN DIAPASON	.	Metal. 8 "
3. GEMSHORNBASS	. .	Metal. 16 "	9. DOPPELFLÖTE	. .	Wood. 8 "
4. SUB-QUINT	. . .	Metal. 10⅔ "	10. CLARABELLA	. . .	Wood. 8 "
5. GRAND PRINCIPAL	.	Metal. 8 "	11. OCTAVE, MAJOR	. .	Metal. 4 "
6. DIAPASON, MAJOR	.	Metal. 8 "	12. CLARIBEL	. . . .	Wood. 4 "

AUXILIARY STOP.

DOLCIANO PROFUNDO, Metal. 32 Feet—61 Notes. From Pedal Organ.

EXPRESSIVE SUBDIVISION.

Inclosed in Swell-box No. 1.

13. QUINTATEN	. .	Wood. 16 Feet.	23. TIERCE	. . . .	Metal. 3⅕ Feet.
14. VIOL DIAPASON	.	Metal. 8 "	24. TWELFTH	. . .	Metal. 2⅔ "
15. GEMSHORN	. . .	Metal. 8 "	25. FIFTEENTH	. .	Metal. 2 "
16. TIBIA PLENA	. .	Wood. 8 "	26. CORNET	. .	Metal. IV. Ranks.
17. OCTATEN	. . .	Wood. 8 "	27. FULL MIXTURE	Metal. VI.&V. "
18. BOURDON	. . .	Metal. 8 "	28. CONTRAFAGOTTO	.	Wood. 16 Feet.
19. TIBIA CLAUSA	.	Wood. 8 "	29. DOUBLE TRUMPET	Metal. 16 "
20. QUINT	. . . .	Metal. 5⅓ "	30. TROMBONE	. . .	Metal. 8 "
21. OCTAVE, MINOR	.	Metal. 4 "	31. HARMONIC TRUMPET	Metal. 8 "
22. HARMONIC FLUTE	.	Metal. 4 "	32. HARMONIC CLARION	Metal. 4 "

The Expressive Subdivision to be brought on and thrown off the clavier by thumb pistons: and to be commanded, when desired, by the Double-touch only of the clavier.

The Swell-box No. 1, to be controlled by Expression Lever No. 1, situated on the left of all the other Expression Levers.

All the labial stops to speak on wind of five inches; and the four lingual stops on wind of twelve inches.

It will be desirable as each division Organ is passed under review, to follow its list of speaking stops with an enumeration of the Couplers directly connected with it. As we have already expressed our disapproval, chiefly on scientific grounds, of the common practice of introducing couplers which act on the same tonal division (or clavier) in the sub-octave and octave, we shall in no case include these couplers. Accordingly, so far as the First Organ, now under consideration, is concerned, there is no necessity for its stops to be extended beyond the compass of 61 notes. In the case of the other manual divisions, commanded by the higher claviers, the stop compass of 73 notes is necessary for legitimate octave coupling, as will be shown in further remarks.

It will be seen that under our system of compound expression, which divides the stop apportionments of the Second, Third, and Fourth Organs, it is necessary for a larger number of couplers, operating between the Organs, to be introduced than is required in instruments of common construction and tonal appointment. No complexity, however, is caused by our new system, which, though simply and clearly systematic, imparts powers of musical expression, and renders possible orchestral effects, absolutely unknown in any Concert-room Organ constructed in the organ-building world up to the present year (1918).

FIRST ORGAN COUPLERS.

Second Organ.... 1st Subdivision.....to First Organ, Unison Coupler.
Second Organ.... 1st Subdivision.....to First Organ, Octave Coupler.
Second Organ.... 2nd Subdivision.....to First Organ, Unison Coupler.
Second Organ.... 2nd Subdivision.....to First Organ, Octave Coupler.
Third Organ..... 1st Subdivision.....to First Organ, Unison Coupler.
Third Organ..... 1st Subdivision.....to First Organ, Octave Coupler.
Third Organ..... 2nd Subdivision.....to First Organ, Unison Coupler.
Third Organ..... 2nd Subdivision.....to First Organ, Octave Coupler.
Fourth Organ.... 1st Subdivision.....to First Organ, Unison Coupler.
Fourth Organ.... 2nd Subdivision.....to First Organ, Unison Coupler.
Fifth Organ..... Undivided ....to First Organ, Unison Coupler.
Fifth Organ..... Undivided ....to First Organ, Octave Coupler.

This may seem a formidable array of couplers connected with an Organ commanded by the First Clavier; but, while some of the octave couplers might be omitted, the entire number is to be recommended. With their rocking-tablets arranged in the order given, and so particolored as to clearly indicate the Organs and Subdivisions coupled no confusion or uncertainty can possibly present itself. The desirability of retaining the full complement will be seen when our entire tonal scheme is realized and understood.

While we have already touched slightly on the greatly increased powers of tone-production given the First Organ by the inclosure of

portion of its voices in a swell-box; we may conclude our remarks, on
this fundamental division, by asking the student of organ matters to
form in his mind some idea of the extent and importance of these
powers, placed at his disposal on a single uncoupled clavier—powers of
tone-production altogether absent in any entirely uninclosed Great Organ
ever constructed.   From the time we entered on a serious study of organ
tonal appointment, we have realized the absolute necessity, if the Great
Organ is to be made an efficient musical division, that an important portion of its tonal forces must be put under control, and rendered flexible
and expressive: and we have just cause to feel proud that we were the
first to point the way to this very important development, by putting it
to practical test, and incontestibly proving its great importance from
every musical point of view.   In fact, we went still further, dividing the
Great or First Organ into three tonal parts, and endowing two of them
with separate powers of flexibility and expression; and this with tonal
results of a character as fascinating as they were previously undreamt
of in connection with the usual circumscribed musical resources of the
ordinary Great Organ.   The first organ-builder to follow our lead, in
imparting flexibility and expressive powers to the Great Organ, was the
late Hilborne L. Roosevelt, of New York City.

Turning to the First Organ as tonally apportioned in our scheme,
the student must realize that without the subdivision and inclosure in
a swell-box of the special portion of its voices, the tonal effects of a
satisfactory character would necessarily be very limited, and, for the
most part, to those of a pronounced intonation.   For instance, were the
entire tonal forces uninclosed, it is obvious that the mutation and harmonic-corroborating stops, comprising fourteen ranks of pipes, could only
be used along with the complete foundation work of the Organ.   Surely
this is an absurd and most undesirable narrowing of the office and utility
of such valuable tonal elements.   With the inclosure of such elements,
and the consequent powers of flexibility imparted to them, their range of
utility and sphere of tone-production are increased a hundred fold.

All the inclosed labial and lingual stops of the Expressive Subdivision
can be used in combination with the labial stops of the Unexpressive
Subdivision, either in graduated stationary tones, forming practically
countless beautiful effects; or, through their powers of expression,
imparting tonal light and shade to the stationary voices of the Unexpressive Subdivision, of the utmost value in artistic organ music.   Just
as a matter of curiosity, it may be stated that omitting the purely
harmonic-corroborating stops, which could not be used alone or in
combination with themselves only, there remain twenty-seven stops which
could produce no fewer than one hundred and thirty-four million, two
hundred and seventeen thousand, and seven hundred different combinations and tonal effects, without resort to the changes due to the swell.

Respecting the tonal character of the foundation stops, it is sufficient to say that they must yield pure organ-tones of the richest and most refined quality, perfectly balanced and regulated. The harmonic-corroborating stops, single and compound, to be formed of full-scaled open metal pipes, also yielding pure organ-tone, so as to assimilate perfectly with the tones of the principal foundation stops. The composition of the FULL MIXTURE, VI. and V. RANKS, to be that given on a preceding page: that of the CORNET to be as follows:—

CORNET—IV. RANKS.

I. SEVENTEENTH	Metal $1\frac{3}{5}$	Feet.
II. NINETEENTH	Metal $1\frac{1}{3}$	"
III. SEPTIÈME	Metal $1\frac{1}{7}$	"
IV. TWENTY-SECOND	Metal 1	"

The DOPPELFLÖTE to be of large scale and carried down to CC in double-mouthed pipes. The CLARABELLA to be of open pipes throughout. The CLARABEL to be a true octave to the CLARABELLA. The metal BOURDON to be of large scale, voiced to yield a full tone, as free from upper partial tones as possible. The newly invented, dual-voiced OCTATEN, valuable on account of its remarkable acoustical properties, is fully described in Chapter XV. The TIBIA PLENA, 8 FT., an open stop of large scale, yielding a powerful unimitative flute-tone; and the TIBIA CLAUSA, 8 FT., a covered stop, yielding a pure and liquid tone, fluty in quality, and of great body, and extremely valuable in combination with the lingual stops, are described in Chapter XV. It is unnecessary to allude to the other stops in any special manner, as their characteristics are well known.

SECOND ORGAN.

In approaching the question of the tonal apportionment of the Second Organ, several important considerations have to be borne in view. First, as to its relation to the tonal apportionment of the First Organ. Secondly, as to its relation to the apportionments of the Third, Fourth, and Fifth Organs. Thirdly, as to its place and office in the complete tonal scheme of the instrument. Fourthly, as to its value as an independent division.

In Organs of to-day this tonal division is termed the Choir Organ; and in its stop apportionment is, as a rule, merely a soft-toned variant of the Great Organ, without any indication of a definite and sharply defined office in the general scheme of the instrument. The stops introduced seem to have been selected at hazard, and some are mere duplications of stops provided in the Great or some other division. This may be pronounced the general rule to which there are few exceptions. For a long time, in all classes of instruments, the so-called Choir Organ was constructed without powers of flexibility and expression; and in this uncontrollable condition it appears to-day in many important Concert-room Organs. In this country, Roosevelt's lead has been followed, and we find the Choir Organ in several important instruments endowed with powers of expression, by having its pipe-work inclosed in the Great Organ swell-box, or, more rarely, in an independent swell. No attempt, however, has been made to impart to this tonal division of the Concert-room Organ compound powers of flexibility and expression.

The conditions of primal importance in the stop apportionment of the Second Organ are three in number. First, that it shall, as a whole, contrast tonally with the stop apportionments of the other Organs. Secondly, that it shall embrace stops which can be effectively separated into two groups or subdivisions of contrasting tonalities. Thirdly, that the subdivisions shall be separately endowed with powers of flexibility and expression; thereby multiplying to a large extent the musical resources and effects of the whole apportionment. These are simple and reasonable conditions against which no valid objections can be taken; yet they have never been carried into effect in the Choir division of a Concert-room Organ: and we fail to see in the stop appointment of lately schemed important instruments any indications of a thought having been given to any departure—save, perhaps, in the direction of size—from old-established methods. Let the reader consult the lists of stops of recently schemed and constructed Concert-room Organs and compare them with those of large Church Organs, and judge for himself.

At the risk of repeating what has already been conveyed, we desire it to be clearly understood that the leading principle in the system of organ appointment we are now advocating, on both artistic and logical grounds, is that each divisional Organ shall have special and well defined tonal characteristics of its own. The present worn-out method of stop apportionment, which to a very large extent makes each manual division (with, perhaps the exception of the Solo Organ, when such a division is provided) little better than a tonal replica of the others, is obviously wrong; and results in a great loss of variety and tonal concentration, and, accordingly, in a serious sacrifice of the beauty and utility of the entire instrument.

The importance and value of having distinctive and contrasting tonal colorings in each of the manual divisions and their subdivisions in the Concert-room Organ must be freely acknowledged by the *musician;* not only on account of the immense facilities given him in painting his most complex and expressive tone-pictures, and in keeping all his special effects of light and shade distinct; but also in leading him to the realization of musical compositions hitherto practically impossible of interpretation through the medium of the present style of Organ. The Organ of the Twentieth Century, constituted as we propose becomes an instrument for the *Virtuoso;* and with its limitless range of tonal combination * and powers of flexibility and expression, is only second to that supreme musical machine—the Grand Orchestra.

It may be accepted, as a first proposition, that tonally the Second Organ will, on account of its principal office in the economy of the instrument, be more closely allied to the First Organ than to any of the others, while it must firmly assert its individuality. The general tone-character of the First Organ, furnished by the voices of the unison and double DIAPASONS and their practically complete harmonic corroborating stops, being what is recognized as pure organ-tone, the remaining voices in the division being introduced with the aim of enriching, relieving, and slightly coloring the organ-tones without impairing their proper fundamental character; the question arises as to what the tonal characteristics of the Second Organ should be. If the Second Organ is to be chiefly of an accompanimental nature, under single expressive control, resembling the best examples of the Choir Organ to be found in the ordinary instruments of to-day, the answer to the question presents very little difficulty to one familiar with stop tonalities. But as it is our desire, for the advancement of the Organ as a musical instrument, to depart both in a tonal and expressive direction from such old-fashioned appointments, the question has to be approached from an entirely different standpoint.

In the first place, the stops apportioned to the Second Organ have to bear, collectively, a certain desirable contrast in their voices to those apportioned to the First Organ. In the second place, they have to be divided into two groups, tonally contrasting, and to which separate powers of flexibility and expression have to be given. This disposition, never systematically adopted, up to the present time, in the Concert-room Organ, involves the questions: What shall the tonalities of the Subdivisions be, and which, if either, shall predominate?

We shall answer these questions from our own point of view; freely admitting that a better answer may be formed. We are of opinion that use should be made, for the most part, of unimitative voices, preference being given to flute organ-tone and viol organ-tone; such lingual stops being introduced as would lend themselves to effective combination with the labial stops of the division; and which would be less desirable in the more assertive manual Organs, while being valuable and conducive to

---

* We may be allowed to use the word *limitless* in this matter, when the fact is that with merely forty stops the following number of combinations can be made—1,099,511,627,735. Some idea can be formed of what this number means, when, allowing a different combination to be made every second, without a single intermission during the twenty-four hours of every day, the time required to execute the entire series of combinations would, in round figures, be thirty-four thousand, eight hundred years.

variety and contrast of tone situated in the Second Organ. On reference to the stop apportionment of the First Organ it will be observed that only a slight resort is there made to stops yielding flute-tone; only two of any pronounced character—the DOPPELFLÖTE and TIBIA PLENA —being introduced, for the purpose of coloring the volume of pure organ-tone, and imparting body to the lingual voices. Therefore, and in accordance with our principles of tonal apportionment, free use can be made of flute-tone in one of the Subdivisions of the Second Organ. For contrast of tone in the other Subdivision, viol organ-tone, with a slight addition of the softer variety of imitative string-tone, will be most desirable. These apportionments will lead to many beautiful combinations of contrasting tones, especially under the control of compound flexibility and expression. The following is a suggestive appointment for the Second Organ.

SECOND ORGAN—SECOND CLAVIER.

FULLY EXPRESSIVE—COMPASS CC TO c⁴—61 NOTES.

FIRST EXPRESSIVE SUBDIVISION.

Inclosed in Swell-box No. 2.

1. LIEBLICHGEDECKT .	Wood. 16 Feet.	7. SPITZFLÖTE . . .	Metal. 8 Feet.
2. KERAULOPHONE . .	Metal. 8 "	8. ROHRQUINTE . . .	Metal. 5⅓ "
3. DULCIANA . . .	Metal. 8 "	9. LIEBLICHFLÖTE . .	Metal. 4 "
4. LIEBLICHGEDECKT .	Wood. 8 "	10. FLAUTO D'AMORE .	Metal. 4 "
5. DOLCAN	Metal. 8 "	11. FLAGEOLET . . .	Metal. 2 "
6. ROHRFLÖTE . . .	Metal. 8 "	12. COR ANGLAIS . .	Metal. 8 "

I. TREMOLANT.

SECOND EXPRESSIVE SUBDIVISION.

Inclosed in Swell-box No. 3.

13. DOUBLE VIOL . .	Metal. 16 Feet.	20. SALICET	Metal. 4 Feet.
14. FLÛTE A PAVILLON	Metal. 8 "	21. DOUBLETTE .	Metal. 2⅔ & 2 "
15. VIOL DIAPASON .	Metal. 8 "	22. DOLCE CORNET .	.Metal. V. Ranks.
16. SALICIONAL . .	Metal. 8 "	23. DULCIAN . . .	Metal. 16 Feet
17. VIOLA DA GAMBA .	Metal. 8 "	24. OBOE D'AMORE . .	Metal. 8 "
18. VOX ANGELICA .	Tin. 8 "	25. CHALUMEAU . .	Metal. 8 "
19. VOX CŒLESTIS . .	Tin. 8 "	26. MUSETTE . . .	Metal. 4 "

II. TREMOLANT.

Both the Subdivisions to be independently brought on and thrown off the Second Clavier by thumb-pistons: and the Second Subdivision only to be commanded, when desired, by the Double-touch of the clavier.

The swell-box No. 2 to be controlled by Expression Lever No. 2, and Swell-box No. 3 to be controlled by Expression Lever No. 3, situated immediately to the right of Expression Lever No. 1.

All the stops of the First Expressive Subdivision to speak on wind of 3½ inches. All the labial stops of the Second Expressive Subdivision to speak on wind of 4 inches, and the four lingual stops on wind of 6 inches.

All the stops of the Second Organ to be planted on wind-chests of 73 notes.

SECOND ORGAN COUPLERS.

Third Organ..... 1st Subdivision..... to Second Organ, Unison Coupler.
Third Organ..... 1st Subdivision..... to Second Organ, Octave Coupler.
Third Organ..... 2nd Subdivision..... to Second Organ, Unison Coupler.
Third Organ..... 2nd Subdivision..... to Second Organ, Octave Coupler.
Fourth Organ.... 1st Subdivision..... to Second Organ, Unison Coupler.
Fourth Organ.... 1st Subdivision..... to Second Organ, Octave Coupler.
Fourth Organ.... 2nd Subdivision..... to Second Organ, Unison Coupler.
Fourth Organ.... 2nd Subdivision..... to Second Organ, Octave Coupler.
Fifth Organ..... Undivided .... to Second Organ, Unison Coupler.

Before passing on to the consideration of the stop apportionment of the important Third organ, we may add a few words to what has already been said regarding the speaking stops of the present Organ; specially with the view of showing our reasons for the insertion of certain voices in the contrasting Subdivisions. The three LIEBLICHGEDECKTS, 16 FT., 8 FT., and 4 FT., forming a valuable family, are introduced on account of their quiet and refined, covered, fluty tones. These stops to be of small scales, voiced to yield tones, as free as practicable from the Twelfth, which will combine well with, and give body to, the more pronounced voices of the other flute-toned stops of the Subdivision. Two half-covered stops, the ROHRFLÖTE, 8 FT., and ROHRQUINTE, 5⅓ FT., add voices of distinctive tonality, building up a solid foundation of covered tone in combination with the LIEBLICHGEDECKTS. Sufficient variety of voices is furnished in this Subdivision by the KERAULOPHONE, 8 FT., voiced to yield a full horn-like tone; the DOLCAN, 8 FT., made, in its correct form, of inverted conical pipes, voiced to yield a bright and singing quality of tone; and the DULCIANA, 8 FT., which introduces pure organ-tone, which will combine perfectly with every other voice in the Organ. The only lingual stop in the Subdivision is the COR ANGLAIS, the quiet tone of which should imitate, as closely as possible, the " melancholy, dreamy, and rather noble voice " of the orchestral instrument. Any one acquainted with the tonal values of organ stops can see how perfectly suited this Subdivision—flexible and expressive—is for accompanimental purposes of a refined character, as well as for the more delicate episodes of descriptive music.

Turning now to the Second Expressive Subdivision the existence of a studied tonal contrast can be seen at a glance, and it will not take the musician long (however long it may take groove-loving organ-builders) to realize its value. Flute-tone is not represented by a single stop; the FLÛTE À PAVILLON, 8 FT., being the French name for the BELL DIA-

PASON, the tone of which is full and more horn-like than that of the true DIAPASON, furnishes the foundation unison tone of the Subdivision. Contrasting viol-tone is amply supplied by the DOUBLE VIOL, 16 FT., VIOL DIAPASON, 8 FT., SALICIONAL, 8 FT., VIOLA DA GAMBA, 8 FT., and SALICET, 4 FT.; all of which have different tonal characters, and values in combination. The VOX ANGELICA, 8 FT., formed of very small-scaled cylindrical pipes, yielding tones much softer than those of the DULCIANA, has a slight string character, which, in combination with its companion stop, the VOX CŒLESTIS, 8 FT., produces the usual delicate *tremolo*, so much admired, and which imparts a certain charm to string-toned combinations. The DOUBLETTE, formed of two ranks of SALICIONAL pipes of 2⅔ ft. and 2 ft., is harmonic-corroborating; its compound voice being similar to, and carrying up, that of the SALICET, 4 FT. The DOLCE CORNET, V RANKS, is not timbre-creating, being formed of small-scaled pipes yielding pure organ-tone of a singing quality, of the greatest value, on account of its harmonic-corroborating property, in combination with the principal stops in both the Subdivisions. Just as a single instance; drawn alone, with swell-box No. 3 closed or very slightly opened, and played with either the DULCIANA or DOLCAN, with expression, in swell-box No. 2, the musical effect produced would be one of fascinating beauty; impossible on a single clavier (if under any conditions) in any Church or Concert-room Organ in existence to-day.* Imagine such an accompaniment to a solo on a VOX HUMANA or any delicately-toned lingual stop in another manual division. The most desirable composition of the DOLCE CORNET is as here given:—

DOLCE CORNET—V. RANKS.

CC to BB	. . . . .	19—22—24—26—29.
C to e¹	. . . . .	12—15—17—19—22.
f¹ to e²	. . . . .	8—12—17—19—22.
f² to c⁴	. . . . .	1— 8—10—12—15.

THIRD ORGAN.

We approach this important Third Division of the Concert-room Organ on the principles we have formulated; namely, contrast in tonal apportionment and compound powers of flexibility and expression. The former prepares a palette of distinct tone-colors, from which the brush of the musician, skilfully manipulated, can paint tone-pictures replete with poetic chiaro-oscuro, fancy and pathos, simplicity and grandeur:

* It is safe to say that this remarkable musical effect has only been heard on our own Chamber Organ. It fascinated every one who performed for the first time on its keys, and who not only had never heard it before, but failed, in every instance, to individualize the stops producing it.

while the latter invests all such pictures with the indescribable charms of expression, which reveal the thoughts of the musician to the mind of his listener.

In the tonal apportionment of the Third Organ due regard must obtain to the apportionments of the First and Second Organs, and also to those of the Fourth and Fifth Organs and such ancillary Divisions as may be embraced in the grand scheme of the instrument. We hold that in a scientifically and artistically schemed Organ, every Division must be dependent on all the others, and occupy a definite and relative position and office, tonally, in the complete appointment of the instrument. Yet a survey of the tonal appointments of important Organs recently constructed or schemed fails to show that any such ideas entered the minds of their designers. It seems impossible to trace any clearly defined aims in their tonal apportionments. Old-fashioned methods are followed; and anything beyond ordinary powers of expression is not ventured on.

As in the Second Organ, so in the Third we adopt compound flexibility and expression; arranging the tonal forces in two Subdivisions, not only contrasting with each other, but also with the Subdivisions of the Second Organ, as already described, and, as will shortly be shown, with the Subdivisions of the Fourth Organ. By such an obviously desirable method of stop apportionment, not only is the musician furnished with the readiest means for effective tone-painting, and striking effects of contrast, assisted by powers of expression; but the objectionable use of coupling, with its attendant crippling of independence in the claviers, is rendered practically unnecessary, save for extraordinary massing of contrasting tones, endowed with either single or compound expression.

In the apportionments of the First and Second Organs, pure organ-tone and unimitative voices have been systematically introduced, laying the foundation, in conjunction with the Pedal Organ, for the entire tonal fabric of the instrument. Accordingly, in the Third Organ, now under consideration, a tonality of a widely different character is called for on artistic and practical grounds. To furnish this tonality, stops having voices imitative of certain orchestral instruments take an important place in the apportionment. The stops selected are those which represent the wood-wind and reed forces of the grand orchestra, associated with such stops as lend themselves to the support of, and desirable combinations with, the imitative voices. Reserving further remarks for the present, we now give our scheme for the stop apportionment of this Organ:—

THIRD ORGAN—THIRD CLAVIER.

FULLY EXPRESSIVE—COMPASS CC to c⁴—61 NOTES.

FIRST EXPRESSIVE SUBDIVISION.

Inclosed in Swell-box No. 2.

1. Double Principal .	Metal. 16 Feet.		9. Contra-Oboe . .	Metal. 16 Feet.
2. Viol Principal .	Metal. 8 "		10. Fagotto . . .	Wood. 8 "
3. Corno Dolce . .	Metal. 8 "		11. Orchestral Oboe	Metal. 8 "
4. Quintaten . . .	Metal. 8 "		12. Orchestral	
5. Doppelrohrgedeckt	Metal. 8 "		Clarinet . .	Metal. 8 "
6. Doppelrohrflöte .	Metal. 4 "		13. Saxophone . .	Metal. 8 "
7. Sesquialtera .	Metal. IV. Ranks.		14. Vox Humana . .	Metal. 8 "
8. Fagottone . . .	Wood. 16 Feet.		15. Octave Oboe . .	Metal. 4 "

III. Tremolant.

SECOND EXPRESSIVE SUBDIVISION.

Inclosed in Swell-box No. 3.

16. Kleingedeckt . .	Wood. 16 Feet.		25. Gedecktquinte .	Wood. 5⅓ Feet.
17. Principal . . .	Metal. 8 "		26. Orchestral Flute	Wood. 4 "
18. Gemshorn . . .	Metal. 8 "		27. Spitzflöte . .	Metal. 4 "
19. Flautone . . .	Wood. 8 "		28. Gedeckt-Tierce .	Metal. 3⅕ "
20. Philomela . .	Wood. 8 "		29. Orchestral	
21. Tierce Flute			Piccolo . .	Metal. 2 "
(Dual) . .	Metal. 8 "		30. Grand Cornet	Metal. IV. Ranks.
22. Orchestral Flute	Wood. 8 "		31. Corno di Bassetto	Metal. 16 Feet.
23. Hohlflöte . .	Wood. 8 "		32. Corno di Bassetto	Metal. 8 "
24. Dolce	Metal. 8 "		IV. Tremolant.	

Both the Subdivisions to be independently brought on and thrown off the Third Clavier by thumb-pistons: and the Second Subdivision only to be commanded, when desired, by the Double-touch of the clavier.

As in the Second Organ, Swell-box No. 2 is to be controlled by Expression Lever No. 2, and Swell-box No. 3 to be controlled by Expression Lever No. 3.

All the labial stops and the Vox Humana of the First Subdivision to speak on wind of 4½ inches; and all the remaining lingual stops to speak on wind of 10 inches.

All the labial stops of the Second Subdivision, with the exception of Nos. 21, 22, and 26, to speak on wind of 6 inches. Stops Nos. 21, 22, 26, 31, 32, to speak on wind of 10 inches.

All the stops of the Third Organ to be planted on wind-chests of 73 notes.

THIRD ORGAN COUPLERS.

Fourth Organ.... 1st Subdivision.....to Third Organ, Unison Coupler.
Fourth Organ.... 1st Subdivision.....to Third Organ, Octave Coupler.
Fourth Organ.... 2nd Subdivision.....to Third Organ, Unison Coupler.
Fourth Organ.... 2nd Subdivision.....to Third Organ, Octave Coupler.
Fifth Organ..... Undivided ....to Third Organ, Unison Coupler.
Fifth Organ..... Undivided ....to Third Organ, Octave Coupler.
Fifth Organ..... Undivided ....to Third Organ, Sub-octave Coupler.

A glance over the lists of stops forming the apportionments of the two Expressive Subdivisions of this Third Organ will be sufficient to convey their purpose in the general tonal scheme of the entire instrument. In the First Subdivision are grouped the representatives—as far as possible in organ-pipes—of the reed instruments of the orchestra; namely, the Oboe, Clarinet, Bassoon, and Saxophone: supplemented by effective additions of both lower and higher pitches, rendered possible in organ pipes—the FAGOTTONE, 16 FT., CONTRA-OBOE, 16 FT., and OCTAVE OBOE, 4 FT. The seven labial stops are selected on account of their good combining qualities, and their value in tone-production in combination with the lingual stops, the VOX HUMANA excepted, which, as a dual stop of a solo character, calls for no further addition. The same may be said of the ORCHESTRAL CLARINET, which is also a dual stop, formed of its proper lingual pipes associated with a DOPPELFLÖTE, 8 FT., of small scale and soft intonation, regulated to blend perfectly. The stop associated with the VOX HUMANA to be a small-scaled and soft-toned MELODIA, 8 FT. The only stop calling for special details is the SESQUIALTERA, which is composed of four ranks of organ-toned pipes of medium scales as follows:—

SESQUIALTERA—IV RANKS.

CC to F,	.	.	.	.	.	15 —19*—22 —24*.
F♯ to f¹,	.	.	.	.	.	12*—15 —17*—19.
f♯¹ to c³,	.	.	.	.	.	8 —12*—15 —17*.
c♯³ to c⁴,	.	.	.	.	.	1 — 5*— 8 —10*.

In the apportionment of the Second Subdivision, the flute voices of the orchestra are represented by the ORCHESTRAL FLUTES, 8 FT., and 4 FT., and the ORCHESTRAL PICCOLO, 2 FT.; completing, along with the two lingual stops,—the CORNO DI BASSETTO, 16 FT., and CORNO DI BASSETTO, 8 FT.,—the wood-wind forces. The family of ORCHESTRAL FLUTES is supported by the several unimitative flute-toned stops; while volume, richness, and variety of tonal coloring are secured by the pure organ-toned PRINCIPAL, 8 FT., and DOLCE, 8 FT., and by the GEMSHORN, three GEDECKTS, and GRAND CORNET. Certain of the stops require comment, so that their position and office in the apportionment may be understood. The FLAUTONE, 8 FT., is an open wood stop of full scale, having a voice of a good mixing and filling-up quality, not quite so powerful as that of the true GROSSFLÖTE. The PHILOMELA, 8 FT., is a small-scaled open wood stop, voiced to yield an extremely sweet and delicate flute-tone. The TIERCE FLUTE, 8 FT., of powerful and penetrating voice, is formed of two ranks of open metal pipes, as described on page 104, Chapter IV. The DOLCE, 8 FT., formed of open metal pipes of smaller scale than the normal DULCIANA, is voiced to yield a soft, singing tone of great value in combination with the less assertive stops. Should a *céleste* effect be desired the DOLCE may be tuned sharp, and drawn with the PHILOMELA, or with the CORNO DOLCE in the First Expressive Division. The GRAND CORNET, IV. RANKS, is timbre-creating and formed as follows:—

GRAND CORNET—IV. RANKS.

I. FLÛTE A CHEMINÉE	. . . . .	Metal. 8 Feet.
II. VIOLETTA	. . . . . .	Tin. 4 "
III. GEMSHORN	. . . . . .	Metal. 2⅔ "
IV. SPITZFLÖTE	. . . . . .	Metal. 2 "

While the thirty-two stops are divided into two apportionments of contrasting tonalities, and are located in the swell-boxes Nos. 2 and 3 (in which the Subdivisions of the Second Organ are also located), collectively they form a single manual Division or Organ, commanded by the Third Clavier. The stops of the Subdivisions can, accordingly, be associated in any desirable combinations, either under simple or compound expression; the former only requiring both expression levers, Nos. 2 and 3 to be operated simultaneously, by placing the foot partly on both; while by operating the levers separately, either by one or both feet, compound expression can be produced. Further, one lever may be moved to obtain any desired strength of tone in the swell-box it controls; while the other lever is being used to impart expression to the voices in the other swell-box.

If reference is made to the stop apportionments of the Second Organ, it will be seen that the stops in its First Expressive Subdivision contrast effectively with the stops of the First Expressive Subdivision of the Third Organ, both of which are inclosed in swell-box No. 2. The same remarks hold good with regard to the Second Expressive Subdivisions of the Second and Third Organs, which are both inclosed in the swell-box No. 3.

If the dispositions of the four contrasting and tonally distinct Subdivisions alluded to are fully considered in their several combinations, some idea may be formed of the absolutely infinite variety of beautiful tonal effects and *nuances* that are possible by the combinations of the numerous contrasting voices, under the control and refining influence of both simple and compound powers of flexibility and expression—tonal effects that have never yet been heard, or are, indeed, possible, on any Organ hitherto constructed; but will be heard, some day, on The Organ of the Twentieth Century.

Now, supposing the unison coupler drawn, connecting the Third Organ to the Second Organ, and the performer's hands are confined, for the time, to the Second Clavier, let us see, by way of example, what can be done, under our system, in the mere combination of the four contrasting Expressive Subdivisions at his disposal. The following statement is eloquent.

LIST OF COMBINATIONS OF CONTRASTING FIRST AND SECOND
EXPRESSIVE SUBDIVISIONS OF THE SECOND AND THIRD ORGANS.

1. 1st. Subdivision of Second Organ with 2nd. Subdivision of Second Organ—
   Compound expression.
2. 1st. Subdivision of Second Organ with 1st. Subdivision of Third Organ—
   Simple expression.
3. 1st. Subdivision of Second Organ with 2nd. Subdivision of Third Organ—
   Compound expression.
4. 1st. Subdivision of Second Organ with 1st. and 2nd. Subdivisions of Third
   Organ—Compound expression.
5. 2nd. Subdivision of Second Organ with 1st. Subdivision of Third Organ—
   Compound expression.
6. 2nd. Subdivision of Second Organ with 2nd. Subdivision of Third Organ—
   Simple expression.
7. 2nd. Subdivision of Second Organ with 1st. and 2nd. Subdivisions of Third
   Organ—Compound expression.
8. 1st. and 2nd. Subdivisions of Second Organ with 1st. Subdivision of Third
   Organ—Compound expression.
9. 1st. and 2nd. Subdivisions of Second Organ with 2nd. Subdivision of Third
   Organ—Compound expression.
10. 1st. and 2nd. Subdivisions of Second Organ with 1st. and 2nd. Subdivisions
    of Third Organ—Compound expression.

It will be seen from the list that with our system of divisional stop
apportionment and the operation of a unison coupler only, the performer
has at his disposal on the Second Clavier ten Swell Organs, each of
which comprises two, three, or four contrasting tonal divisions; eight
of the organs being endowed with compound powers of flexibility and
expression, under the control of two expression levers, which, as has
been stated, can be operated independently or conjointly, as the performer desires. Great and unique as these advantages are, they are
merely a part of those which our scheme for The Organ of the Twentieth
Century places at the disposal of the artist organist.

Should the combinations, under compound expression, just listed,
which are available on the Second Organ Clavier, seem too troublesome
to the timid performer, who desires greater simplicity; he has only to
realize that he can, at any time, have at his disposal a *single* Swell Organ
of 26 stops, 41 stops, 43 stops, or 58 stops. All that is necessary is to
couple the Third Organ to the Second Organ in the unison, perform on
the Second Clavier, and operate simultaneously expression levers No.
2 and 3—a matter of no greater difficulty than operating either lever
alone.

FOURTH ORGAN.

According to our present scheme of tonal apportionment, the chief
office of the Fourth Organ is to furnish, to as full an extent as practic-

able, the representatives of the "brass-wind" forces of the orchestra. With this view, we introduce a series of lingual stops such as has never appeared in a single manual division of any Organ hitherto constructed. These stops are arranged in two groups of dissimilar tonalities—contrasting to as great an extent as possible—and occupy positions, respectively, in the First and Second Expressive Subdivisions of the Organ. Two very important families of stops are introduced. In the First Subdivision is the family of TROMBAS, 16 FT., 8 FT., and 4 FT.; with which are associated the OPHICLEIDES, 16 FT., and 8 FT., the ORCHESTRAL TRUMPET, 8 FT., and FRENCH HORN, 8 FT. In the Second Subdivision is the larger family of the TROMBONES, 16 FT., 8 FT., 5⅓ FT., and 4 FT.; with which are associated the EUPHONIUM, 16 FT., CORNOPEAN, 8 FT., and BARITONO, 8 FT.

The labial stops apportioned to the Subdivisions have been selected chiefly with the view of creating rich and varied tonalities in combination with the lingual voices. In this direction the three compound harmonic-corroborating stops would prove productive of beautiful orchestral effects. The appointment of the Organ is as follows:—

FOURTH ORGAN—FOURTH CLAVIER.

FULLY EXPRESSIVE—COMPASS CC TO c⁴—61 NOTES.

FIRST EXPRESSIVE SUBDIVISION.
Inclosed in Swell-box No. 4.

1. GROSSGEDECKT	.	Wood. 16 Feet.	9. OPHICLEIDE	. . .	Metal. 16 Feet.
2. GRAND DIAPASON	.	Metal. 8 "	10. CONTRA-TROMBA	.	Metal. 16 "
3. DIAPASON	. . .	Wood. 8 "	11. TROMBA MAGNA	.	Metal. 8 "
4. VIOL, MAJOR	. .	Metal. 8 "	12. OPHICLEIDE	. .	Metal. 8 "
5. QUINTATEN	Wood & Metal. 8 "		13. ORCHESTRAL		
6. WALDFLÖTE	. . .	Wood. 4 "	TRUMPET	. .	Metal. 8 "
7. HARMONIC OCTAVE	Metal. 4 "		14. FRENCH HORN	. .	Metal. 8 "
8. GRAND CORNET	. Metal. V. Ranks.		15. TROMBA CLARION	.	Metal. 4 "

V. TREMOLANT.

SECOND EXPRESSIVE SUBDIVISION
Inclosed in Swell-box No. 5.

16. STARKGEDECKT	. .	Wood. 16 Feet.	24. CONTRA-TROMBONE	Metal. 16 Feet.
17. HORN PRINCIPAL	.	Metal. 8 "	25. EUPHONIUM	. .	Metal. 16 "
18. VIOL, MINOR	. .	Metal. 8 "	26. TROMBONE	. . .	Metal. 8 "
19. WALDFLÖTE	. .	Wood. 8 "	27. CORNOPEAN	. .	Metal. 8 "
20. HARMONIC FLUTE	.	Metal. 8 "	28. BARITONO	. . .	Metal. 8 "
21. HARMONIC FLUTE	.	Metal. 4 "	29. TROMBONE QUINT	.	Metal. 5⅓ "
22. DOUBLETTE	.	Metal. 2⅔ & 2 "	30. TROMBONE OCTAVE	Metal. 4 "
23. CYMBAL	. .	Metal. VI. Ranks.	VI. TREMOLANT.

Both the Subdivisions to be independently brought on and thrown off the Fourth Clavier by thumb-pistons.

The Swell-box No. 4 to be controlled by Expression Lever No. 4, and Swell-box No. 5 to be controlled by Expression Lever No. 5.

The labial stops of the First Subdivision to speak on wind of 6 inches; and the lingual stops to speak on wind of 12 inches.

The labial stops of the Second Subdivision to speak on wind of 6 inches. The lingual stops Nos. 24, 26, and 30 to speak on wind of 15 inches; and stops Nos. 25, 27, 28, and 29 to speak on wind of 12 inches.

All the stops of the Fourth Organ to be planted on wind-chests of 73 notes.

FOURTH ORGAN COUPLERS.

Fifth Organ.....Undivided.....to Fourth Organ, Unison Coupler.
Fifth Organ.....Undivided.....to Fourth Organ, Octave Coupler.

While there are only two stops in the apportionments the compositions of which require to be described in detail; namely, the GRAND CORNET, V. RANKS, and CYMBAL, VI. RANKS; it is perhaps desirable that, to more clearly set forth our purpose, a few particulars should be given respecting certain of the more important stops.

It must be obvious that while the labial stops in the Subdivisions can be effectively used alone in many combinations, assisted by contrasting tonalities and powers of flexibility and expression, they have been selected with the special aim of their forming suitable and effective combinations with the several lingual stops; building up orchestral tones —giving volume and weight to some, and imparting force and brilliancy to others.

The GROSSGEDECKT, 16 FT., to be of a scale larger than that usually adopted for the proper LIEBLICHGEDECKT and to have a voice of the same pure quality as, but of much greater volume than, that commonly given to the true LIEBLICHGEDECKT, 16 FT. While this stop would be generally valuable in combination; in conjunction with the GRAND CORNET it would produce majestic tones in combination with the OPHICLEIDES and TROMBAS. The GRAND DIAPASON to be of a large scale and voiced to yield a pure organ-tone of a commanding power. The VIOL MAJOR to be formed of medium scaled pipes having a full unimitative string-tone of good mixing quality. The GRAND CORNET to be composed as follows:—

GRAND CORNET—V. RANKS.

I. GEMSHORN	. . . .	Metal. 8 Feet.
II. SPITZFLÖTE	. . . .	Metal. 5⅓ "
III. GEMSHORN	. . . .	Metal. 4 "
IV. SPITZFLÖTE	. . . .	Metal. 2⅔ "
V. PICCOLO	. . . .	Metal. 2 "

This important stop is both timbre-creating and harmonic-corroborating—belonging to the 16 ft. harmonic series—but in the regulation of its ranks it is not required to follow the strict rule of graduation of tone proper in the ordinary harmonic-corroborating MIXTURES. It is, however, important that its unison and octave ranks should, in strength of tone, dominate the two fifth-sounding ranks. The tones of the GEMSHORNS to be full and rich; and that of the PICCOLO bright, without undue assertiveness.

The OPHICLEIDES to be scaled and voiced to yield full and commanding tones, as free from clang and brassiness as possible; contrasting in this respect with the tones of the TROMBAS and TROMBONES, which have different degrees of brazen clang. The ORCHESTRAL TRUMPET to have a bright and penetrating voice, imitating closely that of the orchestral Slide Trumpet. The desirable HORN will be that which imitates most closely the orchestral instrument in its characteristic tones.

A few remarks only are necessary on the principal stops of the Second Subdivision. The STARKGEDECKT, 16 FT., to be of a larger scale than the GROSSGEDECKT, and to yield a fuller and rounder tone, approximating that of the best type of BOURDON. The HARMONIC FLUTES to be of the larger scales, and voiced to yield full tones of good mixing quality, desirable in combination with the graver voices of the lingual stops. The DOUBLETTE to be formed of open pipes similar to those of the HORN PRINCIPAL, and to have the same quality of tone. The CYMBAL, VI. RANKS, to be formed of open pipes of medium scale, voiced to yield pure organ-tone, free from any coarse or screaming quality. It is to be composed as follows:—

CYMBAL—VI. RANKS.

CC to BB,			12—15—19—22—26—29.
C to B,			8—12—15—19—22—26.
c¹ to g²,			5—8—12—15—19—22.
g♯² to c⁴,			1—5—8—12—15—19.

The complete TROMBONE family, which forms the most distinctive feature in the stop apportionment of this Subdivision, has never, so far as our knowledge extends, been introduced in any manual division of an Organ hitherto constructed or schemed. Indeed, in the present rule-of-thumb, aimless system—or rather want of system—followed by organ-builders and designers of to-day in the stop apportionment of their most important Organs, the value of tonal massing, by means of stop families, is entirely ignored. The grandest effects the Organ is capable of producing are sacrificed by the incongruous and purposeless stop apportionments now universally and thoughtlessly perpetrated. The tones of the four TROMBONES in our present scheme to be bright and assertive, with sufficient brassiness to closely imitate those of the orchestral Trombones played *forte*. The ameliorating effect of the swell will be sufficient to modify the tones until they resemble those of the Trombones played softly. The EUPHONIUM to have a round and clear voice entirely free from any brazen clang, resembling that of the orchestral instrument played by a master. The most satisfactory tone is obtained from a free-reed stop when properly made. It is to be regretted that free-reed stops are totally neglected by organ-builders in this country at the present time. Those we specified for the Organ installed at the Louisiana Purchase Exposition were imported from Germany. The CORNOPEAN to be voiced to yield a tone of a solo character, and of a quality between the tones of the ORCHESTRAL TRUMPET and the FRENCH HORN. The tone should imitate as closely as possible that of the orchestral Cornet à pistons, as played by a master. The BARITONO to have a full tone of perfect mixing quality, resembling that of the Barytone Sax Horn in B♭. This stop to be used chiefly in combination with labial voices of the Subdivision in which it is placed.

FIFTH ORGAN.

This manual Division, strictly belonging to and commanded by the Fifth Clavier, may properly be considered a Solo Organ; its apportionment embracing stops specially adapted for the production of distinct tonal effects of an orchestral and solo character. It is so appointed as to relieve the other manual Organs from having to be inconveniently or suddenly changed, and to render the undesirable resort to coupling unnecessary. As we have already said, every possible arrangement should be made, in the tonal apportionment of the several Organs, to avoid the necessity for a frequent resort to coupling for the production of special and frequently recurring tonal effects. In an artistically schemed instrument, each manual Organ should have its special place and office; and be at all times independent and untrammeled. This principle we have steadily held in view in the tonal apportionments of the four Organs already treated, and shall continue to observe in the apportionments of the Divisions which remain to be considered.

As the office of this Fifth Organ is essentially different from the offices of the other four manual Organs, it is unnecessary to divide its tonal forces and impart to them compound expression. Every stop, however, must be inclosed in the most responsive and perfectly constructed swell-box that art can devise; care being taken to avoid any approach to annihilation of sound when the swell is closed, and to secure a very gradual and even *crescendo* and *diminuendo;* for upon such desirable conditions depend the beauty and sympathetic refinement of the solo effects this Organ places at the command of the musician.

FIFTH ORGAN—FIFTH CLAVIER.

FULLY EXPRESSIVE—COMPASS CC to c⁴—61 notes.

Inclosed in Swell-box No. 6.

1. DOPPELGEDECKT . .	Wood.	16 Feet.	9. CONTRA-TUBA . .	Metal.	16	Feet.
2. VIOL PRINCIPAL .	Metal.	8 "	10. TUBA MAGNA . .	Metal.	8	"
3. STENTORPHONE . .	Metal.	8 "	11. HARMONIC TRUMPET	Metal.	8	"
4. ORCHESTRAL VIOLONCELLO .	Metal.	8 "	12. ORCHESTRAL CLARINET . .	Metal.	8	"
5. VIOLE D'ORCHESTRE .	Metal.	8 "	13. ORCHESTRAL OBOE	Metal.	8	"
6. DOPPELROHRFLÖTE .	Wood.	8 "	14. TUBA QUINT . .	Metal.	5⅓	"
7. ORCHESTRAL FLUTE	Wood.	4 "	15. TUBA CLARION. .	Metal.	4	"
8. ORCHESTRAL PICCOLO	Metal.	2 "	16. CARILLON.			
			VII. TREMOLANT to Labial Stops.			

The Swell-box No. 6 to be controlled by Expression Lever No. 6, located to the right of the other five Levers.

All the labial stops to speak on wind of 8 inches. Stops Nos. 12 and 13 to speak on wind of 10 inches, and stops Nos. 9, 10, 11, 14, and 15 to speak on wind of 20 inches.

All the stops of the Fifth Organ to be planted on wind-chests of 73 notes.

FIFTH ORGAN COUPLERS.

First Organ......to Fifth Organ, Unison Coupler.
Third Organ.....to Fifth Organ, Unison Coupler.

The chief office of this Fifth Organ is to furnish solo voices and combinations of a special and assertive character, that may be required for pronounced musical passages or effects, thereby leaving the other Organs entirely free for their independent and appropriate rôles in the composition that may be under rendition. A long study of organ-stop registration has convinced us of the paramount necessity of holding the Organs, commanded by the different claviers, at all times largely independent. This matter has already been alluded to; but we again desire to urge its importance, which seems not to be fully realized, judging from the absence of any systematic tonal apportionment in Organs constructed at the present time.

This is the Organ in which high pressures of wind may be more legitimately employed than elsewhere, for the production of commanding voices in which power and richness are more required than refinement and sweetness of tone.

The peculiarities of certain of the stops selected for this Organ may be briefly described, so that their tonal values can be better realized. The DOPPELGEDECKT, 16 FT., is a large-scaled, covered stop, the pipes of which have two mouths similar in all respects to those of the ordinary

DOPPELFLÖTE, 8 FT. It is in reality a DOUBLE DOPPELFLÖTE of power-ful voice. The DOPPELROHRFLÖTE, 8 FT., is a large-scaled DOPPELFLÖTE, the stoppers of which have long perforated handles. Properly scaled and voiced, this stop yields a rich tone of good mixing quality. The VIOL PRINCIPAL, 8 FT., to be scaled and voiced to yield a full, unimitative string-tone: while the STENTORPHONE, 8 FT., is a large-scaled, organ-toned stop of powerful voice. The tone of the VIOL D'ORCHESTRE, 8 FT., to be as highly imitative of that of the orchestral Violin as art and skill can accomplish: while that of the VIOLONCELLO, 8 FT., is to be richer and fuller; approaching as closely as practicable to that of the orchestral instrument. The ORCHESTRAL FLUTE and PICCOLO to be strictly imitat-ive. The only lingual stops that call for comment are the ORCHESTRAL CLARINET and OBOE: these, of course, must be imitative; the former being associated with a small-scaled DOPPELFLÖTE, 8 FT., as directed for the ORCHESTRAL CLARINET of the Third Organ. The CARILLON to be of tubular bells having the compass of C to c²—25 notes. To be fur-nished with a damper action that can be brought into play along with the hammer action at the will of the performer. Two draw-stop rock-ing-tablets, knobs, or touches to be provided, and placed side by side in the most convenient place in the console: one to bring on the hammer action alone, and the other to bring on both the hammer and damper actions simultaneously.

PEDAL ORGAN.

Although it would have been more in order to describe the Pedal Organ before treating of the principal manual Divisions, we considered it desirable for the reader to grasp the scheme of tonal appointment and apportionment of the latter before entering on the consideration of the stop appointment of the Pedal Organ. At this point it must be said that certain manual Divisions have yet to be described; but these have not the same direct relationship to the Pedal Organ stop appointment as the main Divisions which strictly belong to the five manual claviers.

The importance in the Concert-room Organ of having a complete and thoroughly independent Pedal Organ cannot be overrated. It is essential that, in its tonal appointment, it should be able to meet every possible call that could be made upon it by the manual Organs. At the present time there is a pernicious system coming to the front in organ-building quarters in this country, which is striking at the root of the true and independent Pedal Organ. What is one to think when one sees in a list of stops for an important Organ, prepared by an established organ-building firm, a Pedal Organ of twelve stops, while in reality all that would strictly belong to this all-important Division would be two separate octaves of grave pipes: all the rest of the Division being derived from stops of the Great, Choir, and Solo Organs? This is obviously an organ-builder's trick to catch the ignorant and unwary purchaser, and should be denounced by every true lover of the Organ. Providing that an adequate Pedal Organ is provided for all reasonable calls upon its tonal forces, then, and then only, may auxiliary stops of some special tonality be derived from the manual Divisions; especially valuable if they are inclosed and expressive. These must not be confounded with the forces of the Pedal Organ proper; but must be distinctly classed, by themselves, as Auxiliary Pedal stops; and are to be used only for special effects, and when not drawn on the manual claviers. On the other hand, the deriving of octave voices from Pedal Organ double or unison stops is admissible, and in most cases desirable when the suitable stops are selected.

As we have urged the necessity of imparting powers of flexibility and expression to the Pedal Organ in the Chapter on The Swell, it is unnecessary to enlarge on the subject here. The following stop appointment will show the method we advocate for the Concert-room Organ.

PEDAL ORGAN.

PARTLY EXPRESSIVE—COMPASS CCC TO G—32 NOTES.

UNEXPRESSIVE SUBDIVISION.

1.	VOX GRAVISSIMA .		64 Feet.	12.	GEMSHORN . . .	Metal.	16 Feet.
2.	DOUBLE PRINCIPAL	Wood.	32 "	13.	GRAND OCTAVE .	Metal.	8 "
3.	CONTRA-VIOL . .	Metal.	32 "	14.	FLÖTENBASS . .	Wood.	8 "
4.	CONTRA-DULCIANA	Metal.	32 "	15.	MAJORFLÖTE . .	Wood.	8 "
5.	SUB-QUINT . .	Wood.	21⅓ "	16.	LIEBLICHGEDECKT		
6.	GRAND PRINCIPAL.	Wood.	16 "		(From No. 10)	Wood.	8 "
7.	PRINCIPAL, MAJOR	Metal.	16 "	17.	GEMSHORN		
8.	PRINCIPAL, MINOR	Metal.	16 "		(From No. 12)	Metal.	8 "
9.	DULCIANA (From			18.	DULCET		
	No. 4) . .	Metal.	16 "		(From No. 4).	Metal.	8 "
10.	LIEBLICHGEDECKT .	Wood.	16 "	19.	COMPENSATING		
11.	GRAND VIOL				MIXTURE .	Metal.	VI. Ranks.
	(From No. 3)	Metal.	16 Feet.	20.	FAGOTTONE . . .	Wood.	32 Feet.

EXPRESSIVE SUBDIVISION.

Inclosed in Swell-Chamber.

21.	CONTRA-BOURDON .	Wood.	32 Feet.	26.	SALICIONAL . .	Metal.	16 Feet.
22.	GEIGENPRINCIPAL .	Metal.	16 "	27.	QUINT	Wood.	10⅔ "
23.	QUINTATEN . .	Wood.	16 "	28.	VIOLONCELLO		
24.	BOURDON (From				(Orchestral) .	Metal.	8 "
	No. 21) . . .	Wood.	16 "	29.	VIOLONCELLO		
25.	CONTRABASSO				(Tuned sharp)	Metal.	8 "
	(Orchestral) .	Wood.	16 "	30.	SUPER-OCTAVE .	Metal.	4 "

31. HARMONIC FLUTE. Metal. 4 "	37. CONTRA SAXOPHONE Metal. 16 "
32. GRAND CORNET. Metal. VI. Ranks.	38. CONTRAFAGOTTO . Wood. 16 "
33. CONTRA-BOMBARDE Metal. 32 Feet.	39. OPHICLEIDE . . Metal. 16 "
34. CONTRA-TROMBONE Metal. 32 "	40. QUINT BOMBARDE. Metal. 10⅔ "
35. BOMBARDON	41. TROMBA
(From No. 33) Metal. 16 "	(Harmonic) . Metal. 8 "
36. TROMBONE	42. CLARION
(From No. 34) Metal. 16 "	(Harmonic) . Metal. 4 "

The Swell-Chamber, inclosing the Expressive Subdivision, to be directly, and at all times, controlled by Expression Lever No. 1, located at the left of all the others. But in addition to this constant control, five Couplers are to be provided, by means of which the Pedal Swell-Chamber may, at the will of the performer, be also controlled by any one or more of the Expression Levers belonging to the manual Organs. This arrangement is necessary for several obvious reasons, and essential to the utility and full office of the expressive Pedal Organ.

All the stops of the Unexpressive Subdivision to speak on wind of five inches. All the labial stops of the Expressive Subdivision to speak on wind of six inches; and all the lingual stops on wind of twelve inches. This latter pressure is permissible only on account of the lingual stops being inclosed and their tonal effects being under control. By inclosure, the tonal values of all the stops of the Expressive Subdivision are increased tenfold.

All the stops of both Subdivisions, with the single exception of the CONTRA-DULCIANA, 32 FT. (No. 4), to be planted on wind-chests of 44 notes. The CONTRA DULCIANA to be planted on a wind-chest of 61 notes; furnishing the auxiliary DOLCIANO PROFUNDO, 32 FT., of the First Organ.

PEDAL ORGAN COUPLERS.

First Organ.......to Pedal Organ, Unison Coupler.
First Organ.......to Pedal Organ, Octave Coupler.
Second Organ.....to Pedal Organ, Unison Coupler.
Third Organ......to Pedal Organ, Unison Coupler.
Fourth Organ.....to Pedal Organ, Unison Coupler.
Fifth Organ......to Pedal Organ, Unison Coupler.
Pedal Organ......on Itself, Octave Coupler.

EXPRESSION LEVER COUPLERS.

Coupler connecting Pedal Organ Swell-action with Expression Lever No. 2.
Coupler connecting Pedal Organ Swell-action with Expression Lever No. 3.
Coupler connecting Pedal Organ Swell-action with Expression Lever No. 4.
Coupler connecting Pedal Organ Swell-action with Expression Lever No. 5.
Coupler connecting Pedal Organ Swell-action with Expression Lever No. 6.

The rocking-tablets or other appliances commanding these Expression Lever Couplers may occupy different situations in the console. They may range with the Pedal Organ Couplers; with the draw-stops of the Expressive Subdivision of the Pedal Organ; with the draw-stops of the Organs to which the several Expression Levers belong; or they may, in the form of thumb-pistons, be located under the respective manual claviers. It would be desirable to have the thumb-pistons in addition to the couplers located elsewhere. Under any conditions, the Expression Lever Couplers should be commanded by toe-levers or touches adjoining the Expression Levers.

The tonal appointment of the Pedal Organ is carefully schemed to furnish a suitable bass, either analogous or contrasting, to any voice or combination of voices in the manual Divisions and Subdivisions of the instrument; and to do this without drawing upon them for any help through auxiliary or borrowed stops: thus leaving the two great tonal departments of the Organ at all times independent. The inclosure of twenty-two important stops in a swell-chamber, and imparting to them powers of flexibility and expression, gives to the Pedal Organ artistic resources absolutely unknown in any Pedal Organ in existence to-day.

To fully explain the tonal scheme it is desirable that the peculiarities of certain of the important stops be described. The Vox GRAVISSIMA, 64 FT., cannot correctly be designated a stop: it is, as its name implies, a very grave voice. This voice results, acoustically, from the combination of the DOUBLE PRINCIPAL, 32 FT., and the SUB-QUINT, 21⅓ FT. It has been formed with its bottom octave only resultant; but we prefer, on scientific grounds, its being resultant throughout. It must be admitted that it is not important in any form.

The voice of the DOUBLE PRINCIPAL, 32 FT., to be as clear and prompt as the voicer's skill can secure; and for these desirable ends we advise the adoption of a moderate scale, and the form of mouth introduced so successfully by Schulze, and illustrated in Fig. LXX., Chapter XV. We do not recommend a larger scale for the CCCC pipe of this important stop than 18 inches by 22 inches internally; while, with proper voicing, a satisfactory tone can be obtained with a scale of 15 inches by 19 inches. The DOUBLE DIAPASON, 32 FT., in the Wanamaker Store Organ has its CCCC pipe measuring 22¾ inches by 27¾ inches, but this is an inordinate and undesirable scale. It must be borne in mind that the 32 ft. pitch is not the foundation or unison pitch of the Pedal Organ. The CONTRA-VIOL, 32 FT., of metal (thick zinc may be used), to have its CCCC pipe 10 inches in diameter. To be voiced to yield a round, unimitative string-tone of good mixing quality. The CONTRA-DULCIANA, 32 FT., of metal, having a compass of 61 notes and a soft and pure organ-tone, is not only valuable in its grave pitch, but also on account of its furnishing the DULCIANA, 16 FT., and the DULCET, 8 FT., in the Pedal Organ, and the auxiliary DOLCIANO PROFUNDO, 32 FT., in the First Organ. The last points the way to a new method of enriching the tonality of the Organs commanded by the manual claviers. The SUB-QUINT, 21⅓ FT., to have its pipes of a scale two pipes less than that of the DOUBLE PRINCIPAL.

The GRAND PRINCIPAL, 16 FT., to have its CCC pipe measuring 14 inches by 17½ inches. Its voice to be full and prompt and of pure organ-tone. The PRINCIPAL, MAJOR, 16 FT., of metal, to have its CCC pipe of 10.72 inches diameter, and its scale ratio 1:2.519. This stop, properly voiced with copious wind at the pressure of five inches, will

yield a commanding pure organ-tone of sufficient volume. The Principal, Minor, 16 ft., of metal, to have its CCC pipe of 9.64 inches
diameter, and its scale ratio 1 : 2.66. Its tone to be softer and brighter
than that of the major stop. The Dulciana, 16 ft., is derived, as
before stated, from the Contra-Dulciana, 32 ft. The Grand Viol,
16 ft., to be voiced to yield a full unimitative string-tone; strictly subordinate, in strength of voice, to the Principals; and of a good mixing
quality, imparting to the foundation organ-tones a life and brightness
they do not naturally possess, owing to the absence of harmonic upper
partial tones. The Gemshorn, 16 ft., to be formed of conical pipes,
having a diameter at top equal to about one-third the diameter at the
mouth line. A suitable scale gives the CCC pipe a diameter at the mouth
of 7.88 inches and at the top a diameter of 2.58 inches, with the ratio
1 : 2.519. The tone characteristic of the stop to be carefully produced.
The Compensating Mixture, V. ranks, is an extremely valuable stop
in a Pedal Organ in which there are so many grave voices of 32 ft.
and 16 ft. pitch, the lower tones of which are naturally indeterminate
and lacking in distinctness. The stop to be formed of medium-scaled
pipes of the Diapason class voiced to yield pure organ-tone. It is not
desirable that this compound harmonic-corroborating stop should impart
any change of timbre to the grave foundation tones. Its office is to give,
to as great an extent as practicable, distinct articulation to the extremely
low voices of the 32 ft. and 16 ft. organ-toned stops without affecting
their pitch. It will be observed, from an examination of the composition
of the Mixture, that it gives a gradually decreasing aid to the stops
with which it may be combined, as their voices rise in pitch. It is
intended that the tones of the ranks forming the Mixture shall decrease
in strength as they rise in pitch until they seem to die away in the normal
volume of pure foundation tone. To accomplish this, in addition to their
gradual decrease in strength of tone, each rank terminates upward on a
different note, in the manner shown in the following scheme :—

COMPENSATING MIXTURE—VI. RANKS.

CCC to G,	Octave, 8 ft.	32 Notes.
CCC to D,	Twelfth, 5⅓ ft.	27 "
CCC to BB,	Fifteenth, 4 ft.	24 "
CCC to GG,	Seventeenth, 3⅕ ft.	20 "
CCC to EE,	Nineteenth, 2⅔ ft.	17 "
CCC to CC,	Twenty-second, 2 ft.	13 "

The great tonal value of a stop of this class has not been realized
by French, English, or American organ-builders. We are not aware of
one ever having been introduced in a French or English Organ; and we
have been the only one to introduce it in this country. The first time

in the Concert-room Organ exhibited at the Louisiana Purchase Exposition; and the second time in the Grand Organ in the Church of Our
Lady of Grace, Hoboken, N. J.   The lingual FAGOTTONE, 32 FT., to
have a voice of Bassoon quality and medium strength.   To be formed
with small-scaled, quadrangular, inverted conical, resonators of wood,
slotted and shaded for perfect regulation.

Only a few of the stops apportioned to the Expressive Subdivision
require special comment.   The first in order is the QUINTATEN, 16 FT.,
a covered stop of wood, of medium scale, voiced to yield its first harmonic upper partial as prominently as practicable along with the prime
tone.   This stop is valuable in combination with the double and unison
lingual stops.   The CONTRABASSO, 16 FT., to be formed on the model of
the Schulze VIOLONBASS, 16 FT., as illustrated in Fig. LXXXIV., Chapter
XV.   This stop, in the Organ of St. Peter's Church, Hindley, England,
imitates in a most remarkable manner the characteristic tones of the
orchestral Double-Bass.   The scale is small; the CCC pipe measuring
only 5½ inches square internally.   A CONTRABASSO of metal may be
introduced if found more imitative.   The VIOLONCELLO, 8 FT., to have
its pipes of high-class alloy; the 8 ft. pipe having the diameter of 3.13
inches.   The scale ratio to be 1:2.519.   This full scale is desirable to
secure as rich and firm a string-tone as possible, closely imitative of that
of the orchestral instrument when played *forte*.   The second VIOLON-
CELLO, 8 FT., to have pipes of a smaller scale, the 8 ft. pipe having the
diameter of 2.79 inches.   The scale ratio to be 1:2.519.   This stop to
be voiced slightly softer and brighter than the first VIOLONCELLO, and
tuned a few beats sharp; not enough, however, to produce an undesirable *céleste* effect, but sufficient to impart a nervous power of an
orchestral character to the combined tones of the two stops.   These
stops under the control of the swell will meet all the requirements for
an artistic and expressive Pedal Organ solo.   The GRAND CORNET, VI.
RANKS, is extremely valuable in this Expressive Subdivision, in which
there are so many grave labial and lingual stops with which it will enter
into effective combination, imparting variety and harmonic brilliancy to
their massive tones.   The stop to be composed of open metal pipes of
DIAPASON form and scale, voiced to yield pure organ-tones, scientifically
reduced in strength as they rise in pitch, as set forth in Chapter III., on
the Compound Harmonic Corroborating Stops.   The desirable composition of the stop is as follows:—

GRAND CORNET—VI. RANKS.

CCC to G	.	OCTAVE	8 Feet.	44 Notes.
"	"	TWELFTH	5⅓ "	" "
"	"	FIFTEENTH	4 "	" "
"	"	SEVENTEENTH	3⅕ "	" "

| CCC to G | . | NINETEENTH | . | . | 2⅔ Feet. | 44 Notes. |
| " | " | . | TWENTY-SECOND | . | 2 | " | " | " |

To have this stop perfectly satisfactory it is necessary, in addition to the gradual reduction of tone upwards in all the ranks, as already mentioned, that the two fifth-sounding ranks be voiced perceptibly softer than the three octave-sounding ranks; and that the third-sounding rank be voiced softest of all. Both science and art are called into play in the tonal adjustment of such a stop as this, and neither should be neglected.

The chief feature in the tonal apportionment of this Subdivision is its great resources in important lingual stops, numbering nine including the two that are derived. There are two of 32 ft., five of 16 ft., one of 8 ft., one of 4 ft., and one of 10⅔ ft. The last, the QUINT BOMBARDE is a stop which has never, to our knowledge, been introduced in an Organ; but its presence in such a Pedal Organ as here set forth would, under the powers of flexibility and expression, be productive of remarkable and hitherto unheard qualities of tone, when in combination with the 32 ft. and 16 ft. lingual stops. The pipes of the QUINT BOMBARDE to be of comparatively small scale, and voiced considerably softer than the double and chief unison lingual stops. It is unnecessary to go into particulars respecting the other lingual stops; their forms and tonalities are well known.

ANCILLARY ORGANS.

We now approach an important tonal extension in connection with the Concert-room Organ, which, apparently, has never been seriously contemplated by the organ-building world; or, if contemplated at all, was in all probability dismissed as unnecessary, because it involved an undesirable, and perhaps unprofitable, departure from the established and " good old-fashioned " way of doing things. However this may be; the fact remains that we were the first to point the way to the introduction of, and demonstrate the tonal value of, the Ancillary Organ. The first Organ strictly of this class, having a distinct tonal coloring and fulfilling a distinct office in the tonal economy of the Concert-room Organ, was the String-toned Division appended to the Third Clavier of the Organ installed in the Festival Hall of the Louisiana Purchase Exposition.

We had long realized the absurdity of depending upon a few string-toned stops, chiefly unimitative and devoid of powers of expression, distributed over all the manual claviers, for the production of anything approaching the tonal effects of the string forces of the orchestra: yet such effects were absolutely necessary for the artistic rendition of transcriptions of orchestral works. On the first opportunity presenting itself, we schemed a special ancillary string-toned Organ and endowed it with independent powers of expression. The introduction of so valuable a tonal element was successful: and now one sees the organ-building world awakening to the necessity of providing, in some form or other, a massing of string-toned stops in important Organs. That was effectively done by us, for the first time in the history of organ-building, in 1904 —fifteen years ago.

We are now going to point the way to further developments in the tonal resources of The Organ of the Twentieth Century, through the agency of Ancillary or Floating Organs, having distinct tonal colorings and special offices in the tonal economy of the instrument. These Organs are permanently attached to none of the Divisions or Subdivisions commanded by the several claviers: while they can instantly be brought, singly or in combination, on any one or more of the claviers. The stop apportionment of these Floating Organs will necessarily be dictated by the main stop appointment of the instrument, and the offices they are required to fulfil in the complete tonal scheme; accordingly no rules respecting them can be formulatd, nor can their number be decided. We introduce three in our present scheme, which seem most desirable additions to the stationary manual Organs. These will be separately commented on.

STRING ORGAN.

FULLY EXPRESSIVE—COMPASS CC to c⁴—61 NOTES.

Inclosed in Swell-box No. 7.

1. CONTRABASSO	Wood.	16 Feet.	10. VIOLA D'AMORE	Metal.	8 Feet.
2. VIOL DIAPASON	Metal.	8 "	11. ORCHESTRAL VIOLIN	Tin.	8 "
3. SALICIONAL	Metal.	8 "	12. VIOLINO SORDO	Tin.	8 "
4. QUINTATEN	Metal.	8 "	13. VIOLINO VIBRATO	Tin.	8 "
5. ORCHESTRAL VIOLONCELLO	Metal.	8 "	14. VIOL QUINT	Metal.	5⅓ "
6. VIOLONCELLO SORDO	Metal.	8 "	15. VIOLETTA	Metal.	4 "
7. VIOLONCELLO VIBRATO	Metal.	8 "	16. VIOL TIERCE	Metal.	3⅕ "
8. VIOLA POMPOSA	Metal.	8 "	17. VIOL TWELFTH	Metal.	2⅔ "
9. VIOLA SORDO	Metal.	8 "	18. VIOL FIFTEENTH	Metal.	2 "
			19. VIOL MIXTURE	Metal.	V. Ranks.
			VIII. TREMOLANT.		

All stops to speak on wind of four inches, unless they are located in any disadvantageous position with respect to the main exposed portion of the Organ, when it may be advisable to increase their strength of tone by employing a higher pressure. This, however, should be avoided if possible.

All the stops to be planted on a wind-chest of 61 notes.

Special care must be taken in the construction of the swell-box for this Ancillary Organ; for much will depend upon it for the desirable powers and refinement of expression. There must be no approach to annihilation of tone when the box is closed.

CLAVIER COUPLERS.

Coupler connecting String Organ with Second Organ—Second Clavier.
Coupler connecting String Organ with Third Organ—Third Clavier.
Coupler connecting String Organ with Fourth Organ—Fourth Clavier.
Coupler connecting String Organ with Fifth Organ—Fifth Clavier.

EXPRESSION LEVER COUPLERS.

Coupler connecting String Organ Swell-action with Expression Lever No. 2.
Coupler connecting String Organ Swell-action with Expression Lever No. 3.
Coupler connecting String Organ Swell-action with Expression Lever No. 4.
Coupler connecting String Organ Swell-action with Expression Lever No. 5.
Coupler connecting String Organ Swell-action with Expression Lever No. 6.

All the Couplers of this and the other Ancillary Organs to be arranged in a separate row, located either above or below the row of principal Couplers.

THUMB-PISTONS.

On and Off Thumb-Pistons, commanding the String Organ, to be located under the Second, Third, Fourth, and Fifth Claviers; and may conveniently occupy positions on the extreme right. With the full complement of Clavier Couplers, the Thumb-Pistons are not absolutely necessary, but they are unquestionably desirable for easy manipulation in rapid playing, and when short string passages or effects are required.

Of all Ancillary Organs likely to be schemed, the String Organ will certainly remain the most important. Indeed, it is quite important enough to have a clavier specially devoted to it; but that would seriously limit its utility and tonal value. As a Floating Organ, capable of being connected, immediately and at the will of the performer, with any desirable clavier, there to be played alone or in combination with the tonal forces of the Organ commanded by that clavier, its usefulness can hardly be overrated. Musical results could be obtained by such simple means, that could never be arrived at were the String Organ confined to a special clavier, as can be readily understood. Again, the musical value of the String Organ is vastly increased by its being endowed with powers of expression; and by the fact that those powers can be commanded, as may be desired, by any of the expression levers—that belonging to the Organ with which the String Organ is coupled, or with any of the other expression levers deemed more conducive to the production of the special musical effects desired. The String Organ can be connected, at the same time, with two or more of the claviers, and, accordingly, with the Organs they command. The countless beautiful combinations of tone rendered possible by such means almost baffle imagination. The importance and musical value of the Floating String Organ, in the rendition of orchestral compositions, cannot be overestimated.

On the examination of the stop apportionment of the Organ now under review, it will be observed that the stops representing the three most important string instruments of the orchestra—the Violoncello, Viola, and Violin—are duplicated: the first class representing these instruments played *forte*—the ORCHESTRAL VIOLONCELLO, 8 FT., VIOLA POMPOSA, 8 FT., and ORCHESTRAL VIOLIN, 8 FT.;—and the second class representing the same orchestral instruments played *con sordini*—the VIOLONCELLO SORDO, 8 FT., VIOLA SORDO, 8 FT., and VIOLINO SORDO, 8 FT. This arrangement not only gives great firmness and fulness, in combination, to the string-tones, by avoiding unison sympathy; but it furnishes two complete qualities and strengths of string-tone of the greatest value; the latter class being voiced softer than the orchestral stops, and with a thinner tone, as imitative as art can achieve. The VIOLONCELLO VIBRATO and VIOLINO VIBRATO to be voiced softer than the orchestral stops, and tuned a few beats sharp, so as to impart an expression of nervous power to a full combination, such as is observable in the combined tones of the full string division of the grand orchestra. This tuning must be very carefully performed—avoiding the effect of the VOX CŒLESTIS. The scales and voicing of the string-toned stops must be nicely graded, so as to impart a decided individuality to the VIOLONCELLOS, VIOLAS, and VIOLINS, such as one recognizes in the tones of the orchestral instruments. No rule-of-thumb, happy-go-lucky, ways of doing things must be followed by the organ-builder if the String Organ is to be a work of science and art. The tonal problem it presents has yet to be solved in The Organ of the Twentieth Century. The remaining unison stops do not call for special comment.

The CONTRABASSO, 16 FT., to be a covered wood stop of a small scale, the CC pipe measuring 4·08 inches square internally, developed on the ratio 1 : 2·66. To be voiced with the harmonic-bridge, so as to yield a rich and full orchestral string-tone. All the octave and mutation stops to be of small scale, voiced to yield singing tones of an unimitative and perfect mixing string quality. The VIOL MIXTURE,—V. RANKS, to be formed of pipes of DULCIANA scale, voiced to yield refined unimitative string-tones. Its desirable composition is as follows :—

VIOL MIXTURE—V. RANKS.

CC	to	BB	. . . . .	19——22——26——29——33.
C	to	B	. . . . .	15——19——22——26——29.
c¹	to	b¹	. . . . .	12——15——19——22——26.
c²	to	b²	. . . . .	8——12——15——19——22.
c³	to	c⁴	. . . . .	1—— 8——12——15——19.

The greatest care must be taken in voicing this compound stop, and in the scientific graduation of the tones of its several ranks. Except extreme refinement and delicacy pervade the entire stop its important office will be imperfectly fulfilled.

HARMONIC ORGAN.

FULLY EXPRESSIVE—COMPASS CC TO c⁴—61 NOTES.

FORTE SUBDIVISION.

Inclosed in Swell-box No. 8.

1. GEDECKT . Wood & Metal. 16 Feet.	6. TIERCE . . . . Metal. 3⅕ Feet.
2. DIAPASON . . . Metal. 8 "	7. OCTAVE QUINT . Metal. 2⅔ "
3. QUINTATEN Wood & Metal. 8 "	8. SUPER-OCTAVE . . Metal. 2 "
4. QUINT . . . . Metal. 5⅓ "	9. MIXTURE . . Metal. IV. Ranks.
5. OCTAVE . . . . Metal. 4 "	

PIANO SUBDIVISION.

Inclosed in Swell-box No. 8.

10. DULCIANA . . . Metal. 8 Feet.	14. DOLCE TIERCE . . Metal. 3⅕ Feet.
11. LIEBLICHGEDECKT	15. DOLCE TWELFTH . Metal. 2⅔ "
Wood & Metal. 8 "	16. DOLCE FIFTEENTH . . 2 "
12. DOLCE QUINT . . Metal. 5⅓ "	17. DOLCE NINETEENTH Metal. 1⅓ "
13. DOLCE OCTAVE . . Metal. 4 "	18. DULCIANA CORNET Metal. V. Ranks.

All the stops of the Forte Subdivision to speak on wind of three inches; and all the stops of the Piano Subdivision to speak on wind of one and a half inches. The stops of both Subdivisions to be planted on wind-chests of 61 notes.

CLAVIER COUPLERS.

Coupler connecting Harmonic Organ with Second Organ—Second Clavier.
Coupler connecting Harmonic Organ with Third Organ—Third Clavier.
Coupler connecting Harmonic Organ with Fourth Organ—Fourth Clavier.
Coupler connecting Harmonic Organ with Fifth Organ—Fifth Clavier.

EXPRESSION LEVER COUPLERS.

Coupler connecting Harmonic Organ Swell-action with Expression Lever No. 2.
Coupler connecting Harmonic Organ Swell-action with Expression Lever No. 3.
Coupler connecting Harmonic Organ Swell-action with Expression Lever No. 4.
Coupler connecting Harmonic Organ Swell-action with Expression Lever No. 5.
Coupler connecting Harmonic Organ Swell-action with Expression Lever No. 6.

It will probably be asked by the reader—organ-builder or organist—who has reached this page in our essay: What is the use of this Harmonic Organ, with its dual series of stops, seeing that each of the five stationary Organs is more or less provided with harmonic-corroborating stops? Under the present universal, systemless, and heterogeneous method of stop apportionment, with its remarkable neglect of harmonic-corroborating stops, which is believed to represent the acme of tonal development, it seems quite reasonable that such a question should be asked by the organist. The fact is, the true value and great importance of the harmonic-corroborating stops—simple and compound—are generally unrealized, and to the great majority of organ-builders and organists absolutely unknown. An open-minded study of musical acoustics is necessary to the proper appreciation of the great tonal value and office of such stops.

Our answer to the question—arrived at after an exhaustive study of tonal problems during half a century and a lengthened practical experience—is, that by means of such an Ancillary Organ as here presented countless tonal effects of a remarkable, beautiful, and almost mysterious character could be produced, in combination with the stationary Organs, that have never yet been heard in organ music, and which could not be produced on any Organ constructed up to the present time. To give the mere outline of what would be possible in this direction would occupy many pages, and would utterly fail to convey any adequate idea of the tonal effects due to the combinations of the stops of the stationary expressive Organs with the series of harmonic stops of the equally expressive Harmonic Organ. They can be better imagined than described.

The musical value of the Harmonic Organ largely depends on the proper scaling, the artistic voicing, and the scientific graduation of the tones of its several stops. The natural laws of compound musical sounds must be recognized and worked to, otherwise disappointment is certain.

We have formed two Subdivisions, designated the Forte and Piano, which provide harmonic series of widely different strengths and characters of tone, produced by pipes of different scales and forms, voiced on winds of different pressures. These two series of tones, controlled by powers of flexibility and expression, enable the Harmonic Organ to meet every demand that can possibly be made upon it in compound-tone production. To fully realize its value, it must be borne in mind that it can be coupled with any one or more of the Second, Third, Fourth, and Fifth Organs; and that its swell-action can be coupled to any of their five expression levers; or left entirely uncoupled, with its swell-box closed, a condition conducive to the production of many fascinating and almost mysterious musical effects. In this closed and unexpressive condition, either of the complete harmonic Subdivisions can be used in combination with any single unison stop in any of the four stationary Organs, which may be played as a solo with expression.

In the Forte Subdivision, the scale of the DIAPASON, 8 FT., dictates the scales of all the other stops of the series. The CC pipe of the DIAPASON to be 4.46 inches in diameter, and the ratio of the scale $1 : \sqrt{8}$. The OCTAVE, 4 FT., and the SUPER-OCTAVE, 2 FT., to be formed of pipes one note less in scale, which will give the CC pipe of the former stop the diameter of 2.44 inches. The QUINT, 5⅓ FT., and the OCTAVE QUINT, 2⅔ FT., to be two notes less in scale; and the TIERCE, 3⅕ FT., to be three notes less in scale than the standard DIAPASON scale. The pipes forming the MIXTURE to be throughout of a scale one note less than that of the TIERCE. The composition of the stop to be as follows:—

MIXTURE—IV. RANKS.

CC	to	F	.	.	.	.	. .	19——22——26——29.
F♯	to	g¹	.	.	.	.	. .	15——19——22——26.
g♯¹	to	c³	.	.	.	.	. .	12——15——19——22.
c♯³	to	c⁴	.	.	.	.	. .	8——12——15——19.

In the Piano Subdivision the scale of the DULCIANA, 8 FT., gives the scale, uniformly, to all the other stops of series. The CC pipe of the DULCIANA to be 2.89 inches in diameter, and the ratio of the scale $1 : 2.3$. The DULCIANA CORNET,—V. RANKS, to be composed in the manner set forth in the Example XXV., given in Chapter III., page 83. The greatest care to be taken in the voicing and regulating of all the stops of this Subdivision. A singing tone of silvery quality is what is required. Great care must also be taken in the construction of the swell-box of this Organ; when closed, the voice of the most delicately toned stop must be clearly audible: this is essential.

AËRIAL ORGAN.

Some apology seems necessary for the introduction of the new term —Aërial Organ—into organ nomenclature. Some difficulty presented itself in finding an expressive name for an Organ of a new and extremely refined and delicate tonality, such as had never before been contemplated in the appointment of any class of Organ. The common term Echo Organ was undesirable, for we had no desire that this new tonal Division should in any way be confused with the old established form of Echo Organ, which depended for its tone-effects upon some position distant from the main Organ, and not on the softness and refinement of its voices. On careful consideration we decided on the name Aërial as the most expressive and appropriate.*

* " AËRIAL—Possessed of a light and graceful beauty; ethereal.
" Some music is above me; most music is beneath me. I like Beethoven and Mozart—or else some of the *aërial* compositions of the older Italians. *Coleridge,* Table-Talk."—
" Century Dictionary."

AËRIAL ORGAN.

FULLY EXPRESSIVE—COMPASS CC to c⁴—61 NOTES.

Inclosed in Swell-box No. 9.

1. BOURDONECHO	.	. Wood. 16 Feet.	12. VOIX CÉLESTE	.	. Tin.	8 Feet.
2. ECHO DIAPASON	.	Metal. 8 "	13. SUAVE FLUTE	.	. Wood. 4 "
3. DULCIANA	. .	. Metal. 8 "	14. CŒLESTINA	.	. . Metal. 4 "
4. GELINDGEDECKT	.	Wood. 8 "	15. FLAGEOLET	.	. . Metal. 2 "
5. MELODIA	. .	. Wood. 8 "	16. HARMONIA-ÆTHERIA	Tin. VI. Ranks.
6 VIOLE SOURDINE	.	Tin. 8 "	17. DULCIAN	.	. . Metal. 8 Feet.
7. FLAUTO D'AMORE	.	Wood. 8 "	18. SCIALUMO	.	. . Metal. 8 "
8. HARMONICA	.	. Metal. 8 "	19. VOX HUMANA	.	. Metal. 8 "
9. ÆOLINA	. .	. Metal. 8 "	20. CELESTA.
10. DOLCISSIMO	.	. Wood. 8 "	21. HARP.
11. VOIX ANGÉLIQUE	.	Tin. 8 "	IX. TREMOLANT.

All the stops of this Organ to speak on wind of one and a half inches.
All the stops to be planted on wind-chests of 61 notes.

CLAVIER COUPLERS.

Coupler connecting Aërial Organ with Second Organ—Second Clavier.
Coupler connecting Aërial Organ with Third Organ—Third Clavier.
Coupler connecting Aërial Organ with Fourth Organ—Fourth Clavier.
Coupler connecting Aërial Organ with Fifth Organ—Fifth Clavier.

EXPRESSION LEVER COUPLERS.

Coupler connecting Aërial Organ Swell-action with Expression Lever No. 2.
Coupler connecting Aërial Organ Swell-action with Expression Lever No. 3.
Coupler connecting Aërial Organ Swell-action with Expression Lever No. 4.
Coupler connecting Aërial Organ Swell-action with Expression Lever No. 5.
Coupler connecting Aërial Organ Swell-action with Expression Lever No. 6.

All the stops of this Organ to be of the smallest scales suitable for the production of extremely delicate and refined qualities of tone, aided by the lowest wind pressure that can be effectively employed. That perfectly satisfactory tones can be produced from stops voiced on wind by one and a half inches has been proved by the Echo Division of the Organ in the Parish Church of Leeds, England, voiced by the great Schulze.

As the metal pipes are all of small scales, those not of tin should be formed of a high-class alloy of tin and lead, or "confluent metal." The scale of the principal unison—the ECHO DIAPASON, 8 FT.,—gives the CC pipe the diameter of 3·96 inches, and the ratio 1 : 2·3. The CC pipe of the DULCIANA, 8 FT., to be 2·52 inches in diameter, and the scale ratio 1 : 2·3. Both these stops to yield pure organ-tone of a singing character, resembling those of the DIAPASONS of the old English builders, when low wind-pressures were in favor. The VIOLE SOURDINE, 8 FT., to be of very small scale, and voiced to yield an imitative string-tone of extreme softness. Its CC pipe to have the diameter of 1·60 inches, and the scale ratio to be as given above. The ÆOLINA, 8 FT., to be voiced to yield a soft and plaintive flute-tone: its CC pipe to be 2·28 inches in diameter. The mouths of the pipes to be narrow and cut up sufficiently to give the required tone. The VOIX ANGÉLIQUE, 8 FT., to be voiced to yield a singing, unimitative string-tone, much softer than the tone of the VIOLE SOURDINE. The CC pipe to be 1·91 inches in diameter. The VOIX CÉLESTE, 8 FT., to be similar in scale and voicing; but tuned sufficiently sharp to produce the *céleste* effect in a manner not too pronounced. The CŒLESTINA, 4 FT., to be the Octave of the VOIX ANGÉLIQUE. The HARMONIA ÆTHERIA,—VI. RANKS, to be formed of pipes, of the scale given for the ÆOLINA, voiced and regulated with the greatest care. The composition of the stop to be as follows:—

HARMONIA ÆTHERIA—VI. RANKS.

CC to F♯,	. . .	15——17——19——22——26——29.
G to f♯¹	. . .	12——15——17——19——22——26.
g¹ to f♯²,	. . .	8——12——15——17——19——22.
g² to c⁴,	. . .	1—— 8——12——15——17——19.

In regulating this unique stop, the third-sounding rank, which appears in every break, should be made slightly softer than the octave- and fifth-sounding ranks. The entire stop belongs to the 8 ft. harmonic series. As such a compound harmonic-corroborating stop, of so small a scale, voiced on a wind of one and a half inches, has never been inserted in a constructed Organ, we cannot expect the reader to realize its value and the wondrous tonal effects it is capable of producing in countless combinations. From our own experience in a kindred direction, and on scientific grounds, we have no difficulty in mentally realizing the effects almost as clearly as if we heard them.

Of the two covered stops the more important is the BOURDONECHO, 16 FT. As in all the others, the scale of this stop is to be extremely small, the CC pipe measuring 3·10 inches in width by 4·10 inches in depth internally, the scale ratio being 1:2·3. The unison covered stop-—GELINDGEDECKT, 8 FT.,—the softest of the GEDECKT family, to have its CC pipe 1·78 inches in width by 2·28 inches in depth internally. Both this stop and the BOURDONECHO to be voiced to yield tones in which the quint is slightly in evidence. The DOLCISSIMO, 8 FT., is the softest flute-toned stop made; and carefully voiced on wind of 1½ inches it yields a voice of pure and beautiful unimitative fluty quality, extremely valuable in combination. It is made of different scales and proportions of width to depth, according to wind pressure and the tone required. For the present stop, the CC, 8 ft., open pipe is to measure 2·05 inches in width by 3·10 inches in depth internally, the scale ratio being 1 : 2·3. The top octave of this stop may be made of metal. The FLAUTO D'AMORE, 8 FT., to be formed of half-covered pipes of small scale, voiced to yield the delicate flute-tone peculiar to the stop. Its top octave may also be made of metal if the small wood pipes prove unsatisfactory. The MELODIA, 8 FT., to be of the ordinary form and of the smallest desirable scale, and to be open throughout. No metal pipes to be introduced.

As in the case of all the labial stops of this Organ, the lingual stops are to be of the softest intonation possible commensurate with perfectly clear and characteristic speech. The DULCIAN, 8 FT., to be constructed with closed-reeds and slender inverted conical resonators, shaded: its tone to be of a Bassoon quality, but lighter and brighter than the orchestral tone. The SCIALUMO, 8 FT., to be of the CLARINET family, constructed with small-scale, cylindrical resonators. The VOX HUMANA, 8 FT., to be of the most desirable form and scale to yield a quiet and refined voice. The low pressure of the pipe-wind will prevent any coarseness in these lingual stops.

It must be said that the low pressure advocated is conditional on the Aërial Organ being properly located, close to the main Organs, and where no obstruction to the free emission of its sound obtains. If, however, there is any danger of the tones of so delicate an Organ being interfered with, a higher pressure of wind may become necessary. Care must be taken, in any case to construct the swell-box of wood of only sufficient thickness to secure a *pianissimo* effect, without in any way impairing the clearness and character of the tones of the inclosed stops, when completely closed. Anything approaching the *annihilating swell* must be here avoided, as in every other Organ.

Perhaps the organist accustomed to the loudly-voiced Organs, in which pipe-winds of high pressures only are used, which are so largely in favor to-day, will, on first thoughts, consider our Aërial Organ undesirable or of little value. Such, at least, will naturally be the verdict of the lovers of musical noise, so numerous in the prevailing school of organists at the present time. To the accomplished musician and organ virtuoso, however, a different view is likely to present itself. As there is no equivalent to our Aërial Organ in existence in any constructed instrument, a certain question as to its value may be looked for. This is likely to be the case among organ-builders, who hate innovations which may disturb the trade methods of doing things, and who have no desire to enter on a new and very exacting school of voicing, in which skill and art of a high order will be necessary at every step. It is to be regretted that organists do not take a much greater interest in the tonal development of the Organ; and that they do not let their imagination go beyond what organ-builders deem sufficient for their musical needs.

As the Aërial Organ can be coupled with any of the Second, Third, Fourth, and Fifth Organs or Claviers, and its swell-action with any of the Expression Levers, it is easy to see into what a new world of tonal combinations it can enter, producing musical effects hitherto undreamt of and impossible on any Organ in existence. Coupled with the String Organ, on any clavier, and under compound expression, tonal effects could be produced never yet heard in organ music. Used alone, the Aërial Organ would be a most sympathetic and expressive accompanimental medium in solo passages of a refined character on any of the solo stops in the stationary Organs. But why continue? Words can convey no idea of the unexhaustible musical resources furnished by three expressive Ancillary Organs in combination with the nine Divisions and Subdivisions of the five main Organs: all of which would be at the ready command of the intelligent and artistic performer.

Such, then, is our suggestive scheme for the tonal appointment and apportionment of the Concert-room Organ of the Twentieth Century. It will, probably, be found to have many shortcomings, which we will be glad to acknowledge and strive to overcome. It should, however, be borne in mind that we have worked alone, opposed by all known precedents. But, such as it is, our scheme deserves, we venture to think, the open-minded study of the musician versed in organ and orchestral music. To the ordinary organist it may not commend itself, for it is new, perhaps somewhat difficult to grasp, and seemingly bristling with difficulties of manipulation, demanding study and practice. However this may be, we consider our Organ would amply repay its mastery. We know its musical resources would be found so great that a new school of organ compositions could be based upon them. "The Beautiful rests on the foundations of the Necessary." *Emerson.*

CHAPTER XII.

THE CHAMBER ORGAN.

AVING treated of the tonal appointment and divisional apportionment of the two leading classes of Organs, to as great a length as is practicable in a treatise of the present size, we have now to consider, necessarily in a brief manner, the similar appointment and apportionment of the Chamber Organ, at the present time a matter of no slight importance.

So far as our observation extends, there seems to have been absolutely no systematic attempts made in the organ-building world, to differentiate, by a special and desirable tonal appointment, the Chamber Organ from the ordinary type of Church Organ. In the face of the fact that numerous instruments of important dimensions have been installed in homes all over the United States and England, this neglect is greatly to be regretted. It must be obvious to every thoughtful music lover, who has any appreciation of the true office and tonal character of the Organ, that there can be no direct and close bond of similarity between an instrument properly appointed and suitable for church services, and an instrument, in like manner, adapted in every way for the refined rendition of chamber music—correctly so called—in which duets, trios, and quartets with the pianoforte, violin, violoncello, and other orchestral instruments take so prominent a place. An instrument which should embrace within itself elements—tonal and expressive—sufficient, in the proper order of things, to win it the title The Orchestra of the Home.

We are able to speak from long and special experience in this direction, as we shall endeavor to show. The first instrument made in Europe, in which any attempt was essayed to produce what could be properly designated a Chamber Organ, was that we constructed, in our own residence in England, between the years 1865 and 1872, and subsequently enlarged. While small—comprising only nineteen speaking stops—this instrument still presents a tonal apportionment, combined with powers of flexibility and compound expression on its First Organ clavier, which has never been duplicated in any other Chamber Organ, however large, constructed up to the present time in any country. Yet it was that very tonal apportionment and its attendant powers of compound expression that won for the instrument the admiration of every accomplished musician who touched its keys; and which called forth from the distinguished English cathedral organist, Dr. Daniel J. Wood, of Exeter, the remark, after having made himself familiar with the special tonal powers it furnished and foreshadowed: " It opened up to my imagination quite a vista of new and previously impossible effects in organ playing."

Although our Organ will appear to the organ-builders and organists of this country, accustomed to large and powerfully-voiced instruments, little better than a toy; it was, none the less, the first instrument formed to practically demonstrate the value of multiple powers of flexibility and expression, at a time when both Church and Concert-room Organs were considered sufficient and complete when furnished with only a single expressive tonal division—the Swell Organ. It may, accordingly, lay claim, on more grounds than one, to be considered a landmark in the history of organ-building, pointing the way to a development not yet fully carried out in any Organ hitherto constructed. As its scheme will to a considerable extent furnish the text for the disquisition now entered upon, it may properly be given at this point.

CHAMBER ORGAN.

FIRST ORGAN.

FIRST CLAVIER—COMPOUND EXPRESSION.

UNEXPRESSIVE SUBDIVISION

1. PRINCIPALE GRANDE   .   .   .   .   .   Metal. 8 Feet.

FIRST EXPRESSIVE SUBDIVISION.
Inclosed in Swell-box No. 1.

2. FLAUTO TEDESCA	. Wood. 8 Feet.	4. PICCOLO	. Metal. 2 Feet.
3. FLAUTO TRAVERSO	. Wood. 4 "	5. OBOE	. Metal. 8 "

SECOND EXPRESSIVE SUBDIVISION.
Inclosed in Swell-box No. 2.

6. FLAUTO PRIMO . .	. Wood. 8 Feet.	10. RIPIENO DI CINQUE	. V. Ranks.
7. FLAUTO SECONDO	. Metal. 8 "	11. TROMBA	. Metal. 8 Feet.
8. VIOLA D'AMORE . .	. Tin. 8 "	12. CLARINETTO . . .	. Metal. 8 "
9. OTTAVA	. Metal. 4 "	13. VOCE UMANA . .	. Metal. 8 "

TREMOLANT.

This Expressive Subdivision is brought on and thrown off the First Clavier by Thumb-pistons, conveniently located, in a central position, under the Clavier.

SECOND ORGAN.
SECOND CLAVIER—SINGLE EXPRESSION.
Inclosed in Swell-box No. 1.

14. PRINCIPALE DOLCE . . . . . Metal. 8 Feet.
15. CORNO DI CACCIA . . . . . . Metal. 8 "
16. FLAUTO D'AMORE . . . . . . Wood. 4 "

PEDAL ORGAN.

17. PRINCIPALE . . . . . Open Wood. 16 Feet.
18. CONTRA-BASSO . . . .Covered Wood. 16 "
19. CONTRA-SAXOPHONE . . . . . Metal. 16 "

Swell-box No. 1 is controlled by Expression Lever No. 1, and Swell-box No. 2 is controlled by balanced Expression Lever No. 2, located side by side toward the right.

The TREMOLANT affects every manual stop in the instrument; but those inclosed in Swell-box No. 1 in a more delicate manner than those inclosed in Swell-box No. 2.

All the stops in the Organ speak on a wind of 2⅜ inches pressure.

MECHANICAL ACCESSORIES.
COUPLERS.
Second Clavier to First Clavier, Unison Coupler.
Second Clavier to First Clavier, Octave Coupler.
Second Clavier to First Clavier, Sub-octave Coupler.
First Clavier to Pedal Clavier, Coupler.
Second Clavier to Pedal Clavier, Coupler.

FOOT LEVERS.
Expression Lever controlling Swell-box No. 1.
Expression Lever controlling Swell-box No. 2.
Lever drawing Forte Combination in Swell No. 1.
Lever drawing Piano Combination in Swell No. 1.

To have the stop nomenclature uniform, Italian names were adopted throughout. As some are not in common use, the stops to which they are given in this Organ may properly be described.

PRINCIPALE GRANDE, 8 FT., is an OPEN DIAPASON, yielding the true old English tone, rendered possible by the low wind pressure.

FLAUTO TEDESCA, 8 FT., is an open stop of the CLARABELLA class, yielding an almost pure organ-tone.

FLAUTO TRAVERSO, 4 FT., is an open wood stop, yielding a tone imitative of that of the orchestral Flute.

FLAUTO PRIMO, 8 FT., is a DOPPELFLÖTE, of a full and mellow tone of perfect mixing quality.

FLAUTO SECONDO, 8 FT., is a metal LIEBLICHGEDECKT, of small scale, yielding an unimitative flute-tone inclining to that of the QUINTATEN.

VIOLA D'AMORE, 8 FT., is a stop yielding a bright string-tone, imitative of that of the old orchestral instrument. The pipes are of tin, of small scale, and voiced with the Gavioli *frein harmonique.*

PRINCIPALE DOLCE, 8 FT., is a true English DULCIANA, having a pure organ-tone of a silvery, singing quality.

CORNO DI CACCIA, 8 FT., is an open metal stop of the KERAULOPHONE class, yielding a full and rich tone resembling that of the orchestral Horn.

FLAUTO D'AMORE, 4 FT., a half-covered stop of wood, yielding an unimitative flute-tone of great delicacy and beauty.

RIPIENO DI CINQUE, V. RANKS, is a harmonic-corroborating stop, of small-scale DULCIANA pipes, carefully voiced and scientifically graduated in strength of tone throughout every rank and break. For combination, with both lingual and labial stops, it is one of the most valuable tonal forces in the Organ. The composition of this stop is given in Chapter III., Example XXV., under the name DULCIANA CORNET, V. RANKS.

TROMBA, 8 FT., is a TRUMPET of medium scale, yielding a bright imitative tone of suitable assertiveness.

VOCE UMANA, 8 FT., is a lingual stop, of singular purity of tone and of special formation. Drawn without the TREMOLANT, it is a beautiful stop which can be used alone in full chords and also in combination; while with the TREMOLANT it becomes a remarkably refined VOX HUMANA.

Of the other manual stops it is unnecessary to speak beyond stating that they are equal in refinement of tone to the other stops described above.

PRINCIPALE, 16 FT., an open wood stop of small scale, yielding a pure organ-tone, prompt and distinctly marked.

CONTRA-BASSO, 16 FT., a covered wood stop of small scale, voiced to yield a tone imitating very closely that of the orchestral Double Bass. This is a most valuable stop in the rendition of orchestral transcriptions and music of that class.

CONTRA-SAXOPHONE, 16 FT., is a free-reed stop of very smooth and beautiful tone; resembling in the lower octave the tone of the Euphonium, softly played, more closely than that of the Double-bass Saxophone.

This instrument was designed with the special aim of furnishing to chamber music an important element which, up to the time of its construction, had never been provided; and it proved eminently successful in its new field. It was the first Chamber Organ ever tuned in accord with the pianoforte in England, and, so far as we can learn, in the world.* As a solo instrument its powers both in legitimate organ music and in orchestral transcriptions proved remarkable, as was freely admitted by every one who had the opportunity of judging; and it was performed on by many of the most distinguished organists of the time —English, French, and American. But, in our opinion, its great and unique office lay in concerted music in which the pianoforte and orchestral instruments took important part. We had numerous opportunities of judging correctly of this office, and always under most favorable circumstances. We may be pardoned, in the desire to point out the

---

* Mace's Table Organ (see page 194), as he quaintly says, was contrived for his own use, " as to the maintaining of Public Consorts, &c." Although no mention is made by him on the subject, it is possible that the Harpsichord, weak in tone though it was, took part in his " Consorts." We find in " L'Art du Facteur d'Orgues," an instrument described and illustrated in which a few organ stops are associated with a Harpsichord.

importance of this office of the properly appointed Chamber Organ, presenting here the program of one of the many Chamber Concerts given in our residences in Liverpool and London; on which occasion the Organ was presided at by Mr. Alfred Hollins—one of England's most refined and accomplished organists and composers of organ music.

CHAMBER CONCERT.

GIVEN AT DEVON NOOK, DUKE'S AVENUE, LONDON, W.
APRIL EIGHTH, 1891.

PART FIRST.

CONCERT OVERTURE........................*Alfred Hollins*
ORGAN SOLO.
SCHERZO CAPRICCIOSO.....................*Alex. Guilmant*
DUET—PIANO AND ORGAN.
ADOREMUS.................................*H. Ravina*
QUARTET—VIOLIN, VIOLONCELLO, PIANO, AND ORGAN.
IMPROVISATION ON THE ORGAN..............*Alfred Hollins*
On a Theme given at the time.
EASTER EVE—*Scene Picturesque*............*Alfred Hollins*
Written specially for, and performed for the first time on, the occasion.
DUET—PIANO AND ORGAN.
SERENADE................................*Ch. M. Widor*
QUINTET—VIOLIN, FLUTE, VIOLONCELLO, PIANO, AND ORGAN.
ANDANTE PASTORALE.......................*C. E. Stephens*
SCHERZO.................................*H. Turner*
ORGAN SOLOS.
LARGO..*Handel*
SESTET—TWO VIOLINS, VIOLONCELLO, HORN, PIANO, AND
ORGAN.

PART SECOND.

TRIUMPHAL MARCH.........................*Franz Liszt*
ORGAN SOLO.
AIR D'ÉGLISE DE STRADELLO................*Lefébure Wély*
TRIO—VIOLIN, PIANO, AND ORGAN.
IMPROVISATION ON THE ORGAN..............*Alfred Hollins*
On an original Theme.
PASTORALE...............................*Alex. Guilmant*
DUET—PIANO AND ORGAN.

Notwithstanding the admiration our Organ engendered in the minds of the many distinguished musicians who heard it or performed upon it, largely on account of the beauty of its tones, but chiefly on account of its unprecedented powers of compound flexibility and expression, and the facilities it provided for the production of *nuances* of the most refined character, no serious attempt, up to the present time, has been made in the organ-building world to differentiate, as we have already said, the Chamber Organ from the ordinary type of Church Organ. Although hundreds of Chamber Organs have been constructed in this and other countries, not one of the many which have come under our observation or to our knowledge shows any evidences of special thought in the all-important matters of divisional tonal apportionment and powers of flexibility and expression. Compound expression has evidently never entered the brains of their designers. Yet there is a very wide field for the scientific and artistic development of the Chamber Organ—a development which must take place before that instrument can occupy its proper position among the Organs of the Twentieth Century.

So long as the appointment of Chamber Organs is left to trade concerns or persons who take no special interest in it, it is hopeless to look for any departure from old-style Church Organ models. Improvements in any important direction will involve trouble and expense, and, accordingly, less profit. They are not entered upon, for the purchaser will not know if anything better can be obtained, and it is not to the builder's profit, in dollars, to tell him that a more useful and effective Chamber Organ can be made and had been made long ago. Considering the numerous golden opportunities that have presented themselves, and the large sums expended on instruments for the home, it is greatly to be regretted that some one of influence in the organ-building world has not devoted serious attention to the construction of a true and perfect Chamber Organ, leading thereby to the fostering of musical accomplishments in the home circle, and the institution of such delightful Chamber Concerts as we instituted in England, with the Organ the central point of attraction round which everything musical gathered.

It will not be out of place or uninteresting to give, as the other side of the picture, at this point of our subject, the most advanced idea respecting the appointment of the Chamber Organ, arrived at by France's most accomplished and painstaking organ-builder, and beyond which, save perhaps in point of size, he never developed it. The following are the particulars of the " Grand Orgue de Salon " exhibited at the Exposition Universelle, Paris, 1878, by M. Aristide Cavaillé-Coll.

"Un Grand Orgue de Salon à double expression (nouveau système), à deux claviers et un pédalier en console, dont la composition suit:

CLAVIER DU GRAND ORGUE.

d'Ut à Sol, 56 notes.

1. Bourdon . . . . . de 16 pieds.	4. Prestant . . . . . de 4 pieds.
2. Principal . . . . 8 "	5. Doublette . . . . 2 "
3. Bourdon . . . . . 8 "	6. Trompette . . . . 8 "

CLAVIER DU RÉCIT.

d'Ut à Sol, 56 notes.

7. Flûte Harmonique	. de 8 pieds.		10. Voix Célestes . . .	de 8 pieds.
8. Viole de Gambe . . .	8 "		11. Basson-Hautbois . .	8 "
9. Flûte Octaviante . .	4 "		12. Voix Humaine . .	8 "

CLAVIER DE PÉDALES.

d'Ut à Fa, 30 notes.

13. Soubasse . . . . de 16 pieds. | 14. Basse Ouverte . . de 8 pieds.

PÉDALES DE COMBINAISON.

1. Effets d'orage.
2. Tirasse du Grand Orgue.
3. Tirasse du Récit.
4. Expression du Grand Orgue.

5. Expression du Récit.
6. Copula des claviers.
7. Tremolo.
8. Prolongement harmonique."

Again, in 1882, M. Aristide Cavaillé-Coll sent another " Grand Orgue de Salon " to the Exposition des Arts Décoratifs. This Organ was in all respects similar to the above, giving an unquestionable proof that he was at that time convinced he could suggest or construct nothing better in the shape of a Chamber Organ. On subjecting both these instruments to a very careful examination, and hearing them repeatedly performed upon, we were forced to the conclusion that they were simply small Organs of the church type, slightly modified in tone but still infinitely better suited for a small church than for a private music-room. They were built on wrong lines, as Chamber Organs, save in one direction. They were instruments of " *double expression,*"—that is, both the manual divisions were rendered expressive by their stops being inclosed in swell-boxes. Beyond this, it is difficult to realize what had been accomplished toward rendering the instruments examples of a " *nouveau système.*"

This treatment was doubtless new in France in 1878; but its novelty could not be extended to England, simply because, eleven years before, we had constructed a Chamber Organ of *triple expression*—the first Organ ever constructed with such extended powers of flexibility and expression. When the distinguished musician M. Saint-Saëns performed on our Organ, he pronounced it unique, and remarked that he wished he had such an instrument at his disposal in Paris.

It can hardly be necessary at this time, one would naturally think, to point out to the musician and organ *virtuoso,* who has paid any serious attention to the subject of differentiation in organ tonal appointments, that the Church Organ, in its proper accompanimental form and office, is not the desirable model on which to scheme a useful and effective Chamber Organ ; especially if it is to be employed in its manifold offices, already alluded to. On the other hand, it is obvious that the closer its general tonal appointment and divisional apportionment approximates to that of the Concert-room Organ, the more generally useful and satisfactory it will prove both in solo and concerted music. The general conditions on which a true Chamber Organ should be schemed may be stated as follows:—

1. All its voices should be pure and refined; and so balanced and carefully regulated that it would be practically impossible to draw an unmusical combination. This perfection would involve scientific scaling and most artistic voicing of all stops.

2. That to secure the necessary refinement and repose of tone, moderate and low pressures of wind must alone be used, and all forced voicing abandoned.

3. That in the tonal apportionments of all its Divisions and Subdivisions contrasts should obtain, so as to secure the maximum value of compound expression.

4. That all its Divisions—manual and pedal—should be flexible and expressive. The Organs commanded by the First, Second, and Third Claviers to be divided, and all the desirable Subdivisions to be made flexible and expressive, by being inclosed in different swell-boxes, as recommended for the Concert-room Organ.

5. That its several swell-boxes should be so constructed that, while the necessary range of expression is secured, there must be no annihilation of tone involved. At all times the tones of the stops, while the swell-boxes are completely closed, must be perfectly audible and clear.

6. That the Pedal Organ should be inclosed in a suitable chamber and rendered flexible and expressive. If of considerable size, the stops calling most for expressive powers may only be inclosed, as set forth in our scheme for the Concert-room Organ.

7. The action will be either tubular-pneumatic or electro-pneumatic; but preference should be given to the latter, especially when the console is detached and located at some distance from the sound-producing portions of the instrument. If the console is movable, the electro-pneumatic action becomes imperative.

8. No special appointment of the console is necessary beyond what will be dictated by the complete scheme of the Organ. Its model, however, should be that of the perfect Concert Organ console. Generally, an extreme compactness and neatness should characterize the Chamber Organ console: and its artistic design and high-class workmanship should not be neglected, for it can be made an effective piece of furniture suitable for any room.

It is practically impossible, as it is unnecessary, to enter into detail concerning the exterior design or displayed case of the Chamber Organ, for that will in all instances depend on the locality and surroundings of the instrument.

It is now a very common practice to bury the Organ in some confined chamber or unsuitable place, and by objectionable expedients to hide or disguise its presence. No true lover of the Organ would tolerate so destructive a mode of treatment. When so buried, its stops have to be loudly and coarsely voiced, and blown to the extreme limit, so that they can be heard; and, accordingly, all refinements of tonality and the expressive *nuances,* on which so much of the beauty and charm of chamber music depends, are destroyed. If the Organ is to be merely a toy, played, inartistically, by means of perforated music-rolls, perhaps the more buried it is the better. But that is far from being our idea of the true and supreme office and value of the Chamber Organ, which we happen to have been the first to practically demonstrate.

In all matters of tonal appointment and divisional apportionment we would direct the expert's attention to our scheme for the Concert-room Organ, in our conviction that, as we have already said, it is the proper model to be humbly followed in scheming the true and resourceful Chamber Organ.

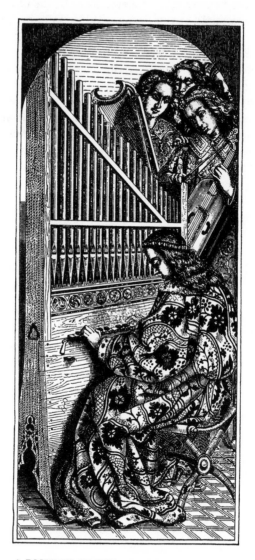

A POSITIVE OF THE FIFTEENTH CENTURY,
FROM A PAINTING BY THE VAN EYCKS.

CHAPTER XIII.

SCALES OF LABIAL PIPES.

ACH pipe in a properly-proportioned stop has, when of metal, a different diameter, or, when of wood, a different internal width and depth, from every other pipe comprised in the several octaves of the stop; or, in other words, the internal transverse area of each pipe differs from that of every other pipe constituting the stop. The standard of measurements by which the correct areas are determined is termed the *scale:* while the proportion which the pipes bear to each other in the successive octaves of the stop is designated the *ratio* of the scale.

The determination of desirable ratios and the subsequent development of accurate scales thereon are matters of the utmost importance in the art of pipe-making and in tone-production. While the general impression obtains that the best ratios have been determined; and organ-builders have found it convenient and time-saving to adopt them unmodified in any direction, we are convinced that the adoption of any one ratio throughout a stop is not necessary and in many stops not desirable. In a few quarters this matter is receiving some attention: and it is time, we venture to say, that serious investigation and careful experiment in compound scaling should be entered upon, in the earnest desire to reach a greater mastery over tone-production and the equalization of power.

There are several old treatises which touch on the subject of pipe scales, but from these nothing of practical value can be learnt. Dom Bedos, in his ponderous treatise, gives numerous scales set out full size. We presume some system was followed in the formation of these scales, but it is so erratic that we have failed to discover it. We allude to the extremely irregular disposition of their ordinates. Töpfer tried

343

the scales given by Dom Bedos, and, as might be expected, found them very unsatisfactory.

The first systematic treatment of this important subject appears to be that of Prof. J. G. Töpfer, whose first work on the Organ was published at Weimar in 1833. In this he recommends for general adoption scales developed on three different ratios; namely, one in the ratio $1 : \sqrt{8}$, wherein the half measure, or half diameter, falls on the sixteenth step; one in the ratio $1 : 2.66$, wherein the half measure falls on the seventeenth step; and one in the ratio $1 : 2.519$, wherein the half measure falls on the eighteenth step. In all these ratios the pipe from which the steps are counted is not included. It is necessary to bear this in mind when referring to the tables given in this Chapter. Of the three ratios, Töpfer claimed $1 : \sqrt{8}$ to be the most satisfactory. This, in the light of recent investigation, we gravely question: it, however, appears to have been very generally adopted by both German and French organ-builders, including Schulze and Cavaillé-Coll.* The distinguished German organ-builders Ladegast and Sauer appear to have followed compound scales for many of their stops: the latter certainly proved the advantage of the variable scale. The following is an example of Sauer's method:

SCALE OF ROHRFLÖTE.

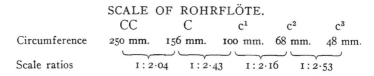

	CC	C	c^1	c^2	c^3
Circumference	250 mm.	156 mm.	100 mm.	68 mm.	48 mm.
Scale ratios		$1 : 2.04$	$1 : 2.43$	$1 : 2.16$	$1 : 2.53$

Instead of blindly following precedent, and confining himself to what has been considered sufficient in the past, the artist in tone-production to-day may find it expedient to develop scales, simple or compound, specially suitable for the stops he employs for the creation of new tonal colors, and for the establishment of a greater balance of power between the lower and upper octaves of the manual compass. The latter is a matter of considerable importance and should receive careful attention. The augmentation of the treble has exercised the minds of several artistically inclined organ-builders. No "rule-of-thumb" method should, however, obtain in scale-formation; and if any departure is made from mathematical gradation it must be systematically and artistically done.

The system of augmentation by means of enlargement of the pipe scales, upward, is one that has been frequently adopted by artistic

---

* On this subject Mr. F. E. Robertson remarks: " Of these Töpfer says: $1 : \sqrt{8}$ is *the* scale, and his reasoning appears to be that, as the ratio of $1 : 2$ is an extreme in one direction, and $1 : 4$ in the other, the geometrical mean $\sqrt{2 \times 4}$ will be the best scale, and we need not quarrel with the logic of this deduction, as the scales have met with general approval, though experienced voicers have their fancy for particular stops."—A Practical Treatise on Organ-Building, p. 34.

builders; and it deserves to be well considered in the stop appointment of all classes and sizes of Organs. It cannot, however, be applied equally to all stops. The OPEN DIAPASON, for instance, in which augmentation of the treble would be most valuable, does not lend itself to anything approaching an extreme treatment; for when its treble pipes are increased in scale beyond a desirable ratio they begin to lose the beautiful diapason-tone, and become objectionably fluty in character. Stops of the flute family generally admit of enlargement of scale without any loss of tonal character. Hill and Willis sometimes used ratios which place the half diameter at the twenty-first and twenty-ninth pipe, counting the starting pipe in both cases. Examples of the former ratio are to be found in certain LIEBLICHGEDECKTS made by Hill; and of the latter ratio in the beautiful CLARIBEL FLUTES and HARMONIC FLUTES made by Willis. This exceptional ratio we are informed by an organ expert is to be found, in the above-named stops, in the Organ in the Church of Hoddesdon, Hertfordshire. Reed stops, under certain limitations, admit of enlargement of scale, and, accordingly, contribute somewhat to the augmentation of the treble.*

Of the different methods of forming scales for labial pipes, suitable for general work, the most correct and satisfactory is that in which a straight base line is drawn and accurately divided into the required number of logarithmic abscissæ, and from each of which an ordinate is drawn perpendicular to the base line. When this has been correctly done, say, in the ordinary ratio $1 : \sqrt{8}$, it is only necessary to mark off the diameter decided on for the CC, or largest pipe of the stop, on the first ordinate, from the base line; and then to mark off in a similar manner the half of that diameter on the sixteenth ordinate (exclusive of the first on which the original diameter has been marked), and, finally, to draw a straight line obliquely from the mark on the first ordinate, onward through that on the sixteenth ordinate, and thence through all the remaining ordinates of the scale, prolonging the oblique line until it strikes the base line. In Diagram 1, in Plate XXVII., is shown a scale drawn in the ratio $1 : \sqrt{8}$—halving on the sixteenth step. A—B is the base line divided into sixty logarithmic abscissæ; and A—C, D—E, etc., are the ordinates determining, in conjunction with the oblique line C—B, the diameters of metal pipes. On a scale so formed, the circumferences of metal pipes may also be correctly determined. It is only necessary to lengthen the ordinates, to mark the circumference of the largest pipe on the first ordinate A—C, and then to draw an oblique line thence to the point B on the base line. All the ordinates, as cut by the oblique line, will give the circumferences of the different pipes correctly to the ratio of the scale. When such a scale is used for the

---

* A dissertation on this subject will be found in " The Art of Organ-Building," Vol. II., Chapter XV.

construction of quadrangular or triangular wood pipes, all that is required is to mark off the internal width and depth of the largest pipe on the first ordinate A—C, and draw two diagonal lines from the marks to the point B on the base line. In like manner, the widths and heights of mouths, and any other dimensions requiring to be accurately graduated may be determined throughout the compass of a stop.

To enable the pipe maker to easily and correctly construct a scale, as above described, and to any of the approved ratios, we give the accompanying Table, in which are set forth the distances—in inches and hundredths of an inch—that separate all the ordinates occurring between the first and last ordinates of each complete series.

TABLE GIVING THE MEASUREMENTS OF THE PROGRESSIVE STEPS
LOCATING THE POSITIONS OF THE ORDINATES IN PIPE
SCALES ACCORDING TO DIFFERENT RATIOS.

STEPS.	HALVING ON 16TH STEP.	HALVING ON 17TH STEP.	HALVING ON 18TH STEP.	HALVING ON 20TH STEP.	HALVING ON 22ND STEP.	HALVING ON 24TH STEP.
0	2·00	2·00	2·00	2·00	2·00	2·00
1	1·91	1·92	1·92	1·93	1·93	1·94
2	1·83	1·84	1·85	1·86	1·87	1·88
3	1·75	1·77	1·78	1·80	1·81	1·83
4	1·68	1·70	1·71	1·74	1·75	1·78
5	1·61	1·63	1·65	1·68	1·70	1·73
6	1·54	1·56	1·59	1·62	1·65	1·68
7	1·47	1·50	1·53	1·56	1·60	1·63
8	1·41	1·44	1·47	1·51	1·55	1·58
9	1·35	1·38	1·41	1·46	1·50	1·54
10	1·29	1·33	1·36	1·41	1·45	1·50
11	1·24	1·28	1·31	1·36	1·40	1·46
12	1·19	1·23	1·26	1·31	1·36	1·42
13	1·14	1·18	1·21	1·26	1·32	1·38
14	1·09	1·13	1·16	1·22	1·28	1·34
15	1·04	1·08	1·11	1·18	1·24	1·30
16	1·00	1·04	1·07	1·14	1·20	1·26
17	—	1·00	1·03	1·10	1·16	1·22
18	—	—	1·00	1·06	1·12	1·18
19	—	—	—	1·03	1·09	1·15
20	—	—	—	1·00	1·06	1·12
21	—	—	—	—	1·03	1·09
22	—	—	—	—	1·00	1·06
23	—	—	—	—	—	1·03
24	—	—	—	—	—	1·00

The measurements given in the Table can be easily laid down by the use of a scale of inches divided and lined in the manner shown in Fig. XXXI. This can be made by accurately scratching its lines on a piece of zinc or pipe-metal. Along the bottom line are read inches and the decimals ·10, ·20, ·30, ·40, ·50, ·60, ·70, ·80, and ·90; on the second

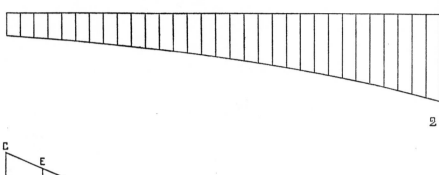

2

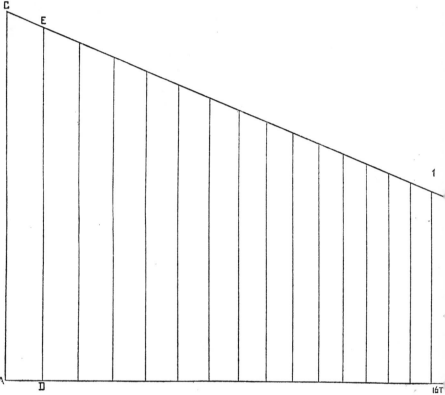

PLATE XXVII

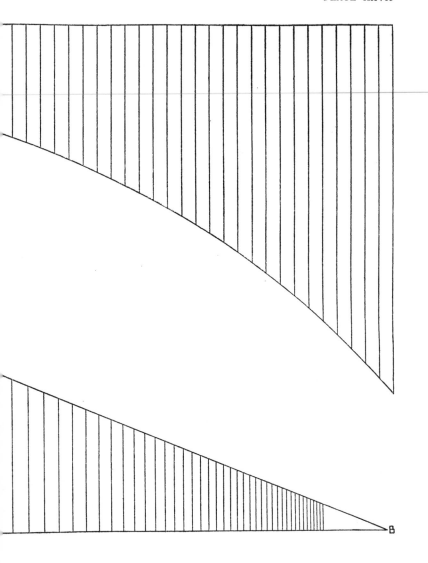

line are read inches and, measured to the diagonal lines, the decimals
·01, ·11, ·21, ·31, ·41, ·51, ·61, ·71, ·81, and ·91; on the third line are
read inches and the decimals ·02, ·12, ·22, ·32, ·42, ·52, ·62, ·72, ·82,
and ·92; and so on until on the ninth line are read inches and the decimals ·09, ·19, ·29, ·39, ·49, ·59, ·69, ·79, ·89, and ·99. By applying a
pair of sharp-pointed compasses to the scale great accuracy can be
secured. When the first series of ordinates have been accurately set

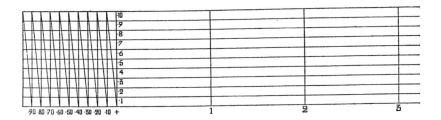

FIG. XXXI.

out on the base line of the pipe-scale the second series is formed by
simply halving the progressive measurements of the first series. To
prevent any accumulation of errors, it is desirable to take all half measurements from the first ordinate to the others, thus: from the first to
the second ordinate; from the first to the third ordinate; from the first
to the fourth ordinate, and so on throughout the series. All the measurements so taken are set out on the base line from the last ordinate of
the primal series, on which the half diameter is given. By this mode
of proceeding, any slight error in any one of the half measurements is
not extended to the others; and the second series of ordinates finishes
correctly, occupying on the base line exactly half the distance covered
by the primal series. The third series is derived from the second, and
the fourth from the third, in precisely the same manner as above described or the setting out of the second series.*

We may now consider another and perhaps quicker method of forming a working pipe-scale. In following this method, it is only necessary
to erect the requisite number of perpendicular ordinates at equidistant
points on a base line, and mark on the several ordinates, which determine the ratio of the scale, the circumferences or diameters of metal
pipes, or the widths and depths of wood pipes. The first ordinate gives
the dimensions of the largest pipe of the stop. When all these details

---

* Having furnished a practically complete set of Tables, to all the useful ratios, in the
present Chapter, we have not considered it necessary to occupy space, more valuable for other
matters, by giving the mathematical formulæ by which the measurements given have been
obtained. To those who desire to study such formulæ, pages 33-38 of Mr. F. E. Robertson's
"Practical Treatise on Organ-Building," and pages 132-149 of Töpfer-Allihn's "Die Theorie
und Praxis des Orgelbaues" will doubtless be of interest.

have been attended to, it only remains to connect all the points marked
on the special ordinates by a perfectly true curve. This can be drawn
with sufficient accuracy by means of a " spline," or slender, elastic strip
of celluloid, constructed for such a purpose; or a thin strip of straight-
grained wood may be used. Needles should be driven into the board (on
which the scale is being drawn) at the points marked on the ordinates,
and the spline bent in concave fashion against all the needles, and held
in that position, by the proper spline weights or by several needles, until
the curve is transferred to the scale. Should any difficulty be experienced in adjusting the spline so that it comes, without local forcing, in
contact with all the needles (on the ordinates) at the same time, or if
the scale is a compound one, it will be necessary to apply the spline
successively to the different sections, always bringing it in contact
with at least three of the needles. In Diagram 2, in Plate XXVII., is
shown a pipe-scale drawn as above described. While this method of
scale-formation is not to be recommended for scales of regular gradation, it certainly is very suitable and convenient for the development
of irregular or compound scales, in which quicker or slower gradations
may be required in their different sections or octaves.

The following six Tables of scale measurements, in different ratios,
will be found useful, either in the formation of working scales, or for
checking the accuracy, or comparing the gradation, of scales developed
on any special lines. It is almost unnecessary to point out the fact
that, as all the calculations have been carried out to only two places
of decimals, the measurements are only approximately correct. They
are, however, sufficiently accurate for practical use; indeed, it would
have been absurd to carry the decimals to three places, and confront
the pipe maker with measurements involving thousandths of an inch.
It is hardly reasonable to expect unvarying accuracy to even one-
hundredth of an inch.

From the several ratios and measurements given in the Tables
innumerable scales may be obtained. The dimensions placed opposite
the notes of the scale are not necessarily fixed in the relations given.
For instance, in Table I. the note CC (8 ft.) has a diameter of 5·80;
but this diameter may be increased or diminished by starting the note
on either a larger or a smaller diameter in the table; all the other note
measurements taking their regular progression from it, downward
and upward. It is not desirable in practice to use a scale having a
gradation quicker than that of the ratio $1 : \sqrt{8}$, which places the half
diameter on the seventeenth pipe,—that is, on the sixteenth step from
any pipe in the scale,—notwithstanding the fact that the French authority, Hamel, advocates the ratio $2 : 3$, which places the half diameter,
according to his series of Tables, practically on the fifteenth step, in
the scales for what he calls the " five principal stops of the Organ."

I. TABLE OF SCALE MEASUREMENTS IN INCHES, RATIO $1:\sqrt{8}$—
HALVING ON THE SIXTEENTH STEP.

NO.	NAMES OF NOTES	DIAMETER	CIRCUMFERENCE	EQUAL SQUARE	WIDTH OF QUAD. PIPE	NO.	NAMES OF NOTES	DIAMETER	CIRCUMFERENCE	EQUAL SQUARE	WIDTH OF QUAD. PIPE
1	CCCC	16·40	51·52	14·56	12·88	45	G♯	2·44	7·66	2·16	1·91
2	CCCC♯	15·72	49·36	13·92	12·32	46	A	2·33	7·32	2·06	1·83
3	DDDD	15·04	47·24	13·32	11·80	47	A♯	2·23	7·01	1·98	1·75
4	DDDD♯	14·40	45·24	12·76	11·32	48	B	2·14	6·72	1·90	1·68
5	EEEE	13·80	43·32	12·24	10·84	49	c^{1}	2·05	6·44	1·82	1·61
6	FFFF	13·20	41·48	11·72	10·36	50	$c\sharp^{1}$	1·96	6·17	1·74	1·54
7	FFFF♯	12·64	39·72	11·20	9·92	51	d^{1}	1·88	5·90	1·66	1·47
8	GGGG	12·12	38·08	10·72	9·52	52	$d\sharp^{1}$	1·80	5·65	1·59	1·41
9	GGGG♯	11·60	36·44	10·28	9·12	53	e^{1}	1·72	5·41	1·53	1·35
10	AAAA	11·12	34·92	9·84	8·72	54	f^{1}	1·65	5·18	1·46	1·29
11	AAAA♯	10·64	33·44	9·44	8·36	55	$f\sharp^{1}$	1·58	4·96	1·40	1·24
12	BBBB	10·20	32·04	9·04	8·00	56	g^{1}	1·51	4·76	1·34	1·19
13	CCC	9·76	30·64	8·64	7·64	57	$g\sharp^{1}$	1·45	4·55	1·28	1·14
14	CCC♯	9·32	29·28	8·24	7·32	58	a^{1}	1·39	4·36	1·23	1·09
15	DDD	8·92	28·04	7·92	7·00	59	$a\sharp^{1}$	1·33	4·18	1·18	1·04
16	DDD♯	8·56	26·88	7·60	6·72	60	b^{1}	1·27	4·00	1·13	1·00
17	EEE	8·20	25·76	7·28	6·44	61	c^{2}	1·22	3·83	1·08	0·95
18	FFF	7·86	24·68	6·96	6·18	62	$c\sharp^{2}$	1·16	3·66	1·03	0·91
19	FFF♯	7·52	23·62	6·66	5·90	63	d^{2}	1·11	3·50	0·99	0·87
20	GGG	7·20	22·62	6·38	5·66	64	$d\sharp^{2}$	1·07	3·36	0·95	0·84
21	GGG♯	6·90	21·66	6·12	5·42	65	e^{2}	1·02	3·22	0·91	0·80
22	AAA	6·60	20·74	5·86	5·18	66	f^{2}	0·98	3·08	0·87	0·77
23	AAA♯	6·32	19·86	5·60	4·96	67	$f\sharp^{2}$	0·94	2·95	0·83	0·74
24	BBB	6·06	19·04	5·36	4·76	68	g^{2}	0·90	2·83	0·79	0·71
25	CC	5·80	18·22	5·14	4·56	69	$g\sharp^{2}$	0·86	2·71	0·76	0·68
26	CC♯	5·56	17·46	4·92	4·36	70	a^{2}	0·82	2·59	0·73	0·65
27	DD	5·32	16·72	4·72	4·18	71	$a\sharp^{2}$	0·79	2·48	0·70	0·62
28	DD♯	5·10	16·02	4·52	4·00	72	b^{2}	0·76	2·38	0·67	0·59
29	EE	4·88	15·32	4·32	3·82	73	c^{3}	0·72	2·28	0·64	0·57
30	FF	4·66	14·64	4·12	3·66	74	$c\sharp^{3}$	0·69	2·18	0·61	0·54
31	FF♯	4·46	14·02	3·96	3·50	75	d^{3}	0·66	2·09	0·59	0·52
32	GG	4·28	13·44	3·80	3·36	76	$d\sharp^{3}$	0·64	2·00	0·56	0·50
33	GG♯	4·10	12·88	3·64	3·22	77	e^{3}	0·61	1·91	0·54	0·48
34	AA	3·93	12·34	3·48	3·08	78	f^{3}	0·58	1·83	0·51	0·46
35	AA♯	3·76	11·81	3·33	2·95	79	$f\sharp^{3}$	0·56	1·75	0·49	0·44
36	BB	3·60	11·31	3·19	2·83	80	g^{3}	0·53	1·68	0·47	0·42
37	C	3·45	10·83	3·06	2·71	81	$g\sharp^{3}$	0·51	1·61	0·45	0·40
38	C♯	3·30	10·37	2·93	2·59	82	a^{3}	0·49	1·54	0·43	0·38
39	D	3·16	9·93	2·80	2·48	83	$a\sharp^{3}$	0·47	1·48	0·42	0·37
40	D♯	3·03	9·52	2·68	2·38	84	b^{3}	0·45	1·41	0·40	0·35
41	E	2·90	9·11	2·57	2·28	85	c^{4}	0·43	1·35	0·38	0·34
42	F	2·78	8·73	2·46	2·18	86	$c\sharp^{4}$	0·41	1·29	0·37	0·32
43	F♯	2·66	8·36	2·36	2·09	87	d^{4}	0·39	1·24	0·35	0·31
44	G	2·55	8·01	2·26	2·00	88	$d\sharp^{4}$	0·38	1·19	0·33	0·29

NO.	NAMES OF NOTES	DIAMETER	CIRCUMFERENCE	EQUAL SQUARE	WIDTH OF QUAD. PIPE	NO.	NAMES OF NOTES	DIAMETER	CIRCUMFERENCE	EQUAL SQUARE	WIDTH OF QUAD. PIPE
89	e^4	0·36	1·14	0·32	0·28	95	$a\#^4$	0·28	0·88	0·25	0·22
90	f^4	0·35	1·09	0·31	0·27	96	b^4	0·27	0·84	0·24	0·21
91	$f\#^4$	0·33	1·04	0·29	0·26	97	c^5	0·26	0·80	0·23	0·20
92	g^4	0·32	1·00	0·28	0·25	98	$c\#^5$	0·24	0·77	0·22	0·19
93	$g\#^4$	0·30	0·96	0·27	0·24	99	d^5	0·23	0·74	0·21	0·18
94	a^4	0·29	0·91	0·26	0·23	100	$d\#^5$	0·22	0·71	0·20	0·17

II. TABLE OF SCALE MEASUREMENTS IN INCHES, RATIO 1 : 2·66— HALVING ON THE SEVENTEENTH STEP.

NO.	NAMES OF NOTES	DIAMETER	CIRCUMFERENCE	EQUAL SQUARE	WIDTH OF QUAD. PIPE	NO.	NAMES OF NOTES	DIAMETER	CIRCUMFERENCE	EQUAL SQUARE	WIDTH OF QUAD. PIPE
1	CCCC	14·52	45·60	12·88	11·40	33	GG#	3·94	12·38	3·49	3·09
2	CCCC#	13·92	43·72	12·36	10·93	34	AA	3·78	11·88	3·35	2·97
3	DDDD	13·36	41·96	11·84	10·49	35	AA#	3·63	11·40	3·22	2·85
4	DDDD#	12·84	40·32	11·36	10·08	36	BB	3·48	10·93	3·09	2·73
5	EEEE	12·32	38·72	10·92	9·68	37	C	3·34	10·49	2·96	2·62
6	FFFF	11·80	37·08	10·48	9·27	38	C#	3·21	10·08	2·84	2·52
7	FFFF#	11·36	35·68	10·08	8·92	39	D	3·08	9·68	2·73	2·42
8	GGGG	10·92	34·32	9·68	8·58	40	D#	2·95	9·27	2·62	2·32
9	GGGG#	10·48	32·92	9·28	8·23	41	E	2·84	8·92	2·52	2·23
10	AAAA	10·04	31·52	8·88	7·88	42	F	2·73	8·58	2·42	2·14
11	AAAA#	9·64	30·28	8·52	7·57	43	F#	2·62	8·23	2·32	2·06
12	BBBB	9·24	29·04	8·16	7·26	44	G	2·51	7·88	2·22	1·97
13	CCC	8·88	27·88	7·84	6·97	45	G#	2·41	7·57	2·13	1·89
14	CCC#	8·52	26·76	7·56	6·69	46	A	2·31	7·26	2·04	1·81
15	DDD	8·20	25·76	7·28	6·44	47	A#	2·22	6·97	1·96	1·74
16	DDD#	7·88	24·76	6·98	6·18	48	B	2·13	6·69	1·89	1·67
17	EEE	7·56	23·76	6·70	5·94	49	c^1	2·05	6·44	1·82	1·61
18	FFF	7·26	22·80	6·44	5·70	50	$c\#^1$	1·97	6·19	1·74	1·54
19	FFF#	6·96	21·86	6·18	5·46	51	d^1	1·89	5·94	1·67	1·48
20	GGG	6·68	20·98	5·92	5·24	52	$d\#^1$	1·81	5·70	1·61	1·42
21	GGG#	6·42	20·16	5·68	5·04	53	e^1	1·74	5·46	1·54	1·36
22	AAA	6·16	19·36	5·46	4·84	54	f^1	1·67	5·24	1·48	1·31
23	AAA#	5·90	18·54	5·24	4·64	55	$f\#^1$	1·60	5·04	1·42	1·26
24	BBB	5·68	17·84	5·04	4·46	56	g^1	1·54	4·84	1·36	1·21
25	CC	5·46	17·16	4·84	4·28	57	$g\#^1$	1·47	4·63	1·31	1·16
26	CC#	5·24	16·46	4·64	4·12	58	a^1	1·42	4·46	1·26	1·11
27	DD	5·02	15·76	4·44	3·94	59	$a\#^1$	1·36	4·29	1·21	1·07
28	DD#	4·82	15·14	4·26	3·78	60	b^1	1·31	4·11	1·16	1·03
29	EE	4·62	14·52	4·08	3·62	61	c^2	1·25	3·94	1·11	0·98
30	FF	4·44	13·94	3·92	3·48	62	$c\#^2$	1·20	3·78	1·06	0·94
31	FF#	4·26	13·38	3·78	3·34	63	d^2	1·15	3·63	1·02	0·90
32	GG	4·10	12·88	3·64	3·22						

NO.	NAMES OF NOTES	DIAMETER	CIRCUMFERENCE	EQUAL SQUARE	WIDTH OF QUAD. PIPE	NO.	NAMES OF NOTES	DIAMETER	CIRCUMFERENCE	EQUAL SQUARE	WIDTH OF QUAD. PIPE
64	d#²	1·11	3·48	0·98	0·87	83	a#³	0·51	1·61	0·45	0·40
65	e²	1·06	3·34	0·94	0·83	84	b³	0·49	1·55	0·44	0·38
66	f²	1·02	3·22	0·91	0·80	85	c⁴	0·47	1·48	0·42	0·37
67	f#²	0·98	3·09	0·87	0·77	86	c#⁴	0·45	1·42	0·40	0·35
68	g²	0·94	2·97	0·84	0·74	87	d⁴	0·43	1·37	0·38	0·34
69	g#²	0·91	2·85	0·80	0·71	88	d#⁴	0·42	1·31	0·37	0·33
70	a²	0·87	2·73	0·77	0·68	89	e⁴	0·40	1·26	0·35	0·31
71	a#²	0·83	2·62	0·74	0·65	90	f⁴	0·38	1·21	0·34	0·30
72	b²	0·80	2·52	0·71	0·63	91	f#⁴	0·37	1·16	0·33	0·29
73	c³	0·77	2·42	0·68	0·60	92	g⁴	0·35	1·11	0·31	0·28
74	c#³	0·74	2·32	0·65	0·58	93	g#⁴	0·34	1·07	0·30	0·27
75	d³	0·71	2·23	0·63	0·56	94	a⁴	0·33	1·03	0·29	0·26
76	d#³	0·68	2·14	0·60	0·53	95	a#⁴	0·31	0·98	0·28	0·25
77	e³	0·65	2·06	0·58	0·51	96	b⁴	0·30	0·95	0·26	0·24
78	f³	0·63	1·97	0·55	0·49	97	c⁵	0·29	0·91	0·25	0·23
79	f#³	0·60	1·89	0·53	0·47	98	c#⁵	0·28	0·87	0·24	0·22
80	g³	0·58	1·81	0·51	0·45	99	d⁵	0·27	0·84	0·23	0·21
81	g#³	0·55	1·74	0·49	0·43	100	d#⁵	0·26	0·80	0·22	0·20
82	a³	0·53	1·67	0·47	0·42						

III. TABLE OF SCALE MEASUREMENTS IN INCHES, RATIO 1 : 2·519— HALVING ON THE EIGHTEENTH STEP.

NO.	NAMES OF NOTES	DIAMETER	CIRCUMFERENCE	EQUAL SQUARE	WIDTH OF QUAD. PIPE	NO.	NAMES OF NOTES	DIAMETER	CIRCUMFERENCE	EQUAL SQUARE	WIDTH OF QUAD. PIPE
1	CCCC	13·00	40·84	11·52	10·20	20	GGG	6·26	19·66	5·54	4·92
2	CCCC#	12·52	39·32	11·08	9·83	21	GGG#	6·02	18·92	5·32	4·73
3	DDDD	12·04	37·84	10·64	9·46	22	AAA	5·80	18·22	5·14	4·56
4	DDDD#	11·60	36·44	10·28	9·11	23	AAA#	5·58	17·52	4·94	4·38
5	EEEE	11·16	35·04	9·88	8·76	24	BBB	5·36	16·84	4·76	4·21
6	FFFF	10·72	33·68	9·52	8·42	25	CC	5·16	16·20	4·58	4·05
7	FFFF#	10·32	32·40	9·16	8·10	26	CC#	4·96	15·58	4·40	3·89
8	GGGG	9·92	31·16	8·80	7·80	27	DD	4·78	15·00	4·24	3·75
9	GGGG#	9·56	30·00	8·48	7·50	28	DD#	4·60	14·44	4·08	3·61
10	AAAA	9·20	28·88	8·16	7·22	29	EE	4·42	13·86	3·92	3·46
11	AAAA#	8·84	27·72	7·84	6·93	30	FF	4·26	13·38	3·78	3·34
12	BBBB	8·52	26·76	7·56	6·69	31	FF#	4·10	12·88	3·64	3·22
13	CCC	8·20	25·76	7·28	6·44	32	GG	3·94	12·38	3·49	3·09
14	CCC#	7·88	24·76	6·98	6·19	33	GG#	3·79	11·91	3·36	2·98
15	DDD	7·58	23·82	6·72	5·95	34	AA	3·65	11·47	3·24	2·87
16	DDD#	7·30	22·94	6·48	5·74	35	AA#	3·51	11·03	3·11	2·76
17	EEE	7·02	22·06	6·22	5·52	36	BB	3·38	10·62	3·00	2·65
18	FFF	6·76	21·24	6·00	5·31	37	C	3·25	10·21	2·88	2·55
19	FFF#	6·50	20·42	5·76	5·10						

NO.	NAMES OF NOTES	DIAM-ETER	CIRCUM-FERENCE	EQUAL SQUARE	WIDTH OF QUAD. PIPE	NO.	NAMES OF NOTES	DIAM-ETER	CIRCUM-FERENCE	EQUAL SQUARE	WIDTH OF QUAD. PIPE
38	C♯	3·13	9·83	2·77	2·46	70	a²	0·91	2·87	0·81	0·72
39	D	3·01	9·46	2·66	2·36	71	a♯²	0·88	2·76	0·78	0·69
40	D♯	2·90	9·11	2·57	2·28	72	b²	0·84	2·65	0·75	0·66
41	E	2·79	8·76	2·47	2·19						
42	F	2·68	8·42	2·38	2·10	73	c³	0·81	2·55	0·72	0·64
43	F♯	2·58	8·10	2·29	2·02	74	c♯³	0·78	2·46	0·69	0·61
44	G	2·48	7·79	2·20	1·95	75	d³	0·75	2·36	0·66	0·59
45	G♯	2·39	7·50	2·12	1·87	76	d♯³	0·72	2·28	0·64	0·57
46	A	2·30	7·22	2·04	1·81	77	e³	0·70	2·19	0·62	0·55
47	A♯	2·21	6·93	1·96	1·73	78	f³	0·67	2·10	0·59	0·52
48	B	2·13	6·69	1·89	1·67	79	f♯³	0·64	2·02	0·57	0·50
						80	g³	0·62	1·95	0·55	0·49
49	c¹	2·05	6·44	1·82	1·61	81	g♯³	0·60	1·87	0·53	0·47
50	c♯¹	1·97	6·19	1·74	1·54	82	a³	0·57	1·80	0·51	0·45
51	d¹	1·89	5·95	1·68	1·49	83	a♯³	0·55	1·73	0·49	0·43
52	d♯¹	1·82	5·73	1·62	1·43	84	b³	0·53	1·67	0·47	0·42
53	e¹	1·75	5·51	1·55	1·38						
54	f¹	1·69	5·31	1·50	1·32	85	c⁴	0·51	1·61	0·45	0·40
55	f♯¹	1·62	5·10	1·44	1·27	86	c♯⁴	0·49	1·55	0·44	0·39
56	g¹	1·56	4·91	1·38	1·23	87	d⁴	0·47	1·46	0·42	0·37
57	g♯¹	1·50	4·73	1·33	1·18	88	d♯⁴	0·46	1·43	0·40	0·36
58	a¹	1·45	4·55	1·28	1·14	89	e⁴	0·44	1·38	0·39	0·34
59	a♯¹	1·39	4·38	1·23	1·09	90	f⁴	0·42	1·32	0·37	0·33
60	b¹	1·34	4·21	1·19	1·05	91	f♯⁴	0·40	1·28	0·36	0·32
						92	g⁴	0·39	1·23	0·35	0·31
61	c²	1·29	4·05	1·14	1·01	93	g♯⁴	0·38	1·18	0·33	0·30
62	c♯²	1·24	3·89	1·10	0·97	94	a⁴	0·36	1·14	0·32	0·28
63	d²	1·19	3·75	1·06	0·94	95	a♯⁴	0·35	1·09	0·31	0·27
64	d♯²	1·15	3·61	1·02	0·90	96	b⁴	0·33	1·05	0·30	0·26
65	e²	1·10	3·46	0·98	0·86						
66	f²	1·06	3·34	0·94	0·83	97	c⁵	0·32	1·01	0·29	0·25
67	f♯²	1·02	3·22	0·91	0·80	98	c♯⁵	0·31	0·97	0·27	0·24
68	g²	0·99	3·09	0·87	0·77	99	d⁵	0·30	0·94	0·26	0·23
69	g♯²	0·95	2·98	0·84	0·74	100	d♯⁵	0·29	0·90	0·25	0·22

IV. TABLE OF SCALE MEASUREMENTS IN INCHES, RATIO 1 : 2.3— HALVING ON THE TWENTIETH STEP.

NO.	NAMES OF NOTES	DIAM-ETER	CIRCUM-FERENCE	EQUAL SQUARE	WIDTH OF QUAD. PIPE	NO.	NAMES OF NOTES	DIAM-ETER	CIRCUM-FERENCE	EQUAL SQUARE	WIDTH OF QUAD. PIPE
1	CCCC	10·76	33·80	9·52	8·45	7	FFFF♯	8·80	27·64	7·80	6·91
2	CCCC♯	10·40	32·68	9·20	8·17	8	GGGG	8·48	26·64	7·52	6·66
3	DDDD	10·08	31·64	8·92	7·91	9	GGGG♯	8·20	25·76	7·28	6·44
4	DDDD♯	9·76	30·64	8·64	7·66	10	AAAA	7·92	24·88	7·02	6·22
5	EEEE	9·44	29·64	8·36	7·41	11	AAAA♯	7·66	24·06	6·78	6·02
6	FFFF	9·12	28·64	8·08	7·16	12	BBBB	7·40	23·24	6·54	5·80

NO.	NAMES OF NOTES	DIAMETER	CIRCUMFERENCE	EQUAL SQUARE	WIDTH OF QUAD. PIPE
13	CCC	7·14	22·42	6·32	5·60
14	CCC♯	6·88	21·62	6·10	5·40
15	DDD	6·64	20·86	5·88	5·22
16	DDD♯	6·42	20·16	5·68	5·04
17	EEE	6·20	19·48	5·48	4·86
18	FFF	5·98	18·80	5·30	4·70
19	FFF♯	5·78	18·16	5·12	4·54
20	GGG	5·58	17·52	4·94	4·38
21	GGG♯	5·38	16·90	4·76	4·22
22	AAA	5·20	16·34	4·60	4·08
23	AAA♯	5·04	15·82	4·46	3·96
24	BBB	4·88	15·32	4·32	3·82
25	CC	4·72	14·82	4·18	3·70
26	CC♯	4·56	14·32	4·04	3·59
27	DD	4·40	13·82	3·90	3·46
28	DD♯	4·24	13·32	3·76	3·32
29	EE	4·10	12·88	3·64	3·22
30	FF	3·96	12·44	3·51	3·11
31	FF♯	3·83	12·03	3·39	3·01
32	GG	3·70	11·62	3·27	2·90
33	GG♯	3·57	11·21	3·16	2·80
34	AA	3·44	10·81	3·05	2·70
35	AA♯	3·32	10·43	2·94	2·61
36	BB	3·21	10·08	2·84	2·52
37	C	3·10	9·74	2·74	2·43
38	C♯	2·99	9·40	2·65	2·35
39	D	2·89	9·08	2·56	2·27
40	D♯	2·79	8·76	2·47	2·19
41	E	2·69	8·45	2·38	2·11
42	F	2·60	8·17	2·30	2·04
43	F♯	2·52	7·91	2·23	1·98
44	G	2·44	7·66	2·16	1·91
45	G♯	2·36	7·41	2·09	1·85
46	A	2·28	7·16	2·02	1·79
47	A♯	2·20	6·91	1·95	1·73
48	B	2·12	6·66	1·88	1·66
49	c^1	2·05	6·44	1·82	1·61
50	$c♯^1$	1·98	6·22	1·75	1·55
51	d^1	1·91	6·01	1·69	1·50
52	$d♯^1$	1·85	5·81	1·63	1·45
53	e^1	1·78	5·60	1·58	1·40
54	f^1	1·72	5·40	1·52	1·35
55	$f♯^1$	1·66	5·21	1·47	1·30
56	g^1	1·60	5·04	1·42	1·26
57	$g♯^1$	1·55	4·87	1·37	1·21
58	a^1	1·49	4·70	1·32	1·17
59	$a♯^1$	1·44	4·54	1·28	1·13
60	b^1	1·39	4·38	1·23	1·09
61	c^2	1·34	4·22	1·19	1·05
62	$c♯^2$	1·30	4·08	1·15	1·02
63	d^2	1·26	3·95	1·11	0·99
64	$d♯^2$	1·22	3·83	1·08	0·95
65	e^2	1·18	3·70	1·04	0·92
66	f^2	1·14	3·58	1·01	0·89
67	$f♯^2$	1·10	3·45	0·97	0·86
68	g^2	1·06	3·33	0·94	0·83
69	$g♯^2$	1·02	3·22	0·91	0·80
70	a^2	0·99	3·11	0·88	0·78
71	$a♯^2$	0·96	3·01	0·85	0·75
72	b^2	0·92	2·90	0·82	0·72
73	c^3	0·89	2·80	0·79	0·70
74	$c♯^3$	0·86	2·70	0·76	0·67
75	d^3	0·83	2·61	0·73	0·65
76	$d♯^3$	0·80	2·52	0·71	0·63
77	e^3	0·77	2·43	0·68	0·61
78	f^3	0·75	2·35	0·66	0·59
79	$f♯^3$	0·72	2·27	0·64	0·57
80	g^3	0·70	2·19	0·62	0·55
81	$g♯^3$	0·67	2·11	0·59	0·53
82	a^3	0·65	2·04	0·57	0·51
83	$a♯^3$	0·63	1·98	0·56	0·49
84	b^3	0·61	1·91	0·54	0·48
85	c^4	0·59	1·85	0·52	0·46
86	$c♯^4$	0·57	1·79	0·50	0·45
87	d^4	0·55	1·75	0·49	0·43
88	$d♯^4$	0·53	1·66	0·47	0·41
89	e^4	0·51	1·61	0·45	0·40
90	f^4	0·49	1·55	0·44	0·39
91	$f♯^4$	0·48	1·50	0·42	0·38
92	g^4	0·46	1·45	0·41	0·36
93	$g♯^4$	0·45	1·40	0·39	0·35
94	a^4	0·43	1·35	0·38	0·34
95	$a♯^4$	0·41	1·30	0·37	0·33
96	b^4	0·40	1·26	0·35	0·31
97	c^5	0·39	1·22	0·34	0·30
98	$c♯^5$	0·37	1·17	0·33	0·29
99	d^5	0·36	1·13	0·32	0·28
100	$d♯^5$	0·35	1·09	0·31	0·27

V   TABLE OF SCALE MEASUREMENTS IN INCHES, RATIO 1 : 2 13—
HALVING ON THE TWENTY-SECOND STEP

NO.	NAMES OF NOTES	DIAM-ETER	CIRCUM-FERENCE	EQUAL SQUARE	WIDTH OF QUAD. PIPE	NO.	NAMES OF NOTES	DIAM-ETER	CIRCUM-FERENCE	EQUAL SQUARE	WIDTH OF QUAD. PIPE
1	CCCC	9·28	29·16	8·24	7·29	45	G$\sharp$	2·32	7·29	2·06	1·82
2	CCCC$\sharp$	9·00	28·28	7·96	7·07	46	A	2·25	7·07	1·99	1·77
3	DDDD	8·72	27·40	7·72	6·85	47	A$\sharp$	2·18	6·85	1·93	1·71
4	DDDD$\sharp$	8·44	26·52	7·48	6·63	48	B	2·11	6·63	1·87	1·66
5	EEEE	8·20	25·76	7·28	6·44						
6	FFFF	7·94	24·96	7·04	6·24	49	c^1	2·05	6·44	1·82	1·61
7	FFFF$\sharp$	7·70	24·20	6·82	6·05	50	c$\sharp^1$	1·98	6·24	1 76	1·56
8	GGGG	7·46	23·44	6·60	5·86	51	d^1	1·92	6·05	1 70	1·51
9	GGGG$\sharp$	7·22	22·68	6·40	5·67	52	d$\sharp^1$	1·86	5·86	1·65	1·46
10	AAAA	7·00	21·98	6·20	5·49	53	e^1	1·80	5·62	1·60	1·41
11	AAAA$\sharp$	6·78	21 30	6·00	5·32	54	f^1	1·75	5·49	1 55	1·37
12	BBBB	6·58	20·66	5·80	5·16	55	f$\sharp^1$	1·69	5·32	1 50	1·33
						56	g^1	1·64	5·16	1·45	1·29
13	CCC	6·38	20·04	5·62	5·01	57	g$\sharp^1$	1·59	5·01	1·40	1·25
14	CCC$\sharp$	6·18	19·40	5·46	4·85	58	a^1	1·54	4·85	1·36	1·21
15	DDD	5·98	18·80	5·30	4·70	59	a$\sharp^1$	1·49	4·70	1·32	1·17
16	DDD$\sharp$	5·80	18·22	5·14	4·55	60	b^1	1·45	4·55	1·28	1·14
17	EEE	5·62	17·64	4·98	4·40						
18	FFF	5·44	17·08	4·82	4·27	61	c^2	1·40	4·41	1 24	1·10
19	FFF$\sharp$	5·28	16·58	4·68	4 14	62	c$\sharp^2$	1·36	4·27	1 20	1·07
20	GGG	5·12	16·08	4 54	4·02	63	d^2	1·32	4·14	1 17	1·03
21	GGG$\sharp$	4·96	15·58	4·40	3·89	64	d$\sharp^2$	1·28	4·02	1 13	1·00
22	AAA	4·80	15·08	4 26	3·77	65	e^2	1·24	3·89	1·10	0·97
23	AAA$\sharp$	4·64	14·58	4·12	3·64	66	f^2	1·20	3·77	1 06	0·94
24	BBB	4·50	14 14	3·98	3·53	67	f$\sharp^2$	1 16	3·64	1·03	0·91
						68	g^2	1 12	3·53	0·99	0·88
25	CC	4·36	13 70	3·86	3·42	69	g$\sharp^2$	1·09	3·42	0·96	0·85
26	CC$\sharp$	4·22	13·26	3·74	3·32	70	a^2	1·05	3·31	0·93	0·83
27	DD	4·10	12·88	3·64	3·22	71	a$\sharp^2$	1·02	3·22	0·91	0·80
28	DD$\sharp$	3·97	12 48	3 52	3·12	72	b^2	0·99	3·12	0·88	0·78
29	EE	3·85	12·10	3 41	3·02						
30	FF	3·73	11·72	3·30	2·93	73	c^3	0·96	3·02	0·85	0`75
31	FF$\sharp$	3·61	11·34	3·20	2·83	74	c$\sharp^3$	0·93	2·93	0·82	0·73
32	GG	3 50	10·99	3·10	2·75	75	d^3	0·90	2·83	0·80	0·71
33	GG$\sharp$	3·39	10·65	3·00	2·66	76	d$\sharp^3$	0·87	2·75	0·77	0·69
34	AA	3·29	10·33	2·90	2·58	77	e^3	0·85	2·66	0·75	0·66
35	AA$\sharp$	3·19	10·02	2·81	2·50	78	f^3	0·82	2·58	0·72	0·64
36	BB	3·09	9·71	2·73	2·43	79	f$\sharp^3$	0·80	2·50	0·70	0·62
						80	g^3	0·77	2·43	0·68	0·61
37	C	2·99	9·40	2·65	2·35	81	g$\sharp^3$	0·75	2 35	0·66	0·59
38	C$\sharp$	2·90	9·11	2·57	2·28	82	a^3	0·72	2·28	0·64	0·57
39	D	2·81	8·82	2·49	2·20	83	a$\sharp^3$	0·70	2·20	0·62	0·55
40	D$\sharp$	2·72	8·54	2·41	2·13	84	b^3	0·68	2·13	0·60	0·53
41	E	2·64	8·29	2·34	2·07	85	c^4	0·66	2·07	0·58	0·52
42	F	2·56	8·04	2·27	2·01	86	c$\sharp^4$	0·64	2·01	0·57	0·50
43	F$\sharp$	2·48	7·79	2·20	1·95	87	d^4	0·62	1·95	0·55	0·49
44	G	2·40	7·54	2·13	1·88	88	d$\sharp^4$	0·60	1·88	0·53	0·47

NO.	NAMES OF NOTES	DIAMETER	CIRCUMFERENCE	EQUAL SQUARE	WIDTH OF QUAD. PIPE	NO.	NAMES OF NOTES	DIAMETER	CIRCUMFERENCE	EQUAL SQUARE	WIDTH OF QUAD. PIPE
89	e⁴	0·58	1·82	0·51	0·45	95	a#⁴	0·48	1·51	0·43	0·38
90	f⁴	0·56	1·77	0·50	0·44	96	b⁴	0·47	1·46	0·41	0·37
91	f#⁴	0·54	1·71	0·48	0·43	97	c⁵	0·45	1·42	0·35	0·35
92	g⁴	0·53	1·66	0·47	0·41	98	c#⁵	0·44	1·37	0·34	0·34
93	g#⁴	0·51	1·61	0·45	0·40	99	d⁵	0·42	1·33	0·33	0·33
94	a⁴	0·50	1·56	0·44	0·39	100	d#⁵	0·41	1·29	0·32	0·32

VI. TABLE OF SCALE MEASUREMENTS IN INCHES, RATIO 1 : 2— HALVING ON THE TWENTY-FOURTH STEP.

NO.	NAMES OF NOTES	DIAMETER	CIRCUMFERENCE	EQUAL SQUARE	WIDTH OF QUAD. PIPE	NO.	NAMES OF NOTES	DIAMETER	CIRCUMFERENCE	EQUAL SQUARE	WIDTH OF QUAD. PIPE
1	CCCC	8·20	25·76	7·28	6·44	33	GG#	3·25	10·21	2·88	2·55
2	CCCC#	7·96	25·02	7·06	6·26	34	AA	3·15	9·90	2·79	2·47
3	DDDD	7·74	24·32	6·86	6·08	35	AA#	3·06	9·61	2·71	2·40
4	DDDD#	7·52	23·62	6·66	5·90	36	BB	2·98	9·36	2·64	2·34
5	EEEE	7·30	22·94	6·48	5·74						
6	FFFF	7·10	22·30	6·30	5·57	37	C	2·90	9·11	2·57	2·28
7	FFFF#	6·90	21·66	6·12	5·42	38	C#	2·82	8·86	2·50	2·21
8	GGGG	6·70	21·04	5·94	5·26	39	D	2·74	8·61	2·43	2·15
9	GGGG#	6·50	20·42	5·76	5·10	40	D#	2·66	8·36	2·36	2·09
10	AAAA	6·30	19·80	5·58	4·95	41	E	2·58	8·10	2·29	2·02
11	AAAA#	6·12	19·22	5·42	4·80	42	F	2·51	7·88	2·22	1·97
12	BBBB	5·96	18·72	5·28	4·68	43	F#	2·44	7·66	2·16	1·91
						44	G	2·37	7·44	2·10	1·86
13	CCC	5·80	18·22	5·14	4·55	45	G#	2·30	7·22	2·04	1·81
14	CCC#	5·64	17·72	5·00	4·43	46	A	2·24	7·03	1·98	1·76
15	DDD	5·48	17·22	4·86	4·30	47	A#	2·17	6·82	1·92	1·71
16	DDD#	5·32	16·72	4·72	4·18	48	B	2·11	6·63	1·87	1·66
17	EEE	5·16	16·20	4·58	4·05						
18	FFF	5·02	15·76	4·44	3·94	49	c¹	2·05	6·44	1·82	1·61
19	FFF#	4·88	15·32	4·32	3·83	50	c#¹	1·99	6·25	1·76	1·56
20	GGG	4·74	14·88	4·20	3·72	51	d¹	1·93	6·08	1·71	1·52
21	GGG#	4·60	14·44	4·08	3·61	52	d#¹	1·88	5·90	1·66	1·47
22	AAA	4·48	14·06	3·96	3·52	53	e¹	1·82	5·73	1·62	1·43
23	AAA#	4·34	13·64	3·84	3·41	54	f¹	1·77	5·57	1·57	1·39
24	BBB	4·22	13·26	3·74	3·32	55	f#¹	1·72	5·41	1·53	1·35
						56	g¹	1·67	5·26	1·48	1·31
25	CC	4·10	12·88	3·64	3·22	57	g#¹	1·62	5·10	1·44	1·27
26	CC#	3·98	12·51	3·53	3·13	58	a¹	1·57	4·95	1·39	1·23
27	DD	3·87	12·16	3·43	3·04	59	a#¹	1·53	4·80	1·35	1·20
28	DD#	3·76	11·81	3·33	2·95	60	b¹	1·49	4·68	1·32	1·17
29	EE	3·65	11·47	3·24	2·87						
30	FF	3·55	11·15	3·15	2·79	61	c²	1·45	4·55	1·28	1·14
31	FF#	3·45	10·83	3·06	2·71	62	c#²	1·41	4·43	1·25	1·10
32	GG	3·35	10·52	2·97	2·63	63	d²	1·37	4·30	1·21	1·07

NO.	NAMES OF NOTES	DIAM- ETER	CIRCUM- FERENCE	EQUAL SQUARE	WIDTH OF QUAD. PIPE	NO.	NAMES OF NOTES	DIAM- ETER	CIRCUM- FERENCE	EQUAL SQUARE	WIDTH OF QUAD. PIPE
64	$d\sharp^2$	1·33	4·18	1·18	1·04	83	$a\sharp^3$	0·76	2·40	0·68	0·60
65	e^2	1·29	4·05	1·14	1·01	84	b^3	0·74	2·34	0·66	0·58
66	f^2	1·25	3·94	1·11	0·98	85	c^4	0·72	2·28	0·64	0·57
67	$f\sharp^2$	1·22	3·83	1·08	0·95	86	$c\sharp^4$	0·70	2·21	0·62	0·55
68	g^2	1·18	3·72	1·05	0·93	87	d^4	0·68	2·15	0·61	0·54
69	$g\sharp^2$	1·15	3·61	1·02	0·90	88	$d\sharp^4$	0·66	2·09	0·59	0·52
70	a^2	1·12	3·51	0·99	0·88	89	e^4	0·64	2·02	0·57	0·50
71	$a\sharp^2$	1·08	3·41	0·96	0·85	90	f^4	0·63	1·97	0·55	0·49
72	b^2	1·05	3·31	0·93	0·83	91	$f\sharp^4$	0·61	1·91	0·54	0·48
73	c^3	1·02	3·22	0·91	0·80	92	g^4	0·59	1·86	0·52	0·46
74	$c\sharp^3$	0·99	3·13	0·88	0·78	93	$g\sharp^4$	0·57	1·81	0·51	0·45
75	d^3	0·97	3·04	0·86	0·76	94	a^4	0·56	1·76	0·49	0·44
76	$d\sharp^3$	0·94	2·95	0·83	0·74	95	$a\sharp^4$	0·54	1·71	0·48	0·43
77	e^3	0·91	2·87	0·81	0·72	96	b^4	0·53	1·66	0·47	0·41
78	f^3	0·89	2·79	0·79	0·70	97	c^5	0·51	1·61	0·45	0·40
79	$f\sharp^3$	0·86	2·71	0·76	0·68	98	$c\sharp^5$	0·50	1·56	0·44	0·39
80	g^3	0·84	2·63	0·74	0·66	99	d^5	0·48	1·52	0·43	0·38
81	$g\sharp^3$	0·81	2·55	0·72	0·64	100	$d\sharp^5$	0·47	1·47	0·42	0·37
82	a^3	0·79	2·47	0·70	0·62						

While we do not recommend any quicker gradation than that given in Table I., we strongly advise the adoption of the slower gradations given in Tables II. and III., for metal foundation stops, mainly because they tend to impart fulness to the treble octaves of the manual compass. For PRINCIPALS, 8 ft., and their relative OCTAVES it would not be wise to follow a slower gradation than that furnished by the ratio 1 : 2.519, halving on the eighteenth step, because an undue enlargement of the treble pipes is certain to affect their relative tone-color.

For flute-toned stops, and especially those of an assertive character, the scales of slower gradations given in Tables IV., V., and VI., will be found useful. Such scales are rarely adopted by conservative builders; but that fact is no argument against their proper use in the hands of the artist, either in their entirety or in compound scaling. Such scales are specially valuable for powerful flute-toned wood stops. For the CLARABELLA, MELODIA, HOHLFLÖTE, WALDFLÖTE, and other wood stops of a kindred character we recommend the scale given in Table IV. Such a scale gives considerable fulness to the treble octaves, and is, accordingly, very valuable.

For string-toned pipes, which to-day are constructed of such varied measurements,—measurements that were never contemplated by Töpfer, or by the organ-builders of his time in any country,—it is quite impossible to advise the adoption of scales of any set ratios. When it is realized that the diameters of the CC (8 ft.) pipes of the purely imitative string-toned stops, as now made by different artists, vary from, say, 3.13 inches, through numerous steps, to only 1.13 inches, one can readily see that it would be impracticable to follow any one or two standard ratios for their scales. It is quite evident that, while the ratio 1 : 2.66 might be properly used for the largest scale, it would be altogether absurd to attempt to use it for the smallest scale, which gives the diameter of 1.13 inches for the CC pipe. The only complete ratio for this very small scale is that given in Table VI., halving on the twenty-fourth step, or the super-octave pipe. We are strongly of opinion in the case of such small stops that compound or irregular scales would be found the most suitable.

From the highly satisfactory results obtained by certain artists in tone-production, we feel justified in strongly advocating the adoption of compound scales; namely, those formed, in the length of their compass, of two or more ratios. It is obvious that in stops in which both wood and metal pipes are associated, different ratios are desirable if not necessary. One English artist in tone-creation has found the advantage of adopting variable scales in wood stops he has introduced. We allude to Mr. Thomas Pendelbury, Organ-builder, of Leigh, Lancashire.* In the unison rank of the timbre-creating dual QUINT FLUTE, 8 FT., in the great Wanamaker Organ, a compound scale is effectively used (See particulars given in Chapter on Timbre-creating Compound Stops).

Compound scales can readily be formed from the measurements given in the Tables. One example will be sufficient to explain our meaning respecting the formation of compound scales. Take in Table I. (ratio $1 : \sqrt{8}$) the gradation from the note CC (8 ft.), having a diameter of 5.80 inches, to the note F♯, having the diameter of 2.66 inches, inclusive. Then, turning to Table III. (ratio 1 : 2.519), find a diameter which is so close to the latter as to be practically the same. This will be found on the note F, having a diameter of 2.68 inches. Follow the gradation from this note upward to the highest note required, inclusive. We form by these means a compound scale having a quick gradation from CC to F♯—19 notes, and a slower gradation thence to the top note of the manual compass.

The true and progressive artist should throw aside all rule-of-thumb methods of scale-production and concentrate his intelligence and experience on the formation of special scales adapted to the requirements of special stops. It is in our opinion, and in view of our own observation, absolutely illogical and unreasonable to expect a scale of any one ratio to be appropriate for stops of varied tonality. We freely admit the difficulty that will beset the introduction of any radical de-

* Particulars and scales of these stops are given in "The Art of Organ-Building," Vol. II., pp. 476-9 and 482-3.

partures from the scales that have hung on the walls of organ-building workshops, for so many years, as sacred heirlooms, handed down by past generations of pipe makers, and as fixed, in their way, as the laws of the Medes and Persians.

While in the six Tables of ratios the first and second columns of dimensions give the diameters and circumferences of metal pipes, the third column furnishes the measurements of the sides of squares having, approximately, the same areas as those inclosed within the corresponding circumferences. The dimensions given in the third column are, accordingly, useful in the scaling of square wood pipes. Schulze used square wood pipes for some of his imitative string-toned wood stops, a noteworthy and very fine example of which obtains in the VIOLONBASS, 16 FT., in the Pedal department of the Organ in the Church of St. Peter, Hindley, Lancashire. From measurements of this stop taken during our survey of the Organ, we found the CCC pipe to be practically 5.46 inches square internally, and the scale of the stop developed in the ratio 1 : 2.66, halving on the seventeenth step or the FF pipe. Schulze has clearly shown the value and excellence of wood basses to metal trebles, especially in his PRINCIPALS or OPEN DIAPASONS, and the lessons he has given to the organ-building world should not be ignored. In scaling wood basses, or any wood pipes designed to carry down an otherwise metal stop, the fourth column of measurements in the several Tables will be found useful. The measurements there given decide the widths, while the diameters given in the first column of figures decide the depths of the wood pipes. For instance, if the lowest metal pipe of a stop is C, having a diameter of 3.45 inches, the BB wood pipe would properly be 2.83 inches in width. (See Table I.) But it has been found in practice that, to obtain a satisfactory junction of the tones yielded by the cylindrical metal and the quadrangular wood pipes, it is desirable to make the wood pipe about two pipes smaller than that arrived at by the method just given. We understand that this was the proportion adopted by Schulze, who was invariably successful in his joining of wood basses to metal tenors.

In using the Tables for scaling wood stops generally, the pipes which are to have a greater depth than width, or a greater width than depth, it is only necessary to find the width decided on for the CC, or the largest pipe, in the column of diameters, in the Table selected, and follow the successive measurements throughout the compass: then, in like manner, find the measurement in the same column that comes closest to the depth required for the CC pipe, and follow the successive measurements for all the higher pipes of the stop. For instance, if we decide that the scale shall be in the ratio 1 : 2.66, and that the CC pipe shall have a width of 5.46 inches, and a depth of 6.42 inches internally; then we shall find the C pipe measuring 3·34 inches in width by 3·94 inches in depth, and the c¹ pipe measuring 2·05 inches in width by 2·41 in depth, and so on. As the measurements in all the columns in the six Tables are in correct (approximately and practically) mathematical progression, it is self-evident that any of the columns can be used for the scaling of wood pipes.

In the fourth column of measurements, in all the Tables, are given, as above mentioned, the internal widths of quadrangular wood pipes, the internal depths of which are understood to be the same as the diameters of the corresponding metal pipes given in the first column of measurements. The internal transverse areas of quadrangular pipes so dimensioned are approximately those of the corresponding cylindrical pipes. The measurements in the fourth column also give the widths of metal-pipe mouths, practically one-fourth of the circumference of the corresponding cylindrical pipes.

The Tables can also be used for the correct scaling of conical or tapered pipes, such as those forming the Spitzflöte, Gemshorn, and Dolce. It is only necessary to find the measurements required for the CC or largest pipe, at the mouth-line and at the open top, and then follow the successive measurements for all the higher pipes of the stop. From what has been said it will be clearly seen that from the six Tables any desirable simple or compound scales (according to the standard ratios) can be derived for cylindrical and tapered metal stops, and for straight quadrangular and triangular and tapered wood stops.

In the foregoing pages no attempt has been made to formulate rules or furnish measurements for those portions of metal and wood pipes which depend entirely on the form and nature of the pipes, the quality and volume of the tone required from them, and the aim and experience of the voicer. We allude to their mouths, their wind-ways, and the wind-holes in their feet. Certain writers on organ-building have essayed to give scale measurements for these portions; but it stands to reason that such measurements are only applicable to pipes of one class, voiced on wind of one pressure, and producing one quality of tone. In short, such definite measurements are practically valueless to the artistic pipe maker and voicer.

The width and height of the mouth, or its area in comparison with that of the cross section of the pipe-body, are important factors in tone-production. In ordinary practice, and especially in purely trade quarters, certain standards are commonly adhered to which naturally foster the dead level of tonality which characterizes the trade Organs of to-day. The widths of the mouths of metal pipes vary, under ordinary practice, from one-fifth to two-sevenths the circumference of the pipes. The medium width, or one-quarter the circumference, appears to be that most frequently adopted; and it is certainly suitable for pipes voiced to yield pure organ-tone. As it is desirable that the widths of the mouths should follow the same ratio as that on which the pipes are scaled, it is only necessary to mark the width of the largest mouth on the first ordinate of the pipe-scale, and draw a diagonal line thence, through all the ordinates, to the vanishing point on the base line. While we say it is *desirable,* we do not assert that it is *necessary* that the same ratio should be adopted in all cases. If an increase in strength of voice is desired in the higher octaves of a stop, the width of mouth may start at one-quarter on the lowest note, and finish at two-sevenths on the highest note. Should such a gradation be decided upon, it will only be necessary to mark the quarter of the circumference on the first ordinate of the pipe-scale, and the two-sevenths of the circumference of the highest pipe on its corresponding ordinate, and then connect the two marks by a diagonal line in the usual manner. In the case of compound scales, to which we have alluded in preceding pages, the width of mouth may, and probably should, follow the varying ratios. All these are matters subject to the taste and experience of artistic voicers; no hard and fast rules are practicable here.

In the generality of wood pipes the widths of their mouths are dictated by the interior widths of their bodies. While this may be accepted as a general rule in wood-pipe construction, and will be found exemplified in more than nine-tenths of the wood pipes introduced in ordinary modern Organs, it has no claim to universal adoption. Indeed, we are led, from our own investigations, to regret, on tonal grounds, the too slavish adherence to the rule; for we are convinced that it has largely retarded the production of many beautiful voices for the Organ. On referring to Chapter on the Forms and Construction of Wood Pipes, the student of the art of organ-building will find some noteworthy examples of successful departures from the general rule, showing, on the one hand, the width of the mouth equal to the larger interior dimension of the pipe; and, on the other hand, the width of the mouth considerably less than the smaller interior width of the pipe, not to mention the circular mouths of the imitative flute-toned pipes. The present vitiated taste for loud tones with their inherent coarseness, and the present craze for high wind-pressures will, we are afraid, seriously retard the development of pure, delicate, and refined tonalities, for the production of which properly-formed and artistically-voiced wood pipes are so admirably suited.

Much that has been said respecting the width of the mouth, applies with equal force to its height; but much greater variety of relative measurements obtains in the adjustment of height, while an entirely new factor in tone-production appears in the form of the upper lip of the mouth.

CHAPTER XIV.

FORMS AND CONSTRUCTION OF METAL PIPES.

LL the more important and numerous speaking stops of the Organ, both labial and lingual, are constructed of metal. It is, accordingly, necessary that care should be taken to employ only the most suitable metals and alloys in their formation, so that the maximum durability and the best tonal results may be secured. In this matter the old builders were very careful, hence the durability of their existing work, as in the Organ in the Cathedral of Haarlem. It was left to modern organ-builders to introduce inferior and objectionable metals and alloys in their pipe-work. A little knowledge, in this direction, on the part of organ purchasers, on the one hand, and the preparers of Organ Specifications, on the other, would have done much to stem the use of inferior and unsuitable alloys. We commend this important matter to the consideration of those interested in the Organ, either as purchasers or performers. It should be borne in mind that there are few matters of more importance in an Organ than the quality of the alloys used in the construction of its pipes.

It is impossible, within the narrow limits of the present manual, to go fully into details connected with the metals and alloys used in pipe-making; but a few remarks are called for before we enter on the principal subject of the Chapter.

The materials suitable for metal pipes are tin, alloys of tin and lead, and pure zinc. The alloys are commonly known under the general term " metal "; but as this term conveys no idea of quality, or of the relative proportions of tin and lead used in their composition, it should invariably be attended by a statement of those proportions. This is certainly necessary on account of the inferior and undesirable material that is too often passed off on the inexperienced purchaser by the cheap organ-builder under the seemingly satisfactory name of "pipe-metal," stuff little better than lead, stiffened sufficiently by the addition of antimony or old type-metal, to enable it to stand in the form of pipes, until the work is well out of the hands of the not over-scrupulous maker. Under these circumstances no reliance can be placed on the term "metal," when it appears in an Organ Specification unaccompanied by any statement or guarantee of quality. Purchasers of Organs should not overlook this fact, and should insist on having the proportions of tin and lead used clearly stated. No honest organ-builder can object to give this information. If any serious question arises, the specific gravity of the alloy will determine the percentage of tin used.

TIN.—Of all the materials employed for the construction of metal pipes, tin, as pure as it can be properly used, is unquestionably the best; and this fact has been recognized by all the great organ-builders. Tin recommends itself by its lightness, firmness, durability, malleability, and ductility; and also on account of its tarnishing very slightly under ordinary atmospheric conditions.

Tin has the specific gravity of about 7·3. It fuses at the temperature of 442° Fahr., and this fact constitutes the only objection, of a practical nature, to its use in a pure state. Its easy fusibility renders the process of soldering difficult and uncertain. Such being the case, it has been found necessary to alloy it with a small percentage of pure lead. In organ nomenclature the term "pure tin" is understood to signify an alloy of 90 parts tin and 10 parts pure lead. This high quality is necessary for burnished and displayed pipe-work, while for inside pipes an alloy of 75 parts tin and 25 parts lead, having a specific gravity of about 7·9942, will be found sufficient. The beautiful silver-like appearance of "pure tin" when burnished is highly effective and refined; it harmonizes with all the richer-tinted woods of which an organ-case may be fabricated, and renders gilding or painting unnecessary. The high price of tin has of late years prevented its use for displayed pipes, a fact much to be regretted: but the recent introduction of a pipe-metal, faced with a substantial layer of pure tin, highly burnished, renders the return to beautiful, polished, displayed pipes a matter of no difficulty on the score of expense or manufacture. This compound metal will be described later on.

LEAD.—In anything approaching a pure and unalloyed state, lead is absolutely worthless for organ-pipes. It has, nevertheless, been frequently used, stiffened and rendered brittle by the addition of some old type-metal or antimony, by unprincipled organ-builders, and palmed off on unsuspecting purchasers under the ambiguous name "pipe-metal."

Lead is a very soft, pliable, and heavy metal. When freshly cut or scraped, it presents a lustrous surface, but this quickly becomes dull from the formation of a film of oxide. It cannot be polished or burnished. Its specific gravity is about 11·4. It fuses at a temperature of about 617° Fahr., or 175° higher than that at which pure tin melts: and it is this fact that renders it a valuable alloy for tin, enabling it to withstand the heat of molten solder and the soldering-iron.

PIPE-METAL.—Under this term, or under the shorter and more usual one of " metal," are included all the alloys of tin and lead used in pipe-making, which do not, in organ nomenclature, receive the more distinguished name of " tin," as already explained. The simple term metal is, accordingly, ambiguous and generally misleading, inasmuch as it is frequently employed to designate an alloy which contains the smallest percentage of tin that the elastic conscience of the cheap organ-builder will allow him to indulge in; while, on the other hand, it may be employed to designate all the other alloys which range from the poorest quality up to the high-class alloy containing 75 per cent pure tin. The term " metal," accordingly, in itself conveys no further idea of quality or character than the presumption that it is an alloy of tin and lead. We use the word presumption because the name has frequently been given to alloys of lead and antimony, innocent of the slightest admixture of tin.

In face of this uncertainty and ambiguity, it is desirable that some certain test should be resorted to to protect the purchasers of Organs against imposition. The most satisfactory test, and one that cannot well be disputed, is furnished by the specific gravity of the alloy in question. As the specific gravity of tin is 7·3, and that of lead is 11·4, it is obvious that all the alloys of tin and lead will have specific gravities ranging between these figures. For this test to be conclusive it must first be ascertained that the metal is an alloy of tin and lead. As the specific gravity of antimony is 6·7, it follows that the specific gravities of alloys of that metal and lead will range between 11·4 and 6·7, so they might easily be confounded with some of the poorer alloys of lead and tin. Antimony metal can, however, always be detected by its brittle character. Type-metal illustrates this in an extreme degree. It is most desirable that antimony metal should never be used for organ-pipes: and to prevent purchasers of Organs being imposed upon by the organ-builder they should demand a guarantee that no antimony metal is used, and also a statement of the quality of the alloys used in the pipe-work.

The following Table gives the specific gravities of twelve different alloys of tin and lead. This will render special calculations unnecessary, for the character of any alloy, the specific gravity of which has been found, may be readily known by reference to the Table.

Plain pipe-metal is an alloy in which the percentage of lead greatly exceeds that of the tin; and unfortunately it does not present any external indications, beyond a dull gray tint, whereby its quality may be readily detected. Experienced persons can, of course, arrive at a fairly accurate estimate of its quality, but the only conclusive proof is its specific gravity. Pipes made of metal having a greater specific gravity than 10.1832—that is, containing less than 20 per cent tin—should never be allowed in an Organ. A fair plain pipe-metal is composed of 35 per cent pure tin and 65 per cent pure lead, having a specific gravity of about 9.65.

THE SPECIFIC GRAVITIES OF ALLOYS OF PURE TIN AND LEAD.

PROPORTIONS OF TIN AND LEAD.		SPECIFIC GRAVITIES.
Pure Tin	————	7.3000
4 parts Tin	1 part Lead	7.8830
3 " "	1 " "	7.9942
5 " "	2 " "	8.1094
2 " "	1 " "	8.2669
3 " "	2 " "	8.4973
1 " "	1 " "	8.8640
2 " "	3 " "	9.2653
1 " "	2 " "	9.5535
2 " "	5 " "	9.7701
1 " "	3 " "	9.9387
1 " "	4 " "	10.1832
————	Pure Lead	11.4000

SPOTTED-METAL.—This is a term so frequently met with in relation to organ-pipes that a few words respecting its signification are called for here. When a certain percentage of fine tin is melted with pure lead and cast in the usual manner, the surface of the sheet develops a richly-mottled or spotted appearance as it sets in cooling. This appearance is a sure guarantee of good quality; for a really fine and bright spot cannot be obtained in an alloy having less than 45 per cent of pure tin, or, say, a greater specific gravity than 9.06. Finer qualities of spotted-metal are produced by larger proportions of tin up to 55 per cent. So rich is the alloy in which this percentage of Cornish tin is introduced, that the term " confluent-metal " has been employed to distinguish it. In this high-class metal the stops are so small and so close together as to present a surface almost uniformly bright, hence the term " confluent-metal." So reliable is this metal that, when of sufficient thickness, it can be safely used for the most important and most delicate stops in the Organ. As in the case of pure tin, the only objection to its use is its high cost.*

HOYT'S TWO-PLY PIPE-METAL.—This material has been recently introduced with the view of furnishing the organ-builder with a metal

---

* Fuller particulars respecting the metals and alloys alluded to will be found in Chapter XXXV., in " The Art of Organ-Building," which is devoted to the subject.

thoroughly reliable and in every way suitable for all classes of both interior and displayed metal pipe-work. This material is formed of a strong and pliable foundation of an alloy of pure lead, tin, and a small and unharmful percentage of antimony; upon which is laid a substantial layer or ply of pure tin. This two-ply metal has the great advantage over the ordinary cast alloys of lead and tin, as made by the organ-builder, in being produced by a process of rolling, which imparts extreme closeness, firmness, and resistance to vibration—all valuable properties in a pipe-metal when combined with durability and sufficient pliability. This beautiful metal once more renders the production of burnished tin displayed pipes, of a perfectly satisfactory and durable nature, as in old work, possible at a reasonable cost. So far as toughness and pliability are concerned, experimental tests have proved that the metal can undergo repeated bending over a sharp edge a hundred per cent better than spotted-metal. This is an unanswerable argument in favor of the adoption of the two-ply metal in all high-class work. Both its surfaces are perfectly smooth and highly polished, another advantage of considerable importance.

The two-ply metal is furnished to the organ-builder in twenty-two regularly graduated thicknesses, ranging from 0·015 of an inch to 0·120 of an inch; saving him all labor and uncertainty in graduating his pipe-metal for the various sizes of pipes and different stops. It is practically impossible for the organ-builder to graduate, by any means, his cast metal in anything approaching the accuracy of the rolled metal now under consideration. It is obvious that owing to the firmness and vibration-resisting property of the rolled metal, it can be used of a thinner gauge than would be possible or desirable in the case of cast confluent-metal or any inferior alloy; hence a saving in weight and cost—not matters of small importance in these times.

The following Table gives the thicknesses in thousandths of an inch, and the weights per square foot in pounds, of the twenty-two standard gauges of the two-ply metal.

ZINC.—The use of zinc in organ-building is of very recent date, no record of its employment in pipe-work by the old masters having been found. Zinc is a dull gray metal, having the specific gravity of about 7·0. It is more tenacious than tin, lead, or any of the alloys of these two metals. In its cold state it is difficult to work, being readily pliable only between the temperatures of 200° and 250° Fahr.: accordingly, in forming pipes it requires to be heated. The sheets, of various thicknesses, from which pipes are made are produced by rolling. Their comparative lightness and cheapness have led to their use by the organ-building world.

Zinc has been largely used of late years in the construction of large pipes and frequently for those forming the bottom octave of labial stops of 8 feet pitch. The only qualities that recommend the use of zinc for organ-pipes (setting aside its comparative cheapness) are its lightness and stiffness. The latter property has led to its abuse in the hands of inferior builders, who, to save money, use it of objectionable thinness. When zinc is used for speaking pipes it should be of ample thickness. Sufficient time has not elapsed to test the durability of zinc pipes; so little of any value can be said on that subject.

TABLE OF STANDARD THICKNESSES AND WEIGHTS OF HOYT TWO-PLY PIPE-METAL.

GAUGE	WEIGHT—SQ. FT.	GAUGE	WEIGHT—SQ. FT.
0·015	0·87	0·070	4·06
0·020	1·16	0·075	4·35
0·025	1·45	0·080	4·64
0·030	1·74	0·085	4·93
0·035	2·03	0·090	5·22
0·040	2·32	0·095	5·51
0·045	2·61	0·100	5·80
0·050	2·90	0·105	6·09
0·055	3·19	0·110	6·38
0·060	3·48	0·115	6·67
0·065	3·77	0·120	6·96

When labial pipes are made of zinc, their languids, lower and upper lips, and the tips or toes of their feet must be formed of good pipe-metal. This is necessary to allow those important parts to be properly manipulated in the process of voicing and regulating. Zinc has been recommended and used by good builders for the tubes or resonators of lingual pipes which are liable to bend or break if made of ordinary pipe-metal. Such tubes should have their upper ends finished with short lengths of pipe-metal so that they may be readily cut or otherwise treated.

To what extent the different metals and alloys used in the formation of organ-pipes affect the tones of pipes is a question that has never been, and probably never will be, satisfactorily answered, and this notwithstanding the statements made by certain writers on the Organ. Many years of careful and unprejudiced observation have had the effect of making us anything but dogmatic on one side or another. We have heard tones in every way satisfactory produced from pipes constructed of practically all classes of pipe-metal and alloys—from the poorest and deadest alloy of lead and antimony to the richest alloy of tin and lead. We have heard the most perfect imitations of the tones of the Violin and Violoncello produced from pipes of spotted-metal;—such imitative and beautiful tones as we have never heard from pipes of tin;—and we have known such choice pipes to be joined in the bass octave by pipes having bodies of zinc, without any perceptible break in tone where the spotted-metal ones ended and the zinc ones began. We have known one voicer to produce a better tone from pipes of almost pure lead than another was able to produce from similar pipes constructed of rich confluent metal. And such experience and observation, extending over a period of more than forty-five years, in connection with French, German, English, and American organ-building, leaves us with the conviction that art has more to do with high-class tone production than has mere material: and although in general and artistic practice certain classes of pipes appear to be most satisfactory in tone when formed of tin or fine spotted metal, their tonal character and excellence depends chiefly, if not altogether, on their correct scaling, proper thickness of material, perfection of formation, the pressures of wind that are used, and, above all, on the skill and musical sense of their voicers. It is on the score of strength, rigidity, and durability that the higher-class alloys of tin and lead are to be advocated for all the metal pipes of the Organ. One has only to look at such a landmark in the art of organ-building as the noble instrument in the Church of St. Bavon, at Haarlem, to realize the value of such materials: its pipe-work—one hundred and sixty-eight years old—is practically as good to-day as when it was made. Whatever alloy is used for the pipe-work of the Organ, care must be taken to have it of ample thickness in all the foundation stops. It is impossible to obtain the grand rolling tones which should characterize the Principals or Open Diapasons from pipes having thin and light walls. No consideration or expense should be allowed to influence the pipe-maker in this matter. Scale, pressure of wind, and the volume of tone required, should alone dictate the thickness and weight of the metal used in pipe construction.

If there is one thing more than another that should be attended to, both by designers and purchasers of Organs, it is the important matter of the thickness of the metal used in the pipe-work. It stands to reason that in these times of high prices of tin, lead, and zinc every endeavor will be made, on the part of pipe-makers and organ-builders, to reduce the thickness of pipe-metal to the greatest possible limit, causing deterioration of tone and a positive lack of durability. Both these serious disqualifications should, in all possible cases, be prevented by a proper specification of, and a careful attention to, the requisite thicknesses of the metal forming the stops. To serve as a guide in this direction we give the following Table, showing the minimum desirable thicknesses of good spotted-metal that should be used for the pipes of the several octaves of the Diapason, its derivatives, and other important stops of the Organ. The thicknesses are given in decimals of an inch, and these are carried through seven octaves—calculated on a wind-pressure not exceeding six inches, and a scale for the CC pipe, 8 feet, not exceeding seven inches in diameter.

TABLE SHOWING MINIMUM THICKNESSES OF GOOD SPOTTED-METAL FOR LABIAL PIPES.

	16′	8′	4′	2′	1′	6″	3″
C	0·110	0·080	0·065	0·055	0·040	0·030	0·025
C♯	0·110	0·080	0·065	0·050	0·040	0·030	0·025
D	0·105	0·080	0·065	0·050	0·040	0·030	0·025
D♯	0·105	0·075	0·060	0·050	0·040	0·030	0·025
E	0·100	0·075	0·060	0·050	0·040	0·030	0·020
F	0·100	0·075	0·060	0·050	0·040	0·030	0·020
F♯	0·095	0·070	0·060	0·045	0·035	0·030	0·020
G	0·095	0·070	0·060	0·045	0·035	0·030	0·020
G♯	0·090	0·070	0·055	0·045	0·035	0·025	0·020
A	0·090	0·070	0·055	0·045	0·035	0·025	0·020
A♯	0·085	0·065	0·055	0·045	0·035	0·025	0·020
B	0·085	0·065	0·055	0·045	0·035	0·025	0·020

These thicknesses substantially agree with those we have obtained from the representative works of old organ-builders in England and on the Continent, which have stood the test of time. They will be found valuable by those preparing Specifications for first-class pipe-work, as their insertion along with the quality of the metal, subject to the specific gravity test, will secure proper attention on the part of the pipe-maker, who will know that his pipes will be liable to rejection if found short of the standards required. It is surprising that so little attention is being paid to these important matters by organists and others who undertake to prepare Specifications for large and expensive Organs. The ordinary organ-builder will naturally neither suggest nor approve of their insertion in Specifications. It is in such matters, among many others equally important, that the knowledge and services of an experienced Organ Architect are of the greatest value. No Organ of any consequence should be built without the supervision of a qualified expert, engaged by the purchaser to watch his interests and to see every detail of the Specification honestly carried out.

THE PRINCIPAL FORMS OF METAL PIPES.

The normal and representative form of the metal organ-pipe is that obtaining in the pipes forming the PRINCIPAL or DIAPASON stops, as shown, in Front View and Longitudinal Section, in Fig. XXXIII. The

pipe is formed of three parts—the foot, the body, and the languid—
formed separately and soldered together. To these, in certain pipes,
are added two small pieces, called ears, attached to the sides of the
mouth for the purpose of confining the wind-stream laterally. In the
accompanying illustration, Fig. XXXII., the three chief parts are
shown, adjoining the mouth of the pipe. A is the upper part of the
conical foot, flattened to form the under lip of the mouth, as shown in
the Section, 4. B is the lower part of the cylindrical body, flattened

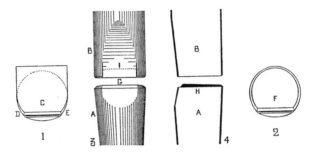

FIG. XXXII.

to form the corresponding upper lip of the mouth, as indicated in the
Section, 4. The languid is shown in each of the Diagrams. It is
shown at C in the Top View, 1, laid in proper position with respect
to the lower lip on the foot, and preparatory to its being cut to the
circular form indicated by the dotted line. In the Top View, 2, it is
shown finished. Its front beveled edge is shown at G in the Front
View, 3, and in section at H in the Section, 4. When all the portions
alluded to have been properly formed, the edges of the body and foot
are accurately brought together and soldered, except, of course, where
the lower and upper lips meet. The opening of the mouth is now cut
in the flattened portion, or upper lip, in the body, to the minimum height
as indicated by the dotted line I, in the Front View, 3. If the pipe is
to have ears, they are now soldered on. At this stage the pipe is ready
for the operations of the voicer.*

PRINCIPALS.—Among all the organ-toned stops the PRINCIPALS or
DIAPASONS stand preëminent. Upon them should be built the tonal
structure of the dominating divisions of the Organ. In the Pedal
Organ the unison PRINCIPAL is of 16 feet pitch, and in the Great Organ
the unison is of 8 feet pitch. From the chief PRINCIPAL, 8 FT., of the

---

* In Chapter XXXVI. of "The Art of Organ-Building" eight pages are devoted to all
the processes involved in the construction of metal labial pipes. In Chapter XXXIX., of the
same work, the processes of voicing are fully described, covering twelve pages.

First or Great Organ the pipes of all the other organ-toned stops in the manual divisions should be scientifically and artistically proportioned both in scale and strength of tone, and especially those octave, mutation, and compound stops which belong to its harmonic series. The PRINCIPAL, 16 FT., of the Pedal Organ, when of Metal, should carry down,

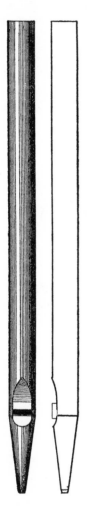

in the same strength of tone, the chief manual PRINCIPAL, 8 FT., to which it furnishes the true bass. In the accompanying illustration, Fig. XXXIII., are given a Front View and Section of a PRINCIPAL or DIAPASON pipe. The body is cylindrical and, accordingly, of the same diameter throughout. The form of the mouth is that commonly designated the " bay-leaf," from the resemblance of its upper portion to the pointed half of the natural leaf. This form, which has long been preferred by English pipe-makers for displayed pipes, is in our opinion the most elegant of all the forms which have been introduced. In Fig. XXXIV. are given Front Views and Sections of the principal forms of mouths used at different times by different builders for their PRINCIPALS or DIAPASONS, MONTRES, and other displayed pipe-work. At A is shown the bay-leaf mouth in its most artistic treatment, in which both its lower and upper portions are gradually raised from the surface of the pipe as they sweep from the lips, as indicated in the Section. At B is a modification of the bay-leaf, the upper portion being defined by straight lines and in no way relieved from the surface of the pipe. This form has been used by both English and Continental builders and is illustrated by Dom Bedos, shown without ears, as at B. The so-called French mouth, in what appears to be its most approved treatment, is shown at C, in which the semicircular parts are curved boldly forward, as indicated in the Section. In simpler examples no projection from the pipe-body or foot appears. This form has always been favored by the French and other Continental pipe-makers.

FIG. XXXIII.

This mouth is fully illustrated by Dom Bedos, without the addition of ears; indeed, the French organ-builders seem to have very rarely used ears on their MONTRES or their derivatives, which may to some extent account for the somewhat harsh tones of these stops. In the remaining example, at D, we find a modified form of the French mouth, in which the upper part terminates in an ogee

treatment having considerable projection: this is also illustrated by
Dom Bedos. In old Organs both in England and on the Continent,
different forms of mouths have been used side by side for the sake
of variety; and there is certainly no objection to the adoption of a
similar course in modern instruments. The only question that should
have any weight in this matter is that relating to tone; and given that
all other conditions are similar in two pipes—namely, thickness and
quality of metal, scale, width and height of mouth, wind-pressure, and
style of voicing—there can be no appreciable difference of tone imparted by the adoption of any two of the artistic treatments of mouth
above described. It is true that the French builders, who almost in-

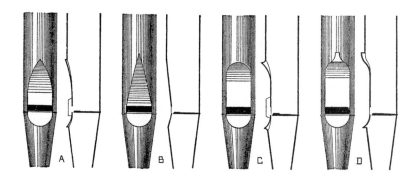

FIG. XXXIV.

variably adopt their favorite form of mouth, as shown at C, for their
MONTRES, fail to produce a satisfactory " Diapason-tone "; but that
this failure lies in the peculiar style of their voicing has, we think, been
clearly proved by certain distinguished English builders who have used
the same form of mouth for their displayed OPEN DIAPASONS, without
sacrificing the dignified, rich, and pure, unimitative organ-tone which
has always distinguished the old English school of voicing.* The

* The following notes from the pen of Professor R. H. M. Bosanquet, a great authority
on tonal matters, will be of interest: "If there is any one stop which in itself represents the
Organ as a whole it is the OPEN DIAPASON. The pipes of this stop are the typical metal pipes
which have always been characteristic of the appearance of the Organ. A single OPEN DIA-
PASON stop is capable of being used as an Organ of sufficient power for many purposes, though
of course without variety. The pipes of this stop are called ' PRINCIPAL ' in German, this
appellation apparently corresponding to the fact that they are the true and original organ pipes.
The English appellation of ' DIAPASON ' has been taken to mean that these are the normal pipes
which run through the whole compass. This, however, does not appear to be the actual deriva-
tion of the term; originally it is technically applied to the organ-builder's rule, which gives the
dimensions of pipes; and it appears that the application to the stop followed on this meaning.
    "The scales, character, and voicing of the OPEN DIAPASON vary with fashion, and are
different in different countries. We may distinguish three principal types. The old English
DIAPASONS of the days before the introduction of Pedal Organs into England were characterized
by a rich sweet tone, and were not very powerful. They were generally voiced on a light
wind, having a pressure equivalent to that of a column of water of from 2 to 2½ inches.
The scale was in some cases very large, as in Green's two OPEN DIAPASONS in the old Organ
at St. George's, Windsor; in these the wind was light and the tone very soft. In other cases
the scale was smaller and the voicing bolder, as in Father Smith's original DIAPASONS in St.
Paul's Cathedral. But on the whole the old English DIAPASONS presented a lovely quality of

mouths of the tenor and higher pipes of the PRINCIPAL, 8 FT., which are planted on the internal wind-chests, do not require to be ornamental, and are usually formed directly by the flattening-tool.

A practice has been introduced of late, whereby, it is claimed, the tone of a pipe of the DIAPASON class is improved. We allude to the practice of thickening the upper lip of the pipe by covering it with a folded strip of leather. The expedient is probably found to improve, for the time being at least, the tone of a pipe constructed of metal of insufficient thickness; but how long the leather will last in good condition has yet to be seen. It is certain, however, that from the hour of its application, it commences to decay. That such a covering is unnecessary is proved by the numerous fine DIAPASONS which have been made by distinguished English and Continental organ-builders; the tones of which have to be surpassed, or even equalled by those with leathered lips. Let pipes with lips of proper thickness be made; and let them be artistically voiced, on a copious supply of wind of a proper pressure, and there will be no necessity to pad their lips with a perishable material, or run any risk of deterioration. Pipes properly made will last a century. How long will leathered lips last?

Several scales have been used by different builders for their PRINCIPALS, OPEN DIAPASONS, or MONTRES, of 8 feet pitch, usually dictated by the class, requirements, and general peculiarities of the instruments in which they are placed. These scales commonly range between 7 inches and 5 inches for the internal diameter of the CC pipe. The largest scales seem to have been used by the English builders, but these have, in artistic work, seldom exceeded 6·75 inches. The German builders appear to have fixed the maximum diameter for the CC PRINCIPAL pipe at 6·25 inches. This is the scale of the large OPEN DIAPASON, by Schulze, in the Great division of the Organ in Leeds Parish Church. The tenor C pipe of this magnificent stop measures 3·69 inches

tone. English travelers of those days, accustomed to these DIAPASONS, usually found foreign Organs harsh, noisy, and uninteresting. And there are many still in England who, while recognizing the necessity of a firmer diapason-tone in view of the introduction of the heavy pedal bass, and the corresponding strengthening of the upper departments of the organ-tone, lament the disappearance of the old diapason-tone. However, it is possible with care to obtain DIAPASONS presenting the sweet characteristics of the old English tone, combined with sufficient fulness and power to form a sound general foundation. And there can be no doubt that this should be one of the chief points to be kept in view in organ design.

"The German DIAPASON was of an entirely different character from the English. The heavy bass of the pedals has been an essential characteristic of the German Organ for at least two or three centuries, or, as it is said, for four. The development of the piercing stops of high pitch was equally general. Thus foundation work of comparatively great power was required to maintain the balance of tone; the ordinary German DIAPASON was very loud, and we may almost say coarse, in its tone when compared with the old English DIAPASON. The German stop was voiced as a rule on from 3½ to 4 inches of wind, not quite twice the pressure used in England.

"The French DIAPASON is a modern variety. It may be described as presenting rather the characteristics of a loud GAMBA than of a DIAPASON. In other words, the tone tends towards a certain quality which may be described as 'tinny' or metallic, or as approaching to that of a string instrument of rather coarse character. Some modern English builders appear to aim at the same model, and not without success.

"The tone of a DIAPASON must be strong enough to assert itself. It is the foundation of the whole organ-tone. It is the voicer's business to satisfy this condition in conjunction with the requirement that the tone shall be full and of agreeable quality."—Encyclopædia Britannica: Ninth edition. Article "ORGAN."

in diameter, and the c^1 pipe 2.19 inches. The dimensions, which are as accurate as could be obtained from the pipes *in situ,* indicate that the scale is in the ratio $1 : \sqrt{8}$, the half diameter of the CC pipe falling on tenor E. The width of the mouth of the CC pipe is 5¼ inches, cutting off practically six-nineteenths of the circumference of the pipe. The height of the mouth is 1½ inches; and the wind-hole in tip is 1¼ inches in diameter. This stop yields its singularly majestic tone on a wind-pressure of 3¾ inches, showing in its voicing the skill of a master-hand. We know of no organ-toned labial stop which surpasses this in dignity and volume of tone on so moderate a wind-pressure. This pressure must be considered moderate when one bears in mind that in their attempts to obtain dominating " diapason-tone " some English organ-builders have resorted to a wind-pressure of 6 inches, completely sacrificing what Professor Bosanquet calls the " lovely quality of tone ; " and forgetting his assurance that " it is possible with care to obtain DIAPASONS presenting the sweet characteristics of the old English tone, combined with sufficient fulness and power to form a sound general foundation. And there can be no doubt that this should be one of the chief points to be kept in view in organ design." These words should be lettered in gold and placed on the walls of every voicing-room.

It is unnecessary save in Organs of the first magnitude, in which several unison PRINCIPALS are inserted, to adopt so large a scale as that represented by the CC pipe of 6.25 inches diameter. For large Church Organs it is, as a rule, undesirable to use a scale exceeding 6 inches for the CC pipe. Schulze advocated the scale of 5.75 inches, in the approved ratio $1 : \sqrt{8}$, for Church Organs of considerable size. For general adoption in Organs of moderate dimensions, placed in buildings of ordinary size, voiced on wind of about 3½ inches, 5.56 inches will be found ample for the CC pipe; the C pipe being 3.30, and the c^1 pipe 1.96 inches in diameter. For a small Church Organ, voiced on 3½ inches wind, the CC pipe of the PRINCIPAL, 8 FT., need not exceed 5.24 inches in diameter, and the ratio 1 : 2.66 is to recommended. This scale is also appropriate for a Chamber Organ voiced on wind of 2½ inches. When small scales are used in conjunction with higher wind-pressures, it is most difficult, if not impossible, to secure the sweet, round, and restful tones which are so desirable in a Chamber Organ. In the PRINCIPALS of Chamber Organs we strongly advocate a return to the refined work of the old English masters. As Professor Bosanquet remarks : " The old English DIAPASONS of the days before the introduction of Pedal Organs into England were characterized by a rich sweet tone, and were not very powerful. They were generally voiced on a light wind, having a pressure equivalent to that of a column of water of from 2 to 2½ inches." In the Chamber Organ we constructed about fifty years ago we inserted a PRINCIPALE, 8 FT., having its CC pipe 5.25 inches in diameter, voiced on wind of 2⅜ inches, the tone of which was ample in volume to dominate and sustain that of all the remaining eighteen stops of the instrument, including the five reeds, while it was so pure and smooth that the ear, placed six inches from the mouths of the larger bass pipes, could hardly realize that they were sounded by wind. This stop was universally admired by the most critical musicians.

In the construction of the PRINCIPAL or OPEN DIAPASON pipe the proportions of the mouth are matters of great importance. In alluding to the scale of the fine OPEN DIAPASON, made by Schulze, in the Organ in Leeds Parish Church, we stated the dimensions of the mouth of the CC pipe to be 5¼ inches wide by 1½ inches high. This mouth cuts off six-nineteenths of the circumference of the pipe, as indicated at B in Fig. XXXV. and, accordingly, its width is slightly in excess of

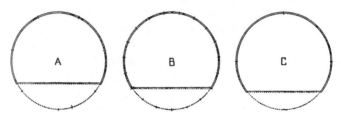

FIG. XXXV.

one-quarter of the circumference of the pipe. Its height is exactly two-sevenths of its width, or a little less than one-fourth the internal diameter of the pipe. As this stop is a remarkable work of an equally remarkable voicer, these proportions deserve careful consideration, remembering that the wind-pressure is 3¾ inches. For PRINCIPALS, of 8 ft. pitch, of much smaller scales Schulze has used mouths of larger proportions with much success. These are in some examples equal in width to two-sevenths of the circumference of their respective pipes, as indicated at A. It will never be found necessary to adopt mouths of greater width. For the normal English OPEN DIAPASON the width of mouth need rarely exceed one-fourth the circumference of the pipe, as indicated at C; and its height should be one-fourth the internal diameter of the pipe. The height may vary, however, when abnormal wind-pressures are employed. For the pure organ-toned PRINCIPAL, 8 FT., of the Chamber Organ, when of good scale and voiced on light wind, the height of the mouth may, with advantage to the tone, be reduced to one-fifth the internal diameter of the pipe, or to one-fourth the width of the mouth. With these proportions, a pure and round tone can be procured without any forcing or objectionable windiness.

DOUBLE PRINCIPAL is a manual stop of 16 ft. pitch, constructed in every respect similarly to the unison PRINCIPALS already described. The chief matter to be carefully considered in connection with the DOUBLE PRINCIPAL, when inserted in any manual division, is its relative scale; and with respect to this opinions naturally differ. In deciding its scale one has to bear in mind that the true and fundamental pitch of all the manual divisions of the Organ is 8 feet, and that no stops of pure organ-tone inserted should be calculated to destroy its predominance. Accordingly we are of opinion that in a division in which there is only one PRINCIPAL, 8 FT., the DOUBLE should be made of a smaller scale than the unison, the 8 ft. pipes of each stop being used for comparison. A scale three or four pipes smaller, combined with appropriate voicing and regulating, will be found satisfactory. When two unison PRINCIPALS are introduced in one division—usually in the Great Organ—the DOUBLE PRINCIPAL may be made of the same scale as the smaller PRINCIPAL.

The Pedal Organ PRINCIPAL, 16 FT., is usually made of larger scale than that adopted for the manual MAJOR PRINCIPAL, 8 FT., and, except, perhaps, in complete Pedal Organs, there can be no serious objection to this practice, provided that the stop is not too powerful in tone. In the properly-appointed Pedal Organ the metal PRINCIPAL, 16 FT., should be scaled and voiced to yield a true bass to the MAJOR PRINCIPAL, 8 FT., of the First or Great Organ: but as in the generality of English and American Organs all ideas of proper tonal appointment so far as the Pedal Organ is concerned are cast aside, the PRINCIPAL, 16 FT., is made of large scale and voiced so as to serve as the bass for the combined unison labial stops of the manual divisions, if not for the Full Organ. It is right to remark that in such instruments the stop is usually of wood. In general form and construction the metal PRINCIPAL, 16 FT., of the Pedal Organ differs in no respect from the DOUBLE PRINCIPAL, 16 FT., of the Great Organ.

The Pedal Organ DOUBLE PRINCIPAL, 32 FT., when of metal, is constructed on the same lines as those above laid down. As might be expected in a stop of this magnitude, the scale varies considerably in different Organs. In the Organ in St. George's Hall, Liverpool, the new lower octave of the metal DOUBLE OPEN DIAPASON, 32 FT., has its CCCC pipe 25 inches in diameter. This octave is of zinc. The CCCC pipe of the SUB-PRINCIPAL, 32 FT., in the celebrated Haarlem Organ, which is of tin, measures only 15 inches in diameter. The corresponding pipe in the Organ in the Monastery Church, at Weingarten, also of tin, is about 15½ inches in diameter. Several metal stops having scales ranging between those above given are to be found in important Organs constructed by different builders. While it is impossible to lay down any rule of universal application for the scaling of this exceptional stop, we can venture to strongly recommend the adoption of the comparatively small scales favored by the German and Dutch masters. If the stop be adequately winded and skilfully voiced, there can be no necessity to exceed the scale of the SUB-PRINCIPAL, 32 FT., in the Haarlem Organ.

OCTAVE and MUTATION STOPS.—All the pure organ-toned octave and mutation stops, properly related to the foundation-work, and which are, or should be, scientifically scaled from the chief PRINCIPAL, have their pipes constructed in precisely the same manner as those of the PRINCIPAL. The most important matter in connection with these harmonic-corroborating or harmonic-creating stops is their relative scaling, and for this unfortunately no rules of universal application have been formulated. This is probably due to the fact that up to the present time few, if any, pipe-makers and voicers have devoted sufficient attention to the science of acoustics, so far, at least, as it defines the character, constituents, and phenomena of compound musical sound. Where traditional and rule-of-thumb methods prevail there is no abiding place for either science or art.

COMPOUND STOPS or MIXTURES.—The pipes forming the MIXTURES or the high-pitched harmonic-corroborating stops, which belong to the pure organ-toned series, are constructed in the same manner as the pipes of the mutation stops. As the compound stops are formed of two, three, or more ranks of pipes of high pitch, the sounds of which are introduced in the tonal structure of the Organ to corroborate or create the higher upper partials of the foundation unison tones, produced by the PRINCIPAL, 8 FT., in the manual department and the PRINCIPAL, 16 FT., in the pedal department, the pipes forming their ranks are properly scaled and voiced in due subordination to the scales and voices of the PRINCIPALS.

DULCIANA and VOX ANGELICA.—In their most desirable and perfect form, the DULCIANA, 8 FT., and the so-called VOX ANGELICA, 8 FT., are pure organ-toned stops, and may, accordingly, be correctly considered diminutives of the PRINCIPAL, 8 FT., both in scale and tone. The pipes of both these stops have cylindrical bodies, and are constructed in the same fashion as those of the PRINCIPAL.

The scale of the DULCIANA varies considerably, being dictated by special circumstances. First, with reference to the scale of the PRINCIPAL or chief unison stop; secondly, by the division of the Organ for which it is designed; and, thirdly, by the strength of tone it is required to yield—either as the softest voice in the Organ, or as a voice intermediate between those of the PRINCIPAL and the VOX ANGELICA, the latter being in this case the softest voice in the instrument. The scale of the normal DULCIANA, 8 FT., commonly ranges between 3·00 inches and 3·65 inches diameter for the CC pipe; but, except in special cases, neither of these scales is to be recommended, for both mark the extreme limits. The most desirable scales under ordinary circumstances range from 3.25 to 3.51 inches diameter for the CC pipe, with the ratio 1 : 2.519, which places the half diameter on the eighteenth step, or F♯. This ratio gives the stop desirable fulness in the treble without, of necessity, increasing its loudness there. The width of the mouth should be one-fifth the circumference of the pipe, while its height is dictated by the wind-pressure and the strength and character of tone desired. For the mouth of the normal DULCIANA pipe an area equal to one-sixth of the transverse area of the body of the pipe has been recommended. The mouths, except, perhaps, in very small pipes, should be furnished with ears of slight projection. Under no consideration should DULCIANA pipes be slotted for tuning purposes; for the slotting destroys the greatest charm of their tone, removing it from pure organ-tone of a clear silvery character to one of a nondescript character. As the DULCIANA in its genuine English form and treatment is worthy of all the care that can be bestowed upon it, we strongly recommend its pipes being furnished with tuning-slides. These will not only prevent the pipes being injured by repeated tuning with the cones, but will secure perfect uniformity in their tonality, their open tops remaining at all times of the correct internal diameters.

The pipes of the VOX ANGELICA, 8 FT., differ in form from those of the DULCIANA, 8 FT., only in their scale, while in strength of tone they bear about the same proportion to those of the DULCIANA as the pipes of the DULCIANA do to those of the PRINCIPAL, 8 FT. Such, at least, should be the case, when both a DULCIANA and a VOX ANGELICA are inserted in the same Organ. With the scale in the same ratio as that above recommended for the DULCIANA, the CC pipe of the VOX ANGELICA may have its diameter ranging from 2.30 to 2.79 inches. When the smaller scale is adopted, the mouth may be of the same proportionate width as that recommended for the DULCIANA; but when the larger scale is used, the mouth may be made slightly narrower, say, two-elevenths of the internal circumference of the pipe. The height of the mouth will, as in the case of the DULCIANA, be dictated by the wind-pressure used and the quality of the tone required. On no account should the pipe be slotted. The VOX ANGELICA should be made of tin, its small scale and light weight rendering the adoption of tin a matter of trifling expense. The Hoyt two-ply metal will be found suitable.

The Pedal Organ DULCIANA, 16 FT., is an invaluable and beautiful stop, yet it is surprising how very seldom it is found in the pedal department of important Organs. It is not too much to say that it should find a place in every Organ of any pretensions to completeness or proper tonal appointment. The pipes of this stop, being of small scale and graceful proportions, are admirably adapted for display, especially when they are made of burnished tin. The freedom given to their voices, when the pipes are mounted in the case-work, is of great value, and renders forced voicing altogether unnecessary. The same remarks apply to the DOUBLE DULCIANA, 16 FT., of the manual department. In intonation both these stops, of 16 ft. pitch, are intended to carry down

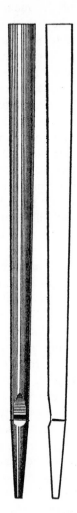

the voice of the DULCIANA, 8 FT.; but in a large instrument, in which both appear, the Pedal Organ stop may with advantage be made to a somewhat larger scale and be voiced to a fuller tone than the manual unison. In form and construction the pipes of the 16 ft. stops differ in no respect from those of the DULCIANA, 8 FT.

DOLCAN.—The pipes forming the DOLCAN, 8 FT., while differing materially in form from those of the PRINCIPAL, yield a voice on the border-land of pure organ-tone. The characteristic tone of the DOLCAN is freer or more open in quality than that of the true English DULCIANA, and has, when produced under skilful voicing, a somewhat plaintive singing character which is valuable and very pleasing, and which renders it highly effective in accompanimental music. The DOLCAN pipe has a body in the form of a slender, inverted, truncated cone, as shown in Fig. XXXVI., which depicts a tenor C, 4 ft., pipe drawn in correct proportions. The scale of the DOLCAN varies according to the volume of tone required: that which, in the ratio 1 : 2·519, gives the CC pipe a mouth-line diameter of 3·38 inches and a top diameter of 4·96 inches may be accepted as generally satisfactory. The width of the mouth is properly two-ninths of the internal circumference of the pipe at the mouth-line; and its height varies from one-fourth to one-third its width according to the wind-pressure and the tone desired. When a very delicate tone is desired, on a wind of 2½ inches, a mouth of one-fifth the circumference may be adopted, having a height about one-fourth its width; the languid should be finely nicked. The bass octave has sometimes been made of wood, the pipes being square and larger at the top than at the mouth to correspond with the metal pipes; but zinc pipes of the correct form are to be preferred. As the DOLCAN pipes should be made of tin, no better substitute is to be found than the hard-rolled, Hoyt two-ply metal, which can be used almost as thin as pure tin. It is interesting in connection with this stop to note the difference of tonality due to its

FIG. XXXVI.

inverted conical pipes, in comparison with the tones produced by the direct conical pipes of the GEMSHORN and SPITZFLÖTE.

METAL PIPES OF FLUTE-TONE.

Although all the labial stops of the Organ may be correctly classified under the generic name *flute stops,* there is a certain class of stops to which the name is specifically given by German, English, and American organ-builders and experts. The stops commonly included in this class receive the name because their voices partake more or less of that quality of tone which we recognize as flute-tone, represented, in its most perfect development and constitution, by the tone of the orchestral Flute. The French experts seem to commonly use the term in its wider sense. As will be seen on reference to the Chapter on the Forms and Construction of Wood Pipes, the more important imitative and unimitative flute-toned stops are formed of wood pipes. The tones of some of these can be successfully imitated by metal pipes; while, on the other hand, there are certain metal flute-toned pipes which have voices that cannot be successfully imitated by wood pipes. These facts clearly show the desirability of including both wood and metal stops in the tonal appointment of the Organ, and of not following the modern practice of ignoring the value of the wood stops, and depending almost entirely on metal stops, constructed largely of zinc to save expense.

FLÛTE À PAVILLON.—This stop, which is called by English builders BELL DIAPASON, is formed of large-scale pipes having cylindrical bodies surmounted by spreading bells, hence the name. The French name is clearly the most appropriate one, because the stop belongs to the flute-work rather than to the principal-work. The main or cylindrical portion of the body of the FLÛTE À PAVILLON pipe is in all essentials similar to that of a large-scale PRINCIPAL pipe, while its upper portion is in the form of a short inverted truncated cone. For facility in tuning, the bell should be attached to a short cylindrical piece fitting closely around the top of the body, its lower edge being cut so as to have a screw-like motion against a small projecting button of solder on the pipe. In tuning the pipe it is only necessary to raise or lower the bell by turning it slightly. The proportion of the *pavillon* or bell varies according to the tone desired; but its usual dimensions are one and one-half the diameter of the pipe in height, and one and two-thirds the diameter of the pipe in its diameter at top. A peculiar horn-like quality can be imparted to the tone by making the bell longer and of less diameter at top, and by cutting a long narrow slot in it: another quality can be given by cutting a circular opening instead of a slot. The mouth of the FLÛTE À PAVILLON pipe is of the same width as that of the MAJOR PRINCIPAL, 8 FT., but it is cut higher; the height depending largely on the wind-pressure used and on the strength of tone desired. In all cases it should be copiously winded. Owing to the labor required in constructing this stop and the space required for its accommodation on the windchest, it has not been and never will be favored by English or American organ-builders. We know of only one example in an English Organ, that in the Town Hall of Leeds, Yorkshire.

STENTORPHONE, 8 FT.—When properly formed and voiced, the STENTORPHONE is one of the most powerful labial stops in the Organ. It is of larger scale than the MAJOR PRINCIPAL and its pipes are made of metal of great thickness, so as to withstand the vibrations caused by the high-pressure wind on which it is voiced. This pressure ranges from seven to ten inches. The pipes have plain, cylindrical bodies, and are constructed in all respects like those of the PRINCIPAL, 8 FT. A suitable scale for the STENTORPHONE, 8 FT., in the ratio $1 : 2.519$, gives the CC pipe 7.02 inches diameter and the tenor C pipe 4.42 inches diameter. The mouths should be two-sevenths the internal circumference of the pipes in width, and their height should not be less than one-third their width. This stop strictly belongs to the flute-work.

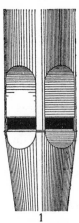

FIG. XXXVII.

SERAPHONPFEIFE.—The stop to which this name has been given is capable of yielding a more powerful voice than the STENTORPHONE. It was invented by Mr. G. F. Weigle, and first introduced in the large Organ in the City Church of Wertheim, Baden, constructed by Messrs. G. F. Steinmeyer & Co. The pipes which form this stop are of large scale and have two mouths, formed in the usual manner, and placed as close together as practicable, as shown in the Front View and Transverse Section of the lower portion of a pipe given in Fig. XXXVII. The large lineal measurement of the combined mouths—about four-tenths of the circumference of the pipe—gives a powerful intonation. The quality of the tone depends on the scale of the pipe, the height and shape of the upper lips of its mouths, the pressure of the wind on which it speaks, and the manner of voicing.*

A stop formed of pipes of so powerful an intonation would be extremely valuable in the Solo division of a large Concert-room Organ, where its prominent voice would add volume and solidity to the high-pressure reed-work there introduced. Voiced so as to yield as closely as possible a pure flute-tone, the SERAPHONPFEIFE, 8 FT., would be an

* Further particulars respecting this stop, patented by Mr. G. F. Weigle, are given in " The Art of Organ-Building," Vol. II., pp. 534-6.

important addition to the Great division of a large Organ. It is practically a metal DOPPELFLÖTE.

SPITZFLÖTE.—The pipes which form the stop usually called the SPITZFLÖTE, or, as rendered in English, SPIRE FLUTE, and in French, FLÛTE À POINT or FLÛTE À FUSEAU, have their bodies in the form of a slender truncated cone open at top, as shown in Fig. XXXVIII. The scale of the stop differs according to the office it is designed to fulfil in the tonal scheme of the Organ. On the one hand it is introduced because its voice possesses good mixing and building-up properties, while on the other hand it is valued on account of its special tonality, which, in good examples, is a pleasing combination of flute- and string-tone. It is extremely valuable in the softer divisions of the Organ, where it furnishes desirable octave and mutation stops. For the former purpose the pipes are made to a somewhat large scale; while for the production of the softer compound tone they are made to a comparatively small scale. In the SPITZFLÖTE pipe made by English organbuilders the upper diameter varies between one-half and two-thirds of the diameter at the mouth-line. The dimensions given by Töpfer, and apparently followed by Friedrich Haas, the rebuilder of the Lucerne Organ, are practically as follows: For the CC, 8 ft., pipe 4·60 inches diameter at the mouth, and 1·50 inches diameter at the top. This is a good medium scale for the production of the most desirable and characteristic bright flute-tone of the true SPITZFLÖTE. The mouth may be made one-fourth or two-ninths the larger circumference, and its height may vary from one-fourth to one-third of its width, according to the wind-pressure and the character of the tone desired: the upper lip may be slightly arched, and the lower lip and languid nicked moderately fine. The pipes must not be slotted at top for tuning.

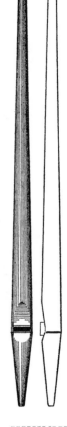

XXXVIII.

ROHRFLÖTE or FLÛTE À CHEMINÉE.—The German ROHRFLÖTE and the French FLÛTE À CHEMINÉE, in their representative forms, are large-scale metal stops, usually of 8 ft. and 4 ft. pitch, formed of labial pipes, having cylindrical bodies fitted at their upper ends with sliding metal caps, to the top flat surface of which are soldered small open cylindrical tubes or "chimneys." The pipes forming these stops are accordingly classified as half-covered or half-stopped, to distinguish them from the covered or stopped pipes of the GEDECKT and BOURDON. The form and correct proportions of a middle c¹ FLÛTE À CHEMINÉE pipe are given in Fig. XXXIX. Diagram 1 is a Front View and Diagram 2 is a Longitudinal Section of the pipe. These have been accurately drawn from a pipe in our possession made by a distinguished French organ-builder. The several dimensions of this pipe are as follows: Internal diameter of body 1·62 inches; length of body from lower lip 10¾ inches; internal diameter of chimney 0·28 inch; length of chimney 3 inches; width of mouth 1⅜ inches; height

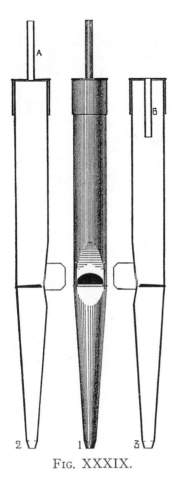

FIG. XXXIX.

of mouth in center ⅝ inch; projection of the ears 1⅜ inches; and wind-hole in foot ¼ inch. Both the languid and lower lip have twenty-two bold nicks. This pipe is roughly tuned by the sliding cap, and then accurately tuned by bending the large ears inward or outward. The latter method of tuning is not always followed.

The distinctive feature of the ROHRFLÖTE pipe is its perforated cap, to which is soldered the open tube or chimney; the perforation, prolonged by the chimney, imparting a certain clearness and brightness to the voice of the pipe. As both the relative diameter and length of the chimney affect the tone, these dimensions vary considerably in examples made by different builders. The larger the diameter, the more the tone approaches that of an open pipe. The diameter of the chimney varies in ordinary examples from one-sixth to one-third of the diameter of the body, while the length of the chimney varies from one-fourth to one-half the speaking length of the body of the pipe. According to Dom Bedos, larger chimneys were sometimes used: but as large ones destroy the desirable and distinctive tonal character of the pipes, their diameter should never exceed one-fourth that of their respective pipes; nor should their length exceed one-half the speaking lengths of the bodies of their respective pipes. In the large representation of the FLÛTE À CHEMINÉE given by Dom Bedos, the chimney is exactly one-third the diameter and one-half the length of the body of the pipe.

The tonal peculiarities of the ROHRFLÖTE, and the acoustical problem involved, appear to have exercised the enquiring minds of organ-builders and others. Professor Helmholtz, however, touches the matter very slightly in his important treatise, "Die Lehre von den Tonempfindungen." He only says: "Narrow stopped pipes let the Twelfth be very distinctly heard at the same time with the prime tone, and have hence been called *Quintaten (quintam tenentes)*. When these pipes are strongly blown, they also give the fifth partial, or higher major Third, very distinctly. Another variety of quality is produced by the ROHRFLÖTE. Here a tube, open at both ends, is inserted in the cover of a stopped pipe, and in the examples I examined its length was that of an open pipe giving the fifth partial tone of the prime tone of the stopped pipe. The fifth partial tone is thus proportionately stronger than the rather weak third partial on these pipes, and the quality of tone becomes peculiarly bright." Here the Professor leaves the subject. It was, accordingly, left to Dr. Robert Gerhardt to dive deeply into the acoustical problem presented by the ROHRFLÖTE, and show the scientific world what the profound mathematical mind could do in the matter. This he did, greatly to his own satisfaction, in his treatise entitled, "Die Rohrflöte, ein Pfeifenregister der Orgel." *

We cannot in these pages enter into the mathematic-aspect of the matter as presented by the learned writer of this treatise, but we may briefly give the practical results of his investigations, which must be evident to any expert who has handled a ROHRFLÖTE pipe. Providing the diameter of chimney be retained, the lengthening of it flattens the pitch of the pipe; while, on the other hand, if the length is retained and the diameter of the chimney is increased, the pitch is sharpened. In all cases the modification of the dimensions of the chimney, in relation to those of the body of the pipe, not only alters the pitch but affects the tone produced, due to the creation of certain enharmonic upper partial tones. The acoustical problem involved is somewhat obscure, and is only increased by the strange fact that the tone of the pipe is in no way affected if the chimney is turned downward into the body of the pipe, as indicated at B, in the Longitudinal Section 3. In the Front View 1 and the Section 2 the chimney is shown in its usual position. The internal position of the chimney is much to be preferred as it protects it effectually from injury.

In the ROHRFLÖTE, 8 FT., it is not necessary to carry the pipes with chimneys below tenor C. The bass octave may be formed of covered pipes of metal or wood,—preferably the former,—voiced to carry down the normal tone of the stop as closely as possible. In the stop of 4 ft. pitch the top octave should be formed of open flute-toned pipes.

The scale of the ROHRFLÖTE, 8 FT., varies considerably in different old examples. Large scales have been employed by both German and

* "Nova Acta der Ksl. Leop.-Carol.-Deutschen Akademie der Naturforscher."—Band XLVII. Nr. 1. Halle, 1884.

French builders, but these are neither necessary nor desirable in a properly-balanced, modern Organ. A good medium scale, in the ratio $1 : \sqrt{8}$, gives the tenor C pipe a diameter of 2·66 inches; the middle c^1 pipe a diameter of 1·58 inches; and the c^2 pipe a diameter of 0·94 inch. This scale is almost identical with that indicated by the French pipe of which the dimensions have been given. Let the chimneys be one-fourth the diameter of the respective bodies, and from one-third to one-half the speaking length of the bodies, according to the quality of tone desired. The proportionate lengths of the chimneys may decrease as the lengths of the bodies increase. No rule of universal application can be given in a matter where art and taste should rule supreme. The proper form of the mouth is accurately represented in Fig. XXXIX.

DOPPELROHRFLÖTE.—Although it appears that the DOPPELROHRFLÖTE has in the majority of cases been made of wood, the pipes of the treble octaves—from c^1 to c^4—may with advantage be formed of metal. As the name implies, the pipes have two mouths; and it is only in this respect that they differ in form and construction from the pipes of the ROHRFLÖTE just described. Instead of having metal caps with chimneys, we would suggest the adoption of perforated wood stoppers. It is not easy to tune the DOPPELROHRFLÖTE pipes by means of large projecting ears, and as it is difficult to accurately tune by means of the metal caps, it becomes advisable to employ stoppers that are easily manipulated. Allowing that the wood stoppers are made of the proper lengths, and are perforated with holes correctly graduated, they will influence the tone in precisely the same manner as the metal chimneys do. Should a very full and filling-up tone be desired, the scale may be slightly increased beyond that given for the ROHRFLÖTE. The mouths should each be one-fifth of the circumference of the pipe, and have arched upper lips of the same form and proportionate height as shown for the ROHRFLÖTE, Fig. XXXIX. The pipes of the tenor octave may be of wood, with double mouths and perforated stoppers, while those of the bass octave (when the stop is of 8 feet pitch) may be of large-scale wood pipes, wholly stopped, and having single mouths. When properly made, this stop becomes a highly valuable tonal variant of the ordinary DOPPELFLÖTE.

GEDECKT, STOPPED DIAPASON, or BOURDON.—In England the name STOPPED DIAPASON is commonly understood to mean a manual covered stop composed of wood pipes, notwithstanding the fact that many fine examples have been made of metal, with the bass octave only of wood pipes. In Germany, while wood pipes are much in favor for the normal GEDECKT, metal pipes are frequently employed for the treble octaves of the stop. A remarkable instance of the use of metal pipes throughout a GEDECKT of 16 feet tone is furnished by the BOURDON in the Great division of the Organ in the Cathedral of St. Bavon, at Haarlem, constructed in the year 1738. In France the term BOURDON is applied to covered stops of 16 ft., 8 ft., and 4 ft. pitch, composed chiefly or entirely of metal pipes of large scale. This was the practice when Dom Bedos wrote.

The metal pipes of the French BOURDONS are of large scale, and are formed of a rich alloy of considerable thickness. They are usually covered with sliding lids or caps of the same material, lined with thin leather, or sliding against paper wound around the tops of the pipes. The mouth of the true BOURDON pipe is about one-fourth or two-sevenths of the internal circumference of the pipe in width, and about two-fifths of its own width in height; but the proportions of the mouth, as well as the form of its upper lip, differ according to the character and volume of the tone desired. For the production of a full, humming flute-tone, proper for the true BOURDON, a mouth one-third its width in height, and having a straight or very slightly arched upper lip, is to be preferred: but in these matters the supply and pressure of the pipe-wind are controlling factors. The scale according to Dom Bedos gives the tenor C pipe a circumference of 10.37 inches, or a diameter of 3.30 inches; and as his scale is evidently based on the common ratio $1 : \sqrt{8}$, the middle c^1 pipe will have a circumference of 6.17 inches, or a diameter of 1.96 inches, and the c^2 pipe will have a circumference of 3.66 inches, or a diameter of 1.16 inches. The minimum scale advocated by this old authority gives the tenor C pipe a diameter of 2.93 inches. A tenor C pipe, according to the larger scale, is represented in Fig. XL.

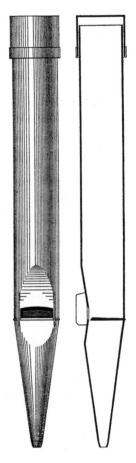

FIG. XL.

The fine BOURDON, 16 FT., in the Great division of the Organ in the Town Hall of Manchester, constructed by A. Cavaillé-Coll, has its two low octaves of wood. The CCC pipe is 6½ inches wide by 8 inches deep. The C pipe,—the largest of metal,—which speaks on the middle c^1 key, is 3.37 inches in diameter, having a mouth 2½ inches wide by 1¾₆ inches high, with upper lips slightly arched, flanked with ears 2½ inches long and 1 inch projection. This pipe and the eleven above it are closed with metal caps; while the upper portion of the stop is formed of FLÛTE À CHEMINÉE pipes. The pipe which speaks on the c^2 key is 2·25 inches in diameter, having a mouth $1\frac{5}{8}$ inches wide by $^{11}\!/_{16}$ inch high, with upper lip slightly arched. The speaking length of its body is $10\frac{1}{4}$ inches; and its chimney is 5 inches long by 0·56 inch in diameter.*

The scales alluded to above are larger than those employed by English organ-builders for the metal STOPPED DIAPASON. The English scale, in the ratio $1 : \sqrt{8}$, seldom exceeds a diameter of 2·55 inches for the tenor C pipe.

In the German GEDECKT, 8 FT., the metal pipes do not, as a general rule, descend below middle c^1. This appears to have been the practice followed by E. Schulze, as exemplified by the GEDECKTS in his remarkable Organ in St. Peter's Church, at Hindley, Lancashire. The scales of these stops vary. The GEDECKT, 8 FT., in the Great Organ has a c^1 pipe of 1·50 inches diameter, with a mouth $1\frac{1}{8}$ inches in width and $\frac{9}{16}$ inch in height; and the GEDECKT, 8 FT., in the Swell Organ has a c^1 pipe of 1·31 inches diameter, with a mouth-width equal to one-fourth the internal circumference of the pipe, cut up equal to three-fifths of its width.† The wind-pressure is $3\frac{1}{2}$ inches in both these manual divisions.

All covered metal pipes should be made of the best spotted-metal, and of sufficient thickness to withstand the pressure of the stoppers for any length of time. The stoppers should not fit too tightly; it is sufficient that they are airtight and have no tendency to drop in the pipes. They should move smoothly in the process of tuning.

LIEBLICHGEDECKT.—The true German LIEBLICHGEDECKT is simply a small-scale GEDECKT, of 16 ft., 8 ft., or 4 ft. pitch, formed of wood, wood and metal, or altogether of metal. The stop of 4 ft. pitch, which is frequently labeled LIEBLICHFLÖTE, should be formed entirely of metal pipes, the top octave of which should be open. The pipes of the LIEBLICHFLÖTE are voiced to yield a bright and singularly pleasing quality of flute-tone, hence its name, which may be rendered *Lovely-toned Stopped Flute*. The tone is best produced on low pressures of wind, ranging from $1\frac{1}{2}$ to $2\frac{1}{2}$ inches. Both the LIEBLICHGEDECKT, 8 FT., and the LIEBLICHFLÖTE in the Choir division of the Organ in St. Peter's Church, Hindley, are on wind of only $1\frac{7}{8}$ inches, while the same stops in the Echo division of the Organ in Leeds Parish Church speak on wind of $1\frac{1}{2}$ inches. All these beautiful stops are by Edmund Schulze. A satisfactory scale for the LIEBLICHGEDECKT, 8 FT., is that which, in the ratio 1 : 2·519, gives the tenor C pipe an internal diameter of 1.97 inches. The scale of Schulze's LIEBLICHGEDECKT, 8 FT., in his fine

---

* We obtained these measurements as accurately as practicable from the pipes in situ.
† The bass and tenor octaves of both these stops are formed of wood pipes. The scale of the CC pipe of the GEDECKT in the Great is 2.87 inches by 3.87 inches, having a mouth 2 inches high. The CC pipe of the stop in the Swell measures 2.12 inches by 3 inches, having a mouth 2 inches high, or slightly more than its width. Moderate scales, high mouths, and copious winding, are characteristics of the true German GEDECKTS, both of wood and metal.

Organ in St. Peter's, Hindley, gives the middle c¹ pipe—the lowest in metal—a diameter of 1.19 inches. The mouth is one-fourth the internal circumference of the pipe, and its arched upper lip is ½ inch high in the center. Other German builders have favored somewhat larger scales.

SPINDELFLÖTE or SPINDLE FLUTE.—The SPINDELFLÖTE is a metal stop of 8 ft., 4 ft., or 2 ft., which derives its name from the peculiar form of its pipes. The SPINDELFLÖTE pipe differs from the SPITZFLÖTE inasmuch as, instead of taper- ing from the mouth line to the top, only portion of its body is conical, as shown in Fig. XLI. The stop appears to have been devised in the early part of the sixteenth century and is now almost a curiosity in organ-building, largely due to the time and trouble involved in its construction. Its tone is not very distinctive, being between the tones of the SPITZ- FLÖTE and the ROHRFLÖTE.

FLÛTE HARMONIQUE or HARMONIC FLUTE.— The FLÛTE HARMONIQUE was invented by MM. Cavaillé-Coll, and first introduced by them in the Grand Organ constructed, in 1841, for the Abbey Church of Saint-Denis, near Paris. The stop de- rives its name from the fact that the pipes form- ing the higher portion of its compass are so constructed and voiced as to yield their first har- monic upper partial tones instead of the tones which normally belong to their full lengths. The pipes which form the harmonic portion of the HARMONIC FLUTE, 8 FT., usually commence on the note f¹ or g¹, although they are occasionally, and desirably, carried down to middle c¹. In the HARMONIC FLUTE, 4 FT., and the HARMONIC PICCOLO, 2 FT., the harmonic pipes are, of course, carried one and two octaves lower than the notes above mentioned. Open pipes of wood or metal of the normal speak- ing lengths, are used for the lower portion of the stops of 8 ft. and 4 ft. pitch. In this place, however, we have to deal only with the form and construction

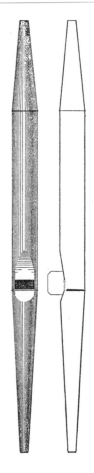

FIG. XLI.

of the harmonic pipes. In selecting a stop for illustration and descrip- tion we cannot do better than take the FLÛTE HARMONIQUE, 8 FT., in the Great division of the Concert-room Organ erected by Cavaillé-Coll in the Town Hall of Manchester. The lowest harmonic pipe of this stop is g¹, shown in correct proportions in the accompanying illustration, Fig. XLII. The pipe is 2.37 inches in diameter and 29½ inches in length from its mouth-line. At the distance of 13 inches from that line a hole ⅛ inch in diameter is drilled, as shown in the illustration. The mouth of the pipe is 1¾ inches in width and ¹¹⁄₁₆ inch in height, having a straight upper lip. Through the agency of the perforation in the body, which prevents the formation of a node in the middle of the internal column of air, and by the pipe being slightly overblown, a note is produced which is about the octave of that which normally belongs to a pipe of the full length of 29½ inches. In addition to its high pitch the note has a peculiar quality and volume, owing largely to the scale of the pipe, which would be excessive in a pipe about half its length, yielding a note of similar pitch under ordinary conditions. The *timbre* of the note is also due to the prominence of certain upper partial tones obtained by special voicing. The bass of the FLÛTE HARMONIQUE, 8 FT., in the Manchester Organ is formed of open wood pipes, the CC one of which has a scale of 5.00 inches by 6.50 inches. The open metal, non-harmonic middle c¹ pipe has a diameter of 2.75 inches and a speaking length of 22 inches, belonging to a very large scale.

Certain organ-builders who are specially careful in tonal matters wisely prefer to construct the HARMONIC FLUTE, 8 FT., entirely of metal, commencing the double-length pipes at f¹. This appears to be the commendable practice of the distinguished builders, Messrs. Casavant Brothers, of St. Hyacinthe, P. Q., Canada. The rule given for determining the position of the perforation in harmonic pipes, as given by these authorities, is as follows: Divide the body of the pipe—the full length of which is calculated to yield the note an octave below that which it is required to yield when rendered harmonic—into nine equal parts, and make the perforation at the height of four of these parts above the languid. The pipe f¹ may be pierced with a hole about one-sixteenth of an inch in diameter. The size must be carefully graduated in the pipes forming the harmonic portion of the stop; but their size varies in different stops according to the strength and quality of the tone desired. As Messrs. Casavant correctly state, a larger hole changes the tone somewhat and permits its strength to be increased. The mouths of the harmonic pipes are one-fourth of the circumference of their respective bodies, and one-third of their own width in height. The nicking of both lower lip and languid should be clean and deep.

FIG. XLII.

In the HARMONIC FLUTE, 4 FT., the open non-harmonic pipes, preferably of metal, extend on the clavier from CC to B—24 notes,—the double-length harmonic pipes, accordingly, commencing on c¹: the HAR-

MONIC PICCOLO, 2 FT., having its harmonic pipes carried down to tenor C. All these HARMONIC FLUTES are extremely valuable voices in the Organ, and repay all the skill and care that can be bestowed upon their construction and voicing.

ZAUBERFLÖTE.—This valuable addition to the voices of the Organ is due to the genius of the late Mr. William Thynne, Organ-builder, of London. The following particulars are derived from the last ZAUBER-FLÖTE, 4 FT., voiced by this great artist in tone-production, and placed in the Organ in St. John's Church, Richmond, Surrey. The stop is formed of wood and metal, and its unique and characteristic feature obtains in the fact that from tenor C to the top note of its compass the pipes are stopped and harmonic, speaking the first possible upper partial tone—the Twelfth—of the ground tone belonging to their speaking length. The reader may be here reminded that the first harmonic of a stopped pipe is the second upper partial tone, not proper to an open pipe capable of yielding the same ground or prime tone under the ordinary conditions. The octave of the stop from CC to BB is formed of open wood pipes, the scale of the CC pipe being 2·13 inches by 2·81 inches. The mouth of this pipe is ⅝ inch in height, and has a straight upper lip, about ⅛ inch thick, and slightly rounded. The wind-way is narrow; and both cap and block have twenty nicks cut in a vertical direction. The cap is set ⅛ inch below the edge of the block. The mouth is of the ordinary form, sloped externally, and without applied ears. The cap is hollowed and cut to a sharp edge at the wind-way. From tenor C to E—5 notes, the pipes are of wood, stopped, and harmonic. The scale of the C pipe is 2·13 inches by 2·75 inches; and its length from its lower lip, including sufficient hold for the stopper, is 2 feet 9½ inches. It is perforated with a hole, ¹⁄₁₆ inch in diameter, 19¼ inches above the lower lip. In all cases the holes are made as small as possible, being just sufficient to prevent the pipes from speaking their ground tone. The mouth is of the same form as in the open pipes, and has a straight upper lip about ¹⁄₁₀ inch thick, cut up ⁷⁄₁₆ inch. The cap, which is set flush with the edge of the block, is sunk on the inside to form the wind-way, and is sloped externally, to correspond with the mouth, leaving ⅛ inch at the wind-way. This treatment, which was used by Schulze in the wood pipes of his PRINCIPALS, 8 FT., allows a free current of air to approach the mouth from below. In the ZAUBER-FLÖTE this sloping of the cap is slightly rounded, and not straight like that of the upper lip of the mouth. Both block and cap have twenty-eight fine nicks, cut vertically as in the open pipes.

We now come to the metal portion of the stop, which commences on tenor F and extends to the top note. The scale of this portion is best given at the middle c¹ pipe. The internal diameter of this pipe is 1·91 inches, and its length is 17 inches from the lower lip, allowing about

1¼ inches for the stopper. The harmonic perforation is about ¹⁄₁₆ th inch in diameter, and is situated 9 inches above the languid. The exact proportions of this pipe are given in Fig. XLIII. The width of the mouth is 1 ⁵⁄₁₆ inches, and its height is a fraction more than one-fourth of its width.

The ZAUBERFLÖTE was made by Mr. Thynne of both 8 ft. and 4 ft. pitch. When of the former pitch, the bass octave was formed of stopped wood pipes, voiced to carry down the characteristic tone of the stop as closely as possible, but by no means satisfactorily, as can be understood. The tone of the stop in its true register is singularly liquid and pure, and valuable on account of its full and good mixing qualities.

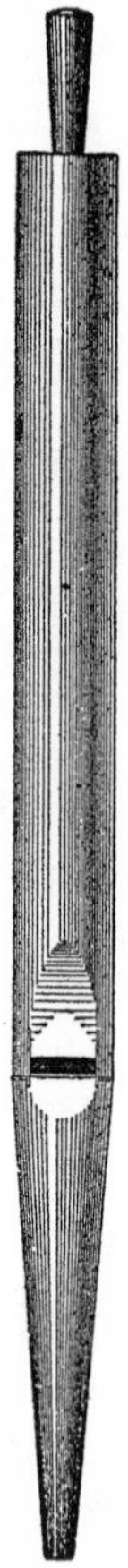

QUINTATEN.—The QUINTATEN of 8 ft. pitch is, in its most satisfactory form, a covered metal stop of rather large scale, the pipes of which are voiced to yield their first upper partial tone—the Twelfth—in addition to their proper ground-tone, hence the name of the stop (from *quintam tenentes*). The form and correct proportions of a middle c^1 pipe of full scale, derived from an eminently satisfactory example, are as follows: The body of the pipe is cylindrical, with a speaking length of 11 inches and an internal diameter of 1·29 inches. It is covered with a sliding cap of 1½ inches long, made air-tight by a lining of soft paper. The pipe is tuned by means of this cap. The width of the mouth is two-ninths of the circumference of the pipe, and is ⁵⁄₁₆ inch in height. The upper lip is straight, and the languid and upper lip have seventeen bold nicks. The pipes forming the lowest octave of the stop from which the above particulars have been derived have mouths furnished with projecting ears carrying cylindrical wood harmonic-bridges. The diameter of the CC pipe is 3·25 inches and the speaking length is 3 feet 10 inches. The ratio of the stop is 1 : 2·519. The mouth of the CC pipe is 2³⁄₁₆ inches in width by ¹¹⁄₁₆ inch in height. The upper lip is straight; and the languid and lower lip are boldly nicked. The stop is voiced on wind of 3⅓ inches.

FIG. XLIII.

The family of QUINTATENS—16 ft., 8 ft., and 4 ft.—is extremely valuable in the tonal appointment of a large Organ; its members, collectively or separately, lending themselves to the creation of a series of fine combinations of a building-up and timbre-creating character, not possible in any Organ in which the complete family is not present. As a manual stop of 16 ft. pitch, the QUINTATEN (under the less desirable name QUINTATON) seems to have been first introduced in England in the Organ in the Albert Hall, Sheffield, constructed by Cavaillé-Coll in 1873, in which it appears in the Positif Expressif, and is the only QUINTATEN in the instrument. The introduction of the complete family of QUINTATENS should not be neglected by designers of important Organs.

ZARTFLÖTE.—Of all the metal stops yielding tones more or less resembling those of the QUINTATENS, the stop now to be considered may be pronounced the most beautiful. The ZARTFLÖTE in its covered form was invented by the distinguished English artist, Mr. John W. Whiteley, in the year 1896. The pipes forming this stop are of small scale, fully stopped, and have narrow mouths furnished with cylindrical harmonic-bridges. In Fig. XLIV. are given a Front View and Longitudinal Section of the chief portions of the tenor C pipe of the ZARTFLÖTE, 8 FT., or the largest pipe of the ZARTFLÖTE, 4 FT. The harmonic-bridge is of aluminium tubing, held, at a considerable distance from the lower lip of the mouth, between strong ears shaped as shown in the Section. The bridge is secured in position by projections, punched from the ears, which enter the tube at both ends. The scale of the stop, in the slow ratio $1 : 2\cdot13$, gives the C (2 ft.) pipe a diameter of $1\cdot24$ inches; the c^1 pipe a diameter of $0\cdot85$ inch; the c^2 pipes a diameter of $0\cdot58$ inch; and the c^3 pipe a diameter of $0\cdot40$ inch. The mouths are unusually small, being about two-elevenths of the circumferences of their respective pipes. It will probably be found desirable to increase the widths of the mouths in the two higher octaves to one-fifth the circumferences of the pipes. The harmonic-bridges vary in diameter from $0\cdot25$ inch at tenor C (2 ft. pipe) to $0\cdot06$ at the c^4 pipe. It is only

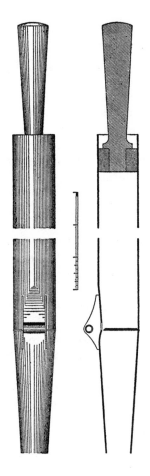

FIG. XLIV.

necessary to have six different sizes, changing them at about equal intervals in the compass. The stoppers are of soft cork rings glued to turned wood handles, as indicated in the Longitudinal Section. In voicing the pipes a greater number of nicks are placed on the languids than

on the lower lips. For instance, in the tenor C pipe the languid has
eight nicks while the lower lip has only five. The nicks are very small
and cleanly cut. In describing this ZARTFLÖTE, its inventor says: " This
stop is a modification of the QUINTATEN, with every suggestion of tonal
coarseness removed. It bears the same relation to the ordinary QUINTA-
TEN that a very refined DULCIANA or SALICIONAL does to an OPEN DIA-
PASON, the result being a light and bright flute-tone, with sufficient reedy
quality to give it a distinctive character."

METAL PIPES OF STRING-TONE.

Of all the classes of metal labial stops which go to complete the tonal
forces of the Organ, there is no one which has been developed during
late times to so remarkable a state of perfection as the class yielding
imitative string-tone. The first stops yielding strongly imitative string-
tone heard in English Organs were the handiwork of the late Edmund
Schulze; and, in some respects, we have yet to hear stops superior, or
even equal, in tone to those he inserted in certain of his Organs still
existing. He was ably followed in this branch of pipe-work by the late
William Thynne and subsequently by John W. Whiteley. Schulze's
work appears to have been unknown to American organ-builders prior
to our placing in the late Hilborne L. Roosevelt's hands models and scale
drawings of Schulze's and Thynne's masterpieces. Pipes producing
unimitative string-tone had long been made by German builders, and
had been imitated and to some degree improved by builders of other
countries. To the more important of these we shall first direct attention.

GEIGENPRINCIPAL.—The GEIGENPRINCIPAL, 8 FT., as properly constructed and voiced by the German organ-builders, yields a rich organ-
tone in which a stringy quality of comparatively little prominence asserts
itself, imparting a tonal-coloring which contrasts in an effective manner
with the full-bodied pure organ-tone of the English OPEN DIAPASON.
The GEIGENPRINCIPAL is a favorite stop of the German builders, appearing in the majority of their important Organs in either the second or
third manual divisions. In the hands of English organ-builders this
stop, either under its proper name or the English equivalent VIOLIN DIA-
PASON, has rarely assumed its true dignity.

The GEIGENPRINCIPAL, 8 FT., is formed of cylindrical pipes of medium
scale, preferably of fine spotted-metal, having mouths one-fourth their
circumference, and between one-fourth and one-third of their own width
in height. The best tonal results are obtained when the mouths are
furnished with the harmonic-bridge; but care must be taken to prevent
too much interference with the foundation-tone, otherwise the stop will
lose its characteristic dignity. Under no circumstances should its pipes
be slotted. The best scale for the normal GEIGENPRINCIPAL, 8 FT., gives

the following diameters in inches: CC, 4.66; C, 2.78; c¹, 1.65; c², 0.98; c³, 0.58; c⁴, 0.35. This is practically the scale advocated by Edmund Schulze, in the ratio 1 : √8. Should a fuller tone be desired in the higher octaves, the scale may be in the ratio 1 : 2.66, starting with the diameter of 4.62 inches for the CC pipe.

GEIGENOCTAVE.—This stop, of 4 ft. pitch, is, as its name implies, the true Octave of the GEIGENPRINCIPAL, 8 FT. Its pipes are of the same form as those of the unison stop above described. As the GEIGENOCTAVE (very commonly termed GEIGENPRINCIPAL, 4 FT.) should never be introduced in the absence of the GEIGENPRINCIPAL, 8 FT., its scale should be subordinate to that of the unison stop: accordingly, it may be made two pipes smaller. The GEIGENOCTAVE should be voiced so as to blend perfectly with the GEIGENPRINCIPAL, 8 FT., enriching without disturbing the unison tone. In our opinion it is undesirable to introduce the Octave stop, except, perhaps, in Organs of the first magnitude.

SALICIONAL.—Secondary in importance to the GEIGENPRINCIPAL is the true SALICIONAL. Properly scaled and voiced, it yields a string-tone of unimitative, but singularly delicate character. It may be said, when voiced by a master, to be one of the most beautiful stops in the Organ. As made by different builders, in different countries, the stop varies considerably in its tonal coloring, the variation appearing chiefly in the amount of string-tone it yields in combination with its subdued organ-tone. The SALICIONAL, 8 FT., is made to several medium scales; but probably that commonly adopted by the late Mr. F. Haas is the most suitable. This scale, in the ratio 1 : 2.66, gives the CC pipe a diameter of 3.21 inches; the C pipe a diameter of 1.97 inches; and the c¹ pipe a diameter of 1.20 inches. The mouths should be one-fifth the circumference of their respective pipes, although they are sometimes made wider; their heights being dictated by the quality of tone desired, the wind-pressure, and, accordingly, the strength of voice. Both larger and smaller scales have been used. The SALICIONAL pipe is usually made with a cylindrical body, but a body of a slightly conical form has been used, as shown in the only drawing of the pipe given in " Die Theorie und Praxis des Orgelbaues " (Plate III., Fig. 16). The mouth of the SALICIONAL pipe is usually fitted with some form of harmonic attachment, calculated to aid the development of a delicate string-tone. A representative example of this is shown in the Front View and Longitudinal Section given in Fig. XLV., which have been accurately drawn from a middle c¹ SALICIONAL pipe kindly furnished us by the late Hilborne L. Roosevelt. The triangular and wavy form of this attachment, which occupies the position of a beard, gives the air free access below the mouth. The diameter of the pipe is 1.25 inches, indicating a medium scale. The mouth is somewhat large, being in width one-fourth the circumference of the body. When a very delicate quality of tone is desired, the mouth, one-fifth the circumference of the pipe, may be bearded in the manner indicated in the Front View and Longitudinal Section given in Fig. XLVI. It will be observed that the beard and ears are formed of a single strip of metal, bent, and soldered (at the ears only) to the sides of the mouth. The pipes should be made of tin or confluent-metal; but they do not require to be heavy, especially if they are to speak on wind of a low pressure. We are of opinion that for all stops of this class the hard-rolled, Hoyt two-ply metal will be found eminently satisfactory and economical. In voicing, both the languids and lower lips should be closely and cleanly nicked. The SALICIONAL is made of 16 ft., 8 ft., and 4 ft. pitch; but it may well appear in mutation-work, forming a very valuable and beautiful family, not yet made full use of.

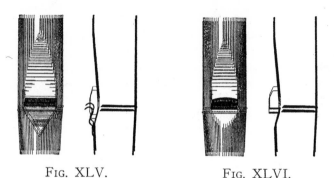

FIG. XLV.   FIG. XLVI.

ÆOLINE.—This stop, properly of 8 ft. pitch, in its most approved labial form may be considered an ECHO SALICIONAL. It is formed of small-scale cylindrical pipes, preferably of tin, the mouths of which are furnished with ears and small, adjustable curved beards after the fashion shown in Fig. XLV. The latter greatly aid the production of the delicate string-tone which is the desirable characteristic of the stop. A suitable scale for this stop, in the ratio $1:2.519$, gives the CC pipe a diameter of 2.51 inches; the C pipe a diameter of 1.54 inches; and the c^1 pipe a diameter of 0.94 inches. The mouths to be one-fifth or two-ninths the circumference of their respective pipes, and kept as low as practicable, consistent with the quality and strength of the tone required. The ÆOLINE is peculiarly suitable for the Chamber Organ.

VIOLA DA GAMBA.—Apparently the first real attempt made by the old German organ-builders to produce imitative string-tone showed itself in the stop called by them VIOLA DA GAMBA. In this they strove to reproduce, as closely as the then state of their art permitted, the tones of the orchestral Viola da Gamba—an instrument held in the highest estimation in Germany and elsewhere during the seventeenth and eighteenth centuries, and for which Johann Sebastian Bach wrote several beautiful compositions. The pipes of the stop, as originally made, were cylindrical and of medium scale; and they were invariably slow of speech, so much so as to be almost valueless when used alone or for rapid passages. This class of stop has been commonly distinguished among English organ-builders by the name German GAMBA; and while it is more stringy than the GEIGENPRINCIPAL, its tone cannot be said to be satisfactory from an imitative point of view. Later essays were more successful, when small-scale pipes were used and greater promptness of speech secured. A radical departure (from the old slow-speaking, cylindrical German GAMBA) in quest of imitative string-tone was made when the stop designated GLOCKENGAMBA or BELL GAMBA was devised and introduced in the Organ. As the voicing of this stop was improved and its tone became more imitative, the above names, which simply alluded to the form of its pipes, gave way to the more desirable and expressive name VIOLA DA GAMBA. This form of stop is now very rarely made, first because its pipes are troublesome to construct properly; and, secondly, because a much better tonal result can be readily obtained from pipes of simpler form. The shape of the old VIOLA DA GAMBA pipe is shown in the accompanying illustration, Fig. XLVII.

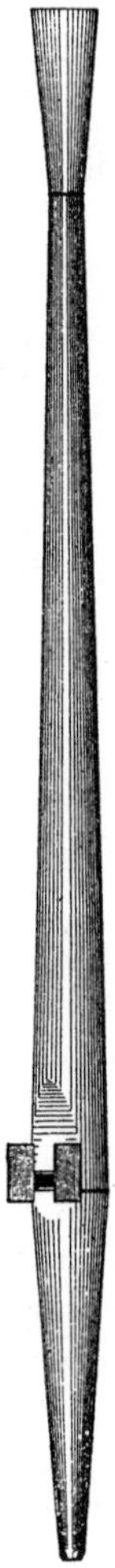

The characteristic tone of the old Viola da Gamba can be closely imitated by small-scale cylindrical or conical pipes, preferably of tin, the mouths of which are small, and furnished with small ears and slender harmonic-bridges.* The VIOLE DE GAMBE, 8 FT., in the Swell division of the Organ in the Town Hall of Manchester, constructed by A. Cavaillé-Coll, is of small-scale, cylindrical tin pipes, the mouths of which, devoid of ears are fitted with a simple form of *frein harmonique,* as shown in Fig. XLVIII. The *frein* here consists of a narrow strip of tin, the ends of which are bent at right angles and soldered to the sides of the pipe. This method is not be recommended, as it renders an absolutely correct initial adjustment a matter of considerable difficulty, and any subsequent easy adjustment practically impossible. The *frein* is omitted in several of the higher pipes. The tone of the stop is pleasing, but lacking in brilliancy and crispness. A better result is obtained by applying the *frein* in the

FIG. XLVII.

---

* The author has had opportunities of studying the tone of the true Viola da Gamba, and does not hesitate to make this assertion.

manner shown in Fig. XLIX. The narrow strip or plate is here inserted in oblique saw-cuts made in the ears, rendering a certain amount of adjustment possible so far as its distance from the mouth is concerned.

It is extremely difficult to convey in writing any clear idea of the tone of the true Viola da Gamba; but as some guide to the pipe voicer we may say that it is considerably thinner and less pungent than the tone of the Violoncello, of which latter instrument the Viola da Gamba was the precursor. Perhaps the best advice we can give the pipe voicer of to-day, is to imitate as closely as practicable the tone of the orchestral Viola (Viola da Braccio), played at medium strength. This treatment will place the tone of the VIOLA DA GAMBA in proper subordination to

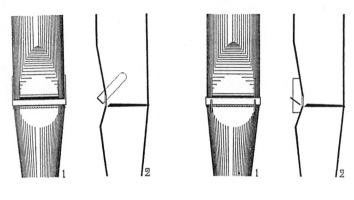

FIG. XLVIII.   FIG. XLIX.

that of the imitative VIOLONCELLO. The VIOLA DA GAMBA when made and voiced by a master hand is a most desirable stop for the true Chamber Organ, in which refinement and delicacy of tone are essential conditions.

VIOLA D'AMORE.—The orchestral Viola d'Amore—now practically an obsolete instrument—is rather larger than the Viola now in use. It is strung with seven catgut stopped strings, and with several metal sympathetic strings, which pass through the bridge and under the finger-board. These metal strings are tuned to the gut strings, and, accordingly, vibrate sympathetically with them, producing a compound tone " full of sweetness and mystery." It is this character of tone that the organ-pipe voicer has to strive to produce. The VIOLA D'AMORE of the Organ is properly formed of small-scale, cylindrical tin pipes, having mouths three-thirteenths their circumference, and about one-fourth their own width in height, furnished either with the *frein harmonique* or some other description of harmonic-bridge. In Fig. L. are given a Front View and Longitudinal Section of the mouth portion of the tenor C pipe of the Viola d'Amore, 8 ft., made by Henri Zimmermann, of Paris, for the author's Chamber Organ. The dimensions of this pipe are as follows: Diameter 1·75 inches; width of mouth 1·24 inches; and height of mouth 0·33 inch; the ratio of the scale being 1:2·519. The *frein harmonique* (system Gavioli), which is adjusted to the mouth in the manner shown, consists of thin brass plate A, 1·44 inches long and 0·44 inch wide, supported by the strip B, attached to the foot of the pipe and adjusted to the mouth by means of the tapped-wires and leather buttons C and D. The strip B is forked and slotted, as indicated in the Front View, to allow the plate A to be raised or lowered, while the strip, acting as a spring, is moved to or from the pipe under the control of the button D. The inclination of the plate or *frein* A can be readily altered by

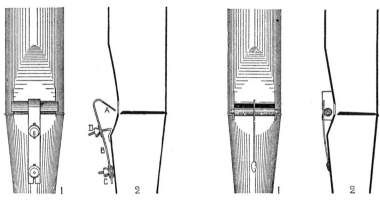

Fig. L.   Fig. LI.

bending the curved portion of the strip. By these means every requisite adjustment can be executed with facility: and the *frein* can be removed should the mouth require manipulation at any time. The top of the pipe has a tuning-slide in which is a slot 1¼ inches long by 9⁄16 inch wide.

Although the pipes of the Viola d'Amore may be said to be invariably cylindrical in modern work, we are strongly of opinion that a more satisfactory tone could be obtained from conical pipes of small scale, unslotted, and having their mouths furnished with small cylindrical harmonic-bridges, fitted so as to be removable, in the manner shown in Fig. LI. The advantage of movable bridges was fully realized by the late Mr. Henry Willis, for we find all the Gambas in the Organ in Glasgow Cathedral furnished with them—those of the larger pipes being of turned hard-wood and those of the smaller pipes of wire of different gauges. All are held in their positions on the ears by wire springs soldered to the pipe-feet, exactly as shown in Fig. LI.

Violin.—We now come to the consideration of the modern string-toned stops, whose voices imitate to a remarkable extent the compound tones of the orchestral string instruments; namely, the Violin and Violoncello. Under the names VIOLIN, CONCERT VIOLIN, and VIOLE D'ORCHESTRE, we find remarkable stops which have been produced by certain artists during recent years, first and most distinguished of whom was the late William Thynne, of London. These artist-voicers have produced stops whose rich compound tones so closely imitate those of the orchestral string instruments as to be positively deceptive. We have, as a matter of curiosity, tested pipes, voiced by Mr. Thynne, alongside the orchestral Violin, and the imitation was so perfect that we could defy listeners in an adjoining room to say whether they heard the pipes or the Violin when one or the other was sounding; or when both were sounding in perfect unison, which of them it was that dropped out of the combination when one or the other was silenced. It is unnecessary to comment on the immense value of imitative voices of this class in artistic organ appointment. It is not too much to say that a Concert-room Organ without a full complement of such high-class imitative string-toned stops is hopelessly insufficient; and the same can now be safely said of a Chamber Organ schemed on our advanced principles of tonal appointment. Such imitative stops are also valuable, but to lesser degree, in large Church Organs, where, judiciously and artistically used, they may produce effective accompanimental combinations and solo effects.

In attempting to treat of the construction of the imitative string-toned stops which have been designed and fabricated by the artists alluded to, we are confronted with difficulties which neither pen nor pencil can adequately cope with. Such being the case, it is only possible for us to state a few general facts relative to scales and mouth treatments derived from representative stops. The range of the scales which have been adopted in the fabrication of the imitative string-toned stops of the VIOLIN and VIOLONCELLO class is greater than the range presented by any other class of organ stops, ancient or modern. This statement is fully supported by the fact that the scales used by Mr. Thynne and other eminent voicers for the CC (8 ft.) pipes of their VIOLIN stops range from a diameter of 3.13 inches to the small diameter of 1.13 inches, the former scale being developed on the ratio 1:2.519, while the latter appears to be on the ratio 1:2. Mr. Thynne did not favor the adoption of very small scales, and our experience leads us to agree with his opinion; for we have yet to hear finer stops than he produced. The thin, rasping, and unduly assertive tones of the over-blown small-scaled VIOLS of to-day are objectionable to the cultivated ear; but they lend their aid to the present craze for high-pressure noise, rather than to refined and reposeful musical sound. But that craze will kill itself in time.

From the accompanying diagram, Fig. LII., some idea may be formed of the extreme scales of the CC pipes given above, in comparison with a

CC pipe of the Principal or Diapason, 8 ft., of normal scale. The respective diameters are as accurately rendered as practical in so small a diagram, while the respective lengths are only approximate. It will be observed that the Viols are slotted near their tops, a treatment apparently invariably adopted in voicing such stops. As slotting has a decided tendency to impart a horn-like character to the tonality of a pipe, unless it is made wider than three-fifths the diameter of the pipe, it must be resorted to with great judgment and always under the guidance of long experience and a sensitive ear for musical tone.

When the slots exceed three-fifths the diameter they assume the form of a tuning-device. We do not approve of tuning by such a method, as there is always a risk of affecting, undesirably, the *timbre* of the pipes. These remarks apply only to such pipes as yield pure organ-tone, flute-tone, and imitative string-tone, all of which tones have no affinity with a hard horny tonality. It must be admitted, however, that slotting, in the hands of an artistic voicer, may be employed to produce valuable varieties of *timbre* in certain classes of stops. As a common tuning expedient it is to be emphatically condemned.

The mouths of the string-toned pipes of which we have given the scales vary slightly in their widths. In the largest scale adopted by Mr. Thynne the mouth of the CC pipe is two-ninths its circumference. This width is graduated to one-third at c^2, that proportion being retained to the top note. In the largest scale favored by the well-known English voicer, Mr. John W. Whiteley, for his series of "small Viols," the mouth of the CC pipe is one-fifth the circumference. This width is gradually increased in the pipes of the bass and two following octaves to one-fourth at c^2, that proportion being retained to the top note. In the smallest scale the mouth of the CC pipe is two-ninths its circumference, while from the c^2 pipe to the top the mouths are two-sevenths the circumferences of the respective pipes. The heights of the mouths in these pipes vary from one-fourth to one-third their widths; but no fixed rules or clear directions can be formulated in this matter, as the pressure of wind employed—ranging between 2½ inches and 15 inches in executed examples—and the character of the tone desired are controlling factors.

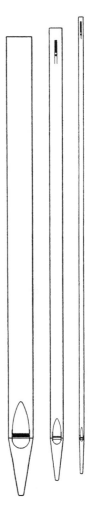

Fig. LII.

In the matter of nicking it is also difficult to lay down directions of general application.   Alluding to his own methods, Mr. Whiteley says: "Wide nicks, placed about the width of the nicks apart, induce fulness of tone.   If this nicking is placed too close together, or made deeper than wide, it will incline the speech toward unsteadiness.   The same tendency obtains if the mouth is too high or too wide.   The lighter the wind-pressure, the fewer and finer the nicks.   In some cases I have nicked the lip only, and in others the languid only.   My general practice is to nick the languid sufficiently to master the dry, acrid quality of the first speech, then to nick the lip in proportion to the amount of bloom I desire for the particular stop in hand.   It is quite easy to obtain a slow, dry, acrid tone; the difficulty is to get rid of it, and maintain the desirable freshness and bloom combined with promptness of speech.   I claim for my works," continues this accomplished voicer, "whether of large or small scales, that they are absolutely perfect in repetition, firmly voiced, and not easily upset.   I have voiced VIOL stops on wind-pressures ranging from 2½ to 15 inches, and in many different degrees of strength, from a bold incisive keenness to the most delicate and characteristic *timbre* possible."

We now come to the indispensable adjunct to the mouths of all the imitative string-toned pipes; namely, the harmonic-bridge—an improvement on the *frein harmonique* already described.   The best form of the harmonic-bridge is the cylindrical, although the semi-cylindrical shape was commonly used by the late Mr. Thynne for pipes from the tenor octave upward.   The shape, however, has not predominant influence; in the production of the proper tone, the position of the harmonic-bridge is practically controlling.   The requisite position with respect to the lower lip of the mouth cannot be fixed by any rule; it has to be determined by actual test in the case of every individual pipe: and as this determination is governed by the musical sense and delicacy of ear on the part of the voicer, one can easily understand why the works of different voicers vary to the great extent they do.   The vast influence the harmonic-bridge exercises over the normal tone of an open pipe can be realized when it is known that it is possible to so place it, with respect to the mouth, that it will cause the pipe to sound the sub-octave as well as its ground tone; while, on the other hand, it can be so adjusted as to invest the ground tone with a complex structure of upper partials, imitative of the compound tones of the orchestral string instruments.   It is in this latter direction that the great value of the harmonic-bridge obtains in pipe construction.   For pipes longer than four feet, and of medium scales, the harmonic-bridges may be of close-grained hard wood, preferably boxwood, turned and highly polished; and for smaller pipes they should be of aluminium tubing, of the several diameters required for the different sizes of pipes.   Instead of such tubing, bridges of hard pipe-metal, cast to graduated sizes, are commonly used. Mr. Thynne used pipe-metal bridges of semi-cylindrical form; but Mr. Whiteley prefers aluminium tubing, and, certainly, nothing could be better from any point of view. Bridges of this material are light, firm, smooth, and do not corrode. No definite measurements can be formulated for the diameters of the bridges, for they depend on the dimensions of the mouths, the wind-pressure employed, and, above all, on the character of tone required, and the peculiar method of the voicer in securing that tone. Accordingly, we find considerable differences both in the diameters and positions of the harmonic-bridges in the imitative string-toned pipes of different makers, just as we find in them marked differences of tone. The bridges are supported between the projecting ears of the mouths, and when accurately adjusted by the voicer, are fixed by screws or pins driven through the ears, by projections punched from

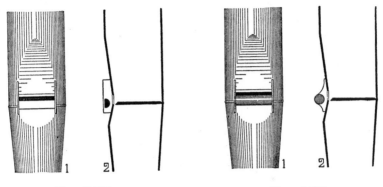

Fig. LIII. Fig. LIV.

the ears, or by solder, as the materials or forms of the bridges dictate. It has been found by expert voicers that the character of the string-tone and promptness of speech are to some extent influenced by the dimensions and form of the pipe-ears which support the harmonic-bridges; but here, again, no hard and fast rules obtain. Mr. Thynne and the generality of voicers have used ears of the ordinary form, as shown in Fig. LIII., while Mr. Whiteley, in his more advanced methods, uses ears cut away above and below the harmonic-bridge in the manner shown in Fig. LIV. Judging by tonal results, there seems to be no question as to the superiority of this latter form of ear for all purely imitative string-toned pipes. If the reader will glance at Plate XXIX., Chapter XV., which represents a VIOLONCELLO pipe as constructed by Mr. Whiteley, he will observe the same cut-away treatment of what are practically ears. There can be no doubt, we venture to think, that as much freedom as possible should be given to the action of the pipe-wind and its induced currents at the mouths of pipes furnished with harmonic-bridges. In the VIOLINS and VIOLONCELLOS voiced by Mr. Thynne, while their tones are very beautiful, they are somewhat slow in rapid repetition. This imperfection is entirely absent from the same stops voiced by Mr. Whiteley: and, probably, the freedom his form of ear gives to the wind at the mouth is a potent factor in securing promptness of articulation.

The Violin of the orchestra does not go below tenor G (commonly called fiddle G), and it would appear proper to stop the downward range of the imitative VIOLIN of the Organ on this note. Such a mode of procedure is certainly not to be recommended, for a short stop in any division of the Organ is an abomination and the father of endless tonal imperfections. To get over this apparent incongruity, it has been suggested to label the complete stop VIOLIN & VIOLONCELLO, 8 FT., but this is undesirable simply because there is another stop, properly called VIOLONCELLO, the tone of which closely imitates that of the orchestral instrument; and this valuable stop will in all likelihood appear along with the VIOLIN, 8 FT., in the same Organ. It should be borne in mind that if it is incorrect to carry the VIOLIN, 8 FT., below G, it is equally incorrect to carry the VIOLONCELLO, 8 FT., above g^2—the highest natural note of the true instrument in ordinary playing.

A most effective orchestral coloring has been given, in some rare cases, to the imitative string-tone forces of the Organ by associating with the correctly-tuned unison VIOLIN one or two VIOLS of similar imitative tone, tuned slightly out of accord. When one VIOL is added, it should be of smaller scale than the solo VIOLIN, and tuned a few beats sharp; and when a second VIOL is added, it should be of a scale a pipe or two larger than the solo VIOLIN, and tuned a few beats flat. When played in combination, these stops produce the effect of a number of Violins played together in unison, just as one hears them in the orchestra.

VIOLE SOURDINE, VIOLINO SORDO, or MUTED VIOLIN.—This stop is formed of small-scale, conical pipes, the mouths of which are treated in precisely the same manner as above described for those of the VIOLIN or VIOLE D'ORCHESTRE. The most approved scale for this stop gives the CC (8 ft.) pipe a diameter of 1.53 inches at its mouth line, and a diameter of 0.51 inch at its top, with the ratio of 1:2 for the complete stop. The tone of the stop imitates that of the muted Violin of the orchestra, and is a most valuable voice for the true Chamber Organ. The pipes of this stop and all the small-scale VIOLINS should be of tin, or an alloy containing not less than 75 per cent pure tin. The slender form of the pipes, especially in the bass and tenor octaves, renders a light and stiff metal imperative, to say nothing of the benefit it affords to the tone.

VIOLINO or OCTAVE VIOLIN.—This stop, of 4 ft. pitch, is properly formed of tin pipes in all respects similar in construction and voicing to the corresponding pipes of the VIOLE D'ORCHESTRE, 8 FT. It has been argued that, as the Violin sounds are sometimes carried above c⁴ of the Organ, it is desirable to provide an imitative string-toned stop of octave pitch for special solo effects. There can be no doubt that such a stop would be extremely valuable in combination with the unison VIOLE D'ORCHESTRE. The pipes of the VIOLINO, 4 FT., should be made one or two pipes smaller in scale than those of the unison stop. For perfect combinational effects, the octave tones should be subordinate to the unison ones. This is a rule of universal application in the tonal structure of the Organ. An octave stop of smaller scale and more delicate intonation, under the name VIOLETTA, is to be highly recommended for the Chamber Organ, where it would produce charming effects both in solo passages and in combination with other stops of the same or different tonality. The pipes of the VIOLETTA, 4 FT., should be of small scale and, preferably, conical in form. Such a stop when softly voiced or muted would form the true OCTAVE to the VIOLINO SORDO, 8 FT.

VIOLONCELLO.—There can be no question, we venture to think, that the rich and broad tones of the orchestral Violoncello can be best imitated by wood pipes, especially in the lower octaves. While we are free to admit that admirable metal VIOLONCELLOS have been made, we strongly advise that all the pipes which are embraced in the true compass of the orchestral instrument be made of wood, while the few remaining pipes may be conveniently made of metal, voiced fuller in tone than the corresponding pipes of the VIOLIN. Full particulars respecting the imitative string-toned pipes constructed of wood will be found in Chapter XV. When the VIOLONCELLO, 8 FT., is made entirely of metal, its pipes should be of comparatively large scale, having their mouths treated in precisely the same manner as those of the VIOLIN. The artistic voicer will proportion the mouths, execute the nicking, and provide and fix in position harmonic-bridges of requisite diameters, so as to produce the rich full tone of the orchestral Violoncello. The stop so treated will yield a tone perfectly distinct in *timbre* from that yielded by the VIOLIN, while it will combine with it in the most satisfactory manner, producing a compound tone of great volume and rich color.

VIOLA.—Speaking of the Viola, Berlioz remarks: " Of all the instruments of the orchestra, the one whose excellent qualities have been longest misappreciated, is the Viola. It is no less agile than the Violin, the sound of its strings is peculiarly telling, its upper notes are distinguished by their mournfully passionate accent, and its quality of tone altogether, of a profound melancholy, differs from that of other instruments played with a bow." These particulars will afford some inspiration to the artistic voicer in creating the VIOLA of the Organ. They point out to him the necessity of imparting to the stop a *timbre* distinct from that of the VIOLIN and VIOLONCELLO. No words, however expressive, can educate the ear sufficiently to enable the voicer to produce a correct imitation. "There is no royal road to learning," so nothing but enthusiastic study and careful observation can lead to good results. Let the voicer call in the aid of a competent Viola player, and, in the quiet of the voicing-room, let him exercise all his knowledge and skill until his pipes yield tones that can hardly be distinguished from those of the orchestral instrument. A similar practice has been followed in producing imitations of the tones of the Violin and Violoncello, and it has been attended with marked success. In constructing and voicing the pipes of the Viola, 8 ft., the methods which have been found successful in connection with the pipes of the Viola and Violoncello will certainly have to be followed. We have not heard during our many years of observation and study in organ matters a single Viola stop which could be said to be strictly imitative. That a stop yielding a tone between the bright and incisive voice of the Orchestral Violin and the richer and fuller voice of the Orchestral Violoncello is called for in the string-toned forces of the Concert Organ of the Twentieth Century, must be evident to everyone who has thoroughly studied the subject of tonal appointment from an artistic point of view.

Contra-Basso or Violone.—Although we are of opinion that the tones of the orchestral Contra-Basso can be best imitated by wood pipes, constructed and voiced on the Schulze system, there is no question that highly satisfactory results can be obtained from metal pipes. To obtain the strictly imitative tones required, the pipes, cylindrical in form, must be of small scale; practically carrying down that of the metal Violoncello, 8 ft., and their mouths must be treated in the same manner as that above described for the unison imitative string-toned stops. When the Contra-Basso, 16 ft., is inserted in a Pedal Organ (its usual place) in which a Violoncello is also inserted, it is desirable to impart a distinctive breadth of tone to it, just as one hears in the orchestra, by making its pipes of larger scale and to a slower ratio than the corresponding pipes of the Violoncello. There is no manner of doubt that an imitative Contra-Basso, 16 ft., is an all-important feature of a complete Pedal Organ. It should in all Concert-room Organs be preferred to the unimitative Violone, 16 ft., so commonly found in modern instruments.

METAL PIPES OF SPECIAL TONALITIES.

There are very few metal labial stops which yield tones which are markedly distinct from those properly classed as organ-tone, flute-tone, and string-tone; but, in saying this, we do not desire to convey the idea that the field in this direction has been thoroughly ploughed and cultivated. Some more workers are wanted in this important field, so soon as they can spare time and thought, from comparatively unimportant mechanical details, to devote to tonal matters. We may point out one direction in which very desirable results await the skilful and pains-taking pipe maker and voicer; we allude to the production of certain classes of tone at present only yielded by brass instruments of the orchestra—notably the Horns. We do not despair of hearing a satis-factory imitation of the tones of the orchestral Horn produced from labial pipes: indeed, we had in our own Chamber Organ a metal stop of the KERAULOPHONE class, from the tenor and middle octaves of which tones were produced closely resembling those of the Horn softly played. It is also very desirable that serious essays be made to produce what is commonly recognized as reed-tone from metal labial pipes. Very satis-factory results in this direction have already been obtained from wood labial pipes: these are recorded in the following Chapter. In the prog-ress of study and experiment, even should complete success not be reached, it is more than probable that some very valuable additions would be made to the timbre-creating forces of the Organ of the Twentieth Century.

Several indeterminate qualities of tone have, during recent times, been added to the voices of the Organ; but these are destined to exert very little, if any, influence on the desirable and artistic tonal appoint-ment of the instrument. Fanciful, inexpressive, and in certain instances ridiculous names have been given to the stops claimed by their makers to be new inventions, whereas they are either slight modifications of old-established forms, or old forms producing modifications of established voices, due to the necessary alterations in voicing and other expedients under the abnormal and undesirable heavy wind-pressures which are now doing so much to sweep refinement, repose, and beauty from the general tonality of the King of Instruments.

As we have already said, there is one very desirable tone which still awaits production in labial pipes; namely, Orchestral Horn-tone. From the little that has already shown itself in certain existing stops, we feel strongly that the peculiar and pathetic voice, and the somewhat mourn-ful and mysterious tones of the " stopped notes " of the orchestral in-strument, if they are ever produced in the Organ, will emanate from labial pipes. We may briefly describe two stops which, as their names imply, have a tendency to yield horn-like sounds.

KERAULOPHONE.—When first made—due to an accident it is said—this stop was observed to produce a peculiar horn-like tone sufficiently pronounced to suggest the distinctive name given to it, derived from the Greek words κέρας—a horn, αὐλός—a pipe, and φωνή—sound.

The pipes of the KERAULOPHONE, 8 FT., are cylindrical and of medium scale. That which, in the ratio 1:2·66, gives the CC pipe a diameter of 3·94 inches; the C pipe a diameter of 2·41 inches; and the c¹ pipe a diameter of 1·47 inches, may be accepted as the largest desirable scale for the stop. Smaller scales have been used by different builders, and should be used when the stop is destined for a Chamber Organ. The mouth of the KERAULOPHONE pipe should be one-fifth the circumference of the pipe in width, and about one-fourth its own width in height. This latter proportion, however, depends on the wind-pressure used and the strength and quality of the tone desired. The upper lip is straight and not pared sharp, and the nicking of the languid is moderately fine. The mouth has small ears without any harmonic attachment. The characteristic feature of the pipe, and that which is the chief factor in imparting the refined horn-like quality to the tone, is its perforated tuning-slide of the form shown in Fig. LV. The length of

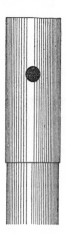

FIG. LV.

the slide is about two and a half times the diameter of the pipe; and the perforation should be made at the distance of the diameter of the slide from the open end. In the CC pipe the diameter of the perforation should be 0·79 inch; in the C pipe 0·56 inch, and diminishing, in the ratio 1 : 2, to the diameter of 0·14 inch in the c⁴ or top pipe of the stop. The slides must be so accurately fitted to the bodies of the pipes as to firmly retain their position while they can be easily tapped up or down in the process of tuning. In our opinion, stops of the KERAULOPHONE class have not yet received the attention they deserve; for there can be no doubt that, skilfully treated, they are capable of giving valuable voices to the Organ.

GEMSHORN.—The tone of the GEMSHORN varies considerably in different existing examples, while in all it seems to be indeterminate. In its most desirable tonality it has a bright horny *timbre,* from which it has evidently earned its name.

The pipes of the GEMSHORN are conical in form, their open tops having diameters equal to one-third of the diameters at their mouth lines. This is the accepted rule, but, like all rules in pipe-proportions, it is open to modification under artistic treatment. The scale of the GEMSHORN, like that of all other stops, varies according to the ideas of different builders and the volume of tone desired. A good scale for a Concert-room or Church Organ stop, in the ratio 1 : 2.519, gives the CC pipe a diameter, at the mouth line, of 4.96 inches and a diameter at the top of 1·62 inches; the C pipe diameters of 3·13 inches and 1·02 inches; and the c¹ pipe diameters of 1·97 inches and 0·64 inch. For a true Chamber Organ the above scale may be made four pipes smaller, the CC pipe being 4.26 inches in diameter at its mouth line. The width of the mouth should be two-ninths of the larger circumference of the pipe, and its height should be one-fourth its width.

CHAPTER XV.

FORMS AND CONSTRUCTION OF WOOD PIPES.

HE subject of the present Chapter is one which has been almost entirely neglected by writers on the Organ and organ construction; yet it is one of great importance and interest, and certainly should be well understood by every one connected with organ designing and tonal appointment. Probably the matters which have prevented other writers from entering at all deeply into the subject is the want of personal experience in actual pipe making, on the one hand, and the difficulty of preparing or obtaining proper and adequate practical illustrations, on the other. Both, however, are absolutely essential to a satisfactory disquisition on the subject of the forms and construction of wood pipes, required for the production of different varieties of tone.

As this question of the production of different qualities of tone is one of paramount importance, it may justly claim attention in this place, and before we enter on purely practical matters of construction.

The sound of a labial organ-pipe is generated at its mouth by the rapid vibratory action of the wind-stream or wind-sheet which rushes from its wind-way across the mouth, setting up shocks, pulses, or tremors throughout the column of air within the pipe. This action we shall attempt to describe as we understand it. This much we know to be the case; but beyond this simple and evident fact we acknowledge we know very little. We leave it to others to be, in their conceit, dogmatic on the subject. The varied opinions held by acousticians and others who seem to have given some attention to the subject, go to prove how unsatisfactory is the present knowledge of the behavior of the air in producing sound of different qualities in pipes of different form and construction. It must be admitted, after an exhaustive study of all

the experiments made and theories advanced by the acousticians who
have written on the subject of organ-pipes, that science has done very
little to help the organ-builder and pipe-voicer, to whom, at the present
time, simple traditional methods and practical experience are of infinitely
more value than all that scientific research has placed at their disposal.

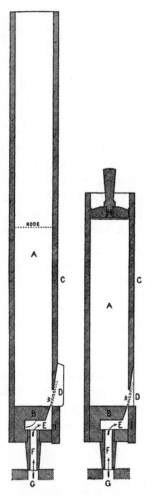

Before proceeding to treat on the
varied forms and modes of construction
of labial pipes, we may properly state,
at this point, that there are three general
families of such pipes—namely, the *open,*
the *covered* or *stopped,* and the *half-
covered* or *partially-stopped.* While the
forms and the methods of construction
of all these pipes differ considerably in
certain directions, it must be understood
that their sounds are generated in precisely the same manner and by the same
means. A brief description may now be
given of the two leading forms—the
open pipe and the *stopped pipe*—which,
though similar in general conformation
in what may be considered the normal
type, produce tones of entirely different
character or timbre.

Fig. LVI. is the Longitudinal Section
of an open wood pipe, the body, A, of
which is quadrangular in form, constructed of four boards glued together at
their edges and to the block B. The face-
board C is shorter than the others, and
thinned at its lower end so as to form the
upper lip of the mouth of the pipe, D.
The block B is cut to the section shown,
in which the throat E is for the free passage of the compressed air, which is sent
from the wind-chest G, through the chan-

Fig. LVI.   Fig. LVII.   nel in the pipe-foot F. The direction of
the wind is indicated by the small arrows.
The front of the block B is covered by the cap I; and between the
upper sharp edge of the block and the inner upper edge of the cap is
a narrow slit, extending the width of the mouth, and forming the wind-
way through which the compressed air rushes upward, in a thin sheet,
across the mouth. The direction of this wind-sheet or -stream, immediately before the pipe speaks, is indicated by the dotted lines at W.

The first fact to be observed is that when the pipe is made to speak its fundamental tone the column of air within its body, A, divides itself into two slightly unequal portions, separated by a stratum of air apparently at rest; both the divisions being in a state of tremor or molecular vibration, the exact nature of which has never been satisfactorily determined. The dividing stratum of air, which is obviously the place of latent energy and opposing force, is commonly designated the node of the pipe; and its position (which is variable under controlling conditions) is hypothetically indicated by the horizontal dotted line marked NODE. It will be shown later on that when a pipe is forced to speak its harmonic upper partial tones, two or more nodes are formed in its vibrating air-column.

In Fig. LVII. is given a Longitudinal Section of a quadrangular stopped or covered pipe, drawn to the same scale as the adjoining open pipe, so as to show, as nearly as practicable, the relative lengths of an open and stopped pipe yielding notes of the same pitch, that is, sounding in unison. It will be observed that the differences which obtain between the pipes lie in their respective lengths, and in the addition to the shorter one of the stopper H. This stopper is formed of wood covered with leather, so as to make it fit air-tight, and yet allow of its being raised or lowered in the process of tuning. The lower portion of the pipe and the construction of the mouth and wind-way are essentially similar to those of the open pipe. When the stopped pipe speaks its fundamental tone, there is no node formed in its internal column of air; the under surface of the stopper fulfilling the same office in tone production as the node in the open pipe. Accordingly, while the pipe speaks its fundamental tone the entire column of air within it is set in vibration by the action of the wind-stream at its mouth.

Before proceeding further, we may briefly allude to the ideas which have been formulated respecting the manner in which the column of air within an organ-pipe, while it yields, by increased wind pressure, its first and second harmonic over-tones, divides itself by means of separating nodes. While we admit that the conclusions are reasonable and to a considerable extent logical, we cannot but look upon them as hypothetical. In Fig. LVIII. are given a series of Longitudinal Sections of an open organ-pipe, in which are indicated the various positions of the nodes, as formulated.

As before stated, the column of air within the body of an open pipe while yielding its fundamental tone is divided, according to the accepted theory, into two parts separated by a node. This primal division is indicated in Sections A and B. The arrows show the supposed direction of the pulses in the process of condensation in the pipe A, and the direction of the pulses in the process of rarefaction in the pipe B; similar motions obtaining from both sides of the node. When the same pipe is

made, by increased wind pressure or other means, to speak the first
upper partial tone—the Octave—of its prime or fundamental tone, the
column of air within it is believed to be divided into three parts, separated by two nodes, in the manner indicated in Sections C and D.
The nodes are at N, N. It will be observed, the central division of the
column is equal in length to both the other parts added together. The
arrows indicate the directions of the pulses in the several divisions.
When the same pipe is made to speak its proper second upper partial
tone, the column of air within it is believed to be divided into four

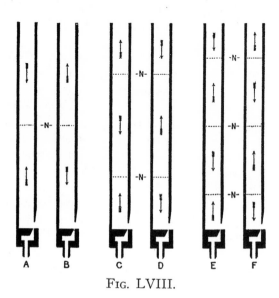

Fig. LVIII.

parts, separated by three nodes, N, N, N, as indicated in the Sections
E and F. The two parts, separated by the node, in Sections A and B,
are termed by acousticians " semi-ventral segments." In the Sections C
and D, the larger central part is termed a " ventral segment," the lower
and upper parts being semi-ventral segments. A similar condition obtains in Sections E and F. Therefore, it will be seen that the mouth of
an open pipe is at all times at the middle of a ventral segment; or, in
other words, that the part of the column of air adjoining the mouth is
a semi-ventral segment.

We may now consider the conditions believed to obtain in the air-
column within a stopped pipe while yielding its fundamental and its first
and second upper partial tones, employing another series of Sections—
Fig. LIX.—to elucidate the subject. When a stopped pipe yields its
fundamental tone no division takes place in the column of air within it,
as indicated in Sections G, H, for in this case the under side of the
stopper occupies the office of the upper semi-ventral segment as it

obtains in an open pipe (A, B, in Fig. LVIII.), and, accordingly, serves
as a node at N.   The pulses due to condensation and rarefaction moving up and down unobstructed within the air-column, as indicated by
the arrows.   The complete column is therefore a semi-ventral segment.
Under controlling conditions it is not possible to make a stopped pipe
speak the Octave of its fundamental tone: its first upper partial tone is
the Twelfth.   When a stopped pipe speaks this upper partial, the column
of air within it is understood to be divided into two parts separated
by a node, as indicated in Sections I and J; the under side of the stopper
continuing to be nodal.   When the same stopped pipe is made to speak

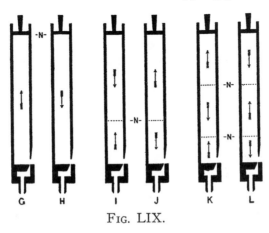

F𝐈G. LIX.

its second upper partial tone—the Seventeenth or Tierce—the column
of air is divided into three parts—a semi-ventral segment and two ventral
segments—separated by two nodes and bounded by the nodal surface of
the stopper, as indicated in Sections K and L.

    It is supposed that theoretically there is no limit to the division of
the column of air in a tube or pipe, either open or stopped; but in
practice its divisions are very limited, as all who are acquainted with
the voicing of organ-pipes are aware.   In an open pipe commencement
is made with two semi-ventral segments, the pipe yielding its prime or
fundamental tone: then the division of the column proceeds in even
numbers of semi-ventral segments; namely, four, six, eight, and so on.
In a stopped pipe commencement is made with one semi-ventral segment,
the pipe yielding its fundamental tone: then the division of the column
proceeds in odd numbers of semi-ventral segments; namely, three, five,
seven, and so on.   Accordingly, when we voice an open pipe to speak
its first harmonic or upper partial tone, we produce the octave of its
prime or fundamental tone; but when we treat a stopped pipe in a
similar manner, we produce a note a twelfth above its prime tone.   No
intermediate modes of vibration are in either case possible.

How is sound produced in organ-pipes? This is a question that has evidently exercised many minds, and it is a remarkable fact that professing acousticians have been among those who have signally failed to answer it in any way approaching a satisfactory manner. Owing to limited space at our disposal we can only, in these pages, treat the question in the briefest manner.* We must, accordingly, confine our remarks to the action that goes on at the mouths of pipes while they are producing their musical tones; for it must be clearly understood that it is at their mouths, and at their mouths only, that their sounds are generated. If open pipes alone produced sound, such a statement might, perhaps, be questioned, but as stopped pipes are equally good sound-producers it admits of no reasonable doubt.

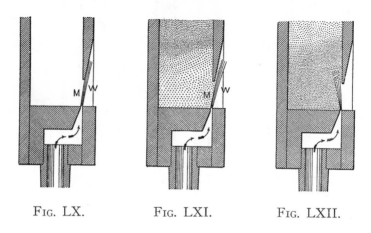

FIG. LX.   FIG. LXI.   FIG. LXII.

At the outset, it must be understood that the compressed air (from the bellows) which issues from the wind-way, between the cap and block of the organ-pipe, ascends across the mouth of the pipe in the form of a thin sheet. This wind-sheet or wind-stream takes a course, directed slightly in an outward direction, so as to escape striking the edge of the upper lip of the mouth. This position of the wind-stream, taken at the first instant of its rush from the wind-way across the mouth, is roughly indicated in the accompanying illustration, Fig. LX., which is a Vertical Section through the mouth and lower portion of an ordinary wood FLUTE pipe. M is the mouth of the pipe where the sound is generated, and W represents the wind-stream, issuing from the wind-way between the cap and block and passing across the mouth in an outward direction so as to escape the edge of the upper lip and glide along the outer sloping surface. When a pipe is properly voiced so as to speak promptly and firmly, this is the initial direction given to the wind-stream.

* The subject is fully discussed in the Chapter on Acoustical Matters Connected with Organ Pipes, in the First Volume of our work—" The Art of Organ-Building "—pp. 357-404.

If it is directed so as to pass a slight distance in front of the sloping surface, the pipe will be slow of speech; and if the wind-stream is directed still farther in the outward direction, the pipe will not speak at all. On the other hand, the pipe will produce no sound if the wind-stream is directed inward, or so as to split against the edge—thin or thick—of the upper lip. These are facts well known to scientific voicers.

While the wind-stream remains in the initial position, indicated in Fig. LX., no sound is created; but it is rapidly instituting a condition in the air-column within the pipe that will enable it to generate a musical note. It is impossible for a rapidly rushing stream of compressed air to be directed immediately across an opening in any tube or vessel, without its exerting a certain power of suction, and of drawing toward and into itself whatever is close to the opening and of a nature capable of being easily moved and carried away. This action of the wind-stream at the mouth of a large organ-pipe is clearly proved by placing on the block or languid, within the mouth and immediately behind the wind-way, some filaments of cotton or down, and then admitting wind to the pipe: the filaments are shot out with considerable energy, showing the suction exerted by the wind-stream.

The first action of the rushing wind-stream is to abstract the air, within the pipe, which is in the immediate neighborhood of the mouth, forming, for the instant, a partial vacuum there. This state of the air within the pipe is diagrammatically shown in Fig. LXI. by the few and widely-spaced dots in the neighborhood of the mouth, M, in comparison with the closer and darker dotting higher in the pipe, which indicates the less disturbed portion of the air-column. As already said, the first effect of the suction exercised by the rushing wind-stream is the creation of a partial vacuum behind the stream; and this being increased by the continuity of the operating force becomes a more and more decided vacuum. To fill this partial vacuum the rest of the air-column in the pipe expands (to make our explanation clear let a stopped pipe be understood), and, in the natural order of things, sets in rapid motion every particle of air within the pipe. The active extraction of the internal air into the rushing wind-stream, and also between it and the outer surface of the upper lip of the pipe, causes the wind-stream to swell in volume and swing in an outward direction. This position of the wind-stream we have attempted to indicate in Fig. LXI. When the wind-stream has reached its outward limit, and has exerted all its power of suction, under the controlling conditions imposed by the nature and proportions of the pipe, a natural reaction sets in, caused by the rarefaction of the internal air, on the one hand, and the pressure of the external air, on the other; the latter pressing on the outer surface of the wind-stream in its attempt to fill, or bring to an equilibrium, the exhausted air within the pipe.

At the second stage of its operation, above alluded to, the wind-stream swings inward, past the edge of the upper lip, first reinstating the equilibrium between the internal and external air, and then, inverting its initial operation, shocking the internal air-column by a sudden and forcible condensation, and creating at the same instant a partial vacuum in the external air immediately adjoining its outer surface. The direction of the wind-stream at this stage is diagrammatically represented in Fig. LXII., in which the supposed condensation is indicated by close and dark dotting. The instant this state of the internal air-column is reached an inevitable reaction takes place, and, relieved from active external pressure, and assisted by the condensed state of the internal column, which naturally seeks the state of equilibrium, the wind-stream swings outward, resuming its original position, with reference to the upper lip, and its active operation on the air within the pipe, now greatly assisted by its condensed condition. The slowness of speech in pipes under certain styles of voicing is probably due to the fact that the wind-stream is at the start unassisted by the air-columns within them, which are not then in a state of disturbance.

It has taken many words and occupied several minutes to outline the operations of a single inward and outward swing of the wind-stream; but it must be realized that in the process of generating a musical tone these operations may have to be repeated many hundreds of times in a second, and that with unvarying precision and regularity. From the description given, it will be realized that the wind-stream at the mouth of an organ-pipe is in reality a rapidly vibrating wind-tongue somewhat resembling the metallic tongue in the free-reed of the harmonium. Mr. Hermann Smith calls the air-stream an " aëro-plastic reed," or simply an " air-reed." He remarks: " The aëro-plastic reed forming with the pipe a *system* of transverse vibration associated with longitudinal vibration, and possibly another phase of vibration across the width of the reed enabling it to synchronize with the harmonic range of the pipe; the principle of action of the whole being termed, in my non-academic phraseology, suction by velocity; but if a more exact expression is found its explanation should imply, or better still, include the axiomatic phrase of Sir William Thomson, ' in a moving fluid the pressure is least where velocity is greatest.' To state the existence of an air-moulded free-reed is to give the key to its nature. . . . Velocity is power, and in every conjunction of reed and pipe the reed in dominant. Most distinctly it should be recognized that the air-reed does *work* and expends power in doing it." *

* The late Mr. Hermann Smith was the first to formulate the theory which we advocate, and which, up to the present time, is the only one that is consistent with all observed phenomena. For a complete presentation of his arguments and views, set forth in extensive quotations from his published writings on the subject, we must refer the interested reader to Chapter IX., on Acoustical Matters connected with Organ Pipes, in our work " The Art of Organ-Building."

There can be no doubt, we venture to say, that some such action as above described takes place at the mouth of an organ-pipe while it is speaking. Considerable force on the part of the wind-stream or air-reed is necessary to set instantaneously into a state of excitement or tremor the column of air in a large organ-pipe; and one can hardly imagine any other motion or action of the wind-stream capable of imparting the necessary disturbance to the resonating and synchronizing air-column within the pipe. While the mode of sound-production at the mouth of the pipe is not easily realized, from analogy we may accept it as due to the intense vibration or molecular disturbance of the air immediately at the mouth, which vibration is influenced by both the form and dimensions of the internal air-column; for, as we have already observed, no positive sound issues from the air-column itself. The exact nature of the synchronizing vibration or disturbance in the air-column cannot well be decided; but while it may have some relation to the velocity of sound conduction in air, its phenomena go to prove that it can have little to do with the hypothetical wave-lengths, as taught by Tyndall and other wave-theorists. That there is a close relationship between the rushing wind-stream at the mouth and the proportions of the responding and resonating column within the pipe, and that they exert a mutual influence, are self-evident; but in exactly what manner this mutual influence is exerted, and what the conditions are that modify it in the way one observes in pipes of different forms, proportions of parts, scales, etc., have never been satisfactorily explained.

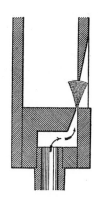

FIG. LXIII.

In concluding these few remarks on this interesting subject, we may direct attention to the accompanying illustration, Fig. LXIII., which is a Vertical Section through the mouth of a pipe, in which the dotted fan-like figure, which issues from the wind-way and curves outward and inward as it sweeps past the upper lip of the mouth, graphically portrays the swing of the stream-reed while the pipe is speaking. Only part of the stream is shown, and its swing is greatly exaggerated for the sake of clearness. Mr. Hermann Smith's investigations and experiments seem to point conclusively to this action of the wind-stream in producing sound in a labial pipe.

Experience and practice, aided by traditional methods, have taught the average organ-builder and organ expert all they know about pipes and sound-production: acoustical science, in its popular aspect, teaching in direct opposition to known and self-evident facts, has given them absolutely no assistance. On the contrary, the modern acoustician has taken pipes from the hands of the organ-builder, and, without careful study and investigation, has endeavored to extract some support to his pet theory from them. He has signally failed, as we have already pointed out. It is time some humility should be learned; and acknowledgment made that in matters of sound-generation and subsequent conduction very little is known beyond what natural phenomena seem to imply.

THE CONSTRUCTION OF WOOD PIPES.

The construction of wood organ pipes is extremely simple, calling for nothing but ordinary skill and the manipulation of the common tools used by the joiner. In large workshops the usual labor-saving machinery and appliances are, of course, resorted to in the preparation of the wood for the subsequent manual processes.

As a suitable starting-point, we shall describe the construction of pipes of the ordinary GEDECKT or so-called STOPPED DIAPASON, 8 FT. A pipe of this stop, so far as the general form of its tube or body and the shape and treatment of its mouth are concerned, may be accepted as the normal type of the quadrangular wood organ-pipe. A pipe so formed may or may not be furnished with a stopper; for, save as regards the proportions of length to transverse scale, there are no essential differences between an *open* CLARABELLA pipe and an ordinary GEDECKT or *stopped* pipe.

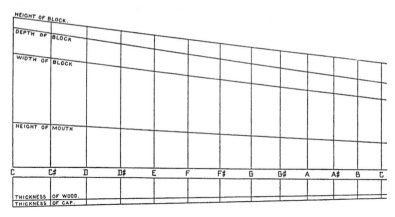

Fig. LXIV.

Before proceeding to construct a stop of wood pipes, it is necessary to procure a correct and well-approved scale, giving dimensions for the blocks, thicknesses of wood, heights of mouths, and sizes of caps; and also a rod with the lengths marked thereon, to which the pipes have to be cut when finished. It is sufficient for our present purpose to give a reduced representation of the scale of one octave, showing the manner in which all the chief finished dimensions are clearly marked for the guidance of the pipe maker. Fig. LXIV. may be considered the scale for the bass or lowest octave, the CC or lowest pipe of which will measure rather more than 4 feet in length, and the rest proportionate, the C pipe being a little over 2 feet in length from its block. In using this scale, measurements must be taken in all cases from the datum line—above it for all the important dimensions, and below it for the approved thicknesses of the pipe sides and caps. The greatest accuracy must be observed in taking off all the important dimensions, for the regularity of tonal coloring in a stop depends to a large extent upon accuracy of workmanship. It is of little use having a correctly developed scale if it is not rigidly adhered to. The only dimensions which are practically matters of taste are the heights of the blocks and caps. These need not be graduated throughout, but may be made of the same height in each octave if preferred.

The blocks are the first portions of the pipes that have to be made. For blocks above 2 inches in depth the wood should be of two or more thicknesses of perfectly dry white pine, placed with the grain in different directions, and faced with some close-grained hard wood, all securely glued together. Blocks so built up stand better than those cut from single pieces of wood. The blocks for the small pipes may advantageously be made of some hard wood, such as cherry or close-grained mahogany. The wood should be glued up in lengths sufficient for six or eight blocks, and extra building-up pieces, of convenient thicknesses, for the tops of the pipes. In some cases it may be desirable to provide for slices, averaging 1½ inches thick, for the stoppers of the larger pipes. Commencing with the CC pipe, the wood should be dressed accurately to the depth and width of its

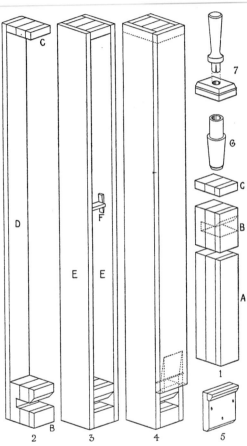

Fig. LXV.

block, having the hard wood on a narrow side, or what will be the face, or exposed side, of the block. The first block must then be carefully and squarely sawn off, in length about an inch more than the scale calls for. This extra length will be cut away when the body of the pipe is finished. A slice should then be sawn from the wood, about an inch thick, to serve as the building-up piece for the top of the pipe. Referring to the accompanying illustration, Fig. LXV., which shows a pipe in the different stages of construction, the block wood is represented at A, in Diagram 1, formed of two thicknesses of white pine with a facing of hard wood, as already described. B is the block cut off, and C is the top building-up piece. When the first block has been thus secured, the piece A must be planed down to the next size on the scale, and the cutting-off process repeated, and so on until all the blocks and building-up pieces have been prepared. The top ends of the blocks must now be smoothed by a plane or sandpaper, the front edges, which form the under lips of the mouths, being left perfectly square and sharp. The next proceeding is the cutting of the throats in the blocks for the passage of the wind, as hereafter described. These should be cut with a fine saw and cleaned with a chisel. The dotted lines in the Block B, in Diagram 1, indicate the direction and form of the cutting; while in the block B, in Diagram 2, the throat is shown finished. The blocks at this stage are ready to be glued to the backs of the pipes.

Measurements taken from the two scales of widths and lengths, with due allowances for the thicknesses of wood and extra length of blocks and building-up pieces, enable the pipe maker to cut the pine boards for the backs and sides, and, subsequently, the hard wood fronts, for the pipe bodies. These should in all cases be sawn slightly in excess of the finished width. When all are thus prepared, they should be dressed to nearly their final thicknesses; and one face of each piece must be planed true and smooth. The back pieces are now taken and one edge of each is shot perfectly straight, and square to the finished face.

We shall at this stage consider the formation of a single pipe, all the pipes of the stop being put together in precisely the same manner. A back is taken, and on one end of its finished face is firmly glued the block, care being taken to accurately adjust one side to the shot edge of the back: at the other end is glued the building-up piece, similarly adjusted. The relative positions of the three pieces, at this stage, are clearly indicated in Diagram 2; B being the finished block, C the building-up piece, and D the back of the pipe. When the glue is thoroughly dry, the undressed edge of the back is planed down until perfectly level with the side of the block and the corresponding side of the building-up piece, care being taken to avoid planing the edge of the back in any way hollow; while if it is very slightly cambered it will be rather an advantage than otherwise. Pipes, and especially large ones, speak more freely when they are a trifle larger, in cross section, in the middle than at the ends. The other edge of the back, which was originally shot, has just a shaving taken from it so as to secure its being perfectly true to the block and the building-up piece. In no case, however, must the block be touched, unless allowance has been made when its width was taken from the scale. Diagram 2, Fig LXV., shows the pipe in the state ready to receive the side boards. These are now taken, and one edge of each is shot straight; they are then adjusted with their shot edges laid in line with the outside of the back board, and small holes are pierced through them close to each end, and into the waste length of the block and the building-up piece. These holes are for small wooden pegs to be used for fixing them in correct position in the necessarily hurried process of gluing up. When the glue is made as hot as possible and is brought to the proper consistency for use, the side boards are warmed at a stove or with a large flat-iron, laid side by side with their finished faces upward and their shot edges close together, and quickly covered with the hot glue at each end, where they will come in contact with the block and building-up piece, and for the necessary width along their faces at the shot edges. One side is quickly placed in position and pegged down, the pipe turned, and the other side immediately manipulated in the same manner. Before the glue has time to set, hand-screws are applied to both ends and at intervals along the back, firmly pressing the sides in contact with the block, back board, and building-up piece.

The pipe having been tightly screwed up, and all the joints examined and found perfectly close, it is turned on its back, and with a brush, dipped in boiling water, the glue that may appear in the inside is washed away locally and spread, in the form of size, all over the inside surfaces of the back, sides, and block. Should the glue in the pipe not be sufficient to size the entire surfaces, some additional weak glue size may be added, for it is desirable that they should be well coated. The pipe is now laid aside to become thoroughly dry.

The hard wood intended for the front of the pipe is carefully dressed, on both sides, to the proper thickness; and one edge and end are shot perfectly straight and square. The inside face of the board is sized like the other inside surfaces, and is then ready for attachment to the pipe.

When the pipe is dry and the hand-screws are removed, it is laid on its back, and the front edges of the sides are planed down until they are level with the faces of the block and building-up piece. There is just a possibility that the sides may have bent inward slightly during the preceding process of gluing, screwing, and sizing, and it is necessary to rectify any inward tendency, and prevent its occuring while the front is being glued on. This is done by taking a small slice from the wood cut from the throat of the block, and wedging it between the sides of the pipe. The slice being the exact width of the block, the wedging has the effect of very slightly pressing the sides outward, a proceeding which is of advantage to the tone of the finished pipe. The condition of things at this stage is distinctly shown in Diagram 3, Fig. LXV., E E being the sides of the pipe, and F the expanding piece wedged in.

The pipe is now taken and the proper height of the mouth, measured from the upper edge of the block, is marked across the edges of the sides, and a pencil line is drawn across the upper part of the block, indicating the position of the top of the cap below the level of the lip or edge of the block. The front board is now laid on the pipe with its squared end accurately adjusted to the pencil line on the block, and the height of the mouth marked upon it. Then, with a square and a sharp knife, a deep cut is made across its inside face, at the mark, to ultimately form the upper lip of the mouth. The next step is the gluing of the front to the sides of the pipe. The edges of the sides are well warmed by passing a hot iron along them, and immediately covered with glue from the line on the block to the top of the pipe. The front, which has also been warmed, is quickly laid in position, pegged to the building-up piece, covered with a piece of straight board to serve as a caul, and pressed to the sides with hand-screws until the joints are perfectly closed.

When the glue has become dry, the pipe is released from the screws, and cleanly dressed on its sides and back until the desired thickness of wood is obtained. The pipe has now reached its complete state so far as its tube is concerned, and is ready to receive its mouth and be cut to its proper length. This stage is shown in Diagram 4, on which are indicated, by dotted lines, the form of the mouth, and the portion to be cut from the top of the pipe. The block end is shown cut to its finished size. The vertical lines at the sides of the mouth, and the horizontal line indicating the height of the mouth externally, are now drawn on the front, and the mouth is carefully cut out until its slope meets the knife-cut previously made on the inside. The slope of the mouth is now accurately formed so as to leave the upper lip of the requisite thickness. When this very simple process is completed, the top and bottom of the pipe are sawn at the lines already marked, and the bottom is dressed square; then the small wedged piece inside is knocked away, and the body of the pipe is finished, ready for the reception of its cap, foot, and stopper. The exterior of the cap is shown in Diagram 5. It is formed of hard wood and furnished with a projecting piece, commonly called a "beard," an adjunct not always necessary, as subsequently explained. The cap is hollowed on the inner side to form the wind-way of the mouth. We treat of this matter fully elsewhere. The foot, a turned piece of wood through which a hole is bored, is shown in Diagram 6: this is inserted in a hole bored in the bottom of the block into the throat, and through it the wind from the wind-chest enters the pipe. The stopper, with its handle detached, is shown in Diagram 7. This may be made of two layers of white pine glued together with their grains running at right angles, or from a slice cut from the wood prepared for the block, such as appears at C in Diagram 1. In either case the stopper is dressed so much smaller than the inside of the pipe as to admit of a covering of thick and soft leather, or of felt and leather combined, for the purpose of making its edges air-tight against the four walls of the pipe, while allowing it to be moved up and down in tuning. The upper edges of the stopper are splayed, as shown, and its lower edges and its corners are very slightly rounded to prevent their cutting the leather. In the accompanying illustration, Fig. LXVI., the pipe, constructed and finished as above described, is clearly represented. It is an ordinary English STOPPED DIAPASON CC pipe of 4 feet speaking length, and, accordingly, of 8 feet tone.

We may properly conclude this portion of our present subject by pointing out the three types of mouths upon which every form of mouth met with in wood pipes is based. These types are shown, in section in Fig. LXVII. At A is represented what, for the sake of distinction, may be called the *English mouth,* from the fact that it was universally adopted by the old English organ-builders, although not exclusively by them. In this type of mouth it will be observed that the upper lip is formed by cutting a slope on the outside of the front-board of the pipe, while the under lip is formed by the edge of the block, and a hollowed cap depressed to a slight extent below the level of the same. The wind-way is made in the inner, thin edge of the cap, as indicated. This is the form of mouth used for the English STOPPED DIAPASON, CLARABELLA, etc. Under ordinary conditions and moderate wind-pressures it produces a soft and singing quality of tone, so much affected by the old English builders.

At B is shown what is commonly known as the *German mouth,* because it has always been a favorite form with the German masters. The upper lip is formed similarly to the preceding, but the lower lip is differently treated. In this type of mouth the cap is flat on the inside and placed level with the upper edge of the block, the block being sloped from its upper edge downward into the throat, and having the wind-way cut in it, and not in the cap as in the preceding type. This treatment, under normal conditions, produces a powerful and somewhat incisive quality of tone, dear to the lovers of loud-voiced stops.

FIG. LXVI.

At C is represented what is called the *inverted mouth,* because the slope forming its upper lip is cut on the inside of the pipe, and its lower lip is formed by the perforation of the front, and not in any way by the block, which latter in this type is almost invariably sunk below the level of the lower lip. The cap is hollowed, and depressed below the lip, having the wind-way cut from it, as in the English mouth. This form of mouth is adopted for the imitative and clear-toned FLUTE stops, and certain others of crisp intonation. The Longitudinal Sections of pipes, drawn in perspective, in Fig. LXVIII., show in a very clear manner the formation of the German and the inverted mouths, and their respective treatments.

Such, then, are the three types of formation which are followed in the construction of the lips and wind-ways of all wood pipes. Outside these, however, there are many modifications and additions which experiment and experience have introduced for the purpose of producing varieties of tonal coloring. So much has been done in this direction, that from quadrangular pipes of wood have been produced pure organ-tones of considerable volume and richness; flute-tones of both normal and highly imitative character; string-tones so closely resembling those of the orchestral Violoncello and Double Bass as to be absolutely deceptive under certain conditions; and tones resembling those of reeds. It is, accordingly, our purpose in the following pages of this Chapter, to lay before the reader particulars

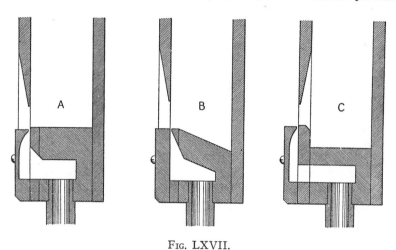

Fig. LXVII.

and illustrations of the several characteristic treatments which have been invented and introduced by artists in pipe-voicing with the aim of furnishing such varieties and qualities of tone as are essential in so large and comprehensive an instrument as a Concert-room Organ.

WOOD PIPES OF ORGAN-TONE.

There are only two or three forms of wood pipes which can be recognized as yielding pure organ-tone, that is, tone produced by the metal stop of large scale, commonly known as the OPEN DIAPASON, and which can be imitated by no other known instrument. That such a tonality can also be produced from properly-formed and voiced quadrangular wood pipes has been practically demonstrated by the celebrated organ-builder, Edmund Schulze, of Paulinzelle, who was probably the greatest artist, in wood pipe formation, of the nineteenth century.

The most important stops of this class are the PRINCIPAL, 16 FT., and the DOUBLE PRINCIPAL, 32 FT., properly belonging to the Pedal Organ. These stops are formed of quadrangular pipes, the CCC and the CCCC pipes having, respectively, the " theoretical speaking lengths " of 16 feet and 32 feet. But their practical lengths vary slightly in accordance with their scales and musical pitches. In Fig. LXIX. is shown the sound-producing portion of a pipe of a PRINCIPAL or OPEN DIAPASON, 16 FT., as commonly formed. This is shown in its complete form, in Longitudinal and Transverse Sections, and dissected. Referring to Diagram 1, it will be seen that, instead of a solid block as previously described for the STOPPED DIAPASON, 8 FT., two horizontal boards are used, placed at a convenient distance apart, and let into grooves cut in the back and sides of the pipe. The space between the boards forms the throat. The grain of both the boards must run from side to side of the pipe; and the upper board, which may be called the languid, should be edged with a piece of maple, or some other hard wood, to form a satisfactory under lip. In such large pipes, the upper lip should be of hard wood with its grain running across the mouth. The manner in which this is attached to the soft wood front, by grooving and tonguing, is clearly shown. The Perspective View, Diagram 2, represents the lower portion of the pipe complete and with all its parts in place. Diagram 3 shows, separately, all the portions which form the mouth. A is the hard wood upper lip, sloped to produce the proper thickness at the mouth; B is the tongue, also of hard wood, required to join the upper lip to the end of the front board, C; D D are the ears, shaped to fit the upper lip, etc.; E is the cap, as seen from the outside; and F is the beard, which is securely glued and screwed

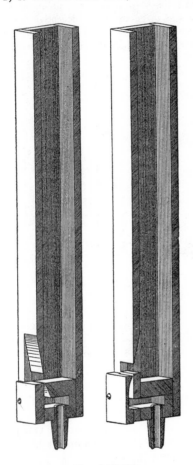

FIG. LXVIII.

to the check in the cap. At G is shown the cap, as seen from the inside, hollowed, and with its wind-way cut; and at H is given a Transverse Section through the mouth, looking toward the languid and cap, the wind-way being indicated by the thick black line. The pipe-foot is shown at I.

Pipes of this class are also made with mouths of the German form, that is, with their languids and caps placed at the same level, and their wind-ways cut from the face of the languids. In some cases, with the view of improving the speech, the wind-way is cut a little short, at both sides, of the width of the mouth. A pipe voiced in this manner can easily have its wind-way extended to the full width if found desirable. It is probable that this shortening of the wind-way steadies the wind-sheet by permitting it to spread slightly before it reaches the upper lip.

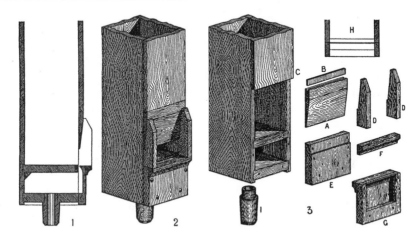

Fig. LXIX.

With respect to the most desirable scales for the Pedal Organ Principals, opinions have differed widely in the past through the different lights in which the office of the Pedal Organ has been viewed by English and Continental builders. The Pedal Organ is not an independent and self-contained department, but one which is entirely dependent on, and dictated by, the contents of the manual divisions of the instrument. All the Pedal Organ stops must be viewed and treated as furnishing true basses for the more important stops of the manual Organs; and their scales must, accordingly, be derived from, or dictated by, the scales of those manual stops. Let this important and surely self-evident fact be recognized, and all becomes a simple matter, no longer subject to ignorant caprice, but governed by reasonable laws. The old, and the greater number of the modern, English organ-builders, in their vain attempts to make a single Open Diapason serve as the bass for twenty or more manual stops, were compelled to use inordinate scales. To this simple fact we owe the construction of 16 ft. pipes with such excessive, and to our mind absurd, internal dimensions as 22 inches in width and 24 inches in depth; or, more frequently, 18 inches in width and 20 inches in depth. Stops formed on such immense scales were unmanageable monsters, tolerable only with the full Organ, and absolutely ridiculous, from an artistic point of view, with softer combinations: and the great floor-space they occupied usually led to the undesirable cramping of every other part of the instrument. The German and other Continental builders, in their appreciation of the true nature and office of the Pedal Organ, never, so far as we have been able to learn, used scales even approaching those above mentioned. The largest scale known to us in German Organs is 12 inches in width and 14 inches in depth, while the generality of Pedal PRINCIPALS, 16 FT., rarely exceed 9 inches in width by 11 inches in depth. Yet from pipes of these scales tones of great purity and power are obtained. High mouths and a copious supply of wind are important factors in the production of such tones. Three scales for the CCC pipe of the PRINCIPAL, 16 FT., may be recommended for general use; namely, 8 inches by 10 inches; 9 inches by 11 inches; and 10 inches by 12 inches. The last scale was that advocated and invariably specified by the late W. T. Best, and he was the best judge of organ-tone in his day. We have proved the smallest scale to be perfectly suitable for a Chamber Organ, even, or the low pressure of 2⅜ inches. It would also be sufficient, if properly voiced on wind of 3 inches to 4 inches, for a small, softly-voiced Church Organ. It must be borne in mind that this stop has to provide a properly balanced bass to the Great Organ PRINCIPAL or DIAPASON, 8 FT.

The most satisfactory scales for the DOUBLE PRINCIPAL, 32 FT., are not proportionately so large as those desirable for the PRINCIPAL, 16 FT. This may be explained, in the light of scientific tonal balance, by the facts that the fundamental unison pitch of the Pedal Organ is 16 ft., and that it is undesirable to have the sub-octave pitch of 32 ft. as pronounced as the fundamental unison.

The most suitable minimum scale may be accepted at 11 inches in width of 13½ inches in depth for the CCCC pipe, halving on the eighteenth pipe. The maximum scale may be that adopted by Schulze for the fine stop in the Organ in the Church of St. Bartholomew, at Armley—namely 14¼ inches in width by 18¼ inches in depth. This scale is larger than that adopted for the DOUBLE PRINCIPALS, by the same celebrated builder, in his Organs in Bremen Cathedral and St. Mary's Church, at Wismar, which measure 12 inches in width by 15 inches in depth. The equally celebrated builder, Ladegast, uses a still smaller scale—11⅛ inches in width by 14⅛ inches in depth—for the DOUBLE PRINCIPAL, 32 FT., in his Organ in Schwerin Cathedral. We can speak from experience of the satisfactory character of this small scale in connection with an Organ constructed to our Specification. Of the inordinate scales that have been used by English builders and others, it is unnecessary to speak.*

* The DOUBLE DIAPASON, 32 FT., in the Wanamaker Organ in Philadelphia, has its CCCC pipe measuring 22¾ inches in width by 27¾ inches in depth. Its construction called for over one thousand square feet of three-inch thick sugar-pine. It weighs 1,735 lbs.

The treatment of the mouths of the pipes of the Armley DOUBLE
PRINCIPAL is interesting from an acoustical point of view. The mouth
of the largest pipe is shown in Section and Front View in Fig. LXX.
It will be observed that a harmonic-bridge, of a peculiar form, is placed
across the mouth, and that the cap is hollowed underneath it, so as to
provide a wind-way under the mouth. This treatment imparts a crisp
and prompt intonation. The practice of adding the harmonic-bridge, of
different forms, to large wood pipes has been successfully followed by
other builders.

PRINCIPAL or OPEN DIAPASON, 8 FT.—Although the PRINCIPAL, 8
FT., of wood, as a manual stop, has very seldom been carried above the
bass octave by German organ-builders, and has, so far as we can learn,
never been introduced by English builders, there are strong reasons in

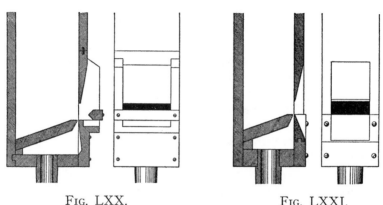

FIG. LXX.   FIG. LXXI.

favor of its being added to the list of stops available for modern use.
That it can be made of a beautiful quality of tone has been satisfactorily
shown by Schulze—that consummate artist in wood-pipe voicing. In his
Organ in Armley Church, the bass octave of the " MAJOR PRINCIPAL "
in the Great Organ—a truly grand stop of pure organ-tone—is carried
down in wood pipes in so perfect a manner that the keenest ear almost
fails to detect the transition from metal to wood. The accompanying
illustration, Fig. LXXI., shows the peculiar construction of the mouths
of these bass pipes. It will be observed that the external lines of the
upper lip and the splayed cap resemble those of an ordinary metal-pipe
mouth. The chief feature here is the recessed and splayed cap, which is
almost brought to a sharp edge at the lower lip. The upper lip is cut
sharp, as shown. In the matter of scale, the most important dimensions
are those of the BB pipe which follows, downward, the metal tenor C
pipe. The metal C pipe is 3⅜ inches in diameter, with a mouth 3 inches
wide and ¾ inch high, and with the wind-hole in the foot ⁹⁄₁₆ inch in

diameter. The BB wood pipe measures 2 ¹³/₁₆ inches in width by 3¾ inches in depth, with a mouth ⅞ inch high. All is of hard pine with the exception of the upper half of the cap, which is of oak. The languid slopes downward toward the back of the pipe. All the details are accurately shown in the illustration. The " MINOR PRINCIPAL," 8 FT., in the Choir Organ, has its bass octave of wood; the " SUB-PRINCIPAL," 16 FT., has its bass and tenor octaves of wood. All are specimens of fine voicing.

WOOD PIPES OF FLUTE-TONE.

The greater number of wood stops introduced in the different divisions of the Organ are those which yield flute-tone either unimitative or imitative: and the pipes which compose such stops present a great variety of scales and treatments; are of several essentially different forms; and are either open, covered, or half-covered.

Flute-toned stops, both of wood and metal, may be grouped into two classes: First, those which yield organ flute-tone; and, secondly, those which yield orchestral flute-tone. The former are unimitative, and may be called normal flute-toned stops; while the latter yield tones closely resembling those of the orchestral Flute and Piccolo, and may, accordingly, be designated imitative flute-toned stops. The term normal is here used to convey the idea that the tone is produced under the ordinary conditions of organ-pipes, and may vary infinitely according to scale, voicing, wind-pressure, etc.: while in the case of the imitative stops, everything is made subservient to the production of an exact quality of tone—that of the orchestral Flutes—and such extraordinary forms and treatments are resorted to as may be found necessary to attain the end in view. With this explanation, it will be understood what is meant when we speak of a FLUTE pipe having a normal unimitative or an imitative tone.

CLARABELLA.—The first stop of normal flute-tone that may be considered here is the modern one known as the CLARABELLA: a stop of 8 ft. pitch belonging to the manual department of the Organ. In its most pleasing and useful form it has a voice of a full and round character, inclining toward pure organ-tone rather than toward flute-tone. Some voicers give it a pronounced flute-tone, resembling that which is characteristic of the HOHLFLÖTE; but in this case the chief charm and musical value of the CLARABELLA are sacrificed. The CLARABELLA pipe is quadrangular and open. It has the English mouth, the height of which should be about one-quarter of its width, without applied ears or beard; and the block is level on its upper surface. The exact treatment is shown in the Longitudinal Section A, Fig. LXVII. The scale may be varied according to the tonal character desired. As both volume and character of tone depend upon the proportion the mouth bears to the internal transverse area of the pipe, it can readily be understood how easy it is for the pipe maker to vary the intonation by altering his scale. For a true CLARABELLA the proportion of width of mouth to depth of pipe may be as 3 to 4, when a comparatively light tone is required: or as 3 to 3½, when a full tone is necessary. It is undesirable to approach nearer to the square than the latter proportion.

STOPPED DIAPASON.—The name of this time-honored stop is certainly misleading, for it does not belong to the DIAPASON family. Its characteristic voice places it in the flute-work, although, like the CLARABELLA, its fluty character is not, in genuine examples, very pronounced. As the form and construction of its pipes have already been described and illustrated, it is unnecessary to add much here. While its tone of necessity differs from that of an open stop like the preceding, its form differs from that of the CLARABELLA, generally considered, only inasmuch as its pipes are about half the speaking length and are stopped or covered. If there is any harmonic upper partial tone heard in the voice of the CLARABELLA pipe, it will be the first, or the octave of the prime tone; while in the STOPPED DIAPASON pipe, the upper partial heard is the second, or Twelfth, of the prime tone—the first "over-tone" of a stopped pipe. Herein lies the distinctive difference between the voices of the CLARA-BELLA (open stop) and the STOPPED DIAPASON (covered stop)—a difference of coloring only in the normal flute-tone yielded by both stops. STOPPED DIAPASON pipes furnish the best bass octave for a tenor C CLARABELLA. They can be scaled and voiced so as to make the break almost imperceptible. The STOPPED DIAPASON should be in all cases carried throughout the manual compass in wood pipes. It should invariably be introduced in a complete form.

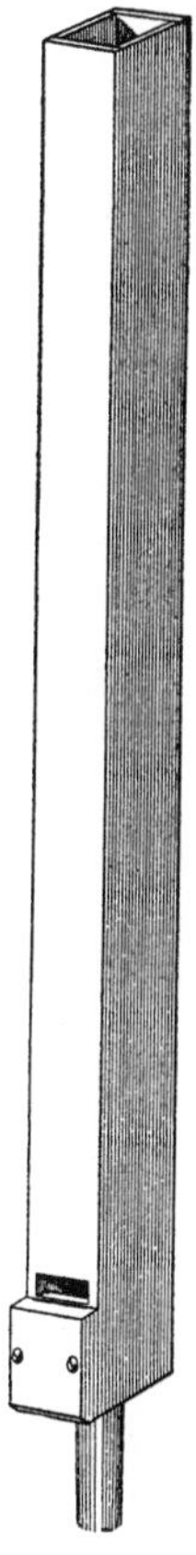

MELODIA.—This stop is of the CLARABELLA class, but owing to difference of scale and form of mouth it yields a tone of more fluty character. The scale

FIG. LXXII.

varies in different examples; but that which gives the CC pipe a width of 3½ inches and a depth of 4¼ inches, halving on the nineteenth pipe (F♯), is probably the most satisfactory. The mouth is inverted, and cut up about one-third its width.

Organ-builders, in their desire to save money, very commonly make the bass octave of the MELODIA of LIEBLICHGEDECKT pipes, but this practice, like too many others indulged in by them, is contrary to the canons of artistic organ-building, a very important one **of** which may read thus: *Each stop in the Organ must be carried throughout the compass of the instrument in pipes of its own class or tonality: and the bass of one stop should never be made to serve for the bass of other stops.* Those interested in the construction or acquisition of an Organ should insist on this canon being strictly observed. More of the grandeur and true beauty of the tonal structure of the Organ depends upon its observance than is commonly realized even by those who prepare specifications for Organs. The MELODIA, 8 FT., in its complete and most perfect form, is a stop of beautiful tone, valuable alike in combination with other stops of all classes and in solo effects. The MELODIA pipe is represented in Fig. LXXII. Like all the smaller-sized open wood flute-toned pipes, it is tuned by a metal shade at top.

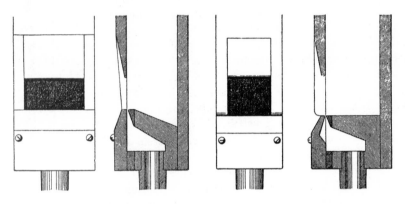

FIG. LXXIII.   FIG. LXXIV.

The DOUBLE MELODIA, 16 FT., should be made of precisely the same form as the MELODIA; but the pipes of the lowest octave may only have their mouths of hard wood, with the rest of their fronts of white pine.

WALDFLÖTE.—This normal flute-toned stop is commonly made of 4 ft. pitch. From its general resemblance, in form and construction, to the MELODIA, it may be looked upon as the OCTAVE, 4 FT., of that stop. Its pipes are made to a slightly larger scale, and voiced to yield a full fluty tone, more pronounced than that of either the CLARABELLA or MELODIA. The mouths of the pipes should be cut up about one-third their width in height; but the proportions will vary according to the wind-pressure, and the quantity and quality of the tone desired. The blocks are properly depressed below the lower lips, the distance being equal to one-third the width of the mouths.

HOHLFLÖTE.—This is a powerful, but rather dull-voiced, stop of normal flute-tone, differing both in the shapes and proportions of its pipes from all the preceding examples. In the wooden varieties of the stop two leading forms obtain—the quadrangular and the triangular. In the most characteristic treatment of the quadrangular form the open pipes have their mouths cut in their wide sides, as in the HOHLFLÖTE in the Organ in the Town Hall, Northampton, constructed by Schulze. In the accompanying illustration, Fig. LXXIII., the mouth portion of a pipe of this treatment is shown in front view and section. The mouth is of the German class, cut up equal to one-half its width, and having its side-pieces and the upper part of the cap sloped toward the opening.

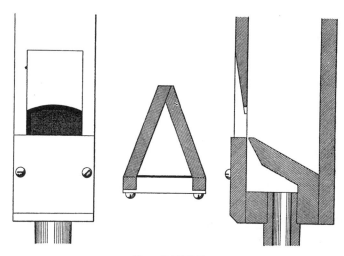

FIG. LXXV.

In Fig. LXXIV. is shown, in front view and section, the mouth portion of an open pipe from the HOHLFLÖTE, in the back Great Organ of the Concert Organ in the Public Halls, Glasgow, constructed by Messrs. Lewis & Company. The C pipe of this fine stop measures $2\frac{1}{8}$ inches in width by $2\frac{11}{16}$ inches in depth. The mouth, cut in the narrow way of the pipe, is nearly square, being $1\frac{7}{8}$ inches high. All these proportions are correctly given in the illustration. As in the preceding example, the cap is sloped toward the lower lip, and is slightly hollowed on the inside, as shown. The upper part of the pipe has a slot, 5 inches long, cut 2 inches from the top. The bass octave is in covered pipes, as is usual in HOHLFLÖTE stops.

Schulze has used triangular open pipes for the HOHLFLÖTE stops in his Organs in the Parish Church of Doncaster, St. Bartholomew's Church, Armley, and St. Peter's Church, Hindley. The illustrations given in Fig. LXXV. are a Transverse Section, a Longitudinal Section, and a Front View of the mouth of the middle c^1 pipe of the HOHLFLÖTE, in the Great division of the Organ in the Church of St. Peter, Hindley. It measures 1⅝ inches in width at the mouth by 2⅛ inches in depth, and its mouth is ⅞ inch in height and arched, as shown. The adoption of the triangular form is for the purpose of obtaining a mouth large in proportion to the transverse area of the pipe: and it is with the same view that Schulze placed the mouth on the wide side of his pipes in his Northampton Organ, as above mentioned. The upper lip of the HOHLFLÖTE is usually finished thick and slightly rounded, favoring the production of its somewhat dull and hollow tone. The pipes should be made of thick wood, fronted with hard wood, and have large feet for the copious supply of wind. We may remark that there is very little gained by the adoption of triangular pipes, notwithstanding the good opinion the great artist in pipe-voicing apparently had of them.

LIEBLICHGEDECKT.—Of all the varieties of covered stops the true LIEBLICHGEDECKTS are the most valuable and beautiful. They form quite a large family, appearing in 16 ft., 8 ft., 4 ft., and 2 ft. pitch, all of which are properly introduced in the manual divisions of the Organ. The English equivalent for the German name may be rendered as *Lovely-toned Covered Stop;* and good examples richly merit such a title. While all the forms in which the LIEBLICHGEDECKTS are made have certain features in common, they present some distinctive treatments which we shall attempt to illustrate and describe.

In the first place, they vary considerably in scale, while all are characterized, in comparison with the other covered stops of the Organ, by smallness: and the scales vary not only in size generally, but also in the proportions of width to depth, the softer varieties being narrow in proportion to their depth, while the stronger-toned have proportionally wider mouths,* reaching their maximum width in the rarely-used square pipes.

The largest scale to be recommended for the unison CC pipe of the true LIEBLICHGEDECKT is 3¼ inches in width by 4 inches in depth; but a smaller scale is more generally useful. The three stops of this class in the Organ in St. Peter's Church, Hindley, are of the following scales: the CC pipe of the Great Organ GEDECKT measures 2⅞ inches by 3⅞ inches, having its mouth 2⅞ inches by 2 inches; the corresponding pipe in the Swell Organ GEDECKT measures 2⅛ inches by 3 inches, having its mouth 2⅛ inches wide by 2¼ inches high; and the LIEBLICHGEDECKT in the Choir Organ measures 2⅛ inches by 3⅛ inches, having its mouth 2⅛ inches by 1½ inches. The range between the maximum given and the smallest of the above scales, as used by Schulze, practically covers

---

* In speaking of the width of a pipe, we invariably allude to the internal dimension of the side in which the mouth is cut. A pipe may, therefore, be described as having a greater depth than width, or greater width than depth, according to the location of its mouth.

all the dimensions suitable for the CC pipe of the stop. From the width
and depth decided on, the scale can be developed by halving on the seventeenth note above, or in the ratio 1 : 2.66.

The height of the mouth is a most important factor in the production
of the characteristic normal flute-tone of the LIEBLICHGEDECKT. In no
case should it be less than half its width in height; and, as in the case
of the stop in the Swell division of the Hindley Organ, it may exceed its
width in height. In the smaller scales, the square mouth may be used
with a perfectly satisfactory result. The accompanying illustration, Fig.
LXXVI., shows the Front View and Section of the mouth and lower
portion of a LIEBLICHGEDECKT pipe, having a square, German mouth.
The thickness of the upper lip is another important factor in the tone
production. This may vary from a
quarter to half an inch (the thicker
producing a rounder tone), and be cut
square or have rounded edges; and the
lip may be straight, as in the illustration, or arched, as the voicer deems
expedient. All these details must be
decided before the pipes are made.
Pipes having mouths of so great a
height in proportion to width require
a copious supply of wind for their
proper speech; and, accordingly, their
feet should have large holes. The CC
pipe should have a hole an inch in
diameter. The stoppers should be made
of slices cut from the block-wood, and
treated as in the case of those for the

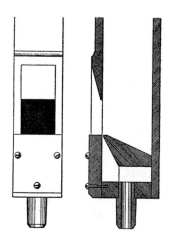

FIG. LXXVI.

so-called STOPPED DIAPASON. It is quite a common practice to use metal
pipes for the higher octaves of the unison LIEBLICHGEDECKT, for it is
found that there the tone of the wood pipes can be closely imitated by
covered metal ones.

Valuable as are the LIEBLICHGEDECKTS of 8 ft. tone, they are not
more so than those of 16 ft. tone. For insertion in Choir and Swell
divisions the latter are in every way suitable. They should be entirely
of wood, or if metal is used it should not go below the top octave. Dr.
Hopkins gives a scale for a Choir or Swell LIEBLICHGEDECKT, 16 FT.,
apparently of German origin. The CCC pipe is 3⅜ inches in width by
5 inches in depth; the CC pipe is 2 9/16 inches in width by 3 inches in
depth; and the C pipe is 1⅜ inches in width by 1⅞ inches in depth.
This scale is remarkable for its irregularity: each octave seems to have
a ratio of its own, if ratios have been used at all in its formation. It
approaches most closely to the standard ratio, 1 : 2.519.

In form and treatment the wood pipes of the LIEBLICHGEDECKT, 4 FT., are similar to those of the unison stop; but it is seldom that more than the lowest octave is made of wood, while it is quite a common practice to form the entire stop of metal.

BOURDON.—The construction of the pipes of the ordinary BOURDON does not differ materially from that of the STOPPED DIAPASON, as above described; and the materials used may be the same. The larger size of the stop, which is of 16 ft. tone, renders the use of solid blocks undesirable save in the upper octaves. The BOURDON proper varies greatly in scale, chiefly because it is inserted in both the pedal and manual departments of the Organ. The most suitable scales for the Pedal Organ stops range from a width of 8½ inches by a depth of 10 inches to a

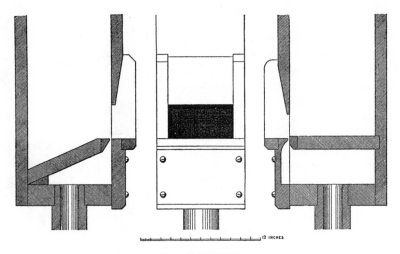

FIG. LXXVII.

width of 5¾ inches by a depth of 8 inches for the CCC pipe, all scales halving on the sixteenth pipe—ratio $1 : \sqrt{8}$. The latter scale has been adopted by Schulze in the Pedal department of the Hindley Organ, the CCC pipe having a mouth 4 inches high. The scale of 6½ inches by 8½ inches is ample for all ordinary Church Organs with properly-apportioned Pedal departments; and 4 inches by 5½ inches is a suitable scale for a true Chamber Organ. Larger scales than the maximum above given have been frequently used; but they are neither necessary nor to be recommended. In most instances the pipes have low mouths, rarely exceeding one-third their width; and their tones are tubby and often unmusical in the extreme. In the accompanying illustration, Fig. LXXVII., are given the Front View and two Sections of the mouth and lower portion of a BOURDON pipe, according to the medium scale above recommended. The Section on the left of the Front View shows the

mouth of the German form, one-half its width in height, with straight
and thick upper lips, ears of medium projection, and a bearded cap.
The Section on the right has the ordinary English mouth. The internal
construction of both forms is clearly shown.

The scales of the manual BOURDON, 16 FT., may range from a width
of 5 inches by a depth of 7 inches to a width of 3⅞ inches by a depth
of 6⅜ inches. The latter are the dimensions of the lowest (CCC) pipe
in the Great division of the Hindley Organ, the mouth of which pipe is
3⅛ inches in height. The LIEBLICHBOURDON in the Swell division of
the same instrument has its lowest pipe measuring 3⅜ inches by 5
inches, with a mouth 3¾ inches high. The tone is round and full.

The mouths of the BOURDONS usually made by English builders are
seldom over one-half their width in height, and are often less than one-
third. Their tones, accordingly,
have the twelfth, or first harmonic of a stopped pipe, more
or less prominent, approaching
in some cases to the QUINTATEN
in tone. These pipes have the
ordinary English mouth, with
the horizontal languid, similar to
that shown in the right Section
in Fig. LXXVII. On the other
hand, the BOURDONS and LIEB-
LICHBOURDONS of the German
builders have their mouths cut
up very high, rising from about
a height of two-thirds their
width to a height exceeding their
width, as exemplified by the stop

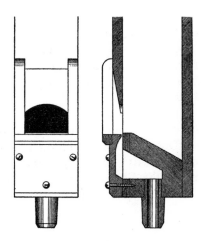

FIG. LXXVIII.

in the Hindley Organ, the dimensions of which have just been given.
It is true that certain English builders have during recent years learnt
valuable lessons in pipe-making and voicing from German work, to the
great improvement of tonal coloring.

The tones produced by small-scaled and high-mouthed BOURDONS are
fuller and purer than those yielded by the large-scaled and low-mouthed
English stops: and this fact, combined with the comparatively small
standing room they require, makes them most suitable for insertion in
the manual divisions of the Organ, and especially those enclosed in swell-
boxes. The tone of the BOURDON pipe is also affected by the thickness
of the upper lip of its mouth, which varies from a quarter of an inch
to nearly an inch in different examples. The lowest pipe of the BOUR-
DON in the Great division of the Concert Organ in the Public Halls,
Glasgow, measures 5⅛ inches in width by 6⅜ inches in depth, having

a mouth 3⅞ inches high, with a square-cut upper lip ¹¹⁄₁₆ inch thick. The tone of the BOURDON pipe is also affected by the form of the upper lip, which may vary, according to the taste of the voicer, from the straight line to an arch approaching a semi-circle. In Fig. LXXVIII. are given a Front View and Section of the lower part of a manual BOURDON pipe. The mouth is of the German class, with sloping languid, and with a thick and arched upper lip. The scale here observed is that of a CCC pipe, 4¼ inches wide by 6 inches deep, with a mouth two-thirds of its width in height. As all the high-mouthed GEDECKTS require a copious supply of wind, care must be taken to provide the BOURDON pipes with large feet: the CCC pipe should have a foot with a hole from 1¼ inches to 2 inches in diameter, according to requirements, and the rest of the pipes in proportion. There must be no stint in the matter of wind.

It is quite a common practice, especially with French and German organ-builders, to insert the upper octaves of the BOURDON in metal. The BOURDON, 16 FT., in the Great division of the Armley Organ is of wood to b¹, and thence to the top—25 notes, in covered pipes of metal. The three manual BOURDONS in the Concert Organ in the Town Hall, Manchester, constructed by Cavaillé-Coll, of Paris, have pipes of wood up to the pipe yielding the 4 ft. note, where they break into large-scale, covered pipes of metal. Numerous other instances could be mentioned.

DOPPELFLÖTE.—We now come to what is probably the most useful and beautiful normal flute-toned stop in the Organ, commonly known under the German name of DOPPELFLÖTE, and which, in English, may be called the DOUBLE-MOUTHED FLUTE. It is somewhat surprising that so fine a stop should have been so systematically neglected by English organ-builders; and it is equally remarkable that in none of the several Organs built for England by the great Schulze is there a single specimen of the stop.

The tone of the DOPPELFLÖTE when properly voiced is singularly full and round, having more filling-up power and better mixing qualities than any other covered stop in use; and these facts are surely sufficient to recommend it for insertion in every Organ of any pretensions toward completeness. But being more troublesome and expensive to make and voice than a single-mouthed stop it is not a favorite with the tradesman organ-builder. The DOPPELFLÖTE is specially useful with lingual stops of all classes, imparting to their voices fulness and firmness without injuring their characteristic tonalities. No other stop in the Organ combines with and improves the CLARINET and CORNO DI BASSETTO in so satisfactory a manner. In the Concert-room Organ of the Twentieth Century a DOPPELFLÖTE, 8 FT., should be inserted in the principal manual divisions.

The DOPPELFLÖTE is invariably of 8 ft. pitch, and is formed of wood throughout. The bass octave is of single-mouthed GEDECKT pipes, of medium scale, voiced to yield a full tone, which carries down the characteristic quality of the more important portion of the stop in a fairly satisfactory manner. From tenor C to the top, each pipe has two mouths, on opposite sides of a block in which a semi-circular depression has been cut. The mouths are otherwise of the English form, having splays cut in their side-pieces, and slightly arched upper lips. These and all other details are accurately shown in the accompanying illustration, Fig. LXXIX. In the drawing A is given a Longitudinal Section of a pipe, cut through the mouths, and showing the forms of the block and caps. Above is given the section of the stopper, edged with cork, and covered with soft leather. A Front View of one of the mouths is given in the drawing B, showing the proportionate height of mouth, the arch of the upper lip, and the lateral splays. At C is a Transverse Section through the mouths, showing the depression in the block, the wind-ways, and the upper ends of the caps. The wind-ways are indicated by the thick black lines. All the parts are drawn in correct proportion.

The pipes of the DOPPELFLÖTE, having the double mouths, require a scale allowing a considerable depth in proportion to width. This can be seen from the following measurements, from the standard scale used by Roosevelt: Tenor

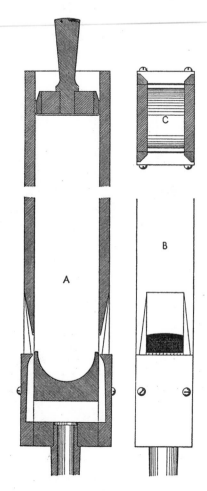

FIG. LXXIX.

C, $2\frac{1}{4}$ inches in width by $3\frac{7}{16}$ inches in depth; middle c^1, $1\frac{3}{8}$ inches by $2\frac{3}{16}$ inches; and c^2, $\frac{3}{4}$ inch by $1\frac{7}{16}$ inches. It will be observed that the proportions of depth to width vary as the scale ascends, the C pipe being a little over one and a half its width in depth, while the c^2 pipe is a little under twice its width in depth. The height of mouth, at the spring of its arched upper lip, ranges between one-third and one-half its width, according to the wind-pressure and strength of tone required.

A powerful-voiced open wood stop of normal flute-tone has been made with double mouths, in a similar manner to the DOPPELFLÖTE, but it has not been commonly approved of or often used. We believe that although the stopped DOPPELFLÖTE appears in every important Organ Roosevelt built, he only introduced the open DOPPELFLÖTE in one instrument, under the somewhat inappropriate name of PHILOMELA. In the three largest suggested Specifications given in his handsome *brochure,*

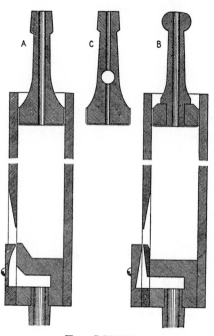

FIG. LXXX.

the PHILOMELA is placed with the Solo Organ stops. Should this stop be used it should bear a more expressive name, for it is difficult to associate its powerful voice with the sweet notes of the Nightingale (*Daulias philomela*). Clarke, in his " Outline of the Structure of the Pipe Organ," describes the PHILOMELA as of " Small-scale, stopped wood pipes, voiced with the sweetest and most delicate quality." The name in this case is about as appropriate as most fancy names can claim to be.

FLAUTO D'AMORE.—This is a small-scale stop of 4 ft. pitch, the pipes of which, in general form, resemble those of the LIEBLICHGEDECKT, but differ from them in having lower mouths and pierced stoppers.

These peculiarities separate the FLAUTO D'AMORE from the true LIEB-LICHGEDECKT and LIEBLICHFLÖTE, 4 FT., and impart a delicate and peculiar tonality to the stop. The FLAUTO D'AMORE can be made with the inverted mouth if desired, its tone being somewhat keener. Both mouths are shown in the Longitudinal Sections given in Fig. LXXX. Two forms of stoppers are also shown: that at A, being cut from solid wood, is the most suitable for the smaller pipes; while that at B, having a turned and inserted handle, is adapted for the larger pipes of the lowest octave. As the perforations in the stoppers affect the quality of the tone, their lengths must of course be graduated regularly throughout the stop: and as this gradation of length would make the stoppers of the higher octaves inconveniently short, if treated as at A, long stoppers must be provided, perforated transversely with as large a hole as possible. At C is shown a Section of such a stopper, with this larger transverse hole shortening the smaller vertical one at the necessary point. The diameters of the vertical perforations may vary in size according to the scale of the pipes and the quality of tone desired. The largest pipes may have a perforation of about ⅜ inch. All the perforations must be cleared and hardened by burning with red-hot wires of proper sizes. The FLAUTO D'AMORE pipes require for their most characteristic tones a comparatively small supply of wind, and speak best on a pressure of about 2½ inches.

FLAUTO DOLCE.—Under such names as FLAUTO DOLCE, FLÛTE DOUCE, SANFTFLÖTE, and ZARTFLÖTE, several forms of stops have been made, producing unimitative flute-tones whose chief characteristic is softness. As the pipes forming the generality of these stops present no special features differing from those already described and illustrated, we pass them over, reserving one form for consideration which does present a feature that has not been mentioned. This may be named, in allusion to the special feature in its construction, the CYLINDER-LIPPED FLUTE, or still more appropriately, with reference to its beautiful voice, the SUAVE FLUTE. The

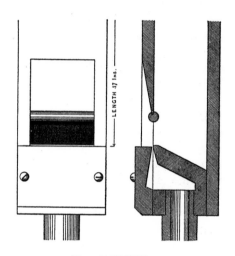

FIG. LXXXI.

formation of its mouth, block, and cap is shown in Fig. LXXXI. It will be observed that the upper lip of the mouth has a cylindrical piece of wood attached to it, against the smooth round surface of which the wind sheet acts in its vibratory motion: and it is evident the peculiarly soft and smooth quality of tone produced is due to the very thick cylindrical lip and its unique position with respect to the wind-way. The pipes of this stop are made five-sixths of their width in depth, as indicated in the illustration; and their mouths are slightly more than one-third their width in height. The illustration was made from a pipe lent us by Mr. August Gern, organ-builder, of London. Beautiful as the stop is, the time and skill required in its construction and voicing will prevent its ever being favored by the organ-builder of to-day.

ORCHESTRAL FLUTE.—As there are only two Flutes used in the

Orchestra; namely, the Flauto Traverso and Flauto Piccolo, the range of imitative flute-tone is naturally circumscribed; and the forms of the organ stops or pipes which have been invented for the purpose of imitating the tones of the orchestral instruments are accordingly few in number. As it was found impossible to produce the pure, liquid, and penetrating tones of the orchestral Flute from pipes of the ordinary form, having quadrangular mouths, the peculiar form of the embouchure and the method of sounding the orchestral instrument were carefully studied with the view of imitating them, to as full an extent as practicable, in the organ-pipe.

There are three forms for the bodies of wood pipes used for the ORCHESTRAL FLUTE or FLAUTO TRAVERSO stops; viz.: cylindrical, quadrangular, and triangular. The first is not uncommon in good German work, but rarely, if ever, used by the builders of other nations, who are content with simpler methods of construction, even though the tones produced are unsatisfactory from the strictly imitative point of view. The quadrangular form is most frequently used, and, under certain treatments, its tones are strongly imitative; and the triangular form of body is that most rarely met with in Organs.

The pipes which have proved the most imitative in their tones are those which most closely resemble the orchestral Flute in form. They are constructed of cylindrical tubes of hard wood, with mouths of small size, placed in relation to their blocked ends just as is the embouchure of the orchestral instrument. The formation of their caps is such that the wind is directed obliquely against the face of their upper lips, just as the wind from the human mouth is directed across the embouchure of the Flute. The cylindrical pipes are invariably harmonic, and accordingly about double their true speaking length; and they are only introduced in the higher octaves of the stop, quadrangular pipes being used for the lower octaves. Fine examples, under the name of FLAUTO TRAVERSO, are to be found in Schulze's work in the Doncaster Parish Church and Leeds Parish Church Organs. As both stops are practically alike, a description of that in the latter Organ will be sufficient. The stop is of 8 ft. pitch but is not carried down below tenor C. The cylindrical, harmonic pipes commence at $a\sharp^1$ and extend to the top. They are of beech wood, carefully and clearly bored, and turned externally. We presume the builder, reasoning on the fact that all the notes of the orchestral Flute are produced from a single tube, considered it unnecessary to graduate, in the usual manner, the diameters as well as the lengths of all his pipes; for we observe in the FLAUTO TRAVERSO under consideration, that several groups of pipes of similar diameters obtain. No apparent irregularity of tone results from this absence of regular gradation, herein showing the skill of the voicer. In the accompanying illustration, Plate XXVIII., are given Front Views of the $a\sharp^1$ and c^2

PLATE XXVIII

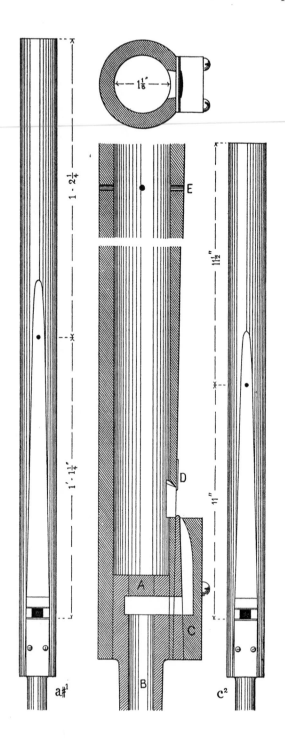

pipes, both of which have the same internal diameter of $1\frac{1}{8}$ inch: all the other important dimensions are furnished. Each pipe has a slant planed off one side, extending from a little above its center to the foot, in which the mouth is cut, and against which the cap is placed. The mouth is a small square perforation cut in the slant; and owing to the difficulty of cutting an internal slope from the outside, the voicer has found it necessary to form the upper lip with a piece of hard cardboard, glued across the slant, and pared thin, and in some cases slightly arched, at the mouth. This is indicated in the drawings. The block and pipe-foot are turned from a single piece of wood, a piece being cut out to form the throat, as shown in the Longitudinal Section. The proper form of cap for this description of pipe is that which directs the wind-sheet in a slanting direction across the mouth, as already mentioned. The cap is constructed of two pieces; namely, the cap proper, hollowed on its inner side, and having the wind-way cut in it; and a thin wedge-shaped piece of wood, slightly longer than the cap proper, and rounded along its thinner edge, used for the purpose of holding the cap in a sloping position slightly above the slanting surface of the pipe. All these details are accurately shown in the two Sections given in Plate XXVIII., both of which are cut through the mouth of the pipe. A is the block; B the pipe-foot; C the cap, constructed of two pieces, as above described; and D is the strip of cardboard forming the upper lip of the mouth. All the cylindrical pipes are harmonic, and, accordingly, are made about twice their true speaking lengths; and to secure their promptly speaking the harmonic notes, they are perforated, near their nodal lines, with four small holes, as indicated in the Front Views and at E in the Longitudinal Section. The pipes are tuned by metal shades at top.

The form of ORCHESTRAL FLUTE we are now going to describe produces, when carefully made and voiced, a quality of tone almost equal to that yielded by the German cylindrical stop. It has the advantage of being more easily constructed, while it admits of being accurately scaled throughout. The pipes are harmonic from F, are quadrangular and nearly square in form, and have circular mouths and compound caps. The construction of the lower portion of a pipe is accurately delineated in Fig. LXXXII., which is drawn from a c^1 pipe made by Roosevelt, the stop being of 4 ft. pitch. The scale of the F pipe is $1\frac{1}{8}$ inches in width by $1\frac{3}{8}$ inches in depth; and that of the c^1 pipe $1\frac{3}{16}$ inch in width by $1\frac{1}{16}$ inches in depth. The former pipe has a mouth $1\frac{1}{16}$ inch in diameter; and its single harmonic perforation, $\frac{1}{8}$ inch in diameter, placed $13\frac{9}{16}$ inches from the top of the mouth. The c^1 pipe has a mouth $\frac{9}{16}$ inch in diameter, and its harmonic perforation, a little under $\frac{1}{8}$ inch in diameter, placed $8\frac{3}{4}$ inches from the top of the mouth. The full length of the c^1 pipe, from the top of the mouth, is $22\frac{1}{4}$ inches, while the total internal length of the pipe, from the sunk block, is 23½ inches. It will be seen on reference to the Longitudinal Section A, in Fig. LXXXII., that the circular mouth is hollowed on the inside so as to leave a thin rim for the wind to play over; and that the construction of the compound cap is such as to direct the wind-sheet across the mouth at a considerable angle. As the form and size of the wind-way has to be carefully adjusted, and so that it shall not alter in moist or dry weather, it is cut in a thin plate of brass, which is pinned to the top of the outer part of the cap. The position of this plate is shown in the Longitudinal Section A; and the form of its wind-way is given in the Transverse Section through the mouth B. The position of the rounded upper edge of the wedge-shaped part of the cap with relation to the circular mouth is accurately delineated both in the Longitudinal Section and in the Front View C. In voicing pipes of this kind, three things have to be considered; namely, the thickness of the wedge piece, the size of the wind-way, and the position of the cap with relation to the circular mouth: all are factors of importance in the production of a perfect intonation. No attempt should be made to fix the cap, either by glue or screws, until the correct position has been determined on the voicing machine.

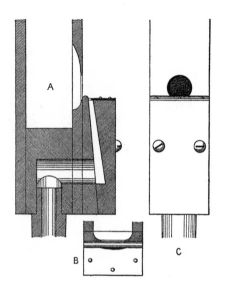

FIG. LXXXII.

The pipes that are harmonic should preferably be made of pear or maple; and on no account should white pine be used for their fronts, although it, or spruce, may be employed for their sides and backs. The caps are best made of beech. As the pipes do not call for a great supply of wind, their feet need not have bores of large size.

A very effective ORCHESTRAL FLUTE, 4 FT., may be made of pipes of quadrangular form, with mouths constructed in the simple manner shown in the accompanying illustration, Fig. LXXXIII. These pipes may vary in scale, be made of greater depth than width, or be made square, according to the strength of tone required. The mouths should be about three-fifths the widths of the pipes, and about three-fifths their widths in height, or of the proportions shown in the drawing. The pipes should be made harmonic from tenor C, 2 ft. pitch—the lowest note of the true orchestral Flute,—but for a soft FLUTE for a Choir or Chamber Organ they may be made non-harmonic throughout. In the latter case a small scale should be adopted.

HARMONIC FLUTE.—The wood stop commonly labeled HARMONIC FLUTE, and occasionally, on account of its strongly imitative tone, FLAUTO TRAVERSO, appears of both 8 ft. and 4 ft. pitch. In the unison stop, the bass octave is generally of LIEBLICHGEDECKT pipes; the seventeen pipes from C to e¹, inclusive, are of open unison lengths; and from f¹ to c⁴, inclusive, the pipes are harmonic, and, accordingly, of double lengths. In the octave stop, from CC to E the pipes are of open unison lengths; from F to c³ the pipes are harmonic; and from c♯³ to c⁴ the pipes are harmonic and made of metal. The scale of the lowest open non-harmonic pipes, in both stops, is 2¼ inches in width by 2¾ inches in depth; and that of the highest non-harmonic pipe is 1 ³⁄₁₆ inches in width by 1 ⁷⁄₁₆ inches in depth. The lowest harmonic pipe, made double length, is 1¼ inches in width by 1½ inches in depth; and the highest harmonic pipes of wood is ⅜ inch in width by ¹⁵⁄₃₂ inch in depth. The mouths of all the pipes are inverted, are of the full widths of the scale, and are one-third of their width in height. Their caps are of the ordinary hollowed-out form and are depressed slightly below the lower lips of the mouths.

ORCHESTRAL PICCOLO.—As the ORCHESTRAL PICCOLO, 2 FT., is

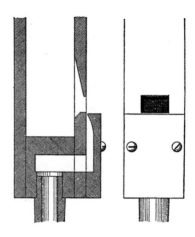

FIG. LXXXIII.

simply an Octave of the ORCHESTRAL FLUTE of 4 ft. pitch, its pipes are constructed in precisely the same manner as those of the imitative flute-toned stops just described. The ORCHESTRAL PICCOLO being, in its proper form, a solo stop, the scale of its pipes should be similar to, or perhaps two pipes smaller than, the scale of the corresponding octaves of the ORCHESTRAL FLUTE. The stop should be of harmonic pipes throughout, the wood pipes extending from the bottom note to e², and metal ones from f² to the top. There will be an advantage in the matter of construction, and no disadvantage in tonal effect, attending this arrangement; for in notes of so high a pitch, the tones from wood are not in any way superior to those produced from metal pipes; and there is more than one practical reason in favor of the adoption of metal pipes in the octaves of high pitch.

The several normal flute-toned stops, to the names of which the

Latin term *tibia* has been prefixed, do not call for illustration or lengthy description. As open or covered stops, they are merely modified forms, so far as their pipes are concerned, of old and established types. The German TIBIA MAJOR is similar to the HOHLFLÖTE, but of a much fuller and heavier tone: it is made of 16 ft. and 8 ft. pitch. The German TIBIA MINOR, of 8 ft. and 4 ft. pitch, appears to be similar so far as tonal character is concerned to the TIBIA MAJOR, differing only from it in being made of higher pitch.

The stops which were first produced by the pipe makers and clever voicers with whom the late Mr. R. Hope-Jones was associated, are variants of a more marked character. The TIBIA CLAUSA, 8 FT., is a very large scaled covered stop, yielding a powerful, normal, covered flute-tone. A suitable scale gives the CC pipe a width of 5·78 inches, and a depth of 7·66 inches, with the ratio of 1 : 2·66. The mouth is about half its width in height. The pipes are copiously winded.

TIBIA PLENA.—An open stop of very large scale and of 8 ft. pitch, yielding a powerful, unimitative flute-tone. The stop in the Organ of Worcester Cathedral has its CC pipe measuring 7 13⁄16 inches by 9 inches; its C pipe 4⅝ by 5 1⁄16 inches; and its c¹ pipe 2 13⁄16 by 3¼ inches. The mouths have their upper lips leathered; but this perishable expedient is as unnecessary as it is undesirable. If the lips are made of sufficient thickness, carefully rounded, and burnished with black-lead, a perfectly satisfactory tone will be obtained.

TIBIA DURA.—The quadrangular pipes of this stop are of inverted pyramidal form; reproducing in wood the inverted conical pipes of the DOLCAN and DOLCE. The tone produced, however, being widely different from that of either metal stop; being, as the name implies, hard and pungent. It is strongly inclined to a flute tonality. We are of opinion that few organ-builders will consider this stop worth the trouble involved in its construction. Of other unimportant and valueless flute-toned variants it is unnecessary to speak.

WOOD PIPES OF STRING–TONE.

Of all the wood stops that have been invented perhaps those which yield imitative string-tone are the most noteworthy and interesting. One can readily understand the production of both pure organ-tone and flute-tone from wood pipes; but the problem of producing sounds from such pipes strongly imitative of the compound and penetrating tones of the orchestral bowed instruments, would appear to be surrounded by insurmountable difficulties. That those who first essayed the task of making and voicing such imitative pipes found it difficult, is amply proved by the small success which attended early efforts. The problem seems to have been first completely solved by the great Schulze. At all events, in our long study of the art of organ-building, and during our personal examination of hundreds of representative Organs distributed throughout Germany, Switzerland, Belgium, Holland, France, Italy, and England, we have discovered no string-toned stops at all comparable to those made and voiced by Edmund Schulze, of Paulinzelle. It is quite certain that wood stops of imitative string-tone were unknown in England prior to the advent of the organs constructed by Schulze: notably those in the Parish Church of Doncaster and St. Peter's Church, Hindley. In the numerous pages of " The Organ," by Hopkins and Rimbault, published in 1870, string-toned wood stops are not even mentioned; indeed the VIOLA DA GAMBA, in its old-fashioned treatment in metal, is the only stop of string-tone described.

This proves that up to a late date English organ-builders and organ experts knew nothing of the nature and powers of wood pipes producing string-tone.

DOUBLE BASS.—Of all the wood stops of string-tone, known to us, that which best deserves the name of DOUBLE BASS is the stop labeled VIOLON-BASS, 16 FT., in the Hindley Organ. The tone of this stop is imitiative to a remarkable degree, extending even to the rasping effect of the bow on the strings. The pipes are of small scale, square in section, and furnished with sunk blocks, caps with an external inclined sinking, and harmonic-bridges.*

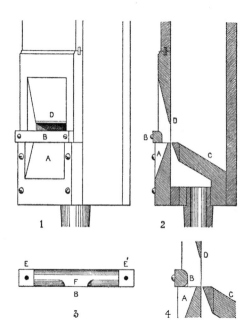

FIG. LXXXIV.

The accompanying illustration, Fig. LXXXIV., shows the forms and arrangement of the several parts constituting the speaking portion of the CCC pipe, accurately drawn to scale. Diagram 1 is a Diagonal View of the lower portion of the pipe, showing all the parts belonging to the mouth in position; Diagram 2 is a Longitudinal Section of the same, through the center of the mouth;

* We have introduced the term *harmonic-bridge*, as being perfectly logical and expressive; and for the purpose of doing away with the incorrect term *beard*, which is one of the several inapplicable and inexpressive terms used by modern organ-builders. A *beard*, in pipe terminology, is something placed immediately *below* the mouth and properly attached to its under lip, of which there are several forms, including those attached to blocks of wood pipes. For a similar reason we have used the term *labial pipe* in preference to the somewhat objectionable term *flue pipe*.

Diagram 3 shows an Enlarged View of the inner face of the harmonic-bridge, and Diagram 4 a Section of the mouth, clearly indicating the position of the bridge with relation to the cap and upper lip. The cap A is a thick piece of hardwood, flat on the side toward the block C, and having a sloping portion sunk on the outside, as shown, to allow a current of the external air to approach the mouth under the harmonic-bridge, while the pipe is speaking. B is the harmonic-bridge, a quadrangular bar of hardwood, notched at either end, E, E', to allow its central portion to approach somewhat nearer the mouth than the thickness of the pipe-front would otherwise permit. The upper inner edge of the bridge is rounded to a quarter circle along its entire length from E to E', while the lower edge is only rounded from each end a certain distance toward the center, where the roundings curve out, leaving the square-edged portion F, Diagram 3. The shape and position of this bridge are matters of considerable nicety, as they affect the quality and promptness of the tone. This we have tested by pipes copied for the purpose. The block C is sunk in the sloping manner shown, having a sharp edge where the wind-way is cut from it. No nicking is used on either cap or block; and the under lip is flush with the top of the cap. The height of the mouth is a little under one-third its width; and its upper lip is filed almost to a sharp edge. The dimensions of the three C pipes of the stop are as follows:

EDMUND SCHULZE'S SCALE OF VIOLONBASS, 16 FT.

PIPE.	WIDTH.	DEPTH.	HEIGHT OF MOUTH.
CCC. 16 ft.	. 5½ inches.	. 5½ inches.	. 1⁷⁄₁₀ inches.
CC. 8 ft.	. 3⅜ "	. 3⅜ "	. 1 inch.
C. 4 ft.	. 2 "	. 2 "	. ⅘ "

VIOLA.—In the Hindley Organ there is a VIOLA, 8 FT., constructed, in all essentials, similar to the stop just considered, except that its pipes are of different scale and deeper than wide. The dimensions of the CC (8 ft.) pipe are 2⅝ inches in width by 3⅝ inches in depth; and its mouth is ¹³⁄₁₆ inch in height: otherwise, the fittings and shaping of the mouth are in the relative proportions rendered in the illustration, Fig. LXXXIV. The stop is placed in the Choir Organ on a wind of about 2 inches pressure, and it is remarkably effective in tonal character.

The form of the harmonic-bridge met with in the two stops of the Hindley Organ, above described, appears to have been specially contrived by Schulze, for we have not found it in the works of any other organ builder. He did not confine himself to it, however, for in a fine string-toned stop, of 16 ft. pitch, in the pedal department of the Armley Organ, we find an entirely new form of harmonic-bridge. This is shown in the accompanying illustration, Fig. LXXXV. This bridge presents an acute-angled edge toward the lower lip of the mouth throughout its width. All other details of the lower part of the pipe are clearly shown. Various other forms of harmonic-bridges are used by different organ builders, but they are, judging by tonal results, in no way an improvement on those used by Schulze.

Violone.—In the Pedal department of the Organ in the Parish Church, Doncaster, there is a Violone, 16 ft., made by Schulze on an entirely different system from that followed by him in the Violonbass of the Hindley instrument. Its tone is full, rich, and imitative; but it is somewhat slow of speech, like a great many German stops of the string-tone class. A Diagonal View and Longitudinal Section of the lower portion of the CCC pipe are given in the accompanying illustration, Fig. LXXXVI. This pipe measures internally 6⅝ inches square, and its mouth is about 1⅝ inches in height. The peculiarity of the construction of the sound-producing portion of this pipe lies chiefly in the hopper-shaped appendage to the mouth, C. This rests on the beard of

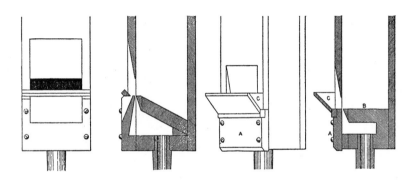

Fig. LXXXV.   Fig. LXXXVI.

the cap A, while its ends form projecting ears to the mouth. The block B is level on the top and flush with the cap, as shown, having the wind-way cut from it. The cap A is flat on the wind side, as common in pipes with German mouths. All the proportions of the several parts are correctly given in the Longitudinal Section from measurements taken from the pipe itself. The distance across the cap, from the wind-way to the start of the inclined front of the hopper, is 1¼ inches; and the inner inclined face of the front and the projection of the hopper both measure 3 inches. In the absence of ocular demonstration, it is extremely difficult to form any conception of the action of the external air on the wind-sheet at the mouth, as it is drawn down the sloping face of the hopper, to fill the partial vacuum caused by the upward rush of the organ-wind from the wind-way. While the action of the external air on the wind-sheet must be similar, to judge from the similarity of tone produced, its mode of approaching the wind-sheet is essentially

different from that which obtains where the sloping cap and the harmonic-bridge are used, as in the VIOLONBASS of the Hindley Organ.
In the one case it rushes downward obliquely, and in the other case it is
drawn upward obliquely, toward the mouth.

We may now leave the above representative German methods of
producing imitative string-tone in wood pipes, and enter on the brief
consideration of those which appear to be due to French ingenuity. Both
the harmonic-bridge and the acoustical-hopper, disappear, and a sloping
or curved plate of metal, called the *frein harmonique,* takes their place
at the mouth of the pipe. The *frein* (literally a *bridle* or *curb*) is most
effective when applied to small-scaled metal pipes;* but, in certain

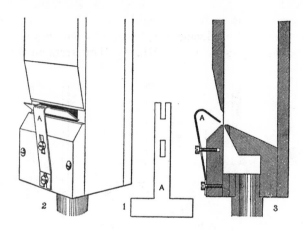

FIG. LXXXVII.

forms, it has proved very effective in connection with small-scaled wood
pipes. The *frein harmonique* was invented and patented by Gavioli, of
Paris.

VIOLIN.—In the accompanying illustration, Fig. LXXXVII., are
diagrams showing the construction of the lower part of an open wood
pipe, the tone of which is strongly imitative of the corresponding note of
the Violin. The drawings are taken from a 4 ft. pipe, the scale of
which is 1¾ inch square, with a mouth ⅜ inch in height. To admit
the use of the *frein harmonique,* the front of the pipe is sloped across
its entire width in forming the upper lip of the mouth; and for the
same purpose the upper part of the cap is splayed to almost a sharp
edge. This treatment brings the mouth, externally, to resemble the
mouth of a metal pipe without ears. The *frein harmonique* is a plate

* The first stop having the *frein harmonique* (system Gavioli) on its pipes introduced in
an English Organ was the VIOLA D'AMORE, 8 FT., made by Henri Zimmermann, of Paris, for
the author's Chamber Organ in the year 1876.

of thin brass, cut to the form shown at A, in Diagram 1, and slotted for the adjusting screws. This plate is bent into the shape indicated in the other Diagrams, and screwed to the face of the cap, as shown. The slots permit the *frein* to be raised or lowered, and the upper screw adjusts its proper distance from the wind-way. The angle at which the plate approaches the mouth is important, and this must be adjusted by bending the shank. All the three adjustments must be exactly right before the pipe will yield the true imitative tone. The block is slanted downward and has the wind-way cut from it, leaving a sharp under lip; the cap is straight on its inner surface and no nicking is used on either, block or cap. The pipes should be made of straight-grained spruce, with pear-tree or maple fronts and caps; and the blocks must be fronted with the same hard wood. Much depends on the sharpness and accuracy of all the edges touched by the wind-sheet. The under lip and inside edge of the cap must be perfectly smooth, and polished with black-lead. The pipes throughout the compass must be made with the greatest accuracy and care; but they amply repay the time and trouble expended on them by the beauty of their tones. This VIOLIN is most satisfactory when voiced on wind of about $3\frac{1}{2}$ inches, but a higher pressure may be used when a very cutting tone is desired.

VIOLONCELLO.—An 8 ft. open stop, producing a string-tone imitative of that of the orchestral Violoncello. It would be impossible, in our opinion, to adopt a better model for a wood stop of this class than that furnished by the fine VIOLONBASS, 16 FT., in the Hindley Organ, already described and illustrated (Fig. LXXXIV.). It would be desirable to reduce the scale slightly, making the CC pipe 3 inches square internal measurement, instead of $3\frac{3}{8}$ inches square as in the case of the 8 ft. pipe of the VIOLONBASS.

We may now describe what may be considered the most successful VIOLONCELLO, 8 FT., constructed by an English organ-builder, that invented by Mr. John W. Whiteley. A fine example of this stop appears in the Solo division of the Concert-room Organ in the Polytechnic Institute, Battersea, London. In the construction and treatment of the pipes of this valuable stop some novel features obtain, as will be seen from the drawings and particulars here given—features which, in our opinion, point the way to further developments of an important character. In the accompanying illustration, Plate XXIX. is shown part of the middle c^1 pipe of this stop, the scale of which is 1 inch in width by 1 $\frac{9}{16}$ inches in depth. It will be observed from the illustration that, while the internal dimensions are the same throughout the length of the pipe, the wood of which it is formed is evenly reduced in thickness toward the top, being $\frac{1}{4}$ inch at the block and only about $\frac{1}{8}$ inch thick at the open end. The result of this unusual treatment goes to prove that the thickness of the wood used in pipe-making exercises an influence on the tone produced; and this very important factor in pipe formation should not be overlooked. The formation of the mouth and all its associated parts deserves careful study. The slopings of the upper lip are carried entirely across the front in a manner similar to that shown in the VIOLIN pipe, Fig. LXXXVII. A similar treatment obtains in the external slopings of the cap, as distinctly shown. The mouth is cut up one-third of its width, and its upper lip is reduced to a fine edge. The lower lip on the block is also sharp, and has no nicking. The cap is slightly hollowed on its inside, also to a somewhat sharp edge, in which a slightly curved wind-way is cut, and finished with seven small nicks, as shown in the Transverse Section through the mouth, Diagram 3. A special peculiarity obtains in the manner in which the cylindrical harmonic-bridge is supported in front of the mouth. This bridge, instead of being simply the length of the mouth, and being attached to small ears, either formed from the wood of the pipe-front or the cap, is carried across the entire width of the pipe, and is supported by two thick spotted-metal plates, which are screwed to the sides of the pipe. The front edges of these plates are sloped away from the bridge so as to free the wind in the neighborhood of the mouth: indeed the entire construction of the mouth portion of the pipe insures perfect freedom to the under stream of air which is generated by the rushing wind-sheet of the mouth. This is essential to the production of the compound tone which so closely imitates that of the orchestral Violoncello. In the larger pipes the harmonic-bridges are made of hard wood, while in the small pipes they are made of aluminium tubing, held in position by points punched inward in the metal side-plates.

In the Organ in the Battersea Polytechnic—the instrument for which this VIOLONCELLO was devised and constructed in 1899—the stop is carried down to CCC (16 ft.), so as to be available in the pedal department under the name of CONTRA-BASS. From the measurements given of the middle c^1 pipe the scale of the entire stop can easily be developed, preferably on the ratio 1 : 2·66. All the pipes have to be considerably longer than the normal speaking lengths, to allow them to be slotted in the manner shown.

WOOD PIPES OF REED-TONE.

Numerous attempts have been made by artistically inclined organ-pipe voicers to produce imitative orchestral brass-tone and reed-tone from labial pipes. In the former case, the desire has been to obtain a tonality imitative of the orchestral Horn, the very peculiar, refined, and expressive voice of which has never been successfully imitated by lingual pipes. Regarding imitative orchestral reed-tone, some remarkable results have been reached in labial wood stops, the formation of the pipes

PLATE XXIX

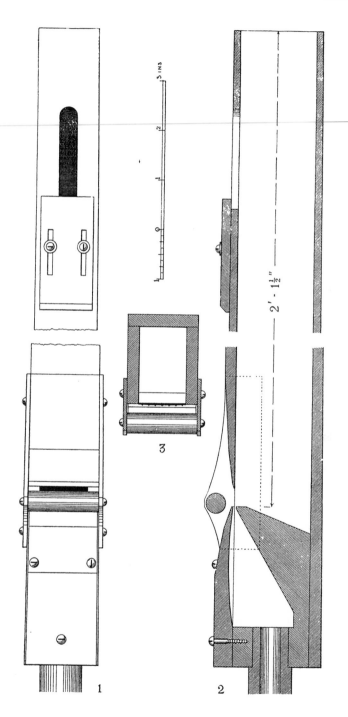

1

2

3

3 INS

2' - 1½"

of two of which we shall describe. Edmund Schulze had evidently directed his attention to this latter problem, with the result of producing the very beautiful stop which, on account of its extremely delicate quality of voice, he called the ECHO OBOE: * but this was not in any marked degree imitative of the orchestral Oboe played softly.

ORCHESTRAL OBOE. — We have now to describe and illustrate a wood labial stop of a noteworthy character, which yields a tone almost identical with that of the orchestral Oboe. This stop is due to the genius of Mr. W. E. Haskell, an American organ-builder of artistic taste and acquirements, who has paid considerable attention to the very important subject of tone production.

The drawings given in Fig. LXXXVIII. clearly show the form and construction of the middle c^1 pipe of this labial OBOE, 8 FT. The body of the pipe measures $\frac{7}{8}$ inch square, internally, at its mouth line, and, while its width remains the same, its depth is gradually reduced to $1\frac{1}{16}$ inch at its open end, the reduction commencing at twelve inches above the mouth and taking a curved form from that point in the front of the pipe, as indicated in the Section, 1. The block is sunk $\frac{3}{8}$ inch below the lower lip of the mouth. The mouth is inverted, and its lower lip is sloped on the inside down to the block level and slightly rounded in the manner shown. The upper lip is filed on the outside so as to produce a sharp edge slightly back from the face of the pipe. All these peculiarities are accurately indicated in the Section. The mouth is a little over $\frac{1}{8}$ inch in height. The cap is made sufficiently long to extend about $\frac{1}{8}$ inch above

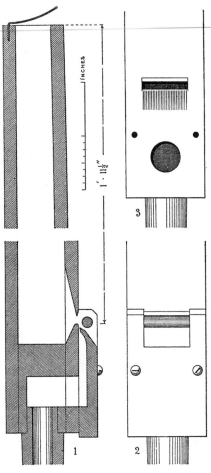

FIG. LXXXVIII.

* This beautiful stop is commented on, and the formation of its pipes illustrated, in "The Art of Organ-Building," vol. ii., pp. 481-2.

the upper lip of the mouth, and is cut away and sloped on the outside so as to support the small cylindrical harmonic-bridge in position, as shown in the Section, 1, and Front View, 2. The cap is hollowed on the inside, and is filed so as to produce a small sharp-edged wind-way, just sufficient to admit the passage of a strip of a playing-card. The cap is not nicked. The under lip of the mouth has twenty-seven straight and cleanly-cut nicks, as depicted in Diagram 3, which shows the mouth and lower part of the pipe with the cap removed. The illustrations are so accurately drawn to scale that further description of the sound-producing portion of the pipe is unnecessary. The pipe is tuned in the usual way by a metal shade at top. The stop is voiced on wind of 3½ inches, the pipes requiring a very small supply. As the orchestral Oboe does not descend below B♭, the stop under review when carried down to CC should certainly be labeled Oboe & Fagotto, 8 ft.

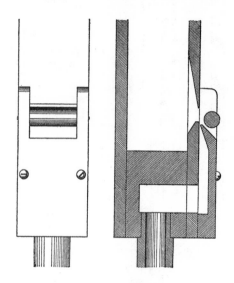

Fig. LXXXIX.

Saxophone.—We may conclude this special branch of our subject with a description of the form and construction of another remarkable imitative wood stop, invented by Mr. W. E. Haskell, the first introduced in the Organ built by Mr. C. S. Haskell for the Church of the Holy Trinity, Philadelphia, Pa., in 1897.

This fine stop is of 8 ft. pitch, and extends throughout the manual compass. Its scale is as follows: CC pipe, 3 ⁵⁄₁₆ inches in width by 4 ³⁄₁₆ inches in depth; C pipe, 2 inches in width by 2 ⁹⁄₁₆ inches in depth; c¹ pipe, 1 ³⁄₁₆ inches in width by 1 ¹⁷⁄₃₂ inches in depth; and c² pipe, ¾ inch in width by ³¹⁄₃₂ inch in depth. The accompanying illustration, Fig. LXXXIX., which gives a Front View and a Longitudinal Section of the sound-producing portion of the middle c¹ pipe, shows a formation almost identical with that in the labial Oboe previously illustrated. The block is sunk ¾ inch below the lower lip. The mouth is inverted, and its lower lip is sloped on the inside of the pipe and slightly rounded. The upper lip is filed to a very thin edge in the same manner as that of the Oboe pipe. The cap and the large cylindrical harmonic-bridge are so clearly shown that it is unnecessary to describe them. Both the face of the lower lip and the opposite edge of the cap are closely and sharply nicked. The mouth is a small fraction over two-sevenths its width in height. The body of the pipe is of the same dimensions throughout its length, and it is unslotted, being tuned by means of a metal shade at top in the usual manner.

Voiced on wind of about 3½ inches, this stop yields a tone exactly imitative of that of the orchestral Saxophones, described by Berlioz as possessing " most rare and precious qualities. Soft and penetrating in the higher part, full and rich in the lower part, their medium has something profoundly expressive. It is, in short, a quality of tone *sui generis,* presenting vague analogies with the sounds of the Violoncello, of the Clarinet, and Corno Inglese, and invested with a brazen tinge which imparts a quite peculiar accent." It seems too much to expect that so peculiar and complex a tone could be produced from wood pipes; but we have satisfied our mind on the subject by testing the stop, as inserted in the Organ above mentioned, by a direct comparison with the orchestral Saxophone, performed upon in the Organ immediately alongside the stop. While the imitation was practically perfect, in certain parts of its compass the SAXOPHONE of the Organ was, if anything, more pleasing than the corresponding tones of the orchestral instrument. The stop is a notable achievement, and great credit is due to its inventor. It certainly goes far to prove that much can still be done through the agency of wood pipes to enrich the imitative voices of the Organ; and we are convinced that they are to enter largely into the formation, in combination with metal pipes, of dual timbre-creating stops, so soon as the true value of such compound stops is realized.

WOOD PIPES OF DUAL TONALITY.

The principal stop of dual tonality, which has hitherto occupied an important place in the Organ, is the QUINTATEN, in the voice of which the second upper partial tone—the Twelfth—is present very prominently along with the prime tone. This stop is extremely valuable in combination and in timbre creation. Very recently another valuable stop of dual intonation has been added to the tonal forces of the Organ. It has already been spoken of in Chapter IV., page 109, and its construction has only to be described and illustrated here. In the accompanying illustration, Fig. XC., are given the Front View and Section of the lower portion of the c¹ pipe, showing the construction of the mouth; and also of the upper portion, showing the slotting and the tuning-slide. All are drawn to scale. The front and back of the pipe are parallel, 1 ³⁄₁₆ inches apart; while the sides are 3 ¹⁄₁₆ inches apart at the mouth and 1 ³⁄₁₆ inches at the top. The chief feature of the mouth is its upper lip A, which is a thick plate of pipe-metal, cut to a sharp edge, as shown. Directly opposite the mouth, and supported by the projecting ears B, B, is the cylindrical harmonic-bridge C. The manner in which the block, D, is sunk and splayed, and the exterior and interior sinkings of the cap E, are clearly shown in the Section, and should be carefully noted. The upper part of the front of the pipe has a long slot, F, about ¼ inch wide,

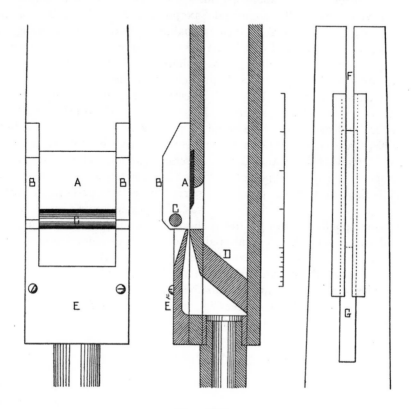

FIG. XC.

cut through to the top edge. The tuning is effected by means of the sliding strip of metal G. As stated in Chapter IV., this pipe yields the Octave, or first upper partial tone almost as strongly as its prime tone, accordingly, its proper name is OCTATEN—holding the Octave. Its inventor is Mr. George W. Till, of Philadelphia, Pa.

CHAPTER XVI.

FORMS AND CONSTRUCTION OF LINGUAL PIPES.

ERTAINLY, it may be safely said, there is no branch of the art of organ-building so difficult to treat by the pen as that embracing the special formation, scaling, and voicing of lingual or reed pipes. This fact appears to have been realized by even the most accomplished writers on the Organ. Certain ingenious authorities, learned in mathematics, have attempted to formulate laws and rules, only to find them upset at every point, and rendered valueless in practice, proving in this, as in many other artistic and tonal matters, that an ounce of hard fact is worth a hundredweight of supposition or theory, however much either may be bolstered up by mathematical formulæ and apparently conclusive demonstration, arrived at, not in the practical atmosphere of the pipe-making and voicing rooms of an organ factory, but in the narrow breathing-space of the physical laboratory, furnished with the usual special and insufficient means of investigation. The writer who has, up to the present time, given the most voluminous dissertation on reed pipes is Max Allihn, in his extension of Töpfer's original treatise, entitled " Die Theorie und Praxis des Orgelbaues." In this work he devotes one hundred and seventeen pages to the subject, bristling with mathematical formulæ, and studded with tables of dimensions. Notwithstanding all such evidences of learning and research, he is forced to say as follows:

" The subject of reed pipes is a question so intricate and obscure that it creates a sensation as of one trying to find a path through a forest with which one is unacquainted, and in which numberless stray paths lead from the right road. If we undertake to offer our guidance to the reader in this realm, we do not presume to transform the rough ways into a smooth road; but with the consciousness of having taken pains in exploring the territory, and in the belief of having found some points from which right views and unprejudiced perspectives are possible. The organ-builder has, at all times, had trouble with reed stops.

" Under such circumstances, the practician justly turns to theory for enlightenment; but in this matter theory is just as helpless as practice. In the case of labial pipes it has been observed that the physical process of their sound-production has by no means been sufficiently grasped; the same is the case with reed pipes, with which very few expert scientists have concerned themselves."

It must be evident to everyone who has paid attention to the subject, and who has studied the writings of Dom Bedos, Töpfer and his latest editor, Max Allihn, Helmholtz, and others of lesser note, that these authorities have failed to establish any theory or rules on which lingual pipes can be designed to produce definite tonal results. Yet their writings are worthy of careful consideration, for they contain the results of their experiments which are not valueless. " Nor," as Mr. F. E. Robertson remarks, " are their labors fruitless, for, if their scales (which are not approved by competent judges) are not the best possible, yet the information they have collected throws a light upon the behavior of reed pipes, and indicates the direction which further research into this most interesting subject should take."

Before going into particulars respecting the usual forms of the several classes of reed pipes introduced in modern Organs, it is desirable that the general reader be made acquainted with the forms and construction of the several parts which constitute the sound-producing and tone-controlling portions of a normal striking-reed pipe. The several constructive and essential parts of a reed pipe are the boot; the block; the reed or *échalote;* the tongue or *languette;* the wedge; the tuning-wire; and the resonator or body. To the last-named part is sometimes added a regulator of some suitable form, as will be described farther on. The parts just mentioned may properly be described in the order adopted.

The boot is that part of a reed pipe which rests directly on the wind-chest, and into the lower end of which the pipe-wind enters on the opening of the corresponding valve or pallet in the wind-chest, and into the upper end of which is inserted the block carrying the sound-producing parts of the pipe. When formed of metal, the boot is round, slightly conical (but not necessarily so), and contracted at its lower end, which rests in the pipe-hole in the upper-board of the wind-chest. The upper and lower ends of a metal boot are shown in Diagram 1, Plate XXX. Boots as above described are properly made of good pipe-metal or stout zinc, and when of the latter material are tipped with pipe-metal. The boots are made much in the same manner as the feet of metal labial pipes, and, accordingly, call for no special details of con-

PLATE XXX

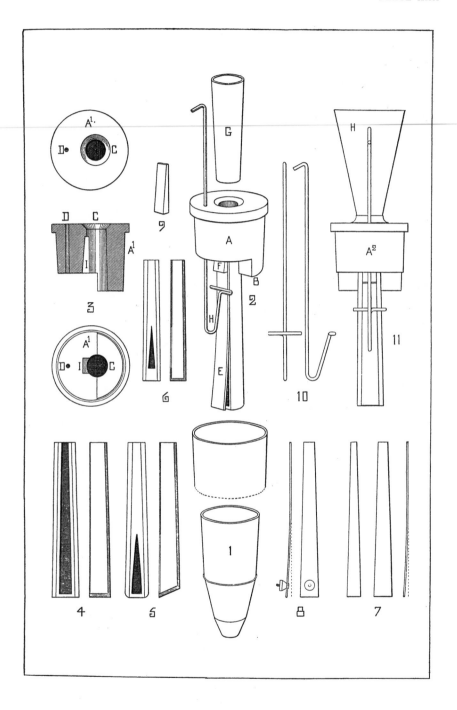

struction here. When made of wood, the boot is quadrangular, open at
its lower end, where it is screwed to, or socketed into, the upper-board
of the wind-chest; and formed at its upper end to receive either a quadrangular wood block or a round metal one. Wooden boots are used
only for very large reed pipes, and have been largely abandoned by pipe
makers since zinc has come into favor. Boots are made of various
lengths in proportion to their diameters, according to the nature of the
pipes with which they are associated. As a rule, a long boot is advantageous to the speech of a reed, and such being the case, they are sometimes used for the pipes of the Vox Humana, the resonators of which
are very short, as will be pointed out later on. We have before us while
we write a middle c^1 pipe of this stop, the boot of which measures 21½
inches in length, while its diameter is only 1⅛ inches. The consequent
elevation of the speaking portion of the pipe is very convenient for
regulating and tuning purposes. Free reeds demand very long and
otherwise large boots; but, while this requirement has been demonstrated by practice, the reason for it has not been clearly arrived at.

The block is that portion of a reed pipe which is inserted in, and
supported by, the upper end of the boot. It carries, pendant from it,
the sound-producing apparatus of the pipe, and receives, and holds in
place, on its upper surface, the lower and contracted end of the resonator
or body of the pipe. In addition, the block has passing through it in a
vertical direction the movable tuning-wire. The block, when of metal,
is usually of the form shown in perspective at A, in Diagram 2, and in
section at A^1, in Diagram 3, Plate XXX. The circular portion, slightly
tapered, fits tightly into the boot, while the lower segmental portion is
for the support of the reed against the pressure of the tuning-wire, as
indicated at B, in Diagram 2. In small blocks, and in those of German
manufacture, this segmental support is frequently omitted, the reed being
simply driven firmly into the perforation in the block. Two perforations
pass vertically through the block: a large and slightly-tapered one for
the reception of the reed and its communication with the resonator,
indicated at C, and a small one for the passage of the tuning-wire,
indicated at D, in Diagram 3. The blocks are of pipe-metal, cast in
metal molds of the requisite graduated sizes. In high-class work they
are subsequently neatly finished in the turning lathe.

The reed or *échalote* is a slightly-tapered tube of soft brass, closed
at its lower and larger end with a disc of the same metal soldered on.
Along the tube a perfectly flat and smooth face is formed by the file,
and in this face an opening of some special form is made. According
to the old method, the reed is formed by beating or swaging a plate of
soft and annealed brass, of the proper size and form, around a tapered
steel mandrel, a grooved iron block and wooden mallet being used in
the process. The plate may require repeated annealing before it is

brought to its required shape.   According to the more satisfactory and expeditious modern method, the reed is made from a drawn tube of soft and annealed brass, expanded into a tapered form by means of a steel mandrel driven into it while it is supported in a tapered hole in an iron block.   By this latter process a seamless tube, perfect in form, is quickly produced.   The face of the reed for the reception of the tongue is now carefully made by filing or grinding, and the opening of the required form is cut in it.   The reed is practically completed by having a disc of soft brass soldered to its lower end, and filed to its external form.   All that remains to be done is the final filing and polishing of the face.   The shape, proportion, and position of the opening in the face of the reed are important factors in tone-production.   The three typical treatments are illustrated in Plate XXX.   In Diagram 4 is shown the " open reed," in which the opening, of a tapered form, extends from the stopped end throughout the length of the tube.   This form of reed is frequently used for TRUMPETS and other loud-toned stops.   In Diagram 5 is represented the so-called " closed reed," in which the opening, of a lancet form, extends from the stopped end only a moderate distance up the face of the tube.   In Diagram 6 is shown a " closed reed " differing from the preceding in having its lancet-shaped opening raised a short distance above the stopped end of the tube.   The proportions which these openings bear to the lengths and diameters of their tubes vary considerably in the different classes of reed pipes, and also in the same classes of pipes made by different organ-builders.   Absolutely no rules of universal application can be given in this matter.   In the case of large pipes belonging to stops of 32 ft. and 16 ft. pitch the reeds are frequently made of some close-grained hardwood, and have their faces against which the tongues beat covered with leather.   The German builders, to overcome the rough-ness which is liable to attend their style of voicing, commonly leather the faces of their larger brass reeds.   This practice is clearly indicated in the illustrations of reed-work given in " Die Theorie und Praxis des Orgelbaues."   The brass reeds are accurately fitted to the perforations in their respective blocks, which are tapered to suit the reeds, and ac-curately dimensioned so as to allow the reeds to enter only the proper distance in all cases.

The tongue or *languette* is a thin and narrow strip of fine elastic brass, shaped so as to accurately cover the face of its corresponding reed.   It is filed perfectly flat on both sides and so as to be uniform in thickness.   Its thickness is accurately adjusted to accord with the size of the reed, and the conditions under which the voicing is conducted.   An accurate gradation in thickness is as essential for the production of uniform tonality as is the gradation in the other dimensions of the tongues belonging to a stop.   Several forms of gauges have been introduced or used by voicers for accurately graduating the lengths, widths, and thicknesses of tongues, and these are very conducive to satisfactory and rapid workmanship.

When the tongue is finished perfectly smooth and level on both its faces, and correctly fitted—in length, width, and form—to the surface of its reed, it is ready to receive its voicing- or speaking-curve. The curving of the tongue is perhaps the most exacting operation in the reed-voicer's art, demanding experience, skill, and delicacy of touch. It is usually performed as follows: The tongue is laid, with its striking-face downward, on a smooth and perfectly flat piece of very hard and close-grained wood, and its narrow or upper end is held firmly by a small block or clamp screwed down to the flat piece. Then, by means of a highly-polished cylindrical steel rod or burnisher, held firmly, by both hands, truly and squarely on the surface of the tongue toward its clamped end, and passed thence to its free end, with a motion and varying degrees of pressure which long experience and practice only can teach, and which words cannot describe, the tongue receives a slight curve upward. This burnishing process is repeated just as often as the voicer finds it necessary; that is, until the exact curvature is obtained which is requisite for the production of the special tone aimed at, combined with promptness of speech. The curvature must be perfectly true, and of such a nature that when the free end of the tongue is gently pressed down to the surface of the wood, the whole tongue will return to an absolutely flat state, just as it lay on the wood before the burnisher was applied. The slightest kink or twist in the tongue will render it useless. Machines have been devised for the curving of large and thick tongues, which have proved more or less successful in their operation. These machines apply the burnisher in a manner imitative of the operation of the hands, as above outlined, but with a degree of force and an accuracy of application that no simple manipulation can approach in the curving of large and thick tongues. The limited space at our disposal prevents our attempting to describe and illustrate these mechanical appliances. The form of the curve given to the tongue exercises not only a controlling influence over promptness of speech, but also on the character of the tone produced while it is in vibration.

The lengths and thicknesses of the tongues are properly dictated by the pitch of the tones they have to yield under certain controlling factors, and require to be accurately graduated throughout the series belonging to a complete stop, in accordance with some approved ratio and thickness-gauge. The widths and forms of the tongues are largely dictated by the general formation and proportions of the pipes, the character and loudness of the tones desired, and the pressure of the wind employed to set them into vibration. With such conditions affecting the formation of tongues suitable for the various classes and pitches of reed pipes, it is quite obvious that no scales of measurements of anything approaching general application can be formulated, and all attempts to produce such scales have ended in failures. Such being the case, special scales or tables of measurements are made or adopted by each reed-pipe maker or voicer for the different classes of stops—measurements which have been arrived at by experiment and experience—yielding the qualities of tone which each voicer affects. We may properly say at this point that whatever proportionate measurements are adopted, they should be based on some logarithmic scale, constructed in the manner set forth in Chapter XIII. on the Scales of Labial Pipes. There can be no question that the smoothness and regularity of the tone of a lingual stop depends, in one important direction at least, on the perfect scaling of its tongues.

In Diagram 7, Plate XXX., are shown the common forms of tongues as used in reed pipes of different classes. At E, in Diagram 2, the tongue is shown adjusted to the reed, and secured to the pipe-block in its proper position.

Up to this point we have been treating of tongues formed of plates of brass, practically of uniform thickness throughout their lengths. We have now to describe what are known as "loaded tongues." To avoid using tongues of inconvenient length for the production of grave tones, organ-builders have adopted tongues, the free ends of which are loaded or weighted in some manner. In loading a tongue, which has been formed and curved in the manner previously described, care must be taken to leave it perfectly free to vibrate and properly strike the face of the reed. A usual and satisfactory method of accomplishing this is to attach to its outer face, near its free end, a conical brass button, the small truncated end of which rests on the tongue without in any manner interfering with its curvature or free vibration. Front and Side Views of a tongue loaded in this fashion are given in Diagram 8, Plate XXX. The conical buttons are graduated in size to accord with the different dimensions of tongues; and they are firmly secured by small screw-pins, which pass through holes drilled in the tongues in the manner indicated. The tongues of the pipes of the CONTRA-OBOE, 16 FT., from CC to f♯[1], in the Swell division of the Organ in Glasgow Cathedral are weighted in this manner. This instrument was constructed by Willis. Other methods of loading striking tongues have been adopted; namely, that of gluing some substance, such as soft leather, to the outer surface of their vibrating portions, but it is questionable if these methods, or loading in any form can be recommended.

The wedge is a small piece of hard wood of the form shown in Diagram 9, Plate XXX. It is used to secure the tongue, at its upper end, in the block and against the face of the reed. It is shown in position at F, in Diagram 2, while the place for its reception is indicated at I, in Diagram 3. When the tongue is held in its correct position against the face of the reed, the wedge is pressed into its place by the blade of a strong knife or any convenient tool. When the tongue has to be removed for alteration or cleaning, the wedge can be easily withdrawn by notching a knife into it and turning the blade so as to bear on the under surface of the block. In the process of voicing the tongue may have to be frequently removed, and a temporary wedge is often used until the tongue is perfected, when the permanent wedge is inserted; which, in high-class work, is made of brass.

The tuning-wire is represented in Front and Side views in Diagram 10, and in Perspective at H, in Diagram 2. The wire is of unannealed steel, hard brass, or phosphor-bronze, but the last-named alloy is much to be preferred. The wire used must be of sufficient size to exert a pressure that will firmly hold the tongue against its reed and retain its position after tuning. Different sizes are employed for the large, medium, and small reeds, Nos. 13, 14, and 15 B. W. G. being suitable for the stops of 8 ft. pitch. Larger sizes are used for reeds of lower pitch. The description of wire employed to some extent dictates its gauge. The wire must be formed so as to bear upon the tongue perfectly true, and must be bent so that it will move smoothly in the process of tuning, and have no disposition to spring into another position after the tuning is finished. Weak and badly-formed tuning-wires are very apt to alter their positions and, accordingly, to throw the pipes out of tune.

The resonator, body, or tube of a lingual pipe is that portion which rises from the upper surface of the block, directly over the perforation in which the reed is inserted. The office of the resonator is, to control the sound produced by the reed and tongue, and translate it into a musical tone of definite pitch and *timbre*. In the form and dimensions of the resonator—matters in connection with which no rules of general application seem to have been formulated—the peculiar acoustical properties of the reed and tongue have to be recognized; and it is evident that upon the scientific relationship of these parts the perfection of the resultant tone of a reed pipe depends. Such being the case, it is hardly to be wondered at that a perfectly satisfactory lingual stop is a rare and a highly-prized possession in any Organ. A striking reed will not yield any note of truly musical character until its resonator is added; and the same reed will generate different qualities of musical tone when associated with resonators of different forms and proportions. But the tones so produced will not be equally good; indeed, it is highly probable that only one form and size of resonator will be found to be perfectly adapted to the peculiar acoustical properties of the reed and tongue, producing a beautiful musical tone. The special and practically-fixed construction of the sound-producing portion of a reed pipe to a large extent dictates the form of its resonator; for instance, whatever the shape of the upper or main portion of the resonator may be, its lower portion, which is joined to the block, has to be (under all usual conditions) tapered to the size dictated by the diameter of the reed below, or the perforation in the block over which it is attached.

As the different forms of resonators are described and illustrated in the following particulars of the various lingual stops introduced in the modern Organ, it is unnecessary to treat of them in any special manner in this place, but their modes of construction may be briefly touched upon here. Resonators are made of both metal and wood: the former being used for those of all forms and dimensions, while the latter is usually confined to resonators of large size and of inverted pyramidal form, such as are commonly used for the pipes of the CONTRAPOSAUNE, 32 FT., and the CONTRA-TROMBONE and CONTRAFAGOTTO, 16 FT.

The materials used in the construction of metal resonators are tin, pipe-metal, and zinc. While the high-class alloys of tin and lead are always to be preferred a good deal may be said in favor of the employment of zinc, especially for resonators which are long and extremely slender, such as those properly used for the ORCHESTRAL OBOE, 8 FT., CONTRA-OBOE, 16 FT., and FAGOTTO, 8 FT. The resonators are formed in precisely the same manner as are the bodies of labial pipes. The sheets of metal are cut to the proper forms and dimensions, according to templates prepared for the stop in hand, and are then rolled up on mandrels of the required shape, and subsequently soldered. While the resonators of certain stops are simply conical in form, and require only single pieces of metal in their formation, those of other stops are compound in form, and require two or more pieces in their construction. In the latter case the component parts are cut out, rolled up, and soldered separately, and finally soldered together. When zinc is employed for plain conical resonators, it must have all parts requiring manipulation in the processes of voicing, regulating, and tuning added in pipe-metal. The resonators of small pipes, or, say, those under two feet in length, are usually soldered directly to their respective blocks; but the larger resonators are properly inserted in sockets of suitable forms and dimensions, which are soldered to their corresponding blocks. This latter method is convenient and to be commended for all practical purposes. A socket suitable for an ordinary conical resonator, such as that of a TRUMPET pipe, is shown at G in Plate XXX., detached from its block A. In the Front View of a block, reed, tongue, and tuning-wire, given in Diagram 11, a socket for the reception of a resonator of a CLARINET pipe is indicated at H. Having briefly detailed the several component parts of a normal striking-reed pipe, we may now proceed to describe the different classes of reed pipes used in the modern Organ.

TRUMPET.—The TRUMPET, 8 FT., may be accepted as the representative of a family of striking-reed stops, the pipes of which extend through seven octaves. The stop of 8 ft. pitch is invariably made of metal, which should be of good quality and of substantial thickness. The resonator of the TRUMPET pipe is of an inverted conical form, as shown in the accompanying illustration, Fig. XCI., of a length nearly that of an open labial pipe of the same pitch, and entirely open at top. In certain high-pressure TRUMPET stops the pipes have resonators of about double the normal speaking lengths. A stop of this class is commonly distinguished by the name HARMONIC TRUMPET, and its voice should be full and brilliant, imitative of that of the orchestral Trumpet played *fortissimo*. The reeds are made both open and closed, according to the character of the tone desired. For the true Chamber Organ, the TRUMPET, 8 FT., should invariably be made with closed reeds, so as to secure a somewhat mellow quality combined with the clang which should distinguish the stop. When closed reeds are used for full-toned pipes, their openings should extend fully half up their respective exposed faces. The scale which determines the diameters of the open ends of the resonators, varies considerably in different TRUMPETS, a wide scale being used for stops of powerful intonation, and a comparatively narrow scale for Chamber Organ stops.

TUBA.—This stop is simply a large-scale TRUMPET, of 8 ft. pitch, and very powerful voice. It is commonly voiced on wind of from 10 to 30 inches, and finds its place in the Solo division of large Organs. When of very large scale, the stop has been designated TUBA MIRABILIS. Its reeds are properly of the open class, and its tongues are both wide and thick. Its resonators are necessarily of large scale, and of thick and firm metal. The most powerful reed stop introduced in the Organ is that called HARMONIC TUBA, 8 FT., the resonators of which are about double the length of those belonging to the ordinary TUBA, 8 FT. The reeds are large and open, and the tongues broad and very thick. The pipes are overblown with wind of not less than 20 inches. The resonators are of large scale, inverted conical in form, and of great thickness. Double tongues have in some rare instances been used, but

FIG. XCI.

there is no need to resort to this extreme practice. Single tongues can be made to produce tones quite as loud as any musical effect can call for. The love for loud, coarse, and blatant sounds in the Organ is a purely modern craze, and can hardly be supported on artistic grounds, we venture to think.

CORNOPEAN.—From the name used to designate this stop, it might be supposed to imitate in tone the brass instrument popularly known by the same name, but in this direction it falls far short of being successful. In too many examples it is simply a bad TRUMPET. The CORNOPEAN, 8 FT., is, however, when made and voiced by a master, both a distinct and agreeable stop. Its resonators are similar in form to those of the TRUMPET; but, in good examples, they are larger in scale, and they are never made harmonic or of double length. The reeds of the CORNOPEAN should invariably be of the closed species; and the tongues should be carefully curved to produce a tone free from the brilliant and somewhat brassy clang of the TRUMPET, while they have a firm and bold character. But, after all that can be done with this stop by the most skilful voicer, we must acknowledge that it holds about the same unsatisfactory position in the tonal forces of the Organ as the true Cornet à pistons does among the instruments of the orchestra, where it too often does duty for the orchestral Trumpet, and does it badly. The CORNOPEAN, 8 FT., should certainly never occupy the place of the TRUMPET in any Organ.

CLARION.—This stop is in its normal form simply an OCTAVE TRUMPET, 4 FT. Its pipes are, in construction and general treatment, precisely similar to those of the TRUMPET, 8 FT. While the latter stop is invariably carried throughout in reed pipes, the CLARION, 4 FT., owing to its high pitch, usually has its top octave of large-scale and loud-toned labial pipes. The tone of the CLARION should in all artistic tonal appointments be subordinate to that of the associated TRUMPET. Its resonators should, accordingly, be of smaller scale. In all ordinary cases it should have closed reeds. When the TRUMPET is harmonic, it is usual and proper, although not absolutely essential, to have a HARMONIC CLARION, 4 FT. The CLARION, when properly voiced and regulated, is a very valuable addition to the reed-work of the Organ, brightening it, and materially enriching its harmonic structure. The stop is, however, rarely introduced in small Organs, where its high-pitched voice would be almost certain to upset the tonal balance.

DOUBLE TRUMPET.—This stop is an unimitative TRUMPET, of 16 ft. pitch, frequently introduced in the Great divisions of large Organs. It is, however, best suited for the most important expressive division, where its grave and commanding voice would be under control and productive of fine effects. When associated with the unison TRUMPET, its voice should be somewhat subordinate, so as to disturb as little as possible the unison pitch. For this purpose, the scale of its corresponding pipes should be smaller than that of the TRUMPET, 8 FT., pipes.

TROMBONE or POSAUNE.—This stop belongs to the TRUMPET family. When introduced in a manual division, it is properly of 8 ft. pitch and constructed entirely of metal, differing from the ordinary TRUMPET,

8 FT., only in having tongues and reeds of more powerful and distinctive intonation and resonators of larger scale. Its tone should closely imitate that of the orchestral Trombone, having the brazen clang of that instrument when played *forte*. This *timbre* distinguishes the TROMBONE, 8 FT., from the other unison reeds of the same family— TRUMPET, TUBA, CORNOPEAN, and HORN—in which brassy tonality is objectionable. The TROMBONE of the Pedal Organ is properly of 16 ft. pitch, and is constructed entirely of metal or of wood and metal. When of metal, its pipes differ in no respect beyond their size from those of the TROMBONE, 8 FT. When chiefly of wood, the pipes differ considerably both in form and mode of construction. It will be sufficient for us to describe the CCC and CC pipes of a Pedal Organ TROMBONE, 16 FT., made by Roosevelt. In Plate XXXI. are given Transverse Sections of the sound-producing portions of these pipes, accurately drawn to scale, and Side Views of the complete pipes, showing the proportions of their resonators. At A, in Diagram 1, is a Longitudinal Section of the boot of the CCC pipe, a quadrangular box of wood 16 inches long and measuring internally $3\frac{1}{2}$ inches by $2\frac{7}{8}$ inches. Its lower end is socketed into the upper-board of the windchest B, and is supplied with pipe-wind through the hole C, $1\frac{1}{8}$ inches in diameter. The upper end of the boot receives the hardwood block D, bored for the reception of the reed E and the passage of the tuning-wire F, and socketed to receive the lower end of the resonator G. The reed E is made of maple, turned, bored, plugged at its lower end, and planed so as to provide a face for the tongue H to strike against. The face is covered throughout the greater portion of its length with close-grained leather, faced with smooth drawing-paper of the finest quality, while its upper portion, against which the tuning-wire presses the tongue, and which enters the block, is covered with a veneer of hardwood, of exactly the same thickness as the leather, over which the paper facing is carried. The leather and veneer are indicated in the diagram between the reed and the tongue. The tongue is of hard rolled brass, about $\frac{1}{32}$ inch thick, $6\frac{7}{8}$ inches long from the under surface of the block, $\frac{13}{16}$ inch wide where it is wedged into the block, and $\frac{15}{16}$ inch wide at its free end. The resonator is of pine, quadrangular and inverted pyramidal in form, having a speaking length of 14 feet 1 inch, and an internal size at top of $8\frac{3}{8}$ inches by $7\frac{1}{2}$ inches. In Diagram 2 is shown, also in correct scale, a Side View of the complete CCC pipe. In Diagram 3 is given a Longitudinal Section of the sound-producing portion of the CC pipe, drawn to the same scale as Diagram 1. Its dimensions are as follows: Length of boot 10 inches, and internal measurements of same $2\frac{5}{8}$ inches by $2\frac{3}{16}$ inches; diameter of wind-hole $\frac{11}{16}$ inch; length of tongue from under surface of block $5\frac{1}{8}$ inches; width of tongue at wedge $\frac{19}{32}$ inch, and at its free end $\frac{11}{16}$ inch; length

of resonator 7 feet, with an internal size at top of 5⅜ inches by 4⅞ inches. In Diagram 4 is shown a Side View of the complete CC pipe drawn to the same scale as Diagram 2. The stop composed of pipes constructed as above described is very suitable for a Pedal Organ of small dimensions, in which it would be the only reed. Its tone is dignified and full, in which the brazen character properly belonging to the manual TROMBONE, 8 FT., is desirably absent. The smoothness of intonation is due to the manner in which the reeds are made and leathered and the fine curvature of the strong tongues. In addition, the large size of the boots favors the production of smooth and prompt speech.

CONTRA-TROMBONE.—This name is employed to designate a TROMBONE, 16 ft. pitch, inserted in the manual department, the tone of which is intended to imitate that of the Bass Trombone of the orchestra; and also to designate a stop of similar character and of 32 ft. pitch, inserted in the pedal department of the Organ. The manual CONTRA-TROMBONE should be constructed entirely of metal, its resonators being made of stout zinc topped with good pipe-metal. Its true tone should resemble that of the TROMBONE, 8 FT., as above described, but be slightly softer. The CONTRA-TROMBONE, 32 FT., of the Pedal Organ, should be similar in tone to the TROMBONE, 16 FT., and be constructed in precisely the same manner.

Certain English organ-builders have used the name CONTRAPOSAUNE for stops having a more powerful and a more brazen tonality than those commonly designated by the name CONTRA-TROMBONE; but in the present unsatisfactory state of organ-stop nomenclature in both England and America, very little weight can be laid on the names used by organ-builders, so far, at least, as fine distinctions of tonality are concerned. Even a brief survey of the tonal appointments and the stop-knobs of English and American Organs may well cause one to ask: " What's in a name? "

OPHICLEIDE.—The tone of this stop is intended to imitate that of the orchestral Ophicleide, but the imitation is far from satisfactory. The OPHICLEIDE of the Organ is an extremely powerful, high-pressure reed, of 8 ft. pitch in the manual department, and of 16 ft. pitch in the Pedal Organ. The resonators of the pipes are inverted conical in form, of large scale, and constructed of thick spotted metal or of zinc and pipe-metal, while the reeds and tongues are made to withstand the action of wind of very high pressure. Otherwise, the construction of the pipes differs in no essential from that of the pipes of the TRUMPET or the TUBA. In the Willis Organ in St. George's Hall, Liverpool, there are two OPHICLEIDES, of 8 ft. pitch, in the manual department, and one, of 16 ft. pitch, in the Pedal Organ. The fine unison stop in the Solo Organ speaks with a commanding voice on wind of 22 inches pressure: this is, so far as our knowledge extends, the grandest speci-

PLATE XXXI

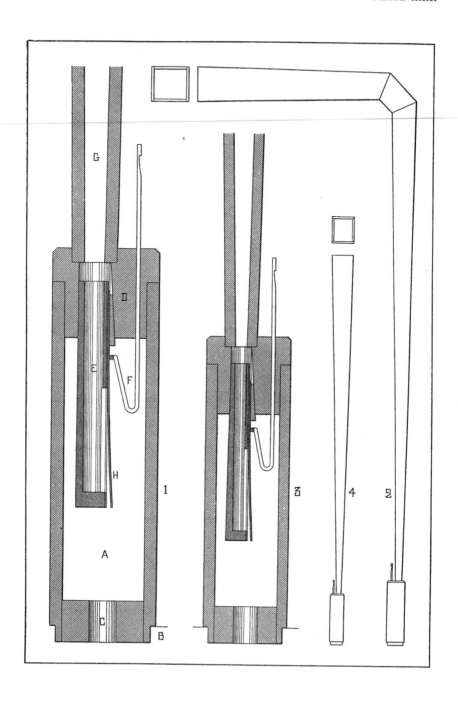

men of the organ OPHICLEIDE, 8 FT., in existence—voiced by a master.

Notwithstanding these facts and all that has been achieved, we are strongly of opinion that the perfect OPHICLEIDE of the Organ has yet to be produced. The orchestral Ophicleide belongs to the Bugle family of wind instruments, being, in fact, the bass correlative of the key or so-called "Kent Bugle." While the usual Ophicleide of the orchestra is of 8 ft. pitch, extending only one semitone below the lowest note of the Violoncello, yet, as a Contra-bass Ophicleide has been made and used in the orchestra,* organ-builders should not hesitate to produce an imitative stop of 16 ft. pitch; forming a special family—CONTRA-BASS OPHICLEIDE, 16 FT., OPHICLEIDE, 8 FT., and BUGLE, 4 FT.—of considerable tonal value in the Concert-room Organ. Let the tone of the orchestral instrument be carefully studied; and we venture to predict that anything but high-pressure wind will be found necessary or desirable.

HORN.—It has long been the ambition of the more accomplished reed voicers to produce a stop, the tones of which would closely imitate those peculiar to the orchestral Horn. The problem has proved a difficult one; and our observations have led us to the conclusion that the somewhat mournful character of the *closed* or "*hand notes,*" which are absolutely free from brassiness or reediness, can best be imitated by labial pipes. Perhaps, however, when the art of forming timbre-creating dual stops is better understood, the Horn may be satisfactorily imitated by the combination of a lingual stop with a sympathetic labial one.

The normal HORN, 8 FT., as found in modern Organs, can lay no claim to have an imitative voice. It has simply a comparatively soft and smooth intonation in best examples; of the inferior examples it is unnecessary to speak. The resonators of the pipes are similar to those of the TRUMPET, but are usually of larger scale. The tones produced should be of a softer and smoother character than those of the CORNOPEAN, as above described. Several expedients have been resorted to, to approach the *closed sounds* of the orchestral Horn, one of which consists of inserting within the resonator a disc of metal perforated with numerous small holes. This to some extent muffles the tone natural to the pipe, but in no way improves it. In other examples the resonators are partly closed at top, or are furnished with adjustable shades, which allow the pipes to be regulated and slightly modified in tone. During recent years, however, considerable attention has been given to the production of an ORCHESTRAL HORN, 8 FT., and some steps toward success may be recorded, in which lingual pipes alone have been employed.

* At the Birmingham Festival in 1834 an Ophicleide and also a Contra-bass Ophicleide were used with such effect that they were noticed in a periodical of the time as "destined to operate a great change in the constitution of the orchestra."

Very recently our attention has been directed to a lingual stop, labeled FRENCH HORN, which imitates the voice of the orchestral instrument more closely than any other organ stop known to us. This stop is the production of the Hook and Hastings Company, the esteemed organ-builders, of Kendal Green, Mass., through whose courtesy we are able to give, in the accompanying illustration, Fig. XCII., a drawing, to scale, of the Tenor G pipe of this important stop. It differs in construction from any HORN pipe we have seen. While the resonator is of the usual TRUMPET form, it is surmounted by a pyramidal cap, soldered on, which is a novelty, so far as our knowledge extends, and which, we can readily understand, exerts a considerable mellowing effect on the tone in conjunction with the slot which admits of adjustment both at bottom and top. The slot is properly made on the side toward the tuning-wire, but is so placed in the illustration that both it and the tuning-wire can be clearly shown. The dimensions of the resonator are as follows: Length, exclusive of the conical capping, 2 feet 3¾ inches; height of capping internally ⅝ inch; diameter at top 3⅜ inches. Dimensions of the slot are: Length of opening 2 1/16 inches; width 9/16 inch; distance of opening from top edge of resonator 1½ inches. It will be observed that the opening is adjustable at both ends, providing for accurate regulation and toning. The dimensions of the sound-producing parts are: The length of the reed or éschalote from the under side of the block is 1¾ inches; the width of the tongue at its free end is 11/32 inch, and where it is wedged into the block 3/16 inch. The reed is closed and its perforation commences 15/16 inch from the lower end. The whole is most carefully finished, a brass wedge being used to fix the tongue. The resonator is of spotted-metal of ample thickness.

FIG. XCII.

It is interesting to observe by what diametrically opposite treatments similar results are aimed at and to some extent obtained in lingual pipes. Comparison between the pipes illustrated in Figures XCII. and XCIII. exemplify this matter. The drawings given in Fig. XCIII. are made, to scale, from the Tenor C pipe of the HORN added to the list of imitative organ stops, some years ago by Mr. E. M. Skinner, of Boston, Mass. It would be difficult to imagine two resonators more widely different, devised to produce the same quality of tone, than those of these two stops. It must not be supposed, however, that they are both equally efficient. In the case of the Horn pipe shown in Fig. XCIII., the resonator, instead of being inverted conical in form and of large scale, after the usual Trumpet model, is extremely slender and, accordingly, only very slightly tapered, open at top, and having a short cylindrical portion carrying an adjustable slide shaded with a disc of metal, as shown. The dimensions of the resonator are: Length 3 feet 3½ inches from the surface of the block, and internal diameter at top 1·63 inches. The dimensions of the sound-producing parts are: The length of the *éschalote* from the under side of the block is 2 ¾₁₆ inches; the width of the tongue at its free end is ⅞₁₆ inch, and where it is wedged into the block ⅞₃₂ inch. The *éschalote* is closed, with a perforation as shown in Diagram 3. In Diagram 1 the form of the pipe is given in correct proportions; in Diagram 2 is given a Longitudinal Section of the sound-producing parts drawn to scale. Diagram 4 shows the treatment of the upper part of the resonator.

We may safely say that a no more acceptable addition to the tonal forces of the Concert-room Organ can well be conceived than a truly imitative Orchestral Horn, 8 ft.

Having outlined the forms and construction of the pipes of all the important stops belonging to the Trumpet family, which are introduced in modern Organs, and which in their tones imitate to some extent the characteristic voices of the brass wind instruments of the orchestra, exclusive of the Saxophones, we may now direct attention to the forms and construction of the pipes of the stops whose tones more or less closely imitate those yielded by the reed instruments of the orchestra, the chief of which remain in use to-day.

Oboe.—Though rarely successful so far as imitative tone is concerned, the Oboe, 8 ft.,

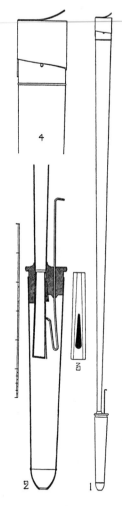

Fig. XCIII.

is a valuable lingual stop, and the one most frequently introduced in Organs of all dimensions. In small instruments it is often the only reed stop inserted: and when it is so, its tone is almost invariably of a bright, unimitative character, being what may be considered normal organ reed-tone. This character renders it generally useful for combination with labial stops of all tonalities. When carefully voiced and regulated, the unimitative OBOE is also very useful as a solo stop. The reeds of this stop are of a smaller scale than those of the normal TRUMPET, 8 FT., and are invariably of the closed class, having comparatively small triangular openings in their faces, which extend upward from the discs which close their lower ends. The tongues are correspondingly slender in form and of medium thickness, and have a slight and finely formed curve, which prevents the production of any coarseness or brassiness in the tone of the pipes. The bodies or resonators of the pipes of the OBOE now under consideration have each a slender tapered tube surmounted by a long inverted conical bell, imitating to some extent the conical and belled tube of the orchestral Oboe. In its most satisfactory construction, the resonator has its bell shaded with a disc of pipe-metal, soldered to the bell so as to allow about one half free to be bent up to any desirable extent in regulating the tone. Shaded OBOES are not invariably introduced, but they are unquestionably the most desirable tonally. The form of the OBOE pipe just described is shown in Diagram 1, Fig. XCIV., which represents a pipe belonging to the lower octaves of a stop. As the pipes become shorter, the relative proportions of their tubes and bells are considerably altered, so much so that in the highest octave the tubes and bells are about the same length.

ORCHESTRAL OBOE.—Voicers realizing the utter impracticability of obtaining what Berlioz describes as the " small acid-sweet voice " of the orchestral Oboe—" especially a melodial instrument, having a pastoral character, full of tenderness "—from the form of pipe above described, numerous attempts have been made, with different forms and proportions of reeds, tongues, and resonators, to arrive at a close imitation of the characteristic tone of the true instrument. Probably the most successful results have been obtained by Willis, who adopted resonators of an extremely slender inverted conical form, devoid of bells, and having closed upper ends and elongated perforations adjoining them. This form of pipe is shown in Diagram 2, Fig. XCIV., which is derived from the Willis ORCHESTRAL OBOE, such as is to be found in the Organs in Durham Cathedral and the Town Hall of Huddersfield. Another example very similar in treatment exists in the Organ, by the same distinguished builder, in Glasgow Cathedral. In the last example the reeds are very small, and have their stopped ends formed at an acute angle upward from the lower edge of their faces. The tongues are very narrow and beautifully curved. Less successful stops have been formed of pipes having very slender tubes carrying small shaded bells, the latter being slotted or pierced with circular holes. In all cases the reeds are closed and of small diameter, and the tongues are thin and very narrow. In the construction of the pipes of this, and, indeed, of all delicate striking-reed stops, the open ends of the reeds, before they are inserted in their blocks, should be covered with very fine silk gauze, stretched over them and glued down on their sides. While this treatment in nowise impairs the tone, it prevents dust falling into the reeds and silencing them.

As the Oboe of the orchestra does not go below tenor B♭, it is obvious that the imitative tones of the ORCHESTRAL OBOE, 8 FT., of the Organ must stop at that note. Below B♭ the pipes should strictly be of the FAGOTTO class, because the true Fagotto provides the proper bass to the Oboe of the orchestra. But it is both unnecessary and undesirable to break the organ stop either in tone or in the form of its pipes. In purely Oboe solo passages, the performer will never be called upon to go beyond the correct compass of the instrument, while in ordinary organ music the complete stop will be extremely valuable in combination with the other tonal forces of the Organ. In the absence of a FAGOTTO, 8 FT., the lower octaves of the OBOE will be found invaluable for certain orchestral effects. The latter stop, on account of the short compass of its strictly imitative portion, has been frequently labeled OBOE & FAGOTTO.

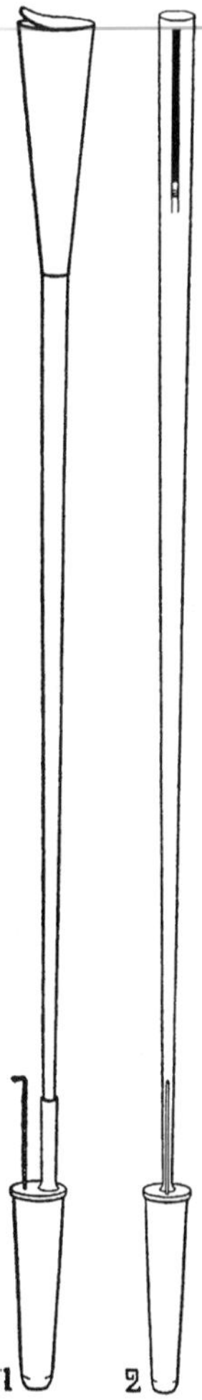

CONTRA-OBOE or CONTRA-HAUTBOY.—This stop, of 16 ft. pitch, is of course unimitative in its tone, carrying down the ordinary unimitative OBOE, 8 FT. Its general construction is similar in all essentials to that of the OBOE above described and its pipes are of the form shown in Diagram 1, Fig. XCIV. The stop is extremely rare; the only examples which have come under our observation are the CONTRA-HAUTBOY, 16 FT., made by Willis, in the Organ in St. George's Hall, Liverpool, and the CONTRA-OBOE, 16 FT., by the same builder, in the Organ in Royal Albert Hall, London.

FAGOTTO.—In all Organs which contain imitative stops of an orchestral character, the FAGOTTO or BASSOON, 8 FT., is an absolute necessity. No Concert-room Organ can be considered complete in which the stop does not appear in the manual department.

FIG. XCIV.

When artistically voiced on wind of moderate pressure, the tone of this stop closely imitates that of the orchestral Fagotto, while it is more uniform in color throughout. Its peculiar color renders it highly valuable in countless tonal combinations. The reeds and tongues of the FAGOTTO are essentially similar to those used for the ORCHESTRAL OBOE, but slightly larger in scale, giving a desirable fulness and solidity to the tone, to distinguish it from the characteristic voice of the OBOE. The resonators commonly used for the FAGOTTO are, when of metal, inverted conical in form; and when of wood, inverted pyramidal in form. We are strongly of opinion that the best tonal results are to be obtained from the resonators of wood. In all cases the resonators are of very small scale: in this respect approaching the conical tube of the orchestral Fagotto. While resonators open at top and provided with metal shades have been frequently employed, those completely closed at top and slotted or otherwise perforated near their closed ends have yielded the most satisfactory imitative tones. This latter treatment has been adopted by Willis in the pipes of some of his stops. In Fig. XCV. is represented the upper portion of the resonator of the CC pipe of the BASSOON, 8 FT., inserted by Willis in the original Organ in Colston Hall, Bristol. The upper end, which is only 2 inches in diameter, is completely closed with a metal disc, soldered on. At a distance of 2⅛ inches below the top is pierced a hole ½ inch in diameter, and below this, at a distance of ¼ inch, is cut a slot ½ inch wide and 1⅝ inches long, provided with a small regulating piece cut from the slot, all as clearly indicated in the illustration. We found the tone of this stop very quiet and refined, but lacking somewhat in the reediness characteristic of the tones of the orchestral Fagotto. This is a fault that could have been easily rectified by an alteration in the curvature of the tongues. A beautiful smoothness has always characterized the Willis reed stops of the best period. Such a FAGOTTO as we have just spoken of would be an admirable voice in a true Chamber Organ.

The wooden tubes or resonators of the FAGOTTO pipes are properly square in transverse section, and must be made of sufficient thickness to withstand the vibrations of the columns of air within them. Their lower ends should be rounded externally so as to fit into the metal socket pieces soldered to the reed-blocks; and they must be bored vertically with holes corresponding in size to the reeds below. These holes will open into the interiors of the resonators, and die out as the latter expand in size. The resonators may be simply shaded by adjustable metal plates; they may be both shaded and slotted; or they may be closed at their upper ends and slotted after the fashion of the metal resonator shown in Fig. XCV.

CONTRAFAGOTTO or DOUBLE BASSOON.—This is a stop, of 16 ft. pitch, formed in all respects like the stop just described. In its only proper form it yields tones imitative of those of the orchestral Contrafagotto. Its resonators should be made of wood when there is sufficient room for their accommodation; but when mitering is necessary, the resonators are properly made of metal. The CONTRAFAGOTTO, 16 FT., is both a manual and a pedal stop. When placed in the Pedal Organ, its tone should be as powerful as its imitative character warrants: and when placed in the manual department, its voice should be of medium strength, and it should invariably be inserted in an expressive division.

CLARINET.—This is one of the most important reed stops of the Organ; while it is, under favorable conditions, the most satisfactory of all in its orchestral or imitative tonality. The CLARINET, 8 FT., of the Organ when voiced by a master hand yields tones which reproduce with remarkable fidelity those of the best registers of the orchestral Clarinets. Speaking of the latter, Berlioz says: *"Single reed* instruments, such as the Clarinet and the Corno di Bassetto, form a family, whose connection with that of the Hautboy is not so near as might be thought. That which distinguishes it especially, is the nature of its sound. The middle notes of the Clarinet are more limpid, more full, more pure than those of *double reed* instruments, the sound of which is never exempt from a certain tartness or harshness, more or less concealed by the player's skill. The high sounds of the last octave, commencing with c^3, partake only a little of the tartness of the Hautboy's loud sounds; while the character of the lower sounds [DD to e^1] approaches, by the roughness of their vibrations, to that of certain notes of the Bassoon." The compass of the orchestral Clarinets is from DD to d^4 inclusive, and including the lower notes of the Bass Clarinet, and is, accordingly, covered by the unison compass of the Organ, with the exception of the two highest and seldom-attempted notes. In voicing the CLARINET, the artist should take for his tonal model the middle register of the orchestral Clarinets. On bb^1 the register known as the *chalumeau* commences and extends downward, having a distinctive tonal coloring; but there is no neces-

FIG. XCV.

sity, we venture to think, for the organ stop to change its quality of tone on this or any other note. It is certainly open to the artistic voicer to carry his imitations to any degree of nicety he may think proper, and we would be the first to commend him for so doing.

The CLARINET pipe differs in form and proportions from all those previously described and illustrated. This will be clearly seen on glancing at Fig. XCVI., which represents a CC pipe, or that yielding a note of 8 ft. pitch. The resonator, instead of being, approximately, the true speaking length of eight feet, is in this case only a little more than four feet in length above the reed-block. The resonator is cylindrical except where it is coned to adapt it to the size of the hole in the block in which the reed is inserted. To this form of resonator is mainly due the imitative character of the tone produced, resembling as it does the cylindrical tube of the orchestral Clarinet, which has the same series of upper partial tones as a stopped labial pipe. Both in the lengths and scale of its resonators the CLARINET differs from all the reed stops belonging to the other families. The following Table of measurements, obtained from a very beautiful CLARINET, 8 FT., made by a distinguished English artist, fully supports what we have just stated:

SCALE OF CLARINET, 8 FT.

PIPES.	DIAMETERS OF RESONATORS.	LENGTHS OF RESONATORS.	STANDARD LENGTHS OF OPEN LABIAL PIPES.
CC	1¾ inches.	4 ft. 3½ inches.	8 ft. 0 inches.
C	1¼ "	2 " 1½ "	4 " 0 "
c¹	1⅛ "	1 " 1¼ "	2 " 0 "
c²	1⁵⁄₁₆ "	0 " 6⅝ "	1 " 0 "
c³	1³⁄₁₆ "	0 " 3⁹⁄₁₆ "	0 " 6 "

The resonators of this stop are furnished with adjustable regulating slides, by means of which they can be slightly altered in length, so as to secure perfect uniformity in strength and character of tone throughout the compass. The form of the regulating slide is shown in Fig. XCVI. This treatment is preferable to any method of shading. The scales adopted by different makers vary considerably, as may be seen by comparing the diameters given in the above Table with the following, derived from a CLARINET made by the late Mr. George Willis: c¹ pipe, diameter of resonator, 1 ³⁄₁₆ inches; c² pipe, 1⅛ inches; and c³ pipe, 1 ¹⁄₃₂ inches. The lengths of the resonators are practically the same as those given in the Table. The resonators which are of sufficient length to admit of being mitered should be so treated near their open ends, to prevent dust readily finding its way into the reeds. Under any circumstances the upper ends of the reeds may be covered with fine silk gauze. The reeds of the CLARINET are of medium size and invariably of the closed kind, their triangular perforations extending directly from the discs which stop their lower ends. These discs commonly slope upward from the faces of the reeds, but only to a small extent.

While the resonators of the CLARINET are at the present time invariably made of metal, they have in a few instances been formed of hard wood, cylindrical in form, and carried in metal sockets, which are soldered to the reed-blocks in the usual manner. These resonators can be made by boring and turning single pieces of wood; or they can be formed of two pieces glued together, each piece having exactly half the bore of the resonator worked in it. When glued together, the resonators can be turned in the lathe to the requisite thickness and size to fit their respective metal sockets. We are strongly of opinion that admirable resonators could be made of good tough paper, glued, and rolled around mandrels of the proper sizes. The tubes so formed can be rendered hard and durable, and quite unsusceptible to atmospheric influences, by being thoroughly saturated with shellac varnish, applied internally and externally. Resonators so formed would have to be carried in metal sockets, as in the case of the wooden resonators above mentioned.

We have proved entirely to our own satisfaction that to produce what may be justly named an ORCHESTRAL CLARINET, specially suitable for solo and melodic effects, the dual method must be followed. The lingual stop, as usually made, should be associated with a labial rank of unison pitch, preferably a small-scaled and softly-toned DOPPELFLÖTE, regulated so as to combine and be in perfect sympathy in tone with the voice of the CLARINET. Personally, we would never specify, for an important Concert-room Organ, an ORCHESTRAL CLARINET, 8 FT., save in the dual form, as set forth above. Dual stops will occupy no unimportant place in the Organ of the Twentieth Century.

CORNO DI BASSETTO.—This fine stop belongs to the CLARINET family, and when made by a master hand is hardly equaled by any other reed stop of the Organ. The orchestral instrument from which it derives its name is practically a Tenor Clarinet furnished with a prolonged bore and additional keys, which give it a compass from FF to c³. The tone of the Corno di Bassetto is fuller and more reedy than that of the Alto Clarinet, and, accordingly, the tone of the CORNO DI BASSETTO, 8 FT., should be richer and nobler than that of the CLARINET, 8 FT. To secure this desirable result, the reeds should be somewhat larger in their diameters and have longer perforations in their faces, and the tongues should be both wider and thicker than the corresponding parts of the pipes of the CLARINET. The resonators should also be of larger scale. While they are usually made cylindrical like those of the CLARINET, our experiments with resonators have inclined us to favor a modification of the simple open cylindrical form. The scale should be somewhat larger than that given for the CLARINET, and instead of the resonators being merely furnished with straight, cylindrical regulators at top, as shown in Fig. XCVI., we recommend the resonators to be surmounted with heads of the form shown in Fig. XCVII. This treatment has a special effect on the tone, which goes far to add character to it and to differentiate it, in a desirable manner, from the voice of the CLARINET.

XCVI.

Although there is no authority furnished by the orchestra, we are strongly in favor of adding a valuable voice to the Concert-room Organ in the form of a CONTRA-BASSET-HORN, 16 FT. We are not aware if any essay has already been made in this direction, but such a stop would seem as desirable as the CONTRAFAGOTTO, 16 FT., is found to be; and it would furnish a pleasing contrast to that valuable stop. By the further addition of an OCTAVE BASSET-HORN, 4 FT., a most effective family of stops could be added to the Organ.

Vox Humana.—This is another stop belonging strictly to the Clarinet family, the chief peculiarity in its construction obtaining in the shortness of the cylindrical resonators of its pipes. The resonators are in some good examples of the stop only about half the length of those of the Clarinet; and, accordingly, are approximately one-fourth the length of open labial pipes yielding tones of the same pitch. The strained relations which exist between the reeds and the resonators create a tone of false character, which is generally accepted as imitating the human voice, the slight resemblance to which is increased by the addition of a *tremolo* effect. The finest Vox Humana that has come under our observation, and one that did not require distance to lend enchantment to it, was a perfect stop of refined tone, which could be used in full chords, alone or in combination, when the Tremolant was not drawn with it. It was about as imitative of a human voice as one could possibly expect from organ-pipes, when a slow and delicate *tremolo* was imparted to its sounds. Such a Vox Humana is widely different in its construction and tone from the much-vaunted stops of the same name in certain European Organs, and notably in the Organ of Lucerne Cathedral, the sole beauty of which consists in their being located so far away from the ear of the listener, and so ameliorated by existing acoustical conditions, that they can be tolerated. Such stops when heard in their immediate neighborhood are coarse and vulgar in the extreme. It is extremely rare to find a Vox Humana, 8 ft., having anything approaching a rich and refined tone in an English or American Organ; even the great Willis has not scored a marked success in this direction. The Vox Humana which we have alluded to as the finest which has come under our observation was made by Mr. E. Franklin Lloyd, of Liverpool. The resonators of this stop have a different treatment from those we have found in the other Vox Humanas we have examined. In Diagram 1, Fig. XCVII., is represented the c^1 pipe of this stop accurately drawn to scale. The resonator is 8⅝ inches in length from the surface of the block, and 1⅛ inches in diameter. It is completely closed at top, and is slotted close to its upper end, as indicated in Diagram 2. The effective length of this slot is determined by the regulating slide A, which is made of tin-plate sprung tightly around the resonator. This form of resonator produces a smoother and more refined voice than seems possible to be

XCVII.

obtained from the ordinary open-topped and shaded forms. All the resonators of this stop are much longer than those commonly made; that of the CC pipe measuring 34½ inches in length. The common shaded form of Vox Humana pipe is shown in Diagram 3. Stops composed of such pipes invariably require the refining effect of distance and more or less inclosure. In the case of the Lloyd Vox Humana, the tone was perfectly agreeable, with or without the *tremolo*, at a distance of ten feet, and while speaking in an open swell-box, and under no special acoustical conditions.*

The *éschalotes* of the Vox Humana are closed, of medium size, and are pierced with very narrow triangular openings. The *éschalote* of the c¹ pipe usually measures about 1⅜ inches in length from the under surface of the block, having a diameter at its lower end of about ¹³⁄₃₂ inch. The corresponding tongue at its free end seldom exceeds ¼ inch in width, and is thin and slightly curved. The largest tongue, that of the CC pipe, rarely exceeds ¹¹⁄₃₂ inch in width. In the *éschalotes* of some makers, the triangular openings start from the plates which are soldered to their ends, while in those of other makers, the openings start a short distance above their stopped ends, as shown in Diagram 3, Fig. XCIII. We are in favor of the latter treatment, which is conducive to refinement of tone, a virtue which the usual Vox Humana is markedly innocent of.

The boots of Vox Humana pipes vary greatly in length, dictated by the stop's position on the wind-chest, and with the aim of its being made easy of access for tuning when crowded by larger pipes. While no boot of the Lloyd stop measured more than 7 inches in length, we have found examples measuring 20½ inches. A long boot is shown in Diagram 3, Fig. XCVIII. While large boots are desirable for free-reeds, they do not seem to be of much value in the case of striking-reeds.

The Vox Humana is another stop which calls aloud for a dual treatment: this is due to the artificial char-

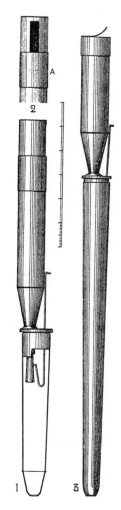

FIG. XCVIII.

---

* Writing of this stop and its accessory, Mr. Clarence Eddy says: " It would be difficult to find so satisfactory a Vox Humana, while its accessory, the Tremolo, is absolutely perfect."

acter of its voice, resembling in this direction the CLARINET. We have found the most desirable associated stop to be a unison, open wood, stop of the MELODIA class. This imparts to the voice of the Vox HUMANA a full and sonorous character naturally absent in the lingual stop; while it covers much of the disagreeable nasal intonation so objectionable in the Vox HUMANAS as almost universally made. While the Lloyd stop did not imperatively call for duality, it was greatly enhanced in its imitative character by the addition of a softly-toned CLARABELLA, 8 FT.

Other forms of resonators than those mentioned above have been tried for the pipes of the Vox HUMANA, but little success has apparently attended them; perhaps the most satisfactory of these have cylindrical bodies surmounted by short truncated cones, having openings at top of about half the diameter of their respective bodies; or have their cylindrical bodies furnished with regulating slides covered with discs of metal soldered on and pierced with holes in their centers for the necessary emission of the air and sound.

COR ANGLAIS.—Although this stop has been made, by German and French organ-builders, with free-reeds, it is now commonly and successfully constructed with striking-reeds. The Cor Anglais of the orchestra is a double-reed instrument belonging to the Oboe family; indeed, it has commonly been classed as the Alto of the Oboe, and was sometimes called Oboe da caccia. The compass of the instrument is from E to b² inclusive; accordingly, the true imitative portion of the organ COR ANGLAIS, 8 FT., lies in this range. Speaking of the Cor Anglais, Berlioz remarks: " Its quality of tone, less piercing, more veiled, and deeper than that of the Oboe, does not so well as the latter lend itself to the gaiety of rustic strains. Nor could it give utterance to anguished complainings; accents of keen grief are almost interdicted to its powers. It is a melancholy, dreamy, and rather noble voice, of which the sonorousness has something of vague,—of *remote*,—which renders it superior to all others, in exciting regret, and reviving images and sentiments of the past, when the composer desires to awaken the secret echo of tender memories." To the reed voicer who has not had any opportunity of studying the tone of the orchestral instrument—now very rarely seen or heard—these particulars will be helpful and interesting. While the reeds are generally similar to those of the OBOE, the form of the resonators of the COR ANGLAIS is different. Their bodies are slender inverted conical tubes, surmounted by double truncated cones, having a comparatively small opening at top, which produce the " more veiled and deeper " quality of tone than that of the OBOE.

CHAPTER XVII.

THE ORGAN SPECIFICATION.

F all documents connected with the expenditure of considerable sums of money—often running into tens of thousands of dollars—with which we have had any connection in our long professional practice, the most superficial, inadequate, and practically value-less one is the so-called Organ Specification, which is commonly, or, indeed, one may say universally, produced by the competing organ-builder or the ordinary non-expert organist.

The term Specification is a misnomer when applied to what is merely a list of stops and mechanical appliances, such as constitute the accepted and practically invariable Organ Specification of to-day. This latter statement is in no way inaccurate; for among the hundreds of so-called Specifications, produced by modern organ-builders and organists in this country and Great Britain, which are in our possession, not one shows the slightest attempt to go beyond what is a dry list of the names of the speaking stops, commonly with the addition of their pitch and compass, and sometimes with the further addition of the words "metal" and "wood," indicating the material to be used in the construction of the pipes; to which is appended a list of the mechanic-appliances. To a very large extent such a dry list is valueless from both a musical and constructional point of view; while, accordingly, it goes only a small way towards the assurance of a perfectly satisfactory musical instrument. For instance, the term "DIAPASON" does not assure the purchaser of the Organ that he is to receive the rich, pure, and commanding tone that properly belongs to the best examples of this beautiful foundation stop. As there is no standard of tonality that every organ-builder recognizes and adheres to; it follows that unless the desired quality is provided for and carefully described in the Specification, the organ-builder is left to his own devices and prejudices; and, accordingly, the Diapasons of Brown, Jones, and Robinson are all different and in the majority of cases unsatisfactory. The difference in tonality is caused by different scales; different proportions of mouth; different wind-pressure and supply; skill and taste of the voicer; and, to a certain extent, on the metal used in the fabrication of the stop, its thickness, etc. Now, none of these important matters should be left to the tender mercies of the tradesman organ-builder; but should be carefully and fully provided for in the Specification by the expert writer. Yet, in the usual Organ Specification of to-day, all one finds respecting this all-important stop is, at most:—

DIAPASON   .   .   .   Metal. 8 Feet. 61 Pipes.

No instructions being given in the document regarding the nature or quality of the metal or alloy to be used,—whether it is to be tin, spotted-metal, common pipe-metal, or zinc,—it is, accordingly, left to the organ-builder to decide what he considers desirable; who will, as a profit-loving tradesman, naturally select the cheapest that has any reasonable chance of being accepted by the purchaser or his adviser—probably an organist who does not know the composition of spotted-metal or the difference between it and base pipe-metal. Zinc will certainly be selected for the pipes of the lowest (8 ft.) octave, which if made of a proper alloy of tin and lead would cost as much as all the other four octaves of the stop.

In a properly written and legally-binding Organ Specification, not only the DIAPASON but every speaking stop in the instrument should have its form, scale, material, and desired tonality clearly and fully set forth; so that the organ-builder may thoroughly understand what he is required to produce, and what the purchaser insists on receiving in exchange for his money. Beyond the pipe-work, every other portion and detail of the Organ should have its materials, workmanship, and all necessary particulars relating to its construction fully specified: nothing of any importance should be left to the option of the organ-builder. Such a businesslike method never obtains in Specifications prepared by organ-builders, and for a very obvious reason: and very few organists of to-day have sufficient technical knowledge to enable them to write fully detailed and descriptive Specifications from which organ-builders could work with the certainty of giving satisfaction.

What would one think of an Architect's specification for the erection of a church or dwelling-house, if it merely gave a list of so many thousands of bricks; so many cubic feet of stone; so many thousand feet of timber; so many barrels of cement; so many loads of sand; so many hundredweights of plaster; so many squares of slating; so many square feet of glass, etc., etc., without stating kinds, qualities, forms, and dimensions; or in what manner the several materials are to be used? Yet such a specification would hardly be more absurd than the usual Organ Specification of the present day.

There lies before us as we write a so-called Specification cleverly prepared by a well-known organ-building firm, for an Organ presenting an ostensible list of sixty speaking stops, but which in reality would comprise less than forty. For instance, the Pedal Organ, which in all properly schemed instruments is a complete and perfectly independent division, is in this deceptive Specification listed to comprise twelve stops, while in reality all that would strictly belong to this important division would be two separate octaves of pipes.* All the rest of this Division being borrowed or derived from the stops of the Great, Choir, and Solo Organs. Such a list of stops is calculated, if it is not intended, to deceive the unwary purchaser; and is a flagrant example of a false and pernicious system of building up a Pedal Organ, now too often adopted, to the outrage of true art and sound and honest organ construction.

Again it may be noted: in this Specification the Solo Organ is listed to comprise thirteen stops, while in fact it has only three special stops. Eight stops are borrowed, in their entirety, from the Choir Organ. The special reed stop provided, yielding, by the two-octave extension of its compass, the 8 ft. and 4 ft. derivatives. By this method the brass-tone, provided by this single long-compass reed stop, is carried without any change of tonality or strength of voice throughout the three stops—furnishing a notable example of unscientific and inartistic tonal appointment. It may also be noted that this reed stop and its two derivatives furnish the only reed stops in both the Great and Pedal Organs, being borrowed in both cases.

In not a single instance, in this Specification, are any particulars respecting the scale of a stop given; in no case is the nature or quality of the " metal " or " wood," of which the pipes are to be made, described; and in no instance is any information regarding the tonality of a stop given, beyond what its name is supposed to indicate, and, accordingly, it may be good or bad, characteristic or otherwise, as the voicer's skill or want of skill may render it. The mere name of a stop is no guarantee as to its tonality: for it is well known that stops bearing the same name in Organs built by different builders, frequently, and indeed commonly, vary considerably in the quality and strength of their voices.

* A properly appointed Pedal Organ of twelve stops should comprise 384 pipes. The Pedal Organ as set forth in the Specification under review contains nothing strictly belonging to it save 24 pipes required to furnish the bottom octaves to two borrowed stops. So much for artistic organ-building in the twentieth century.

Such being the case, the expert, in scheming an Organ Specification, should so far as is possible in words define the tonality of every stop or, at least, every important stop; thereby removing from the organ-builder the power—which according to the loose Specification under review he has—of serving up any class of tonality which may suit his voicer's ideas or his own pocket.

Under this Specification, the purchaser is, in the matter of materials, largely, if not entirely, at the mercy of the builder; who is at liberty to translate the terms "metal" and "wood" to be just what he thinks proper to provide. Such being the case, it is safe to surmise that he will use the cheapest materials that will prove passable, and which he could reasonably expect to be accepted without demur by the purchaser or his adviser. Zinc would of course be used for the pipe-work to the extreme limit possible; all the rest of the pipes being made of ordinary pipe-metal—lead with the addition of tin (or perhaps antimony) just sufficient to prevent the pipes sinking out of shape by their own weight. No information is given respecting the wood or woods to be used for the pipes of the several wood stops, while this is a matter of considerable importance as all organ experts know. In a properly detailed Specification, the woods for the pipe-work and all the other portions of the Organ would be clearly named and their qualities defined. The same remark holds good with respect to the metals to be used for the different metal stops. Alloys containing different proportions of tin and lead are desirable for different classes of pipes, hence the necessity of clearly specifying them.

For the constructional portions of the Organ no materials are specified: accordingly, the building-frame, wind-reservoirs, wind-chests, and the numerous other portions of the structure, can be made of just such materials as the builder may think proper to use; he being bound only by such a clause as this in the Specification:—"All materials to be of the first quality." A departure is made from this general ambiguousness in favor of the organ-case, which is specified to be of American oak or some wood of equal value: but as no design for the case is furnished, this important matter is, as in the others, entirely at the mercy of the organ-builder. One well knows what organ-builders' cases are like—usually little more than flat framed-and-paneled screens, surmounted by flats of apparently unsupported pipes, bronzed or painted. The cost of the casework and the displayed pipes is not to exceed six per cent of the total cost of the Organ; so one can form some idea of what such a case, with its displayed pipes, would be like. The console is to be of the same wood as the case; but no further details respecting it are given.

No particulars are specified respecting the form or character of the blowing plant, beyond its being of ample size and electrically driven.

Nor is any information vouchsafed respecting the wind-pressures to be provided, so that some idea could be formed as to the qualities and strengths of the voices produced by the various stops: this is a remarkable omission. Of equal importance are matters relating to the nature and construction of the swell-boxes (of which there are two only, controlled by three expression-levers), but respecting which not a single word appears in the Specification.

It must be admitted, we venture to think, that the Specification thus briefly commented on is a very ingenious document, and one very much, if not entirely, in the organ-builder's favor. In our opinion it is rather too ingenious, and totally insufficient as a just and reliable base for a satisfactory agreement between the purchaser and the builder. It is evident that it is so framed as to give considerable license and advantage to the builder; while it leaves the purchaser very insufficiently protected. It is, in short, an organ-builder's Specification in the usual sense of the term. Everything connected with the Organ, specified and left unspecified, may be justly said to depend on the honor and business honesty of the builder; for the Specification, as written, unquestionably gives a wide field for money-saving, in material and labor, on his side; and much room for disappointment and dissatisfaction on the part of the purchaser, who is especially at the mercy of the builder in the extremely important matter of tonality and all that affects it. In this direction the purchaser has no power to object to what the organ-builder chooses to give him. This, it must be admitted, is a very serious condition of affairs; for the true glory of the Organ, as a musical instrument, depends essentially on the tonality and harmonious balance of all its stops, and largely on their perfect regulation. Unless this last matter is clearly stipulated in the Specification, it is almost certain to be largely neglected; for accurate tonal regulation requires considerable time and attention at the completion of the Organ. It has not yet, in our half century of experience, been our good fortune to see a Specification, written by an organ-builder or organist, in which tonal matters were touched upon beyond what the mere names of the stops listed implied. Can one wonder, under such a state of affairs, at the unsatisfactory condition of so many modern Organs? One is seldom invited to hear a new Organ without one's attention being directed to some of its stops which have specially pleasing or even beautiful voices. Why some of the stops only? In a properly scaled and carefully made and voiced stop appointment, every stop throughout it should be equally satisfactory in its special class; and it is only by such a pervading excellence that a perfect Organ can be secured. A properly prepared Specification—not written by an interested organ-builder—would go far to secure this desirable result.

Following what has been already said in this Chapter, it is only proper that some idea should be given of what may be considered a practical and sufficient Specification for an Organ; so prepared as to fully instruct the organ-builder in all important matters, constructional and tonal; and to give adequate protection to the purchaser, either directly if he is sufficiently experienced, or through the services of an expert or organ architect. In this direction we perhaps cannot do better than give the Specification prepared for the Organ erected in the Church of Our Lady of Grace, Hoboken, N. J., an instrument unique, at the present time, in its tonal apportionment and powers of expression and flexibility.

SPECIFICATION
OF THE GRAND ORGAN

(AUDSLEY SYSTEM—QUINTUPLE EXPRESSION)

FOR THE

CHURCH OF OUR LADY OF GRACE,
HOBOKEN, N. J.

—— FIRST ORGAN—FIRST CLAVIER. ——

Compass CC to c⁴—61 Notes.

First Subdivision—Unexpressive.

1.	Double Principal	. . .	Metal.	16 Feet.
2.	Grand Principal .	. . .	Metal.	8 "
3.	Major Principal .	. . .	Metal.	8 "
4.	Grand Viol .	. . . .	Metal.	8 "
5.	Major Octave	. . .	Metal.	4 "

Second Subdivision—Expressive.

Inclosed in Swell-Box No. 1.

6.	Major Flute	. . . .	Wood.	8 Feet.
7.	Minor Flute	. . . .	Wood.	4 "
8.	Octave Quint	. . . .	Metal.	2⅔ "
9.	Super-Octave	. . . .	Metal.	2 "
10.	Grand Cornet	. . . .	Metal.	V. Ranks.
11.	Double Trumpet .	. . .	Metal.	16 Feet.
12.	Trumpet	. . . . .	Metal.	8 "
13.	Clarion .	. . . . .	Metal.	4 "

—— SECOND ORGAN—SECOND CLAVIER. ——

Compass CC to c⁴—61 Notes.

FIRST SUBDIVISION—EXPRESSIVE.

Inclosed in Swell-Box No. 2.

14.	LIEBLICHGEDECKT	Wood.	16 Feet.
15.	GEIGENPRINCIPAL	Metal.	8 "
16.	LIEBLICHGEDECKT	Wood.	8 "
17.	LIEBLICHFLÖTE	Metal.	4 "
18.	DOLCE CORNET	Metal.	V. Ranks.

SECOND SUBDIVISION—EXPRESSIVE.

Inclosed in Swell-Box No. 3.

19.	DULCIANA	Metal.	8 Feet.
20.	VIOLA DA GAMBA	Tin.	8 "
21.	VIOLA D'AMORE	Tin.	8 "
22.	ORCHESTRAL CLARINET . .	Metal.	8 "
23.	VOX HUMANA	Metal.	8 "
I.	TREMOLANT.		

—— THIRD ORGAN—THIRD CLAVIER. ——

Compass CC to c⁴—61 Notes.

FIRST SUBDIVISION—EXPRESSIVE.

Inclosed in Swell-Box No. 2.

24.	DOLCE	Metal.	8 Feet.
25.	FLAUTO D'AMORE	Wood.	8 "
26.	ORCHESTRAL FLUTE . . .	Wood.	4 "
27.	ORCHESTRAL PICCOLO . . .	Metal.	2 "
28.	ORCHESTRAL OBOE . . .	Metal.	8 "
II.	TREMOLANT.		

SECOND SUBDIVISION—EXPRESSIVE.

Inclosed in Swell-Box No. 3.

29.	MINOR PRINCIPAL	Metal.	8 Feet.
30.	VIOLONCELLO	Tin.	8 "
31.	CONCERT VIOLIN	Tin.	8 "
32.	CORNO DI BASSETTO . . .	Metal.	8 "
33.	CONTRAFAGOTTO	Metal.	16 "
III.	TREMOLANT.		

—— PEDAL ORGAN. ——

Compass CCC to G—32 Notes.

34. DOUBLE PRINCIPAL . . . Wood. 32 Feet.
35. GRAND PRINCIPAL (44 pipes) . Wood. 16 "
36. CONTRA-BASSO (44 pipes) . . Wood. 16 "
37. DULCIANA (44 pipes) . . . Metal. 16 "
38. BOURDON . . . . . . Wood. 16 "
39.* GRAND OCTAVE (Derived from No. 35) . 8 "
40.* DOLCE (Derived from No. 37) . . . 8 "
41.* VIOLONCELLO (Derived from No. 36) . . 8 "
42. COMPENSATING MIXTURE . . Metal. III. Ranks.
43. TROMBONE . . . . . Metal. 16 Feet.

—— AUXILIARY PEDAL ORGAN. ——

EXPRESSIVE

44.* LIEBLICHGEDECKT (Derived from No. 14) 16 Feet.
45.* DOUBLE TRUMPET (Derived from No. 11) 16 "
46.* CONTRAFAGOTTO (Derived from No. 33) . 16 "

WIND PRESSURES.

The First Organ to be supplied with Wind of 4 inches.
The Second Organ to be supplied with Wind of 3 inches.
The Third Organ to be supplied with Wind of 4½ inches.
The Pedal Organ to be supplied with Wind of 5 inches.

—— MECHANICAL ACCESSORIES. ——

COUPLERS.

1. Second Organ.... 1st Subdivision..... to First Organ, Unison Coupler.
2. Second Organ.... 2nd Subdivision..... to First Organ, Unison Coupler.
3. Second Organ.... 1st Subdivision..... to First Organ, Octave Coupler.
4. Third Organ..... 1st Subdivision..... to First Organ, Unison Coupler.
5. Third Organ..... 2nd Subdivision..... to First Organ, Unison Coupler.
6. Third Organ..... 2nd Subdivision..... to First Organ, Sub-octave Coupler.
7. Third Organ..... 1st Subdivision..... to Second Organ, Unison Coupler.
8. Third Organ..... 2nd Subdivision..... to Second Organ, Unison Coupler.
9. First Organ...... 1st Subdivision..... to Pedal Organ.
10. First Organ...... 2nd Subdivision..... to Pedal Organ.
11. Second Organ.... 1st Subdivision..... to Pedal Organ.
12. Third Organ..... 2nd Subdivision..... to Pedal Organ.

DIVISIONAL PISTONS.

I. Two Thumb-pistons, bringing on and throwing off 2nd Subdivision of First
Organ, on First Clavier.

II. Two Thumb-pistons, bringing on and throwing off 1st Subdivision of Second
Organ, on Second Clavier.

III. Two Thumb-pistons, bringing on and throwing off 2nd Subdivision of Second Organ, on Second Clavier.

IV. Two Thumb-pistons, bringing on and throwing off 1st Subdivision of Third
Organ, on Third Clavier.

V. Two Thumb-pistons, bringing on and throwing off 2nd Subdivision of Third
Organ, on Third Clavier.

The above Thumb-pistons to be conveniently located beneath their respective
claviers.

ADJUSTABLE COMBINATION PISTONS.

1-2-3-4-0.....Operating on all Stops of First Organ and Pedal Organ, and
manual to pedal Coupler.

1-2-3-4-5-0...Operating on all Stops of Second Organ and Pedal Organ, and
Couplers.

1-2-3-4-5-0...Operating on all Stops of Third Organ and Pedal Organ, and
Couplers.

This Adjustable Combination Action to be so constructed as to allow any
combinations of the Stops and Couplers of the different divisions of the Organ
to be connected with their respective Thumb-pistons, or to be changed or released,
by the Performer while seated at the keys. The Pistons to be conveniently
located beneath their respective claviers.

TREMOLANT PISTONS.

A. Double-acting Thumb-piston for TREMOLANT I.
B. Double-acting Thumb-piston for Tremolant II.
C. Double-acting Thumb-piston for Tremolant III.

These Pistons to be placed immediately to the right of the respective groups
of Combination Pistons.

EXPRESSION LEVERS.

1. Balanced Expression lever to Swell-box No. 1.
2. Balanced Expression lever to Swell-box No. 2.
3. Balanced Expression lever to Swell-box No. 3.
4. Crescendo lever operating on Full Organ from First Clavier.

FOOT-LEVERS.

1. Lever opening all Swell-boxes.
2. Lever closing all Swell-boxes.
3. Double-acting Lever for First Organ to Pedal Organ Coupler.

THE GENERAL LAY-OUT.

The Organ to be carefully planned with every portion disposed to
the best advantage with reference to the free emission of sound; and

conveniently arranged for easy access to all parts for tuning and regulating, and to allow of any necessary mechanical adjustment or repairs. The manual divisions of the Organ to extend the entire width of the choir gallery, and to be carried forward from the end wall of the nave only so far as is absolutely necessary. Here, also, are to be planted the lower octave of the Pedal DOUBLE PRINCIPAL, 32 ft., and such other large pipes of the Pedal Organ as room will permit. In the Architect's design for the case, the pipes of the First Organ DOUBLE PRINCIPAL, 16 ft., and the larger pipes of the GRAND PRINCIPAL, 8 ft., and MAJOR PRINCIPAL, 8 ft., will be accommodated; all the other pipes required to complete the design being dummies, made as called for in the design. The remainder of the Pedal Organ stops to be located in the large chamber which opens from the gallery and into the side aisle of the nave. In this chamber is to be placed the complete Blowing Plant, actuated by an electromotor automatically governed by a rheostat of the most efficient design.

The Organ-builder to prepare the complete lay-out according to the disposition given above, and submit the same for the Architect's approval.

THE ACTION.

The Action throughout the Organ to be tubular-pneumatic of the most perfect description, having instantaneous attack and rapid repetition. In these respects it must be entirely satisfactory to the Architect. To be constructed of the best materials of their respective kinds, and finished in all details in the most careful and workmanlike manner. All unnecessary complexity of construction to be avoided; and all parts to be conveniently disposed for ready access for adjustment, repairs, etc. All must be carried out to the Architect's entire satisfaction.

THE CONSOLE.

The Console to be of a neat plain design, and of the smallest dimensions practicable: to be constructed externally of quartered oak, stained and varnished—cabinet finish.

The Console to be detached, located close to the gallery-front and directly in front of the center of the Organ, and so placed that the organist faces the instrument. The pneumatic tubes and all the necessary mechanical movements are to pass from the Console, under a narrow platform raised from the gallery floor, into the Organ.

The Manual Claviers to be of the overhanging pattern, set as close together as practicable and convenient. The natural keys to be plated with ivory one-tenth of an inch thick, and the sharp keys to be of best black ebony.

The Draw-stop knobs to be of the oblique-faced form. Those belonging to each division of the Organ to be clearly distinguished by being turned from choice wood of a special color. The name-plates to be boldly lettered and figured with the name and pitch of the stops, and any further information that may be necessary, and as directed. Each group of these draw-stop knobs to be conveniently arranged in stepped jambs; and to have engraved ivory name-plates, stating the Organs and their Divisions clearly, with the addition of the numbers of the swell-boxes—1st., 2nd., or 3rd.—in which the five Subdivisions are inclosed.

The Couplers to be commanded by draw-stop knobs or rocking-tablets, as the action may render necessary, boldly lettered, and located in a row above, and as close to as practicable, the third clavier.

The Thumb-pistons and the Adjustors of the Adjustable Combination Action to be of ivory, numbered and inscribed as required.

The interior exposed parts of the Key-case to be of best mahogany, richly stained, highly finished, and French polished.

The Pedal Clavier to be of the Audsley-Willis pattern, carefully made of oak, having the sharp keys mounted with ebony or rosewood—32 notes.

The Expression Levers to be of cast malleable iron, faced with beech or other approved hard wood, shaped to accommodate the foot, and to be well made in every respect. To be so placed that one foot can operate two adjoining ones at the same time. The Crescendo Lever to be similarly formed. The Expression Levers to occupy a central position directly over the pedal clavier, while the Crescendo Lever is to be placed at a convenient angle toward the right end of the clavier. The three Foot Levers to be of neat form and conveniently placed.

The Console and all its necessary fittings, and all details specified and implied, are to be executed in the most substantial and artistic manner to the entire satisfaction of the Architect.

MATERIALS AND WORKMANSHIP.

WOODWORK.

All the materials used in the construction of every part of the Organ are to be of the best quality of their respective kinds, and only used in their perfectly suitable conditions.

All the soft wood used in the construction of the wind-chests, pneumatic appliances, wood pipes, swell-shutters, bellows, reservoirs, and wind-trunks, to be of clear white pine free from imperfections of any kind. Straight-grained mahogany to form the top layer of the upper-boards of the wind-chests: and mahogany or maple is to be used for the fronts of the manual wood pipes of two feet in length and under. The wood pipes of the Pedal Organ and bass pipes of the manual wood stops, to have their mouths, facings of their languids, and caps made of a suitable hard wood, and as may be directed. Hard wood of the proper description to be used where required for the proper construction of any other portions of the Organ.

The workmanship of all the portions alluded to above, to be of the highest class; and all the woodwork is to be sized and to be well varnished with spirit or oil varnish, so as to resist the action of the atmosphere.

No whitewood or other inferior wood is to be used for any of the portions of the Organ enumerated above, or in any other portion where it is considered unsuitable by the Architect.

The Building-frames of both the Organ proper and the blowing plant to be constructed of clear yellow pine, cleanly dressed, and well varnished with hard-drying oil varnish.

The back, sides, and tops of the three Swell-boxes to be of clear yellow pine. To be strongly constructed with frames 6 inches wide and 1⅞ inches thick (finished dimensions), filled in with double panels ⅞ inch thick, rebated to frames, leathered, and securely screwed on, flush on outside and inside, and having a layer of coarse felt between them, in the manner indicated in the accompanying Section. The vertical shutters to be of the finest light, clear white pine, built up so as to

—— Section of Wall of Swell-box. ——

prevent warping or bending, and to have double rebated and felted edges, as approved. All to be pivoted on steel centers, resting in gunmetal sockets.

The insides of the Swell-boxes to have three coats of hard-drying white-lead oil paint, finished with one coat of white enamel and one coat of the best quality oil varnish, as approved by the Architect. This internal painting to be executed when the boxes are put together in place. The external surfaces of the Swell-boxes to be sized and varnished with three coats of durable exterior oil varnish. The shutters to be similarly varnished on both faces. Means of access to the Swell-boxes, for tuning and other purposes, must be provided, without interfering with the sound-resisting qualities of their walls. Every matter and thing must be done to render the Swell-boxes perfect in every respect to the satisfaction of the Architect.

The Bellows or Feeders for the different pressures of wind, and the necessary Reservoirs for their distribution to the wind-chests and pneumatic action, to be made of ample size to meet the most exacting tests— to supply at all times a copious supply of wind, absolutely steady and uniform in the different pressures. All the woodwork to be cleanly dressed and well sized and varnished with good hard-drying oil varnish. All the Bellows and Reservoirs to be jointed with the best bellows-leather, and put together in the most workmanlike manner. The Reservoirs to have direct and inverted ribs; to be properly valved, and weighted by cast-iron blocks or coiled steel springs. All the Wind-trunks to be capacious and as short and direct as practicable.

All the other portions of the interior woodwork not particularly mentioned, but which enter into the construction of the Organ, are to be executed in strict accord with what is specified above, and with the letter and spirit of this Specification, and to the satisfaction of the Architect.

THE ORGAN-CASE.

As the Case is to be richly decorated with colors and gold, to accord with the decoration of the church, all its portions not liable to injury are to be carefully executed in clear white pine, thoroughly seasoned, and free from imperfections. The pillars supporting the towers, the base-board, and other portions in the lower part of the case to be of oak or some equally good hard wood. All the moldings, arch- and tracery-work, the exposed pipe-staybars, and all the carving to be most accurately and carefully executed to the Architect's detail drawings. The entire case to be made to the design furnished, and put together in the most substantial and workmanlike manner, to the Architect's entire satisfaction. The organ-builder will not be called upon to decorate the Case or the displayed pipes.

METALWORK.

All the Metalwork throughout the Organ proper and the blowing plant to be accurately and carefully made and finished; and to be well painted and protected from corrosion.

All the metal pipes throughout the Organ, unless otherwise specified, are to be formed of rich spotted-metal—an alloy of 45 parts tin and 55 parts lead, specific gravity 9.06—and as approved by the Architect. The pipes of the Viola da Gamba, Viola d'Amore, and Concert Violin to be formed of the alloy having 90 per cent. of pure tin and

10 per cent. of pure lead. All the pipes so specified to be of the full desirable thickness, approved by the Architect.

The feet and bodies of the pipes of the two lower octaves of the DOUBLE PRINCIPAL, 16 ft., of the First Organ (No. 1), and of the entire DULCIANA, 16 ft., of the Pedal Organ (No. 37), are to be of thick zinc. The languids, mouths, and toes of these zinc pipes are to be of spotted-metal. The mouths of all displayed speaking and dummy pipes are to be of the French form, carefully made and accurately proportioned. Such pipes, shown in the design of the case, as cannot conveniently and properly be used as speaking pipes are to be made to correspond in all particulars of form with the speaking pipes with which they are associated.

Every matter and thing required to make the metal pipe-work perfect must be done to the entire satisfaction of the Architect, whose instructions must be fully carried out.

SCALING, VOICING, AND REGULATING.

All the metal and wood stops are to be made to scales which will be given or approved by the Architect. The Builder to accurately develop the scales to the dimensions and ratios given or approved.

Full instructions will be given to the Builder respecting qualities and strengths of the tones of all the stops, and these must be carefully observed. The Architect reserves the right to reject any stop, or portion of any stop, which does not fully come up to the defined tonal character; and his verdict on all such tonal matters is to be final and binding on the Builder.

Every stop throughout the Organ must be so carefully regulated that no inequality can be observed in any note or part of its compass. The compound harmonic-corroborating stops must have their several ranks most accurately adjusted in relative strength of tone, as instructed by the Architect and approved by him. Great stress will be laid on this matter of scientific and artistic regulation, for very much of the beauty and mixing quality of the stops depend upon it.

ERECTION AND COMPLETION.

The Builder to erect the Organ in the Church without in any way interfering with the services therein. To coöperate with, and give all necessary assistance to the case-maker while erecting the case and joining it to the woodwork of the Organ.

The Builder to do every matter and thing necessary for the completion of his work in a thoroughly substantial and artistic manner, and to leave everything clean and perfect.

The Builder to keep the instrument in every part in perfect condition, making any repairs, additions, or alterations incident on his own workmanship, neglect, or departure from the letter or spirit of this Specification, for a period of twelve months after the instrument is provisionally certified as complete by the Organ Architect.

PARTICULARS OF THE STOPS.

The following particulars and instructions respecting the scaling and the tonality of the several stops are to be strictly observed by the organ-builder, unless a departure, for any sufficient reason, is sanctioned by the Architect.

METAL STOPS.

Double Principal, 16 ft.—The tone of this important foundation stop to be of the true English Diapason quality, smooth, and as free from harmonics as possible. In strength of voice it must resemble that of the Major Principal, 8 ft. The scale to be to the ratio 1 : 2·66—halving on the eighteenth pipe :—

Scale of Double Principal.

CC——10·04 inches diameter.   31·52 inches circumference.
C —— 6·16   "   "   19·36   "   "
F —— 5·02   "   "   15·76   "   "
c^4 —— 0·87   "   "   2·73   "   "

The mouths to be flattened two-sevenths the circumference of the pipes, and to be cut up not more than one-fourth the diameter of the pipes. The pipes of the bass and tenor octaves to be of thick zinc, with lips, languids, and toes of spotted-metal, and as approved. Such pipes as are required to be displayed in the organ-front, to be made of the required over-lengths to suit the design.

Grand Principal, 8 ft.—This, the chief unison foundation stop of the Organ, calls for a voice of extreme fulness and dignity, dominating effectively the voices of all the other unison stops of the Diapason family. It must have a pure organ-tone, practically free from perceptible upper partial tones, so as to mix with any combination of tones that may be built upon it. The organ-builder must pay special attention to all matters connected with the formation and voicing of this all-important stop. The scale to be to the ratio 1 : 2·66—halving on the eighteenth pipe :—

Scale of Grand Principal.

CC——6·68 inches diameter.   20·98 inches circumference.
C ——4·10   "   "   12·88   "   "
F ——3·34   "   "   10·49   "   "
c^4 ——0·58   "   "   1·81   "   "

The mouths to be flattened five-fourteenths the circumference, and in height not to greatly exceed one-fourth the diameter of the pipes. All the pipes of this stop to be of spotted-metal of the alloy already specified and of the proper thicknesses, and as approved.

MAJOR PRINCIPAL, 8 FT.—The tone of this stop to be that of the true old English DIAPASON—pure, full, and silvery in quality. It may have a slight trace of harmonics, but must be absolutely free from any string tonality. In strength of voice, this stop must be markedly subordinate to that of the GRAND PRINCIPAL, 8 FT. The scale to be to the ratio 1 : 2·66—halving on the eighteenth pipe :—

SCALE OF MAJOR PRINCIPAL.

CC——6·16 inches diameter. 19·36 inches circumference.
C ——3·78 "   "   11·88 "   "
F ——3·8 "   "   9·68 "   "
c⁴ ——0·53 "   "   1·67 "   "

The mouths to be flattened two-sevenths the circumference, and in height not to exceed one-fourth the diameter of the pipes. All the pipes of this stop to be of spotted-metal of the proper and approved thickness.

GRAND VIOL, 8 FT.—The tone of this stop to be, as its name implies, of an unimitative string-character; more pronounced than that of the ordinary VIOLIN DIAPASON, but not approaching an imitative quality rich in upper partial tones. This stop is required to add to, and enrich, the voices of the three PRINCIPALS specified above. The scale to be to the ratio of 1 : 2·66—halving on the eighteenth pipe :—

SCALE OF GRAND VIOL.

CC——4·26 inches diameter. 13·38 inches circumference.
C ——2·62 "   "   8·28 "   "
F ——2·13 "   "   6·69 "   "
c⁴ ——0·37 "   "   1·16 "   "

The mouths to be flattened one-fourth the circumference, and in height as necessary to produce the required tone: to have harmonic-bridges. All the pipes of this stop to be of spotted-metal of the necessary and approved thickness.

MAJOR OCTAVE, 4 FT.—The tone of this stop to be similar to that of the MAJOR PRINCIPAL, 8 FT., but somewhat less powerful, so that it can be used with that stop alone without unduly affecting its pitch, while enriching its voice by corroborating firmly its first and most important upper partial tone. The scale to be to the ratio 1 : 2·66—halving on the eighteenth pipe :—

SCALE OF MAJOR OCTAVE.

CC——3·48 inches diameter. 10·19 inches circumference.
C ——2·13 "   "   6·69 "   "
F ——1·74 "   "   5·46 "   "
c⁴ ——0·30 "   "   0·95 "   "

The mouths to be flattened two-sevenths the circumference of the pipes, and to be cut up not more than one-fourth the diameter of the pipes. All pipes to be of spotted-metal.

OCTAVE QUINT, 2⅔ FT.—As the voice of this mutation stop corroborates the second upper partial tone of the foundation unison, its tone must be similar to that of the MAJOR OCTAVE, 4 FT., but perceptibly softer, as dictated by the natural laws of sound. The scale to be to the ratio 1 : 2·66.

SCALE OF OCTAVE QUINT.

CC——2·41 inches diameter. 7·57 inches circumference.
C ——1·47 " " 4·63 " "
F ——1·20 " " 3·78 " "

The mouths to be flattened one-fourth the circumference of the pipes, and to be of the height necessary to obtain the pure organ-tone required. All pipes to be of spotted-metal.

SUPER-OCTAVE, 2 FT.—The tone of this stop to be similar to that specified for the two preceding stops but to be slightly softer than that of the OCTAVE QUINT. The scale to be to the ratio 1 : 2·3—halving on the twenty-first pipe :—

SCALE OF SUPER-OCTAVE.

CC——1·91 inches diameter. 6·01 inches circumference.
C ——1·26 " " 3·95 " "
G♯——0·96 " " 3·01 " "

The mouths to be flattened one-fourth the circumference of the pipes. The pipes to be of spotted-metal.

GRAND CORNET.—This important compound harmonic-corroborating stop to be composed of five complete ranks of pipes as follows :—
First Rank—A ROHRFLÖTE, 4 FT., yielding a flute organ-tone of medium strength in its lowest octave, and gradually and slightly decreasing in strength as it rises in pitch, until at c⁴ it is perceptibly softer in tone.
Second Rank—A TWELFTH, 2⅔ FT., formed of medium-scaled pipes; the pure organ-tone of which must be subordinate to that of the ROHRFLÖTE; and must, correspondingly, be reduced in strength upwards.
Third Rank—A FIFTEENTH, 2 FT., formed of pipes of a scale two pipes smaller than that of the TWELFTH. To be voiced slightly softer than the TWELFTH, and similarly reduced in strength upwards.
Fourth Rank—A SEVENTEENTH, 1⅗ FT., formed of pipes of small scale, voiced to yield a pure organ-tone similar in strength to that of the usual small-scaled DULCIANA. To be reduced in strength upwards, so as to be almost inaudible in the top octave.
Fifth Rank—A NINETEENTH, 1⅓ FT., formed of pipes of DULCIANA scale, softly voiced and reduced in strength upwards until the tone, when in combination, becomes almost inaudible in the top notes.
All the ranks to be carefully regulated and graduated so as to produce a perfectly combined tone throughout the compass. If properly made and finished, the stop will yield a tone resembling, in the middle octaves, a finely voiced reed in character. This tonality must be obtained. All the pipes to be of spotted-metal.

GEIGENPRINCIPAL, 8 FT.—The tone of this stop to be of a quality in which the tones of the old English DIAPASON and the VIOL are pleasantly blended. The string quality must be markedly subordinate to that of the pure organ-tone, while it must be sufficient to impart a bright singing tonality to the stop, highly desirable in combination with flute organ-tones.

The scale to be to the ratio 1 : 2·66—halving on the eighteenth pipe :—

SCALE OF GEIGENPRINCIPAL.

CC——4·62 inches diameter.   14·52 inches circumference.
C ——2·84   "   "   8·92   "   "
F ——2·31   "   "   7·26   "   "
c⁴ ——0·40   "   "   1·26   "   "

Mouths to be flattened two-sevenths the circumference of the pipes, and of the height necessary to obtain the tone required. All the pipes to be of spotted-metal.

DOLCE CORNET.—This stop to be composed of five ranks of pipes of DULCIANA scale as here given :—

DOLCE CORNET—V. RANKS.

CC to BB	.	.	.	.	.	19——22——24——26——29.
C to B	.	.	.	.	.	12——15——17——19——22.
c¹ to b¹	.	.	.	.	.	8——12——17——19——22.
c² to c⁴	.	.	.	.	.	1—— 8——10——12——15.

The regulation of this harmonic-corroborating MIXTURE is a matter of great importance and must be carefully performed.

The first rank to commence with a full DULCIANA tone, which must be slightly and gradually reduced in strength as it proceeds throughout the compass to the top note. The second rank to commence slightly softer than the first rank, and to be graduated in tone upwards in like manner. The third rank to commence slightly softer than the second rank, and to be graduated in tone upwards in like manner. The fourth rank to commence slightly softer than the third rank, and to be graduated in tone upwards in like manner. The fifth rank to commence softer than the fourth rank, and to be gradually reduced in strength of tone upwards to the top note of the compass, as in the other four ranks. Such a system of tonal regulation is requisite in a compound harmonic-corroborating stop to conform with the phenomena of musical sounds. All the pipes to be of spotted-metal.

DULCIANA, 8 FT.—This stop to have a pure organ-tone of a singing quality, characteristic of the true English DULCIANA: it must be absolutely free from any trace of string-tone. The scale to be to the ratio 1 : 2·519—halving on the nineteenth pipe :—

SCALE OF DULCIANA.

CC——3·51 inches diameter.   11·03 inches circumference.
C ——2·21   "   "   6·93   "   "
F ——1·75   "   "   5·51   "   "
c⁴ ——0·35   "   "   1·09   "   "

The mouths to be flattened two-ninths the circumference of the pipes, and kept as low as the proper voicing will permit. The pipes throughout to be of spotted-metal.

DOLCE, 8 FT.—This stop to have a delicate intonation inclining toward a string quality, in this respect differing from the pure organ-tone of the DULCIANA. The pipes to be inverted conical, their diameters being larger at top than at the mouth. The scale to be to the ratio 1·519—halving on the nineteenth pipe:—

SCALE OF DOLCE.

		Diameter at Mouth.					Diameter at Top.
CC	———	2·90	.	.	.	.	3·65
C	———	1·82	.	.	.	.	2·30
F♯	———	1·45	.	.	.	.	1·82
c⁴	———	0·29	.	.	.	.	0·36

The mouths to be flattened two-ninths the circumference and to be cut low. The pipes to be of spotted-metal.

MINOR PRINCIPAL, 8 FT.—The tone of this stop to be of DIAPASON character, but to have a slight horn-like intonation combined with a sufficient brightness to render it effective in a swell-box. The scale to be to the ratio 1 : 2·66—halving on the eighteenth pipe:—

SCALE OF MINOR PRINCIPAL.

CC	5·24 inches diameter.	16·46 inches circumference.
C	3·21 " "	10·08 " "
F	2·62 " "	8·23 " "
c⁴	0·45 " "	1·42 " "

The mouths to be flattened one-fourth or two-ninths the circumference, as may be found best for the production of the desired tonality. All pipes to be of spotted-metal.

VIOLONCELLO, 8 FT.—This stop, which is an important member of the Orchestral String-tone group, must yield a tone as strongly imitative of that of the orchestral Violoncello as the pipe-maker's and voicer's art can produce. The scale here given is one adopted with satisfactory results by distinguished voicers using cylindrical metal pipes. The scale to be to the ratio 1 : 2·519—halving on the nineteenth pipe:—

SCALE OF VIOLONCELLO.

CC	2·48 inches diameter.	7·78 inches circumference.
C	1·56 " "	4·91 " "
F♯	1·24 " "	3·89 " "
c⁴	0·23 " "	0·75 " "

The mouths to be of the width and height considered most suitable by the voicer, and to be furnished with harmonic-bridges. All pipes to be of 90 per cent. tin.

VIOLA DA GAMBA, 8 FT.—The tone of this stop must be of a rounder and less pungent string quality than that of the VIOLONCELLO. As its name implies, it is intended to imitate the tones of the old Viola da Gamba or English Bass Viol —precursors of the Violoncello. The scale of the cylindrical pipes of this stop, to the ratio 1 : 2·519, to be as follows:—

SCALE OF VIOLA DA GAMBA.

CC——3·51 inches diameter. 11.03 inches circumference.
C ——2·21   "   "   6·93   "   "
F♯——1·75   "   "   5·51   "   "
c⁴——0·35   "   "   1·09   "   "

The mouths to be flattened two-ninths the circumference, and of the height desirable, with the aid of harmonic-bridges, to produce the tone required. All the pipes to be made of an alloy of 90 per cent. tin and 10 per cent. pure lead; and of a sufficient and approved thickness.

VIOLA D'AMORE, 8 FT.—The tone of this stop to resemble that of the VIOLA DA GAMBA, but to be softer and brighter in its string quality. The pipes to be conical in form, their diameters at top being one-half of those at the mouth. The scale at the mouth to be the same as that given above for the VIOLA DA GAMBA. All the pipes to be of tin, slightly alloyed as above specified. The stop to be tuned a few beats sharp, as directed and approved.

CONCERT VIOLIN, 8 FT.—This stop is the most important member of the Orchestral String-tone group, and must yield a tone as closely imitative of that of the orchestral Violin as the voicer's art can achieve. The scale to be to the ratio 1·2·13—halving on the twenty-third pipe. This comparatively slow diminution tends to secure a desirable fulness in the treble octaves.

SCALE OF CONCERT VIOLIN.

CC——2·05 inches diameter. 6·44 inches circumference.
C ——1·40   "   "   4·41   "   "
A♯——1·02   "   "   3·22   "   "
c⁴——0·25   "   "   0·78   "   "

The mouths to be of the width and height considered by the voicer as most conducive to the production of the imitative tone required, and to be fitted with harmonic-bridges. The pipes to be slotted for tuning. All the pipes to be of tin, as above specified.

ORCHESTRAL PICCOLO, 2 FT.—The tone of this stop to be as clear and liquid as possible, without being unduly assertive. The pipes to be double length—harmonic—from tenor C to c⁴. The diameter of the CC pipe to be 1·47 inches, ratio 1 : 2·66.

DULCIANA, 16 FT.—Pedal Organ—The tone of this stop to be similar to, and a little fuller than, that of the DULCIANA, 8 FT., of the Second Organ. The scale to be to the ratio 1 : 2·519—halving on the nineteenth pipe. 44 pipes.

SCALE OF PEDAL ORGAN DULCIANA.

CCC——6·26 inches diameter. 19·66 inches circumference.
CC ——3·94   "   "   12·38   "   "
FF ——3·13   "   "   9·83   "   "
G ——1·89   "   "   5·95   "   "

The mouths to be flattened two-ninths the circumference of the pipes, and to have their lips and languids of spotted-metal of substantial thickness. The toes of the pipes to be of thick spotted-metal. All the rest of the pipes to be of stout zinc. In case a portion of this stop should be required for the organ-front, its pipes to be finished in all respects similar to those displayed therein, and as directed by the Architect.

COMPENSATING MIXTURE—This compound harmonic-corroborating stop to be composed of three ranks of full-scaled PRINCIPAL pipes, yielding pure organ-tone, graduated in strength as proper in all MIXTURES. The scale to be to the ratio $1 : \sqrt{8}$—halving on the seventeenth pipe.

First Rank—A SUPER-OCTAVE, 4 FT. Compass CCC to G—32 notes. Scale of CCC pipe 4·10 inches in diameter. The tone at this note to be equal to that of the Tenor C pipe of the GRAND PRINCIPAL, 8 FT., and to be gradually decreased in strength upwards until at G it is not much louder than the tone of the ordinary DULCIANA pipe of the same pitch.

Second Rank—A NINETEENTH, 2⅔ FT. Compass CCC to D—27 notes. Scale of CCC pipe 3·03 inches in diameter. The tone at this note to be equal to that of the corresponding pipe of the GRAND PRINCIPAL, 8 FT., and to be decreased in strength as directed for the first rank.

Third Rank—A TWENTY-SECOND, 2 FT. Compass CCC to GG—20 notes. Scale of CCC pipe 2·44 inches in diameter. The tone at this note to be equal to that of the corresponding pipe of the GRAND PRINCIPAL, 8 FT., and to be decreased in strength as directed for the first rank.

All the pipes of this stop to be of spotted-metal.

LIEBLICHFLÖTE, 4 FT.—The tone of this stop to be a bright flute organ-tone of medium strength. The diameter of the CC pipe to be 2·05 inches, and the ratio of the scale 1 : 2·66. The pipes to be of spotted-metal.

WOOD STOPS.

DOUBLE PRINCIPAL, 32 FT.—Pedal Organ—The tone of this important stop to be full and round with a leaning toward a string quality, created by the application of harmonic-bridges, which also aid the promptness of speech. The scale to be to the ratio 1·2·66. Inside measurements :—

SCALE OF DOUBLE PRINCIPAL.

CCC——11·40 inches in width.	14·52 inches in depth.			
CC —— 6·97 "	"	8·88	"	"
FF —— 5·70 "	"	7·26	"	"
G —— 3·22 "	"	4·10	"	"

The pipes to be of clear white pine, not less than 1¾ inches thick in the CCC pipe. The mouths, caps, and harmonic-bridges to be of hard wood.

GRAND PRINCIPAL, 16 FT.—Pedal Organ—This stop to yield a pure organ-tone, sonorous and prompt. To comprise 44 pipes, to allow the GRAND OCTAVE, 8 FT., to be derived from it. Scale to be to the ratio $1 : 1\sqrt{8}$; inside measurements :—

SCALE OF GRAND PRINCIPAL.

CCC——10·08 inches in width.	12·84 inches in depth.			
CC —— 6·18 "	"	7·88	"	"

FF —— 5·04 inches in width. 6·42 inches in depth.
G —— 2·97   "   "   3·78   "   "
g¹ —— 1·81   "   "   2·31   "   "

The pipes to be of clear white pine, not less than 1⅜ inches thick in the CCC pipe. The mouths and caps to be of hard wood.

CONTRA-BASSO, 16 FT.—Pedal Organ—The tone of this important stop to be of orchestral quality, imitating as closely as possible in its lower register the tone of the orchestral Contra-Basso, and in its higher register that of the orchestral Violoncello. To comprise 44 pipes, to allow the VIOLONCELLO, 8 FT., to be derived from it. Scale to be to the ratio 1 : 2·66. Inside measurements :—

SCALE OF CONTRA-BASSO.

CCC——5·70 inches in width. 7·26 inches in depth.
CC ——3·48   "   "   4·44   "   "
FF ——2·85   "   "   3·63   "   "
G ——1·61   "   "   2·05   "   "
g¹ ——0·98   "   "   1·25   "   "

The pipes from CCC to EE to be of clear white pine, with mouths, caps, and harmonic-bridges of hard wood. The pipes from FF to g¹ to have fronts of maple, with caps and harmonic-bridges of the same.

BOURDON, 16 FT.—Pedal Organ—The tone of this covered stop to be smooth and sonorous, with its first upper partial slightly audible along with the dominant prime, rendering its tone valuable in combination and as a unison bass of medium strength. Scale to the ratio of 1 : 2·66 :—

SCALE OF BOURDON.

CCC——7·26 inches in width. 9·25 inches in depth.
CC ——4·46   "   "   5·68   "   "
FF ——3·63   "   "   4·62   "   "
G ——2·06   "   "   2·62   "   "

The pipes to be of clear white pine of sufficient thickness to secure a perfectly steady tone and withstand the pressure of the stoppers. The mouths and caps to be of hard wood. Great care must be taken in voicing this stop, and in regulating its tone perfectly.

MAJOR FLUTE, 8 FT.—This stop to yield a full and bold flute organ-tone, secured in its higher register by its pipes having double mouths from Tenor F♯ to c⁴. The scale in both portions of the compass to be to the ratio 1 : 2·66 :—

SCALE OF MAJOR FLUTE.

Single Mouths	CC——3·34 inches in width.	4·26 inches in depth.		
	C ——2·05 "	"	2·62 "	"
	F ——1·67 "	"	2·13 "	"
Double Mouths	F♯——1·60 "	"	3·34 "	"
	c¹ ——1·25 "	"	2·62 "	"
	c⁴ ——0·29 "	"	0·60 "	"

The pipes from CC to F to be of clear white pine, with mouths and caps of hard wood. The pipes from F♯ to c⁴ to have their narrower sides, in which their mouths are formed, of mahogany or maple, and their caps of similar wood. Their wider sides to be of pine. Every care must be taken in voicing to cover the break in tone between the single- and double-mouthed pipes.

LIEBLICHGEDECKT, 16 FT.—The tone of this stop to be of medium power and of a sweet and singing quality, naturally inclining to the covered-flute intonation. It must not be blown and voiced to dominate assertively over the unison voices of the Subdivision in which it is placed. The scale to be to the ratio $1 : 2.66$:—

SCALE OF LIEBLICHGEDECKT.

CC——4·10 inches in width.   4·62 inches in depth.
C ——2·51   "   "   2·84   "   "
F ——2·05   "   "   2·31   "   "
c⁴ ——0·35   "   "   0·40   "   "

The pipes from CC to b¹ to be of clear white pine, having mouths and caps of hard wood; and the pipes from c¹ to c⁴ to have their mouthed sides of mahogany or maple, and caps of the same.

LIEBLICHGEDECKT, 8 FT.—The tone of this stop to be similar in quality to that already specified for the LIEBLICHGEDECKT, 16 FT., but to be decidedly more powerful so as to assert the dominance, along with the GEIGENPRINCIPAL, 8 FT., of the unison pitch of the Subdivision. The scale to be to the ratio $1 : 2.3$, halving on the twenty-first pipe:—

SCALE OF LIEBLICHGEDECKT.

CC——2·20 inches in width.   3·21 inches in depth.
C ——1·44   "   "   2·12   "   "
G♯——1·10   "   "   1·60   "   "
c⁴ ——0·26   "   "   0·40   "   "

The pipes from CC to B to be of clear white pine, having mouths and caps of hard wood; and the pipes from c¹ to c⁴ to have their mouthed sides of mahogany or maple, and caps of the same. From c³ to c⁴ metal pipes may be used.

MINOR FLUTE, 4 FT.—The tone of this stop to be full and assertive, only subordinate to the MAJOR FLUTE, 8 FT. The pipes to be open. The scale to be to the ratio $1 : 2.66$:—

SCALE OF MINOR FLUTE.

CC——2·22 inches in width.   2·84 inches in depth.
C ——1·36   "   "   1·74   "   "
F ——1·11   "   "   1·42   "   "
c⁴ ——0·18   "   "   0·25   "   "

The pipes from CC to B to be of clear white pine, having mouths and caps of hard wood; and the pipes from c¹ to c⁴ to have their mouthed sides of mahogany or maple and caps of the same.

Flauto d'Amore, 8 ft.—The tone of this stop to be of a delicate and singing flute quality, and about the same strength of voice as the Dolce, 8 ft., in the same Subdivision. The scale to be to the ratio 1 : 2·519 :—

Scale of Flauto d'Amore.

CC——2·05 inches in width.　2·58 inches in depth.
C ——1·29 　"　　　"　1·62　"　　"
F♯——1·02 　"　　　"　1·29　"　　"
c⁴ ——0·20 　"　　　"　0·26　"　　"

The pipes to be "half-covered," having pierced stoppers. From CC to B the pipes to be of clear white pine, having mouths and caps of hard wood; and the pipes from c¹ to c⁴ to have their mouthed sides of mahogany or maple. The top-octave may be of metal pipes, stopped.

Orchestral Flute, 4 ft.—The tone of this stop to be a close imitation of that of the orchestral instrument. Although the mode of constructing the pipes here specified has been found satisfactory for the production of the required tone, under skilful voicing, the organ-builder is at liberty to suggest any improvement his experience may have taught him. The stop to be partly harmonic, the lower portion from CC to E to be of open pipes of the ordinary speaking lengths, while from F to c⁴ the pipes are to be double lengths and harmonic. The scale of the F pipe to be 1·13 inches in width by 1·39 inches in depth. The mouths of these harmonic pipes to be circular and splayed inside. The caps to have wedge-shaped under pieces, so as to direct the wind-stream obliquely across the mouth. The lower pipes to be of clear white pine or straight-grained spruce, fronted with maple: the harmonic pipes to be of maple throughout. Metal pipes may be substituted for wood in the top octave.

Generally—All the wood pipes specified above to be made in the most workmanlike manner, and to be well finished in every respect. To be cleanly glue-sized internally, and to be sized and receive two coats of best copal varnish externally. Every matter and thing to be done to render this pipe-work perfect to the entire satisfaction of the Architect.

LINGUAL STOPS.

Trombone, 16 ft.—The tone of this stop to be full and sonorous, in imitation of that of the orchestral Bass Trombone played by a master, and just short of *fortissimo,* as an extreme blare is undesirable in a dignified Church Organ. The resonators, of the usual form, to be of ample scale, and constructed of stout zinc or white pine, as the voicer may decide as most favorable to the production of the required tone. Every means must be adopted to secure prompt speech throughout the stop.

Double Trumpet, 16 ft.—As this is an inclosed stop, its voice must be clear and of sufficient strength to be effective in a *crescendo.* In its Tenor and higher octaves it must not dominate the voice of the unison Trumpet, with which it is associated. The resonators, of the usual form, to be of medium scale: the two lower octaves to be of stout zinc and the remaining three octaves of spotted-metal.

CONTRAFAGOTTO, 16 FT.—The tone of this stop to be as imitative as practicable of that of the orchestral instrument of the same name. The resonators to be inverted conical in form and of small scale, the top of that of the CC pipe not to exceed 4½ inches square. The resonators from CC to b¹ to be of yellow pine, as thin as is suitable; and from c² to c⁴ to be of zinc. This important stop must be carefully voiced and regulated.

ORCHESTRAL CLARINET, 8 FT.—The tone of this stop to be strictly imitative of the tones of the orchestral Clarinets. It is desirable that the voice of this stop should be rather brighter and clearer than that which commonly obtains in the CLARINETS usually made. The stop to be of spotted-metal. To have adjustable regulating slides.

CORNO DI BASSETTO, 8 FT.—This stop to have a tone of the same quality as that of the ORCHESTRAL CLARINET, but of much greater body and richness. Its resonant tubes to be cylindrical, and of larger scale than those of the latter stop. All to be of spotted-metal. To have adjustable regulating slides.

TRUMPET, 8 FT.—The tone of this stop to be bright and full, resembling as closely as possible the voice of the orchestral Trumpet played *forte*. As this is the dominant brass-toned stop in the manual department, its scale must be sufficiently large to yield the volume of sound required. All of spotted-metal.

CLARION, 4 FT.—As this stop is, strictly considered, an OCTAVE TRUMPET, its voice must resemble, but be much softer than that of the TRUMPET. Care must be taken to avoid coarseness of intonation or too great assertiveness. All to be of spotted-metal.

ORCHESTRAL OBOE, 8 FT.—Great care and skill must be exercised in the formation and voicing of this exacting stop, so as to produce a satisfactory imitation of the tone of the orchestral instrument. As voicers of any special skill have their own methods of forming and voicing the pipes of this stop, it is undesirable to give any suggestions here beyond those conveyed in the preceding few words. All to be of spotted-metal.

VOX HUMANA, 8 FT.—This is the only stop in the Organ that presents apparently insuperable difficulty in the matter of formation and voicing, with the view of producing a desired tonality. While the tones of the orchestral instruments can be more or less closely imitated, those of the cultivated human voice, in its several registers, have defied satisfactory imitation by artificial means. Such being the case, all details respecting the formation and voicing of the VOX HUMANA must be left to the skill of the voicer. It must, however, be approved of and accepted by the Architect.

GENERALLY.—The Organ-builder to do every matter and thing required to render the reed stops, described above, complete and perfect in every respect, to the entire satisfaction of the Architect, whose decision shall be final and binding on all parties concerned.

G. A. AUDSLEY,
ORGAN ARCHITECT.

PLATE XXXII

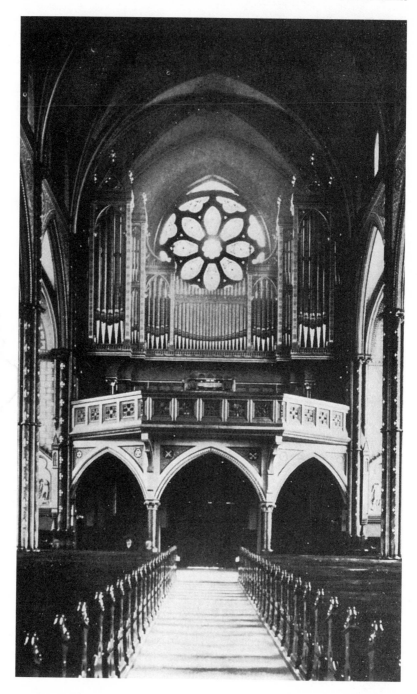

GRAND ORGAN IN THE CHURCH OF OUR LADY OF GRACE, HOBOKEN, N. J.

APPENDIX.

GRAND CONCERT ORGAN.

INSTALLED IN THE FESTIVAL HALL
OF THE LOUISIANA PURCHASE EXPOSITION
ST. LOUIS, 1904.

AS ORIGINALLY SCHEMED BY G. A. AUDSLEY.

—— PEDAL ORGAN ——

Compass CCC to G—32 Notes.

FIRST SUBDIVISION—UNEXPRESSIVE.

1. GRAVISSIMA . .	Wood. 64 Feet.		7. QUINT . . .	Wood. 10⅔ Feet.
2. DOUBLE OPEN			8. OCTAVE . . .	Metal. 8 "
DIAPASON . .	Wood. 32 "		9. BASS FLUTE . .	Wood. 8 "
3. OPEN DIAPASON .	Wood. 16 "		10. COMPENSATING	
4. OPEN DIAPASON .	Metal. 16 "		MIXTURE . .	Metal. VI. Ranks.
5. GAMBA	Metal. 16 "		11. CONTRA-	
6. CONTRAFLAUTO .	Wood. 16 "		BOMBARDE .	Wood. 32 Feet.

SECOND SUBDIVISION—EXPRESSIVE.

Inclosed in a Swell-chamber.

12. CONTRA-BOURDON .	Wood. 32 Feet.		20. OFFENFLÖTE . .	Wood. 4 Feet.
13. VIOLONE . . .	Metal. 16 "		21. CONTRA-POSAUNE	Metal. 16 "
14. BOURDON . . .	Wood. 16 "		22. BOMBARDE . . .	Metal. 16 "
15. QUINTATEN . .	Wood. 16 "		23. EUPHONIUM	
16. DOLCE	Metal. 16 "		(Free-reed) .	Metal. 16 "
17. VIOLONCELLO . .	Metal. 8 "		24. TROMBA . . .	Metal. 8 "
18. WEITGEDECKT . .	Wood. 8 "		25. FAGOTTO . . .	Metal. 8 "
19. SUPER-OCTAVE .	Metal. 4 "		26. CLARION . . .	Metal. 4 "

THIRD DIVISION—AUXILIARY.

27. DOUBLE PRINCIPAL (From First Organ, No. 31) . . . . Metal. 32 Feet.
28. DULCIANA (Expressive, from Second Organ, No. 57) . . Metal. 16 "
29. LIEBLICHGEDECKT (Expressive, from Third Organ, No. 77) . Wood. 16 "
30. CONTRAFAGOTTO (Expressive, from Third Organ, No. 91) . Wood. 16 "

—— FIRST ORGAN ——
Compass CC to c⁴—61 Notes.
FIRST SUBDIVISION—UNEXPRESSIVE.

31. SUB-PRINCIPAL . Metal. 32 Feet.	37. OPEN DIAPASON,	
32. DOUBLE OPEN	MINOR . . . Metal. 8 Feet.	
DIAPASON . . Metal. 16 "	38. OPEN DIAPASON . Wood. 8 "	
33. CONTRA-GAMBA . Metal. 16 "	39. GRAND FLUTE . . Wood. 8 "	
34. SUB-QUINT . . Wood. 10⅔ "	40. DOPPELFLÖTE . . Wood. 8 "	
35. GRAND PRINCIPAL. Metal. 8 "	41. GAMBA . . . . Tin. 8 "	
36. OPEN DIAPASON,	42. OCTAVE, MAJOR . Metal. 4 "	
MAJOR . . . Metal. 8 "	43. GAMBETTE . . . Metal. 4 "	

SECOND SUBDIVISION—EXPRESSIVE.
Inclosed in Swell-box No. I.

44. GROBGEDECKT . . Wood. 8 Feet.	51. SUPER-OCTAVE . Metal. 2 Feet.
45. HARMONIC FLUTE . Metal. 8 "	52. GRAND CORNET (17th,
46. QUINT . . . . Metal. 5⅓ "	19th, Septième, 22nd) IV. Ranks.
47. OCTAVE, MINOR . Metal. 4 "	53. GRAND MIXTURE Metal. VII. "
48. HARMONIC FLUTE . Metal. 4 "	54. DOUBLE TRUMPET . Metal. 16 Feet.
49. TIERCE . . . . Metal. 3⅕ "	55. HARMONIC TRUMPET Metal. 8 "
50. OCTAVE QUINT . . Metal. 2⅔ "	56. HARMONIC CLARION Metal. 4 "

—— SECOND ORGAN ——
Compass CC to c⁴—61 Notes.
ENTIRELY EXPRESSIVE.
Inclosed in Swell-box No. 1.

57. DOUBLE DULCIANA Metal. 16 Feet.	68. FLAUTO D'AMORE . W.&M. 4 Feet.
58. OPEN DIAPASON . Metal. 8 "	69. SALICET . . . Tin. 4 "
59. GEIGENPRINCIPAL . Metal. 8 "	70. PICCOLO . . . Metal. 2 "
60. SALICIONAL . . Metal. 8 "	71. DULCIANA CORNET
61. KERAULOPHONE . Metal. 8 "	Metal VI. Ranks.
62. DULCIANA . . . Metal. 8 "	72. CONTRA-SAXOPHONE Metal. 16 Feet.
63. VOX ANGELICA . Metal. 8 "	73. SAXOPHONE . . Metal. 8 "
64. VOX CŒLESTIS . Metal. 8 "	74. CORNO INGLESE . Metal. 8 "
65. QUINTADENA . . Metal. 8 "	75. MUSETTE . . . Metal. 4 "
66. GEDECKT . . . Wood. 8 "	76. CARILLON (Tubular Bells) 25 Notes.
67. CONCERT FLUTE . Wood. 8 "	

The CORNO INGLESE, 8 FT., and the MUSETTE, 4 FT., are free-reed stops, made by A. Laukhuff, of Weikersheim, Germany.

The Second Organ is commanded by the Second Clavier and also by the First Clavier through its Double-touch.

——— THIRD ORGAN ———

Compass CC to c⁴—61 Notes

FIRST SUBDIVISION—EXPRESSIVE.

Inclosed in Swell-box No. II.

77. LIEBLICHGEDECKT .	Wood.	16 Feet.	89. HARMONIC PICCOLO	Metal.	2 Feet.
78. HORN DIAPASON .	Metal.	8 "	90. FULL MIXTURE	Metal.	VI. Ranks.
79. VIOLIN DIAPASON.	Metal.	8 "	91. CONTRAFAGOTTO .	Wood.	16 Feet.
80. GROSSFLÖTE . .	Wood.	8 "	92. CONTRA-OBOE . .	Metal.	16 "
81. CLARABELLA . .	Wood.	8 "	93. FAGOTTO Wood &	Metal.	8 "
82. DOPPELROHRGEDECKT	Wood.	8 "	94. ORCHESTRAL OBOE	Metal.	8 "
83. MELODIA . . .	Wood.	8 "	95. CLARINET . . .	Metal.	8 "
84. HARMONIC FLUTE	Metal.	8 "	96. CORNO DI BASSETTO	Metal.	8 "
85. DOLCE	Metal.	8 "	97. HORN	Metal.	8 "
86. GEDECKTQUINT .	Metal.	5⅓ "	98. VOX HUMANA .	Metal.	8 "
87. OCTAVE . . .	Metal.	4 "	99. OCTAVE OBOE . .	Metal.	4 "
88. HARMONIC FLUTE	Metal.	4 "			

The FULL MIXTURE, VI. RANKS, is timbre-creating—composed of metal and wood pipes of different tonalities.

This Subdivision is brought on and thrown off the Third Clavier by means of thumb-pistons.

SECOND SUBDIVISION—EXPRESSIVE.

Inclosed in Swell-box No. III.

100. CONTRA-BASSO .	Wood.	16 Feet.	107. OCTAVE VIOL . . .	Tin.	4 Feet.
101. VIOLONCELLO . .	Tin.	8 "	108. VIOLETTE	Tin.	4 "
102. VIOLA	Tin.	8 "	109. VIOL ⎰ VIOL, Muted.	Tin.	2⅔ "
103. VIOLINO . . .	Tin.	8 "	CORNET, ⎰ VIOL, "	Tin.	2 "
104. VIOLINO (Tuned			IV. ⎱ VIOL, "	Tin.	1⅗ "
sharp) . . .	Tin.	8 "	Ranks. ⎰ VIOL, "	Tin.	1 "
105. TIERCINO . . .	Tin.	8 "	110. CORROBORATING MIXTURE		
106. QUINT VIOL . .	Tin.	5⅓ "		Tin.	V. Ranks.

This Subdivision—String-toned throughout—is brought on and thrown off the Third Clavier by means of thumb-pistons. It is also commanded by the Double-touch of the Clavier.

This Subdivision furnishes the first instance, in the history of organ-building, of the introduction of an independent string-toned division, representng the string division of the Orchestra: no attempt having been previously made to furnish an ancillary addition of the class.

——— FOURTH ORGAN ———

Compass CC to c⁴—61 Notes.

ENTIRELY EXPRESSIVE.

Inclosed in Swell-box No. IV.

111. DOUBLE DIAPASON	Metal.	16 Feet.	114. GROSSGAMBE . .	Tin.	8 Feet.
112. FLÛTE A PAVILLON	Metal.	8 "	115. DOPPELOFFENFLÖTE	Wood.	8 "
113. STENTORPHONE .	Metal.	8 "	116. GROSSFLÖTE . .	Wood.	8 "

117. ORCHESTRAL FLUTE Wood. 8 Feet.	124. OPHICLEIDE . . Metal. 8 Feet.
118. HARMONIC FLUTE Metal. 4 "	125. ORCHESTRAL
119. OCTAVE . . . Metal. 8 "	TRUMPET . . Metal. 8 "
120. GRAND CORNET	126. ORCHESTRAL
Metal. IV., V., & VI. Ranks.	CLARINET . . Metal. 8 "
121. BASS TROMBONE . Metal. 16 Feet.	127. HARMONIC
122. BASS TUBA . . Metal. 16 "	CLARION . . Metal. 4 "
123. TROMBONE . . Metal. 8 "	128. DRUMS.

The ORCHESTRAL CLARINET, 8 FT., is a dual stop, the reed having associated with it a DOPPELFLÖTE, 8 FT., of medium scale.

This Organ is commanded by the Fourth Clavier.

—— FIFTH ORGAN ——

Compass CC to c⁴—61 Notes.

ENTIRELY EXPRESSIVE.

Inclosed in Swell-box No. V.

129. STILLGEDECKT . Wood. 16 Feet.	135. UNDA MARIS . . Metal. 8 Feet.
130. ECHO DIAPASON . Metal. 8 "	136. FLAUTO D'AMORE . Wood. 4 "
131. NACHTHORN . . Metal. 8 "	137. GEMSHORN . . Metal. 4 "
132. SPITZFLÖTE . . Metal. 8 "	138. ECHO CORNET . Metal. V. Ranks.
133. VIOLA D'AMORE . Tin. 8 "	139. ECHO TRUMPET . Metal. 8 Feet.
134. HARMONICA . . Wood. 8 "	140. VOX HUMANA . Metal. 8 "

The VOX HUMANA, 8 FT., is a dual stop, the reed having associated with it an open wood, flute-toned, unison stop of the MELODIA class, imparting to the reed-tone a desirable firmness and body.

This Organ is commanded by the Fifth Clavier.

—— MECHANICAL ACCESSORIES ——

PEDAL COUPLERS.

1. First Organ...... 1st Subdivision......to Pedal Organ.
2. First Organ...... 2nd Subdivision......to Pedal Organ.
3. Second Organ.... Undivided ....to Pedal Organ.
4. Third Organ..... 1st Subdivision......to Pedal Organ.
5. Third Organ..... 2nd Subdivision......to Pedal Organ.
6. Fourth Organ.... Undivided ....to Pedal Organ.
7. Fifth Organ...... Undivided ....to Pedal Organ.
8. Pedal Organ......Octave Coupler on itself.

MANUAL COUPLERS.

9. Second Organ...... Undivided ....to First Organ, Unison Coupler.
10. Second Organ...... Undivided ....to First Organ, Sub-octave Coupler.
11. Second Organ...... Undivided ....to First Organ, Octave Coupler.
12. Third Organ....... 1st Subdivision....to First Organ, Unison Coupler.
13. Third Organ....... 2nd Subdivision....to First Organ, Unison Coupler.
14. Third Organ....... 1st Subdivision....to First Organ, Octave Coupler.
15. Third Organ....... 2nd Subdivision....to First Organ, Octave Coupler.

16. Fourth Organ......Undivided.........to First Organ, Unison Coupler.
17. Fourth Organ......Undivided.........to First Organ, Octave Coupler.
18. Fifth Organ.......Undivided.........to First Organ, Unison Coupler.
19. Third Organ.......1st Subdivision....to Second Organ, Unison Coupler.
20. Third Organ.......2nd Subdivision....to Second Organ, Unison Coupler.
21. Fourth Organ......Undivided.........to 1st Subdivision of Third
     Organ, Unison Coupler.
22. Fourth Organ......Undivided.........to 2nd Subdivision of Third
     Organ, Unison Coupler.
23. Fourth Organ......Undivided.........to Second Organ, Unison Coupler.
24. Fifth Organ........Undivided.........to Second Organ, Unison Coupler.
25. Fifth Organ........Undivided.........to Second Organ, Octave Coupler.
26. Fifth Organ........Undivided.........to 1st Subdivision of Third
     Organ, Unison Coupler.
27. Fifth Organ........Undivided.........to 2nd Subdivision of Third
     Organ, Unison Coupler.
28. Fifth Organ........Undivided.........to Fourth Organ, Unison Coupler.

TREMOLANTS.

I. TREMOLANT to Second Organ.
II. TREMOLANT to 1st Subdivision of Third Organ.
III. TREMOLANT to 2nd Subdivision of Third Organ.
IV. TREMOLANT to Fourth Organ.
V. TREMOLANT to Fifth Organ.

ADJUSTABLE COMBINATION ACTION

Commanded by thumb-pistons located under the several Manual Claviers.

1–2–3–4–0   Operating on stops of 1st Division of First Organ and Pedal Organ, and Couplers.
1–2–3–4–0   Operating on stops of 2nd Division of First Organ and Pedal Organ, and Couplers.
1–2–3–4–5–0   Operating on stops of 1st Division of Third Organ and Pedal Organ, and Couplers.
1–2–3–4–5–0   Operating on stops of 2nd Division of Third Organ and Pedal Organ, and Couplers.
1–2–3–4–5–6–0   Operating on stops of Second Organ and Pedal Organ, and Couplers.
1–2–3–4–5–0   Operating on stops of Fourth Organ and Pedal Organ, and Couplers.
1–2–3–4–0   Operating on stops of Fifth Organ and Pedal Organ, and Couplers.
1–2–3–4–5–6   Operating on combinations of stops of the several Organs or on solo stops.

EXPRESSION LEVERS, ETC.

1. Balanced Expression Lever to Swell-box No. 1.
2. Balanced Expression Lever to Swell-box No. 2.
3. Balanced Expression Lever to Swell-box No. 3.
4. Balanced Expression Lever to Swell-box No. 4.
5. Balanced Expression Lever to Swell-box No. 5.

6. Balanced Crescendo Lever, operating on each Manual Division separately.
7. Balanced Crescendo Lever, operating on Full Organ from First Clavier.
8. Locking Lever, connecting all Swell-boxes to Expression Lever No. 1, so that all may be operated simultaneously with coupled claviers.
9. Locking Lever, reducing the Pedal Organ from forte to piano.
10. Reversible Lever, operating First Organ to Pedal Organ coupler.

This Organ—the most important Concert-room Organ in existence at the time of its construction—was carried out in accordance with the original tonal scheme, with the exception of the appointment of the Pedal Organ, in which the imparting of flexibility and expression to the Second Subdivision was abandoned, being too great an innovation to be recognized according to the old-fashioned ideas of its builders. This was much to be regretted on several grounds: one of which was that the Organ, as schemed, presented the first opportunity of placing on record, in the History of the Organ, the imparting of flexibility of tone and expressive powers to the Pedal Organ.

The Organ now forms the foundation of the Instrument in the great Wanamaker Store, in Philadelphia, Pa., in which the Pedal Organ proper still retains its unexpressive condition; and in which the independent expression of the original String-toned Subdivision has been destroyed. Truly great improvements move slowly in the organ-building world. The History of the Organ is one continued record of slow developments in construction, and misconceptions in tonal matters. To-day history is repeating itself in more than one direction.

INDEX

152-153 (Plate XXII., 152). Touch of the, 152. Formation of the, 153. In the Concert-room Organ, 280-281. In the Church Organ, 486.

MAJOR FLUTE—In the Concert-room Organ, 317. In the Church Organ, 482. Specification for the, 498-499.

MAJOR OCTAVE—In the Concert-room Organ, 297. In the Church Organ, 482. Specification for the, 492.

MAJOR PRINCIPAL—In the Church Organ, 482. Specification for the, 492.

MELODIA—In the Ancillary Aërial Organ, 329, 331. Form and tone of the, 427-428 (Fig. LXXII., 427).

Metal Pipes—Forms and Construction of Metal Pipes, Chapter XIV., 361-406. Suitable metals and alloys to be used for, 361-362. Tin used for, 362. Lead unsuitable for, 362-363. Pipe-metal an ambiguous term, 363. Antimony metal objectionable for, 363. Table of Specific Gravities of alloys of tin and lead, 363. Spotted-metal for, 364. Hoyt's Two-ply Pipe-metal for, 364-365. Table of thicknesses and weights of Hoyt's pipe-metal, 366. Zinc used for, 365-366. Do different metals and alloys affect the tones of pipes? 366-367. Importance of the thickness of the metal used for, 367-368. Table of thicknesses of spotted-metal for, 368. Principal forms of metal labial pipes, 368-406. Construction of, 368-369. Component parts of, 369 (Fig. XXXII., 369). Of organ-tone, 369-379 (Figs. XXXIII., 370; XXXIV., 371; XXXV., 374; XXXVI., 378). Of flute-tone, 379-392 (Figs. XXXVII., 380; XXXVIII., 381; XXXIX., 382; XL., 385; XLI., 387; XLII., 388; XLIII., 390; XLIV., 391). Of string-tone, 392-404 (Figs. XLV., XLVI., 394; XLVII., 395; XLVIII., XLIX., 396; L., LI., 397; LII., 399; LIII., LIV., 401). Of special tonalities, 404-406 (Fig. LV., 406).

MINOR FLUTE—In the Church Organ, 482. Specification for the, 499.

MINOR OCTAVE—In the Concert-room Organ, 297, 504.

MINOR PRINCIPAL—In the Church Organ, 483. Specification for the, 495.

MIXTURE—Formed of II., III., and IV. ranks, 75. On the formation of, 75-78. Seidel's remarks on the, 88. Examples with one break, 76, 78. Examples with two breaks, 76, 77. Examples with three breaks, 76, 77. Examples with four breaks, 77. High upper partial tones furnished by the, 55-56. A fertile field for the exercise of acoustical knowledge, 91. Value of the, discussed, 97-98.

Formed of pipes of different tonalities, 89. Pedal Organ, in Riga Cathedral Organ, 70. Pedal Organ, of VI. and X. ranks, 71. In the Pedal Organ, 72. Four methods of forming Pedal Organ, 72. Pipes forming the, 376. In the Concert-room Organ, 297, 317, 320, 323, 325, 326, 328, 503, 504, 505. In the Church Organ, 241-242, 484, 497.

MUSETTE—In the Concert-room Organ, 303, 504.

Musical Sounds, Limits of the ear in the perception of, 65-66.

Nag's-head Swell, 196.

NACHTHORN—Variation of the FLÛTE À CHIMINÉE, 117, 506.

NASARD FLUTE—Dual stop, 104-105.

NASARD GAMBA—Dual stop, 105-106.

OBOE, HAUTBOY—Tonality of the, 130. In the Church Organ, 131, 246. The family of the, 131. Form of the, 467-468 (Fig. XCIV., 469): See ORCHESTRAL OBOE.

OBOE D'AMORE—In the Concert-room Organ, 303.

OCTATEN—Formation and tonality of the, 451-452 (Fig. XC., 452). Of dual intonation, 109.

OCTAVE—Rôle played by the, in the acoustics of the Organ, 60. Relation to the chief unison voice, 376.

Octave Coupler—Acting on the same manual, objectionable, 284-285. Acting between different manuals, 285.

OCTAVE OBOE—In the Concert-room Organ, 131, 307, 505. In the Church Organ, 131.

OCTAVE QUINT—In the Concert-room Organ, 326, 504. In the Church Organ, 482. Specification for the, 492-493.

OPEN DIAPASON, PRINCIPAL—See DIAPASON.

OPHICLEIDE—Compass of the orchestral, 136. Comparison of the tones of the orchestral instrument with those of the organ stops, 136. In the Concert-room Organ, 136-137, 311, 313, 318, 506. Form of the, 464-465.

Orchestral Brass-tone—Remarks on its production by organ lingual stops, 134-139.

ORCHESTRAL CLARINET—As a dual stop, 99-100. In the Concert-room Organ, 307, 308, 315, 316, 516. In the Church Organ, 483. Specification for the, 501.

ORCHESTRAL FLUTE—Varieties of the, 128. The best forms of the, 128. Proper place in the Concert-room Organ, 129, 307, 308, 315, 506. Forms, construction, and scales of

INDEX